Intermediate Accounting

SEVENTH CANADIAN EDITION

Intermediate Accounting

Donald E. Kieso, PhD, CPA
KPMG Peat Marwick Emeritus Professor of Accounting
Northern Illinois University
DeKalb, Illinois

Jerry J. Weygandt, PhD, CPA
Arthur Andersen Alumni Professor of Accounting
University of Wisconsin
Madison, Wisconsin

Terry D. Warfield, PhD
PricewaterhouseCoopers Research Scholar
University of Wisconsin
Madison, Wisconsin

Nicola M. Young, MBA, FCA
Saint Mary's University
Halifax, Nova Scotia

Irene M. Wiecek, CA
University of Toronto
Toronto, Ontario

John Wiley & Sons Canada, Ltd.

National Library of Canada Cataloguing in Publication Data

Intermediate accounting / Donald E. Kieso... [et al.]—7th Canadian ed.

Includes index.
ISBN 0-470-83372-6 (v. 1).—ISBN 0-470-83373-4 (v. 2)

1. Accounting. I. Kieso, Donald E.

HF5635.I573 2004   657′.044   C2003-905287-7

Production Credits
Editorial Manager: Karen Staudinger
Publishing Services Director: Karen Bryan
Sr. Marketing Manager: Janine Daoust
New Media Editor: Elsa Passera
Developmental Editors: Leanne Rancourt and Amanjeet Chauhan
Formatting: Quadratone Graphics Ltd. (Heidi Palfrey)
Cover Design: Interrobang Graphic Design
Cover Photo: Kitchin and Hurst/Firstlight
Printing & Binding: Tri-Graphic Printing Limited

Printed and bound in Canada
10 9 8 7 6 5 4 3 2

 John Wiley & Sons Canada, Ltd.
6045 Freemont Blvd.
Mississauga, Ontario   L5R 4J3
Visit our website at: www.wiley.com/canada

Dedicated to our husbands

       John and George

and to our children

       Hilary

       Tim

       Megan

       Nicholas, and

       Katherine

for their support, encouragement, and tolerance throughout the writing of this book; and to the many wonderful students who have passed through our Intermediate Accounting classrooms. We, too, have learned from you.

About the Authors

Canadian Edition

Nicola M. Young, MBA, FCA is a Professor of Accounting in the Sobey School of Business at Saint Mary's University in Halifax, Nova Scotia where her teaching responsibilities have varied from the introductory offering to final year advanced financial accounting courses to the survey course in the Executive MBA program. She is the recipient of teaching awards, and has contributed to the academic and administrative life of the university through chairing the Department of Accounting, membership on the Board of Governors, the Pension and other Committees. Professor Young has been associated with the Atlantic School of Chartered Accountancy for over twenty-five years in a variety of roles, including program and course development, teaching, and program reform. In addition to contributions to the accounting profession at the provincial level, Professor Young has served on national boards of the Canadian Institute of Chartered Accountants (CICA) dealing with licensure and education. For the last twelve years, she has worked with the CICA's Public Sector Accounting Board (PSAB) as an Associate, as a member and chair of the Board, and as chair and member of PSAB Task Forces.

Irene M. Wiecek, CA is a faculty member of the Joseph L. Rotman School of Management at the University of Toronto where she teaches accounting courses at all levels in various programs including the Commerce Program, the Master of Management & Professional Accounting Program (MMPA) and the MBA Program. The Associate Director of the MMPA Program for many years, she was recently appointed Co-Director of the ICAO/Rotman Centre for Innovation in Accounting Education. Irene is involved in professional accounting education both at the Institute of Chartered Accountants of Ontario and the CICA, teaching and developing case/program material in various programs including the ICAO School of Accountancy and the CICA In-depth GAAP course. In the area of standard setting, she is Chair of the Canadian Academic Accounting Association Financial Accounting Exposure Draft Response Committee. Irene is a member of the CICA Qualifications Committee which provides leadership, direction and standards for admission into the CA profession.

U.S. Edition

Donald E. Kieso, Ph.D., C.P.A., received his bachelor's degree from Aurora University and his doctorate in accounting from the University of Illinois. He has served as chairman of the Department of Accountancy and is currently the KPMG Peat Marwick Emeritus Professor of Accountancy at Northern Illinois University. He has done postdoctorate work as a Visiting Scholar at the University of California at Berkeley and is a recipient of NIU's Teaching Excellence Award and four Golden Apple Teaching Awards. Professor Kieso has served as a member of the Board of Directors of the Illinois CPA Society, the AACSB's Accounting Accreditation Committees, the State of Illinois Comptroller's Commission, as Secretary-Treasurer of the Federation of Schools of Accountancy, and as Secretary-Treasurer of the American Accounting Association. He served as a charter member of the national Accounting Education Change Commission. He received the Outstanding Accounting Educator Award from the Illinois CPA Society, in 1992 he received the FSA's Joseph A. Silvoso Award of Merit, and the NIU Foundation's Humanitarian Award for Service to Higher Education.

Jerry J. Weygandt, Ph.D., C.P.A., is Arthur Andersen Alumni Professor of Accounting at the University of Wisconsin-Madison. He holds a Ph.D. in accounting from the University of Illinois. Articles by Professor Weygandt have appeared in the *Accounting Review, Journal of Accounting Research, Accounting Horizons, Journal of Accountancy,* and other academic and professional journals. These articles have examined such financial reporting issues as accounting for price-level adjustments, pensions, convertible securities, stock option contracts, and interim reports. He has served on numerous committees of the American Accounting Association and as a member of the editorial board of the *Accounting Review*; he also has served as President and Secretary-Treasurer of the American Accounting Association. In addition, he has been actively involved with the American Institute of Certified Public Accountants and has been a member of the Accounting Standards Executive Committee (AcSEC) of that organization. He has served on the FASB task force that examined the reporting issues related to accounting for income taxes and is presently a trustee of the Financial Accounting Foundation. Professor Weygandt has received the Chancellor's Award for Excellence in Teaching and the Beta Gamma Sigma Dean's Teaching Award. He is on the board of directors of M & I Bank of Southern Wisconsin and the Dean Foundation. He is the recipient of the Wisconsin Institute of CPA's Outstanding Educator's Award and the Lifetime Achievement Award. In 2001, he received the American Accounting Association's Outstanding Accounting Educator Award.

Terry D. Warfield, Ph.D., is Associate Professor of Accounting at the University of Wisconsin-Madison. He received a B.S. and M.B.A. from Indiana University and a Ph.D. in accounting from the University of Iowa. Professor Warfield's area of expertise is financial reporting, and prior to his academic career, he worked for five years in the banking industry. He served as the Academic Accounting Fellow in the Office of the Chief Accountant at the U.S. Securities and Exchange Commission in Washington, D.C., from 1995-1996. While on the staff, he worked on projects related to financial instruments and financial institutions, and he helped coordinate a symposium on intangible asset financial reporting. Professor Warfield's primary research interests concern financial accounting standards and disclosure policies. He has published scholarly articles in *The Accounting Review, Journal of Accounting and Economics, Research in Accounting Regulation,* and *Accounting Horizons,* and he has served on the editorial boards of *The Accounting Review, Accounting Horizons,* and *Issues in Accounting Education.* He has served on the Financial Accounting Standards Committee of the American Accounting Association (Chair 1995-1996) and the AAA-FASB Research Conference Committee. Professor Warfield has received teaching awards at both the University of Iowa and the University of Wisconsin, and he was named to the Teaching Academy at the University of Wisconsin in 1995.

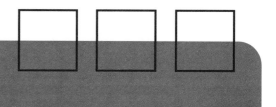

Preface

The first Canadian edition of *Intermediate Accounting* made its appearance over twenty years ago. Over the years it has changed, as have the many students who have used it. This edition represents another step in the metamorphosis of the textbook, with changes that reflect the way accounting is currently practised and the way in which students come to understand these concepts and procedures.

As always, we have aimed for a balanced discussion of the concepts and the procedures so that these elements reinforce one another. We have focused on the rationale behind transactions before discussing the accounting and reporting for those transactions. As with previous editions, we have thoroughly updated and revised every chapter to include coverage of all of the latest developments in the accounting profession and practice. In addition, we have included features to make all of this coverage even more understandable and relevant to today's accounting student. We have completely updated the look of the text, added new pedagogical features, enhanced the technology package that accompanies the text, and we continue to emphasize the use of company data and examples so that students easily relate what they are learning to the real world of business.

Based on extensive reviews and interactions with intermediate accounting instructors and students from across the country, we have introduced new features to help students learn and made content changes to ensure that Kieso, Weygandt, Warfield, Young, Wiecek, *Intermediate Accounting* sets the standard for currency, continuing to reflect the most up-to-date standards and reasons for their evolution.

NEW FEATURES

Student-friendly Design

We are pleased to present the concepts of intermediate accounting in an all-new four-colour design. We believe this student-friendly look will help to ease the transition into this more complex course. The use of colour also allows us to better highlight the pedagogical features and provide clear scans of the financial statements we use to illustrate the concepts presented thereby enhancing the realism even further and ensuring accuracy.

Enhanced Pedagogical Structure

Four new features have been introduced to the text's already solid pedagogical structure. We have enhanced our chapter opening even further with the introduction of new feature stories that introduce students to the concepts about to be discussed through real Canadian business situations. Throughout each chapter students are asked "What do the Numbers Mean?" and are presented with discussions applying accounting concepts to business contexts. These short breaks in the text will help students fully appreciate, from a business perspective, the impact of accounting on decision-making. In addition, a "Perspectives" section has been added to most chapters. This section discusses the effect on the financial statements of many of the accounting choices made by corporate management, alerting students to look behind the numbers. Finally, the accounting equation has been inserted in the margin next to key journal entries to help students understand the impact of each transaction on the financial position and cash flows of the company.

What do the Numbers Mean?

New Cases

New case material has been incorporated to reinforce the importance of in-context, applied decision-making. In addition to understanding the mechanics and theory of accounting, students also need to be sensitized to the fact that accounting decisions are not made in a vacuum. They involve businesses and people with biases, problems, and complexities. The cases feature both real companies and fictitious scenarios. The former allows us to expose students to reading and interpreting real financial statement excerpts. The latter allows us to develop the financial reporting environment scenario more fully, giving students insight into the thought processes that might occur behind the scenes in financial reporting. The "Integrative Cases" that appear in many of the chapters incorporate several issues in each case. These issues draw from material in other chapters in order to help students build issue identification skills. Finally, we have added a "Case Primer" on the Digital Tool which provides a framework for case analysis.

Integration of Ethics Coverage

Rather than featuring ethics coverage and problem material in isolation, we have introduced a new ethics icon to highlight ethical issues as they are discussed within each chapter. This icon also appears beside each exercise, problem, or case where ethical issues must be dealt with in relation to all kinds of accounting situations.

Increased Technology

Kieso continues to provide the most comprehensive and useful technology package available for the intermediate course. With this edition, there are three key components to the technology package.

Interactive Homework is available to all students at the text website. This new feature allows them to work the problems indicated in the text with the Interactive Homework icon on-line. They will be able to try the questions an unlimited number of times as the variables presented will change with each try. They will also get instant feedback so they know how they are doing.

Interactive Homework

eGrade is an expanded version of Interactive Homework that provides instructors with all of the end-of-chapter exercises and problems, allowing them to create the assignments they want. With this added instructor involvement, attempts at completing the assignments are recorded in a gradebook where the progress of each student can be tracked.

We have enhanced the *Digital Tool*. This collection of useful tools is now accessed from the text website using the password provided in the back of each text. New to this edition are interactive tutorials on the accounting cycle, interest capitalization, and more. Also featured are a case primer, demonstration problems, and expanded ethics coverage.

CONTINUING FEATURES

Many things have contributed to the success of Kieso over the last twenty years. Chief among these are its real-world emphasis and its currency and accuracy.

Real-World Emphasis

Since intermediate accounting is a course in which students must understand the application of accounting principles and techniques in practice, we strive to include as many real-world examples as possible.

Currency and Accuracy

Accounting changes at a rapid pace—a pace that has increased in recent years. An up-to-date book is more important than ever. As in past editions, we have endeavored to make this edition the most up-to-date and accurate text available.

The following list outlines the revisions and improvements made in the chapters in **Volume Two**.

Chapter 14

- New *CICA Handbook*/Exposure Draft/EIC material on Disclosure of Guarantees, Separately Priced Extended Warranty Contracts, and Asset Retirement Obligations.
- Section on Property Taxes Payable deleted.
- Discussion of operating lines of credit and section on asset retirement obligations added.
- Material on product guarantees and warranties reordered and rewritten to clarify the cash/accrual discussion. Update on separately priced extended warranties.
- Expansion of Income Taxes Payable section to include entries.
- Days payables outstanding ratio added.

Chapter 15

- Discussion of complex financial instruments moved to new chapter 17. This leaves traditional financial instruments such as bonds and notes in chapter 15.
- Off-balance sheet financing discussion rewritten to incorporate references to Special Purpose/Variable Interest Entities and operating leases.
- Extinguishment of debt discussion expanded to incorporate material on defeasance transactions and exchanges of debt instruments.

Chapter 16

- Material from sixth edition chapter 17 and 17A combined with chapter 16 so that all basic shareholders' equity material is in the same place.
- More complex material relating to financial instruments moved to new chapter 17.
- Reference made to proposed *Handbook* section on Other Comprehensive Income (material covered in chapters 4 and 5).

Chapter 17

- This new chapter has been created so that the more complex material on financial instruments is pulled together. The structure of the chapter is modular for ease of use and includes the following:
  - Updated material from the new *CICA Handbook*/Exposure Draft/EIC material on Financial Instruments, Hedges and Stock Based Compensation.
  - Section on Hybrid/Compound Instruments moved from Chapters 15, 16 and 18 and expanded to include dealing with uncertainty and special features of these instruments.
  - Section on Basic Derivatives with a risk management focus—material moved from Chapter 18 and expanded to include a new framework for understanding options as well as accounting for futures contracts.
  - Section on Stock Compensation Plans—material moved from Chapter 18 and updated. Material linked into new options framework.
  - Appendix on Hedging moved from Chapter 18 and expanded to include material on cash flow hedges.

Chapter 18

- Material on dilutive securities and compensation plans moved from chapter 18 and appendix 18A to chapter 17.
- Derivatives moved from appendix 18B to chapter 17.
- More complex earnings per share example brought back from Digital Tool.

Chapter 19

- New *Handbook* material on Differential Accounting.
- New section added on differential accounting for income taxes.
- Increased emphasis on the differences between balance sheet book and tax values.
- New section added on using a valuation allowance for Future Tax Assets.

Chapter 20

- New *Handbook* material on disclosure requirements for Employee Future Benefits.
- Short sections added on the funding of pension plans and the extent of measurement uncertainty associated with the pension amounts recognized and disclosed.
- Introduction of a simplified one-person pension arrangement as a basis for explaining basic pension terminology (Appendix).

Chapter 21

- Section on real estate leases added in Appendix.

Chapter 22

- New *CICA Handbook*/Exposure Draft material on Accounting Changes and Generally Accepted Accounting Principles.
- Overview of the revised GAAP hierarchy and new Section 1100's relationship to revised Section 1506.
- Fuller explanation of reporting retroactive changes with restatement.
- Expanded discussion of financial statement analysis issues related to accounting changes.
- Section on changes in the accounting entity deleted.

Chapter 23

- New *Handbook* material on Cash Flow per Share Information.
- Increased emphasis on interpreting the cash flow statement.
- Examples of companies who use the direct method in the operating cash flow section.
- Section added on free cash flow.

Chapter 24

- New *Handbook* material on Differential Reporting.
- Increased emphasis on related party transactions.
- Updated section on continuous reporting.
- Increased discussion on measurement uncertainty including reference to executory contracts.
- New material on partnerships.

ACKNOWLEDGMENTS

We thank the users of our sixth edition, including the many students who contributed to this revision through their comments and instructive criticism. Special thanks are extended to the reviewers of and contributors to our seventh edition manuscript and supplements.

Manuscript Reviewers for this seventh edition were:

Cécile Ashman
Algonquin College

Dominique Lecocq
York University

Maria Belanger
Algonquin College

Valorie Leonard
Laurentian University

David T. Carter
University of Waterloo

Cameron Morrill
University of Manitoba

Johan De Rooy
University of British Columbia

Clifton Philpott
Kwantlen University College

Esther Deutsch
Ryerson University

Joe Pidutti
Durham College

Carolyn Doni
Cambrian College

Wendy Roscoe
Concordia University

David Fleming
George Brown College

Jo-Anne Ryan
Nipissing University

H.T. Hao
McMaster University

David J. Sale
Kwantlen University College

Mary A. Heisz
University of Western Ontario

Helen Vallee
Kwantlen University College

Darrell Herauf
Carleton University

Betty Wong
Athabasca University

Johnny Jermias
Simon Fraser University

Appreciation is also extended to colleagues at the Rotman School of Management, University of Toronto and Saint Mary's University who provided input, suggestions and support, especially Joel Amernic and Dick Chesley—who have provided inspiration through many high-spirited debates on financial reporting theory and practice—and Peter Thomas, who has shared many teaching insights over the years!

Many thanks to the staff at John Wiley and Sons Canada, Ltd. who are superb: Publisher John Horne and Editorial Manager Karen Staudinger who have been so supportive throughout; Karen Bryan, Publishing Services Director, for her incredible efforts; Elsa Passera, New Media Editor who took on the Digital Tool; Carl Comeau and Darren Lalonde, Sales Managers; Janine Daoust, Sr. Marketing Manager; and of course all the sales representatives who introduce us and the text to the many talented instructors across the country. They are a committed group of capable people who feed back concerns, questions, and kudos to help us continually improve. The editorial contributions of Laurel Hyatt and Alan Johnstone were also appreciated. Thanks also go to Alison Arnot, for researching and writing the opening vignettes for each chapter. We are particularly grateful to Leanne Rancourt and Amanjeet Chauhan who dealt with us on an almost daily basis and kept everything on track.

Special thanks also to Margaret Forbes, Ann Bigelow, Sibongile Mukandi, and Sophie (Zhi Hua) He for their contributions to the Digital Tool and research services, as well as Cécile Ashman, Maria Belanger, Lynn deGrace, Brock Dykeman, Ian Farmer, Majidul Islam, Gabriela Schneider, Enola Stoyle, and Lisa White who contributed to the related supplements.

We appreciate the co-operation of the staff of the Accounting Standards Board of the Canadian Institute of Chartered Accountants, especially that of its Director, Ron Salole, as well as that of the CICA itself in allowing us to quote from their materials. We thank Intrawest Corporation for permitting us to use its 2003 Annual Report for our specimen financial statements.

Finally, we would like to thank Bruce Irvine and Harold Silvester who, through twenty years of association with and five editions of this text, provided such a strong foundation. Their enthusiasm for intermediate accounting and their sharing of this with so many students set a standard for the rest of us to follow.

If this book helps teachers instill in their students an appreciation of the challenges, value, and limitations of accounting, if it encourages students to evaluate critically and understand financial accounting theory and practice, and if it prepares students for advanced study, professional examinations, and the successful and ethical pursuit of their careers in accounting or business, then we will have attained our objective.

Suggestions and comments from users of this book are always appreciated. We have striven to produce an error-free text, but if anything has slipped through the variety of checks undertaken, please let us know so that corrections can be made to subsequent printings.

Irene M. Wiecek   Nicola M. Young
TORONTO, ONTARIO   HALIFAX, NOVA SCOTIA

June 2004

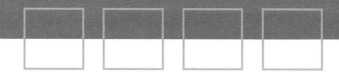

BRIEF CONTENTS

CONTENTS

Tracking Points

Sears Canada credit card holders automatically enter a club: the Sears Club, whose members earn one point for every dollar they charge to their card. When they have a minimum 1,000 points, they can redeem them for Sears Club Certificates, which are as good as cash at any Sears store. However, the points do have an expiry date and must be redeemed within 30 months.

Sears has a high redemption rate, says David Merkley, vice-president and corporate comptroller at Sears Canada. Still, there are some cardholders who redeem points for certificates but then don't cash the certificates, and others never redeem their points at all.

So how does Sears track and account for its potential obligation to these various point collectors? The liability inherent in the points program is tracked at the time of sale, Merkley explains. Sears keeps track of six-month, 12-month, 24-month, and 36-month rolling average redemption rates. The six-month figures are good for seasonal comparisons, since, for example, December is typically a busy time for point redemption. With the 24-month average, however, Sears can get a good estimate of how many points will be redeemed in the future by looking at past redemption patterns.

Sears tracks the sales charged to its credit card, which amount to approximately 60% of its total sales. Since these purchases garner points for the card holder, a percentage of the sale is recorded in a liability account with the offset noted as a marketing expense. "As people use coupons to buy merchandise in the store, we then debit that liability account," Merkley says.

The expiry date allows for easy accounting of the current liability. "Canadian accounting allows you to bring that 'leakage' back into your income, but it does require that you have some means of quantifying it," Merkley says. Once the points have expired, Sears can debit the liability account for that amount and credit the income statement for the expense that had been set up 30 months earlier. ■

CHAPTER 14

Current Liabilities and Contingencies

Learning Objectives

After studying this chapter, you should be able to:

1. Define liabilities and differentiate between financial and other liabilities.
2. Define current liabilities, describe how they are valued, and identify common types of current liabilities.
3. Explain the classification issues of short-term debt expected to be refinanced.
4. Identify and account for the major types of employee-related liabilities.
5. Explain the accounting for common estimated liabilities.
6. Explain the recognition, measurement, and disclosure requirements for asset retirement obligations.
7. Explain the accounting and reporting standards for loss contingencies and commitments.
8. Indicate how current liabilities, and contingencies and commitments are presented and analysed.

Preview of Chapter 14

The purpose of this chapter is to explain the basic principles underlying accounting and reporting for current liabilities, asset retirement obligations, and contingent liabilities, commitments, and guarantees. Chapter 15 addresses issues related to long-term liabilities. The content and organization of this chapter are as follows:

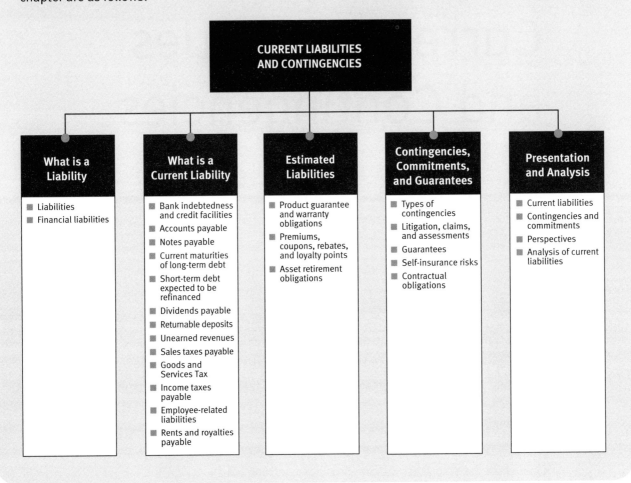

CURRENT LIABILITIES AND CONTINGENCIES

What is a Liability
- Liabilities
- Financial liabilities

What is a Current Liability
- Bank indebtedness and credit facilities
- Accounts payable
- Notes payable
- Current maturities of long-term debt
- Short-term debt expected to be refinanced
- Dividends payable
- Returnable deposits
- Unearned revenues
- Sales taxes payable
- Goods and Services Tax
- Income taxes payable
- Employee-related liabilities
- Rents and royalties payable

Estimated Liabilities
- Product guarantee and warranty obligations
- Premiums, coupons, rebates, and loyalty points
- Asset retirement obligations

Contingencies, Commitments, and Guarantees
- Types of contingencies
- Litigation, claims, and assessments
- Guarantees
- Self-insurance risks
- Contractual obligations

Presentation and Analysis
- Current liabilities
- Contingencies and commitments
- Perspectives
- Analysis of current liabilities

WHAT IS A LIABILITY?

The question, "What is a liability?" is not easy to answer. For example, one might ask whether preferred shares are a liability or an ownership claim. The first reaction is to say that preferred shares are in fact an ownership claim and should be reported as part of shareholders' equity. In fact, preferred shares have many elements of debt.[1] The issuer (and in some cases the holder) often has the right to call in the shares within a specific

---

[1] This illustration is not just a theoretical exercise. In practice, there are a number of preferred share issues that have all the characteristics of a debt instrument, except that they are called—and legally classified as—preferred shares. In some cases, Canada Revenue Agency (CRA) has even permitted the dividend payments to be treated as interest expense for tax purposes.

period of time, making it similar to a repayment of principal. The dividend is often cumulative, making it almost guaranteed and similar to interest. Preferred shares are only one of many financial instruments that are difficult to classify.[2]

Liabilities

To help resolve controversies, the Accounting Standards Board defines liabilities in Section 1000 of the *CICA Handbook* as "**obligations of an enterprise arising from past transactions or events, the settlement of which may result in the transfer of assets, provisions of services or other yielding of economic benefits in the future.**"[3] In other words, a liability has three essential characteristics.

1. It is an obligation to others that entails settlement by future transfer or use of cash or other assets, provision of goods or services on a determinable date, or on the occurrence of some specified event.

2. The entity has little or no discretion to avoid the obligation.

3. The transaction or other event creating the obligation has already occurred.[4]

Because liabilities involve future disbursements of assets or services, one of the most important features is when they are payable. Currently maturing obligations represent a demand on the enterprise's current assets—a demand that must be satisfied promptly and in the ordinary course of business if operations are to continue. Liabilities with a more distant due date do not, as a rule, represent a claim on the enterprise's current resources and are therefore in a different category. This feature gives rise to the basic division of liabilities into (1) current liabilities and (2) long-term liabilities.

1 Objective
Define liabilities and differentiate between financial and other liabilities.

Financial Liabilities

A distinction is also made between financial liabilities and those that are not financial in nature. Financial liabilities are contractual obligations to deliver cash or other financial assets to another party, or to exchange financial instruments with another party under conditions that are potentially unfavourable.[5] The significance of such a distinction becomes greater as the profession begins to apply an accounting model where certain financial assets and financial liabilities are measured in terms of their fair value rather than historic (amortized) cost.[6] Some financial liabilities that historically have not been measured require recognition and measurement under the revised model. In this chapter, most current liabilities are financial in nature, although obligations to be met by the delivery of goods or services (e.g., unearned revenue and warranty obligations) are not financial liabilities.

WHAT IS A CURRENT LIABILITY?

The definition of a current liability is directly related to the definition of a current asset. Current assets are cash or other assets that can reasonably be expected to be converted into

2 Objective
Define current liabilities, describe how they are valued, and identify common types of current liabilities.

---

[2] *CICA Handbook* Section 3860, "Financial Instruments," addresses the issues involved in distinguishing between financial liabilities and equity instruments. Chapter 17 provides a fuller discussion of this issue.

[3] *CICA Handbook* Section 1000.32.

[4] *CICA Handbook* Section 1000.33.

[5] *CICA Handbook* Section 3860.05(c).

[6] Refer to Chapters 10, 15, and 17 for a summary of the steps taken to this text's publication date relative to the use of fair values.

International Insight

In France, the balance sheet does not show current liabilities in a separate category. Rather, debts are disclosed separately by maturity in the notes.

cash, sold, or consumed in operations within a year from the balance sheet date or within a single operating cycle if a cycle is longer than a year. Current liabilities, although not defined in the *CICA Handbook*, are described as including "**amounts payable within one year from the date of the balance sheet or within the normal operating cycle where this is longer than a year**" and it is specified that the normal operating cycle should correspond with that used for current assets.[7] This description has gained wide acceptance because it recognizes operating cycles of varying lengths in different industries and takes into consideration the important relationship between current assets and current liabilities.

The operating cycle is the period of time elapsing between the acquisition of goods and services involved in operations (such as the manufacturing process) and the final cash realization resulting from sales of goods and services and their subsequent collections. Industries that manufacture products requiring an aging process and certain capital-intensive industries have an operating cycle of considerably more than one year. On the other hand, most retail and service establishments have several operating cycles within a year.

There are many different types of current liabilities. The following ones are covered in this section in the order indicated.

1. Bank indebtedness and credit facilities

2. Accounts payable

3. Notes payable

4. Current maturities of long-term debt

5. Short-term debt expected to be refinanced

6. Dividends payable

7. Returnable deposits

8. Unearned revenues

9. Sales taxes

10. Goods and Services Tax

11. Income taxes

12. Employee-related liabilities

13. Rents and royalties

Bank Indebtedness and Credit Facilities

Closely allied with a company's cash position is its bank indebtedness for current operating purposes and its associated line-of-credit or revolving debt arrangements. Instead of having to negotiate a new loan every time the company needs funds, it generally enters into an agreement with its bank to make multiple borrowings up to a negotiated limit. As portions of previous borrowings are repaid, the company is permitted to reborrow under the same contract.[8] Because the financial institution commits itself to making money available to the borrower, the bank often charges a fee for this service over and above interest on the funds actually advanced. In addition, the financial institution usually requires collateral and often imposes restrictions on the company's activities or financial statement ratios.

While the amount of bank indebtedness is reported on the balance sheet, the total funds available to be drawn under the credit arrangement and any restrictions imposed by the financial institution are disclosed in the notes.

---

[7] *CICA Handbook* Section 1510.03.

[8] *Emerging Issues Committee Abstract* EIC-101.

Rapid growth must be carefully managed! **Pacific Safety Products Inc. (PSP)**, based in British Columbia, enjoyed a 69% increase in sales in its fiscal year ended June 30, 2002 and along with it, suffered liquidity problems that often accompany such success. The company's 2002 annual report indicates that its major challenges included managing its cash flow to ensure that its suppliers continued to supply raw materials so that the manufacturing process could continue to meet customer orders on a timely basis. Maintaining close working relationships with customers, banks, suppliers, and other creditors was central to getting through the crunch.

At June 30, 2002, PSP reported bank indebtedness of almost $3 million in its current liabilities. A note to the financial statements indicated a maximum operating line of credit of $3 million with the Bank of Nova Scotia, secured by accounts receivable, inventory, and an assignment of insurance. It also reported that the company was not in compliance with the covenants imposed by the bank regarding the level of the current ratio and tangible net worth, but that the Bank of Nova Scotia was allowing PSP to operate outside its covenants.

One year later, for the company's year ended June 30, 2003, PSP's sales were 75% of those reported for the preceding fiscal year, but its cash flow from operating activities was 189% of that reported for 2002! The uncollected receivables from one year earlier were collected and allowed the company to get over the cash crunch. Bank indebtedness was reported at only $102,417 at June 30, 2003, the operating line was reduced to $2 million, and the company was once again in compliance with the covenants imposed by the bank.

Accounts Payable

Accounts payable, or trade accounts payable, are balances owed to others for goods, supplies, or services purchased on open account. Accounts payable arise because of the time lag between the receipt of services or acquisition of title to assets and the payment for them. This period of extended credit is usually found in the terms of sale (and purchase), for example, 2/10, n/30 or 1/10, E.O.M. and is commonly 30 to 60 days.

Most accounting systems are designed to record liabilities for purchases of goods when the goods are received or, practically, when the invoices are received. Frequently there is some delay in recording the goods and the related liability on the books. If title has passed to the purchaser before the goods are received, the transaction should be recorded at the time of title passage. Attention must be paid to transactions occurring near the end of one accounting period and the beginning of the next to ensure that the record of goods or services received (the inventory or expense) is in agreement with the liability (accounts payable) and that both are recorded in the proper period. Chapter 8 discussed this cut-off issue at more length.

Measuring the amount of an account payable poses no particular difficulty because the invoice received from the creditor specifies the due date and the exact outlay in money terms that is necessary to settle the account. The only calculation that may be necessary concerns the amount of cash discount. Again, refer to Chapter 8 for illustrations of entries related to accounts payable and purchase discounts.

Notes Payable

Notes payable are written promises to pay a certain sum of money on a specified future date and may arise from purchases, financing, or other transactions. In some industries, notes (often referred to as trade notes payable) are required as part of the sales/purchases transaction in lieu of the normal extension of open account credit. Notes payable to banks or loan companies generally arise from cash loans. Notes may be classified as short-term or long-term, depending on the payment due date. Notes may also be interest-bearing or noninterest-bearing (i.e., zero-interest-bearing).

Interest-Bearing Note Issued

Assume that the Provincial Bank agrees to lend $100,000 on March 1, 2005 to Landscape Corp. if the company signs a $100,000, 12%, four-month note. The entry to record the cash received by Landscape Corp. on March 1 is:

A   =   L   + SE
+100,000   +100,000

Cash flows: ↑ 100,000 inflow

March 1		
Cash	100,000	
Notes Payable		100,000
To record the issue of 12% four-month note to Provincial Bank.		

If Landscape Corp. has a December 31 year end but prepares financial statements semiannually, an adjusting entry is required to recognize interest expense and interest payable of $4,000 ($100,000 × 12% × 4/12) on June 30. The adjusting entry is:

A   =   L   +   SE
+4,000   −4,000

Cash flows: No effect

June 30		
Interest Expense	4,000	
Interest Payable		4,000
To accrue interest for four months on Provincial Bank note.		

If Landscape prepares financial statements monthly, the adjusting entry at the end of each month is $1,000 ($100,000 × 12% × 1/12).

At maturity (July 1), Landscape Corp. must pay the note's face value of $100,000 plus $4,000 interest ($100,000 × 12% × 4/12). The entry to record payment of the note and accrued interest is as follows.

A   =   L   + SE
−104,000   −104,000

Cash flows: ↓ 104,000 outflow

July 1		
Notes Payable	100,000	
Interest Payable	4,000	
Cash		104,000
To record payment of Provincial Bank note and accrued interest at maturity.		

Zero-Interest-Bearing Note Issued

A zero-interest-bearing note, previously discussed in Chapters 7 and 10 from the perspective of the lender, may be issued instead of an interest-bearing note. Contrary to its name, a **zero-interest-bearing note does have an interest component,** it is just not added on top of its face or maturity value. Instead, the interest is included in the face amount. It is the difference between the amount of cash received when the note is signed and the face amount payable at maturity. The borrower receives the note's present value in cash and pays back the larger maturity value.

To illustrate, assume that Landscape Corp. issues a $104,000, four-month, zero-interest-bearing note to the Provincial Bank. The note's present value is $100,000.[9] Landscape's entry to record this transaction is as follows.

A   =   L   + SE
+100,000   +100,000

Cash flows: ↑ 100,000 inflow

March 1		
Cash	100,000	
Discount on Notes Payable	4,000	
Notes Payable		104,000
To record issuance of zero-interest-bearing note to Provincial Bank.		

[9] The bank discount rate used in this example to find the present value is 11.538%.

The Notes Payable account is credited for the note's face value, which is $4,000 more than the actual cash received. The difference between the cash received and the note's face value is debited to Discount on Notes Payable. **Discount on Notes Payable is a contra account to Notes Payable and therefore is subtracted from Notes Payable on the balance sheet**. The balance sheet presentation on March 1 is provided in Illustration 14-1.

Current liabilities		
Notes payable	$104,000	
Less: Discount on notes payable	4,000	$100,000

Illustration 14-1

Balance Sheet Presentation of Discount

The amount of the discount, $4,000 in this case, represents the cost of borrowing $100,000 for four months. Accordingly, the discount is charged to interest expense over the life of the note. That is, the debit balance in the Discount on Notes Payable account represents interest expense chargeable to future periods. Instead of reporting it as a current asset, however, it is reported netted against the Note Payable. Additional accounting issues related to long-term notes payable are discussed in Chapter 15.

Current Maturities of Long-Term Debt

Bonds, mortgage notes, and other long-term indebtedness that mature within 12 months from the balance sheet date—current maturities of long-term debt—are reported as current liabilities. When only part of a long-term obligation is to be paid within the next 12 months, as in the case of serial bonds that are to be retired through a series of annual instalments, **only the maturing portion of long-term debt is reported as a current liability**. The balance is reported as a long-term liability.

Long-term debts maturing currently should not be included as current liabilities if they are to be:

1. retired by assets accumulated for this purpose that properly have not been shown as current assets,

2. refinanced or retired from the proceeds of a new debt issue (see next topic), or

3. converted into share capital.

In these situations, the use of current assets or the creation of other current liabilities does not occur. Therefore, classification as a current liability is inappropriate. The plan for liquidation of such a debt is disclosed in a note to the financial statements.

However, a liability that is **due on demand** (callable by the creditor) or will be due on demand within a year, or operating cycle if longer, should be classified as a current liability. Liabilities often become callable by the creditor when there is a violation of the debt agreement. For example, most debt agreements specify a given level of equity to debt that must be maintained, or as illustrated in the Pacific Safety Products situation described above, specify that working capital be of a minimum amount.

If an agreement is violated, classification of the debt as current is required because it is a reasonable expectation that existing working capital will be used to satisfy the debt. The liability can be classified as noncurrent only if the creditor waives the covenant requirements or the violation has been cured within the grace period usually given in these agreements **and it is likely** that the company will not violate the covenant requirements within a year from the balance sheet date.[10]

---

[10] *EIC-59* "Long-Term Debt with Covenant Violations" provides a more detailed discussion of the specific requirements.

Short-Term Debt Expected to Be Refinanced

Objective 3

Explain the classification issues of short-term debt expected to be refinanced.

Short-term obligations are those debts that are scheduled to mature within one year from the date of an enterprise's balance sheet or within its operating cycle, if longer. **Short-term obligations expected to be refinanced** on a long-term basis, however, are not expected to require the use of working capital during the next year or operating cycle.[11]

At one time, the accounting profession generally supported the exclusion of short-term obligations from current liabilities if they were "expected to be refinanced." Because the profession provided no specific guidelines, however, determining whether a short-term obligation was "expected to be refinanced" was usually based solely on management's **intent** to refinance on a long-term basis. A company could obtain a five-year bank loan but, because the bank prefers it, handle the actual financing with 90-day notes, which it keeps turning over or renewing. It was then unclear whether the loan was a long-term or a current liability.

Refinancing Criteria

As a result of these classification problems, authoritative criteria have been developed for determining the circumstances under which short-term obligations may properly be excluded from current liabilities. *CICA Handbook* Section 1510 requires the exclusion of short-term obligations from current liabilities "to the extent that contractual arrangements have been made for settlement from other than current assets."[12] *EIC-122* further addresses this issue by requiring a company to meet **both of the following criteria** in order to exclude amounts from the current category.[13]

1. The entity must **intend to refinance** the obligation on a long-term basis so that the use of working capital will not be required during the following year or operating cycle, if longer.

2. The entity must **demonstrate an ability** to consummate the refinancing. This could be demonstrated by:

   a) actually refinancing the obligation by issuing a long-term obligation or issuing shares after the balance sheet date but before the financial statements are issued; or

   b) entering into a financing agreement that clearly permits the refinancing on a long-term basis on terms that are readily determinable.

If an actual refinancing occurs, the portion of the short-term obligation to be excluded from current liabilities may not exceed the proceeds from the new obligation or equity securities that are applied to retire it. For example, assume Montavon Winery, with $3 million of short-term debt, issued 100,000 common shares subsequent to the balance sheet date but before the balance sheet was issued, intending to use the proceeds to liquidate the short-term debt at its maturity. If the net proceeds from the sale of the 100,000 shares totalled $2 million, only the amount of the short-term debt can be excluded from current liabilities.

An additional question relates to whether a short-term obligation should be excluded from current liabilities if it is paid off after the balance sheet date and subsequently replaced by long-term debt before the balance sheet is issued. To illustrate, assume Marquardt Limited pays off short-term debt of $40,000 on January 17, 2006 and issues long-term debt of $100,000 on February 3, 2006. Marquardt's financial statements dated December 31, 2005 are to be issued March 1, 2006. Because repayment of the short-term obligation

---

[11] Refinancing a short-term obligation on a long-term basis means either replacing it with a long-term obligation or with equity securities, or renewing, extending, or replacing it with short-term obligations for an uninterrupted period extending beyond one year (or the operating cycle, if longer) from the date of the enterprise's balance sheet.

[12] *CICA Handbook* Section 1510.06.

[13] *EIC-122*, "Balance Sheet Classification of Callable Debt Obligations and Debt Obligations Expected to be Refinanced." October 31, 2001: amended July 24, 2002. (CICA).

before funds were obtained through long-term financing required the use of **existing** current assets, the profession requires that the short-term obligation be included in current liabilities at the balance sheet date. This is shown graphically in Illustration 14-2.

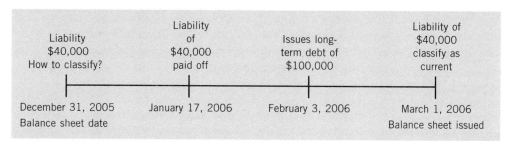

Illustration 14-2

Short-Term Debt Paid off after Balance Sheet Date and Later Replaced by Long-Term Debt

The Canadian standards in this area are expected to get even tighter in the next couple of years. In 2004, FASB was in process of converging with the IASB position that classifies liabilities being refinanced as current liabilities if the refinancing agreement is not completed **by the balance sheet date**. Liabilities due on demand due to violations of debt covenants would also be classified as current unless the lender has agreed **on or before the balance sheet date** to conditions that would allow a non-current classification. The Canadian AcSB is likely to harmonize its standards with the IASB and FASB after both have their standards in place—likely in 2005.

Dividends Payable

A **cash dividend payable** is an amount owed by a corporation to its shareholders resulting from an authorization by the board of directors. At the dividend declaration date, the corporation assumes a liability that places the shareholders in the position of creditors in the amount of dividends declared. Because cash dividends are normally paid within one year of declaration (generally within three months), they are classified as current liabilities.

Accumulated but undeclared dividends on cumulative preferred shares **are not recognized as a liability** because **preferred dividends in arrears** are not an obligation until formal action is taken by the board of directors to authorize the earnings' distribution. Nevertheless, the amount of cumulative dividends unpaid is required to be disclosed, usually in a note to the financial statements.

Dividends payable in the form of additional shares **are not recognized as a liability.** Such stock dividends (discussed in Chapter 16) do not meet the definition of a liability because they do not require future outlays of assets or services. In addition, they are revocable by the board of directors at any time prior to issuance. Undistributed stock dividends are generally reported in the shareholders' equity section because they represent retained earnings in the process of transfer to contributed capital.

Underlying Concept

Preferred dividends in arrears represent a probable future economic sacrifice, but the expected sacrifice does not result from a past transaction or past event. The sacrifice will result from a future event (declaration by the board of directors). Note disclosure improves the predictive value of the financial statements.

Returnable Deposits

A company's current liabilities may include **returnable cash deposits** received from customers and employees. Deposits may be received from customers to guarantee performance of a contract or service or as guarantees to cover payment of expected future obligations. For example, telephone companies often require a deposit when installing a phone. Deposits may also be received from customers or tenants as guarantees for possible damage to property left with the customer. Some companies require their employees to make deposits for the return of keys or other company property. The classification of these items as current or noncurrent liabilities is dependent on the time between the date of the deposit and the termination of the relationship that required the deposit.

Unearned Revenues

A magazine publisher such as **Golf Digest** may receive a customer's cheque when magazines are ordered, and an airline, such as **Air Canada**, often sells tickets for future flights. Restaurants may issue meal tickets that can be exchanged or used for future meals. (Who hasn't received or given a **McDonald's** gift certificate?) Retail stores may issue gift certificates that are redeemable for merchandise. How do these companies account for unearned revenues that are received before goods are delivered or services rendered?

1. When the advance is received, Cash is debited, and a current liability account identifying the source of the unearned revenue is credited.

2. When the revenue is earned, the unearned revenue account is reduced (debited), and an earned revenue account is credited.

To illustrate, assume that the Rambeau Football Club sells 5,000 season football tickets at $50 each for its five-game home schedule. The entry for the sales of season tickets is:

A	=	L	+ SE			
+250,000		+250,000		Cash	250,000	
				Unearned Football Ticket Revenue		250,000

Cash flows: ↑ 250,000 inflow

To record the sale of 5,000 season tickets.

As each game is completed, the following entry is made.

A	=	L	+	SE			
		−50,000		+50,000	Unearned Football Ticket Revenue	50,000	
					Football Ticket Revenue		50,000

Cash flows: No effect

To record football ticket revenues earned.

The balance in the Unearned Football Ticket Revenue account, therefore, is unearned revenue and is reported as a current liability in the balance sheet. As revenue is earned, a transfer from unearned revenue to earned revenue occurs. Unearned revenue is material for some companies. In the airline industry, tickets sold for future flights represent a significant portion of total current liabilities. **WestJet**'s unearned ticket revenue represented 33.5% of its current liabilities at September 30, 2003, up from 25.2% at December 31, 2002. This change might be expected due to the different times of year. **Air Canada** reported advance ticket sales relative to current liabilities of 20.7% and 19.5%, respectively, at the same dates.

Illustration 14-3 indicates specific unearned and earned revenue accounts that might be used in selected industries.

<table>
<tr><td rowspan="2">Industry Type</td><td colspan="2" align="center">Account Title</td></tr>
<tr><td>Unearned revenue</td><td>Earned revenue</td></tr>
<tr><td>Airline</td><td>Advance Ticket Sales</td><td>Passenger Revenue</td></tr>
<tr><td>Magazine publisher</td><td>Deferred Subscription Revenue</td><td>Subscription Revenue</td></tr>
<tr><td>Hotel</td><td>Advance Room Deposits</td><td>Room Revenue</td></tr>
<tr><td>Auto dealer</td><td>Unearned Warranty Revenue</td><td>Warranty Revenue</td></tr>
</table>

Illustration 14-3

Unearned and Earned Revenue Accounts

The balance sheet reports liabilities for any obligations that are redeemable in goods and services; the income statement reports revenues earned during the period.

Sales Taxes Payable

Sales taxes on transfers of tangible property and on certain services must be collected from customers and remitted to the tax authority. The Sales Taxes Payable account reflects the liability for sales taxes collected from customers but not yet remitted to the appropriate government.[14] The entry below illustrates the accounting for a sale on account of $3,000 when a 4% sales tax is in effect.

Accounts Receivable	3,120	
Sales		3,000
Sales Taxes Payable		120

A = L + SE
+3,120 +120 +3,000
Cash flows: No effect

In some companies, however, the sales tax and the sale amount are not segregated at the time of sale; both are credited to the Sales account. In that case, to reflect the actual sales amount and the correct liability for sales taxes, the Sales account must be reduced (debited) for the amount of the sales taxes due the government on these sales and the Sales Taxes Payable account credited for the same amount. As an illustration, assume that the Sales account balance is $150,000, including sales taxes of 4%. Because the amount recorded in the Sales account is equal to sales plus 4% of sales, or 1.04 times the sales total, the sales are $150,000 divided by 1.04, or $144,230.77. The sales tax liability is $5,769.23 ($144,230.77 × 0.04; or $150,000 − $144,230.77), and the following entry is made to record the amount due the taxing authority.

| Sales | 5,769.23 | |
| Sales Taxes Payable | | 5,769.23 |

A = L + SE
+5,769.23 −5,769.23
Cash flows: No effect

Goods and Services Tax

Most businesses in Canada are subject to a Goods and Services Tax (GST). The GST is a tax on the value added by each taxable entity. The amount payable is determined by deducting the amount of GST paid to suppliers on goods and services purchased from the amount of GST collected on sales to customers.

Accounting for GST involves setting up a liability account—GST Payable—to be credited with GST charged on sales, and an asset account—GST Recoverable—which is debited for GST paid to suppliers. Normally, the amount collected on sales exceeds the amount paid on purchases so that a net remittance is made. Since GST is also paid on purchases of capital assets, it is possible for the GST Recoverable account to have a larger balance. In these instances, a claim for reimbursement is made to Canada Revenue Agency (CRA).

Purchases of taxable goods and services are recorded by debiting the GST Recoverable account for the amount of GST and debiting the appropriate account(s) for the purchase price. Since the amount of GST paid is a recoverable amount, the cost of items acquired should not normally include this tax. As an example, Bateman Limited purchases merchandise for $150,000 plus GST of 7% ($10,500). The entry to record this transaction if a perpetual inventory system is used follows.

Inventory	150,000	
GST Recoverable	10,500	
Accounts Payable		160,500

A = L + SE
+160,500 +160,500
Cash flows: No effect

---

[14] In New Brunswick, Newfoundland and Labrador, and Nova Scotia, the provincial retail sales tax has been combined with the federal Goods and Services Tax and named the Harmonized Sales Tax (HST). The HST is administered for the most part by CRA and is accounted for on the same basis as the GST for the other provinces and territories.

If these goods are sold for $210,000 plus GST of 7% ($14,700), the sale entry is:

A   =   L   +   SE
+224,700   +14,700   +210,000

Cash flows: No effect

Accounts Receivable	224,700	
Sales		210,000
GST Payable		14,700

Because companies are permitted to offset the recoverable and payable amounts, only the net balance of the two accounts is reported on the balance sheet. Until net credit balances are remitted to the Receiver General for Canada, they are reported as a current liability. A net debit balance, on the other hand, is reported as a current asset.

Income Taxes Payable

Federal and provincial income taxes vary in proportion to the amount of annual income. Some consider the amount of income tax on annual income as an estimate because the calculation of income (and the tax thereon) is subject to CRA review and approval. The meaning and application of numerous tax rules, especially new ones, are debatable and often dependent on a court's interpretation. Using the best information and advice available, a business must prepare an income tax return at the end of its fiscal year and calculate the income tax payable resulting from the operations of the current period. Assuming Forest Ltd. determines an income tax liability of $21,000 based on its taxable income for the year and no accruals have been made during the year, the following entry is required at year end.

A   =   L   +   SE
+21,000   -21,000

Cash flows: No effect

| Current Income Tax Expense | 21,000 | |
| Income Taxes Payable | | 21,000 |

Most corporations are required to make periodic tax instalments (payments) throughout the year based on last year's or estimates of their current year's income tax. Assume Forest Ltd. made entries summarized as follows.

A   =   L   +   SE
-20,000   -20,000

Cash flows: ↓ 20,000 outflow

| Income Taxes Payable | 20,000 | |
| Cash | | 20,000 |

Forest Ltd. reports an Income Taxes Payable balance of $1,000 in the current liability section of its year-end balance sheet ($21,000 − $20,000). Alternatively, if the company had made payments of $23,000, there would be a $2,000 debit balance in the Income Taxes Payable account ($23,000 − $21,000). This is reported as Income Taxes Receivable and included with the current assets.

An alternative method often used charges (debits) the instalment payments to expense. When the tax return is completed at year end and the actual amount of taxes for the year is known, the expense is adjusted. This series of entries is provided below.

Instalment payments of $20,000			**Instalment payments of $23,000**		
Current Income Tax Expense 20,000			Current Income Tax Expense	23,000	
Cash		20,000	Cash		23,000
Income taxes per tax return: $21,000			**Income taxes per tax return: $21,000**		
Current Income Tax Expense	1,000		Income Taxes Receivable	2,000	
Income Taxes Payable		1,000	Current Income Tax Expense		2,000

Regardless of which method is used, the resulting financial statements are identical.

If in a later year CRA assesses an additional tax on an earlier year's income, Income Taxes Payable is credited and the expense is charged to current operations.

Unlike corporations, proprietorships and partnerships are not taxable entities. Because the individual proprietor and the members of a partnership are subject to personal income taxes on their share of the business's taxable income, income tax liabilities do not appear on the financial statements of proprietorships and partnerships.

Differences between taxable income **under the tax laws** and accounting income **under generally accepted accounting principles** are common. Because of these differences, the amount of income tax payable to the government in any given year may differ substantially from the income tax expense that relates to income before taxes, as reported on the financial statements. Chapter 19 is devoted solely to the problems of accounting for income tax and presents an extensive discussion of related complex and interesting issues.

Employee-Related Liabilities

Amounts owed to employees for salaries or wages at the end of an accounting period are reported as a current liability. In addition, the following items related to employee compensation are often reported as current liabilities:

1. payroll deductions,
2. compensated absences, and
3. bonuses.

4 Objective
Identify and account for the major types of employee-related liabilities.

Payroll Deductions

The most common types of payroll deductions are income taxes, Canada (Quebec) Pension Plan, employment insurance, and miscellaneous items such as other insurance premiums, employee savings, and union dues. **To the extent the amounts deducted have not been remitted to the proper authority by the end of the accounting period, they are recognized as current liabilities along with any matching amounts required of the employer.**

Canada (Quebec) Pension Plan (CPP/QPP). The Canada and Quebec pension plans are financed by the imposition of taxes on both the employer and the employee. All employers are required to collect the employee's share of this tax. They deduct it from the employee's gross pay and remit it to the government along with the employer's share. Both the employer and the employee are taxed at the same rate, currently 4.95% each (2003) based on the employee's gross pay up to maximum contributory earnings of $36,400. This is a function of the maximum amount of pensionable earnings of $39,900 and a basic yearly exemption of $3,500. The maximum annual contribution for each of the employee and employer is $1,801.80 in 2003.

Employment Insurance. Another payroll tax levied by the federal government provides a system of employment insurance (EI). This tax is levied on both employees and employers. Employees must pay a premium of 1.98% (2004) of insurable earnings to an annual maximum contribution of $772 while the employer is required to contribute 1.4 times the amount of employee premiums. Insurable earnings are gross wages above a prescribed minimum and below a maximum amount of $39,000. Both the premium rates and insurable earnings are adjusted periodically.

Income Tax Withholding. Income tax laws require employers to withhold from each employee's pay an amount approximating the applicable income tax due on those wages. The amount of income tax withheld is calculated by the employer according to a government-prescribed formula or a government-provided income tax deduction table and is dependent on the length of the pay period and each employee's wages, marital status, claimed dependents, and other permitted deductions.

Illustration. Assume a weekly payroll of $10,000 entirely subject to CPP (4.95%), employment insurance (1.98%), income tax withholdings of $1,320, and union dues of $88.

The entry to record the wages and salaries paid and the employee payroll deductions is:

A   =   L   +   SE
−7,899 +2,101 −10,000

Cash flows: ↓ 7,899 outflow

Wages and Salaries Expense	10,000	
Employee Income Tax Deductions Payable		1,320
CPP Contributions Payable		495
EI Premiums Payable		198
Union Dues Payable		88
Cash		7,899

The required employer payroll taxes are recognized as compensation-related expenses in the same accounting period as the payroll is recorded. The entry for the required employer contributions follows.

A   =   L   +   SE
        +772   −772

Cash flows: No effect

Payroll Tax Expense	772	
CPP Contributions Payable ($495 × 1.0)		495
EI Premiums Payable ($198 × 1.4)		277

The employer is required to remit to the Receiver General for Canada the employees' income tax, CPP, and EI deductions as well as the employer's required contributions for CPP and EI. The entry to record the payment to CRA for the payroll above is:

A   =   L   +   SE
−2,785 −2,785

Cash flows: ↓ 2,785 outflow

Employee Income Tax Deductions Payable	1,320	
CPP Contributions Payable ($495 + $495)	990	
EI Premiums Payable ($198 + $277)	475	
Cash		2,785

Until remitted to the government, these amounts are all reported as current liabilities. In a manufacturing enterprise, all payroll costs (wages, payroll taxes, and fringe benefits) are allocated to appropriate cost accounts such as Direct Labour, Indirect Labour, Sales Salaries, Administrative Salaries, and the like. This abbreviated and somewhat simplified discussion of payroll costs and deductions is not indicative of the volume of records and clerical work that are involved in maintaining a sound and accurate payroll system.

Compensated Absences

Compensated absences are absences from active employment such as statutory holidays, vacation, and illness for which employees are paid. Vested rights to these benefits exist when an employer is legally required to pay the employee for these benefits even if the employee's employment is terminated; thus, vested rights are not contingent on an employee's continued service. For example, assume that you have earned four days of vacation pay as of December 31, the end of your employer's fiscal year. In a province where vacation pay is prescribed by statute, your employer will have to pay you for these four days even if you resign from your job. In this situation, your four days of vacation pay are considered vested and the costs are accrued by the employer company **in the period in which the benefit is earned by the employee**.

Employers are required under provincial statutes to give each employee vacation equal to a stipulated number of days or compensation in lieu of the vacation. As a result, employers have an obligation for vacation pay that accrues to the employees. Usually this obligation is satisfied by paying employees their regular salaries for the period that they are absent from work while taking an annual vacation.

Now assume that your vacation days **are not vested**, but that they can be carried forward to future periods if not used in the period earned. If you continue in the company's employ, you are entitled to the vacation days, but if you leave the company, they are lost. Although the rights are not vested, they are accumulated rights for which the employer should measure and recognize an accrual, allowing for estimated forfeitures due to turnover. Accumulated rights are those that can be carried forward to future periods if not used in the period in which earned, but are not necessarily vested.

Entitlement to **sick pay** varies considerably among employers. In some companies, sick pay vests and employees are allowed to accumulate unused sick time. They can take compensated time off from work even though they are not ill or they are compensated for the unused sick days when they leave the company. In other companies, employees receive sick pay only if they are absent because of illness, but the number of days they are entitled to accumulates with time. In the first case, an obligation exists to pay future amounts; therefore, **the estimated liability is accrued.** In the second case, it is very difficult to determine in advance the expense associated with the benefits earned by the employees. In this case, no accrual is usually made. Because of measurement problems, most companies account for non-vesting sick pay on a pay-as-you-go basis.

In summary, **the expense and related liability for compensated absences should be recognized in the year in which they are earned by employees whenever a reasonable estimate can be made of amounts expected to be paid out in the future.**

What rate should be used to accrue the compensated absence expense: the current rate or an estimated future rate? Most companies use the current rather than future rate, which is less certain and raises issues concerning the discounting of the future amount. To illustrate, assume that Amutron Limited began operations on January 1, 2005.

- The company employed 10 individuals who were paid $480 per week.

- A total of 20 weeks' vacation was earned by all employees in 2005, but none was used during this year.

- In 2006, the vacation weeks earned in 2005 were used when the current rate of pay was $540 per week for each employee.

The entry at December 31, 2005 to accrue the vacation pay entitlement earned by the employees is as follows.

Wages Expense	9,600	
Vacation Wages Payable ($480 × 20)		9,600

A = L + SE
 +9,600 −9,600
Cash flows: No effect

At December 31, 2005, the company reports a current liability of $9,600 on its balance sheet. In 2006, the vacation pay taken (earned in 2005) is recorded as follows.

Vacation Wages Payable	9,600	
Wages Expense	1,200	
Cash ($540 × 20)		10,800

A = L + SE
−10,800 −9,600 −1,200
Cash flows: ↓ 10,800 outflow

In 2006, the vacation weeks were used and the liability extinguished. Note that the difference between the cash paid and the reduction in the liability account is recorded as an adjustment to Wages Expense in the period when paid. This difference arises because the liability account was accrued at the rate of pay in effect during the period compensated time was earned. The cash paid, however, is based on the rates in effect when the compensated time is used. If the future rates of pay had been estimated accurately and used to calculate the accrual in 2005, then the cash paid in 2006 would be equal to the liability.[15]

Bonus Agreements

For various reasons, many companies give a bonus to certain or all officers and employees in addition to their regular salary or wage. Often the bonus amount is dependent on the company's yearly profit. From the enterprise's standpoint, **bonus payments to employees** are considered additional wages and are an expense in determining the net income for

International Insight

In Japan, bonuses to members of boards of directors and to the Commercial Code auditors are not treated as expenses. They are considered a distribution of profits and charged against retained earnings.

---

[15] Many companies have obligations for benefits payable to employees after they retire. The accounting and reporting standards for post-retirement benefit payments are complex and relate primarily to pensions and post-retirement health care and life insurance benefits. These and other issues of employee future benefits are discussed in Chapter 20.

the year. In a note to its financial statements for the year ending December 31, 2002, **Tesma International Inc.** reports the following.

Tesma International Inc.

Note 21 (partial)

The Company's Corporate Constitution requires that a portion of the Company's profits be distributed or used for certain purposes, including, but not limited to the following:

- allocation or distribution of 10% of pre-tax profits to employees and/or the Tesma Employee Equity Participation and Profit Sharing Program (including the Tesma International Inc. [Canadian] Deferred Profit Sharing Plan and the Tesma International of America, Inc. U.S. Employees' Deferred Profit Sharing Plan forming part thereof);
- allocation of a minimum of 7% of pre-tax profits to R&D; and
- payment of dividends to shareholders based on a formula of after-tax profits.

To illustrate the entries for an employee bonus, assume a company whose income for 2005 is $100,000 will pay out bonuses of $10,700 in January 2006. An adjusting entry dated December 31, 2005, is made to record the bonus as follows.

A = L + SE
+10,700 −10,700

Cash flows: No effect

| Employees' Bonus Expense | 10,700 | |
| Bonus Payable | | 10,700 |

The expense account appears in the income statement as an operating expense. The accrued liability, usually payable within a short time period, is generally included as a current liability in the balance sheet. In January 2006, when the bonus is paid, the entry is:

A   =   L   + SE
−10,700   −10,700

Cash flows: ↓ 10,700 outflow

| Bonus Payable | 10,700 | |
| Cash | | 10,700 |

Care has to be taken in calculating bonus amounts. The formula may specify that the bonus is a given percentage of after-tax income. Because the bonus itself is a tax-deductible expense, simultaneous equations may have to be set up and solved to determine both the bonus and tax amounts.

Rents and Royalties Payable

Similar to bonus arrangements are **contractual agreements covering rents or royalty payments conditional on the amount of revenues earned or the quantity of product produced or extracted**. For example, franchisees usually are required to pay franchise fees calculated as a percentage of sales to the franchisor, tenants in shopping centres may be obligated to pay additional rents on sales above a predetermined amount, and manufacturers may have licencing agreements whereby they pay the holder of a patent a royalty fee per unit produced.

Conditional expenses based on revenues or units produced are usually less difficult to calculate than bonus arrangements. For example, if a lease calls for a fixed rent payment of $500 per month and 1% of all sales over $300,000 per year, the annual rent obligation amounts to $6,000 plus $0.01 of each dollar of revenue over $300,000. Or a royalty agreement may require the accrual of $1.00 for every tonne of product resulting from the patented process, or the accrual of $0.50 on every barrel of oil extracted to benefit the owner of the mineral rights. As each additional unit of product is produced or extracted, an additional obligation, usually a current liability, is created.

ESTIMATED LIABILITIES

Most liabilities that companies incur can be measured fairly accurately at the amount of cash or the cash equivalent value of other assets likely to be given up to discharge the obligation. However, others don't lend themselves to such certain measurement. Obligations under product guarantees and warranties and those that require providing premiums and price reductions in the future, **all related to revenue recognized in the current period**, usually depend on estimation. Another estimated obligation, although not usually a current liability, relates to asset retirement obligations.

5 Objective
Explain the accounting for common estimated liabilities.

Product Guarantee and Warranty Obligations

A warranty or product guarantee is a promise made by a seller to a buyer to make good on a product's deficiency in quantity, quality, or performance. It is commonly used by manufacturers as a sales promotion technique. Automakers, for example, hype their sales by extending the length of their new-car warranty. For a specified period of time following the date of sale to the consumer, a manufacturer may promise to bear all or part of the cost of replacing defective parts, to perform any necessary repairs or servicing without charge, to refund the purchase price, or even to double your money back. Warranties and product guarantees entail future costs that are sometimes called "after costs" or "post-sale costs." They are often significant.

Two different situations may arise with warrantees. If the warranty is provided with the product or service and no additional fee is charged for it, the costs of making good on the warranty must be covered by the sales revenue received for the product sold. Alternatively, a warranty could be sold separately from the product or service. In this case, the proceeds on the separate sale of the product guarantee are used to cover the costs of subsequent repairs and servicing. Consider the purchase of a DVD player. Assume the electronic equipment comes with a one-year warranty. In addition, no doubt you will be offered the opportunity to purchase an extended warranty for an additional charge. The one-year warranty embedded in the sales price will be accounted for by the store differently than the extended warranty product sold separately.

Warranty Embedded in Sales Price of Product

Although the future cost is indefinite in amount, due date, and even customer, **a liability is recognized in the accounts if it is likely that future costs will be incurred as a result of sales reported and the amount can be reasonably estimated.** The liability is measured as an estimate of all the costs that are likely to be incurred after sale and delivery as a result of the warranty provisions. **When the warranty is an integral and inseparable part of the sale,** the accrual-based expense warranty method is used. Under this method, warranty costs are charged to operating expense **in the year of sale** and a warranty liability is recognized for the likely claims.

Illustration of Expense Warranty Method. Assume that the Denson Machinery Corporation begins production of a new machine in July 2005, and sells 100 units for $5,000 each by its year end, December 31, 2005. Each machine is under warranty for one year and the company has estimated, from experience with a similar machine, that the warranty cost will probably average $200 per unit. As a result of parts replacements and services rendered in compliance with machinery warranties related to the units of the new machine sold in 2005, the company incurs $4,000 in warranty costs in 2005 and $16,000 in 2006. Two equally valid series of entries could be made to record these events.

Illustration 14-5
Warranty Expense and Liability Entries

METHOD A		METHOD B	
1. Sale of 100 machines at $5,000 each, July-December, 2005			
Cash/Accounts Receivable 500,000		Cash/Accounts Receivable 500,000	
Sales	500,000	Sales	500,000
2. Recognition of estimated warranty expense at $200/unit for sales, July-December, 2005			
No entry		Warranty Expense	20,000
		Estimated Liability	
		Under Warranty	20,000
3. Actual warranty costs incurred, July-December, 2005			
Warranty Expense	4,000	Estimated Liability	
Cash/Inventory/		Under Warranty	4,000
Accrued Payroll	4,000	Cash/Inventory/	
		Accrued Payroll	4,000
4. Year-end adjusting entry to accrue outstanding warranty obligations at December 31, 2005			
Warranty Expense	16,000	No entry	
Estimated Liability			
Under Warranty	16,000		
5. December 31, 2005 financial statement amounts reported			
Warranty Expense (I/S)	$20,000	Warranty Expense (I/S)	$20,000
Estimated Liability		Estimated Liability	
Under Warranty (B/S)	$16,000	Under Warranty (B/S)	$16,000
6. Actual warranty costs incurred, 2006			
Warranty Expense	16,000	Estimated Liability	
Cash/Inventory/		Under Warranty	16,000
Accrued Payroll	16,000	Cash/Inventory/	
		Accrued Payroll	16,000
7. Adjusting entry, December 31, 2006, to adjust liability account to correct balance of $0			
Estimated Liability		No entry	
Under Warranty	16,000		
Warranty Expense	16,000		
8. December 31, 2006 financial statement amounts reported			
Warranty Expense (I/S)	$ 0	Warranty Expense (I/S)	$ 0
Estimated Liability		Estimated Liability	
Under Warranty (B/S)	$ 0	Under Warranty (B/S)	$ 0

I/S: income statement   B/S: balance sheet

Underlying Concept

Accounting for warranties is a direct application of the matching principle.

Under Method A, the actual warranty costs are charged to expense as incurred. At the end of the accounting period, a further expense and liability are accrued for warranty costs to be incurred in the future relative to current period sales. Alternatively, with Method B the entire expected warranty costs related to current period sales are charged to expense and the related obligation recognized as a liability. As the actual warranty costs are incurred, the liability is reduced. Either series of entries is acceptable: **both result in the same reported amounts on the income statement and the balance sheet**.

In situations **where the warranty costs are immaterial** or **when the warranty period is relatively short**, the product guarantee can be accounted for on a cash basis. Under the **cash method**, warranty costs are charged to expense as they are incurred; that is, **in the period in which the seller or manufacturer complies with the warranty**. No liability is recognized for future costs arising from warranties, nor is the expense necessarily recognized in the period of the related sale. This method is required for income tax purposes. The cash basis is also legitimate if future costs are not likely to be incurred.

If the cash basis method is applied to the facts in the Denson Machinery Corporation example, $4,000 is recorded as warranty expense in 2005 and $16,000 as warranty expense in 2006, with the total sales being recorded as revenue in 2005. In most instances, application of the cash basis method does not match the warranty expense with the associated revenue derived from such products, therefore violating the matching principle. Where similar warranty policies exist year after year, the differences between the cash and the accrual methods on an ongoing basis probably would not be significant, although there would be a mismatch in the early and final years.

Warranty Sold Separately

When an extended warranty or product maintenance contract is sold as a separate product or service, it is accounted for under a different method: the sales warranty method.[16] **The revenue on the sale of the extended warranty or contract is deferred** and is generally recognized in income on a straight-line basis over the life of the contract. Revenue is deferred because the warranty seller has an obligation to perform services over the life of the contract. Any incremental direct acquisition costs related to the sale of the contract, such as commissions, are deferred and amortized on the same basis as the revenue. All other costs are expensed as incurred. [17]

Illustration of Sales Warranty Method.   To illustrate, assume you have just purchased a new automobile from Hanlin Auto for $20,000. In addition to the regular warranty on the auto (all repairs will be paid by the manufacturer for the first 60,000 km or three years, whichever comes first), you purchase an extended warranty for $600 that protects you for an additional three years or 60,000 km. The entry to record the automobile sale (with the regular warranty) and the extended warranty sale on January 2, 2005 on Hanlin Auto's books is:

Cash	20,600	
Sales		20,000
Unearned Warranty Revenue		600

A = L + SE
+20,600 +600 +20,000
Cash flows: ↑ 20,600 inflow

The warranty embedded in the sales revenue is accounted for under the expense warranty method described previously. The entry to recognize revenue and amortize the deferred revenue **on the extended warranty at the end of each of the fourth, fifth, and sixth years** (using straight-line amortization) is as follows.

Unearned Warranty Revenue	200	
Warranty Revenue		200

A = L + SE
−200 +200
Cash flows: No effect

Because the extended warranty contract does not start until after the regular warranty expires, revenue is not recognized until the fourth year. If the costs of performing services under the extended warranty contract are incurred on other than a straight-line basis (as historical evidence might indicate), revenue is recognized over the contract period in proportion to the costs expected to be incurred in performing services under the contract. In addition, if the costs of providing services under the contract (plus any unamortized contract acquisition costs) are expected to be greater than the related unearned revenue, the unamortized acquisition costs are charged to expense, and if necessary, a loss and liability recognized for any further shortfall.[18]

---

[16] *EIC-142*, "Revenue Arrangements with Multiple Deliverables" indicates that this method is also appropriate when the warranty is embedded in the sales price of the product but it is separable, has standalone value, and its value can be objectively and reliably measured.

[17] *EIC-143*, "Accounting for Separately Priced Extended Warranty and Product Maintenance Contracts," CICA, December 17, 2003.

[18] *EIC-143*.

Underlying Concept

Consistent with the accounting for warranties, obligations for premiums and coupons meet the definition of a liability. In addition, matching requires the related expense to be reported in the same period in which the sale is recognized.

What do the Numbers Mean?

Premiums, Coupons, Rebates, and Loyalty Points

Numerous companies offer premiums and other benefits to customers on either a limited or continuing basis in return for boxtops, certificates, coupons, labels, wrappers, or the accumulation of loyalty "points." The **premiums** may be silverware, dishes, a small appliance, toys, free transportation, or cash values against future purchases.[19] Customer loyalty programs, such as the one described by **Sears** in the chapter-opening vignette and that offered by **Shoppers Drug Mart**, all promise future benefits to the customer in exchange for current sales.

Printed coupons that can be redeemed for a cash discount on items purchased are extremely popular marketing tools, as is the cash rebate, which the buyer can obtain by returning the store receipt, a rebate coupon, and Universal Product Code (UPC label or bar code) to the manufacturer. **Contests** have also been widely used to get consumers' attention and their sales dollars, with the **Tim Hortons'** "Roll Up The Rim To Win" promotion being one of the most successful contests in Canadian history. A wide variety of prizes are offered, including automobiles, vacations, major sporting events tickets, and sweepstake winnings!

The costs associated with these marketing tools are not inconsequential. For example, the Coupon Industry Association of Canada reports that Canadian consumers redeemed 110 million coupons in 2002, with an average value of $1.07 each. This represents a redemption rate of 4.7% of the coupons distributed by consumer packaged goods manufacturers to Canadian households.

With the life of many contests running a few months and the average coupon being valid for an average of 201 days, many companies have the practical problem of accounting for these marketing costs, as they affect more than one fiscal period. The practical accounting issue relates to the fact that while these promotions **increase current sales**, the associated costs are often incurred **in future periods**. That is, companies have current obligations that meet the definition of a liability, and also have to match expenses with the related revenue.

Source: Coupon Industry Association of Canada website at www.couponscanada.org.

These premiums, coupon offers, frequent flyer miles, rebates, and prizes are made to stimulate sales, and their costs **should be charged to expense in the period** that benefits from the premium plan: the period of the sale. This is key to understanding the accounting for the costs associated with these various plans. At the end of the accounting period, many of these premium offers may be outstanding and, when presented for redemption in subsequent periods, require an outflow of company assets. **The cost of outstanding promotional offers that will be presented for redemption must be estimated in order to reflect the existing current liability and to match costs with revenues.** The cost of premium offers should be charged to an expense account such as Premium Expense, and the outstanding obligations should be included in a liability account such as Estimated Liability for Premiums or Estimated Premium Claims Outstanding.

---

[19] Premium plans that have widespread adoption are the frequent flyer programs used by all major airlines. On the basis of mileage or number of trips accumulated, frequent flyer members are awarded discounted or free airline tickets. Airline customers can earn miles toward free travel by making long-distance phone calls, staying in hotels, and charging groceries and gasoline on a credit card. Those free tickets represent an enormous potential liability because people using them may displace paying passengers.

When airlines first started offering frequent flyer bonuses, everyone assumed that they could accommodate the free ticket holders with otherwise-empty seats. That made the additional cost of the program so minimal that airlines didn't accrue or report the small liability. But, as more and more paying passengers have been crowded off flights by frequent flyer awardees, the loss of revenue has grown enormously. Although the accounting for this transaction has been studied by the profession, no authoritative guidelines have been issued.

The following example illustrates the accounting treatment accorded a premium offer. Fluffy Cakemix Corporation offered its customers a large nonbreakable mixing bowl in exchange for $1.00 and 10 boxtops. The mixing bowl costs Fluffy Cakemix Corporation $2.25, and the company estimates that 60% of the boxtops will be redeemed. The premium offer began in June 2005 and resulted in the following transactions and entries during 2005.

1. To record the purchase of 20,000 mixing bowls at $2.25 each:

Inventory of Premium Mixing Bowls	45,000	
Cash		45,000

A = L + SE
0   0   0

Cash flows: ↓ 45,000 outflow

2. To record sales of 300,000 boxes of cake mix at $1.50:

Cash	450,000	
Sales		450,000

A   = L +   SE
+450,000   +450,000

Cash flows: ↑ 450,000 inflow

3. To record the redemption of 60,000 boxtops, receipt of $1.00 per 10 boxtops, and delivery of the mixing bowls:

Cash [(60,000 ÷ 10) × $1.00]	6,000	
Premium Expense	7,500	
Inventory of Premium Mixing Bowls		13,500
[Calculation: (60,000 ÷ 10) × $2.25 = $13,500]		

A   = L +   SE
−7,500   −7,500

Cash flows: ↑ 6,000 inflow

4. To record the end-of-period adjusting entry for the estimated liability for outstanding premiums:

Premium Expense	15,000	
Estimated Liability for Premiums		15,000
Calculation:		
Total boxtops sold in 2005	300,000	
Total estimated redemptions (60%)	180,000	
Boxtops redeemed in 2005	60,000	
Estimated future redemptions	120,000	
Cost of estimated claims outstanding		
(120,000 ÷ 10) × ($2.25 − $1.00) =	$15,000	

A =   L   +   SE
    +15,000   −15,000

Cash flows: No effect

The December 31, 2005 balance sheet of Fluffy Cakemix Corporation reports an Inventory of Premium Mixing Bowls of $31,500 as a current asset and Estimated Liability for Premiums of $15,000 as a current liability. The 2005 income statement reports a $22,500 Premium Expense among the selling expenses.

Asset Retirement Obligations

In many industries the construction and operation of long-lived assets involve obligations associated with the retirement of those assets. For example, when a mining company opens up a strip mine, it may also make a commitment to restore the land on which the mine is located once the mining activity is completed. Similarly, when an oil company erects an offshore drilling platform, it may be legally obligated to dismantle and remove the platform at the end of its useful life.

6 Objective
Explain the recognition, measurement, and disclosure requirements for asset retirement obligations.

A company must recognize the existing legal obligation associated with the retirement of a tangible long-lived asset that results from its acquisition, construction, development, or normal operations, **in the period it is incurred**, provided a reasonable estimate can be made of its fair value.[20] This liability is known as an asset retirement obligation (ARO), and its associated costs are added to the carrying value of the underlying asset. If the fair value cannot be reasonably estimated, this fact and the reasons must be reported.

Obligating Events

Examples of existing legal obligations that would require recognition of a liability and asset cost include, but are not limited to:

1. decommissioning nuclear facilities,

2. dismantling, restoring, and reclaiming oil and gas properties,

3. certain closure, reclamation, and removal costs of mining facilities, and

4. closure and post-closure costs of landfills.

In order to capture the benefits of these long-lived assets, the company is generally legally obligated for the costs associated with retirement of the asset. AROs occur in a variety of ways. For example, the obligation may arise from acquisition at the outset of the asset's use (e.g., erection of an oil rig), or it may build over time through normal operations (e.g., a landfill that expands over time).

Measurement

The liability is initially measured at its fair value, which is defined as the amount that the company would be required to pay in an active market to settle the ARO. Although active markets do not exist for many AROs, an estimate of fair value should be based on the best information available. Such information could include market prices of similar liabilities, if available. Alternatively, fair value can be estimated based on present value techniques.

Recognition and Allocation

As explained in Chapter 11, the estimated costs associated with the ARO are added to the carrying amount of the related long-lived asset in the same amount as the liability recognized. An asset retirement cost is recorded as part of the related asset because these costs are considered necessary to operate the asset and to prepare the asset for its intended use. The specific asset (e.g., mine, drilling platform, nuclear power plant) should be increased because the future economic benefit comes from the use of this productive asset. **The capitalized asset retirement costs should not be recorded in a separate account because there is no future economic benefit that can be associated with these costs alone**.

In subsequent periods, the cost of the ARO is allocated to expense over the period of the related asset's useful life. While the straight-line method is acceptable for this allocation, other systematic and rational allocations also are permitted.

Note that environmental remediation required after such events as a major oil spill or accidental run-off of chemicals into a water table **does not result in an asset retirement obligation and addition to the cost base** of the underlying asset. These catastrophes do not result from the normal operations of the entity and an increase in the asset's cost cannot be justified.

---

[20] *CICA Handbook* Section 3110, "Asset Retirement Obligations."

Illustration of Accounting for Initial Recognition of AROs

To illustrate the accounting for AROs, assume that on January 1, 2005, Wildcat Oil Corp. erected an oil platform off the Newfoundland coast. Wildcat is legally required to dismantle and remove the platform at the end of its five-year useful life. It is estimated that the total cost of dismantling and removal will be $1 million. Based on a 10% discount rate, the present value of the asset retirement obligation is $620,920 ($1 million × .62092). Wildcat makes the following entry to recognize the ARO.

January 1, 2005		
Drilling Platform	620,920	
Asset Retirement Obligation		620,920

A   =   L   + SE
+620,920   +620,920
Cash flows: No effect

During the life of the asset, the asset retirement cost is allocated to expense. Using the straight-line method, Wildcat makes the following entries to record this expense.

December 31, 2005, 2006, 2007, 2008, 2009		
Amortization Expense ($620,920 ÷ 5)	124,184	
Accumulated Amortization		124,184

A   = L +   SE
−124,184   −124,184
Cash flows: No effect

In addition, because the liability is measured at its discounted cash flows, interest on the liability must be accrued each period and the liability increased. *CICA Handbook* Section 3110 indicates that the expense should be classified as an operating expense, **but that it not be reported as interest expense**. The entry at December 31, 2005 to record the expense and the related increase or accretion in the carrying amount of the liability is as follows.

December 31, 2005		
Accretion Expense ($620,920 × 10%)	62,092	
Asset Retirement Obligation		62,092

A = L   +   SE
+62,092   −62,092
Cash flows: No effect

On January 10, 2010, Wildcat contracts with Rig Reclaimers, Inc. to dismantle the platform at a contract price of $995,000. Wildcat makes the following entry to record settlement of the liability.

January 10, 2010		
Asset Retirement Obligation	1,000,000	
Gain on Settlement of ARO		5,000
Cash		995,000

A   =   L   + SE
−995,000 −1,000,000 +5,000
Cash flows: ↓ 995,000 outflow

Subsequent Recognition and Measurement of AROs

CICA Handbook Section 3110 explains the accounting complexities when the estimated amount of the obligation changes or additional costs and liabilities need to be recognized due to operating activity. In short, the accretion expense representing the interest element is calculated first. This is followed by the addition or decrease in the carrying amount of the Asset Retirement Obligation account for any increase or decrease in the cost estimates. This latter amount also adjusts the carrying value of the underlying long-lived asset to which it relates and, of course, the annual amortization.

Reporting and Disclosure Requirements

Most asset retirement obligations are long-term in nature and therefore are shown outside current liabilities. As well as providing a description of the AROs and associated long-lived assets, companies are also required to provide:

1. specific information about the assumptions used in determining the reported amounts,

2. a reconciliation of the beginning and ending balance of the liability, and

3. the fair value of assets legally restricted for purposes of settling such obligations.[21]

CONTINGENCIES, COMMITMENTS, AND GUARANTEES

Types of Contingencies

Objective 7

Explain the accounting and reporting standards for loss contingencies and commitments.

A contingency is defined in *CICA Handbook* Section 3290 as an existing condition or situation involving uncertainty as to possible gain (gain contingency) or loss (loss contingency) to an enterprise that will ultimately be resolved when one or more future events occur or fail to occur.[22] As discussed in Chapter 5, **gain contingencies are not recorded** and are disclosed in the notes only when it is likely that a gain will be realized. As a result, it is unusual to find information about contingent gains in the financial statements and the accompanying notes.

Loss contingencies are **existing situations** (i.e., at the balance sheet date) involving uncertainty as to possible loss. A liability recognized as a result of a loss contingency is by definition a contingent liability. Contingent liabilities are obligations that are dependent upon the occurrence or nonoccurrence of one or more future events to confirm either its existence or the amount payable.

When a loss contingency exists, the likelihood that the future event or events will confirm the incurrence of a liability can range from highly probable to only slightly probable. The *CICA Handbook* uses the terms **"likely," "unlikely,"** and **"not determinable"** to identify the range of probability outcomes and assigns the following meanings.

Likely: The chance of occurrence (or nonoccurrence) of the future event is high.

Unlikely: The chance of the occurrence (or nonoccurrence) of the future event is slight.

Not determinable: The chance of the occurrence (or nonoccurrence) of the future event cannot be determined.

An estimated loss from a loss contingency is accrued by a charge to expense and a credit to the liability only if both the following conditions are met:[23]

1. information available prior to the issuance of the financial statements indicates that **it is likely** that a future event will confirm that an asset has been impaired or a liability incurred as of the date of the financial statements and

2. the loss amount can be **reasonably estimated.**

Neither the exact payee nor the exact date payable need be known to record a liability. **What must be known is whether it is likely that a liability has been incurred.**

The second criterion indicates that an estimate of the liability can be reasonably determined; otherwise, it should not be accrued as a liability. Evidence to determine a reasonable

---

[21] *CICA Handbook* Section 3110.21.

[22] *CICA Handbook* Section 3290.02.

[23] Loss contingencies that result in the incurrence of a liability are most relevant to the discussion in this chapter. Loss contingencies that result in the impairment of an asset (e.g., collectibility of receivables or threat of expropriation of assets) are discussed more fully in other chapters of this textbook.

estimate of the liability may be based on the company's own experience, experience of other companies in the industry, engineering or research studies, legal advice, or educated guesses by personnel in the best position to know. Often, **a range of possible amounts** may be determined. If a specific amount within the range is a better estimate than others, this amount should be accrued. If no one amount is more likely than another, the bottom of the range is usually accrued with the amount of the remaining exposure disclosed.

The table in Illustration 14-6, based on *CICA Handbook* Section 3290, summarizes the accounting and reporting standards for contingencies in a variety of circumstances.

IAS Note

In measuring the amount of provision to recognize, IAS37 uses an "expected value" method whereby the possible outcomes are weighted by their associated probabilities.

Illustration 14-6

Accounting and Reporting Standards for Loss Contingencies

	Loss can be reasonably estimated?	
Probability	Yes	No
Likely	Accrue. Report exposure to loss in excess of amount accrued in Notes to Financial Statements*	Report in Notes to Financial Statements*
Not likely	Disclosure not required	Disclosure not required
Not determinable	Report in Notes to Financial Statements*	Report in Notes to Financial Statements*

*Disclose the nature of the contingency and either an estimate of the amount or that an estimate cannot be made.

Illustration 14-7 from the 2003 annual report of **Clearly Canadian Beverage Corporation** is an example of an accrual related to a loss contingency.

Illustration 14-7

Disclosure of Accrual Related to a Loss Contingency

Clearly Canadian Beverage Corporation
Note 17 Commitments and Contingencies (partial)

e) Dispute with D. Bruce Horton and Continental Consulting Ltd.
In August 1999, a claim was filed against the Company in the Supreme Court of British Columbia by D. Bruce Horton and his company, Continental Consulting Ltd. (Continental). Mr. Horton is claiming compensation from the Company for allegedly constructively dismissing him as an officer of the Company. Continental is claiming compensation from the Company alleging that the Company terminated its management agreement without cause. Mr. Horton and Continental are claiming an aggregate of CA$2.4 million plus interest and costs. The Company does not accept Mr. Horton's and Continental's allegations, and has filed statements of defence and has further filed counterclaims against Mr. Horton and Continental for monies owed and damages. The Company has made an accrual based on its expected costs.

Using the terms "likely" and "unlikely" as a basis for determining the accounting for contingencies involves judgement and subjectivity. The items in Illustration 14-8 are examples of loss contingencies and the accounting treatment generally accorded them.

Illustration 14-8

Accounting Treatment of Loss Contingencies

Loss Related to	Not Accrued	May Be Accrued*
1. Risk of loss or damage of enterprise property by fire, explosion, or other hazards	X	
2. General or unspecified business risks	X	
3. Risk of loss from catastrophes assumed by property and casualty insurance companies including reinsurance companies	X	
4. Threat of expropriation of assets		X
5. Pending or threatened litigation		X
6. Actual or possible claims and assessments**		X
7. Guarantees of indebtedness of others		X
8. Obligations of commercial banks under standby letters of credit		X
9. Agreements to repurchase receivables (or the related property) that have been sold		X

* Should be accrued when both criteria are met (likely and reasonably estimable).
** Estimated amounts of losses incurred prior to the balance sheet date but settled subsequently should be accrued as of the balance sheet date.

International Insight

In Germany, company law allows firms to accrue losses for contingencies as long as they are possible and reasonable. Such provisions are one means of smoothing income.

The accounting concepts and procedures relating to contingent items are relatively unsettled. Practising accountants express concern over the diversity that exists in the interpretations of likely and unlikely. Current practice relies heavily on the exact language used in responses received from lawyers, such language being necessarily biased and protective rather than predictive. As a result, accruals and disclosures of contingencies vary considerably in practice. Some of the more common loss contingencies discussed in this chapter are:

1. litigation, claims, and assessments,

2. guarantees, and

3. self-insurance risks.

Note that general risk contingencies that are inherent in business operations, such as the possibility of war, strike, uninsurable catastrophes, or a business recession, are not reported in the notes to the financial statements.

Litigation, Claims, and Assessments

The following factors, among others, must be considered in determining whether a liability should be recorded with respect to pending or threatened **litigation** and actual or possible **claims** and **assessments**:

1. the **time period** in which the underlying cause of action occurred,

2. the **probability** of an unfavourable outcome, and

3. the ability to make a **reasonable estimate** of the loss amount.

To report a loss and a liability in the financial statements, **the cause for litigation must have occurred on or before the date of the financial statements**. It does not matter that the company did not become aware of the existence or possibility of the lawsuit or claims until after the date of the financial statements but before they are issued. To evaluate the likelihood of an unfavourable outcome, consider the nature of the litigation, the progress of the case, the opinion of legal counsel, the experience of the company and others in similar cases, and any management response to the lawsuit.[24]

The outcome of pending litigation, however, can seldom be predicted with any assurance. And, even if the evidence available at the balance sheet date does not favour the defendant, it is hardly reasonable to expect the company to publish in its financial statements a dollar estimate of the probable negative outcome. Such specific disclosures could weaken the company's position in the dispute and encourage the plaintiff to intensify its efforts. A typical example of the wording for litigation disclosure is the note to the financial statements of **RONA Inc.** for its year ended December 29, 2002 as shown in Illustration 14-9.

With respect to **unfiled suits** and **unasserted claims and assessments**, a company must determine (1) the likelihood or probability that a suit may be filed or a claim or assessment may be asserted and (2) the likelihood or probability of an unfavourable outcome. For example, assume that a company is being investigated by the federal government for possible violations of anti-competition legislation, and that enforcement proceedings have been instituted. Such proceedings may be followed by private claims. In this case, the company must determine the probability of the claims being asserted and the likelihood of damages being awarded. If both are likely, if the loss is reasonably

---

[24] For some companies, litigation presents significant costs in employee time and legal fees, even if the outcomes are positive. For example, in 2003, U.S. giant Wal-Mart Stores Inc. reported that it was the target of 6,649 active lawsuits of all sorts (Associated Press).

RONA Inc.

19. Contingencies (partial)

The Company has instituted proceedings against a third party for failure to comply with a contract for the acquisition of land. The third party responded to the Company's claim with a counterclaim for $20,000,000. In the opinion of management, this counterclaim is unfounded.

Moreover, other lawsuits have been filed against the Company totalling $18,000,000 relating to various claims, the outcome of which cannot currently be determined. The Company's insurers have taken up the Company's defense in these matters for an amount of $9,833,000. Management did not deem it necessary to account for an allowance.

Illustration 14-9

Disclosure of Litigation

estimable, and if the cause for action took place on or before the date of the financial statements, the liability is accrued.

Guarantees

Effective 2003, *CICA Handbook Guideline* AcG-14, "Disclosure of Guarantees" requires expanded disclosures by all guarantors about a variety of specific types of guarantees they have provided, **even where the likelihood of having to meet the guarantees is remote**. The *Guideline* is intended to supplement existing requirements related to Contingencies (Section 3290), Contractual Obligations (Section 3280) and Financial Instruments (Section 3860).

The purpose of the expanded disclosures is to give readers better information about the entity's obligations and **particularly about the risks taken on by virtue of issuing the guarantees**. While many specific types of guarantees have been excluded from the *Guideline*, the following types of agreements or contracts have been scoped in: those that require payments to be made if there are changes in a specific interest rate, security or commodity price, foreign exchange rate index of prices or rates, or other variable (sometimes called the "underlying") related to a guaranteed party; those based on another entity's failure to perform; certain indemnification agreements; and indirect guarantees of the indebtedness of others.[25]

Examples include a lessee's guarantee of the residual value of leased property under an operating lease, a standby letter of credit guaranteeing another's payment of a loan, and an agreement to hold another party blameless in the event of an adverse judgement in a lawsuit.

AcG-14 requires the following disclosures.

- the nature of the guarantee, how it arose, and circumstances requiring performance under the guarantee;

- the maximum potential amount of future payments that the guarantor could be required to make, without reduction for any recoverable amounts;

- the nature and extent of any recourse provisions or collateral held; and

- the carrying amount of the liability, if any.

AcG-14 and this chapter do not address recognition and measurement issues for guarantees. These aspects are incorporated in new *Handbook* Section 3855 on "Financial Instruments." Under Section 3855, it is proposed that financial guarantee contracts be measured initially and remeasured subsequently at their fair value.[26]

RONA Inc.'s Note 5 to its financial statements for the third quarter ended September 28, 2003 illustrates its compliance with AcG-14.

---

[25] *Accounting Guideline*, AcG-14, para. 4(a) and (b).

[26] Section 3855 was not yet released as this text went to print. It is expected to be released for application in 2005.

Instructions

(a) Prepare the journal entries that should be made in 2005 and 2006 to record the transactions related to the premium plan of the Hernandez Candy Corporation.

(b) Indicate the account names, amounts, and classifications of the items related to the premium plan that would appear on the balance sheet and the income statement at the end of 2005 and 2006.

(c) For any liabilities identified in (b), indicate whether the account is a financial liability. Explain.

P14-9   Paris Airlines is faced with two situations that need to be resolved before the financial statements for the company's year ended December 31, 2005 can be issued.

1. The airline is being sued for $4 million for an injury caused to a child as a result of alleged negligence while the child was visiting the airline maintenance hangar in March 2005. The suit was filed in July 2005. Paris' lawyer states that it is likely that the airline will lose the suit and be found liable for a judgement costing anywhere from $400,000 to $2 million. However, the lawyer states that the most probable judgement is $800,000.

2. On November 24, 2005, 26 passengers on Flight No. 901 were injured upon landing when the plane skidded off the runway. Personal injury suits for damages totalling $5 million were filed on January 11, 2006 against the airline by 18 injured passengers. The airline carries no insurance. Legal counsel has studied each suit and advised Paris that it can reasonably expect to pay 60% of the damages claimed.

Instructions

(a) Prepare any disclosures and journal entries required by GAAP for the airline in preparation of the December 31, 2005 financial statements.

(b) Ignoring the 2005 accidents, what liability due to the risk of loss from lack of insurance coverage should Paris Airlines record or disclose? During the past decade, the company has experienced at least one accident per year and incurred average damages of $3.2 million. Discuss fully.

P14-10   The Vice-President, Finance of Shoyo Corporation, in preparing its December 31, 2005 financial statements, is attempting to determine the proper accounting treatment for each of the following situations.

1. As a result of uninsured accidents during the year, personal injury suits for $350,000 and $60,000 have been filed against the company. It is the judgement of Shoyo's legal counsel that an unfavourable outcome is unlikely in the $60,000 case but that an unfavourable verdict approximating $225,000 will probably result in the $350,000 case.

2. In early 2005, Shoyo received notice from the provincial environment ministry that a site the company had been using to dispose of waste was considered toxic, and that Shoyo would be held responsible for its clean-up under provincial legislation. The Vice-President, Finance discussed the situation over coffee with the Vice-President, Engineering. The engineer stated that it would take up to three years to determine the best way to remediate the site and that the cost would be considerable, perhaps as much as $500,000 to $2 million or more. The engineering vice-president advocates recognizing at least the minimum estimate of $500,000 in the current year's financial statements, while the financial vice-president advocates just disclosing the situation and the inability to estimate the cost in a note to the financial statements.

3. Shoyo Corporation owns a subsidiary in a foreign country that has a book value of $5,725,000 and an estimated fair value of $8.7 million. The foreign government has communicated to Shoyo its intention to expropriate the assets and business of all foreign investors. On the basis of settlements other firms have received from this same country, Shoyo expects to receive 40% of the fair value of its properties as final settlement.

4. Shoyo's chemical product division, consisting of five plants, is uninsurable because of the special risk of injury to employees and losses due to fire and explosion. The year 2005 is considered one of the safest (luckiest) in the division's history because no loss due to injury or casualty was suffered. Having suffered an average of three casualties a year during the rest of the past decade (ranging from $60,000 to $700,000), management is certain that next year the company will probably not be so fortunate.

Instructions

(a) Prepare the journal entries that should be recorded as of December 31, 2005 to recognize each of the situations above.

(b) Indicate what should be reported relative to each situation in the financial statements and accompanying notes. Explain why.

(c) Are there any ethical issues involved in this discussion?

P14-11 Mosaic Music Limited (MML) carries a wide variety of musical instruments, sound reproduction equipment, recorded music, and sheet music. MML uses two sales promotion techniques—warranties and premiums—to attract customers.

Musical instruments and sound equipment are sold with a one-year warranty for replacement of parts and labour. The estimated warranty cost, based on experience, is 2% of sales.

A premium is offered on the recorded and sheet music. Customers receive a coupon for each dollar spent on recorded music or sheet music. Customers may exchange 200 coupons and $20 for a CD player. MML pays $34 for each CD player and estimates that 60% of the coupons given to customers will be redeemed.

MML's total sales for 2005 were $7.2 million: $5.4 million from musical instruments and sound reproduction equipment, and $1.8 million from recorded music and sheet music. Replacement parts and labour for warranty work totalled $164,000 during 2005. A total of 6,500 CD players used in the premium program were purchased during the year and there were 1.2 million coupons redeemed in 2005.

The accrual method is used by MML to account for the warranty and premium costs for financial reporting purposes. The balances in the accounts related to warranties and premiums on January 1, 2005 were:

Inventory of Premium CD Players	$ 39,950
Estimated Premium Liability	44,800
Estimated Liability for Warranties	136,000

Instructions

MML is preparing its financial statements for the year ended December 31, 2005. Determine the amounts that will be shown on the 2005 financial statements for the following.

1. Warranty Expense
2. Estimated Liability for Warranties
3. Premium Expense
4. Inventory of Premium CD Players
5. Estimated Premium Liability

(CMA adapted)

P14-12 Rodriguez Inc., a publishing company, is preparing its December 31, 2005 financial statements and must determine the proper accounting treatment for the following situations; the company has retained your group to assist it in this task.

(a) Rodriguez sells subscriptions to several magazines for a one-year, two-year, or three-year period. Cash receipts from subscribers are credited to magazine subscriptions collected in advance, and this account had a balance of $2.3 million at December 31, 2005. Outstanding subscriptions at December 31, 2005, expire as follows.

During 2006	$600,000
During 2007	500,000
During 2008	800,000

(b) On January 2, 2005, Rodriguez discontinued collision, fire, and theft coverage on its delivery vehicles and became self-insured for these risks. Actual losses of $50,000 during 2005 were charged to delivery expense. The 2004 premium for the discontinued coverage amounted to $80,000 and the controller wants to set up a reserve for self-insurance by a debit to delivery expense of $30,000 and a credit to the reserve for self-insurance of $30,000.

(c) A suit for breach of contract seeking damages of $1 million was filed by an author against Rodriguez on July 1, 2005. The company's legal counsel believes that an unfavourable outcome is likely. A reasonable estimate of the court's award to the plaintiff is in the range between $300,000 and $700,000. No amount within this range is a better estimate of potential damages than any other amount.

(d) Rodriguez' main supplier, Ball Ltd., has been experiencing liquidity problems over the last three quarters. In order for Ball's bank to continue to extend credit, Ball has asked Rodriguez to guarantee its indebtedness. The bank loan stands at $500,000 at December 31, 2005, but the guarantee extends to the full credit facility of $900,000.

(e) Rodriguez' landlord has informed the company that its warehouse lease will not be renewed when it expires in six months' time. Rodriguez entered into a $2 million contract on December 15, 2005 with Construction Company Ltd., committing the company to build an office and warehouse facility.

(f) During December 2005, a competitor company filed suit against Rodriguez for industrial espionage claiming $1.5 million in damages. In the opinion of management and company counsel, it is reasonably possible that damages will be awarded to the plaintiff. However, the amount of potential damages awarded to the plaintiff cannot be reasonably estimated.

Instructions

For each of the above situations, provide the journal entry that should be recorded as of December 31, 2005, or explain why an entry should not be recorded. For each situation, identify what disclosures are required, if any.

P14-13 Henrik Inc. has a contract with its president, Ms. Sarrat, to pay her a bonus during each of the years 2005, 2006, and 2007. Assume a corporate income tax rate of 40% during the three years. The profit before deductions for bonus and income taxes was $250,000 in 2005, $308,000 in 2006, and $350,000 in 2007. The president's bonus of 12% is deductible for tax purposes in each year and is to be calculated as follows.

(a) In 2005, the bonus is to be based on profit before deductions for bonus and income tax.

(b) In 2006, the bonus is to be based on profit after deduction of bonus but before deduction of income tax.

(c) In 2007, the bonus is to be based on profit before deduction of bonus but after deduction of income tax.

Instructions

Calculate the amounts of the bonus and the income tax for each of the three years.

P14-14 Haida Corp. has manufactured a broad range of quality products since 1985. The following information is available for the company's fiscal year ended February 28, 2005.

1. The company has $4 million of bonds payable outstanding at February 28, 2005 that were issued at par in 1997. The bonds carry an interest rate of 7% payable semi-annually each June 1 and December 1.

2. Haida has several notes payable outstanding with its primary banking institution at February 28, 2005 as follows. In each case, the annual interest is due on the anniversary date of the note each year (same as the due dates listed).

Due Date	Amount Due	Interest Rate
April 1, 2005	$150,000	8%
January 31, 2006	200,000	9%
March 15, 2006	500,000	7%
October 30, 2007	250,000	8%

3. Haida has a two-year warranty on selected products, with an estimated cost of 1% of sales being returned in the 12 months following the sale, and a cost of 1.5% of sales being returned in months 13 to 24 following sale. The warranty liability outstanding at February 28, 2004 was $5,700. Sales of warranteed products in the year ended February 28, 2005 were $154,000. Actual warranty costs incurred during the current fiscal year are as follows.

Warranty claims honoured on 2003–2004 sales	$4,900
Warranty claims honoured on 2004–2005 sales	1,100
	$6,000

4. Regular trade payables for supplies and purchases of goods and services on open account are $414,000 at February 28, 2005. Included in this amount is a loan of $23,000 owing to an affiliated company.

5. The following information relates to Haida's payroll for the month of February 2005. The company's required contribution for EI is 1.4 times that of the employee contribution and for CPP is 1.0 times that of the employee contribution.

Salaries and wages outstanding at February 28, 2005	$220,000
EI withheld from employees	9,500
CPP withheld from employees	16,900
Income taxes withheld from employees	48,700
Union dues withheld from employees	21,500

6. Haida regularly pays GST owing to the government on the 15th of the month following the charging of GST to customers and by suppliers. During February 2005, purchases attracted $28,000 of GST, while the GST charged on invoices to customers totalled $39,900. At Jan. 31, 2005 the balances in the GST Recoverable and GST Payable accounts were $34,000 and $60,000 respectively.

7. Other miscellaneous liabilities included $50,000 of dividends payable on March 15, 2005; $25,000 of bonuses payable to company executives (75% payable in September, 2005 and 25% payable the following March); $75,000 accrued audit fee covering the year ended February 28, 2005; and $330,000 of unearned revenue, one-third of which will be earned in July of each of the next three years.

Instructions

(a) Prepare the current liability section of the February 28, 2005 balance sheet of Haida Corp. Identify any amounts that require separate presentation or disclosure under GAAP.

(b) For each item included as a current liability, identify whether the item is a financial liability. Explain.

(c) If you have excluded any items from the presentation of current liabilities, explain why you have done so.

Writing Assignments

WA14-1 You are the independent auditor engaged to audit ProVision Corporation's December 31, 2005 financial statements. ProVision manufactures household appliances. During the course of your audit, you discover the following contingent liabilities.

1. ProVision began production on a new dishwasher in June 2005, and by December 31, 2005, sold 100,000 to various retailers for $500 each. Each dishwasher is sold with a one-year warranty included. The company estimates that its warranty expense per dishwasher will amount to $25. At year end, the company had already paid out $1 million in warranty expenditures. ProVision's income statement shows warranty expenses of $1 million for 2005. ProVision accounts for warranty costs on the accrual basis.

2. ProVision's retail division rents space from Meadow Malls, which charges ProVision a rental fee of $6,000 per month plus 5% of yearly retail profits over $500,000. ProVision's accountant, Burt Wilson, tells you that he has been instructed to increase the estimate of bad debt expense and warranty costs in order to keep the retail division's profits at $475,000.

3. ProVision's lawyer, Robert Dowski, QC, has informed you that ProVision has been cited for dumping toxic waste into the Salmon River. Clean-up costs and fines amount to $3,330,000. Although the case is still being contested, Dowski is certain that ProVision will most probably have to pay the fine and clean-up costs. No disclosure of this situation was found in the financial statements.

4. ProVision is the defendant in a patent infringement lawsuit by Heidi Golder over ProVision's use of a hydraulic compressor in several of its products. Dowski claims that, if the suit goes against ProVision, the loss may be as much as $5 million; however, Dowski advises that he has insufficient information at this point to determine what might happen as a result of this action. Again, no mention of this suit occurs in the financial statements.

As presented, you question whether these items may create problems in issuing an unqualified audit report. You feel you should note these problems in the working papers.

Instructions

(a) Write a brief narrative about each of the above issues in the form of a memorandum to be incorporated in the audit working papers. Explain what led to the discovery of each problem, what the problem really is, and what you advise your client to do (along with any appropriate journal entries) in order to bring the financial statements in accordance with GAAP.

(b) Identify any issues that you consider unethical and suggest what should be done.

WA14-2 Antigonish Corporation includes the following items in its liabilities at December 31, 2005.

1. Accounts payable, $420,000, due to suppliers in January 2006
2. Notes payable, $1.5 million, maturing on various dates in 2006
3. Deposits from customers on equipment ordered by them from Antigonish, $250,000
4. Salaries payable, $37,500, due January 14, 2006
5. Bonds payable, $2.5 million, maturing July 1, 2006

Instructions

(a) What are the essential characteristics that make an item a liability?

(b) What distinguishes a current liability from a long-term liability?

(c) What distinguishes a financial liability from a non-financial liability?

(d) Indicate under what circumstances, if any, each of the liabilities listed above might be excluded from the current liabilities section of the December 31, 2005 balance sheet.

WA14-3 Eshkol Corporation reports in the current liability section of its balance sheet at December 31, 2005 (its year end) short-term obligations of $15 million, which includes the current portion of 12% long-term debt in the amount of $11 million that matures in March 2006. Management has stated its intention to refinance the 12% debt whereby no portion of it will mature during 2006. The financial statements are issued on March 25, 2006.

Instructions

(a) Is management's intent enough to support long-term classification of the obligation in this situation?

(b) Assume that Eshkol Corporation issues $13 million of 10-year debentures to the public in January 2006 and that management intends to use the proceeds to liquidate the $11 million debt maturing in March 2006. Furthermore, assume that the debt maturing in March 2006 is paid from these proceeds prior to the issuance of the financial statements. Will this have any impact on the balance sheet classification at December 31, 2005? Explain your answer.

(c) Assume that Eshkol Corporation issues common shares to the public in January and that management intends to entirely liquidate the $11 million debt maturing in March 2006 with the proceeds of this equity securities issue. In light of these events, should the $11 million debt maturing in March 2006 be included in current liabilities at December 31, 2005?

(d) Assume that Eshkol Corporation, on February 15, 2006, entered into a financing agreement with a commercial bank that permits Eshkol Corporation to borrow at any time through 2007 up to $15 million at the bank's prime rate of interest. Borrowings under the financing agreement mature three years after the loan date. The agreement is not cancellable except for violation of a provision with which compliance is objectively determinable. No violation of any provision exists at the financial statement's date of issuance. Assume further that the current portion of long-term debt does not mature until August 2006. In addition, management intends to refinance the $11 million obligation under the terms of the financial agreement with the bank, which is expected to be financially capable of honouring the agreement.

   1.   Given these facts, should the $11 million be classified as current on the balance sheet at December 31, 2005?

   2.   Is disclosure of the refinancing method required?

WA14-4   On February 1, 2006, one of the huge storage tanks of Magen Manufacturing Limited exploded. Windows in houses and other buildings within a one-kilometre radius of the explosion were severely damaged, and a number of people were injured. As of February 15, 2006 (when the December 31, 2005 financial statements were completed and sent for printing and public distribution), no suits had been filed or claims asserted against the company as a consequence of the explosion. The company fully anticipates that suits will be filed and claims asserted for injuries and damages. Because the casualty was uninsured and the company considered at fault, Magen Manufacturing will have to cover the damages from its own resources.

Instructions
Discuss fully the accounting treatment and disclosures that should be accorded the casualty and related contingent losses in the financial statements dated December 31, 2005.

WA14-5   Conduit Corporation has a bonus arrangement that grants the financial vice-president and other executives a $15,000 cash bonus if net income exceeds the previous year's by $1 million. Noting that the current financial statements report an increase of $950,000 in net income, Charles Dickinson, the VP Finance, meets with Don Street, the controller, to see what can be done.

   Dickinson suggests to Street that the estimate of warranty expense could be reduced by $25,000 and still be a reasonable estimate as the current $500,000 warranty expense that has been recognized is known to be a fairly "soft" estimate. In addition, he suggests instead of recognizing the $250,000 "most likely" estimate of a contingent loss that has already been recorded in relation to outstanding litigation, that the loss be adjusted to $150,000, the lower number in the range of possible outcomes. Because of the uncertainty in estimating the extent of the expected loss, Conduit would disclose in a note the amount recognized and the total additional exposure to loss.

Instructions

(a) Should Street lower his estimate of the warranty liability?

(b) Should Street lower the amount of contingent loss that has been recognized?

(c) What ethical issue is at stake? Is anyone harmed?

(d) Is Dickinson acting ethically?

WA14-6   Presented below is a note disclosure for Frank Corporation.

   Litigation and Environmental: The Company has been notified, or is a named or a potentially responsible party in a number of governmental (federal, provincial, and local) and private actions associated with environmental matters, such as those relating to hazardous wastes, including certain Canadian sites. These actions seek clean-up costs, penalties and/or damages for personal injury or to property or natural resources.

   In 2005, the Company recorded a pre-tax charge of $56,229,000, included in the Other Expense (Income) Net caption of the Company's Consolidated Statement of Income, as an additional provision for environmental matters. These expenditures are expected to take place over the next several years and are indicative of the company's commitment to improve and maintain the environment in which it operates. At December 31, 2005, environmental accruals amounted to $69,931,000, of which $61,535,000 are considered noncurrent and are included in the Deferred Credits and Other Liabilities caption of the Company's Consolidated Balance Sheet.

While it is impossible at this time to determine with certainty the ultimate outcome of environmental matters, it is management's opinion, based in part on the advice of independent counsel (after taking into account accruals and insurance coverage applicable to such actions) that when the costs are finally determined they will not have a material adverse effect on the financial position of the Company.

Instructions
Answer the following questions.

(a) What conditions must exist before a loss contingency must be recorded in the accounts?

(b) Suppose that Frank Corporation could not reasonably estimate the amount of the loss, although it could establish with a high degree of probability the minimum and maximum loss possible. How should this information be reported in the financial statements?

(c) If the loss amount is uncertain, how would the loss contingency be reported in the financial statements?

(d) If the likelihood of any loss resulting from the litigation is unknown, how would the loss contingency be reported in the financial statements?

Cases

Refer to the Case Primer on the Digital Tool to help you with these cases.

CA14-1 Environmental accounting is one of the most controversial current trends in accounting. It is not controversial in the sense that professionals disagree as to whether it is important; rather, it is controversial because implementation of any environmental accounting model requires us to go outside the traditional GAAP model. It essentially involves a form of social accounting whereby an attempt is made to measure the impact on the environment (usually negative) of running a business. What is the cost of polluting the air and water or of destroying rain forests?

Digital Tool

www.wiley.com/canada/kieso

Envirocompany Limited (EL) is a pulp and paper company that has been in operation for 50 years. Its shares trade on a major stock exchange. It is situated in a small town in Northern Ontario and employs thousands of people. In fact, the town exists primarily because of the jobs created by EL. Its equipment is fairly antiquated and pollutes the surrounding water and air with chemicals that have been shown to be carcinogens. The old equipment is part of the reason for the "success" of the company since it is all paid for and requires little maintenance. For the employees, the pollution is tolerated because EL provides them with jobs and keeps the local economy going.

Last year, a new Chairman of the Board of Directors was appointed to EL. Charles Champion first became aware of the extent of the pollution prior to being appointed to the Board and felt that he would like to do something about it. He took this mission as a personal challenge and in the first year of his appointment, commissioned several in-depth studies as to how EL might reduce or eliminate the pollution. He wanted to be careful to protect himself and the other members of the Board because directors were increasingly held personally liable for the actions of companies.

Most studies pointed to the old machinery and recommended that it be replaced by new state-of-the-art equipment. Cost estimates ran into the millions of dollars and the Board of Directors felt that the company would not be able to survive that type of expenditure. One study proved that the company should not even be in business any more given the cost of new environmentally friendly equipment, declining demand for un-recycled newsprint, and increasing competition from abroad. That study was quickly shelved.

Recent environmental studies had shown that the pollutants were seeping into the water table and finding their way south to where major cities were situated. The studies showed that there were increasing incidences of birth defects in animals and humans in the areas in question, including increases in sterility for certain aquatic and marine life. This caused a number of politicians to start grandstanding and calling for tighter pollution controls and steep fines.

Recently, there had been reports of people living downstream getting sick, apparently from the chemical pollutants from EL. One had threatened to sue, and EL's lawyers were privately acknowledging the potential for a class action suit. EL has insurance that would cover up to $1 million in damages.

Meanwhile, the accountants were struggling with how to account for the problem for the year-end statements. Charles has requested that two sets of financial statements be drafted. He would like to know how the problem should be reflected for the external statements that will be presented at the shareholders' meeting and he would also like a set of financial statements that looks at the problem from a broader, all-encompassing perspective, for management decision making. Specifically, he wants to know if there is a liability, exactly what it is, and when it arose (or arises), if at all.

Pension Funding

TEACHERS'
PENSION PLAN

The **Ontario Teachers' Pension Plan** values the investment potential of real estate. Its subsidiary **Cadillac Fairview Corporation Ltd.** owns more than 100 of Canada's best retail and office properties, including the Toronto Eaton Centre, the Toronto-Dominion Centre, and the Pacific Centre in Vancouver. "Our pension plan guarantees inflation protection. So we look for investments that will give us good exposure to inflation. And real estate is one of those areas that tends to perform well if inflation rises," says Teachers' communications director Lee Fullerton.

To help finance Cadillac Fairview's real estate operations, Teachers' subsidiary **Ontrea Inc.** has issued bond debentures on two occasions. Most recently, in March 2003, Ontrea issued debentures worth $600 million. Teachers' has unconditionally guaranteed payment of principal, premiums, and interest by the bond's maturity date in 2013. This bond issue follows another $600 million of debentures issued in 2001, which was the first time a Canadian pension plan had guaranteed a debenture issue.

Teachers' bought Cadillac Fairview in 2000; the following year the investment restrictions under the *Pension Benefits Act* changed to allow pension plans to provide guarantees to their subsidiaries. A year later, the mortgage for the Toronto Eaton's Centre was coming due, and Teachers' issued a guaranteed debenture.

The most recent bond is unsecured and was issued through private placement. The coupon, or interest rate, on the bond is 5.57%. Interest will be paid semi-annually in arrears. As part of the agreement, Ontrea will not issue additional debentures guaranteed by Teachers' before 2008.

"Our intent was to make it look and act like a standard public bond, with all the requisite pricing benefits associated with a liquid public issue, despite the fact that it came with the less onerous reporting responsibilities of a private issue," says Sean Rogister, Teachers' vice-president, fixed income.■

Long-Term Financial Liabilities

Learning Objectives

After studying this chapter, you should be able to:

1. Describe the formal procedures associated with issuing long-term debt.
2. Identify various types of long-term debt.
3. Explain the initial measurement of bonds/notes at date of issuance.
4. Apply the methods of bond discount and premium amortization.
5. Value bonds and consideration in special situations.
6. Describe the accounting procedures for extinguishment of debt.
7. Explain the issues surrounding off-balance-sheet financing arrangements.
8. Indicate how long-term debt is presented and analysed.

After studying Appendix 15A, you should be able to:

9. Account for impairments on notes and loans receivable.
10. Distinguish between and account for debt restructurings resulting in extinguishment versus debt continuation.

simply for the cash proceeds and the bond's face value. To illustrate, if 10-year term bonds with a par value of $800,000, dated January 1, 2004 and bearing interest at an annual rate of 10% payable semiannually on January 1 and July 1, are issued on January 1 at par, the entry on the books of the issuing corporation would be:

A   =   L   + SE
+800,000   +800,000

Cash flows: ↑ 800,000 inflow

| Cash | 800,000 | |
| Bonds Payable | | 800,000 |

The entry to record the first semiannual interest payment of $40,000 ($800,000 × 0.10 × 1/2) on July 1, 2004 would be as follows.

A   = L +   SE
−40,000   −40,000

Cash flows: ↓ 40,000 outflow

| Bond Interest Expense | 40,000 | |
| Cash | | 40,000 |

The entry to record accrued interest expense at December 31, 2004 (year end) would be as follows.

A = L   +   SE
   +40,000   −40,000

Cash flows: No effect

| Bond Interest Expense | 40,000 | |
| Bond Interest Payable | | 40,000 |

In Chapter 10, we discussed the recognition of a $10,000, three-year note issued at face value by Scandinavian Imports to Bigelow Corp. In this transaction, the stated rate and the effective rate were both 10%. The time diagram and present value calculation in Chapter 10 (see page 500) for Bigelow Corp. would be the same for the issuer of the note, Scandinavian Imports, in recognizing a note payable. Because the note's present value and its face value are the same ($10,000) no premium or discount is recognized. The issuance of the note is recorded by Scandinavian Imports as follows.

A   =   L   + SE
+10,000   +10,000

Cash flows: ↑ 10,000 inflow

| Cash | 10,000 | |
| Notes Payable | | 10,000 |

Discounts and Premiums

The issuance and marketing of bonds to the public does not happen overnight. It usually takes weeks or even months. Underwriters must be arranged, Securities Commission approval must be obtained, audits and issuance of a prospectus may be required, and certificates must be printed. Frequently, the terms in a bond indenture are established well in advance of the bond sale. Between the time the terms are set and the bonds are issued, the market conditions and the issuing corporation's financial position may change significantly. Such changes affect the bonds' marketability and thus their selling price.

A bond's selling price is set by supply and demand of buyers and sellers, relative risk, market conditions, and the state of the economy. The investment community values a bond at the **present value of its future cash flows**, which consist of (1) **interest** and (2) **principal**. The rate used to calculate the present value of these cash flows is the interest rate that provides an acceptable return on an investment commensurate with the issuer's risk characteristics.

The interest rate written in the terms of the bond indenture (and ordinarily printed on the bond certificate) is known as the stated, coupon, or nominal rate. This rate, which is set by the bond issuer, is expressed as a percentage of the bond's face value, also called the par value, principal amount, or maturity value. If the rate employed by the investment community (buyers) differs from the stated rate, the bond's present value calculated by the buyers (and the current purchase price) will differ from its face value. The difference between the face value and the bond's present value is either a discount or premium.[4] If the bonds sell for less than face value, they are sold at a discount. If the bonds sell for more than face value, they are sold at a premium.

The interest rate actually earned by the bondholders is called the effective yield or market rate. If bonds sell at a **discount**, the **effective yield is higher than the stated rate**. Conversely, if bonds sell at a **premium**, the **effective yield is lower than the stated rate**. While the bond is outstanding, its price is affected by several variables, most notably the market rate of interest. There is an inverse relationship between the market interest rate and the bond price.

To illustrate the calculation of the present value of a bond issue, consider Discount Limited, which issues $100,000 in bonds, due in five years with 9% interest payable annually at year end. At the time of issue, the market rate for such bonds is 11%. Illustration 15-2 depicts both the interest and the principal cash flows.

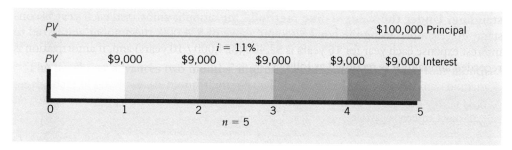

Illustration 15-2

Present Value Calculation of Bond Selling at a Discount

The actual principal and interest cash flows are discounted at an 11% rate for five periods as follows.

International Insight

Valuation of long-term debt varies internationally. In Canada and the United States, discount and premium are booked and amortized over the life of the debt. In some countries (e.g., Japan) it is permissible to write off the discount and premium immediately.

Present value of the principal: $100,000 × .59345	$59,345
Present value of the interest payments: $9,000 × 3.69590	33,263
Present value (selling price) of the bonds	$92,608

By paying $92,608 at the date of issue, the investors will realize an **effective rate or yield** of 11% over the five-year term of the bonds. These bonds would sell at a discount of $7,392 ($100,000 − $92,608). The price at which the bonds sell is typically stated as a percentage of their face or par value. For example, the Discount Limited bonds sold for 92.6 (92.6% of par). If Discount Limited had received $102,000, we would say the bonds sold for 102 (102% of par).

When bonds sell below face value, it means that investors demand a rate of interest higher than the stated rate. The investors are not satisfied with the stated rate because they can earn a greater rate on alternative investments of equal risk. They cannot change the stated rate, so they refuse to pay face value for the bonds. Thus, **by changing the amount**

---

[4] Until the 1950s, it was common for corporations to issue bonds with low, even-percent coupons (such as 4%) to demonstrate their financial solidarity. Frequently, the result was larger discounts. More recently, it has become acceptable to set the stated rate of interest on bonds in more precise terms, e.g., 6 7/8%. Companies usually attempt to align the stated rate as closely as possible with the market or effective rate at the time of issue. While discounts and premiums continue to occur, their absolute magnitude tends to be much smaller; many times it is immaterial. Professor Bill N. Schwartz (Virginia Commonwealth University) studied the 685 new debt offerings in the United States in 1985. Of these, none were issued at a premium. Approximately 95% were issued either with no discount or at a price above 98. Now, however, zero-interest (deep discount) bonds are more popular, which causes substantial discounts.

Illustration 15-7

Bond Premium Amortization Schedule

SCHEDULE OF BOND PREMIUM AMORTIZATION
Effective Interest Method–Semiannual Interest Payments
5-Year, 8% Bonds Sold to Yield 6%

Date	Cash Paid	Interest Expense	Premium Amortized	Carrying Amount of Bonds
1/1/04				$108,530
7/1/04	$ 4,000ᵃ	$ 3,256ᵇ	$ 744ᶜ	107,786ᵈ
1/1/05	4,000	3,234	766	107,020
7/1/05	4,000	3,211	789	106,231
1/1/06	4,000	3,187	813	105,418
7/1/06	4,000	3,162	838	104,580
1/1/07	4,000	3,137	863	103,717
7/1/07	4,000	3,112	888	102,829
1/1/08	4,000	3,085	915	101,914
7/1/08	4,000	3,057	943	100,971
1/1/09	4,000	3,029	971	100,000
	$40,000	$31,470	$8,530	

ᵃ$4,000 = $100,000 × 0.08 × 6/12   ᶜ$744 = $4,000 − $3,256
ᵇ$3,256 = $108,530 × 0.06 × 6/12   ᵈ$107,786 = $108,530 − $744

The entry to record the issuance of Master bonds at a premium on January 1, 2004 is:

A   =   L   + SE
+108,530   +108,530

Cash flows: ↑ 108,530 inflow

Cash	108,530	
Premium on Bonds Payable		8,530
Bonds Payable		100,000

The journal entry to record the first interest payment on July 1, 2004 and amortization of the premium is:

A   =   L   +   SE
−4,000   −744   −3,256

Cash flows: ↓ 4,000 outflow

Bond Interest Expense	3,256	
Premium on Bonds Payable	744	
Cash		4,000

The discount or premium should be amortized as an adjustment to interest expense over the life of the bond such that it results in a **constant interest rate** when applied to the carrying amount of debt outstanding at the beginning of any given period.

Accruing Interest

In our previous examples, the interest payment dates and the date the financial statements were issued were the same. For example, when Master sold bonds at a premium, the two interest payment dates coincided with the financial reporting dates. However, what happens if Master wishes to report financial statements at the end of February 2004? In this case, the premium is prorated by the appropriate number of months to arrive at the proper interest expense, as follows in Illustration 15-8.

Illustration 15-8

Calculation of Interest Expense

Interest accrual ($4,000 × 2/6)	$1,333.33
Premium amortized ($744 × 2/6)	(248.00)
Interest expense (Jan.–Feb.)	$1,085.33

The journal entry to record this accrual is as follows.

Bond Interest Expense	1,085	
Premium on Bonds Payable	248	
Bond Interest Payable		1,333

A = L + SE
+1,085 + −1,085

Cash flows: No effect

If the company prepares financial statements six months later, the same procedure is followed; that is, the premium amortized would be as follows in Illustration 15-9.

Premium amortized (March–June) ($744 × 4/6)	$496.00
Premium amortized (July–August) ($766 × 2/6)	255.33
Premium amortized (March–August 2004)	$751.33

Illustration 15-9

Calculation of Premium Amortization

The calculation is much simpler if the straight-line method is employed. For example, in the Master situation, the total premium is $8,530, which is allocated evenly over the five-year period. Thus, premium amortization per month is $142 ($8,530/60 months).

Deep Discount or Zero-Interest-Bearing Bonds/Notes

If a zero-interest-bearing (noninterest-bearing) note or bond is issued solely for cash, its present value is measured by the cash received by the note or bond's issuer. The implicit interest rate is the **rate that equates the cash received with the present value of the amounts received in the future.** The difference between the face amount and the present value (cash received) is recorded as **a discount and amortized to interest expense over the life of the note.**

To illustrate the entries and the amortization schedule, assume that your company is the one that issued the 3-year, $10,000, zero-interest-bearing note to Jeremiah Company as illustrated on page 501 of Chapter 10 (notes receivable). The implicit rate that equated the total cash to be paid ($10,000 at maturity) to the present value of the future cash flows ($7,721.80 cash proceeds at date of issuance) was 9%. (The present value of $1 for three periods at 9% is $0.77218.) The time diagram depicting the one cash flow is shown below.

Underlying Concept

Even though deep discount bonds have little or no interest attached to them legally, interest is imputed and the payout on maturity is viewed as part principal and part interest, reflecting the economic substance of the bond and the time value of money.

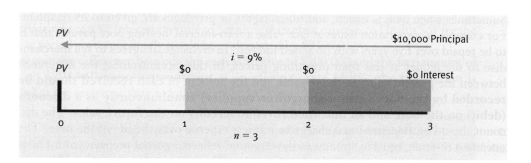

Your entry to record issuance of the note is as follows.

Cash	7,722	
Discount on Notes Payable	2,278	
Notes Payable		10,000

A = L + SE
+7,722 +7,722

Cash flows: ↑ 7,722 inflow

	December 31, 2005	
A = L + SE		
−24,500 −24,500	Bond Issue Expense	24,500	
Cash flows: No effect	Unamortized Bond Issue Costs		24,500
	(To amortize one year of bond issue costs, straight-line method)		

A = L + SE
−24,500   −24,500
Cash flows: No effect

December 31, 2005

Bond Issue Expense	24,500	
Unamortized Bond Issue Costs		24,500
(To amortize one year of bond issue costs, straight-line method)		

EXTINGUISHMENT OF DEBT OR DERECOGNITION

Objective 6
Describe the accounting procedures for extinguishment of debt.

Payment of debt is often referred to as extinguishment of debt. When debt is repaid or extinguished—i.e., when the obligation is discharged, cancelled, or expires—it is **derecognized** from the financial statements.[10] If the bonds (or any other form of debt security) are held to maturity, **no gain or loss is calculated**. Any premium or discount and any issue costs will be fully amortized at the date the bonds mature. As a result, the carrying amount will be equal to the bond's maturity (face) value. As the maturity or face value is also equal to the bond's market value at that time, no gain or loss exists.

Repayment Prior to Maturity Date

In some cases, debt is extinguished before its maturity date. The amount paid on extinguishment or redemption before maturity, including any call premium and expense of reacquisition, is called the **reacquisition price**. On any specified date, the bond's **net carrying amount** is the amount payable at maturity, adjusted for unamortized premium or discount, and cost of issuance. Any excess of the net carrying amount over the reacquisition price is a **gain from extinguishment**, whereas the excess of the reacquisition price over the net carrying amount is a **loss from extinguishment**. At the time of reacquisition, the **unamortized premium or discount and any costs of issue applicable to the bonds must be amortized up to the reacquisition date**.

To illustrate, assume that on January 1, 1997, General Bell Corp. issued bonds with a par value of $800,000 at 97, due in 20 years. Bond issue costs totalling $16,000 were incurred. Eight years after the issue date, the entire issue is called at 101 and cancelled. The loss on redemption (extinguishment) is calculated as follows in Illustration 15-13 (straight-line amortization is used for simplicity).

Illustration 15-13

Calculation of Loss on Redemption of Bonds

Reacquisition price ($800,000 × 1.01)		$808,000
Net carrying amount of bonds redeemed:		
Face value	$800,000	
Unamortized discount ($24,000* × 12/20)	(14,400)	
Unamortized issue costs ($16,000 × 12/20)		
(both amortized using straight-line basis)	(9,600)	776,000
Loss on redemption		$ 32,000

*[$800,000 × (1 − 0.97)]

---

[10] Proposed *CICA Handbook* Section 3855.

The entry to record the reacquisition and cancellation of the bonds is:

Bonds Payable	800,000	
Loss on Redemption of Bonds	32,000	
Discount on Bonds Payable		14,400
Unamortized Bond Issue Costs		9,600
Cash		808,000

A   =   L   +   SE
−817,600 −785,600 −32,000

Cash flows: ↓ 808,000 outflow

Note that it is often advantageous for the issuing corporation to acquire the entire outstanding bond issue and replace it with a new bond issue bearing a lower rate of interest. As an example, in June of 2001, **Aliant Telecom Inc.** redeemed its 10.25% First Mortgage Bonds, Series AC, which were originally due August 2006. The bonds were redeemed at 102% of the principal amount plus $0.28 per $1,000 principal amounts representing accrued interest. The premium of 2% was paid due to the fact that the stated interest rate on the bonds is greater than the current market rate and therefore, holders would need to be induced to part with the bonds.

What do the Numbers Mean?

Exchange of Debt Instruments

The replacement of an existing issuance with a new one is called refunding. Generally, an exchange of debt instruments between a borrower and lender with **substantially different terms** is viewed as an extinguishment of the old debt (and issuance of new debt).[11] Alternatively, if the terms under the new debt are not substantially different, it is viewed as a **renegotiation or modification of the old debt**.

Underlying Concept

If the new debt is substantially the same as the old debt, the economic substance is that it is a continuation of the old debt, even though legally, the old debt may have been settled.

Professional judgement is applied in making this determination. The debt would be viewed as being substantially different when:

- the discounted present value of the cash flows under the new terms (discounted using the original effective interest rate) is at least 10% different from the discounted present value of the remaining cash flows under the old debt or,

- there is a change in creditor and the original debt is legally discharged.[12]

If the debt is considered settled, the liability and related accounts relating to the old debt are derecognized and a gain or loss results. The new debt is then recognized on the balance sheet.

Alternatively, if the debt is viewed as a **modification or renegotiation**, the debt is left on the balance sheet and a new effective interest rate is calculated that equates the cash flows under the new terms to the carrying value of the existing debt. [13]

Appendix 15A looks at modification of debt instruments in more detail, dealing with the scenario where the debt is renegotiated under **troubled debt restructuring conditions**.

Defeasance

Sometimes, a company may wish to extinguish or pay off debt prior to its due date but economic factors such as early repayment penalties may preclude this. One option open to the company in this type of situation is to set aside the money in a trust or other arrangement and allow the trust to repay the original debt (principal and interest) as it becomes due

---

[11] Proposed *CICA Handbook* Section 3855.

[12] Proposed *CICA Handbook* Section 3855.

[13] *CICA Handbook, EIC Abstract #88* and proposed *CICA Handbook* Section 3855.

ules in the accompanying notes. Long-term debt that **matures within one year** should be reported as a **current liability**, unless retirement is to be accomplished with other than current assets.[16] If the debt is to be refinanced, the company must treat it as long-term unless the refinancing has occurred prior to the release of the financial statements or a refinancing agreement is in place.[17]

Debt versus Equity

As financial instruments become more and more complex, the line between what is debt and what is equity is becoming more blurred. As noted above, there is significant pressure on companies to watch their debt levels. The debt versus equity issue will be dealt with in Chapter 17 when more complex financial instruments are addressed.

Classification of Discount and Premium

Conceptually, Discount on Bonds Payable is **not an asset** because it does not provide any **future economic benefit**. The enterprise has the use of the borrowed funds, but for that use it must pay interest. A bond discount means that the company borrowed less than the bond's face or maturity value and therefore is faced with an actual (effective) interest rate higher than the stated (nominal) rate. Discount on Bonds Payable is a **liability valuation account**; that is, it is a reduction of the face or maturity amount of the related liability. This account is referred to as a **contra** account.

Premium on bonds payable has no existence apart from the related debt. The lower interest cost results because the proceeds of borrowing exceed the debt's face or maturity amount. Conceptually, premium on bonds payable is a liability valuation account; that is, it is an addition to the face or maturity amount of the related liability. This account is referred to as an **adjunct** account. In practice, the unamortized portion of discount is frequently shown on the balance sheet as Deferred Charges under assets.[18] Correspondingly, unamortized premium is frequently shown as a deferred credit under liabilities. This is conceptually less appealing for the above noted reasons.

Note Disclosures

Note disclosures generally indicate the **nature of the liabilities, maturity dates, interest rates, call provisions, conversion privileges, restrictions imposed by the creditors, and assets designated or pledged as security**. Any assets **pledged as security** for the debt should be shown in the assets section of the balance sheet. **The fair value** of the long-term debt should also be disclosed if it is practical to estimate fair value. Finally, disclosure is required of **future payments** for sinking fund requirements and maturity amounts of long-term debt during each of the next five years.[19] The purpose of these disclosures is to **aid financial statement users in evaluating the amounts and timing of future cash flows**. An example of the type of information provided is shown in the **Intrawest** financial statements in Chapter 5.

---

[16] *CICA Handbook*, Section 1510.06.

[17] *CICA EIC Abstract # 122* requires the following: i) the loan under the refinancing agreement must be for more than one year, ii) the company must be in compliance with all terms, and iii) the lender must be financially capable of honouring the agreement.

[18] *CICA Handbook* Section 3070.02 makes reference to this treatment.

[19] *CICA Handbook*, Sections 3210 and 3860.

PERSPECTIVES

The level of debt that a company holds is a very high profile number. How much debt is the right amount of debt? Some debt is good to take advantage of leverage; however, too much debt increases the risk to the company. The higher the debt, the greater the risk that the company may not be able to repay it. Capital markets acknowledge this additional solvency risk by increasing the cost of capital and making it more difficult for companies with high debt levels to access additional capital.

Lenders insert covenants into lending agreements as a safeguard to ensure that companies manage their cash flow risks. Although debt holders assume that the covenants will protect them, covenants are often written in a manner that can be interpreted (or misinterpreted) in a number of different ways. Therefore, covenants may provide little or no protection at all. Note further that covenants normally incorporate references to certain financial tests and ratios that must be met or the debt will become payable. **Because of this, the existence of restrictive covenants creates situations where reporting bias may exist.** Most companies must ensure that these tests are met or face the consequences (be prepared to repay the debt). This may provide an environment where the company feels compelled to meet the test even if it means using aggressive accounting to do so.

Users of financial statements must be aware of the existence of covenants so that they understand the potential for misstating the financial statements. Whenever these stipulations are important to completely understand the financial position and the results of operations, they should be described in the body of the financial statements or the notes thereto. Ratio analysis will be revisited at the end of the chapter.

Long-term creditors and shareholders are interested in a company's long-run **solvency**, particularly its ability to pay interest as it comes due and to repay the debt's face value at maturity. Therefore, many debt agreements include covenants that stipulate that certain ratios be met. **Debt-to-total-asset and times interest earned** are two ratios that provide information about debt-paying ability and long-run solvency. Companies have a vested interest in assuring that debt levels are managed so as not to degrade the company's solvency position. The debt-to-total-asset ratio measures the percentage of the total assets provided by creditors. It is calculated as shown in the following formula by dividing total debt (both current and long-term liabilities) by total assets.

$$\text{Debt to total assets} = \frac{\text{Total debt}}{\text{Total assets}}$$

The **higher the percentage** of debt to total assets, the **greater the risk** that the company may be unable to meet its maturing obligations.

The times interest earned ratio indicates the company's ability to meet interest payments as they come due. It is calculated by dividing income before interest expense and income taxes by interest expense.

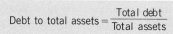

$$\text{Times interest earned} = \frac{\text{Income before income taxes and interest expense}}{\text{Interest expense}}$$

To illustrate these ratios, we will use data from Talisman Energy Inc.'s 2000 annual report, which disclosed total liabilities of $5,012.1 million, total assets of $8,675.7 million, interest of $135.9 million, income taxes of $679.6 million, and net income of $906.3 million. Talisman's debt-to-total-asset ratio is calculated as follows.

$$\text{Debt to total assets} = \$5012.1/8675.7 = 57.8\%$$

Talisman's times interest earned ratio is calculated as follows.

$$\text{Times interest earned} = 1721.80/135.9 = 12.7 \text{ times}$$

Even though Talisman has a relatively high debt-to-total asset percentage of 57.8%, its interest coverage of 12.7 times appears very safe. Note that when capitalized interest is included, the ratio drops to 10.4.

Digital Tool

Glossary

www.wiley.com/canada/kieso

KEY TERMS

Summary of Learning Objectives

1 Describe the formal procedures associated with issuing long-term debt.

Incurring long-term debt is often a formal procedure. Corporation bylaws usually require approval by the board of directors and the shareholders before bonds can be issued or other long-term debt arrangements can be contracted. Generally, long-term debt has various covenants or restrictions. The covenants and other terms of the agreement between the borrower and the lender are stated in the bond indenture or note agreement. Notes are similar in substance to bonds but do not trade as readily in capital markets, if at all.

2 Identify various types of long-term debt.

(1) Secured and unsecured bonds. (2) Term, serial, perpetual, and callable bonds or notes. (3) Convertible, commodity-backed, and bonds that may be settled in common shares. (4) Registered and bearer (coupon) bonds. (5) Income, revenue, and deep discount bonds. The variety in the types of bonds is a result of attempts to attract capital from different investors and risk takers and to satisfy the issuers' cash flow needs.

3 Explain the initial measurement of bonds/notes at date of issuance.

The investment community values a bond at the present value of its future cash flows, which consist of interest and principal. The rate used to calculate the present value of these cash flows is the interest rate that provides an acceptable return on an investment commensurate with the issuer's risk characteristics. The interest rate written in the terms of the bond indenture and ordinarily appearing on the bond certificate is the stated, coupon, or nominal rate. This rate, which is set by the issuer of the bonds, is expressed as a percentage of the bond's face value, also called the par value, principal amount, or maturity value. If the rate employed by the buyers differs from the stated rate, the bond's present value calculated by the buyers will differ from the bond's face value. The difference between the bond's face value and the present value is either a discount or premium.

4 Apply the methods of bond discount and premium amortization.

The discount (premium) is amortized and charged (credited) to interest expense over the period of time that the bonds are outstanding. Bond interest expense is increased by amortization of a discount and decreased by amortization of a premium. GAAP requires the effective interest method; however, in practice, the straight-line method is used where GAAP is not a constraint or where the results are not substantially different. Under the effective interest method, (1) bond interest expense is calculated by multiplying the bond's carrying value at the beginning of the period by the effective interest rate, and (2) the bond discount or premium amortization is then determined by comparing the bond interest expense with the interest to be paid.

5 Value bonds and consideration in special situations.

Bonds may be issued for cash and other rights or for non-monetary consideration. Measurement of the bonds and the consideration must reflect the underlying substance of the transaction. In particular, unearned revenues for future services should be accrued and reasonable interest rates must be imputed. The fair value of the debt as well as non-monetary consideration should be used to value the transaction.

6 Describe the accounting procedures for extinguishment of debt.

At the time of reacquisition, the unamortized premium or discount and any costs of issue applicable to the debt must be amortized up to the reacquisition date. The amount paid on extinguishments or redemption before maturity, including any call premium and expense of reacquisition, is the reacquisition price. On any specified date, the debt's net carrying amount is the amount payable at maturity, adjusted for unamortized premium or discount, and cost of issuance. Any excess of the net carrying amount over the reacquisition price is a gain from extinguishment, whereas the excess of the reacquisition price over the net carrying amount is a loss from extinguishment. Legal defeasance results in debt extinguishment.

7 Explain the issues surrounding off-balance-sheet.

Off-balance-sheet financing is an attempt to borrow funds in such a way that the obligations are not recorded. One type of off-balance-sheet financing occurs with certain variable interest entities.

8 Indicate how long-term debt is presented and analysed.

Companies that have large amounts and numerous issues of long-term debt frequently report only one amount in the balance sheet and support this with comments and schedules in the accompanying notes. Any assets pledged as security for the debt should be shown in the assets section of the balance sheet. Long-term debt that matures within one year should be reported as a current liability, unless retirement is to be accomplished with other than current assets. If the debt is to be refinanced, converted into shares, or is to be retired from a bond retirement fund, it should continue to be reported as noncurrent and accompanied with a note explaining the method to be used in its liquidation. Disclosure is required of future payments for sinking fund requirements and maturity amounts of long-term debt during each of the next five years. Debt-to-total-asset and times interest earned are two ratios that provide information about debt-paying ability and long-run solvency.

a **cash forecast**. A dividend should not be paid unless both the present and future financial position appear to warrant the distribution. Directors must also consider the effect of inflation and replacement costs before making a dividend commitment. During a period of significant inflation, some costs charged to expense under historical cost accounting are understated in terms of **comparative purchasing power**. Income is thereby **overstated** because certain costs have not been adjusted for inflation.

What do the Numbers Mean?

Non-payment of dividends may significantly impact the company as well. For instance Torstar Corporation has Class B shares that are normally non-voting. However, if the company does not pay dividends for eight consecutive quarters, the shares then have voting rights.

Not all shares carry the right to receive dividends. For example, the Saskatchewan Wheat Pool has two classes of shares. Class B shares trade on the TSE and have dividend rights while Class A voting shares are held by farmer-members and are not eligible for dividends. This is presumably due to the fact that the farmers receive other benefits from the Wheat Pool, which is operated as a co-op.

Types of Dividends

Objective 7
Explain the accounting for various forms of dividend distributions.

There are basically two classes of dividends:

1. Those that are a return **on** capital (a share of the earnings), and

2. Those that are a return **of** capital, referred to as liquidating dividends.

The natural expectation of any shareholder who receives a dividend is that the corporation has operated successfully and that he or she is receiving a share of its earnings. A liquidating dividend should therefore be adequately described in the financial statements. This type of dividend will be discussed in greater depth later in the chapter.

Dividends are commonly paid in cash but occasionally are paid in shares or other assets. **Dividends generally reduce the total shareholders' equity in the corporation**, because the equity is reduced, either through an immediate or promised future distribution of assets. Stock dividends are different, however. When a stock dividend is declared, the corporation does not pay out assets or incur a liability. It issues additional shares to each shareholder and nothing more. Stock dividends will be looked at in more detail later in the chapter.

Dividends—Cash or Other Assets

The board of directors votes on the declaration of dividends and if the resolution is properly approved, the dividend is declared. Before it is paid, a current list of shareholders must be prepared. For this reason, there is usually a time lag between declaration and payment. A resolution approved at the January 10 (**date of declaration**) meeting of the board of directors might be declared payable February 5 (**date of payment**) to all shareholders of record January 25 (**date of record**).[22]

Underlying Concept

A declared dividend is a liability because once declared, the company cannot avoid paying it.

The period from January 10 to January 25 gives time for any transfers in process to be completed and registered with the transfer agent. The time from January 25 to February 5 provides an opportunity for the transfer agent or accounting department, depending on who does this work, to prepare a list of shareholders as of January 25 and to prepare and mail dividend cheques.

---

[22] Theoretically, the ex-dividend date is the day after the date of record. However, to allow time for the transfer of shares, the stock exchanges generally advance the ex-dividend date two to four days. Therefore, the party who owns the shares on the day prior to the expressed ex-dividend date receives the dividends, and the party who buys the stock on or after the ex-dividend date does not receive the dividend. Between the declarations date and the ex-dividend date, the market price of the shares includes the dividend.

The following entries are required to record the declaration and payment of an ordinary dividend payable in cash. For example, Rajah Corp. on June 10 declared a cash dividend of 50 cents a share on 1.8 million shares payable July 16 to all shareholders of record June 24.

At date of declaration (June 10)		
Retained Earnings (Cash Dividends Declared)	900,000	
Dividends Payable		900,000
At date of record (June 24)		
No entry		
At date of payment (July 16)		
Dividends Payable	900,000	
Cash		900,000

A = L + SE
  +900,000 −900,000
Cash flows: No effect

A = L + SE
−900,000 −900,000
Cash flows: ↓ 900,000 outflow

To set up a ledger account that shows the amount of dividends declared during the year, Cash Dividends Declared might be debited instead of Retained Earnings at the time of declaration. This account is then closed to Retained Earnings at year end. Dividends may be declared either as a certain percent of par or stated value, such as a 6% dividend, or as an amount per share, such as 60 cents per share. In the first case, the rate is multiplied by the par or stated value of outstanding shares to get the total dividend; in the second, the amount per share is multiplied by the number of shares outstanding. **Cash dividends are not declared and paid on treasury shares since the shares are owned by the company itself.**

Dividends in Kind

Dividends payable in corporation assets other than cash are called property dividends or *dividends in kind*. Property dividends may be merchandise, real estate, or investments, or whatever form the board of directors designates. Because of the obvious difficulties of dividing units and delivering to shareholders, the usual property dividend is in the form of securities of other companies that the distributing corporation holds as an investment.

A property dividend is a nonreciprocal transfer of nonmonetary assets between an enterprise and its owners. These dividends should be measured at the fair value of the asset given up[23] unless they are considered to represent a spin-off or other form of restructuring or liquidation, in which case, they should be recorded at the carrying value of the non-monetary assets or liabilities transferred.[24] No gain or loss would be recorded in the second instance.

When **DuPont's** 23% investment in **General Motors** was held by the U.S. Supreme Court to be in violation of antitrust laws, DuPont was ordered to divest itself of the GM shares within 10 years. The shares represented 63 million shares of GM's 281 million shares then outstanding. DuPont couldn't sell the shares in one block of 63 million, nor could it sell 6 million shares annually for the next 10 years without severely depressing the value of the GM shares. At that time the entire yearly trading volume in GM shares did not exceed 6 million shares. DuPont solved its problem by declaring a property dividend and distributing the GM shares as a dividend to its own shareholders.

The **fair value** of the nonmonetary asset distributed is measured by the amount that would be realizable in an outright sale at or near the time of the distribution. Such an amount should be determined by referring to estimated realizable values in cash transactions of the same or similar assets, quoted market prices, independent appraisals, and other available evidence.

What do the Numbers Mean?

---

[23] *CICA Handbook*, Section 3830.05.

[24] *CICA Handbook*, Section 3830.11.

Stock Dividends.

If the management wishes to capitalize part of the earnings (i.e., reclassify amounts from earned to contributed capital) and thus retain earnings in the business on a permanent basis, it may issue a stock dividend. In this case, **no assets are distributed**, and each shareholder has exactly the same proportionate interest in the corporation and the same total book value after the stock dividend was issued as before it was declared. The book value per share is lower because an increased number of shares are held.

There is no clear guidance as to how to account for stock dividends. The big picture issue is whether they are to be treated in the same manner as other dividends or not.[25] As a dividend they should be **recognized** as such and therefore Retained Earnings should be debited and Share Capital credited. If booked as a dividend, how should the transaction be **measured**? One option is to measure the shares issued at their market value at the declaration date.

Where the stock dividends give the option to the holder to receive them in cash or shares, the stock dividend is a nonmonetary transaction and must be treated as a regular dividend, valued at fair value.[26] Where there is no option to receive the dividend in cash, GAAP is unclear; however, the CBCA states that for stock dividends, the declared amount of the dividend shall be added to the stated capital account. The CBCA does not allow shares to be issued until they are fully paid for in an amount not less than the fair equivalent of money that the corporation would have received had the shares been issued for cash. Therefore, if the company is incorporated under the CBCA, stock dividends should be recorded as dividends and measured at fair value.

To illustrate a stock dividend, assume that a corporation has outstanding 1,000 common shares and retained earnings of $50,000. If the corporation declares a 10% stock dividend, it issues 100 additional shares to current shareholders. If it is assumed that the shares' fair value at the time of the stock dividend is $130 per share and that the shareholders had the option to take the dividend in cash but chose not to, the entry is:

$$A = L + SE$$
$$-13,000$$
$$+13,000$$

Cash flows: No effect

At date of declaration		
Retained Earnings (Stock Dividend Declared)	13,000	
Common Stock		13,000

Note that no asset or liability has been affected. The entry merely reflects a reclassification of shareholders' equity.

No matter what the fair value is at the time of the stock dividend, each shareholder retains the same proportionate interest in the corporation. Illustration 16-3 proves this point.

Illustration 16-3

Effects of a Stock Dividend

Before dividend:	
Common shares, 1,000 shares	$100,000
Retained earnings	50,000
Total shareholders' equity	$150,000
Shareholders interests:	
(a) 400 shares, 40% interest, book value	$ 60,000
(b) 500 shares, 50% interest, book value	75,000
(c) 100 shares, 10% interest, book value	15,000
	$150,000

---

[25] From a tax perspective, CCRA treats stock dividends received the same as other dividends. The dividends are measured at paid up capital (legal capital, which is equal to fair value at the date of dividend declaration for no par shares).

[26] *CICA Handbook*, Section 3830 pars. .04 (ii) and .05.

Illustration 16-3

Effects of a Stock Dividend
continued

After declaration and distribution of 10% stock dividend:
If fair value ($130) is used as basis for entry

Shareholders' Common shares, 1,100 shares	$113,000
Retained earnings ($50,000 − $13,000)	37,000
Total shareholders' equity	$150,000

Shareholders' interest:

(a) 440 shares, 40% interest, book value	$ 60,000
(b) 550 shares, 50% interest, book value	75,000
(c) 110 shares, 10% interest, book value	15,000
	$150,000

Note in Illustration 16-3 that the total shareholders' equity has not changed as a result of the share dividend. Also note that the proportion of the total shares outstanding held by each shareholder is unchanged.

Liquidating Dividends

Some corporations use contributed surplus as a basis for dividends. Without proper disclosure of this fact, shareholders may erroneously believe the corporation has been paying dividends out of profits. We noted in Chapter 12 that companies in the extractive industries may pay dividends equal to the total of accumulated income and depletion. The portion of these dividends in excess of accumulated income represents a return of part of the shareholder's investment.

For example, McChesney Mines Inc. issued a dividend to its common shareholders of $1.2 million. The cash dividend announcement noted that $900,000 should be considered income and the remainder a return of capital. The entries are:

At date of declaration		
Retained Earnings	900,000	
Contributed Surplus	300,000	
Dividends Payable		1,200,000

A = L + SE
    +1,200,000   −$1,200,000

Cash flows: No effect

In some cases, management may simply decide to cease business and declare a liquidating dividend. In these cases, liquidation may take place over a number of years to ensure an orderly and fair sale of assets.

Effects of Dividend Preferences

The examples given below illustrate the effects of various dividend preferences on dividend distributions to common and preferred shareholders. Assume that in a given year, $50,000 is to be distributed as cash dividends, outstanding common shares have a value of $400,000, and 1,000 $6 preferred shares are outstanding (issued at $100,000). Dividends would be distributed to each class as shown below, employing the assumptions given.

8 Objective
Explain the effect of different types of dividend preferences.

1. If the preferred shares are noncumulative and nonparticipating:

	Preferred	Common	Total
$6 × 1,000	$6,000	$0	$ 6,000
The remainder to common	0	$44,000	44,000
Totals	$6,000	$44,000	$50,000

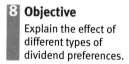

Illustration 16-4

Dividend Distribution, Noncumulative and Nonparticipating Preferred

2. If the preferred shares are cumulative and nonparticipating, and dividends were not paid on the preferred shares in the preceding two years:

Illustration 16-5

Dividend Distribution, Cumulative and Nonparticipating Preferred, with Dividends in Arrears

	Preferred	Common	Total
Dividends in arrears, $6 × 1,000 for 2 years	$12,000	$0	$12,000
Current year's dividend, $6 x 1,000	6,000	0	6,000
The remainder to common	0	$32,000	32,000
Totals	$18,000	$32,000	$50,000

3. If the preferred shares are noncumulative and are fully participating:[27]

Illustration 16-6

Dividend Distribution, Noncumulative and Fully Participating Preferred

	Preferred	Common	Total
Current year's dividend, $6	$ 6,000	$24,000	$30,000
Participating dividend—pro rata	4,000	16,000	20,000
Totals	$10,000	$40,000	$50,000

The participating dividend was determined as follows.

Current year's dividend:	
Preferred, $6 × 1,000 = $ 6,000	
Common, 6% of $400,000 = $24,000 (= a like amount)	$ 30,000
NB the 6% represents $6,000 on pref shares/ $100,000	
Amount available for participation ($50,000 − $30,000)	$ 20,000
Carrying value of shares that are to participate ($100,000 + $400,000)	$500,000
Rate of participation ($20,000/$500,000)	4%
Participating dividend:	
Preferred (4% of $100,000)	$ 4,000
Common (4% of $400,000)	16,000
	$ 20,000

4. If the preferred shares are cumulative and fully participating, and if dividends were not paid on the preferred shares in the preceding two years (the same procedure as described in example (3) is used in this example to effect the participation feature):

---

[27] When preferred shares are participating, there may be different agreements as to how the participation feature is to be executed. However, in the absence of any specific agreement, the following procedure is recommended:

　(a) After the preferred shares are assigned their current year's dividend, the common shares will receive a "like" percentage. In example (3), this amounts to 6% of $400,000.

　(b) If there is a remainder of declared dividends for participation by the preferred and common shares, this remainder will be shared in proportion to the carrying value in each share class. In example (3), this proportion is:

　　Preferred $100,000/500,000 × $20,000 = $4,000

　　Common $400,000/500,000 × $20,000 = $16,000

	Preferred	Common	Total
Dividends in arrears,			
$6 × 1,000 for 2 years	$12,000	$0	$12,000
Current year's dividend, $6	6,000	$24,000	30,000
Participating dividend, 1.6%			
($8,000/$500,000)	1,600	$ 6,400	8,000
Totals	$19,600	$30,400	$50,000

Illustration 16-7

Dividend Distribution, Cumulative and Fully Participating Preferred, with Dividends in Arrears

Stock Splits

If a company has undistributed earnings over several years and accumulated a sizeable balance in retained earnings, the market value of its outstanding shares is likely to increase. Shares that were issued at prices less than $50 a share can easily attain a market value in excess of $200 a share. The higher the share's market price, the less readily it can be purchased by some investors. The managements of many corporations believe that for better public relations, wider ownership of the corporation's shares is desirable. They wish, therefore, to have a market price sufficiently low to be within range of the majority of potential investors.

To reduce the market value of shares, the common device of a stock split is employed.[28] From an accounting standpoint, no entry is recorded for a stock split; a memorandum note, however, is made to indicate that the number of shares has increased.

9 Objective
Distinguish between stock dividends and stock splits.

Stock Split and Stock Dividend Differentiated

From a **legal** standpoint, a stock split is distinguished from a **stock dividend**, because a stock split results in an increase in the number of shares outstanding with no change in the share capital or the retained earnings amounts. As noted earlier, legally, the **stock dividend** may result in an increase in both the number of shares outstanding and the share capital while reducing the retained earnings (depending on the legal jurisdiction).

A stock dividend, like a stock split, also may be used to increase the share's marketability. If the stock dividend is large, it has the same effect on market price as a stock split. In the United States, the profession has taken the position that whenever additional shares are issued to reduce the unit market price, then the distribution more closely resembles a stock split than a stock dividend. **This effect usually results only if the number of shares issued is more than 20–25% of the number of shares previously outstanding.**[29] A stock dividend of more than 20–25% of the number of shares previously outstanding is called a large stock dividend.

In Canada, there is no specific GAAP guidance. In principle, it must be determined whether the large stock dividend is more like a stock split or a dividend (from an economic perspective). Professional judgement must be used in the determination.

Legal requirements must be considered as a constraint. As noted earlier, for instance, companies incorporated under the CBCA must measure any newly issued shares at market (including those issued as stock dividends—large overall). Therefore, all stock dividends would be treated as dividends and measured at market.

On the other hand, in jurisdictions where legal requirements as to stated share capital values are not a constraint, the following options would be available.

---

[28] Some companies use reverse stock splits. A reverse stock split reduces the number of shares outstanding and increases the per share price. This technique is used when the share price is unusually low. Note that a company's debt covenants or listing requirement's might require that the company's shares trade at a certain level. A reverse stock split might assist in getting the price up to where the company needs it to be.

[29] *Accounting Research and Terminology Bulletin No. 43*, par. 13.

(1) Treat as dividend (debit retained earnings and credit common shares) and measure at market value of shares or par or stated value of shares.

(2) Treat as stock split (memo entry only).

The SEC supports the latter for large stock dividends in excess of 25%.

Illustration 16-8 summarizes and compares the effects of dividends and stock splits.

Illustration 16-8

Effects of Dividends and Stock Splits

Effect on:	Declaration of Cash Dividend	Payment of Cash Dividend	Declaration and Distribution of		
			(Small) Stock Dividend	(Large) Stock Dividend	Stock Split
Retained earnings	Decrease	0	Decrease[a]	Decrease[b]	0
Common shares	0	0	Increase	Increase	0
Contributed surplus	0	0	0	0	0
Total shareholders' equity	Decrease	0	0	0	0
Working capital	Decrease	0	0	0	0
Total assets	0	Decrease	0	0	0
Number of shares outstanding	0	0	Increase	Increase	Increase

a Generally equal to market value of shares.

b May be equal to, par, stated value of shares or market value. Note that some companies may choose to interpret GAAP such that another account, e.g., contributed surplus, is debited or that the dividend be treated as a stock split. In Canada, this is a matter of judgement and is governed by legal requirements regarding the value of stated capital and economic substance.

OTHER COMPONENTS OF SHAREHOLDERS' EQUITY

Contributed Surplus

Objective 10

Understand the nature of other components of shareholders' equity.

The term "surplus" is used in an accounting sense to designate the excess of net assets over the total paid-in par or stated value of a corporation's shares.[30] As previously mentioned, this surplus is further divided between earned surplus (retained earnings) and contributed surplus. Contributed surplus may be derived from a variety of transactions or events noted in Illustration 16-9.

Illustration 16-9

Transactions that May Affect Contributed Surplus

- Par value shares issue and/or retirement (see Appendix 16A)
- No par shares repurchase and/or retirement (see Appendix 16A)
- Liquidating dividends
- Financial reorganizations (see Appendix 16B)
- Stock options and warrants (Chapter 17)
- Issue of convertible debt (Chapter 17)
- Share subscriptions forfeited
- Donated shares
- Redemption or conversion of shares

Accumulated Other Comprehensive Income

Accumulated other comprehensive income is the cumulative change in equity due to revenues, expenses, gains, and losses that result from nonshareholder transactions which

---

[30] *CICA Handbook*, Section 3250.01.

are excluded from the calculation of Net Income. It is a catchall account. Comprehensive income was discussed in Chapters 4 and 5.

PRESENTATION AND DISCLOSURE

Various disclosures are required under the *CICA Handbook*.[31] For example, basic disclosures include authorized share capital, issued share capital, and changes in capital since the last balance sheet date. In many corporations, restrictions on retained earnings or dividends exist and should be disclosed. The note disclosure should reveal the source of the restriction, pertinent provisions, and the amount of retained earnings subject to restriction, or the amount not restricted.[32]

11 Objective
Indicate how shareholders' equity is presented.

Restrictions may be based on the retention of a certain retained earnings balance, the corporation's ability to observe certain working capital requirements, additional borrowing, and on other considerations. The following example from the annual report of **Methanex Corporation** illustrates a note disclosing potential restrictions on retained earnings and dividends.

---

9. Capital stock:

(a) The authorized share capital of the Company is comprised as follows:
25,000,000 preferred shares without nominal or par value; and Unlimited number of common shares without nominal or par value.

(b) Under covenants set out in certain debt instruments, the Company can pay cash dividends or make other shareholder distributions to the extent that shareholders' equity is equal to or greater than $850 million.

The following would normally be disclosed in note form:

1. Authorized number of shares or a statement noting that this is unlimited,

2. Existence of unique rights (e.g., dividend preference and amount of such dividends, redemption and/or retraction privileges, conversion rights, whether or not they are cumulative),

3. Number of shares issued and amount received,

4. Whether par value or no par value,

5. Amount of any dividends in arrears,

6. Details of changes during the year, and

7. Restrictions on Retained earnings.

Note that, per *CICA Handbook* Section 1300, enterprises qualifying under differential reporting (non-public companies where owners consent) need only disclose the above for issued shares.

Section 3860 of the *CICA Handbook* requires additional disclosures of any significant terms and conditions of equity instruments that might affect the amount, timing, and uncertainty of future cash flows.[33] Illustration 16-10 is an example of a shareholders' equity section on the balance sheet.

Statements of shareholders' equity are frequently presented in a tabular format in the notes showing the change during the year in each shareholders' equity category.

---

[31] *CICA Handbook*, Section 3240, pars. .02-.05.

[32] *CICA Handbook*, Section 3250.10.

[33] *CICA Handbook*, Section 3860.52.

FROST CORPORATION
Shareholders' Equity
December 31, 2005

Share Capital

Preferred shares, $7 cumulative, 100,000 shares authorized, 30,000 shares issued and outstanding	$ 3,000,000
Common shares, no par, stated value $10 per share, 500,000 shares authorized, 400,000 shares issued	4,000,000
Common shares dividend distributable, 20,000 shares	200,000
Total share capital	7,200,000
Contributed surplus	990,000
Total paid-in capital	8,190,000
Retained earnings	2,200,000
Accumulated Other Comprehensive Income	2,160,000
Total shareholders' equity	$12,550,000

Special Presentation Issues

Preferred shares generally have no maturity date, and therefore no legal obligation exists to pay the preferred shareholder. As a result, preferred shares have historically been classified as part of shareholders' equity. Recently, more and more issuances of preferred share have features that make the security more like a debt instrument (legal obligation to pay) than an equity instrument. As mentioned earlier, these will be covered in Chapter 17.

PERSPECTIVES

Financial Analysis Primer

Objective 12

Analyse shareholders' equity.

Digital Tool

Analyst Toolkit—
Financial
Statement
Analysis Primer

www.wiley.com/canada/kieso

Several ratios use shareholders' equity-related amounts to evaluate a company's **profitability** and **long-term solvency**. The following four ratios are discussed and illustrated below: (1) rate of return on common shareholders' equity, (2) payout ratio, (3) price earnings ratio, and (4) book value per share.

Rate of Return on Common Shareholders' Equity

A widely used ratio that measures profitability from the common shareholders' viewpoint is rate of return on common shareholders' equity. This ratio shows how many dollars of net income were earned for each dollar invested by the owners. It is calculated by dividing net income less preferred dividends by average common shareholders' equity. For example, assume that Garber Inc. had net income of $360,000, declared and paid preferred dividends of $54,000, and average common shareholders' equity of $2,550,000. Garber's ratio is calculated in this manner:

$$\text{Rate of return on common shareholders' equity} = \frac{\text{Net income} - \text{preferred dividends}}{\text{Average common shareholders' equity}}$$

$$= \frac{\$360,000 - 54,000}{\$2,550,000}$$

$$= 12\%$$

As evidenced above, because preferred shares are present, preferred dividends are deducted from net income to calculate income available to common shareholders. Similarly the carrying value of preferred shares is deducted from total shareholders' equity to arrive at the amount of common shareholders' equity used in this ratio.

When the rate of return on total assets is lower than the rate of return on the common shareholders' investment, the company is said to be trading on the equity at a gain. Trading on the equity describes the practice of using borrowed money at fixed interest rates or issuing preferred shares with constant dividend rates in hopes of obtaining a higher rate of return on the money used (sometimes also referred to as **leverage**). These debt issues must be given a prior claim on some or all of the corporate assets. Thus, the advantage to common shareholders of trading on the equity must come from borrowing at a lower rate of interest than the rate of return obtained on the assets borrowed. If this can be done, the capital obtained from bondholders or preferred shareholders earns enough to pay the interest or preferred dividends and to leave a margin for the common shareholders. When this condition exists, trading on the equity is profitable.

Payout Ratio

Another measure of profitability is the payout ratio, which is the ratio of cash dividends to net income. If preferred shares are outstanding, this ratio is calculated for common shareholders by dividing cash dividends paid to common shareholders by net income available to common shareholders. Assuming that Troy Corp. has cash dividends of $100,000 and net income of $500,000, and no preferred shares outstanding, the payout ratio is calculated in the following manner.

$$\text{Payout Ratio} = \frac{\text{Cash Dividends}}{\text{Net income} - \text{Preferred dividends}}$$

$$= \frac{\$100,000}{500,000}$$

$$= 20\%$$

It is important to some investors that the payout be sufficiently high to provide a good yield on the shares.[34] However, payout ratios have declined for many companies because many investors view appreciation in the share value as more important than the dividend amount.

Price Earnings Ratio

The price earnings (P/E) ratio is an oft-quoted statistic used by analysts in discussing the investment possibility of a given enterprise. It is calculated by dividing the share's market price by its earnings per share. For example, Soreson Corp. has a market price of $50 and earnings per share of $4. Its price earnings ratio is calculated as follows.

$$\text{Price Earnings Ratio} = \frac{\text{Market price of share}}{\text{Earnings per share}}$$

$$= \$50/4$$

$$= 12.5$$

---

[34] Another closely watched ratio is the dividend yield: the cash dividend per share divided by the share's market price. This ratio affords investors some idea of the rate of return that will be received in cash dividends from their assessment.

Book Value Per Share

A much-used basis for evaluating net worth is found in the **book value** or **equity value per share**. Book value per share is the amount each share would receive if the company were liquidated **on the basis of amounts reported on the balance sheet**. However, the figure loses much of its relevance if the valuations on the balance sheet do not approximate fair market value of the assets. **Book value per share** is calculated by dividing common shareholders' equity by number of outstanding common shares. Assuming that Chen Corporation's common shareholders' equity is $1 million and it has 100,000 shares outstanding, its book value per share is calculated as follows.

$$\text{Book Value Per Share} = \frac{\text{Common shareholders' equity}}{\text{number of outstanding shares}}$$

$$= \frac{\$1,000,000}{100,000}$$

$$= \$10 \text{ per share}$$

When preferred shares are present, an analysis of the covenants involving the preferred shares should be studied. If preferred dividends are in arrears, the preferred shares are participating, or if preferred shares have a redemption or liquidating value higher than their carrying amount, retained earnings must be allocated between the preferred and common shareholders in calculating book value.

To illustrate, assume that the following situation exists.

Shareholders' equity	Preferred	Common
Preferred shares, 5%	$300,000	
Common shares		$400,000
Contributed surplus		37,500
Retained earnings	0	162,582
Totals	$300,000	$600,082
Shares outstanding		4,000
Book value per share		$150.02

In the preceding calculation, it is assumed that no preferred dividends are in arrears and that the preferred is not participating. Now assume that the same facts exist except that the 5% preferred is cumulative, participating up to 8%, and that dividends for three years before the current year are in arrears. The common shares' book value is then calculated as follows, assuming that no action has yet been taken concerning dividends for the current year.

Shareholders' equity	Preferred	Common
Preferred shares, 5%	$300,000	
Common shares		$400,000
Contributed surplus		37,500
Retained earnings:		
Dividends in arrears (3 years at 5% a year)	45,000	
Current year requirement at 5%	15,000	20,000
Participating additional 3%	9,000	12,000
Remainder to common	0	61,582
Totals	$369,000	$531,082
Shares outstanding		4,000
Book value per share		$132.77

In connection with the book value calculation, the analyst must know how to handle the following items: the number of authorized and unissued shares; the number of treasury shares on hand; any commitments with respect to the issuance of unissued shares or the reissuance of treasury shares; and the relative rights and privileges of the various types of shares authorized.

Digital Tool

Glossary

www.wiley.com/canada/kieso

Summary of Learning Objectives

1 Discuss the characteristics of the corporate form of organization.

Three main forms of organizations are proprietorship, partnership, and corporation. Incorporation affords shareholders protection against claims on their personal assets and allows greater access to capital markets.

2 Identify the rights of shareholders.

In the absence of restrictive provisions, each share carries the following rights: (1) to share proportionately in profits and losses; (2) to share proportionately in management (the right to vote for directors); and (3) to share proportionately in corporate assets upon liquidation. An additional right to share proportionately in any new issues of share of the same class (called the preemptive right) may also be attached to the share.

3 Describe the major features of preferred shares.

Preferred shares are a special class of share that possess certain preferences or features not possessed by the common share. The features that are most often associated with preferred share issues are preference as to dividends and preference as to assets in the event of liquidation. Many other preferences may be attached to specific shares. Preferred shareholders give up some or all of the rights normally attached to common shares.

4 Explain the accounting procedures for issuing shares.

Shares may be issued on a subscription basis, in which case, they are not considered legally issued until they are paid up. Shares may also be issued as a bundle with other securities. The cost must be allocated between the securities. The incremental or proportional methods may be used to allocate the cost.

5 Identify the major reasons for repurchasing shares.

The reasons corporations purchase their outstanding share are varied. Some major reasons are: (1) to increase earnings per share and return on equity; (2) to provide shares for employee share compensation contracts or to meet potential merger needs; (3) to thwart takeover attempts or to reduce the number of shareholders; (4) to make a market in the shares; or (5) to return excess cash to shareholders.

6 Explain the accounting for reacquisition and retirement of shares.

If the acquisition cost of the shares is greater than the original cost, the difference is allocated to share capital, then contributed surplus, then retained earnings. If the cost is less, the cost is allocated to share capital (to stated or assigned cost) and to the contributed surplus.

7 Explain the accounting for various forms of dividend distributions.

Dividends are generally paid out of earnings or are a return of capital. Those paid out of earnings are normally cash, property, or stock dividends. They are recorded at fair value and debited to Retained Earnings. Dividends that are a return of capital are known as liquidating dividends and reduced contributed capital.

KEY TERMS

accumulated other comprehensive income, 862
basic or inherent rights, 845
book value per share, 866
callable/redeemable (preferred shares), 847
capital maintenance, 843
common shares, 845
contributed (paid-in) capital, 843
convertible (preferred shares), 847
cumulative (preferred shares), 847
dividends, 854
dividends in kind, 857
earned capital, 843
large stock dividend, 861
legal capital, 854
leveraged buyout, 852
limited liability, 848
liquidating dividends, 856
lump sum sales, 850
par value shares, 848
participating (preferred shares), 847
payout ratio, 865
preemptive right, 845
preferred shares, 846
price earnings ratio, 865
rate of return, 864
retained earnings, 853
retractable (preferred shares), 847
shareholders' (owners') equity, 842
stock dividends, 858
stock split, 861
subscribed shares, 849
trading on equity, 865
treasury shares, 852

Treasury Shares

Objective 14
Explain accounting for treasury shares.

Treasury shares occur when a company repurchases its own shares but does not cancel them. As previously mentioned, this is not allowed under the CBCA; however, it is allowed in the United States and in certain provinces and therefore will be covered briefly here. Treasury shares may be resold. The *CICA Handbook* notes that the single transaction method should be used to account for treasury shares. The method treats the repurchase and resale as a single transaction. In essence, the repurchase of treasury shares is the initiation of a transaction that is consummated when shares are resold. Consequently, the holding of treasury shares is viewed as a transition phase between the beginning and end of a single activity.

When shares are purchased, the total cost is debited to Treasury Shares on the balance sheet. This account is shown as a deduction from the total of the components of shareholders' equity in the balance sheet. An example of such disclosure follows.

Shareholders' equity:	
Common shares, no par value; authorized 24,000,000	
Shares; issued 19,045,870 shares, of which 209,750	
are in treasury	$ 27,686,000
Retained earnings	253,265,000
	$280,951,000
Less: Cost of treasury shares	(7,527,000)
Total shareholders' equity	$273,424,000

When the shares are sold, the Treasury Shares account is credited for their cost. If they are sold at more than their cost, the excess is credited to Contributed Surplus. If they are sold at less, the difference is debited to Contributed Surplus (if related to the same class of shares) and then to Retained Earnings. If the shares are subsequently retired, the journal entries as noted in the body of the chapter would be followed.

Dividends on treasury shares should be reversed since a company cannot receive dividend income on its own shares (dr. Dividends Payable, cr. Retained Earnings).

Summary of Learning Objectives for Appendix 16A

13 Explain accounting for par value shares.

These shares may only be valued at par value in the common or preferred share accounts. The excess goes to contributed surplus. On repurchase or cancellation, par value is removed from the common or preferred share accounts with the excess or deficit being booked to contributed surplus or retained earnings as discussed for no par shares.

14 Explain accounting for treasury shares.

Treasury shares occur when a company repurchases its own shares and does not cancel or retire them at the same time, i.e., they remain outstanding. The single-transaction method is used when treasury shares are purchased. This method treats the purchase and subsequent resale or cancellation as part of the same transaction.

Financial Reorganization

A corporation that consistently suffers net losses accumulates negative retained earnings, or a deficit. The general presumption of shareholders is that dividends are paid out of profits and retained earnings. In addition, certain laws in some jurisdictions provide that no dividends may be declared and paid so long as a corporation's paid-in capital has been reduced by a deficit. In these cases, a corporation with a debit balance of retained earnings must accumulate sufficient profits to offset the deficit before dividends may be paid.

This situation may be a real hardship on a corporation and its shareholders. A company that has operated unsuccessfully for several years and accumulated a deficit may have finally turned the corner. Development of new products and new markets, a new management group, or improved economic conditions may point to much improved operating results. But, if the law prohibits dividends until the deficit has been replaced by earnings, the shareholders must wait until such profits have been earned, which may take a considerable period of time. Furthermore, future success may depend on obtaining additional funds through the sale of shares. If no dividends can be paid for some time, the market price of any new share issue is likely to be low, if such shares can be marketed at all.

Thus, a company with excellent prospects may be prevented from accomplishing its plans because of a deficit, although present management may have had nothing whatever to do with the years over which the deficit was accumulated. To permit the corporation to proceed with its plans might well be to the advantage of all interests in the enterprise; to require it to eliminate the deficit through profits might actually force it to liquidate.

A procedure that enables a company that has gone through financial difficulty to proceed with its plans without the encumbrance of having to recover from a deficit is called a financial reorganization. A financial reorganization is defined as a substantial realignment of an enterprise's equity and non-equity interests such that the holders of one or more of the significant classes of non-equity interests and the holders of all of the significant classes of equity interests give up some (or all) of their rights and claims upon the enterprise.[35]

A financial reorganization results from negotiation and culminates with an eventual agreement between non-equity and equity holders in the corporation. These negotiations may take place under the provisions of a legal act (e.g., Companies Creditors Arrangement Act) or a less formal process.[36] The result gives the companies a fresh start and the accounting is often referred to as fresh start accounting.

15 Objective
Describe the accounting for a financial reorganization.

---

[35] *CICA Handbook*, Section 1625.03.

[36] *CICA Handbook*, Section 1625.03, par .15.

Comprehensive revaluation

When a financial reorganization occurs, where the same party does not control the company both before and after the reorganization, and where new costs are reasonably determinable, the company's assets and liabilities should undergo a **comprehensive revaluation**.[37] This entails three steps:

1. The deficit balance (retained earnings) is brought to zero. Any asset writedowns or impairments that existed prior to the reorganization should be recorded first. The deficit is reclassified to Share Capital, Contributed Surplus, or a separately identified account within Shareholders' Equity.

2. The changes in debt and equity as negotiated are recorded. Often debt is exchanged for equity, reflecting a change in control.

3. The assets and liabilities are comprehensively revalued. This step assigns appropriate going concern values to all assets and liabilities as per the negotiations. The difference between the carrying values prior to the reorganization and the new values after is known as a **revaluation adjustment**. The revaluation adjustment and any costs incurred to carry out the financial reorganization are accounted for as capital transactions and are closed to Share Capital, Contributed Surplus, or a separately identified account within Shareholders' Equity. Note that the new costs of the identifiable assets and liabilities must not exceed the entity's fair value if known.[38]

Entries Illustrated

The series of entries shown below illustrates the accounting procedures applied in a financial reorganization. Assume New Horizons Inc. shows a deficit of $1 million before the reorganization is effected on June 30, 2005. Under the terms of the negotiation, the creditors are giving up rights to payment for the $150,000 debt in return for 100% of the common shares. The original shareholders agree to give up their shares.

1. **Restate impairments of assets that existed prior to the reorganization**

Deficit	750,000	
Inventories (loss on writedown)		225,000
Intangible Assets (loss on writedown)		525,000

A   =   L   +   SE
−750,000   −750,000
Cash flows: No effect

Elimination of deficit against contributed surplus

Common shares	1,750,000	
Deficit		1,750,000

A   =   L   +   SE
0   0   0
Cash flows: No effect

2. and 3. **Restatement of assets and liabilities to recognize unrecorded gains and losses and to record the negotiated change in control**

Plant Assets (gain on write-up)	400,000	
Long-term Liabilities (gain on writedown)	150,000	
Common shares		550,000

A   =   L   +   SE
+400,000 −150,000 +550,000
Cash flows: No effect

---

[37] *CICA Handbook*, Section 1625.03, pars. .04 and .05.

[38] *CICA Handbook*, Section 1625 pars. .39 to .49.

Note that where there is no change in control, GAAP does not allow a comprehensive revaluation.

Disclosure

When a financial reorganization is effected, the following requirements must be fulfilled.

1. The proposed reorganization should receive the **approval** of the corporation's shareholders before it is put into effect.

2. The new asset and liability valuations should be **fair** and not deliberately understate or overstate assets, liabilities, and earnings.

3. After the reorganization, the corporation must have a zero balance of retained earnings, although it may have contributed surplus arising from the reorganization.

4. In the period of the reorganization, the following must be disclosed:

   (a) The date of the reorganization

   (b) A description of the reorganization

   (c) The amount of the change in each major class of assets, liability of description, and shareholders' equity resulting from the reorganization

5. In subsequent reports for a period of at least three years from the reorganization date, the following must be disclosed:

   (a) The date of the reorganization

   (b) The revaluation adjustment amount and the shareholders' equity account in which it was recorded

   (c) The amount of the deficit that was reclassified and the account to which it was reclassified

   (d) The measurement bases for the assets and liabilities that were revalued

Summary of Learning Objectives for Appendix 16B

Digital Tool

Glossary

www.wiley.com/canada/kieso

15 Describe the accounting for a financial reorganization.

A corporation that has accumulated a large debit balance (deficit) in retained earnings may enter into a process known as a financial reorganization. During a reorganization, creditors and shareholders negotiate a deal to put the company on a new footing. This generally involves a **change in control** and a **comprehensive revaluation** of assets and liabilities. The procedure consists of the following steps: (1) The deficit is reclassified such that the ending balance in Retained Earnings is zero. (2) The change in control is recorded. (3) All assets and liabilities are comprehensively revalued at current values so the company will not be burdened with excessive inventory or fixed asset valuations in following years.

KEY TERMS

comprehensive
   revaluation, 872
financial
   reorganization, 871
fresh start
   accounting, 871
revaluation
   adjustment, 872

Note: All asterisked assignment material relate to the appendices to the chapter.

Brief Exercises

*BE16-1   Shinobi Limited issued 600 shares of no par value common shares for $20,400. Prepare Shinobi's journal entry if (a) the stock has no par value, and (b) the stock has a par value of $2 per share.

BE16-2   Rambo Inc. sells 500 common shares on a subscription basis at $55 per share. On June 1, Rambo accepts a 45% down payment. On December 1, Rambo collects the remaining 55% and issues the shares. Prepare the company's journal entries.

BE16-3   Lufia Corporation has the following account balances at December 31, 2005.

Common shares subscribed	$ 250,000
Common shares, no par value	310,000
Subscriptions receivable	80,000
Retained earnings	1,340,000
Contributed Surplus	320,000

Prepare the December 31, 2005 shareholders' equity section of the balance sheet.

BE16-4   Powerdrive Corporation issued 3,000 shares of its common shares for $70,000. The company also incurred $1,500 of costs associated with issuing the shares. Prepare the journal entry to record the issuance of the company's share.

BE16-5   Maverick Inc. has 10,000 common shares outstanding. The shares have an average cost of $20 per share. On July 1, 2004, Maverick reacquired 100 shares at $45 per share and retired them. Prepare journal entry to record this transaction.

BE16-6   Rangers Corporation has 50,000 common shares outstanding with an average value of $5. On August 1, 2005, the company reacquired and cancelled 500 shares at $35 per share. Contributed Surplus of $2 per share existed at the time of the reacquisition (total $100,000). Prepare the journal entry to record this transaction.

BE16-7   Machines Inc. declared a cash dividend of $ 0.50 per share on its 2 million outstanding shares. The dividend was declared on August 1, payable on September 9 to all shareholders of record on August 15. Prepare all journal entries necessary on those three dates.

BE16-8   Ren Inc. owns shares of Stahl Corporation that are classified as part of the company's trading portfolio. At December 31, 2005, the securities were carried in Ren's accounting records at their cost of $575,000, which equals their market value. On September 21, 2006, when the securities market value was $1.4 million, Ren declared a property dividend whereby the Stahl securities are to be distributed on October 23, 2006, to shareholders of record on October 8, 2006. Prepare all journal entries necessary on those three dates.

BE16-9   Rex Mining Corp. declared, on April 20, a dividend of $500,000 payable on June 1. Of this amount, $200,000 is a return of capital. Prepare the April 20 and June 1 entries for Rex.

BE16-10   Gren Football Corporation has outstanding 500,000 common shares. The corporation declares a 6% stock dividend when the shares' fair value is $35 per share (carrying value is $20 per share). Prepare the journal entries for the company for both the date of declaration and the date of distribution.

BE16-11   Piggs Corporation has outstanding 200,000 common shares with a carrying value of $10 per share. Piggs declares a 2-for-1 stock split. How many shares are outstanding after the split? What is the carrying value per share after the split? What is the total carrying value after the split? What journal entry is necessary to record the split?

*BE16-12   Truck Corporation went through a financial reorganization by writing down plant assets by $105,000 and eliminating its deficit, which was $144,000 prior to the reorganization. As part of the reorganization, the creditors agreed to take back 55% of the common shares in lieu of payment of the debt of $2.3 million. Prepare the entries to record the financial reorganization.

Exercises

E16-1   (Recording the Issuance of Common and Preferred Shares)   Battle Corporation was organized on January 1, 2004. It is authorized to issue 100,000 preferred shares with a $7 dividend, and 400,000 common shares. The following share transactions were completed during the first year.

Interactive
Homework

Jan.	10	Issued 100,000 common shares for cash at $5 per share.
Mar.	1	Issued 5,000 preferred shares for cash at $103 per share.
Apr.	1	Issued 25,000 common shares for land. The land's asking price was $70,000; its fair value was $60,000.
May	1	Issued 100,000 common shares for cash at $7 per share.
Aug.	1	Issued 10,000 common shares to lawyers in payment of their bill of $50,000 for services rendered in helping the company organize.
Sept.	1	Issued 10,000 common shares for cash at $9 per share.
Nov.	1	Issued 1,000 preferred shares for cash at $112 per share.

Instructions

Prepare the journal entries to record the above transactions.

E16-2 (Subscribed Shares) Galway Inc. intends to sell shares to raise additional capital to allow for expansion in the rapidly growing service industry. The corporation decides to sell these shares through a subscription basis and publicly notifies the investment world. 30,000 shares are offered at $20 a share. The terms of the subscription are 30% down and the balance at the end of six months. All shares are subscribed for during the offering period.

Instructions

Give the journal entry for the original subscription, the collection of the down payments, the collection of the balance of the subscription price, and the issuance of the shares.

E16-3 (Share Issuances and Repurchase) Kao Corporation is authorized to issue 500,000 shares of common shares. During 2005, the company took part in the following selected transactions.

Interactive Homework

1. Issued 5,000 shares at $35 per share, less costs related to the issuance of the shares totalling $3,000.

2. Issued 2,000 shares for land appraised at $150,000. The shares were actively traded on a national stock exchange at approximately $46 per share on the date of issuance.

3. Purchased and retired 500 of the company's shares at $43 per share. The shares repurchased have an average per share amount of $40 per share.

Instructions

Prepare the journal entries to record the three transactions.

*E16-4 (Shareholders' Equity Section) Radler Corporation's charter authorized 1 million shares of $11 par value common shares, and 300,000 shares of 6% cumulative and nonparticipating preferred shares, par value $100 per share. The corporation engaged in the following share transactions through December 31, 2005: 300,000 common shares were issued for $3.6 million and 10,000 preferred shares were issued for machinery valued at $1,475,000. Subscriptions for 10,500 common shares have been taken, and 30% of the subscription price of $16 per share has been collected. The shares will be issued upon collection of the subscription price in full. 10,000 common shares have been purchased for $15 and retired. The Retained Earnings balance is $180,000.

Instructions

Prepare the shareholders' equity section of the balance sheet in good form.

E16-5 (Correcting Entries for Equity Transactions) Rae Inc. recently hired a new accountant with extensive experience in accounting for partnerships. Because of the pressure of the new job, the accountant was unable to review what he had learned earlier about corporation accounting. During the first month, he made the following entries for the corporation's capital shares.

May	2	Cash	192,000	
		Common Shares		192,000
		(Issued 12,000 common shares at $16 per share)		
	10	Cash	600,000	
		Common Shares		600,000
		(Issued 10,000 preferred shares at $60 per share)		
	15	Common Shares	15,000	
		Cash		15,000
		(Purchased and retired 1,000 common shares at $15 per share)		
	31	Cash	8,500	
		Common Shares		5,000
		Gain on Sale of Shares		3,500
		(Issued 500 shares at $17 per share)		

Instructions

On the basis of the explanation for each entry, prepare the entries that should have been made for the capital share transactions. Explain your reasoning.

E16-6   (Equity Items on the Balance Sheet)   The following are selected transactions that may affect shareholders' equity.

1. Recorded accrued interest earned on a note receivable.

2. Declared a cash dividend.

3. Effected a stock split.

4. Recorded the expiration of insurance coverage that was previously recorded as prepaid insurance.

5. Paid the cash dividend declared in item 2 above.

6. Recorded accrued interest expense on a note payable.

7. Recorded an increase in value of a Available for Sale investment that will be distributed as a property dividend.

8. Declared a property dividend (see item 7 above).

9. Distributed the investment to shareholders (see items 7 and 8 above).

10. Declared a stock dividend.

11. Distributed the stock dividend declared in item 10.

Instructions

In the table below, indicate the effect each of the 11 transactions has on the financial statement elements listed. Use the following codes:

I = Increase   D = Decrease   NE = No effect

Item	Assets	Liabilities	Shareholders' Equity	Share Capital	Retained Earnings	Comprehensive Income	Net Income

E16-7   (Preferred Dividends)   The outstanding share capital of Millay Corporation consists of 2,000 shares of preferred and 5,000 common shares for which $250,000 was received. The preferred shares carry a dividend of $8 per share and have $100 stated value.

Instructions

Assuming that the company has retained earnings of $90,000, all of which is to be paid out in dividends, and that preferred dividends were not paid during the two years preceding the current year, state how much each class of shares should receive under each of the following conditions.

(a) The preferred shares are noncumulative and nonparticipating.

(b) The preferred shares are cumulative and nonparticipating.

(c) The preferred shares are cumulative and participating.

E16-8   (Preferred Dividends)   MacLeish Limited's ledger shows the following balances on December 31, 2005.

Preferred shares outstanding: 15,000 shares	$ 300,000
Common shares outstanding: 40,000 shares	3,000,000
Retained earnings	980,000

Instructions

Assuming that the directors decide to declare total dividends in the amount of $566,000, determine how much each class of shares should receive under each of the conditions stated below. One year's dividends are in arrears on the preferred shares, which pay a dividend of $0.80 per share.

(a) The preferred shares are cumulative and fully participating.

(b) The preferred shares are noncumulative and nonparticipating.

(c) The preferred shares are noncumulative and are participating in distributions in excess of a 10% dividend rate on the common shares.

E16-9   (Stock Split and Stock Dividend)   The common shares of Hamilton Inc. are currently selling at $143 per share. The directors wish to reduce the share price and increase share volume prior to a new issue. The per share carrying value is $34. Nine million shares are issued and outstanding.

Instructions

Prepare the necessary journal entries assuming:

(a) The board votes a 2-for-1 stock split.

(b) The board votes a 100% stock dividend.

Briefly discuss the accounting and securities market differences between these two methods of increasing the number of shares outstanding.

E16-10 (Entries for Stock Dividends and Stock Splits) The shareholders' equity accounts of Chesterton Inc. have the following balances on December 31, 2005.

Common shares, 700,000 shares issued and outstanding	$10,000,000
Contributed surplus	3,200,000
Retained earnings	7,600,000

Common shares are currently selling on the Prairie Stock Exchange at $57.

Instructions

Prepare the appropriate journal entries for each of the following cases.

(a) A stock dividend of 5% is declared and issued.

(b) A stock dividend of 100% is declared and issued.

(c) A 2-for-1 stock split is declared and issued.

E16-11 (Dividend Entries) The following data were taken from the balance sheet accounts of Masefield Corporation on December 31, 2005.

Current assets	$1,040,000
Investments—Held to Maturity	824,000
Common shares (no par value, no authorized limit,	
500,000 shares issued and outstanding)	6,000,000
Contributed surplus	350,000
Retained earnings	1,840,000

Instructions

Prepare the required journal entries for the following unrelated items.

(a) A 5% stock dividend is declared and distributed at a time when the shares' market value is $39 per share.

(b) A 5-for-1 stock split is effected.

(c) A dividend in kind is declared January 5, 2005 and paid January 25, 2005, in bonds that were classified as held to maturity. The bonds have a carrying value of $100,000 (equal to cost) and a fair market value of $135,000.

*E16-12 (Shareholders' Equity Section) Bruno Corporation's post-closing trial balance at December 31, 2005, was as follows.

BRUNO CORPORATION
Post-Closing Trial Balance
December 31, 2005

	Dr.	Cr.
Accounts payable		$ 310,000
Accounts receivable	$ 480,000	
Accumulated amortization—building and equipment		185,000
Accumulated other comprehensive income		100,000
Contributed surplus common		1,460,000
Allowance for doubtful accounts		30,000
Bonds payable		300,000
Building and equipment	1,450,000	
Cash	190,000	
Common shares		200,000
Dividends payable on preferred shares cash		4,000
Inventories	360,000	
Investments—available for sale	200,000	
Land	400,000	
Preferred shares		500,000
Prepaid expenses	40,000	
Retained earnings		31,000
Totals	$3,120,000	$3,120,000

At December 31, 2005, Bruno had the following number of common and preferred shares:

	Common	Preferred
Authorized	600,000	60,000
Issued	200,000	10,000
Outstanding	190,000	10,000

The dividends on preferred shares are $5 cumulative. In addition, the preferred shares have a preference in liquidation of $50 per share.

Instructions

Prepare the shareholders' equity section of Bruno's balance sheet at December 31, 2005.

(AICPA adapted)

Interactive Homework

E16-13   (Participating Preferred and Stock Dividend)   The following is the shareholders' equity section of Sakamoto Corp. at December 31, 2005.

Preferred shares,* authorized 100,000 shares; issued 25,000 shares	$ 750,000
Common shares, authorized 200,000 shares; issued 60,000 shares	1,800,000
Contributed surplus	1,150,000
Total paid-in capital	3,700,000
Retained earnings	2,470,500
Total shareholders' equity	$6,170,500

* The preferred shares have a $5 dividend rate, are cumulative, and are participating in distributions in excess of a $3 dividend on the common shares.

Instructions

(a) No dividends have been paid in 2003 or 2004. On December 31, 2005, Sakamoto wants to pay a cash dividend of $4 a share to common shareholders. How much cash would be needed for the total amount paid to preferred and common shareholders?

(b) Instead, the company will declare a 15% stock dividend on the outstanding common shares. The shares' market value is $105 per share. Prepare the entry on the date of declaration.

(c) Instead, the company will acquire and cancel 10,500 common shares. The current market value is $105 per share. Prepare the entry to record the retirement, assuming contributed surplus arose from previous cancellations of common shares.

E16-14   (Dividends and Shareholders' Equity Section)   Feller Corp. reported the following amounts in the shareholders' equity section of its December 31, 2004 balance sheet.

Preferred shares, $8 dividend (10,000 shares authorized, 2,000 shares issued)	$200,000
Common shares (100,000 shares authorized, 25,000 shares issued)	100,000
Contributed surplus	155,000
Retained earnings	250,000
Total	$705,000

During 2005, the company took part in the following transactions concerning shareholders' equity.

1. Paid the annual 2005 $8 per share dividend on preferred shares and a $3 per share dividend on common shares. These dividends had been declared on December 31, 2004.

2. Purchased 3,700 shares of its own outstanding common shares for $35 per share and cancelled them.

3. Issued 1,000 shares of preferred shares at $105 per share (at the beginning of the year).

4. Declared a 10% stock dividend on the outstanding common shares when the shares are selling for $45 per share.

5. Issued the stock dividend.

6. Declared the annual 2005 $8 per share dividend on preferred shares and the $2 per share dividend on common shares. These dividends are payable in 2006.

The contributed surplus arose from past common share transactions.

Instructions

(a) Prepare journal entries to record the transactions described above.

(b) Prepare the December 31, 2005 shareholders' equity section. Assume 2005 net income was $450,000.

E16-15 (Comparison of Alternative Forms of Financing) Shown below is the liabilities and shareholders' equity section of the balance sheet for Kingston Corp. and Benson Corp. Each has assets totalling $4.2 million.

Kingston Corp.		Benson Corp.	
Current liabilities	$ 300,000	Current liabilities	$ 600,000
Long-term debt, 10%	1,200,000	Common shares	2,900,000
Common shares (100,000 shares issued)	2,000,000	(145,000 shares issued)	
Retained earnings		Retained earnings	
(Cash dividends, $220,000)	700,000	(Cash dividends, $328,000)	700,000
	$4,200,000		$4,200,000

For the year, each company has earned the same income before interest and taxes.

	Kingston Corp.	Benson Corp.
Income before interest and taxes	$1,200,000	$1,200,000
Interest expense	120,000	0
	1,080,000	1,200,000
Income taxes (45%)	486,000	540,000
Net income	$ 594,000	$ 660,000

At year end, the market price of Kingston's shares was $101 per share and Benson's was $63.50.

Instructions

(a) Which company is more profitable in terms of return on total assets?

(b) Which company is more profitable in terms of return on shareholders' equity?

(c) Which company has the greater net income per share? Neither company issued nor reacquired shares during the year.

(d) From the point of view of income, is it advantageous to Kingston's shareholders to have the long-term debt outstanding? Why?

(e) What is each company's price earnings ratio?

(f) What is the book value per share for each company?

*E16-16 (Financial Reorganization) The following account balances are available from the ledger of Glamorgan Corporation on December 31, 2004.

Common Shares 20,000 shares authorized and outstanding	$1,000,000
Retained Earnings (deficit)	(190,000)

As of January 2, 2005, the corporation gave effect to a shareholder-approved reorganization by agreeing to pass the common shares over to the creditors in full payment of the $250,000 debt, writing up plant assets by $85,600, and eliminating the deficit.

Instructions

Prepare the required journal entries for the financial reorganization of Glamorgan Corporation.

*E16-17 (Financial Reorganization) The condensed balance sheets of Regina Limited immediately before and one year after it had completed a financial reorganization appear below.

	Before Reorg	One Year After		Before Reorg	One Year After
Current assets	$ 300,000	$ 420,000	Common shares	$2,400,000	$1,550,000
Plant assets (net)	1,700,000	1,290,000	Contributed Surplus	220,000	
	–0–	–0–	Retained earnings	(620,000)	160,000
	$2,000,000	$1,710,000		$2,000,000)	$1,710,000

For the year following the financial reorganization, the company reported net income of $190,000, amortization expense of $80,000, and paid a cash dividend of $30,000. As part of the reorganization, the company wrote down inventories by $120,000 in order to reflect circumstances that existed prior to the reorganization. Also, the deficit and any revaluation adjustment was accounted for by charging amounts against contributed surplus until it was eliminated, with any remaining amount being charged against common shares. The common shares are widely held and there is no controlling interest. No purchases or sales of plant assets and no share transactions occurred in the year following the reorganization.

Instructions

Prepare all the journal entries made at the time of the reorganization.

Problems

P16-1 Nells Corp. had the following shareholders' equity on January 1, 2005.

Common shares, 200,000 shares authorized, 100,000 shares issued and outstanding	$ 200,000
Contributed Surplus	300,000
Retained earnings	2,800,000
Total shareholders' equity	$3,300,000

The following transactions occurred, in the order given, during 2005.

1. Subscriptions were sold for 10,000 common shares at $38 per share. The first payment was for $16 per share.

2. The second payment was for $22 per share. All payments were received on the second payment except for 1,000 shares.

3. Per the subscription contract, which requires that defaulting subscribers have all their payments refunded, the company sends a refund cheque to the defaulting subscribers. At this point, common shares are issued to subscribers that have fully paid on the contract.

4. 20,000 common shares were repurchased at $20 per share. They were then retired.

5. 2,000 preferred shares and 3,000 common shares were sold together for $290,000. The common shares had a market value of $27 per share.

Instructions

Prepare the journal entries to record the transactions for the company for 2005.

P16-2 Amado Limited has two classes of shares outstanding: preferred ($6 dividend) and common. At December 31, 2004, the following accounts were included in shareholders' equity.

Preferred Shares, 300,000 shares issued (authorized, 1 million shares)	$ 3,000,000
Common Shares, 1,000,000 shares (authorized, unlimited)	10,000,000
Contributed Surplus Preferred	200,000
Contributed Surplus Common	17,000,000
Retained Earnings	5,500,000

The following transactions affected shareholders' equity during 2005.

Jan.	1	25,000 preferred shares issued at $25 per share.
Feb.	1	50,000 common shares issued at $20 per share.
June	1	2-for-1 stock split (common shares).
July	1	30,000 common shares purchased and retired at $15 per share.
Dec. 31		Net income is $2,100,000.
Dec. 31		The preferred dividend is declared, and a common dividend of $0.50 per share is declared.

Instructions

Prepare the shareholders' equity section for the company at December 31, 2005. Show all supporting calculations.

P16-3 Shikai Corporation's charter authorized issuance of 1 million common shares and 500,000 preferred shares. The following transactions involving the issuance of shares were completed. Each transaction is independent of the others.

1. Issued a $100,000, 8% bond payable at par and gave as a bonus 10 preferred shares, which at that time were selling for $106 a share.

2. Issued 500 common shares for machinery. The machinery had been appraised at $7,100; the seller's book value was $6,200. The common shares' most recent market price is $15 a share.

3. Voted an $11 dividend on both the 10,000 shares of outstanding common and the 2,000 shares of outstanding preferred. The dividend was paid in full.

4. Issued 375 shares of common and 100 shares of preferred for a lump sum amounting to $11,300. The common had been selling at $14 and the preferred at $65.

5. Issued 200 shares of common and 50 shares of preferred for furniture and fixtures. The common had a fair market value of $16 per share and the furniture and fixtures were appraised at $6,200.

Instructions

Record the transactions listed above in journal entry form.

P16-4 Before Polska Corporation engages in the share transactions listed below, its general ledger reflects, among others, the following account balances (average cost of its share is $30 per share). The Contributed Surplus relates to the common shares.

Contributed Surplus	Common Shares	Retained Earnings
Balance $9,000	Balance $270,000	Balance $80,000

Instructions

Record the journal entries for the transactions noted below.

(a) Bought and cancelled 380 shares at $39 per share.

(b) Bought and cancelled 300 shares at $43 per share.

(c) Sold 3,500 shares at $42 per share.

(d) Sold 1,200 shares at $48 per share.

(e) Bought and cancelled 1,000 shares at $60.

*P16-5 Heinrich Corporation had the following shareholders' equity at January 1, 2005.

Preferred shares, 8%, $100 par value, 10,000 shares authorized,	
4,000 shares issued	$ 400,000
Common shares, $2 par value, 200,000 shares authorized,	
80,000 shares issued	160,000
Common shares subscribed, 10,000 shares	20,000
Contributed Surplus preferred	20,000
Contributed Surplus common	940,000
Retained earnings	780,000
	2,320,000
Less: Common share subscriptions receivable	40,000
Total shareholders' equity	$2,280,000

During 2005, the following transactions occurred.

1. 100 shares of common share were exchanged for equipment. The share's market value on the exchange date was $12 per share.

2. 1,000 shares of common share and 100 shares of preferred share were sold for the lump sum price of $24,500. The common shares had a market price of $14 at the time of the sale.

3. 2,000 shares of preferred share were sold for cash at $102 per share.

4. All of the subscribers paid their subscription prices into the firm.

5. The common shares were issued.

6. 1,000 common shares were repurchased and retired by the corporation at $15 per share.

7. Income for 2002 was $246,000.

Instructions

Prepare the shareholders' equity section for the company as of December 31, 2005. (The use of T accounts may help you organize the material.)

P16-6 Transactions of Kalila Corporation are as follows.

1. The company is granted a charter that authorizes issuance of 150,000 preferred shares and 150,000 common shares without par value.

2. 10,000 common shares are issued to founders of the corporation for land valued by the board of directors at $210,000 (based on an independent valuation).

3. 15,200 preferred shares are sold for cash at $110 each.

Common Shares

Prior to the 2004–05 fiscal year, the company had 110,000 shares of outstanding common issued as follows.

1. 95,000 shares were issued for cash on July 1, 2002 at $31 per share.

2. On July 24, 2002, 5,000 shares were exchanged for a plot of land, which cost the seller $70,000 in 1992 and had an estimated market value of $220,000 on July 24, 2002.

3. 10,000 shares were issued on March 1, 2003; the shares had been subscribed for $42 per share on October 31, 2003.

During the 2004–05 fiscal year, the following transactions regarding common shares took place.

October 1, 2004	Subscriptions were received for 10,000 shares at $46 per share. Cash of $92,000 was received in full payment for 2,000 shares and share certificates were issued. The remaining subscription for 8,000 shares was to be paid in full by September 30, 2005, at which time the certificates were to be issued.
November 30, 2004	The company purchased 2,000 shares of its own common on the open market at $39 per share. These shares were restored to the status of authorized but unissued shares.
December 15, 2004	The company declared a 5% stock dividend for shareholders of record on January 15, 2005, to be issued on January 31, 2005. The company was having a liquidity problem and could not afford a cash dividend at the time. The company's common shares were selling at $52 per share on December 15, 2004.
June 20, 2005	The company sold 500 shares of its own common for $21,000.

Preferred Shares

The company issued 50,000 shares of preferred at $44 per share on July 1, 2003.

Cash Dividends

The company has followed a schedule of declaring cash dividends in December and June with payment being made to shareholders of record in the following month. The cash dividends, which have been declared since the company's inception through June 30, 2005, are shown below.

Declaration Date	Common Shares	Preferred Shares
12/15/03	$0.30 per share	$3.00 per share
6/15/04	$0.30 per share	$1.00 per share
12/15/04	—	$1.00 per share

No cash dividends were declared during June 2005 due to the company's liquidity problems.

Retained Earnings

As of June 30, 2004, the company's retained earnings account had a balance of $690,000. For the fiscal year ending June 30, 2005, the company reported net income of $40,000.

In March of 2004, the company received a term loan from Manitoba Bank. The bank requires the company to establish a sinking fund and restrict retained earnings for an amount equal to the sinking fund deposit. The annual sinking fund payment of $50,000 is due on April 30 each year; the first payment was made on schedule on April 30, 2005.

Instructions

Prepare the shareholders' equity section of the company's balance sheet, including appropriate notes, as of June 30, 2005, as it should appear in its annual report to the shareholders.

(CMA adapted)

Writing Assignments

WA16-1   Algonquin Corporation sold 50,000 common shares on a subscription basis for $40 per share. By December 31, 2004, collections on these subscriptions totalled $1.3 million. No subscriptions have yet been paid in full.

Instructions

(a) Discuss the meaning of the account Common Share Subscribed and indicate how it is reported in the financial statements.

(b) Discuss the arguments in favour of reporting Subscriptions Receivable as a current asset.

(c) Discuss the arguments in favour of reporting Subscriptions Receivable as a contra equity account.

(d) Indicate how these 50,000 shares would be presented on Algonquin's December 31, 2004 balance sheet under the method discussed in (c) above.

WA16-2 It has been said that (1) the use of the LIFO inventory method during an extended period of rising prices and (2) the expensing of all human resource costs are among the accepted accounting practices that help create secret reserves (i.e., hidden value in the company).

Instructions

Discuss.

WA16-3 *CICA Handbook* Section 1000 defines various elements of financial statements.

Instructions

Answer the following questions based on Section 1000.

(a) Define and discuss the term "equity."

(b) What transactions or events change owners' equity?

(c) What are examples of changes within owners' equity that do not change the total amount of owners' equity?

WA16-4 The directors of Amman Corporation are considering issuing a stock dividend. They have asked you to discuss the proposed action by answering the following questions.

Instructions

(a) What is a stock dividend? How is a stock dividend distinguished from a stock split: from a legal standpoint and from an accounting standpoint?

(b) For what reasons does a corporation usually declare a stock dividend? A stock split?

(c) Discuss the amount, if any, of retained earnings to be capitalized in connection with a stock dividend.

(AICPA adapted)

*WA16-5 Henning Inc, a medium-sized manufacturer, has been experiencing losses for the five years that it has been in business. Although the operations for the year just ended resulted in a loss, several important changes resulted in a profitable fourth quarter, and the company's future operations are expected to be profitable. The treasurer, Peter Henning, suggests that there be a financial reorganization to eliminate the accumulated deficit of $650,000.

Instructions

(a) What are the characteristics of a financial reorganization? In other words, what does it consist of?

(b) List the conditions under which a financial reorganization generally is justified.

(c) Discuss the propriety of the treasurer's proposals to eliminate the deficit of $650,000.

(AICPA adapted)

Cases

*CA16-1 "You can't write up assets," said Nick Toby, internal audit director of Nadir International Inc., to his boss, Jim Coffin, vice-president and chief financial officer. "Nonsense," said Jim, "I can do this as part of a quasi-reorganization of our company." For the last three years, Nadir International, a farm equipment manufacturing firm, has experienced a downturn in its profits resulting from stiff competition with overseas firms and increasing direct labour costs. Though the prospects are still gloomy, the company is hoping to turn a profit by modernizing its property, plant, and equipment (PP&E). This will require Nadir International to raise a lot of money.

Digital Tool

Refer to the Case Primer on the Digital Tool to help you answer these cases.

www.wiley.com/canada/kieso

Over the past few months, Jim tried to raise funds from various financial institutions. They are unwilling to consider lending capital, however, because the company's net book value of fixed assets on the balance sheet, based on historic cost, was not ample to sustain major funding. Jim attempted to explain to bankers and investors that these assets were more valuable than their recorded amounts, given that the company used accelerated amortization methods and tended to underestimate the useful lives of assets. Jim also believes that the company's land and buildings are substantially undervalued because of rising real estate prices over the past several years.

Jim's proposed solution to raise funds is a simple one: First, declare a large dividend to company shareholders such that Retained Earnings would have a large debit balance. Then, write up the fixed assets of Nadir International to an amount equal to the deficit in the Retained Earnings account.

Instructions

Adopt the role of the internal auditor and discuss the financial reporting issues.

Building on Complexity

TD Securities

TD Securities' "structured finance" department focuses on the equity derivative business. Much of its clientele are institutional businesses looking for swaps, options, or customized derivatives. Todd Hargarten, vice-president and director of TD Securities Inc., describes his work with complex financial instruments as reactive, rather than proactive. "A lot of structured derivatives are bought, not sold," he says.

When working with corporate clients, Hargarten and his colleagues provide information on possible solutions to a business's situation. Often these structures are created for a specific large business; there may occasionally be broadly applicable solutions, but that's rare in Canada, Hargarten says.

Institutional investors make their own decisions. Most large pension plans have in-house expertise to develop their own product. By doing all the pieces themselves and breaking it down to a commodity, the pension funds are isolating the risk, Hargarten adds.

Retail demand for exposure to hot sectors also drives structured products. For example, during the telecom heyday, some financial institutions offered a "custom telecom basket." This principal-protected, equity-linked note would compete with bank-offered, equity-linked GICs. The main difference is the term: a note's term can be up to seven years, while a GIC is generally capped at five years. One shortcoming of these structured notes is they are linked to the financial institution, since brokers are reluctant to push a competitor's branded product. As a result, they are limited in size, often ranging from $5 to $25 million.

Adding a bit more structure and flexibility to these instruments can become complicated. For example, covered call-writing funds were first developed in the early 1990s. Then principal protection was added. "Since then, a lot of these structures morphed into other areas," Hargarten says. The complexity of these and other financial instruments continues to increase.∎

CHAPTER 17

Complex Financial Instruments

Learning Objectives

After studying this chapter, you should be able to:

1. Describe the presentation and measurement issues related to various complex financial instruments.
2. Explain the accounting for issuance, conversion, and retirement of convertible securities.
3. Understand the nature of derivatives and why they exist.
4. Explain the various types of financial risks, including how they arise.
5. Understand the nature of options, forwards, and futures.
6. Describe the recognition, measurement, and presentation issues relating to options, forwards, and futures.
7. Describe the various types of stock compensation plans.
8. Explain the differences between employee and compensatory option plans and other options.
9. Describe the accounting for compensatory stock option plans.

After studying the appendices, you should be able to:

10. Understand how derivatives are used in hedging.
11. Explain what hedge accounting is and identify the qualifying hedge criteria.
12. Explain the difference between a fair value and cash flow hedge.
13. Calculate the impact on net income using hedge accounting for both types of hedges.
14. Account for stock appreciation rights plans.
15. Explain the nature of performance-related plans.

Preview of Chapter 17

Complex financial instruments, once uncommon, are now used by companies in many different industries.[1] Companies use these instruments in an effort to manage risk, access pools of financing, and minimize cost of capital and taxes. In response to this trend, the accounting profession has developed a new framework for dealing with these instruments in the financial statements. Earlier in the text, accounting for basic financial instruments such as accounts and notes receivable/payable, investments, loans, and shares was discussed. This chapter focuses on complex financial instruments, including derivatives, which will be discussed separately. Since employee compensation plans often include derivatives such as stock options, this topic will also be discussed in this chapter. The content and organization of the chapter are as follows:

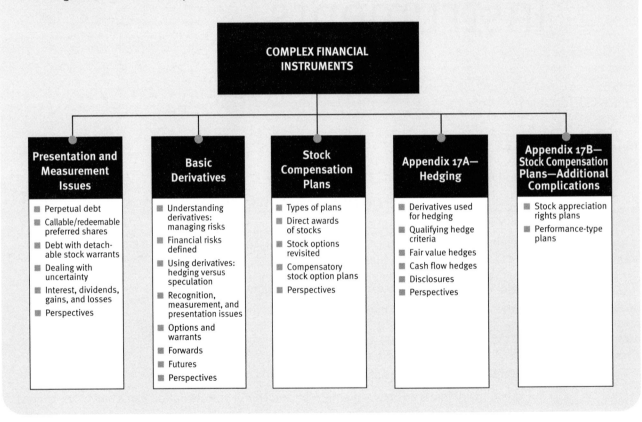

PRESENTATION AND MEASUREMENT ISSUES

Objective 1

Describe the presentation and measurement issues related to various complex financial instruments.

Compound financial instruments have attributes of both equity and debt. They are sometimes referred to as **hybrid instruments** because of these dual attributes. Convertible and perpetual debt are examples. With these instruments, the main accounting complexity

---

[1] *Financial Reporting in Canada 2002* reported that 197 out of 200 companies surveyed provided separate disclosures about financial instruments.

lies in determining how to classify these instruments on the balance sheet. This is a **presentation issue** that must ultimately be determined by examining the economic substance of the instrument. Currently we divide the balance sheet up into at least three major elements: assets, debt, and equity. Many users rely on the classification between debt and equity to assess liquidity and solvency, among other things. Thus, the classification issue is significant. As these types of instrument proliferate, financial statement preparers and analysts are faced with the increasingly difficult task of classifying instruments that do not fit neatly into either the debt or equity category.

Recall from Chapters 15 and 16 the definitions of financial liabilities and equity instruments as follows.

A financial liability is any liability that is a contractual obligation:

(a) to deliver cash or another financial asset to another party; or

(b) to exchange financial instruments with another party under conditions that are potentially unfavourable.

An equity instrument is any contract that evidences a residual interest in the assets of an entity after deducting all of its liabilities.

These definitions are critical in determining how to present the instruments.

Measurement of these instruments is also made complicated by the fact that sometimes the economic value of these instruments is attributable to **both** the debt and equity components (i.e., the instrument is neither 100% debt nor 100% equity but rather **part debt and part equity**). How should these two components be measured? We will review various types of instruments, noting first the nature of the instrument and then the accounting. The chapter will also present two measurement tools: the **incremental or residual method** and the **proportional method**. These tools may be used to allocate the value of an instrument between its debt and equity components.

Underlying Concept

In determining whether to classify as debt, consider the definition of a financial liability. In determining whether to classify as equity, consider the definition of equity instruments.

Underlying Concept

Well-defined measurement tools help reduce measurement uncertainty. These tools ultimately help in preparing financial information that is more reliable.

Perpetual Debt

Perpetual debt is debt that will never be repaid. Even though **legally, it is debt**, economically speaking, it is similar to equity in that it represents permanent capital for the company. Should perpetual debt be presented as debt or equity? To determine this, we must take a closer look at how it derives its value. Traditional debt is valued by taking the present value of the principal and interest payments, discounted at market interest rates. Assume that Jiang Limited issues a $1,000 three-year bond that carries a coupon rate of 10%. If market rates are 10%, the value of the bond will be $1,000, derived as follows.

Underlying Concept

Perpetual debt is debt in legal form and upon closer examination is debt in economic substance as well, since it derives its value from the interest obligation.

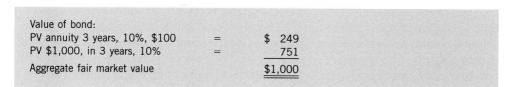

Value of bond:		
PV annuity 3 years, 10%, $100	=	$ 249
PV $1,000, in 3 years, 10%	=	751
Aggregate fair market value		$1,000

Illustration 17-1

Economic Value of a Three-year Bond

Now assume that these bonds are 40-year bonds. The present value of the interest would be as follows.

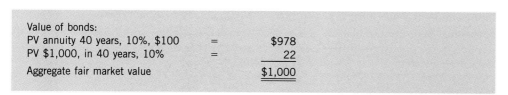

Value of bonds:		
PV annuity 40 years, 10%, $100	=	$978
PV $1,000, in 40 years, 10%	=	22
Aggregate fair market value		$1,000

Illustration 17-2

Economic Value of a 40-year Bond

Note that the value of the bond stems primarily from the interest and as the life of the bond increases, the economic value attributed to the repayment of principal decreases significantly. Now, assume that the bonds are perpetual bonds, i.e., they will never be repaid. The value of the interest will be equal to the bond value. **Therefore, a perpetual bond's value is driven solely by the contractual obligation to pay interest. As such it is a liability.**[2]

Callable/Redeemable Preferred Shares

Preferred shares have traditionally been treated as equity since they normally represent permanent financing. However, what if the shares have a fixed term and will be redeemed by the company at a set point in time? These instruments, often called term or mandatorily redeemable preferred shares (although legally equity), meet the definition of a liability since there is an **obligation for the company to pay cash**. When the term expires, the company is obligated to buy back the shares from the holder. **These shares are therefore presented as liability on the balance sheet.**

Sometimes, even though the shares do not require redemption, the terms of the share agreement are such that redemption is highly probable. For instance, assume Hope Inc. issued preferred shares that carry a dividend of 4%. According to the terms of the share agreement, the dividend rate will double in 5 years and again in 10 years. In this case, although the company is not contractually obligated to redeem the shares, the accelerating dividend will result in an unreasonably high cost of capital for the company, and Hope Inc. will be compelled from an economic point of view to redeem them. Therefore, **Hope has little or no discretion to avoid paying out cash and it could be argued that this obligation to deliver cash creates a liability.**[3] **Therefore, again, these shares would be presented as liabilities.**

What do the Numbers Mean?

Succession Planning and Complex Financial Instruments

Redeemable shares are often used in tax and succession planning. Many small businesses are created and run by individuals who at some point decide they would like to hand the company over to their children. One way of doing this in an orderly manner that minimizes taxes is through the use of redeemable preferred shares, sometimes referred to as **high/low preferred shares**. The business assets may be transferred to a new company using special tax provisions to minimize taxes and the owner takes as part of the consideration, redeemable preferred shares. The children buy the common shares in the new company for a nominal amount, allowing them to share in subsequent increases in the company's value. This also gives them some or all of the voting control since the common shares would normally be voting shares.

The redemption amount of the preferred shares is set at the company's fair value at the time of the transaction. Thus the fair value is frozen for the individual at a point in time (hence the label "estate freeze," which is sometimes given to this type of transaction). All subsequent increases in value will attribute to the offspring through ownership of the common shares. The owner will eventually get his or her money out (which represents the fair value of the assets that he/she put in) at a future point by redeeming the shares. This is a good example of yet another business reason to use complex financial instruments. Note that the redemption feature causes this instrument to be recorded as a (huge) liability since the company has an obligation to deliver cash. Many small business owners are not happy with this accounting since it makes the company look highly leveraged when in fact, the shares will normally not be redeemed in the short- or mid-term. Treating the shares as liabilities in the balance sheet may also cause the company to be offside on pre-existing debt covenants. As a result of this, the CICA allows certain small businesses that qualify for differential reporting to treat these particular instruments as equity.

---

[2] *CICA Handbook*, Section 3860.A19.

[3] *CICA Handbook*, Section 3860.22 and A20.

What if a company issues preferred shares and there is a requirement to use its best efforts to repurchase a certain number of shares each year: does this represent an obligation to the company? It really depends on the exact terms of the share agreement. Professional judgement must be applied in making this determination.[4]

Debt with Detachable Stock Warrants

Debt may be issued with a detachable warrant (option to buy common shares of the company[5]). The warrants give the holder the right to buy common shares at a fixed price (the exercise or strike price) for a specified period of time (the exercise period). Because the warrants are detachable or removable, a market often exists to buy and sell these instruments. **The warrants are equity instruments[6] and therefore, the instrument is part debt and part equity. How much of the value of the instrument is due to the debt portion and how much is due to the warrant portion?**

Invisible Value

On August 22, 2002 **Orbital Sciences Corporation** issued four-year secured notes plus warrants. The debt was issued for net proceeds of $123.1 million (face value $135 million). Each unit consisted of a $1,000 note plus a warrant to purchase up to 122.23 shares at $3.86 per share within four years. At the time of the agreement, the exercise price was 10% higher than the market value of the shares. The warrants were recorded based on their fair value of $28.8 million. Why did the warrants have value when the exercise price was actually greater than the fair value of the shares? This is because investors are willing to pay for the right to buy shares. **The value attributed to the warrant takes into account the possibility that the share price might increase in value over the exercise period.**

The proceeds from the sale of debt with detachable stock warrants should be allocated between the two securities since this instrument includes two distinct and separable components:[7]

1. the note or financial liability portion, and

2. the warrant or equity instrument portion.

Various alternatives exist to measure these items and there is no prescribed way to measure the individual components. Two options are as follows.[8]

1. Proportional method: Determine the market values of similar straight debt (i.e., with no warrants) and tradable options or warrants. This would be facilitated if markets existed for both these instruments as separate items. Measurement of the debt portion may also be done by a PV calculation, discounting at the market rate for

What
do the
Numbers
Mean?

---

[4] *CICA Handbook*, EIC Abstract #74 provides some guidance, noting that if there is an unavoidable obligation to repurchase, an obligation exists.

[5] Options are derivative instruments. These will be discussed in further depth in the next section on derivatives.

[6] The definition of equity instruments may not appear to include options and warrants since they are only rights to obtain a residual interest in the company (not actual residual interests); however, the appendix to *CICA Handbook* Section 3860.A7 specifically includes warrants and options as examples of equity instruments.

[7] *CICA Handbook*, Section 3860.18 and .24.

[8] Although the *CICA Handbook* and Canadian GAAP do not mandate specific measurement techniques, Section 3860.29 and A25 refer to two possible ways to value the equity component: residual valuation (like the incremental method above) and option pricing valuation (like the proportional method above). The *CICA Handbook* presumes that the liability component may generally be valued with little measurement uncertainty using discounting techniques and readily available information about interest (discount) rates.

premiums. These are the **direct**, visible costs charged by an intermediary or the other party to the transaction. Then there are **indirect**, less visible costs. The activity of researching, analysing, and executing these transactions absorbs a significant amount of employee time. Managing risk sometimes results in limiting the potential for gain and thus there is a **hidden cost**: the **opportunity cost**. **Use of too many instruments such as derivatives increases the complexity of financial statements and thus contributes to lack of transparency and understandability.** Given the current climate, capital markets may penalize such companies with higher costs of capital and/or limit or deny access to capital. This latter aspect also represents a **hidden cost** to the company. Companies must consider all of the costs associated with derivatives and weigh them against the benefits.

The growth in use of derivatives has been aided by the development of powerful calculating and communication technology, which provides new ways to analyse information about markets as well as the power to process high volumes of payments. Many corporations therefore use derivatives extensively and successfully.

Underlying Concept

As always, the benefits of entering into certain transactions, especially complex ones, must exceed the costs, otherwise the company will be reducing shareholder value rather than creating it.

What do the Numbers Mean?

Risky Business

As shown in the graph below, use of derivatives has grown steadily in the past several years. Over $3 trillion in derivative contracts were in play at the end of 2001. The primary players in the market for derivatives—large companies and various financial institutions—continue to find new uses for derivatives for speculation and risk management.

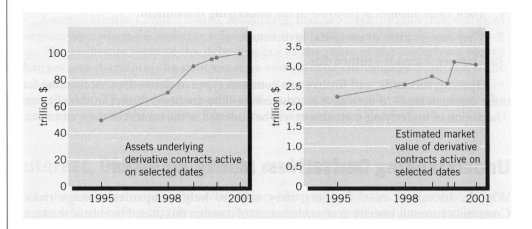

However, as financial engineers develop new uses for derivatives—many times through the use of increasingly complex webs of transactions, spanning a number of markets—the financial system as a whole can be dramatically affected. As a result, some market watchers are concerned about the risk that a crisis in one company or sector could bring the entire financial system to its knees.

This concern was illustrated when **Long-Term Capital Management**, a venerable hedge fund in the United States, experienced big losses on some of its derivative investments and had to be bailed out by a consortium of large banks. In cases like this, there is the possibility that even big market players would rush to cut their losses, resulting in a shortage of cash that could paralyse the system. Stock markets could tumble and banks could close, thereby putting the savings of even households at risk. And if that were to happen, even people with no money directly invested in the derivatives markets could be negatively affected. Thus the growing use of derivatives and their potential impact on the entire financial system highlights the need for transparency in accounting and reporting of derivative transactions.

Source: Adapted from Daniel Altman, "Contracts So Complex They Imperil the System," *New York Times on the Web* (February 24, 2002).

Sp

In s
pur
max
that
incr
forv
take
proi
tion
was
risk,

inef
into
futu
hop
beca
info
kets
eacl
exist

mar

Re

In C
ativ
Mar
Fina
becc
mod

(a)

(b)

(c)

(d)

(e)

tradi

arm'
pulsi
whic
dete

30 EI(

31 Prc

Financial Risks Defined

As mentioned above, companies use derivatives to manage risks, especially financial risks. Financial risks include price risk, credit risk, liquidity risk, and cash flow risk. These are briefly defined as follows.[27]

1. **Price risk**: the **risk that an instrument's price or value will change**. The price or value may vary due to change in currency (**currency risk**), interest rate (**interest rate risk**), or other capital market forces (**market risk**). An example of market price risk is the risk of change in value of an investment in common shares of another company, either due to demand for the common shares or general stock market conditions.

2. **Credit risk**: the **risk that one of the parties to the contract will fail to fulfill its obligation** under the contract and cause the other party loss. For example, credit risk is usually associated with collection (accounts receivable have credit risk associated with them).

3. **Liquidity risk**: the **risk that the company itself will not be able to honour the contract and fulfill its obligation**. The more debt a company has, the greater the risk that it will not be able to repay the debt and the higher the liquidity risk. Additional liabilities, by definition, increase liquidity risk.

4. **Cash flow risk**: the **risk that cash flows related to a contract (e.g., a monetary financial instrument) will change over time**. An example of this is a debt instrument with a variable interest rate. The variable interest rate will cause the interest payments to change when interest rates change.

It is important to identify and understand which risks a company currently has and how it plans to manage these risks using derivatives. Keep in mind that derivatives often expose the company to additional risks. As long as the company identifies and manages these risks, this is not a problem. **The problem arises when stakeholders do not understand the risk profile of derivative instruments.** The use of derivatives can be dangerous, and it is critical that all parties involved understand the risks and rewards associated with these contracts.[28]

Using Derivatives: Hedging versus Speculation

Managing risk may involve reducing pre-existing risks (normally referred to as hedging) and/or increasing risks (speculating). Both are acceptable strategies and depend on the company's risk tolerance profile. Accounting for speculative transactions is more straightforward than accounting for hedging transactions. Although hedging will be discussed in the body of the chapter, **hedge accounting** will be discussed in Appendix 17A due to its added complexity.

What types of business models and processes generate financial risk? Virtually all business models generate financial risks. The following are some examples.

- Any business that purchases commodities such as fuel, agricultural products, or renewable resources as inputs has a **cash flow risk** associated with these inputs. These companies know that commodity prices vary significantly depending on supply and demand. This affects the company's profitability and may lead to volatile net income.

4 Objective

Explain the various types of financial risks, including how they arise.

Underlying Concept

Remember from finance courses that increased risk may bring the opportunity for increased rewards. Thus some companies expose themselves to increased risks in order to maximize shareholder value.

---

[27] *CICA Handbook*, Section 3860.44.

[28] There are some well-publicized examples of companies that have suffered considerable losses using derivatives. For example, companies such as Showa Shell Sekiyu (Japan), Metallgesellschaft (Germany), Proctor & Gamble (United States), and Air Products & Chemicals (United States) have incurred significant losses from investments in derivative instruments.

Illustration 17A-4

Effect of Hedge on Cash Flows

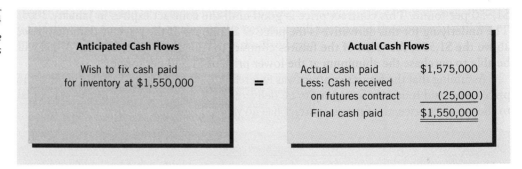

Anticipated Cash Flows		Actual Cash Flows	
Wish to fix cash paid for inventory at $1,550,000	=	Actual cash paid	$1,575,000
		Less: Cash received on futures contract	(25,000)
		Final cash paid	$1,550,000

There are no income effects at this point. The gain on the futures contract is accumulated in equity as part of Accumulated Other Comprehensive Income until the period when the inventory is sold and earnings is affected through cost of goods sold.

For example, assume that the aluminum is processed into finished goods (cans). The total cost of the cans (including the aluminum purchases in January 2005) is $1.7 million. Allied sells the cans in July 2005 for $2 million. The entry to record this sale is as follows.

A   = L +   SE
+300,000   +300,000

Cash flows: ↑ 2,000,000 inflow

July 2005		
Cash	2,000,000	
Sales Revenue		2,000,000
Cost of Goods Sold	1,700,000	
Inventory (Cans)		1,700,000

Since the effect on the anticipated transaction has now affected earnings, Allied makes the following entry related to the hedging transaction.

A   = L +   SE
0   0   0

Cash flows: No effect

July 2005		
Unrealized Holding Gain or Loss— Other Comprehensive Income	25,000	
Cost of Goods Sold		25,000

The gain on the futures contract, which was reported as part of Other Comprehensive Income, now reduces cost of goods sold. As a result, the cost of aluminum included in the overall cost of goods sold is $1,550,000. The futures contract has worked as planned to manage the cash paid for aluminum inventory and the amount of cost of goods sold. Note that this entry could also be made at the date the inventory was acquired except the credit would be booked to Inventory. Thus, the cost of goods sold in July 2005 would be $1,675,000.

Disclosures

Current disclosure provisions for all financial instruments are significant and focus on risks, including:

1. terms and conditions of instrument

2. interest rate risk

3. credit risk, including significant concentrations

4. fair value of all financial instruments, both recognized and unrecognized

5. hedges of anticipated future transactions, description of hedge, and instrument used.[53]

[53] *CICA Handbook*, Section 3860, pars. .43 .95.

Exercises

E17-1 **(Issuance and Conversion of Bonc**

Instructions

Present the entry(ies) required to record eac

(a) Grand Corp. issued $10 million par va
company's investment banker estimates

(b) Hussein Limited issued $20 million pa
with each $100 par value bond. At the ti

(c) On July 1, 2004, Tien Limited called its
were converted into 1 million common
the bonds, and the company paid an ad
The company records the conversion
Surplus—Conversion Rights was $200,0

E17-2 **(Conversion of Bonds)** Aubrey In
accrued interest. The bonds were dated April
tized semi-annually on a straight-line basis. Bo
    On April 1, 2005, $1.5 million of these I
in cash at the time of conversion.

Instructions

(a) Prepare the entry to record the interest
ited when the bonds were issued. (Roun

(b) Prepare the entry(ies) to record the conv
to record amortization of the bond disco

E17-3 **(Conversion of Bonds)** Vargo Li
Premium on Bonds Payable account has a bal.
bonds are converted into preferred shares. Th

Instructions

Assuming that the book value method was us

E17-4 **(Conversion of Bonds)** On Janu
Corp. issued $10 million of 8% convertible d
$1,000 bond to convert the bond into five co
ment's present value at the time of issuance w.
ent value and the amount paid is attributable
shares were split 2 for 1, and the conversion
corporation's common shares were selling for
conversion options. The corporation uses the

Instructions

(a) Prepare in general journal form the entr

(b) Prepare in general journal form the en
method. Show supporting calculations in

(c) How many shares were issued as a result

E17-5 **(Conversion of Bonds)** An excerp
lowing balances.

10% Callable, Convertible Bonds Payable
    (semi-annual interest dates April 30 and O
    convertible into six common shares per $1,
    bond principal; maturity date April 30, 200
Discount on Bonds Payable

Contributed Surplus—Conversion Rights

Perspectives

The new accounting standards for financial instruments, other comprehensive income, and hedge accounting represent the accounting profession's effort to develop accounting guidance for derivatives. Many believe that these new rules are needed to properly measure and report derivatives in financial statements. Others argue that reporting derivatives at fair value results in unrealized gains and losses that are difficult to interpret. Concerns also were raised about the complexity and cost of implementing the standards, since prior to these new proposed standards, many derivatives were not recognized in financial statements.

The profession, as part of its due process, worked to respond to these concerns, holding numerous meetings and receiving comments from hundreds of constituents or constituent groups. The authors believe that the long-term benefits of this standard will far outweigh any short-term implementation costs. As the volume and complexity of derivatives and hedging transactions continues to grow, the risk that investors and creditors will be exposed to unexpected losses arising from derivative transactions also increases. Without this standard, statement readers do not have comprehensive information in financial statements concerning many derivative financial instruments and the effects of hedging transactions using derivatives.

Summary of Learning Objectives for Appendix 17A

Digital Tool

Glossary

www.wiley.com/canada/kieso

KEY TERMS

cash flow hedge, 922
fair value hedge, 921
interest rate swap, 923
settlement date, 924
swap contract, 923

10 Understand how derivatives are used in hedging.

Any company or individual wanting to insure against different types of business risks often uses derivative contracts to achieve this objective. In general, where the intent is to manage and reduce risk, these transactions involve some type of hedge. Derivatives are useful tools for this since they have the effect of transferring risks and rewards between the parties to the contract. Derivatives are used primarily to hedge a company's exposure to fluctuations in interest rates, foreign currency exchange rates, and commodity prices.

11 Explain what hedge accounting is and identify the qualifying hedge criteria.

Hedge accounting is optional accounting that seeks to acknowledge that properly hedged positions will not affect net income. It seeks to match gains and losses from hedged positions with those of the hedging items so that they may be offset. Since this is special accounting, companies must ensure that a real hedge exists in the first place (that is insulated from economic loss or undesirable consequences) and that it remains effective. Proper documentation of the risks and risk management strategy is important.

12 Explain the difference between a fair value and cash flow hedge.

A fair value hedge reduces risks relating to fair value changes of recorded assets and liabilities as well as purchase commitments. Cash flow hedges protect against future losses due to future cash flow changes relating to exposures that are not captured on the balance sheet.

13 Calculate the impact on net income using hedge accounting for both types of hedges.

Properly hedged positions where hedge accounting is used do not affect net income. All gains and losses offset and so the impact on net income is zero. For cash flow hedges, the gains and losses on the hedging items are booked through Other Comprehensive Income.

Note: All asterisked assignmen

Brief Exercises

BE17-1 Verbitsky Corporation h
are converted on December 31, 2(
share. Record the conversion usin

BE17-2 Selly Corporation issu
shares were originally issued at $6
Record the conversion of the pref

BE17-3 Divac Corporation issu
After issuance, the bonds were sel
tional method to record the issuar

BE17-4 Ceballos Corporation i:
rant. After issuance, the bonds w
determined. Use the incremental :

BE17-5 On January 1, 2005, Jol
to purchase one share of Johnson
market price is $55 per share on th
January 1, 2005 and December 31
Assume that the options' fair

BE17-6 Jamieson Limited issuec
how the instrument should be pre

BE 17-7 Silky Limited has rede
redeemed within five years, the divi

BE 17-8 Refer to BE 17-7. Hov

BE 17-9 During 2005, Genoa L
by the holder for redemption afte

BE17-10 Pseudo Inc. purchased c
The premium (cost) related to the c

BE 17-11 Refer to BE17-10. Inst
from Alter Limited as the option |

BE 17-12 On January 1, 2005, (
days. On January 15, the U.S. doll
on January 15. Prepare any necess

BE 17-13 Refer to BE 17-12. As
the Futures Exchange. Ginseng w:
asked Ginseng to deposit an addi
tional margin call as well as the ch

***BE17-14** Tinsdale Limited wol
month to reflect the current excha
ing losses. Explain whether the co

***BE17-15** Perkins, Inc. establish
utives to receive cash at the date
price of $20 on 5,000 SARs. The
2005 and $29 on December 31, :
expense for 2005 and 2006.

---

items has the effect of also reducing net income without affecting the amount of the extraordinary item. The final amount is referred to as income available to common shareholders.

Illustration 18-13

Calculation of Income Available to Common Shareholders

	(A) Income Information	(B) Weighted Shares	(C) Earnings per Share (A ÷ B)
Income before discontinued operations and extraordinary items available to common shareholders	$480,000	480,000	$1.00
Extraordinary gain (net of tax)	240,000	480,000	.50
Income available to common shareholders	$720,000	480,000	$1.50

Disclosure of the per share amount for the extraordinary item (net of tax) must be reported either on the face of the income statement or in the notes to the financial statements. Income and per share information reported would be as follows.

Illustration 18-14

Earnings per Share, with Extraordinary Item

Income before extraordinary item	$580,000
Extraordinary gain, net of tax	240,000
Net income	$820,000
Earnings per share:	
Income before extraordinary item	$1.00
Extraordinary item, net of tax	.50
Net income	$1.50

DILUTED EARNINGS PER SHARE

Complex Capital Structure

One problem with a basic EPS calculation is that it fails to recognize the potentially dilutive impact on outstanding shares when a corporation has dilutive securities in its capital structure. **Dilutive securities present a serious problem because conversion or exercise often has an adverse effect on earnings per share.** This adverse effect can be significant and, more important, unexpected, unless financial statements call attention to the potential dilutive effect in some manner.

A **complex capital structure** exists when a corporation has potential common shares such as convertible securities, options, warrants, or other rights that upon conversion or exercise could dilute earnings per share. **Therefore, as noted earlier, when a company has a complex capital structure, both basic and diluted earnings per share are generally reported.** The calculation of diluted EPS is similar to the calculation of basic EPS. The difference is that diluted EPS includes the effect of all dilutive potential common shares that were outstanding during the period. The formula in Illustration 18-15 shows the relationship between basic EPS and diluted EPS.

Note that companies with complex capital structures will not report diluted EPS if the securities in their capital structure are antidilutive. Antidilutive securities are securities that, upon conversion or exercise, increase earnings per share (or reduce the loss per share). **The dual presentation's purpose is to inform financial statement users of situations that will likely occur and to provide worst case dilutive situations.** If the

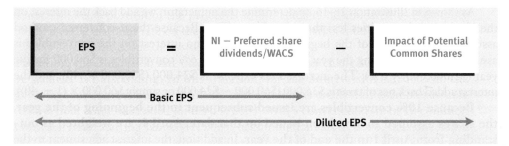

Illustration 18-15

Relationship between Basic and Diluted EPS

securities are antidilutive, the likelihood of conversion or exercise is considered remote. **Thus, companies that have only antidilutive securities are not permitted to increase earnings per share and are required to report only the basic EPS number.**[9]

The calculation of basic EPS was illustrated in the prior section. The discussion in the following sections addresses the effects of convertible and other dilutive securities on EPS calculations.

Convertible Securities

At conversion, convertible securities are exchanged for common shares. Thus convertible securities are potential common shares and may be dilutive. The method used to measure the dilutive effects of potential conversion on EPS is called the if-converted method.

If-Converted Method

The if-converted method for convertible debt or preferred shares assumes:

1. the conversion of the convertible securities at the **beginning of the period** (or at the time of the security issuance, if issued during the period),[10] and

2. **the elimination of related interest, net of tax** or preferred share dividend. If the debt/equity had been converted at the beginning of the period, there would be no bond interest expense/preferred dividend. No tax effect is calculated because preferred dividends generally are not tax deductible.

Thus the denominator—the weighted average number of shares outstanding—is increased by the additional shares assumed issued. The numerator—net income—is increased by the amount of interest expense, net of tax, associated with those potential common shares.

As an example, Field Corporation has net income for the year of $210,000 and a weighted average number of common shares outstanding during the period of 100,000 shares. The basic earnings per share is therefore $2.10 ($210,000 ÷ 100,000). The company has two convertible debenture bond issues outstanding.[11] One is a 6% issue sold at 100 (total $1,000,000) in a prior year and convertible into 20,000 common shares. The other is a 10% issue sold at 100 (total $1,000,000) on April 1 of the current year and convertible into 32,000 common shares. The tax rate is 40%.

International Insight

The provisions in Canadian and U.S. GAAP are currently being revised to ensure they are substantially the same as those in International Accounting Standard No. 33, Earnings per Share, issued by the IASB.

5 Objective

Calculate diluted earnings per share using the if-converted method.

---

[9] *CICA Handbook*, Section 3500.30.

[10] *CICA Handbook*, Section 3500.35.

[11] To simplify, the consequences of measuring and presenting the debt and equity components of the convertible debentures separately have been ignored for this example. As previously noted in the chapter, part of the proceeds would be allocated to the equity component. The interest expense would be calculated using the market interest rate for straight debt, i.e., without the conversion feature.

tracts would be included in the calculations if they represent a liability, i.e., if the forward purchase price is higher than the average market price. Similarly, written call options are the same as **forward sales contracts**. Forward sales contracts would have to be included in the calculations if they represent a liability, i.e., if the forward selling price is lower than the market price.

Purchased Options

Purchased options, on the other hand, do not obligate the company (as opposed to written options, which do). When the company buys options, it obtains the right but not the obligation to buy (call) or sell (put) its own shares. When will it exercise these options? Like any option holder, it is assumed that the company will exercise the options when they are **in the money**. Thus, when the underlying shares in a purchased call option have a market value that is greater than the exercise price, they are in the money. Alternatively, when the underlying shares in a purchased put option have a market value that is less than the exercise price, the options are in the money and it is assumed that they will be exercised.

Illustration 18-19 summarizes this.

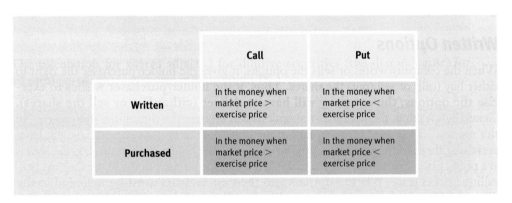

Illustration 18-19

In the Money Options

	Call	Put
Written	In the money when market price > exercise price	In the money when market price < exercise price
Purchased	In the money when market price > exercise price	In the money when market price < exercise price

Purchased options will always be antidilutive since they will only be exercised when they are in the money and this will always be favourable to the company. They are thus not considered in the calculation.[14]

Treasury Stock Method

Objective 6
Calculate diluted earnings per share using the treasury stock method.

Written options and warrants and their equivalents are included in earnings per share calculations through the treasury stock or reverse treasury stock method.

The treasury stock method applies to **written call options and equivalents** and assumes that:

1. the options/warrants or equivalents are exercised **at the beginning of the year** (or date of issue if later), and

2. the proceeds are used to purchase common shares for the treasury at the **average market price** that exists during the year.

If the exercise price is lower than the average market price, then the proceeds from exercise are not sufficient to buy back all the shares. This will result in more shares being issued than purchased and will be dilutive. **The excess number of the shares issued over the number of shares purchased is added to the weighted average number of**

[14] *CICA Handbook*, Section 3500.45.

shares outstanding for purposes of calculating diluted earnings per share. Note that no adjustment is made to the numerator.

Assume 1,500 (written) call options are outstanding at an exercise price of $30 for a common share. The average common share market price per share is $50. Because the market price is greater than the exercise price, the options are considered in the money and the holder is assumed to exercise them. They can buy the shares for a price that is less than market price—a bargain. By applying the treasury stock method, there would be 600 incremental shares outstanding, calculated as follows.[15]

Proceeds from exercise of 1,500 options (1,500 × $30)	$45,000
Shares issued upon exercise of options	1,500
Treasury shares purchasable with proceeds ($45,000 ÷ $50)	900
Incremental shares outstanding (additional potential common shares)	600

Illustration 18-20

Calculation of Incremental Shares

Thus, if the exercise price of the call option or warrant is lower than the shares' market price, dilution occurs because on a net basis, there are more common shares assumed to be outstanding after the exercise. If the exercise price of the call option or warrant is higher than the shares' market price, the options would not be exercised and are therefore irrelevant in the EPS calculation.[16] As a practical matter, a simple average of the weekly or monthly prices is adequate, so long as the prices do not fluctuate significantly.

Comprehensive Illustration—Treasury Stock Method

To illustrate the application of the treasury stock method, assume that Kubitz Industries, Inc. has net income for the period of $220,000. The average number of shares outstanding for the period was 100,000 shares. Hence, basic EPS, ignoring all dilutive securities, is $2.20. The average number of shares under outstanding written call options (although not exercisable at this time) at an option price of $20 per share is 5,000 shares. The average market price of the common shares during the year was $28. The calculation is shown below.

	Basic Earnings per Share	Diluted Earnings per Share
Average number of shares under option outstanding:		5000
Option price per share		× $20
Proceeds upon exercise of options		$100,000
Average market price of common shares		$28
Treasury shares that could be repurchased with proceeds ($100,000 ÷ $28)		3,571
Excess of shares under option over the treasury shares that could be repurchased (5,000 − 3,571)— Potential common incremental shares		1,429
Average number of common shares outstanding	$100,000	$100,000
Total average number of common shares outstanding and potential common shares	$100,000 (A)	$101,429 (C)
Net income for the year	$220,000 (B)	$220,000 (D)
Earnings per share	$2.20 (B ÷ A)	$2.17 (D ÷ C)

Illustration 18-21

Calculation of Earnings per Share—Treasury Stock Method

---

[15] The incremental number of shares may be more simply calculated: (Market price − option price) ÷ market price × number of options = number of shares ($50 − $30) ÷ $50 × 1,500 options = 600 shares

[16] It might be noted that options and warrants have essentially the same assumptions and calculational problems, although the warrants may allow or require the tendering of some other security such as debt in lieu of cash upon exercise. In such situations, the accounting becomes quite complex and is beyond the scope of this book.

Reverse Treasury Stock Method

Objective 7
Calculate diluted earnings per share using the reverse treasury stock method.

The **reverse treasury stock method** is used for (written) put options and forward purchase contracts. It assumes that:

1. the company will issue sufficient common shares **at the beginning of the year** in the marketplace (at the average market price) to generate sufficient funds to buy the shares under the option/forward, and

2. the proceeds from the above will be used to buy back the shares under the option/forward at the beginning of the year.

If the options are in the money, the company will have to buy the shares back under the options/forward at a higher price than the market price. Thus it will have to issue more shares at the beginning of the year to generate sufficient funds to meet the obligation under the option/forward.

Assume 1,500 (written) put options are outstanding at an exercise price of $30 for a common share. The average common share market price per share is $20. Because the market price is less than the exercise price, the options are considered in the money and the holder is assumed to exercise them. They can sell the shares for a price that is higher than market price—again, a bargain. By applying the reverse treasury stock method, there would be 750 additional (incremental) shares outstanding, calculated as follows.

Illustration 18-22

Calculation of Incremental Shares

Amount needed to buy 1,500 shares under put option (1,500 × $30)	$45,000
Shares issued in market to obtain $45,000 ($45,000 ÷ $20)	2,250
Number of shares purchased under the put options	1,500
Incremental shares outstanding (potential common shares)	750

This is dilutive because there will be 750 more shares outstanding. If the market price is higher than the exercise price, the options would never be exercised (the holder could sell the shares in the marketplace for a higher amount). Thus, options that are not in the money are ignored for purposes of the diluted EPS calculation. Likewise, forward purchase contracts where the forward purchase price is lower than the market would be antidilutive because the company would theoretically have to issue fewer shares in the marketplace in order to generate sufficient money to honour the forward contract. Therefore, they would issue fewer than they buy back, resulting in fewer common shares outstanding (not more).

Contingently Issuable Shares

Contingently issuable shares are potential common shares, as previously noted. If these shares are issuable upon the mere passage of time, they are not considered contingently issuable as the passage of time is a certainty.[17] These shares would be considered outstanding for basic EPS when time has passed and they are issuable. They would be included in the diluted EPS calculations as at the beginning of the year (or later if the agreement was made during the year).

If the shares are issuable upon attaining a certain earnings or market price level, for instance, and this level is met at the end of the year, they should be considered as out-

---

[17] *CICA Handbook*, Section 3500.21.

standing from the beginning of the year for the calculation of diluted earnings per share.[18] If the conditions have not been met, the diluted EPS may still be affected. The number of contingently issuable shares included in the diluted EPS calculation would be based on the number of shares (if any) that would be issuable if the end of the reporting period were the end of the contingency period and if the impact were dilutive.[19]

For example, assume that Walz Corporation purchased Cardella Limited in 2003 and agreed to give the shareholders of Cardella 20,000 additional shares in 2005 if Cardella's net income in 2004 is $90,000; in 2003, Cardella's net income is $100,000. Because the 2004 stipulated earnings of $90,000 are already being attained, diluted earnings per share of Walz for 2003 would include the 20,000 contingent shares in the shares outstanding calculation.

Antidilution Revisited

In calculating diluted EPS, the aggregate of all dilutive securities must be considered. But first we must determine which potentially dilutive securities are in fact individually dilutive and which are antidilutive. Any security that is antidilutive should be excluded and cannot be used to offset dilutive securities.

Recall that antidilutive securities are securities whose inclusion in earnings per share calculations **would increase earnings per share (or reduce net loss per share).** Convertible debt is antidilutive if the addition to income of the interest (net of tax) causes a greater percentage increase in income (numerator) than conversion of the bonds causes a percentage increase in common and potentially dilutive shares (denominator). In other words, convertible debt is antidilutive if conversion of the security causes common share earnings to increase by a greater amount per additional common share than earnings per share was before the conversion.

To illustrate, assume that Kohl Corporation has a 6%, $1 million debt issue that is convertible into 10,000 common shares. Net income for the year is $210,000, the weighted average number of common shares outstanding is 100,000 shares, and the tax rate is 40%. In this case, assume conversion of the debt into common shares at the beginning of the year requires the following adjustments of net income and the weighted average number of shares outstanding.

Objective 8
Identify antidilutive potential common shares.

Net income for the year	$210,000	Average number of shares outstanding	100,000
Add: Adjustment for interest (net of tax) on 6% debentures $60,000 × (1 − .40)	36,000	Add: Shares issued upon assumed conversion of debt	10,000
Adjusted net income	$246,000	Average number of common and potential common shares	110,000

Basic EPS = $210,000 ÷ 100,000 = $2.10
Diluted EPS = $246,000 ÷ 110,000 = $2.24 (Antidilutive)

Illustration 18-23

Test for Antidilution

As a shortcut, the convertible debt also can be identified as antidilutive by comparing the incremental EPS resulting from conversion, $3.60 ($36,000 additional earnings ÷ 10,000 additional shares), with EPS before inclusion of the convertible debt, $2.10.

With options or warrants, whenever the option or warrant is not in the money, it is irrelevant because the holder will not exercise.

---

[18] *CICA Handbook*, Section 3500.49. In addition to contingent issuances of stock, other types of situations that might lead to dilution are the issuance of participating securities and two class common shares. The reporting of these types of securities in EPS calculations is beyond the scope of this textbook.

[19] *CICA Handbook*, Section 3500.49.

Additional Disclosures

Complex capital structures and dual presentation of earnings require the following additional disclosures in note form:

1. adjustments to income before discontinued operations and extraordinary items for returns on senior equity instruments in arriving at income available to common shareholders,

2. a reconciliation of the numerators and denominators of basic and diluted per share calculations for income before discontinued operations and extraordinary items (including individual income and share amount of each class of securities that affect EPS), and

3. securities that could dilute basic EPS in the future but were not included in the calculations due to antidilutive features.

Illustration 18-24 presents the reconciliation and the related disclosure that is needed to meet this standard's disclosure requirements.

Illustration 18-24

Reconciliation for Basic and Diluted EPS Basic EPS

	For the Year Ended 2005		
	Income (Numerator)	Shares (Denominator)	Per Share Amount
Income before extraordinary item and accounting change	$7,500,000		
Less: Preferred stock dividends	(45,000)		
Basic EPS			
Income available to common shareholders	7,455,000	3,991,666	$1.87
Warrants		30,768	
Convertible preferred shares	45,000	308,333	
4% convertible bonds (net of tax)	60,000	50,000	
Diluted EPS			
Income available to common shareholders + assumed conversions	$7,560,000	4,380,767	$1.73

Stock options to purchase 1 million shares of common shares at $85 per share were outstanding during the second half of 2005 but were not included in the calculation of diluted EPS because the options' exercise price was greater than the average market price of the common shares. The options were still outstanding at the end of year 2005 and expire on June 30, 2015.

Comprehensive Earnings per Share Exercise

The purpose of this exercise is to illustrate the method of calculating dilution when many securities are involved. The following section of the balance sheet of Andrews Corporation is presented for analysis; assumptions related to the capital structure follow.

ANDREWS CORPORATION
Selected Balance Sheet Information
At December 31, 2005

Illustration 18-25

*Balance Sheet for
Comprehensive Illustration*

Long-term debt:

Notes payable, 14%	$1,000,000
7% convertible bonds payable	2,000,000
9% convertible bonds payable	3,000,000
Total long-term debt:	$6,000,000

Shareholders' equity:

$10 cumulative dividend, convertible preferred shares, no par value; 100,000 shares authorized, 20,000 shares issued and outstanding	$2,000,000
Common shares, no par value; 5,000,000 shares authorized, 400,000 shares issued and outstanding	400,000
Contributed surplus	2,100,000
Retained earnings	9,000,000
Total shareholders' equity	$13,500,000

Notes and Assumptions
December 31, 2005

1. Options were granted/written in July 2003 to purchase 30,000 common shares at $15 per share. The average market price of Andrews' common shares during 2005 was $25 per common share. The options expire in 2013 and no options were exercised during 2005.

2. The 7% bonds were issued in 2004 at face value. The 9% convertible bonds were issued on July 1, 2005 at face value. Each convertible bond is convertible into 50 common shares (each bond has a face value of $1,000).

3. The $10 cumulative, convertible preferred shares were issued at the beginning of 2005. Each share of preferred is convertible into four common shares.

4. The average income tax rate is 35%.

5. The 400,000 common shares were issued at $1 per share and were outstanding during the entire year.

6. Preferred dividends were not declared in 2005.

7. Net income was $1.2 million in 2005.

8. No bonds or preferred shares were converted during 2005.

Instructions

(a) Calculate basic earnings per share for Andrews for 2005.

(b) Calculate diluted earnings per share for Andrews for 2005, following these steps.

   1. Determine, for each dilutive security, the per share effect assuming exercise/conversion. Rank the results from smallest to largest earnings effect per share; that is, rank the results from most dilutive to least dilutive.

   2. Beginning with the earnings per share based upon weighted average of common shares outstanding, recalculate earnings per share by adding the smallest per share effects from the first step. If the results from this recalculation are less than EPS in the prior step, proceed to the next smallest per share effect and recalculate earnings per share. This process is continued so long as each recalculated earn-

ings per share is smaller than the previous amount. The process will end either because there are no more securities to test or a particular security maintains or increases earnings per share (is antidilutive).

(c) Show the presentation of earnings per share for Andrews for 2005.

Solution to Comprehensive EPS Exercise

(a) Basic earnings per share

The calculation of basic earnings per share for 2005 starts with the amount based upon the weighted common shares outstanding, as shown in Illustration 18-25.

Net Income	$1,200,000
Less: $10 cumulative, convertible preferred shares dividend requirements	200,000
Income applicable to common shareholders	$1,000,000
Weighted average number of common shares outstanding	400,000
Earnings per common share	$2.50

Note the following points concerning the calculation above.

1. When preferred shares are cumulative, the preferred dividend is subtracted to arrive at income applicable to common shares whether the dividend is declared or not.

2. The earnings per share of $2.50 must be calculated as a starting point because it is not the per share amount that is subject to reduction due to the existence of convertible securities and options.

(b) Diluted earnings per share

The steps are now applied to the Andrews Corporation. (Note that net income and income available to common shareholders are not the same if preferred dividends are declared or cumulative.) The Andrews Corporation has four securities (options, 7% and 9% convertible bonds, and the convertible preferred shares) that could reduce EPS.

The first step in the calculation of diluted earnings per share is to determine a per share effect for each potentially dilutive security. Illustrations 18-26 through 29 demonstrate these calculations.

Illustration 18-26

Incremental Impact of Options

Number of shares under option	30,000
Option price per share	× $15
Proceeds upon assumed exercise of options	$450,000
Average 2005 market price of common	$25
Treasury shares that could be acquired with proceeds ($450,000 ÷ $25)	18,000
Excess shares under option over treasury shares that could be repurchased (30,000 − 18,000)	12,000
Per share effect: Incremental Numerator Effect: None Incremental Denominator Effect: 12,000 shares	$0
Therefore dilutive	

Interest expense for year ($2,000,000 × 7%)	$140,000
Income tax reduction due to interest (35% × $140,000)	49,000
Interest expense avoided (net of tax)	$ 91,000
Number of common shares issued assuming conversion of bonds (2,000 bonds × 50 shares)	100,000
Per share effect:	
Incremental Numerator Effect:	$91,000
Incremental Denominator Effect: 100,000 shares	$0.91
Therefore dilutive	

Illustration 18-27

Incremental Impact of 7% Convertible Bonds

Interest expense for year ($3,000,000 × 9%)	$270,000
Income tax reduction due to interest (35% × $270,000)	94,500
Interest expense avoided (net of tax)	$175,500
Number of common shares issued assuming conversion of bonds (3,000 bonds × 50 shares)	150,000
Per share effect (outstanding ½ year):	
Incremental Numerator Effect: $175,500 × 0.5 = $87,750	
Incremental Denominator Effect: 150,000 shares × 0.5 = 75,000	$1.17
Therefore dilutive	

Illustration 18-28

Incremental Impact of 9% Convertible Bonds

Dividend requirement on cumulative preferred (20,000 shares × $10)	$200,000
Income tax effect (dividends not a tax deduction)	none
Dividend requirement avoided	$200,000
Number of common shares issued assuming conversion of preferred (4 × 20,000 shares)	80,000
Per share effect:	
Incremental Numerator Effect: $200,000	
Incremental Denominator Effect: 80,000 shares	$2.50
Therefore neutral	

Illustration 18-29

Incremental Impact of Convertible Preferred Shares

Illustration 18-30 shows the ranking of all four potentially dilutive securities.

	$ Effect Per share
Options	0
7% convertible bonds	0.91
9% convertible bonds	1.17
$10 convertible preferred	2.50

Illustration 18-30

Ranking of Potential Common Shares (most dilutive first)

The next step is to determine earnings per share giving effect to the ranking in Illustration 18-30. Starting with the earnings per share of $2.50 calculated previously, add the incremental effects of the options to the original calculation, as follows.

Illustration 18-31

Step by Step Calculation of Diluted EPS Adding Options First (Most Dilutive)

Options	
Income applicable to common shareholders	$1,000,000
Add: Incremental numerator effect of options	none
Total	$1,000,000
Weighted average number of common shares outstanding	400,000
Add: Incremental denominator effect of options— Illustration 18-26	12,000
Total	412,000
Recalculated earnings per share ($1,000,000 ÷ 412,000 shares)	$2.43

Since the recalculated earnings per share is reduced (from $2.50 to $2.43), the effect of the options is dilutive. Again, this effect could have been anticipated because the average market price exceeded the option price ($15).

Recalculated earnings per share, assuming the 7% bonds are converted, is as follows.

Illustration 18-32

Step by Step Calculation of Diluted EPS Adding 7% Bonds Next (Next Most Dilutive)

Numerator from previous calculation	$1,000,000
Add: Interest expense avoided (net of tax)	91,000
Total	$1,091,000
Denominator from previous calculation (shares)	412,000
Add: Number of common shares assumed issued upon conversion of bonds	100,000
Total	512,000
Recalculated earnings per share ($1,091,000 ÷ 512,000)	$2.13

Since the recalculated earnings per share is reduced (from $2.43 to $2.13), the effect of the 7% bonds is dilutive.

Next, earnings per share is recalculated assuming the conversion of the 9% bonds.

Illustration 18-33

Step by Step Calculation of Diluted EPS Adding 9% Bonds Next (Next Most Dilutive)

Numerator from previous calculation	$1,091,000
Add: Interest expense avoided (net of tax)	87,750
Total	$1,178,750
Denominator from previous calculation (shares)	512,000
Add: Number of common shares assumed issued upon conversion of bonds	75,000
Total	587,000
Recalculated earnings per share ($1,178,750 ÷ 587,000)	$2.01

Since the recalculated earnings per share is reduced (from $2.13 to $2.01), the effect of the 9% convertible bonds is dilutive.

The final step is the recalculation that includes the 10% preferred shares. This is shown below.

Numerator from previous calculation		$1,178,750
Add: Dividend requirements avoided		200,000
Total		$1,378,750
Denominator from previous calculation (shares)		587,000
Add: Number of common shares assumed issued upon conversion of preferred		80,000
Total		667,000
Recalculated earnings per share ($1,378,750 ÷ 667,000)		$2.07

Illustration 18-34

Step by Step Calculation of Diluted EPS Adding Preferred Shares Next (Least Dilutive)

The effect of the $10 convertible preferred is not dilutive because the per share effects of the convertible preferred shares result in a higher EPS of $2.07. Since the recalculated earnings per share is not reduced, effects of the convertible preferred are not used in the calculation. Diluted earnings per share to be reported is therefore $2.01.

(c) Presentation of EPS

The disclosure of earnings per share on the income statement for Andrews Corporation is shown in Illustration 18-35.

Net Income	$1,200,000
Basic earnings per common share (Note X)	$2.50
Diluted earnings per common share	$2.01

Illustration 18-35

Presentation of EPS

PERSPECTIVES

Usefulness of EPS

Many companies are reporting additional non-GAAP EPS numbers along with U.S. GAAP-based EPS numbers in the financial information provided to investors. The earnings generally exceed GAAP earnings because the non-GAAP EPS numbers exclude such items as restructuring charges, impairments of assets, R&D expenditures, and stock compensation expense. Here are some examples.

What do the Numbers Mean?

Company	U.S. GAAP EPS	Pro Forma EPS
Adaptec Inc.	$(0.62)	$0.05
Corning Inc.	(0.24)	$0.09
General Motors Corp	(0.41)	$0.85
Honeywell International Inc.	(0.38)	$0.44
International Paper Co.	(0.57)	$0.14
QUALCOMM Inc.	(0.06)	$0.20
Broadcom Corp.	(6.36)	$0.13
Lucent Technologies Inc.	(2.16)	$0.27

The SEC has expressed concern that the non-GAAP EPS disclosures may be misleading. For example, Trump Hotels and Casino Resorts Inc. (DJT) was cited for abuses related to its 1999 third-quarter pro forma EPS release. The SEC noted that the firm misrepresented its operating results by excluding a material, one-time $81.4 million charge in its pro forma EPS statement and including an undisclosed nonrecurring gain of $17.2 million. The gain enabled DJT to post a profit in the quarter. The SEC emphasized that DJT's pro forma EPS statement deviated from conservative U.S. GAAP reporting. Therefore, it was "fraudulent" because it created a "false and misleading impression" that DJT had actually (1) recorded a profit in the third quarter of 1999 and (2) exceeded consensus earnings expectations by enhancing its operating fundamentals.

The Sarbanes-Oxley Act of 2002 requires the SEC to develop regulations on pro forma reporting. As a consequence, the SEC now requires companies that provide pro forma financial information to make sure that the information is not misleading. In addition, a reconciliation between pro forma and GAAP information is required. In Canada, effective June 2003, the disclosure of these non-GAAP EPS numbers is prohibited unless required by a *CICA Handbook* section other than Section 3500.

Sources: SEC Accounting and Enforcement Release No. 1499 (January 16, 2002); "SEC Proposed Rules to Implement Sarbanes-Oxley Act Reforms," SEC Press Release 2002-155 (October 30, 2002).

EPS is one of the most highly visible metrics that is used to assess management stewardship and also to predict the company's future value. It is therefore a very important number and thus GAAP pertaining to the calculation is very specific.

Underlying Concept

There is a tradeoff here between using more relevant information such as sustainable income (which is not as reliable) and information such as EPS, which is more reliable (but perhaps less relevant) because there are stringent standards for calculating EPS.

When companies or their shares are valued, "earnings" are often discounted to arrive at an estimated value. Numerous methods are used; however, discounted cash flows (with earnings often used as a proxy for the calculation) or NPV (net present value) calculations are commonly employed to estimate company or share value. Ideally, a **normalized or sustainable cash flow or earnings** number should be used in the valuation calculation since earnings or net income may be of higher or lower quality (as noted in Chapter 4). Calculating normalized or sustainable cash flows and earnings requires significant judgement, however, and therefore, when valuing common shares, the EPS number may be used since it is felt to be more reliable.

The price earnings ratio divides the price of the share by the earnings per share number. The result is often called the **multiplier**. The multiplier shows the per share value that each dollar of earnings generates. For example, if the share value is $10 and EPS is $1, the multiplier is 10 (10/1). **Therefore each additional dollar of earnings is felt to generate an additional $10 in share price.** This is a very rough calculation only, especially when you think of the judgement that went into calculating that EPS number in the first place. Consider the hundreds of financial reporting choices such as accounting methods, measurement uncertainty, bias, and other judgements. This is a main reason why preparers of financial statements must be aware of the impact of all financial reporting decisions on the bottom line.

Summary of Learning Objectives

Digital Tool

Glossary

www.wiley.com/canada/kieso

1 Understand why EPS is an important number.

Earnings per share numbers give common shareholders an idea of the earnings attributable to each common share. This information is often used to predict future cash flows from the shares and to value companies.

2 Understand when and how EPS is required to be presented.

EPS must be presented for all public companies or companies that are intending to go public. The calculations must be presented on the face of the income statements for net income from continuing operations and net income for both basic EPS and diluted EPS (complex capital structures). Where discontinued operations or extraordinary items are present, the per share impact of this must also be shown but may be shown either on the face of the income statement or in the notes. Comparative calculations must be shown.

3 Identify potential common shares.

Potential common shares include convertible debt and preferred shares, options/warrants, contingently issuable shares, and other instruments that may result in additional common shares being issued by the company. They are relevant because they may cause the present common shareholder interests to become diluted.

4 Calculate earnings per share in a simple capital structure.

Basic earnings per share is an actual calculation that takes income available to common shareholders and divides it by the weighted average number of common shares outstanding during the period.

5 Calculate diluted earnings per share using the if-converted method.

Diluted earnings per share is a "what if" calculation that considers the impact of potential common shares. The if-converted method considers the impact of convertible securities such as convertible debt and preferred shares. It assumes that the instruments are converted at the beginning of the year and that related interest or dividend is thus avoided.

6 Calculate diluted earnings per share using the treasury stock method.

The treasury stock method looks at the impact of written call options on EPS numbers. It assumes that the options are exercised at the beginning of the year and that the money from the exercise is used to buy back shares in the open market at the average common share price.

7 Calculate diluted earnings per share using the reverse treasury stock method.

The reverse treasury stock method looks at the impact of written put options. It assumes that the options are exercised at the beginning of the year and that the company must first issue shares in the market (at the average share price) to obtain sufficient funds to buy the shares under the option.

8 Identify antidilutive potential common shares.

Antidilutive potential common shares are irrelevant since they result in diluted EPS calculations that are higher than the basic EPS; thus, these numbers are antidilutive. Diluted EPS must show the worst possible EPS number. Note that purchased options and written options that are not in the money are ignored for purposes of calculating diluted EPS because they are either antidilutive or will not be exercised.

KEY TERMS

antidilutive securities, 958
basic EPS, 951
call options, 961
complex capital
    structure, 952
contingently issuable
    shares, 952
diluted EPS, 951
exercise price, 961
if-converted method, 959
income available
    to common
    shareholders, 953
in the money, 961
potential common
    share, 952
put options, 961
reverse treasury stock
    method, 964
senior equity
    instruments, 953
simple capital
    structure, 952
treasury stock
    method, 962
weighted average number
    of shares, 955

Brief Exercises

BE18-1   Haley Corporation had 2005 net income of $1.2 million. During 2005, Haley paid a dividend of $2 per share on 100,000 preferred shares. During 2005, Haley had outstanding 250,000 common shares. Calculate Haley's 2005 earnings per share.

BE18-2   Assume the same as BE18-1 except that the preferred shares are noncumulative and the dividend has not been declared or paid.

BE18-3   Assume the same as BE18-1 except that the preferred shares are cumulative and the dividends have not yet been declared or paid.

BE18-4   Barkley Corporation had 120,000 common shares outstanding on January 1, 2005. On May 1, 2005, Barkley issued 55,000 shares. On July 1, Barkley purchased and cancelled 20,000 shares. Calculate Barkley's weighted average number of shares outstanding for the year ended December 31, 2005.

BE18-5   Green Corporation had 500,000 common shares outstanding on January 1, 2005. On May 1, Green issued 130,000 shares.

1. Calculate the weighted average number of shares outstanding for the year ended December 31, 2005 if the 130,000 shares were issued for cash.

2. Calculate the weighted average number of shares outstanding for the year ended December 31, 2005 if the 30,000 shares were issued in a stock dividend.

BE18-6   Strickland Corporation earned net income of $500,000 in 2005 and had 100,000 shares of common outstanding throughout the year. Also outstanding all year was $400,000 of 10% bonds, which are convertible into 16,000 common shares. Strickland's tax rate is 40%. Calculate Strickland's 2005 diluted earnings per share.

BE18-7   Sabonis Corporation reported net income of $1.4 million in 2004 and had 150,000 shares of common outstanding throughout the year. Also outstanding all year were 10,000 shares of cumulative preferred shares, each convertible into two shares of common. The preferred shares pay an annual dividend of $5 per share. Sabonis' tax rate is 40%. Calculate Sabonis' 2004 diluted earnings per share.

BE18-8   Sarunas Corporation reported net income of $700,000 in 2006 and had 300,000 shares of common outstanding throughout the year. Also outstanding all year were 60,000 (written) options to purchase common shares at $12 per share. The average market price for the common shares during the year was $15. Calculate diluted earnings per share.

BE18-9   The 2006 income statement of Schrempf Corporation showed net income of $1,480,000 and an extraordinary loss of $220,000. Schrempf had 50,000 common shares outstanding all year. Prepare Schrempf's income statement presentation of earnings per share.

BE 18-10   Ghenghis Limited purchased $40,000 call options during the year. The options give the company the right to buy its own common shares for $10. The average market price during the year is $12. How should the options be treated for purposes of the diluted EPS calculation?

BE 18-11   Ghenghis also wrote put options that allow the holder to sell Ghenghis shares to Ghenghis at $11. Assume the other information in BE18-10 is the same. How should these options be treated for purposes of the diluted EPS calculation?

BE 18-12   Lee Limited has 100,000 common shares outstanding throughout the year. On June 30, Lee issued 10,000 convertible preferred shares, which are convertible into 1 common share each. Calculate the weighted average common shares for purposes of the diluted EPS calculations. Assume the preferred shares are dilutive.

Exercises

E18-1   (Weighted Average Number of Shares)   Newton Inc. uses a calendar year for financial reporting. The company is authorized to issue 9 million common shares. At no time has Newton issued any potentially dilutive securities. Listed below is a summary of Newton's common share activities.

Number of common shares issued and outstanding at December 31, 2004	3,000,000
Shares issued as a result of a 10% stock dividend on September 30, 2005	300,000
Shares issued for cash on March 31, 2006	2,000,000
Number of common shares issued and outstanding at December 31, 2006	5,300,000

A 3-for-1 stock split of Newton's common shares took place on March 31, 2007.

Instructions

(a) Calculate the weighted average number of common shares used in calculating earnings per common share for 2005 on the 2006 comparative income statement.

(b) Calculate the weighted average number of common shares used in calculating earnings per common share for 2006 on the 2006 comparative income statement.

(c) Calculate the weighted average number of common shares to be used in calculating earnings per common share for 2006 on the 2007 comparative income statement.

(d) Calculate the weighted average number of common shares to be used in calculating earnings per common share for 2007 on the 2007 comparative income statement. (CMA adapted)

E18-2 (EPS: Simple Capital Structure)   On January 1, 2006, Portmann Corp. had 580,000 common shares outstanding. During 2006, it had the following transactions that affected the common share account.

Interactive
Homework

February 1	Issued 180,000 shares
March 1	Issued a 10% stock dividend
May 1	Acquired 200,000 common shares (and retired them)
June 1	Issued a 3-for-1 stock split
October 1	Issued 60,000 shares

The company's year end is December 31.

Instructions

(a) Determine the weighted average number of shares outstanding as of December 31, 2006.

(b) Assume that Portmann earned net income of $3,456,000 during 2006. In addition, it had 100,000 shares of 9%, $100 par nonconvertible, noncumulative preferred shares outstanding for the entire year. Because of liquidity considerations, however, the company did not declare and pay a preferred dividend in 2006. Calculate earnings per share for 2006, using the weighted average number of shares determined in part (a).

(c) Assume the same facts as in part (b), except that the preferred shares were cumulative. Calculate earnings per share for 2006.

(d) Assume the same facts as in part (b), except that net income included an extraordinary gain of $864,000 and a loss from discontinued operations of $432,000. Both items are net of applicable income taxes. Calculate earnings per share for 2006.

E18-3 (EPS: Simple Capital Structure)   Valaderez Inc. had 350,000 common shares outstanding on December 31, 2005. During the year 2006, the company issued 18,000 shares on May 1 and retired 14,000 shares on October 31. For the year 2006, the company reported net income of $449,690 after an extraordinary gain of $30,600 (net of tax).

Instructions

What earnings per share data should be reported at the bottom of Valaderez Inc.'s income statement?

E18-4 (EPS: Simple Capital Structure)   Flagstad Inc. presented the following data.

Net income	$5,500,000
Preferred shares: 50,000 shares outstanding,	
$100 par, 8% cumulative, not convertible	$5,000,000
Common shares: Shares outstanding 1/1	650,000
Issued for cash, 5/1	100,000
Acquired treasury stock for cash, 8/1 (shares cancelled)	150,000
2-for-1 stock split, 10/1	

Instructions

Calculate earnings per share for the year ended December 31.

E18-5   (EPS: Simple Capital Structure)   A portion of the combined statement of income and retained earnings of Seminole Inc. for the current year ended December 31, follows.

Income before extraordinary item		$22,000,000
Extraordinary loss, net of applicable income tax (Note 1)		1,340,000
Net income		20,660,000
Retained earnings at the beginning of the year		93,250,000
		113,910,000
Dividends declared:		
On preferred shares $6.00 per share	$ 300,000	
On common shares $1.75 per share	14,875,000	15,175,000
Retained earnings at the end of the year		$98,735,000

Note 1. During the year, Seminole Inc. suffered a loss of $1,340,000 after applicable income tax reduction of $1.2 million. This was booked as an extraordinary item.

At the end of the current year, Seminole Inc. has outstanding 8.5 million common shares and 50,000 shares of 6% preferred.

On April 1 of the current year, Seminole Inc. issued 1 million common shares for $32 per share to help finance the loss.

Instructions

Calculate the earnings per share on common shares for the current year as it should be reported to shareholders.

E18-6   (EPS: Simple Capital Structure)   On January 1, 2005, Le Phong Limited had shares outstanding as follows.

6% cumulative preferred shares, $100 par value, issued and outstanding 10,000 shares	$1,000,000
Common shares issued and outstanding 200,000 shares	2,000,000

To acquire the net assets of three smaller companies, the company authorized the issuance of an additional 260,000 common shares. The acquisitions took place as follows.

Date of Acquisition	Shares Issued
Company A: April 1, 2005	150,000
Company B: July 1, 2005	80,000
Company C: October 1, 2005	30,000

On May 14, 2005, Le Phong realized a $90,000 (before taxes) insurance gain on the government expropriation of land originally purchased in 1991.

On December 31, 2005, the company recorded income of $600,000 before tax and exclusive of the gain.

Instructions

Assuming a 50% tax rate, calculate the earnings per share data that should appear on the company financial statements as of December 31, 2005. Assume that the expropriation is extraordinary.

E18-7   (EPS: Simple Capital Structure)   At January 1, 2006, Michael Limited's outstanding shares included:

280,000 shares of $50 par value, 7% cumulative preferred shares
900,000 common shares

Net income for 2006 was $2,130,000. No cash dividends were declared or paid during 2006. On February 15, 2007, however, all preferred dividends in arrears were paid, together with a 5% stock dividend on common shares. There were no dividends in arrears prior to 2006.

On April 1, 2006, 550,000 common shares were sold for $10 per share and on October 1, 2006, 310,000 common shares were purchased for $20 per share.

Instructions

Calculate earnings per share for the year ended December 31, 2006. Assume that financial statements for 2006 were issued in March 2007.

E18-8   (EPS with Convertible Bonds, Various Situations)   In 2003, Ben Lo Inc. issued, at par, 60 $1,000, 8% bonds, each convertible into 50 common shares. The company had revenues of $47,500 and expenses other than interest and taxes of $28,400 for 2004 (assume that the tax rate is 45%). Throughout 2004, 2,000 common shares were outstand-

ing; none of the bonds were converted or redeemed. (Assume, for simplicity's sake, that the convertible bond's equity element is not recorded.)

Instructions

(a) Calculate diluted earnings per share for the year ended December 31, 2004.

(b) Assume the same facts as those assumed for part (a), except that the 60 bonds were issued on September 1, 2004 (rather than in 2003), and none have been converted or redeemed.

(c) Assume the same facts as assumed for part (a), except that 20 of the 60 bonds were actually converted on July 1, 2004.

E18-9 (EPS with Convertible Bonds) On June 1, 2003, Mowbray Corp. and Surrey Limited merged to form Lancaster Inc. A total of 800,000 shares were issued to complete the merger. The new corporation reports on a calendar-year basis.

Interactive Homework

On April 1, 2005, the company issued an additional 400,000 shares for cash. All 1.2 million shares were outstanding on December 31, 2005. Lancaster Inc. also issued $600,000 of 20-year, 8% convertible bonds at par on July 1, 2005. Each $1,000 bond converts to 40 shares of common at any interest date. None of the bonds have been converted to date. If the bonds had been issued without the conversion feature, the annual interest rate would have been 10%.

Lancaster Inc. is preparing its annual report for the fiscal year ending December 31, 2005. The annual report will show earnings per share figures based upon a reported after-tax net income of $1,540,000 (the tax rate is 40%).

Instructions

Determine for 2005:

(a) The number of shares to be used for calculating:

 1. basic earnings per share

 2. diluted earnings per share

(b) The earnings figures to be used for calculating:

 1. basic earnings per share

 2. diluted earnings per share

(CMA adapted)

E18-10 (EPS with Convertible Bonds and Preferred Shares) The Shengru Corporation issued 10-year, $5 million par, 7% callable convertible subordinated debentures on January 2, 2005. The debentures have a face value of $1,000, with interest payable annually. The current conversion ratio is 14:1, and in two years it will increase to 18:1. At the date of issue, the bonds were sold at 98. Bond discount is amortized on a straight-line basis. Shengru's effective tax was 35%. Net income in 2005 was $9.5 million, and the company had 2 million shares outstanding during the entire year. For simplicity's sake, ignore the requirement to record the debentures' debt and equity components separately.

Instructions

(a) Prepare a schedule to calculate both basic and diluted earnings per share for the year ended December 31, 2005.

(b) Discuss how the schedule would differ if the security were convertible preferred shares.

E18-11 (EPS with Convertible Bonds and Preferred Shares) On January 1, 2005, Sharif Limited issued 10-year, $2 million face value, 6% bonds, at par. Each $1,000 bond is convertible into 15 shares of common. Sharif's net income in 2005 was $300,000, and its tax rate was 40%. The company had 100,000 common shares outstanding throughout 2005. None of the bonds were exercised in 2005. For simplicity's sake, ignore the requirement to record the bonds' debt and equity components separately.

Interactive Homework

Instructions

(a) Calculate diluted earnings per share for the year ended December 31, 2005.

(b) Calculate diluted earnings per share for 2005, assuming the same facts as above, except that $1 million of 6% convertible preferred shares was issued instead of the bonds. Each $100 preferred share is convertible into five shares of common.

E18-12 (EPS with Options, Various Situations) Viens Corp.'s net income for 2005 is $50,000. The only potentially dilutive securities outstanding were 1,000 call options issued during 2004, each exercisable for one share at $6. None has been exercised, and 10,000 shares of common were outstanding during 2005.

The average market price of the company's shares during 2005 was $20.

Instructions

(a) Calculate diluted earnings per share for the year ended December 31, 2005 (round to nearest cent).

(b) Assume the same facts as those assumed for part (a), except that the 1,000 call options were issued on October 1, 2005 (rather than in 2004). The average market price during the last three months of 2005 was $20.

(c) How would your answer change if in addition to the information for parts (a) and (b), the company issued (wrote) 1,000 put options with an exercise price of $10?

E18-13   (EPS with Contingent Issuance Agreement)   Winsor Inc. recently purchased Holiday Corp., a large home painting corporation. One of the terms of the merger was that if Holiday's income for 2005 were $110,000 or more, 10,000 additional shares would be issued to Holiday's shareholders in 2006. Holiday's income for 2004 was $120,000.

Instructions

(a) Would the contingent shares have to be considered in Winsor's 2004 earnings per share calculations?

(b) Assume the same facts, except that the 10,000 shares are contingent on Holiday achieving a net income of $130,000 in 2005. Would the contingent shares have to be considered in Winsor's earnings per share calculations for 2004?

E18-14   (EPS with Warrants)   Howat Corporation earned $360,000 during a period when it had an average of 100,000 common shares outstanding. The common shares sold at an average market price of $15 per share during the period. Also outstanding were 15,000 warrants that could be exercised to purchase one share of common for $10 for each warrant exercised.

Instructions

(a) Are the warrants dilutive?

(b) Calculate basic earnings per share.

(c) Calculate diluted earnings per share.

Problems

P18-1   Diane Leto, controller at Yaeger Pharmaceutical Industries, a public company, is currently preparing the calculation for basic and diluted earnings per share and the related disclosure for Yaeger's external financial statements. Below is selected financial information for the fiscal year ended June 30, 2005.

YAEGER PHARMACEUTICAL INDUSTRIES
Selected Statement of Financial Position Information
June 30, 2005

Long-term debt	
Notes payable, 10%	$ 1,000,000
7% convertible bonds payable	5,000,000
10% bonds payable	6,000,000
Total long-term debt	$12,000,000
Shareholders' equity	
Preferred Shares, $4.25 cumulative,	100,000
shares authorized, 25,000 shares issued and outstanding	$ 1,250,000
Common Shares, unlimited number of shares authorized,	
1,000,000 shares issued and outstanding	4,500,000
Contributed Surplus—Conversion Rights	500,000
Retained earnings	6,000,000
Total shareholders' equity	$12,250,000

The following transactions have also occurred at Yaeger.

1. Options were granted by the company in 2003 to purchase 100,000 shares at $15 per share. Although no options were exercised during 2005, the average price per common share during fiscal year 2005 was $20 per share.

2. Each bond was issued at face value. The 7% convertible debenture will convert into common shares at 50 shares per $1,000 bond. It is exercisable after five years and was issued in 2004. Ignore any requirement to record the bond's debt and equity components separately.

3. The $4.25 preferred shares were issued in 2003.

4. There are no preferred dividends in arrears; however, preferred dividends were not declared in fiscal year 2005.

5. The 1 million shares of common shares were outstanding for the entire 2005 fiscal year.

6. Net income for fiscal year 2005 was $1.5 million, and the average income tax rate was 40%.

Instructions

For the fiscal year ended June 30, 2005, calculate Yaeger Pharmaceutical Industries':

(a) basic earnings per share

(b) diluted earnings per share

P18-2   As auditor for Banquo & Associates, you have been assigned to check Duncan Corporation's calculation of earnings per share for the current year. The controller, Mac Beth, has supplied you with the following calculations.

Net income	$3,374,960
Common shares issued and outstanding:	
Beginning of year	1,285,000
End of year	1,200,000
Average	1,242,500
Earnings per share	

$$\frac{\$3,347,960}{1,242,500} = \$2.72 \text{ per share}$$

You have developed the following additional information.

1. There are no other equity securities in addition to the common shares.

2. There are no options or warrants outstanding to purchase common shares.

3. There are no convertible debt securities.

4. Activity in common shares during the year was as follows.

Outstanding, Jan. 1	1,285,000
Shares acquired, Oct. 1	(250,000)
	1,035,000
Shares issued, Dec. 1	165,000
Outstanding, Dec. 31	1,200,000

Instructions

(a) Based on the information above, do you agree with the controller's calculation of earnings per share for the year? If you disagree, prepare a revised calculation of earnings per share.

(b) Assume the same facts as those in (a), except that call options had been issued for 140,000 shares of common shares at $10 per share. These options were outstanding at the beginning of the year and none had been exercised or cancelled during the year. The average market price of the common shares during the year was $20 and the ending market price was $25. Prepare a calculation of earnings per share.

P18-3   Hillel Corporation is preparing the comparative financial statements for the annual report to its shareholders for fiscal years ended May 31, 2004 and May 31, 2005. The income from operations for each year was $2.8 million and $3.5 million, respectively. In both years, the company incurred a 9% interest expense on $2.4 million of debt, an obligation that requires interest-only payments for five years. The company experienced a loss of $400,000 from a fire in its Scotsland facility in February 2005, which was determined to be an extraordinary loss. The company uses a 45% effective tax rate for income taxes.

The capital structure of Hillel Corporation on June 1, 2003 consisted of 3 million shares of common shares outstanding and 120,000 shares of $50 par value, 8%, cumulative preferred shares. There were no preferred dividends in arrears, and the company had not issued any convertible securities, options, or warrants.

On October 1, 2003, Hillel sold an additional 500,000 shares of the common shares at $20 per share. Hillel distributed a 20% stock dividend on the common shares outstanding on January 1, 2004. On December 1, 2004, Hillel was able to sell an additional 800,000 shares of the common shares at $22 per share. These were the only common share transactions that occurred during the two fiscal years.

Instructions

(a) Identify whether the capital structure at Hillel Corporation is a simple or complex capital structure, and explain why.

(b) Determine the weighted average number of shares that Hillel Corporation would use in calculating earnings per share for the fiscal year ended:

   1. May 31, 2004.

   2. May 31, 2005.

(c) Prepare, in good form, a comparative income statement, beginning with income from operations, for Hillel Corporation for the fiscal years ended May 31, 2004 and May 31, 2005. This statement will be included in Hillel's annual report and should display the appropriate earnings per share presentations.

(CMA adapted)

P18-4 Edmund Halvor of the controller's office of East Aurora Corporation was given the assignment of determining the basic and diluted earnings per share values for the year ending December 31, 2005. Halvor has compiled the information listed below.

   1. The company is authorized to issue 8 million common shares. As of December 31, 2004, 5 million shares had been issued and were outstanding.

   2. The per share market prices of the common shares on selected dates were as follows.

	Price per Share
July 1, 2004	$30.00
January 1, 2005	21.00
April 1, 2005	25.00
July 1, 2005	11.00
August 1, 2005	10.50
November 1, 2005	9.00
December 31, 2005	11.00

   3. A total of 900,000 shares of an authorized 1.2 million shares of convertible preferred shares had been issued on July 1, 2004. The shares were issued at $25, and have a cumulative dividend of $4 per share. The shares are convertible into common shares at the rate of one share of convertible preferred for one share of common. The rate of conversion is to be automatically adjusted for stock splits and stock dividends. Dividends are paid quarterly on September 30, December 31, March 31, and June 30.

   4. East Aurora Corporation is subject to a 42% income tax rate.

   5. The after-tax net income for the year ended December 31, 2005 was $13,550,000.

The following specific activities took place during 2005.

   1. January 1: A 5% common stock dividend was issued. The dividend had been declared on December 1, 2004 to all shareholders of record on December 29, 2004.

   2. April 1: A total of 200,000 shares of the $4 convertible preferred shares was converted into common shares. The company issued new common shares and retired the preferred shares. This was the only conversion of the preferred shares during 2005.

   3. July 1: A 2-for-1 split of the common shares became effective on this date. The board of directors had authorized the split on June 1.

   4. August 1: A total of 300,000 shares of common shares were issued to acquire a factory building.

   5. November 1: A total of 24,000 shares of common shares were purchased on the open market at $9 per share and cancelled.

   6. Cash dividends to common shareholders were declared and paid as follows:

April 15:	$0.40 per share
October 15:	$0.50 per share

   7. Cash dividends to preferred shareholders were declared and paid as scheduled.

Instructions

(a) Determine the number of shares used to calculate basic earnings per share for the year ended December 31, 2005.

(b) Determine the number of shares used to calculate diluted earnings per share for the year ended December 31, 2005.

(c) Calculate the adjusted net income to be used as the numerator in the basic earnings per share calculation for the year ended December 31, 2005.

P18-5 The following information pertains to Prancer Limited for 2005.

Net income for the year	$2,200,000
8% convertible bonds issued at par ($1,000 per bond)	
Each bond is convertible into 30 common shares	1,000,000
6% convertible, cumulative preferred shares, $100 par value	
Each share is convertible into 3 common shares	3,000,000
Common shares (600,000 shares outstanding)	6,000,000
Stock options (granted in a prior year) to purchase 50,000	
of common shares at $20 per share	500,000
Tax rate for 2005	42%
Average market price of common shares	$27 per share

There were no changes during 2005 in the number of common shares, preferred shares, or convertible bonds outstanding. To simplify, ignore the requirement to book the convertible bonds' equity portion separately.

Instructions

(a) Calculate basic earnings per share for 2005.

(b) Calculate diluted earnings per share for 2005.

P18-6 Cordelia Corporation is preparing the comparative financial statements to be included in the annual report to shareholders. Cordelia employs a fiscal year ending May 31.

Income from operations before income taxes for Cordelia was $1.4 million and $660,000, respectively, for fiscal years ended May 31, 2005 and 2004. Cordelia experienced an extraordinary loss of $500,000 because of an earthquake on March 3, 2005. A 41% combined income tax rate pertains to any and all of Cordelia Corporation's profits, gains, and losses.

Cordelia's capital structure consists of preferred shares and common shares. The company has not issued any convertible securities or warrants and there are no outstanding stock options.

Cordelia issued 150,000 shares of $100 par value, 6% cumulative preferred shares in 1997. All of these shares are outstanding, and no preferred dividends are in arrears.

There were 1.5 million common shares outstanding on June 1, 2003. On September 1, 2003, Cordelia sold an additional 300,000 common shares at $17 per share. Cordelia distributed a 15% stock dividend on the common shares outstanding on December 1, 2004. These were the only common share transactions during the past two fiscal years.

Instructions

(a) Determine the weighted average number of common shares that would be used in calculating earnings per share on the current comparative income statement for:

  1. The year ended May 31, 2005

  2. The year ended May 31, 2004

(b) Starting with income from operations before income taxes, prepare a comparative income statement for the years ended May 31, 2005 and 2004. The statement will be part of Cordelia Corporation's annual report to shareholders and should include appropriate earnings per share presentation.

(c) A corporation's capital structure is the result of its past financing decisions. Furthermore, the earnings per share data presented on a corporation's financial statements are dependent upon the capital structure.

  1. Explain why Cordelia Corporation is considered to have a simple capital structure.

  2. Describe how earnings per share data would be presented for a corporation that has a complex capital structure.

(CMA adapted)

P18-7 Fernandez Corporation, a new audit client of yours, has not reported earnings per share data in its annual reports to shareholders in the past. The treasurer, Angelo Balthazar, requested that you furnish information about the reporting of earnings per share data in the current year's annual report in accordance with generally accepted accounting principles.

Instructions

(a) Define the term "earnings per share" as it applies to a corporation with a capitalization structure composed of only one class of common shares. Explain how earnings per share should be calculated and how the information should be disclosed in the corporation's financial statements.

(b) Discuss the treatment, if any, that should be given to each of the following items in calculating earnings per share of common shares for financial statement reporting:

  1. Outstanding preferred shares issued at a premium with a par value liquidation right

Cases

Refer to the Case Primer on the Digital Tool to help you answer these cases.

Digital Tool

www.wiley.com/
canada/kieso

CA18-1 The **Thomson Corporation** describes itself as a global leader in providing integrated information solutions to business and professional customers. Revenues come primarily from the United States. Common shares are held primarily by the Thomson family (69%) and trade on the TSE and NYSE.

Because of the dual listing, the company provides a reconciliation between Net Income and EPS under U.S. and Canadian GAAP. Below is an excerpt from the 2003 financial statements note 27.

Note 27: Reconciliation of Canadian to U.S. Generally Accepted Accounting Principles

The consolidated financial statements have been prepared in accordance with Canadian GAAP, which differ in some respects from U.S. GAAP. The following schedules present the material differences between Canadian and U.S. GAAP.

	For the year ended December 31	
	2003	2002
Net earnings under Canadian GAAP	867	605
Differences in GAAP increasing (decreasing) reported earnings:		
Development costs	12	24
Pension adjustments	–	–
Business combinations	15	(4)
Related party transactions (notes 24 and 25)	(55)	(2)
Derivative instruments and hedging activities	18	(5)
Income taxes	(11)	(8)
Earnings under U.S. GAAP, before cumulative effect of change in accounting principle	846	610
Cumulative effect of change in accounting principle, net of tax	–	(182)
Net income under U.S. GAAP	846	428
Other comprehensive income:		
Foreign currency translation	319	167
Minimum pension liability (net of taxes in 2003 – $2 million and 2002 – $3 million)	(13)	(28)
Net unrealized gains (losses) on cash flow hedges (net of taxes in 2003 and 2002 – $0 million)	52	(72)
Other comprehensive income	358	67
Comprehensive income	1,204	495
Earnings under U.S. GAAP from continuing operations, before cumulative effect of change in accounting principle	819	552
Cumulative effect of change in accounting principle, net of tax	–	(182)
Earnings under U.S. GAAP from discontinued operations	27	58
Net income under U.S. GAAP	846	428
Basic and diluted earnings (loss) per common share, under U.S. GAAP, from:		
Continuing operations, before cumulative effect of change in accounting principle, net of tax	$1.27	$ 0.83
Cumulative effect of change in accounting principle, net of tax	–	(0.28)
Discontinued operations, net of tax	0.04	0.09
Basic and diluted earnings per common share[1]	$1.31	$ 0.64

1 Earnings per common share is calculated after taking into account dividends declared on preference shares and the gain recognized in connection with the redemption of the Series V preference shares.

The Thomson Corporation
Notes to Consolidated Financial Statements

	As at December 31	
	2003	*2002*
Shareholders' equity as reported under Canadian GAAP	9,200	8,966
Differences in GAAP increasing (decreasing) reported shareholders' equity:		
Development costs	–	(12)
Business combinations	(647)	(658)
Minimum pension liability	(53)	(38)
Derivative instruments and hedging activities	(33)	(103)
Income taxes	171	180
Shareholders' equity under U.S. GAAP	8,638	8,335

Descriptions of the nature of the reconciling differences are provided below:

Development Costs

Under Canadian GAAP, certain costs classified as development are deferred and amortized over their estimated useful lives. Under U.S. GAAP, all development costs are expensed as incurred.

Business Combinations

Prior to January 1, 2001, various differences existed between Canadian and U.S. GAAP for the accounting for business combinations, including the establishment of acquisition-related liabilities. The $15 million increase to income ($4 million decrease – 2002) primarily relates to (i) costs that are required to be recorded as operating expenses under U.S. GAAP which, prior to January 1, 2001 were capitalized under Canadian GAAP; (ii) overall decreased amortization charges due to basis differences; and (iii) differences in gain or loss calculations on business disposals resulting from the above factors.

The $647 million decrease in Shareholders' equity as of December 31, 2003 ($658 million – December 31, 2002) primarily relates to basis differences in intangible assets and goodwill due to the factors discussed above, as well as a gain of $54 million recorded for U.S. GAAP resulting from a 1997 disposal mandated by the U.S. Department of Justice, which was required to be recorded as a reduction of goodwill under Canadian GAAP. On a U.S. GAAP basis, goodwill was $7,856 million at December 31, 2003 (2002 – $7,605 million). On the same basis, identifiable intangible assets, net of accumulated amortization, were $4,113 million at December 31, 2003 (2002 – $4,213 million).

Related Party Transactions

During the years ended December 31, 2003 and 2002, in accordance with Canadian GAAP, the Company recognized gains on transactions with entities associated with its controlling shareholder in its net earnings. Under U.S. GAAP, such related party gains are not recognizable in net earnings, but must be reflected as equity transactions. In 2003, the related party transaction was the sale of the Company's 20% interest in BGM to a company that is owned by the Thomson family which resulted in a gain of $55 million.

Derivative Instruments and Hedging Activities

Under Canadian GAAP, the fair values of derivative instruments are disclosed in the notes to the consolidated financial statements as at and for the year ended December 31, 2003, but not recorded in the consolidated balance sheet. Under U.S. Statement of Financial Accounting Standards ("SFAS") No. 133, *Accounting for Derivative Instruments and Hedging Activities* as amended by SFAS 138, *Accounting for Certain Derivative Instruments and Certain Hedging Activities*, all derivative instruments are recognized in the balance sheet at their fair values, and changes in fair value are recognized either immediately in earnings or, if the transaction qualifies for hedge accounting, when the transaction being hedged affects earnings. Accordingly, under U.S. GAAP as at December 31, 2003, prepaid expenses and other current assets were $6 million higher (2002 – unchanged), accounts payable and accruals were unchanged (2002 – $4 million higher), current portion of long-term debt was unchanged (2002 – $6 million higher), long-term debt was $37 million higher (2002 – $31 million higher) and other non-current liabilities were $2 million higher (2002 – $62 million higher) as compared to Canadian GAAP.

Income Taxes

The income tax adjustment for each period is comprised of the tax effect of the U.S. GAAP reconciling items. The adjustment to shareholders' equity relates entirely to deferred tax liabilities.

Employee Future Benefits

PENSION ADJUSTMENT

In accordance with Canadian GAAP, prior to 2002, the Company recorded a pension valuation allowance for plans that had an excess of the adjusted benefit asset over the expected future benefits, and recognized changes in the pension valuation allowance in earnings. As U.S. GAAP did not specifically address pension valuation allowances, this was not treated as a difference between Canadian and U.S. GAAP in prior periods. Due to a clarification of accounting guidance on this matter in 2002, changes in the valuation allowance must be treated as a GAAP difference. In order to reconcile earnings under Canadian GAAP to earnings under U.S. GAAP in 2002, earnings under Canadian GAAP were reduced by $22 million, representing the after-tax effect of the change in the valuation allowance. This difference was offset by the elimination of the valuation allowance for U.S. GAAP purposes, which increased earnings by $22 million.

MINIMUM PENSION LIABILITY

Certain of the Company's defined benefit pension plans have accumulated benefit obligations in excess of the fair market value of assets available to fund such obligations as of the annual measurement date for those plans. With respect to those plans, U.S. accounting standards require the recognition of an "additional minimum liability" of $53 million (2002 – $38 million), with a corresponding reduction in shareholders' equity. If, at a subsequent date, the fair market value of the pension assets exceeds the accumulated benefit obligations, the equity adjustment would be reversed. This adjustment has no impact on income or cash flow. Because the concept of an additional minimum liability does not exist in Canadian GAAP, the liability and the reduction in equity resulted in a reconciling item.

The accumulated benefit obligation of funded pension plans that had accumulated benefit obligations that exceeded plan assets at December 31, 2003 was $150 million (2002 – $125 million). These plans had related fair values of plan assets of $113 million (2002 – $92 million).

Comprehensive Income

SFAS No. 130, *Reporting Comprehensive Income*, requires companies to disclose comprehensive income, which includes, in addition to net income, other comprehensive income consisting primarily of unrealized gains and losses which bypass the traditional income statement and are recorded directly into shareholders' equity on a U.S. GAAP basis. In 2003 and 2002, the components of other comprehensive income consist of unrealized gains and losses relating to the translation of foreign currency financial statements, minimum pension liabilities, hedging activity and certain investment securities. Accumulated other comprehensive income as at December 31, 2003 was a gain of $194 million (2002 – loss of $164 million).

Change in Accounting Principle

The cumulative effect of change in accounting principle represents the transitional impairment charge relating to adopting the U.S. GAAP equivalent of CICA 3062, SFAS 142, *Goodwill and Other Intangible Assets*. Under U.S. GAAP, this charge is required to be recorded net of tax as a cumulative effect of a change in accounting principle, which is a component of net income, as compared with a charge to opening retained earnings under Canadian GAAP. See Note 7.

Instructions

Analyse the impact of the GAAP differences on EPS. Many of these issues are complex. Rather than analysing the issues in depth, try to explain the underlying business transaction (i.e., what are they trying to account for) and then identify how the item is treated under Canadian GAAP and then U.S. GAAP. In other words, you will identify and articulate the issue and identify the alternatives. What are the largest reconciling items?

Integrated Cases

IC18-1 Canadian Utilities Limited (CUL) is based in Alberta and is involved in power generation, utilities, logistics, and energy services and technologies. The company was incorporated in 1927 and its shares trade on the TSE. Pricewaterhouse-Coopers are the current auditors.

According to the notes to the 2002 financial statements:

"In December 2000, the Province of Alberta issued regulations providing for the deferral of price and volume variance in excess of forecast amounts in respect of the supply of electricity by distributors to their customers for the year ended December 31, 2000. In June 2002, … a decision … was issued approving the collection by … the company … of its deferred costs from customers over a period that is expected to end in July 2003, and permitting … the company … to sell these deferred costs and related rights.

On August 14, 2002, … the company… sold deferred costs of $81 million to an unrelated purchaser for equivalent cash consideration. GAAP requires that this transaction be accounted for as a financing arrangement rather than a sale. Accordingly, the cash received results in the recording of a deferred electricity cost obligation rather than a reduction of deferred electricity costs. The obligation bears interest at 3.3975%, which approximates the interest earned on the deferred costs. The obligation principal and interest incurred will be paid to the purchaser as the deferred costs and interest earned are collected from customers."

The company has Class A and B shares outstanding. Class A shares are non-voting whereas Class B shares are voting. Both shares are entitled to share equally on a share for share basis in all dividends declared on either of the shares as well as remaining property upon dissolution of the company. The company has a stock option plan under which 3,200,000 Class A shares are reserved for issuance. Under the plan, options may be granted to directors, officers, and key employees at an exercise price equal to the weighted average of the trading price of the shares in the TSE for the five trading days immediately preceding the date of the grant.

Instructions

Adopt the role of the auditor and discuss any financial reporting issues.

Research and Analysis

RA18-1   Hudson's Bay Company versus Sears Canada Inc.

Instructions

Go to the Digital Tool and, using the respective annual reports for the Hudson's Bay Company and Sears Canada Inc., answer the following questions.

(a) Comment on the capital structure of each company (simple or complex) and why it exists. List the dilutive securities for each. Which one is more complex?

(b) How significant are the dilutive securities in terms of potential dilution?

(c) What employee stock option compensation plans are offered by both companies?

(d) Compare the exercise price of the option plans with the company share price at year end. Comment on the likelihood of the options expiring or being exercised based on this information.

(e) How have the companies accounted for these plans?

(f) Compare EPS with diluted EPS for each company and comment on the differences between the two.

RA18-2   Molson

Instructions

Go to the Digital Tool and obtain the annual report for Molson. Answer the following.

(a) Does the company have a complex or simple capital structure?

(b) Identify the Potential Common Shares.

(c) What is the impact of the Potential Common Shares on the EPS calculations?

(d) In 2001, the company approved a 2-for-1 stock split. How were the EPS calculations affected by this?

RA18-3   Telus Corporation

Instructions

Go to the Digital Tool and access the annual report for Telus Corporation. Answer the following.

(a) Comment on the capital structure of the company.

(b) Identify Potential Common Shares.

(c) The company presented basic and diluted EPS in 2002. They were both the same. Why would diluted EPS be the same as basic EPS given the capital structure?

RA18-4   Cash Flow per Share and other per Share Amounts

In April of 2002, the CICA issued an Exposure Draft relating to proposed revisions to Cash Flow Statements and EPS. Currently, presentation of cash flow per share and other income per share amounts outside of *CICA Handbook* Section 3500 are no longer allowed.

Instructions

Go to the CICA website and research the issue of presenting additional per share amounts that are outside *CICA Handbook* Section 3500 (i.e., anything besides basic and diluted EPS). Write a short essay on the pros and cons of allowing alternate per share amounts to be included in the annual report by companies.

RA18-5 EPS Harmonization

As of the time of writing of this text, FASB had issued an Exposure Draft to revise the EPS GAAP in the United States. Below is an excerpt.

This proposed Statement would amend the computational guidance in FASB Statement No. 128, *Earnings per Share*, for calculating the number of incremental shares included in diluted shares when applying the treasury stock method. Also, this proposed Statement would eliminate the provisions of Statement 128 that allow an entity to rebut the presumption that contracts with the option of settling in either cash or stock will be settled in stock. In addition, this proposed Statement would require that shares that will be issued upon conversion of a mandatorily convertible security be included in the weighted average number of ordinary shares outstanding used in computing basic earnings per share from the date when conversion becomes mandatory.

Summary

This proposed Statement would amend the computational guidance of FASB Statement No. 128, *Earnings per Share*. When applying the treasury stock method for year-to-date diluted earnings per share (EPS), Statement 128 requires that the number of incremental shares included in the denominator be determined by computing a year-to-date weighted average of the number of incremental shares included in each quarterly diluted EPS computation. Under this proposed Statement, the number of incremental shares included in year-to-date diluted EPS would be computed using the average market price of common shares for the year-to-date period. This proposed Statement also would eliminate the provisions of Statement 128 that allow an entity to rebut the presumption that contracts with the option of settling in either cash or stock will be settled in stock.

Also, this proposed Statement would require that shares to be issued upon conversion of a mandatorily convertible security be included in the computation of basic EPS from the date that conversion becomes mandatory.

Reasons for Issuing This Proposed Statement

In 1991, the FASB issued a plan for international activities (which was updated in 1995) that proposed steps to increase the range and intensity of its international activities. An objective of that plan was to make financial statements more useful for investors and creditors by increasing the international comparability of accounting standards concurrent with improving the quality of accounting standards. Statement 128 and IAS 33, *Earnings per Share*, were issued as a result of the first technical project undertaken jointly by the FASB and the International Accounting Standards Committee (IASC) (the predecessor of the International Accounting Standards Board [IASB]).

In October 2002, the FASB and the IASB undertook a joint project to achieve more comparability in cross-border financial reporting through convergence to a single set of high-quality accounting standards. Each Board reviewed its pronouncements for areas of its generally accepted accounting principles (GAAP) that could be improved by converging with the other Board's GAAP. Since the issuance of Statement 128 and IAS 33, the IASB reexamined IAS 33 and proposed changes to enhance its computational guidance. Therefore, EPS was identified as an area in which the FASB and the IASB could improve accounting by converging their standards. This proposed Statement would reaffirm the Board's conclusion in Statement 128 that ". . . financial statements could be improved by simplifying the existing computational guidance, . . . and increasing the comparability of EPS data on an international basis" (paragraph 75). The Board also noted that under the IASB approach, the denominator used for year-to-date computations of EPS will not be affected by the frequency of interim reporting.

How the Changes in This Proposed Statement Would Improve Financial Reporting
By converging with the IASB's method of calculating year-to-date EPS and by clarifying guidance on mandatorily convertible securities in a way that would be consistent with IAS 33, this proposed Statement would enhance the comparability of financial statements prepared under U.S. GAAP and those prepared under the proposed International Financial Reporting Standard. This is in accordance with the Board's goal of promoting the international convergence of accounting standards concurrent with improving the quality of financial reporting.

Instructions
Discuss the issues raised and comment on whether the changes will result in better financial reporting. Hint: use the conceptual framework to frame your arguments.

Taxing Changes

Oil and gas company EnCana Corporation is the product of the 2002 merger of Alberta Energy Company Ltd. and PanCanadian Energy Corporation. Based in Calgary, the merged entity has an approximate enterprise value of $30 billion.

Forecasting taxes is challenging because of the many unpredictable variables. "Three primary factors influence the amount of tax we can expect to pay," explains John Watson, EnCana's chief financial officer. "First, the business's cash flow, which is directly impacted by commodity prices; second, the magnitude and type of capital expenditures; and third, unusual events such as a major business transaction or significant changes in tax laws that affect us." For example, the 2000 federal budget introduced a gradual reduction in the general corporate tax rate, from 28% to 21% over five years.

Since EnCana's creation, oil and gas prices have fluctuated significantly, which affects cash flow. On the capital expenditure side, Watson provides the example of drilling an exploration well, which results in a rapid write-off, rather than a development well, where the cost is deducted for tax purposes over a longer period. "Also influencing cash tax expense estimates is where the company invests. The tax rates on income and the treatment of expenditures can be quite different in Canada than in, say, Ecuador."

An acquisition, sale, or merger—activity that EnCana engaged in during 2002–2003—can cause changes to an organization's taxable income and cash tax expense. "Add to those variables the changes in federal and provincial tax rates and you have a multitude of contributors to the volatility of our cash tax expense," Watson says. ■

CHAPTER 19

Income Taxes

Learning Objectives

After studying this chapter, you should be able to:

1. Explain the difference between accounting income and taxable income.

2. Explain what a taxable temporary difference is and why a future tax liability is recognized.

3. Explain what a deductible temporary difference is and why a future tax asset is recognized.

4. Differentiate among timing, temporary, and permanent differences.

5. Prepare analyses and related journal entries to record income tax expense when there are multiple temporary differences.

6. Explain the effect of various tax rates and tax rate changes on future income tax accounts.

7. Apply accounting procedures for a tax loss carryback.

8. Apply accounting procedures and disclosure requirements for a tax loss carryforward.

9. Explain why the future income tax asset account is reassessed at the balance sheet date.

10. Explain the need for and be able to apply intraperiod tax allocation.

11. Identify the reporting and disclosure requirements for corporate income taxes.

12. Describe the differential reporting option for income taxes.

13. Describe the key aspects of the asset-liability method and identify outstanding issues with this approach.

Preview of Chapter 19

As part of prudent management, companies are expected to manage all costs in order to maximize shareholder value. For example, good managers look for the best prices for raw materials and supplies that go into making their products, and are expected to be savvy bargainers in negotiating labour and other service contracts to minimize the overall cost of doing business. Other costs that companies manage are those related to taxes. For example, by using accelerated amortization methods for capital assets, companies can defer paying taxes. With faster tax write-offs on plant and equipment, companies report lower taxable income and pay lower taxes in the early years of the assets' lives, thereby managing tax costs. As the opening story about EnCana illustrates, it is the required tax payments that get the most attention!

Income taxes are a major cost to most corporations. As a result, companies spend a considerable amount of time and effort to minimize their tax payments. This chapter discusses the standards that companies follow in accounting for and reporting income taxes.

The chapter's content and organization are as follows:

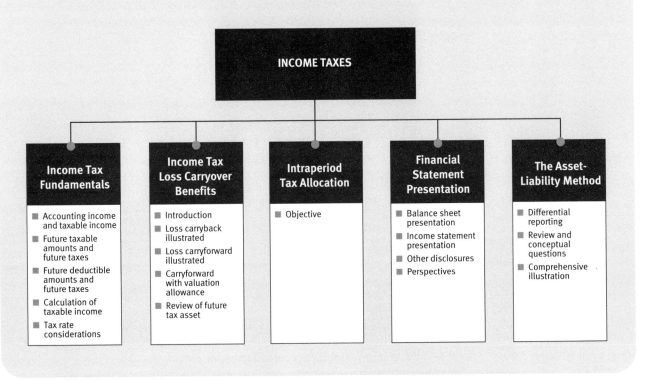

INCOME TAX FUNDAMENTALS

Up to this point, you have learned the basic principles that corporations use to report information to investors and creditors. You also recognize that corporations must file income tax returns following the Income Tax Act (and related provincial legislation) administered by the Canada Revenue Agency or CRA.[1] Because GAAP and tax regulations are different in a number of ways, pretax income on the financial statements (accounting income) and taxable income often differ. Consequently, the amount that a company reports as income tax expense differs from the amount of income taxes payable to the CRA. Illustration 19-1 highlights these differences. This chapter explains the application of GAAP in accounting for income taxes—the asset-liability method (or liability method).

IAS Note

IAS 12 also requires application of the liability method.

Illustration 19-1

Fundamental Differences between Financial and Tax Reporting

Accounting Income and Taxable Income

Accounting income is a financial reporting term often referred to as income before taxes, income for financial reporting purposes, or income for book purposes. In this chapter, it is a pre-tax concept. Accounting income is determined according to GAAP and is measured with the objective of providing useful information to investors and creditors. Taxable income (income for tax purposes) is a tax accounting term used to indicate the amount on which income tax payable is calculated. Taxable income is determined according to the Income Tax Act and Regulations, which is designed to raise money to support government operations.

1 Objective

Explain the difference between accounting income and taxable income.

To illustrate how differences in GAAP and tax rules affect financial reporting and taxable income, assume that Chelsea Inc. reported revenues of $130,000 and expenses of $60,000 in each of its first three years of operation. Illustration 19-2 shows the (partial) income statements over these three years.

---

[1] Proprietorships and partnerships are not subject to income taxes as separate legal entities. Instead, their income is taxable in the hands of the proprietor or partners as individuals. Also note that responsibility for the customs program was transferred to another agency in December 2003, and the Canada Customs and Revenue Agency (CCRA) became the Canada Revenue Agency (CRA).

Illustration 19-2

Accounting Income

CHELSEA INC.
GAAP Reporting

	2005	2006	2007	Total
Revenues	$130,000	$130,000	$130,000	
Expenses	60,000	60,000	60,000	
Accounting income	**$ 70,000**	**$ 70,000**	**$ 70,000**	**$210,000**
Income tax expense (40%)	**$ 28,000**	**$ 28,000**	**$ 28,000**	**$ 84,000**

For tax purposes (following tax regulations), Chelsea reported the same expenses to the CRA in each of the years. However, taxable revenues were $100,000 in 2005, $150,000 in 2006, and $140,000 in 2007, as shown in Illustration 19-3.

Illustration 19-3

Taxable Income

CHELSEA INC.
Tax Reporting

	2005	2006	2007	Total
Revenues	$100,000	$150,000	$140,000	
Expenses	60,000	60,000	60,000	
Taxable income	**$ 40,000**	**$ 90,000**	**$ 80,000**	**$210,000**
Income tax payable (40%)	**$ 16,000**	**$ 36,000**	**$ 32,000**	**$ 84,000**

In reality, companies do not submit revised income statements for the tax return, listing only taxable revenues and deductible expenses. Instead they prepare a schedule that begins with the accounting income and then adjusts for each area of difference between GAAP income and taxable income, ending with taxable income. Chelsea's schedules would appear as in Illustration 19-4.

Illustration 19-4

*Schedule to Reconcile
Accounting Income to
Taxable Income*

CHELSEA INC.

	2005	2006	2007
Accounting income	**$70,000**	**$70,000**	**$70,000**
Less revenue taxable in a future period	(30,000)		
Add revenue recognized in previous period, taxable in current period		20,000	10,000
Taxable income	**$40,000**	**$90,000**	**$80,000**
Taxes payable (40%)	$16,000	$36,000	$32,000

Income tax expense and income tax payable (a 40% tax rate is assumed) differ in each of the three years but in total are the same, as shown in Illustration 19-5.

Illustration 19-5

*Comparison of Income Tax
Expense to Income Tax Payable*

CHELSEA INC.
Income Tax Expense and Income Tax Payable

	2005	2006	2007	Total
Income tax expense	$28,000	$28,000	$28,000	$84,000
Income tax payable	16,000	36,000	32,000	84,000
Difference	$12,000	($8,000)	($4,000)	$ 0

The differences between income tax expense and income tax payable arise because the full accrual method is used to report revenues for financial reporting, whereas in some areas, a method closer to a modified cash basis is used for tax purposes.[2] As a result, Chelsea reports accounting income of $70,000 and income tax expense of $28,000 for each of the three years. Taxable income, however, fluctuates. For example, in 2005, taxable income is only $40,000, which means that just $16,000 is owed to the CRA that year.

As indicated in Illustration 19-5, the $12,000 ($28,000 − $16,000) difference between income tax expense and income tax payable in 2005 reflects taxes that will become payable in future periods. This $12,000 difference is often referred to as a deferred or **future tax amount**. In this case it is a **future tax liability**. In cases where taxes will be lower in the future, Chelsea records a deferred or **future tax asset**. The measurement of and accounting for future tax liabilities and assets are explained in the following sections.

International Insight

In some countries, taxable income and accounting income are the same. As a consequence, accounting for differences between tax and book income is not an issue.

Future Taxable Amounts and Future Taxes

The example summarized in Illustration 19-5 shows how income tax payable can differ from income tax expense. This happens when there are temporary differences between the amounts reported for tax purposes and those reported in the accounts. A *temporary difference* is the difference between the tax basis of an asset or liability and its reported (carrying or book) amount in the balance sheet that will result in taxable amounts or deductible amounts in future years.[3] **Taxable amounts** or *taxable temporary differences* will increase taxable income in future years, and **deductible amounts** or *deductible temporary differences* will decrease taxable income in future years.

In Chelsea Inc.'s situation, the only difference between the book basis and tax basis of the assets and liabilities relates to accounts receivable that arose from revenue recognized for book purposes. Illustration 19-6 indicates that accounts receivable are reported at $30,000 in the December 31, 2005 GAAP-basis balance sheet, but the receivables have a zero tax basis. They have a zero tax value because all revenues reported in taxable income have been received.

2 Objective

Explain what a taxable temporary difference is and why a future tax liability is recognized.

Carrying value	12/31/05	Tax Basis	12/31/05
Accounts receivable	$30,000	Accounts receivable	$–0–

Illustration 19-6

Temporary Difference, Sales Revenue

What will happen to this $30,000 temporary difference that originated in 2005 for Chelsea Inc.? Assuming that Chelsea expects to collect $20,000 of the receivables in 2006 and $10,000 in 2007, this will result in taxable amounts of $20,000 in 2006 and $10,000 in 2007. These future taxable amounts will cause taxable income to exceed accounting income in both 2006 and 2007.

An assumption inherent in a company's GAAP balance sheet is that the assets and liabilities will be recovered and settled, respectively, at their reported amounts (carrying amounts). This assumption creates a requirement under accrual accounting to recognize the future tax consequences of temporary differences in the current year; that is, the amount of income taxes that will be payable (or refundable) when the assets' reported amounts are recovered or the liabilities are settled. The following diagram illustrates the reversal or turnaround of the temporary difference described in Illustration 19-6 and the resulting taxable amounts in future periods.

---

[2] At the risk of oversimplification, the *Income Tax Act* follows a principle of having the tax follow the cash flow. While taxable income is based primarily on income reported under GAAP, in cases where the timing of cash flows differs significantly from the timing of GAAP recognition, revenues tend to be taxable as they are received in cash and expenses are allowable as deductions when paid.

[3] *CICA Handbook*, Section 3465.09(c).

Future Income Tax Asset

A **future income tax asset** is the future tax consequence of deductible temporary differences. In other words, a future income tax asset represents the reduction in taxes payable or increase in taxes refundable in future years as a result of deductible temporary differences existing at the end of the current year.[5] **Future income tax assets are recognized only to the extent that it is more likely than not that the future tax asset will be realized.** This is contingent on earning sufficient taxable income in the future against which the temporary differences can be deducted. *CICA Handbook* Section 3465 defines more likely than not as a probability of greater than 50%.[6]

To illustrate the future income tax asset and income tax benefit, the Cunningham example is continued. The warranty expense recognized on the income statement in 2005 is not deductible for tax purposes until the period the actual warranty costs are incurred, expected to be $300,000 in 2006 and $200,000 in 2007. As a result, a deduction will be allowed for tax purposes in 2006 and again in 2007 as the liability—Estimated Liability for Warranties—is settled, causing taxable income in those years to be lower than accounting income. The future income tax asset at the end of 2005 (assuming a 40% tax rate for 2006 and 2007) is as follows.

Illustration 19-15

Calculation of Future Income Tax Asset, End of 2005

Book basis of warranty liability	$500,000
Tax basis of warranty liability	–0–
Deductible temporary difference at the end of 2005	500,000
Tax rate	40%
Future income tax asset at the end of 2005	$200,000

Another way to calculate the future tax asset is to prepare a schedule that indicates the deductible amounts scheduled for the future as a result of deductible temporary differences. This schedule is shown in Illustration 19-16.

Illustration 19-16

Schedule of Future Deductible Amounts

	Future Years		
	2006	2007	Total
Future deductible amounts	$300,000	$200,000	$500,000
Tax rate	40%	40%	
Future income tax asset at the end of 2005	$120,000	$ 80,000	$200,000

Assuming that 2005 is the company's first year of operations and that income tax payable is $600,000, income tax expense is calculated as follows.

Illustration 19-17

Calculation of Income Tax Expense, 2005

Current tax expense, 2005		
Taxable income × tax rate (given)		$600,000
Future tax expense/benefit, 2005		
Future tax asset, end of 2005	$200,000	
Less: Future tax asset, beginning of 2005	–0–	(200,000)
Income tax expense (total) for 2005		$400,000

---

[5] *CICA Handbook* Section 3465.09(d) indicates that future income tax assets also include the income tax benefits that arise in respect of the carryforward of unused tax losses and unused income tax reductions, excluding investment tax credits. These are discussed later in the chapter.

[6] *CICA Handbook* Section 3465.09(i).

The future income tax benefit results from the increase in the future tax asset from the beginning to the end of the accounting period. The future tax benefit captures the warranty costs' future tax deductibility and recognizes this in the current period when the expense is reported for financial reporting purposes. The total income tax expense of $400,000 on the income statement for 2005 is therefore made up of two elements: current tax expense of $600,000 and the future tax benefit of $200,000. For Cunningham Inc., the following journal entries are made at the end of 2005 to recognize income taxes.

Current Income Tax Expense	600,000	
Income Tax Payable		600,000
Future Income Tax Asset	200,000	
Future Income Tax Expense/Benefit		200,000

A = L + SE
       +600,000 −600,000
Cash flows: No effect

A = L + SE
+200,000   +200,000
Cash flows: No effect

At the end of the second year, 2006, the difference between the carrying value of the Estimated Liability for Warranties of $200,000 and its tax basis of zero is $200,000. Therefore, the future tax asset at this date is 40% of $200,000, or $80,000. Assuming income tax payable for 2006 is $440,000, the calculation of income tax expense for 2006 is as shown below.

Illustration 19-18
Calculation of Income Tax Expense, 2006

Current tax expense, 2006		
Taxable income × tax rate (given)		$440,000
Future tax expense/benefit, 2006		
Future tax asset, end of 2006	$ 80,000	
Less: Future tax asset, beginning of 2006	(200,000)	120,000
Income tax expense (total) for 2006		$560,000

As expected, a reduction in the tax asset account, as with assets in general, results in an increase in the expense recognized. The journal entries to record income taxes in 2006 follow.

Current Income Tax Expense	440,000	
Income Tax Payable		440,000
Future Income Tax Expense	120,000	
Future Income Tax Asset		120,000

A = L + SE
       +440,000 −440,000
Cash flows: No effect

A = L + SE
−120,000   −120,000
Cash flows: No effect

The total income tax expense of $560,000 on the income statement for 2006 is composed of two elements: current tax expense of $440,000 and future tax expense of $120,000.

Note that the future income tax expense of $120,000 recognized in 2006 **is not related to future events at all.** It represents the using up or reversal of a future income tax benefit recognized at the end of the preceding year. While a third component of income tax expense for the current year, such as Utilization of Previously Recognized Future Tax Assets or Reduction in Future Income Tax Assets, could be given separate recognition, the authors have chosen to incorporate this as a component of future income tax expense or benefit. **In all cases, the future income tax expense or benefit measures the change in the future income tax liability or asset account over the period.** As such, it is a combination of increased future tax liabilities, reversals of taxable temporary differences, recognition of future tax assets, and the use of future tax benefits recognized in the past.

At the end of 2007, the Future Income Tax Asset is further reduced by $80,000, as shown in the T account in Illustration 19-19. Future income tax expense in 2007 is $80,000.

Illustration 19-19
*Future Income Tax Asset
Account after Reversals*

Future Income Tax Asset			
2005	200,000	2006	120,000
		2007	80,000
Balance	–0–		

What do the Numbers Mean?

A key issue in accounting for income taxes is whether a future tax asset should be recognized in the accounts. Based on the conceptual definition of an asset in *CICA Handbook* Section 1000, a future income tax asset meets the three main conditions for an item to be recognized as an asset.

1. *It will contribute to future net cash flows.* Taxable income is higher than accounting income in the current year (2005). However, in the next year the opposite occurs, with taxable income lower than income reported for financial statement purposes. Because the deductible temporary difference reduces taxes payable in the future, a future benefit exists at the end of the year.

2. *Access to the benefits is controlled by the entity.* Cunningham has the ability to obtain the benefit of existing deductible temporary differences by reducing its taxes payable in the future. The company has the exclusive right to that benefit and can control others' access to it.

3. *It results from a past transaction or event.* In the Cunningham example, the sale of the product with the two-year warranty is the past event that gives rise to a future deductible temporary difference.

Market analysts' reaction to the write-off of future income taxes supports their treatment as assets, as does management's treatment of them. **Air Canada** reduced its $400 million future income tax asset account at the end of 2001 to zero in 2002. The reason? The uncertainty of generating sufficient taxable income in the future brought into question the ability to realize any benefits from future deductible amounts. Therefore, this asset, like others with uncertain benefits, is written down.

Note that when the future tax asset is recognized, the balance sheet at the end of each accounting period reports the economic resources needed to settle the warranty liability. The following table illustrates this relationship.

	End of 2005	End of 2006
Economic resources needed to settle the obligation:		
Future resources needed to settle the liability	$500,000	$200,000
Future tax savings as liability is settled	200,000	80,000
Net future economic resources needed	$300,000	$120,000
Net assets reported on the balance sheet:		
Warranty liability (in liabilities)	$500,000	$200,000
Future income tax asset (in assets)	200,000	80,000
Net assets reported	$300,000	$120,000

In the absence of interperiod tax allocation (that is, if the future income tax asset is not recognized at the end of 2005), liabilities of $500,000 would be reported on the balance sheet, which require only $300,000 of economic resources to settle. Similarly, the $200,000 liability at the end of 2006 would also be overstated.

Calculation of Taxable Income

Temporary and Permanent Differences

To calculate income taxes currently payable, companies must first determine taxable income. As indicated previously, rather than preparing a "tax income statement" of taxable revenues and deductible expenses, companies begin with the income reported on the income statement and then make whatever adjustments are necessary to convert it to the amount that is taxable.

4 Objective
Differentiate among timing, temporary, and permanent differences.

The major reasons for differences between accounting and taxable income, most of which result in or affect the amount of a temporary difference, are provided below.

A. ***Revenues or gains are taxable after they are recognized in accounting income.*** An asset, such as a receivable, may be recognized on the balance sheet as revenues or gains are recognized on the income statement; however, these amounts may not be included in taxable income until future years when the asset is recovered or realized. Examples include:

- instalment sales accounted for on the accrual basis for financial reporting purposes and on the cash basis for tax purposes, and

- contracts accounted for under the percentage-of-completion method for financial reporting purposes with some or all of the related gross profit deferred for tax purposes.

B. ***Expenses or losses are deductible after they are recognized in accounting income.*** A liability (or contra asset) may be recognized on the balance sheet when expenses or losses are recognized for financial reporting purposes; however, amounts are not deductible in calculating taxable income until future periods when the liability is settled. Examples include:

- product warranty liabilities
- estimated losses and liabilities related to restructurings
- litigation accruals, and
- accrued pension costs.

C. ***Revenues or gains are taxable before they are recognized in accounting income.*** A liability (e.g., unearned revenue) may be recognized for an advance payment for goods or services to be provided in future years. For tax purposes, the advance payment may be included in taxable income when cash is received. When the entity recognizes revenue in the future as the goods or services are provided that settle the liability, these amounts are deducted in calculating taxable income. Examples include:

- subscriptions, royalties, and rentals received in advance, and
- sales and leasebacks, including the deferral of profit on the sale for financial reporting purposes, but reported as realized for tax purposes.

D. ***Expenses or losses are deductible before they are recognized in accounting income.*** An asset's cost may be deducted faster for tax purposes than expensed for financial reporting purposes. As the excess carrying value is subsequently amortized when calculating accounting income, the excess amortization must be added back to calculate taxable income. The result is future taxable income that is higher than accounting income. Examples include:

- depreciable property and depletable resources
- deductible pension funding exceeding pension expense recognized, and
- prepaid expenses that are deducted in calculating taxable income in the period paid.

If a loss is carried back, it is usually applied against the earliest available income—2002 in the example above. The **benefit from a loss carryback** is the **recovery of some or all of the taxes** paid in those years. The tax returns for the preceding years are refiled, the current year tax loss is deducted from the previously reported taxable income, and a revised amount of income tax payable for each year is determined. This is compared with the taxes paid for each applicable preceding year, and the government is asked to refund the difference.[12]

If a corporation elects to carry the loss forward instead, or if the full amount of the loss could not be absorbed in the carryback period, **the tax loss can be used to offset taxable income in the future, thereby reducing or eliminating taxes that would otherwise be payable** in those years.

The decision on how to use a tax loss depends on factors such as its size, results of the previous years' operations, past and anticipated future tax rates, and other factors in which management sees the greatest tax advantage.

Tax losses are relatively common and can be substantial.[13] Companies that have suffered substantial losses are often attractive merger candidates because, in certain cases, the acquirer may use these losses to reduce its taxable income and, therefore, its income taxes. In a sense, a company that has suffered substantial losses may find itself worth more "dead" than "alive" because of the economic value related to the tax benefit that may be derived from its losses by another company. The following sections discuss the accounting treatment of loss carrybacks and carryforwards recommended in *CICA Handbook* Section 3465.

Objective 7

Apply accounting procedures for a tax loss carryback.

Loss Carryback Illustrated

To illustrate the accounting procedures for a tax loss carryback, assume that Groh Inc. has no temporary or permanent differences. Groh experiences the following.

Illustration 19-30

*Income and Loss Data—
Groh Inc.*

Year	Taxable Income or Loss	Tax Rate	Tax Paid
2001	$75,000	30%	$22,500
2002	50,000	35%	17,500
2003	100,000	30%	30,000
2004	200,000	40%	80,000
2005	(500,000)	—	–0–

In 2005, Groh Inc. incurs a tax loss that it elects to carry back. The carryback is applied first to 2002, the third year preceding the loss year. Any unused loss is then carried back to 2003 and then to 2004. Accordingly, Groh would file amended tax returns for each of the years 2002, 2003, and 2004, receiving refunds for the $127,500 ($17,500 + $30,000 + $80,000) of taxes paid in those years.

---

[12] Within certain limits, the company can also increase the amount of taxable income for these earlier years. For example, it could reduce the CCA claimed on its capital assets for those years. This has the effect of increasing prior years' taxable income, permitting more of its current taxable loss to be absorbed. If prior years' CCA claimed is reduced, this increases the undepreciated capital cost (UCC) pool—the amount that can be claimed as CCA in the future. This complexity is the reality, but is not illustrated here nor examined in the assignment material at the end of the chapter.

[13] *Financial Reporting in Canada -2003* (CICA) indicates that of the 200 companies surveyed from 1999 to 2002, between 35 and 49 companies each year disclosed tax recoveries from the carryback of current year's losses. As well, 100 companies in 2002 (96 in 2001) provided disclosures of unrecognized loss carryforward benefits.

For accounting purposes, the $127,500 represents the **tax benefit of the loss carryback**. The tax benefit is recognized in 2005, the loss year, because the tax loss gives rise to a refund (an asset) that is both measurable and currently realizable.

The following journal entry is prepared in 2005.

Income Tax Refund Receivable	127,500	
Current Income Tax Benefit		127,500

A　=　L　+　SE
+127,500　　　　+127,500
Cash flows: No effect

The Income Tax Refund Receivable is reported on the balance sheet as a current asset at December 31, 2005. The tax benefit is reported on the income statement for 2005 as follows.

<table>
<tr><td colspan="2" align="center">GROH INC.
Income Statement (partial) for 2005</td></tr>
<tr><td>Loss before income taxes</td><td>$(500,000)</td></tr>
<tr><td>Income tax benefit</td><td></td></tr>
<tr><td>　Current benefit due to loss carryback</td><td>127,500</td></tr>
<tr><td>Net loss</td><td>$(372,500)</td></tr>
</table>

Illustration 19-31

Recognition of Benefit of the Loss Carryback in the Loss Year

If the tax loss carried back to the three preceding years is less than the taxable incomes of those three years, the only entry required is similar to the one indicated above. In the Groh Inc. example, however, the $500,000 tax loss for 2005 exceeds the $350,000 total taxable income from the three preceding years; **the remaining $150,000 loss remains to be carried forward**.

Loss Carryforward Illustrated

If a net operating loss is not fully absorbed through a carryback or if the company decides not to carry the loss back, then **it can be carried forward for up to seven years**. Because carryforwards are used to offset future taxable income, the tax benefit associated with a loss carryforward is represented by future tax savings: reductions in taxes in the future that would otherwise be payable. Realization of the future tax benefit depends upon the existence of future taxable income, the prospect of which may be highly uncertain.

The accounting issue, then, is whether the tax benefit of a loss carryforward should be recognized in the loss year when the potential benefits arise, or in future years when the benefits are actually realized. The AcSB, in Section 3465, takes the position that the potential benefit associated with unused tax losses meets the definition of an asset and that **the benefit should be recognized in the loss year** to the extent that **it is more likely than not** that future taxable income will be available against which the losses and reductions can be applied.

When a tax loss carryforward is more likely than not to result in future economic benefits, it should be accounted for in the same manner as a deductible temporary difference: a future income tax asset is recognized equal to the expected benefit.

Future Taxable Income More Likely Than Not

To illustrate the accounting for an income tax loss carryforward, the Groh Inc. example is continued. In 2005, after carrying back as much of the loss as possible to the three preceding years, the company has a $150,000 tax loss available to carry forward. Assuming the company determines **it is more likely than not to generate sufficient taxable income**

8 **Objective**
Apply accounting procedures and disclosure requirements for a tax loss carryforward.

International Insight

In the United States, companies may opt for either a two-year carryback plus a 20-year carryforward or use only the 20-year carryforward option for net operating losses.

in the future so that the benefit of the loss will be realized, Groh records a future tax asset to recognize the benefit of the loss. If a rate of 40% is expected to apply to future years, the amount of the asset recognized is $60,000 ($150,000 × 40%). The journal entries to record the benefits of the carryback and the carryforward in 2005 are as follows.

A = L + SE
+127,500 +127,500
Cash flows: No effect

To recognize benefit of loss carryback		
Income Tax Refund Receivable	127,500	
Current Income Tax Benefit		127,500

A = L + SE
+60,000 +60,000
Cash flows: No effect

To recognize benefit of loss carryforward		
Future Income Tax Asset	60,000	
Future Income Tax Benefit		60,000

The income tax refund receivable of $127,500 will be realized immediately as a refund of taxes paid in the past. The Future Income Tax Asset account measures the benefit of the future tax savings. The two accounts credited are "negative" or **contra income tax expense** items, and appear on the 2005 income statement as follows.

Illustration 19-32

Recognition of the Benefit of the Loss Carryback and Carryforward in the Loss Year

GROH INC. Income Statement (partial) for 2005		
Loss before income taxes		$(500,000)
Income tax benefit		
Current benefit due to loss carryback	127,500	
Future benefit due to loss carryforward	60,000	187,500
Net loss		$(312,500)

The $60,000 **future tax benefit** for the year results from an **increase in the future tax asset account**.

For 2006, assume that Groh Inc. returns to profitability and has taxable income of $200,000 from the year's operations, subject to a 40% tax rate. In 2006, Groh Inc. **realizes** the benefits of the entire $150,000 tax loss carryforward that was **recognized** for accounting purposes in 2005. The income tax payable for 2006 is calculated as follows.

Illustration 19-33

Calculation of Income Tax Payable in Year the Loss Carryforward Is Realized

Taxable income before loss carryforward, 2006	$200,000
Loss carryforward deduction	(150,000)
Taxable income for 2006	50,000
Tax rate	40%
Income tax payable for 2006 and current tax expense	$ 20,000
Future income tax asset, opening balance ($150,000 × .4)	$60,000
Future income tax asset, December 31, 2006 ($0 × .4)	–0–
Future income tax expense, 2006	$60,000

The journal entries to record income taxes in 2006 are:

A = L + SE
+20,000 −20,000
Cash flows: No effect

Current Income Tax Expense	20,000	
Income Tax Payable		20,000

A = L + SE
−60,000 −60,000
Cash flows: No effect

Future Income Tax Expense	60,000	
Future Income Tax Asset		60,000

The first entry records income taxes payable for 2006 and, therefore, current income tax expense. The second entry records the use of the tax benefit captured in the future income tax asset the previous year.

The 2006 income statement below illustrates that the 2006 total income tax expense is based on 2006's reported income. The benefit of the tax loss is not reported in 2006; the benefit was previously reported in 2005.

GROH INC.
Income Statement (partial) for 2006

Income before income taxes		$200,000
Income tax expense		
Current	$20,000	
Future	60,000	80,000
Net income		$120,000

Illustration 19-34

Presentation of the Benefit of Loss Carryforward Realized in 2006, Recognized in 2005

Future Taxable Income Not Likely

Return to the Groh Inc. example and 2005. A tax asset (Income Tax Refund Receivable) was recognized in 2005 because the ability to carry back the loss and recover income taxes paid in the past provides evidence that benefits related to $350,000 of the loss will be realized. Assume now that the company's future is uncertain and it is determined at December 31, 2005 that there is insufficient evidence about the possibility of future taxable income to recognize an income tax asset and benefit related to the remaining $150,000 of income tax losses. In this case, the only 2005 income tax entry is:

Income Tax Refund Receivable	127,500	
Current Income Tax Benefit		127,500

A = L + SE
+127,500   +127,500

Cash flows: No effect

The presentation in the following income statement indicates that **only the benefit related to the loss carryback is recognized.** The unrecognized potential tax benefit and related unrecognized future income tax asset associated with the remaining $150,000 of tax losses is relevant information for financial statement readers. **Therefore the amounts and expiry dates of unrecognized (i.e., unbooked) income tax assets related to the carryforward of unused tax losses must be disclosed.** Such information is useful as it makes readers aware of the possibility of future benefits (reduced future income tax outflows) from the loss, even though the likelihood of realizing these benefits is not sufficient to accord them formal recognition in the body of the statements.

GROH INC.
Income Statement (partial) for 2005

Loss before income taxes	$(500,000)
Income tax benefit	
Current benefit due to loss carryback	127,500
Net income	$(372,500)

Illustration 19-35

Recognition of Benefit of Loss Carryback Only

In 2006, assume the company performs better than expected, generating taxable income of $200,000 from its annual operations. After applying the $150,000 loss carry-

Illustration 19-40

*Loss Carryforward Note—
MAAX Inc.*

MAAX Inc.

Excerpts from Note 9, Income Taxes
(tabular amounts in thousands)

9. Income taxes (continued)

The tax effects of significant items comprising the Company's net future tax liabilities are as follows:

	2004	2003
Operating losses carried forward	**$ 4,637**	$ 7,016
Difference in accounting and tax basis for:		
Current assets and liabilities	**4,683**	4,438
Property, plant and equipment	**(12,830)**	(12,774)
Goodwill	**(7,156)**	(8,047)
Other assets	**(554)**	(221)
Other	**50**	(651)
Valuation allowance on operating losses carried forward	**$ (2,798)**	$ (5,195)
Future income taxes	**$(13,968)**	$(15,434)

Tax losses carried forward:
The losses carried forward for tax purposes available to reduce future income taxes amount to $27,512,000.
The company can apply these losses against future taxable income within the following periods:

	Total
2007	$ 454
2008	877
2009	2,461
2011	7,491
Indefinitely	16,229
	27,512
Tax losses on which a tax benefit has been accounted for as a future tax asset	(6,125)
Tax losses on which no tax benefit has been accounted for as a future tax asset	$21,387

In this note, MAAX provides information about both future tax assets and liabilities. The tax effects of operating losses carried forward of $4,637 and differences between the accounting and tax basis for current assets and liabilities of $4,683 result in future income tax assets. The company also reports a valuation allowance of $2,798, which relates to the future tax assets. Total tax losses available to carryforward are $27,512, but a tax benefit has been recognized only on $6,125 of these. This leaves tax losses of $21,387 where no benefit has been recognized in the accounts. Presumably these are capital losses that are available to be carried forward indefinitely.

INTRAPERIOD TAX ALLOCATION

Objective

Objective 10

Explain the need for
and be able to apply
intraperiod tax
allocation.

Another objective of accounting for income taxes is identified in *CICA Handbook* Section 3465.07: **to reflect the cost or benefit related to income tax assets and liabilities in a manner consistent with the transaction or event giving rise to the asset or liability.** In general, this refers to the fact that the current and future income tax expense (benefit) of the current period related to **discontinued operations, extraordinary items, adjustments reported in retained earnings, and capital transactions should be reported with the item to which it relates.** This approach to allocating taxes **within** the financial statements of the current period is referred to as intraperiod tax allocation. **Interperiod tax allocation**, on the other hand, reflects the appropriate allocation of taxes **between** years.

To illustrate, assume that Copy Doctor Inc. has an ordinary loss from continuing operations of $500,000. The tax rate is 35%. In addition, the company has an extraordinary gain of $900,000, of which $210,000 is not taxable. Accounting and taxable income and income taxes payable are calculated below.

	Ordinary Income (Loss)	Extraordinary Gain (Loss)	Total
Accounting income (loss)	($500,000)	$900,000	$400,000
Less nontaxable gain	—	(210,000)	(210,000)
Taxable income (loss)	($500,000)	$690,000	$190,000
Tax rate	35%	35%	
Income tax payable	($175,000)	$241,500	$ 66,500

Illustration 19-41

Tax Calculations with Extraordinary Item

Whenever income tax is required to be separately reported with a particular component of the income or other statement, prepare your analysis as indicated throughout the chapter, but set up a separate column for each component that attracts tax, as illustrated above. The income tax amounts can then be taken directly from the analysis and reported in the correct place on the appropriate financial statement. Copy Doctor Inc.'s taxes are reported as follows on the company's income statement.

Loss before income taxes and extraordinary item	($500,000)
Current income tax benefit from operating loss	175,000
Loss before extraordinary item	(325,000)
Extraordinary gain ($900,000 less income tax of $241,500)	658,500
Net income	$333,500

Illustration 19-42

Income Statement Presentation— Extraordinary Item

For its year ended September 30, 2003, **CGI Group Inc.** reported income tax expense separately for earnings from continuing operations and for earnings from discontinued operations. **RONA Inc.** reported income tax effects in three places on its 2002 financial statements: on the income statement, in the statement of retained earnings (related to costs of issuing shares), and on the statement of contributed surplus (related to a gain on disposal of the company's shares by its subsidiaries.)

FINANCIAL STATEMENT PRESENTATION

Balance Sheet Presentation

Because of the unique nature of income taxes, income tax assets and liabilities are required to be reported separately from other assets and liabilities on the balance sheet. In addition, **current** tax assets and liabilities are reported separately from **future** tax assets and liabilities.[19]

Where an entity classifies its balance sheet into current and noncurrent amounts, future income tax assets and liabilities, in general, are classified and reported as **one net current amount** and **one net noncurrent amount**. That is, the current future tax assets and liabilities are netted as are the long-term accounts. This offset is required, provided the accounts relate to the same taxable entity and the same taxation authority. **The classification of an individual future tax liability or asset as current or noncurrent is determined by the classification of the related asset or liability for financial reporting purposes.**[20]

Most companies engage in a large number of transactions that give rise to future income taxes. The balances in the future income tax accounts must be analysed and classified

11 Objective

Identify the reporting and disclosure requirements for corporate income taxes.

IAS Note

IAS 12 requires that all future (deferred) tax assets and liabilities be reported outside of current assets and liabilities.

---

[19] *CICA Handbook*, Section 3465.86.

[20] *CICA Handbook*, Section 3465.87-.88.

recurring. For example, one year **Wang Laboratories** reported net income of $3.3 million, or 82 cents a share, versus $3.1 million, or 77 cents a share, in the preceding period. The entire increase in net income and then some resulted from a lower effective tax rate, not from improvements in operations.

What do the Numbers Mean?

An area that requires considerable judgement and that therefore may be open to abuse is the accounting for future tax assets. It takes only a minimum of optimism for management to expect flows of taxable income in the future to apply tax losses and other future deductible amounts against to justify the recognition of future income tax assets on the balance sheet and tax benefits on the income statement. Valuation of future income tax assets, either directly or through an adjustment of the valuation allowance account, affects bottom line income on a dollar for dollar basis.

Stelco Inc., "Canada's largest and most diversified steel producer," presents an interesting example. In 2001 the company's loss of $217 million was reduced by $81 million of future income tax benefits and $139 million of future income tax assets were reported on its balance sheet. In 2002, the company's $9 million of income was increased by an $11 million future tax benefit and $161 million of net future tax assets were reported on the balance sheet, **with $74 million classified as a current asset**. The future deductible amounts underlying the tax asset accounts related to the recognition of employee retirement benefit expenses in excess of amounts paid, and income tax losses carried forward.

To have classified $74 million of the future tax asset as a current asset, management must have expected 2003 to be an excellent year for the company! As it turned out, sales volume and prices were down, costs increased, and the cash position deteriorated, resulting in Stelco obtaining an order to initiate a court-supervised restructuring under the Companies' Creditors Arrangement Act early in 2004.

Regardless of management's motivations in assessing the value of future income tax assets, readers of the financial statements should be aware of the extent to which judgement plays a part in these measurements.

Better Predictions of Future Cash Flows

Examining the future portion of income tax expense provides information as to whether taxes payable are likely to be higher or lower in the future. A close examination may disclose the company's policy regarding capitalization of costs, recognition of revenue, and other policies giving rise to a difference between income reported on the financial statements and taxable income. As a result, it may be possible to predict upcoming reductions in future tax liabilities leading to a loss of liquidity because actual tax payments will be higher than the tax expense reported on the income statement.[26]

Helpful in Setting Governmental Policy

Understanding the amount companies currently pay and the effective tax rate is helpful to government policymakers. In the early 1970s, when the oil companies were believed to have earned excess profits, many politicians and other interested parties attempted to determine their effective tax rates. Unfortunately, at that time such information was not available in published annual reports.

---

[26] An article by R. P. Weber and J. E. Wheeler, "Using Income Tax Disclosures to Explore Significant Economic Transactions," *Accounting Horizons*, September 1992, discusses how deferred (future) tax disclosures can be used to assess the quality of earnings and to predict future cash flows.

THE ASSET-LIABILITY METHOD

Differential Reporting

In assessing the costs and benefits of financial reporting, accounting standard setters have concluded that:

Objective 12
Describe the differential reporting option for income taxes.

- the more widespread the ownership of a company and the wider the separation between management and owners, **the greater the benefits** that are derived from information in financial statements,

- the fewer the users of the financial statements and the greater their ability to get information other than financial statements, **the smaller the benefits** derived from the information in financial statements, and

Underlying Concept

Differential reporting is an example of the cost-benefit constraint discussed in Chapter 2.

- the fewer the users benefiting and the higher the costs of compiling the required accounting information relative to the number of users, **the less likely it is that the benefits of providing the information in the financial statements will exceed its costs.**[27]

This reasoning has resulted in the Canadian standard setters allowing qualifying entities—those that are non-publicly accountable and whose owners unanimously consent to the application of an approved alternative—to apply a different method and still be in accordance with GAAP. **The allowed alternative for income taxes is the taxes payable basis.**[28]

The taxes payable method recognizes income tax expense (benefit) equal to income taxes currently payable (receivable). That is, the expense falls into the period the revenues and expenses are recognized for tax purposes. No future tax assets and liabilities are recognized. While considerably less complex an approach to accounting for taxes, *CICA Handbook* Section 3465.106 requires the following income tax-specific disclosures:

International Insight

Nations that recognize future or deferred taxes using the liability method include the United States, Australia, Germany, the UK, and Spain. The European Directives do not specify the accounting for future taxes.

1. income tax expense (benefit) included in each of income before discontinued operations and extraordinary items, discontinued operations, extraordinary items, and capital transactions reported in equity;

2. a reconciliation of the tax rate (or expense) from the statutory rate to the effective rate (or expense) related to income before discontinued operations and extraordinary items, including the nature and amounts of the reconciling items;

3. the amount and expiry date of losses carried forward and unused income tax credits; and

4. the amount of any capital gain reserves to be included in taxable income in the next five years.

Chapter 24 discusses the topic of differential reporting in more detail, including other areas where *CICA Handbook* Section 1300, "Differential Reporting," permits a less complex accounting method.

Review and Conceptual Questions

North American standard setters believe that the asset-liability method (sometimes referred to as the liability approach) is the most consistent method of accounting for income taxes. One objective of this approach is to recognize the amount of taxes payable

---

[27] *CICA Handbook*, Section 1300.04.

[28] *CICA Handbook*, Section 1300.06 and 3465.105.

|Illustration| 19-49

*Determination of Future
Income Tax Expense—2004*

	Carrying Amount	Tax Basis	Taxable (Deductible) Temporary Differences
Assets			
Accounts receivable (Gross profit included therein)	$448,000	–0–	$448,000
Plant and equipment	450,000	$486,000	(36,000)
Liabilities			
Liability for warranties	156,000	–0–	(156,000)
Net taxable (deductible) temporary difference			$256,000
Future income tax liability: $448,000 at 40%			$179,200
Future income tax asset: ($36,000 + $156,000) at 40%			(76,800)
Net future income tax liability, December 31, 2004			102,400
Net future income tax asset/liability, opening balance			–0–
Future income tax expense (benefit)—2004			$102,400

Income Tax Accounting Entries—2004. The entries to record current and future income taxes for 2004 are as follows.

A = L + SE
+77,000 –77,000

Cash flows: No effect

Current Income Tax Expense	77,000	
Income Tax Payable (Illustration 19-47)		77,000

A = L + SE
+102,400 –102,400

Cash flows: No effect

Future Income Tax Expense	102,400	
Future Income Tax Liability[29]		102,400

Financial Statement Presentation—2004. Future tax assets and liabilities are classified as current and noncurrent on the balance sheet based on the classifications of related assets and liabilities that underlie the temporary differences. They are then summarized into one net current and one net noncurrent amount. The classification of Allman's future tax account at the end of 2004 is shown below.

|Illustration| 19-50

*Classification of Future Tax
Asset/Liability Account*

Balance Sheet Account	Balance Sheet Classification	Temporary Difference	Resulting Future Tax (Asset)	Liability	Classification of Future Tax Account Current	Long-term
Instalment receivables	mixed	$448,000		$179,200	$44,800	$134,400
Depreciable assets	LT	(36,000)	(14,400)			(14,400)
Liability for warranties	mixed	(156,000)	(62,400)		(22,400)	(40,000)
			$(76,800)	$179,200	$22,400(L)	$ 80,000(L)

For the first temporary difference, the related asset on the balance sheet is the instalment accounts receivable. This asset is classified partially as a current asset and partially as

---

[29] Two accounts could have been used here: a debit to a Future Income Tax Asset of $76,800 and a credit to a Future Income Tax Liability of $179,200. The entry given above assumes that only one control account is used with the details about the individual temporary differences kept separately in subsidiary accounts or in a file outside the ledger accounts.

long-term. Because $112,000 of the receivable is due in 2005, this portion is a current asset and the current portion of the future tax liability is $112,000 × 40% = $44,800. The remainder of the $179,200 ($179,200 − $44,800 = $134,400) is long-term.

The plant assets are classified as long-term; therefore, the resulting future tax asset is classified as noncurrent. The balance sheet account related to the $62,400 future tax asset is the Warranty Liability account. This account, like the instalment receivables, is split between the current and long-term categories. The current portion relates to the $56,000 of warranty costs expected to be incurred in 2005. Therefore, $56,000 × 40% = $22,400 of the future tax asset is classified as current; the remainder is long-term.

Once the analysis is completed for each future tax asset and liability, determine one amount that will be classified as current, and one as noncurrent. In the Allman example, one net current amount of $22,400 will be reported as a current liability and one net long-term amount of $80,000 will be reported as a long-term liability, as illustrated below.

<table>
<tr><td colspan="2" align="center">**BALANCE SHEET, DECEMBER 31, 2004 (PARTIAL)**</td></tr>
<tr><td>Current liabilities</td><td></td></tr>
<tr><td> Income tax payable</td><td align="right">$77,000</td></tr>
<tr><td> Future income tax liability</td><td align="right">22,400</td></tr>
<tr><td>Long-term liabilities</td><td></td></tr>
<tr><td> Future income tax liability</td><td align="right">$80,000</td></tr>
</table>

Illustration 19-51

Financial Statement Presentation—2004

<table>
<tr><td colspan="3" align="center">**INCOME STATEMENT, YEAR ENDED DECEMBER 31, 2004 (PARTIAL)**</td></tr>
<tr><td>Income before income tax</td><td></td><td align="right">$412,000</td></tr>
<tr><td>Income tax expense</td><td></td><td></td></tr>
<tr><td> Current</td><td align="right">$77,000</td><td></td></tr>
<tr><td> Future</td><td align="right">102,400</td><td align="right">179,400</td></tr>
<tr><td>Net income</td><td></td><td align="right">$232,600</td></tr>
</table>

Second Year 2005

1. During 2005, the company collected one-fifth of the sales price from customers for the receivables arising from contracts completed in 2004. Recovery of the remaining receivables is still expected to result in taxable amounts of $112,000 in each of the following three years.

2. In 2005, the company completed four new contracts with a total selling price of $1 million (to be paid in five equal instalments beginning in 2005) and gross profit of $320,000. For financial reporting purposes, the full $320,000 is recognized in 2005, whereas for tax purposes the gross profit is deferred and taken into taxable income as the cash is received; that is, one-fifth or $64,000 in 2005 and one-fifth in each of 2006 to 2009.

3. During 2005, Allman continued to amortize the assets acquired in 2004 according to the amortization and CCA schedules that appear on page 1028. Therefore, amortization expense amounted to $90,000 and CCA of $97,200 was claimed for tax purposes.

4. Information about the product warranty liability account and timing of warranty expenditures at the end of 2005 is reported below.

Illustration 19-52

Warranty Liability and Expenditure Information

Balance of liability at beginning of 2005	$156,000
Expense for 2005 income statement purposes	180,000
Amount paid for contracts completed in 2004	(62,000)
Amount paid for contracts completed in 2005	(50,000)
Balance of liability at end of 2005	$224,000
Estimated warranty expenditures:	
$ 94,000 in 2006 due to 2004 contracts	
$ 50,000 in 2006 due to 2005 contracts	
$ 80,000 in 2007 due to 2005 contracts	
$224,000	

5. During 2005, nontaxable dividend revenue was $24,000.

6. A loss of $172,000 was accrued for financial reporting purposes because of pending litigation. This amount is not tax deductible until the period the loss is realized, which is estimated to be 2010.

7. Accounting income for 2005 is $504,800.

8. The tax rate in effect for 2005 is 40%; tax rate increases have been enacted for 2006 and subsequent years at 42%.

Taxable Income, Income Tax Payable, Current Income Tax Expense—2005. The calculation of taxable income, income tax payable, and current income tax expense for 2005 is illustrated below.

Illustration 19-53

Calculation of Taxable Income and Taxes Payable—2005

Accounting income for 2005	$504,800
Permanent difference:	
Nontaxable revenue—dividends	(24,000)
Timing differences:	
Collection on 2004 instalment sales	112,000
Excess gross profit per books—2005 contracts ($320,000 − $64,000)	(256,000)
Excess CCA ($97,200 − $90,000)	(7,200)
Payments on warranties from 2004 contracts	(62,000)
Excess warranty expense per books—2005 contracts ($180,000 − $50,000)	130,000
Loss accrual per books	172,000
Taxable income for 2005	$569,600
Income tax payable (current income tax expense) for 2005: $569,600 × 40%	$227,840

Future Income Tax Assets and Liabilities at December 31, 2005, and 2005 Future Income Tax Expense. The next step is to determine the correct balance of the net future income tax asset or liability account at December 31, 2005. The amount required to adjust this account to its correct balance is the future income tax expense/benefit for 2005.

The following schedule is helpful in summarizing the temporary differences existing at the end of 2005 and the resulting future taxable and deductible amounts.

	Future Years				
	2006	2007	2008	2009+	Total
Future taxable (deductible) amounts:					
Instalment sales—2004	$112,000	$112,000	$112,000		$336,000
Instalment sales—2005	64,000	64,000	64,000	$ 64,000	$256,000
Amortization	12,240	27,792	40,234	(109,066)	(28,800)
Warranty costs	(144,000)	(80,000)			(224,000)
Loss accrual				(172,000)	(172,000)
Net taxable (deductible) amount	$ 44,240	$123,792	$216,234	$(217,066)	$167,200
Tax rate enacted for year	42%	42%	42%	42%	
Net future tax liability (asset)	$ 18,581	$ 51,993	$ 90,818	$ (91,168)	$ 70,224

Illustration 19-54

Future Taxable/Deductible Amounts and Future Tax Liability, December 31, 2005

The temporary difference caused by the use of the accrual method for financial reporting purposes and the instalment method for tax purposes results in future taxable amounts; hence, a future tax liability exists. A taxable temporary difference of $336,000 remains on the contracts completed in 2004, and $256,000 relates to the 2005 contracts.

To the end of 2005, $28,800 less CCA has been claimed than amortization. In the future there will be $28,800 more CCA deductible for tax purposes than amortization taken on the books. The temporary difference due to warranty costs will result in deductible amounts in each of 2006 and 2007 as this difference reverses, and the $172,000 loss not deductible for tax purposes this year will be deductible in the future.

Again, because the future tax rates are identical, the future tax liability could have been calculated by simply applying the 42% rate to the net taxable amount at the end of 2005 of $167,200. For those who prefer to calculate the future tax asset and the future tax liability balances separately, the calculations are shown on the following schedule along with the determination of the future income tax expense for the year.

	Carrying Amount	Tax Basis	Taxable (Deductible) Temporary Differences
Assets			
Accounts receivable (Gross profit			
included therein)—from 2004 sales	$ 336,000	–0–	$336,000
—from 2005 sales	256,000	–0–	256,000
Plant and equipment	360,000	$388,800	(28,800)
Liabilities			
Liability for warranties			
—from 2004 sales	94,000	–0–	(94,000)
—from 2005 sales	130,000	–0–	(130,000)
Litigation liability	172,000	–0–	(172,000)
Net taxable (deductible) temporary difference			$167,200
Future income tax liability:			
($336,000 + $256,000) at 42%			$248,640
Future income tax asset:			
($28,800 + $94,000 + $130,000 + $172,000)			
at 42%			(178,416)
Net future income tax liability,			
December 31, 2005			70,224
Net future income tax liability,			
opening balance			102,400
Decrease in liability account, and future			
income tax expense (benefit)—2005			$(32,176)

Illustration 19-55

Determination of Future Income Tax Expense/Benefit—2005

Income Tax Accounting Entries—2005.   The entries to record current and future income taxes for 2005 are as follows.

A = L + SE
    +227,840   −227,840
Cash flows: No effect

| Current Income Tax Expense | 227,840 | |
| Income Tax Payable (Illustration 19-53) | | 227,840 |

A = L + SE
   −32,176   +32,176
Cash flows: No effect

| Future Income Tax Liability | 32,176 | |
| Future Income Tax Benefit[30] | | 32,176 |

Financial Statement Presentation—2005.   The classification of Allman's future tax account at the end of 2005 is shown below.

Illustration 19-56

Classification of Future Tax Asset/Liability Account

Balance Sheet Account	Balance Sheet Classification	Temporary Difference	Resulting Future Tax (Asset)	Liability	Classification of Future Tax Account Current	Long-term
Instalment receivables	mixed	$592,000		$248,640	$73,920	$174,720
Depreciable assets	LT	(28,800)	(12,096)			(12,096)
Liability for warranties	mixed	(224,000)	(94,080)		(60,480)	(33,600)
Loss accrual	LT	(172,000)	(72,240)			(72,240)
		$167,200	$(178,416)	$248,640	$13,440(L)	$ 56,784(L)

The future tax accounts related to the instalment receivables and the warranties are, once again, allocated as current based on the portion of each of the balance sheet accounts that is reported in the current category: $176,000 × 42% = $73,920 for the receivables, and $144,000 × 42% = $60,480 for the warranties. The depreciable assets are long-term assets. The new temporary difference introduced in 2005 due to the litigation loss accrual results in a litigation obligation that is classified as a long-term liability. Therefore, the related future tax asset is noncurrent. The balance sheet at the end of 2005 and the 2005 income statement report the following amounts.

Illustration 19-57

Financial Statement Presentation—2005

BALANCE SHEET, DECEMBER 31, 2005 (PARTIAL)

Current liabilities	
Income tax payable	$227,840
Future income tax liability	13,440
Long-term liabilities	
Future income tax liability	$56,784

INCOME STATEMENT, YEAR ENDED DECEMBER 31, 2005 (PARTIAL)

Income before income tax		$504,800
Income tax expense		
Current	$227,840	
Future	(32,176)*	195,664
Net income		$309,136

*Components may be disclosed

---

[30] Two accounts could have been used here if separate future tax asset and liability accounts were used: a debit of $101,616 to a Future Income Tax Asset (i.e., $178,416 − $76,800) and a credit to a Future Income Tax Liability of $69,440 (i.e., $248,640 − $179,200). See footnote 29 for 2005 opening balances of these accounts.

As the major components of income tax expense are required to be disclosed in some cases and are desirable in others, a further analysis can determine how much of the future tax expense is due to a change in the rate of tax used to measure the net future tax liability and how much is due to a change in temporary differences. Because the tax rate for measuring the net future tax **liability** increased from 40% to 42%, the change in rate results in an increase in both the liability and the future tax expense. The analysis to explain the $32,176 benefit is as follows.

Future income tax expense (benefit) due to:		
• **Increase in tax rate**		
Opening future tax liability at 40%	$102,400	
Opening future tax liability at 42% ($256,000 × .42)	107,520	$5,120
• **Originating and reversing timing differences during 2005**		
Opening future tax liability at 42%	107,520	
Ending future tax liability at 42%	70,224	
Decrease in net future tax liability		(37,296)
Change in future income tax liability, and future income tax expense (benefit) for 2005		$(32,176)

Illustration 19-58

Analysis of Future Income Tax Benefit—2005

Summary of Learning Objectives

1 Explain the difference between accounting income and taxable income.

Accounting income (income reported on the income statement before income taxes) is calculated in accordance with generally accepted accounting principles. Taxable income is calculated in accordance with prescribed tax legislation and regulations. Because tax legislation and GAAP have different objectives, accounting income and taxable income often differ.

2 Explain what a taxable temporary difference is and why a future tax liability is recognized.

A taxable temporary difference is the difference between the carrying value of an asset or liability and its tax basis such that when the asset is recovered or liability is settled in the future for an amount equal to its carrying value, taxable income of that future period will be increased. Because taxes arise in the future as a result of temporary differences existing at the balance sheet date, the future tax consequences of these taxable amounts are recognized in the current period as a future tax liability.

3 Explain what a deductible temporary difference is and why a future tax asset is recognized.

A deductible temporary difference is the difference between the carrying value of an asset or liability and its tax basis such that when the asset is recovered or a liability is settled in the future for an amount equal to its carrying value, taxable income of that future period will be reduced. Because tax reductions arise in the future as a result of temporary differences existing at the balance sheet date, the future tax consequences of these deductible amounts are recognized in the current period as a future tax asset.

4 Differentiate among timing, temporary, and permanent differences.

Temporary differences are differences between the carrying values of assets and liabilities in the accounts and the values of the same assets and liabilities for tax purposes. The differences originate and change whenever a revenue or expense is

Digital Tool

Glossary

www.wiley.com/canada/kieso

KEY TERMS

accounting income, 993
asset-liability method, 993
deductible temporary
    difference, 995
effective tax rate, 1007
future income tax
    asset, 1000
future income tax
    liability, 996
future tax expense, 997
interperiod tax
    allocation, 999
intraperiod tax
    allocation, 1018
liability method, 993
loss carryback, 1009
loss carryforward, 1009
loss for income tax
    purposes, 1009
more likely than not, 1000
originating timing
    difference, 1004
permanent
    differences, 1004
reversing timing
    difference, 1004
taxable income, 993
taxable temporary
    difference, 995
tax loss, 1009
taxes payable
    method, 1025
temporary difference, 995
timing differences, 1004
valuation allowance, 1014

recognized in a different accounting period for tax purposes than for financial reporting purposes. In any given year, there are usually differences between income reported on the financial statements and taxable income on the tax return. Those that had no past and have no future tax consequences are known as permanent differences. Their effect is confined to the current period. Those that relate to recognizing revenues and expenses in different periods for book and tax purposes are known as timing differences. Timing differences, therefore, initiate and cause changes in the amount of temporary differences.

5 Prepare analyses and related journal entries to record income tax expense when there are multiple temporary differences.

With multiple differences, the following steps are followed: (1) calculate taxable income and taxes payable; (2) identify all temporary differences between carrying and tax values at the balance sheet date; (3) calculate the net future income tax asset or liability at the end of the period; (4) compare the opening future tax asset or liability with that at the balance sheet date, the difference being the future tax expense; (5) prepare the journal entries based on the tax payable or receivable (the current tax expense or benefit) and the change in the amount of the net future tax asset or liability (the future tax expense or benefit).

6 Explain the effect of various tax rates and tax rate changes on future income tax accounts.

Tax rates other than the current rate may be used only when the future tax rates have been enacted into legislation or substantively enacted. When there is a change in the future tax rate, its effect on the future income tax accounts should be recognized immediately. The effects are reported as an adjustment to future income tax expense in the period of the change.

7 Apply accounting procedures for a tax loss carryback.

A company may carry a taxable loss back three years and receive refunds to a maximum of the income taxes paid in those years. Because the economic benefits related to the losses carried back are certain, they are recognized in the period of the loss as a tax benefit on the income statement and as an asset, Income Tax Refund Receivable, on the balance sheet.

8 Apply accounting procedures and disclosure requirements for a tax loss carryforward.

A tax loss can be carried forward and applied against the taxable incomes of the succeeding seven years. If the economic benefits related to the tax loss are more likely than not to be realized because of the likelihood of generating sufficient taxable income during the carryforward period, they can be recognized in the period of the loss as a tax benefit in the income statement and as a future tax asset on the balance sheet. If the economic benefits are not more likely than not to be realized, they should not be recognized in the financial statements. Alternatively, they may be recognized in the accounts along with a contra valuation allowance account. Disclosure is required of the amounts of tax loss carryforwards and their expiry dates. If previously unrecorded tax losses are subsequently used to benefit a future period, the benefit is recognized in that future period.

9 Explain why the future income tax asset account is reassessed at the balance sheet date.

Consistent with asset valuation principles in general, every asset must be assessed to ensure it is not reported at an amount in excess of the economic benefits expected to be received from the use or sale of the asset. The economic benefit to be received from the future income tax asset is the reduction in future income taxes payable. If it is unlikely that sufficient taxable income will be generated in the future to allow the entity to benefit from future deductible amounts, the income tax asset may have to be written down. If previously unrecognized amounts are now expected to be realizable, a future tax asset is recognized. These entries may be made directly to the future tax asset account or through a valuation allowance contra account.

10 **Explain the need for and be able to apply intraperiod tax allocation.**

Because the income statement is classified into income before discontinued operations and extraordinary items, discontinued operations, and extraordinary items, the income taxes associated with each component are reported with that component. Taxes related to items reported in retained earnings and those associated with share capital should also be reported with the related items in the financial statements.

11 **Identify the reporting and disclosure requirements for corporate income taxes.**

Income taxes currently payable (or receivable) are reported separately as a current liability (or current asset) on the balance sheet. Future income tax assets and liabilities are classified as one net current and one net noncurrent amount based on the classification of the asset or liability to which the temporary difference relates. If a future tax asset or liability arose from other than an existing balance sheet account, it is classified according to when the temporary differences are expected to reverse. On the income statement, current and future tax expense is disclosed for income before discontinued operations and extraordinary items. Separate disclosure is required of the amounts and expiry dates of unused tax losses, the amount of deductible temporary differences for which no future tax asset has been recognized, and any tax expense related to items charged or credited to equity. For companies that have outstanding financing from public markets, additional disclosures are required about temporary differences and unused tax losses, about the major components of income tax expense, and the reasons for the difference between the statutory tax rate and the effective rate indicated on the income statement.

12 **Describe the differential reporting option for income taxes.**

For qualifying companies—non-publicly accountable entities whose owners all agree—the simpler taxes payable method of accounting is permitted for income taxes. This is one area where differential reporting is allowed within GAAP.

13 **Describe the key aspects of the asset-liability method and identify outstanding issues with this approach.**

The following basic principles are applied in accounting for income taxes under the asset-liability approach at the date of the financial statements: (1) a current tax liability or asset is recognized for the estimated taxes payable or received on the tax return for the current year; (2) a future tax liability or asset is recognized for the estimated future tax effects attributable to temporary differences and carryforwards; (3) the measurement of current and future tax liabilities and assets is based on provisions of enacted tax law; (4) the measurement of future tax assets is reduced, if necessary, by the amount of any benefits that, based on available evidence, are not expected to be realized. Those who agree with this method of comprehensive tax allocation are not all agreed on issues related to whether the future tax amounts should be measured at their discounted present values, the basis on which future tax assets and liabilities are classified, and the degree of certainty that should exist before the benefits of future deductible amounts and tax losses should be given accounting recognition.

Brief Exercises

BE19-1   In 2005, Gonzales Corporation had accounting income of $168,000 and taxable income of $110,000. The difference is due to the use of different amortization methods for tax and accounting purposes. The effective tax rate is 40%. Calculate the amount to be reported as income taxes payable at December 31, 2005.

BE19-2   At December 31, 2005, Thunderforce Inc. owned equipment that had a book value of $80,000 and a tax basis of $48,000 due to the use of different amortization methods for accounting and tax purposes. The enacted tax rate is 35%. Calculate the amount Thunderforce should report as a future tax liability at December 31, 2005.

BE19-3   At December 31, 2004, Serbius Corporation had a future tax liability of $25,000. At December 31, 2005, the future tax liability is $42,000. The corporation's 2005 current tax expense is $43,000. What amount should Serbius report as total 2005 income tax expense?

BE19-4   Merridit Corp. began operations in 2005 and reported accounting income of $225,000 for the year. Merridit's CCA exceeded its book amortization by $30,000. Merridit's tax rate for 2005 and years thereafter is 30%. In its December 31, 2005 balance sheet, what amount of future income tax liability should be reported?

BE19-5   Using the information from BE19-4, assume this is the only difference between Merridit's accounting income and taxable income. Prepare the journal entry(ies) to record the current income tax expense, future income tax expense, income taxes payable, and the future income tax liability.

BE19-6   At December 31, 2005, Spacene Corporation had an estimated warranty liability of $125,000 for accounting purposes and $0 for tax purposes. (The warranty costs are not deductible until paid.) The tax rate is 40%. Calculate the amount Spacene should report as a future tax asset at December 31, 2005.

BE19-7   At December 31, 2004, Next Inc. had a future tax asset of $35,000. At December 31, 2005, the future tax asset is $59,000. The corporation's 2005 current tax expense is $61,000. What amount should Next report as total 2005 tax expense?

BE19-8   Jazman Inc. had accounting income of $154,000 in 2005. Included in the calculation of that amount is insurance expense of $4,000, which is not deductible for tax purposes. In addition, the CCA for tax purposes exceeds accounting amortization by $14,000. Prepare Jazman's journal entry to record 2005 taxes, assuming a tax rate of 45%.

BE19-9   Using the information from BE19-8, calculate the effective rate of income tax for Jazman Inc. for 2005. Reconcile from the statutory rate to the effective rate, using percentages.

BE19-10   Using the information from BE19-8, prepare Jazman's journal entry to record 2005 taxes. Assume a tax rate of 45% and that Jazman's shareholders have decided to use the taxes payable method of accounting for income taxes as a permitted differential accounting option.

BE19-11   Steagal Corporation had income before income taxes of $175,000 in 2005. Steagal's current income tax expense is $40,000, and future income tax expense is $30,000. Prepare Steagal's 2005 income statement, beginning with income before income taxes.

BE19-12   Minator Corporation has a taxable temporary difference related to amortization of $630,000 at December 31, 2005. This difference will reverse as follows: 2006, $42,000; 2007, $294,000; and 2008, $294,000. Enacted tax rates are 34% for 2006 and 2007, and 40% for 2008. Calculate the amount Minator should report as a future tax asset or liability at December 31, 2005.

BE19-13   At December 31, 2004, Ricks Corporation had a future tax asset of $680,000, resulting from future deductible amounts of $2 million and an enacted tax rate of 34%. In May 2005, new income tax legislation is signed into law that raises the tax rate to 36% for 2005 and future years. Prepare the journal entry for Ricks to adjust the future tax account.

BE19-14   Valquois Corporation had the following tax information.

Year	Taxable Income	Tax Rate	Taxes Paid
2002	$300,000	35%	$105,000
2003	$325,000	30%	$ 97,500
2004	$400,000	30%	$120,000

In 2005, Valquois suffered a net operating loss of $450,000, which it elected to carry back. The 2005 enacted tax rate is 29%. Prepare Valquois' entry to record the effect of the loss carryback.

BE19-15 Zoopler Inc. incurred a net operating loss of $500,000 in 2005. Combined income for 2002, 2003, and 2004 was $400,000. The tax rate for all years is 40%. Prepare the journal entries to record the benefits of the carryback and the carryforward, assuming it is more likely than not that the benefits of the loss carryforward will be realized.

BE19-16 Use the information for Zoopler Inc. given in BE19-15. Assume that it is more likely than not that the entire tax loss carryforward will not be realized in future years. Prepare all the journal entries necessary at the end of 2005 assuming (a) Zoopler does not use a valuation allowance account, and (b) Zoopler uses a valuation allowance account.

BE19-17 Use the information for Zoopler Inc. given in BE19-16. Assume that Zoopler earns taxable income of $25,000 in 2006 and at the end of 2006, there is still too much uncertainty to recognize a future tax asset. Prepare all the journal entries necessary at the end of 2006 assuming (a) Zoopler does not use a valuation allowance account, and (b) Zoopler uses a valuation allowance account.

BE19-18 At December 31, 2005, Stargat Corporation has a future tax asset of $200,000. After a careful review of all available evidence, it is determined that it is more likely than not that $80,000 of this future tax asset will not be realized. Prepare the necessary journal entry assuming (a) Stargat does not use a valuation allowance account, and (b) Stargat uses a valuation allowance account.

BE19-19 LePage Inc. reported income from continuing operations of $66,000, a loss from discontinued operations of $10,000, and an extraordinary gain of $23,000 in 2005, all before income taxes. All items are fully taxable and deductible for tax purposes. Prepare the bottom of the income statement for LePage Inc. beginning with income from continuing operations before income taxes and extraordinary items, assuming a tax rate of 40%.

BE19-20 Vector Corporation has temporary differences at December 31, 2005 that result in the following balance sheet future tax accounts.

Future tax liability current	$38,000
Future tax asset current	$52,000
Future tax liability noncurrent	$96,000
Future tax asset noncurrent	$27,000

Indicate how these balances will be presented in Vector's December 31, 2005 balance sheet.

Exercises

E19-1 **(Identify Temporary or Permanent Differences)** Listed below are items that are commonly accounted for differently for financial reporting purposes than they are for tax purposes.

Instructions

For each item below, indicate whether it involves:

(a) A timing difference that will result in future deductible amounts and, therefore, will usually give rise to a future income tax asset.

(b) A timing difference that will result in future taxable amounts and, therefore, will usually give rise to a future income tax liability.

(c) A permanent difference.

Use the appropriate letter to indicate your answer for each.

_____ 1. CCA, a declining-balance method, is used for tax purposes, and the straight-line amortization method is used for financial reporting purposes for some plant assets. A 20% rate is used for both. Ignore the half-year rule.

_____ 2. A landlord collects rents in advance. Rents are taxable in the period when they are received.

_____ 3. Non-deductible expenses are incurred in obtaining tax-exempt income.

_____ 4. Costs of guarantees and warranties are estimated and accrued for financial reporting purposes.

_____ 5. Instalment sales are accounted for by the accrual method for financial reporting purposes and the cash basis for tax purposes.

_____ **6.** For some assets, straight-line amortization is used for both financial reporting purposes and tax purposes but the assets' lives are shorter for tax purposes.

_____ **7.** Pension expense is reported on the income statement before it is funded. Pension costs are deductible only when funded.

_____ **8.** Proceeds are received from a life insurance company because of the death of a key officer (the company carries a policy on key officers).

_____ **9.** The tax return reports no revenue for the dividends received from taxable Canadian corporations. The company reports the dividends received as investment income on its income statement.

_____ **10.** Estimated losses on pending lawsuits and claims are accrued for financial reporting purposes. These losses are tax deductible in the period(s) when the related liabilities are settled.

E19-2 (Terminology, Relationships, Calculations, Entries)

Instructions

Complete the following statements by filling in the blanks.

(a) In a period in which a taxable temporary difference reverses, the reversal will cause taxable income to be _____ (less than, greater than) accounting income.

(b) If a $76,000 balance in Future Tax Asset was calculated by use of a 40% rate, the underlying temporary difference amounts to $_____.

(c) Future taxes _____ (are, are not) recorded to account for permanent differences.

(d) If a taxable temporary difference originates in 2005, it causes taxable income of 2005 to be _____ (less than, greater than) accounting income for 2005.

(e) If total tax expense is $50,000 and future tax expense is $65,000, then the current portion of the expense is referred to as current tax _____ (expense, benefit) of $_____.

(f) If a corporation's tax return shows taxable income of $100,000 for Year 2 and a tax rate of 40%, how much will appear on the December 31, Year 2 balance sheet for "Income tax payable" if the company has made estimated tax payments of $36,500 for Year 2? $_____

(g) An increase in the Future Tax Liability account on the balance sheet is recorded by a _____ (debit, credit) to the Future Income Tax Expense account.

(h) An income statement that reports current tax expense of $82,000 and future tax benefit of $23,000 will report total income tax expense of $_____.

(i) A valuation account may be used whenever it is judged to be _____ that a portion of a future tax asset _____ (will be, will not be) realized.

(j) If the tax return shows total taxes due for the period of $75,000 but the income statement shows total income tax expense of $55,000, the difference of $20,000 is referred to as future tax _____ (expense, benefit).

E19-3 (One Temporary Difference, Future Taxable Amounts, One Rate, No Beginning Future Taxes)   South Shore Corporation has one temporary difference at the end of 2005 that will reverse and cause taxable amounts of $55,000 in 2006, $60,000 in 2007, and $65,000 in 2008. South Shore's accounting income for 2005 is $300,000 and the tax rate is 30% for all years. There are no future tax accounts at the beginning of 2005.

Instructions

(a) Calculate taxable income and income taxes payable for 2005.

(b) Prepare the journal entries to record income taxes for 2005.

(c) Prepare the income tax expense section of the income statement for 2005, beginning with the line "Income before income taxes."

E19-4 (One Temporary Difference, Future Taxable Amounts, One Rate, Beginning Future Taxes)   Use the information for South Shore Corporation in E19-3. Assume the company reports accounting income of $300,000 in each of 2006 and 2007, but no other temporary differences than identified in E19-3.

Instructions

(a) Calculate taxable income and income taxes payable for 2006 and 2007.

(b) Prepare the journal entries to record income taxes for 2006 and 2007.

(c) Prepare the income tax expense section of the income statements for 2006 and 2007, beginning with the line "Income before income taxes."

E19-5 (One Temporary Difference through Three Years, One Rate) Odessa Corporation reports the following amounts in its first three years of operations.

	2005	2006	2007
Taxable income	160,000	139,000	140,000
Accounting income	200,000	120,000	125,000

The difference between taxable income and accounting income is due to one temporary difference. The tax rate is 40% for all years and the company expects to continue with profitable operations in the future.

Instructions

(a) For each year, (1) identify the amount of the temporary difference originating or reversing during that year, and (2) indicate the amount of the temporary difference at the end of the year.

(b) Indicate the balance in the related future tax account at the end of each year and identify it as either a future tax asset or liability.

E19-6 (One Temporary Difference, Future Deductible Amounts, One Rate, No Beginning Future Taxes) North River Corporation has accrued $100,000 of restructuring charges at the end of 2005 that are deductible only when the costs are incurred. This temporary difference will reverse and cause deductible amounts of $40,000 in 2006, $35,000 in 2007, and $25,000 in 2008. North River's accounting income for 2005 is $120,000 and the tax rate is 25% for all years. There are no future tax accounts at the beginning of 2005.

Interactive Homework

Instructions

(a) Calculate taxable income and income taxes payable for 2005.

(b) Prepare the journal entries to record income taxes for 2005.

(c) Prepare the income tax expense section of the income statement for 2005, beginning with the line "Income before income taxes."

E19-7 (One Temporary Difference, Future Deductible Amounts, One Rate, Beginning Future Taxes) Use the information for North River Corporation in E19-6. Assume the company reports accounting income of $120,000 in each of 2006 and 2007, but no other temporary differences than identified in E19-6.

Instructions

(a) Calculate taxable income and income taxes payable for 2006 and 2007.

(b) Prepare the journal entries to record income taxes for 2006 and 2007.

(c) Prepare the income tax expense section of the income statements for 2006 and 2007, beginning with the line "Income before income taxes."

E19-8 (Permanent and Timing Differences, Calculate Taxable Income, Entry for Taxes) Geneva Inc. reports accounting income of $70,000 for 2005. The following items cause taxable income to be different than income reported on the financial statements.

Interactive Homework

1. Amortization on the tax return is greater than amortization on the income statement by $16,000.

2. Rent reported on the tax return is greater than rent earned on the income statement by $22,000.

3. Non-deductible fines for pollution appear as an expense of $11,000 on the income statement.

4. Geneva's tax rate is 30% for all years and the company expects to report taxable income in all future years. There are no future taxes at the beginning of 2005.

Instructions

(a) Calculate taxable income and income taxes payable for 2005.

(b) Prepare the journal entries to record income taxes for 2005.

(c) Prepare the income tax expense section of the income statement for 2005, beginning with the line "Income before income taxes."

(d) Reconcile the statutory and effective rates of income tax for 2005.

E19-9 **(Timing and Permanent Differences, Calculate Taxable Income, Three Years)** In 2005 to 2007, Cheng Corporation's first three years of operations, the company reported accounting incomes of $10,000, $15,000, and $17,000, respectively. The following differences existed between accounting income and taxable income over this three-year period, all but two of the differences reversing by the end of the three years. The tax rate for all three years remained at 25%.

	2005	2006	2007
Depreciation reported in income	$9,000	$9,000	$9,000
CCA reported on tax return	6,000	8,500	12,500
Nontaxable dividends	2,500	2,600	2,700
Gross profit reported in income	8,700	5,300	2,000
Gross profit reported on tax return	4,500	4,500	7,000
Non-deductible tax penalty for late filing		750	
Product loss recognized in income	11,000	2,000	
Product loss recognized on tax return			13,000

Instructions

(a) Determine the amount of taxable income for each of 2005, 2006, and 2007.

(b) Prepare the journal entry to record current income taxes in each year.

E19-10 **(Two Differences, No Beginning Future Taxes, Tracked through Two Years)**   The following information is available for Wenger Corporation for 2005.

1. Excess of tax amortization over book amortization, $40,000. This $40,000 difference will reverse in equal amounts over the years 2006 to 2009.

2. Deferral, for book purposes, of $20,000 of rent received in advance. The rent will be earned in 2006, but is taxable in 2005.

3. Accounting income, $300,000.

4. Tax rate for all years, 40%.

Instructions

(a) Calculate taxable income for 2005.

(b) Prepare the journal entries to record income taxes for 2005.

(c) Prepare the journal entries to record income taxes for 2006, assuming taxable income of $325,000 and no temporary differences except those referred to above.

E19-11 **(Two Temporary Differences, One Rate, Beginning Future Taxes)**   The following facts relate to Kumar Corporation.

1. Future tax liability, January 1, 2005, $40,000.

2. Future tax asset, January 1, 2005, $0.

3. Taxable income for 2005, $95,000.

4. Accounting income for 2005, $200,000.

5. Temporary difference at December 31, 2005, giving rise to future taxable amounts, $240,000.

6. Temporary difference at December 31, 2005, giving rise to future deductible amounts, $35,000.

7. Tax rate for all years, 40%.

8. The company is expected to operate profitably in the future.

Instructions

(a) Calculate income taxes payable for 2005.

(b) Prepare the journal entry(ies) to record income taxes for 2005.

(c) Prepare the income tax expense section of the income statement for 2005, beginning with the line "Income before income taxes."

Interactive Homework

E19-12 **(Two Temporary Differences, One Rate, Beginning Future Taxes)**   The following facts relate to Sabrinad Corporation.

1. Temporary difference at January 1, 2005, giving rise to future taxable amounts, $150,000.

2. Temporary difference at December 31, 2005, giving rise to future taxable amounts, $230,000.

3. Temporary difference at January 1, 2005, giving rise to future deductible amounts, $50,000.

4. Temporary difference at December 31, 2005, giving rise to future deductible amounts, $95,000.

5. Accounting income for 2005, $140,000.

6. Tax rate for all years, 40%. No permanent differences exist.

7. The company is expected to operate profitably in the future.

Instructions

(a) Calculate the amount of taxable income for 2005.

(b) Prepare the journal entries to record income taxes for 2005.

(c) Prepare the income tax expense section of the income statement for 2005, beginning with the line "Income before income taxes."

(d) Calculate the effective tax rate for 2005. Comment.

E19-13 (Three Differences, Classification of Future Taxes)   At December 31, 2005, Surya Corporation had a net future tax liability of $375,000. An explanation of the items that make up this balance follows.

Temporary Differences	Resulting Balances in Future Tax Account
1. Accumulated excess of tax amortization over book amortization	$200,000
2. Accrual, for book purposes, of estimated loss contingency from pending lawsuit that is expected to be settled in 2006. The loss will be deducted on the tax return when paid.	(50,000)
3. Accrual method used for book purposes and instalment method used for tax purposes for an isolated instalment sale of an investment.	225,000
	$375,000

Instructions

Indicate the manner in which future taxes should be presented on Surya Corporation's December 31, 2005 balance sheet.

E19-14 (Amortization, Temporary Difference over Five Years, Determine Taxable Income, Taxes Payable Method)   Patrician Corp. purchased depreciable assets costing $600,000 on January 2, 2004. For tax purposes, the company uses CCA in a class that has a 40% rate. For financial reporting purposes, the company uses straight-line amortization over five years. The enacted tax rate is 34% for all years. This amortization difference is the only temporary difference the company has. Assume that Patrician has income before taxes of $340,000 in each of the years 2004 to 2008 and that all remaining CCA in 2008 can be deducted in that year.

Instructions

(a) Determine the amount of taxable income in each year from 2004 to 2008.

(b) Determine the amount of future income taxes that should be reported in the balance sheet for each year from 2004 to 2008 and indicate where the account(s) should be reported.

(c) Prepare the journal entries to record income taxes for each year from 2004 to 2008.

(d) Prepare the income tax entry(ies) to record income taxes for each year assuming the shareholders have decided on the differential accounting option (taxes payable basis).

E19-15 (One Difference, Multiple Rates, Beginning Future Taxes, Change in Rates)   At the end of 2004, McNevil Corporation reported a Future Tax Liability of $22,000. At the end of 2005, the company has $180,000 of temporary differences that will result in reporting future taxable amounts as follows.

2006	$ 60,000
2007	50,000
2008	40,000
2009	30,000
	$180,000

Tax rates enacted as of the beginning of 2004 are: 2004 and 2005—40%; 2006 and 2007—30%; 2008 and later—25%. McNevil's taxable income for 2005 is $320,000. Taxable income is expected in all future years.

Instructions

(a) Prepare journal entries for McNevil to record income taxes for 2005.

(b) Early in 2006, after the 2005 financial statements were released, new tax rates were enacted as follows: 2006—29%; 2007 and later—27%. Prepare the journal entry for McNevil to recognize the change in tax rates.

Interactive
Homework

E19-16   (Future Tax Liability, Change in Tax Rate)   Notkovich Inc.'s only temporary difference at the beginning and end of 2005 is caused by a $3 million future gain for tax purposes on an instalment sale of a plant asset. The related receivable (only one-half of which is classified as a current asset) is due in equal instalments in 2006 and 2007. The related future tax liability at the beginning of the year is $1.2 million. In the third quarter of 2005, a new tax rate of 34% is enacted into law and is scheduled to become effective for 2007. Taxable income for 2005 is $5 million and taxable income is expected in all future years.

Instructions

(a) Determine the amount reported as a future tax liability at the end of 2005. Indicate proper classification(s).

(b) Prepare the journal entry (if any) necessary to adjust the future tax liability when the new tax rate is enacted into law.

(c) Draft the income tax expense portion of the income statement for 2005. Begin with the line "Income before income taxes." No permanent differences exist.

E19-17   (Two Differences, Multiple Rates, No Beginning Future Taxes)   In 2004, Wolff Corporation reported amortization expense of $200,000 in its income statement. On its 2004 income tax return, Wolff reported CCA of $320,000. Wolff's income statement also included $80,000 accrued warranty expense that will be deductible for tax purposes when paid. Wolff reported accounting income of $300,000 in 2004. The enacted tax rates are 35% for 2004 and 2005, and 40% for 2006 and subsequent years. The amortization difference and warranty expense will reverse over the next four years as follows.

	Amortization Difference	Warranty Expense
2005	$40,000	$10,000
2006	35,000	15,000
2007	25,000	25,000
2008	20,000	30,000
	$120,000	$80,000

Instructions

(a) Calculate income taxes payable for 2004.

(b) Prepare journal entries to record income taxes for 2004.

(c) Prepare the income tax expense section of the income statement for 2004, beginning with the line "Income before taxes."

(d) Prepare the income tax expense section of the income statement for 2004, beginning with the line "Income before taxes," assuming the differential reporting option was chosen (taxes payable method).

E19-18   (Three Differences, Multiple Rates)   During 2005, Nicole Corp.'s first year of operations, the company reports accounting income of $250,000. Nicole's enacted tax rate is 45% for 2005 and 40% for all later years. Nicole expects to have taxable income in each of the next five years. The effects on future tax returns of temporary differences existing at December 31, 2005 are summarized below.

	Future Years					
	2006	2007	2008	2009	2010	Total
Future taxable (deductible) amounts:						
Instalment sales	$32,000	$32,000	$32,000			$96,000
Amortization	6,000	6,000	6,000	$6,000	$6,000	30,000
Unearned rent	(50,000)	(50,000)				(100,000)

Instructions

(a) Complete the schedule below to calculate future taxes at December 31, 2005.

(b) Calculate taxable income for 2005.

(c) Prepare the journal entries to record income taxes for 2005.

Temporary Difference	Future Taxable (Deductible) Amounts	Tax Rate	December 31, 2005 Future Tax Asset	Liability
Instalment sales	$ 96,000			
Amortization	30,000			
Unearned rent	(100,000)			
Totals	$			

E19-19 (Taxes Payable Method—Differential Reporting Disclosures)   Refer to the information in E19-18 for Nicole Corp. Assume that the company is not publicly accountable and its shareholders have agreed that the taxes payable method of accounting will be used for income taxes.

Instructions

(a) Prepare the journal entry(ies) to record income taxes at December 31, 2005.

(b) Prepare the additional disclosures necessitated by the choice of the taxes payable method.

E19-20 (Carryback and Carryforward of Tax Loss)   The accounting income (or loss) figures for Spangler Corporation are as follows.

2000	$160,000
2001	250,000
2002	80,000
2003	(160,000)
2004	(380,000)
2005	120,000
2006	100,000

Accounting income (or loss) and taxable income (loss) were the same for all years involved. Assume a 45% tax rate for 2000 and 2001 and a 40% tax rate for the remaining years.

Instructions

Prepare the journal entries for the years 2002 to 2006 to record income tax expense and the effects of the tax loss carrybacks and carryforwards assuming Spangler Corporation uses the carryback provision first. All income and losses relate to normal operations and it is more likely than not that the company will generate substantial taxable income in the future.

E19-21 (Loss Carryback)   Beilman Inc. reports the following accounting income (loss) for both book and tax purposes (assume the carryback provision is used where possible).

Year	Accounting Income (Loss)	Tax Rate
2003	$120,000	40%
2004	90,000	40%
2005	(80,000)	45%
2006	(40,000)	45%

The tax rates listed were all enacted by the beginning of 2003.

Instructions

(a) Prepare the journal entries for years 2003 to 2006 to record income taxes.

(b) Prepare the income tax section of the income statements for the years 2003 to 2006 beginning with the line "Income (loss) before income taxes."

E19-22 (Loss Carryback and Carryforward)   Spamela Inc. reports the following pretax income (loss) for both financial reporting purposes and tax purposes.

Year	Accounting Income (Loss)	Tax Rate
2003	$120,000	34%
2004	90,000	34%
2005	(280,000)	38%
2006	220,000	38%

The tax rates listed were all enacted by the beginning of 2003.

Instructions

(a) Prepare the journal entries for the years 2003 to 2006 to record income taxes, assuming the tax loss is first carried back, and that at the end of 2005, the loss carryforward benefits are judged more likely than not to be realized in the future.

(b) Using the assumption in (a), prepare the income tax section of the 2005 and 2006 income statements beginning with the line "Income (loss) before income taxes."

(c) Prepare the journal entries for 2005 and 2006, assuming that based on the weight of available evidence, it is more likely than not that 25% of the carryforward benefits will not be realized. A valuation allowance is not used by this company.

(d) Using the assumption in (c), prepare the income tax section of the 2005 and 2006 income statements beginning with the line "Income (loss) before income taxes."

E19-23 (Loss Carryback and Carryforward Using a Valuation Allowance)   Refer to the information provided about Spamela Inc. in E19-22 (c) and (d).

Instructions

(a) Assuming Spamela Inc. uses a valuation allowance in accounting for future tax assets. Prepare the journal entries for 2005 and 2006, assuming that based on the weight of available evidence, it is more likely than not that 25% of the carryforward benefits will not be realized.

(b) Based on your entries in (a), prepare the income tax section of the 2005 and 2006 income statements beginning with the line "Income (loss) before income taxes."

(c) Indicate how the future tax asset account will be reported on the December 31, 2005 and 2006 balance sheets.

E19-24 (Future Tax Asset—Different Amounts to Be Realized)   Scapriati Corp. had a future tax asset account with a balance of $150,000 at the end of 2004 due to a single temporary difference of $375,000. At the end of 2005, this same temporary difference has increased to $450,000. Taxable income for 2005 is $820,000. The tax rate is 40% for all years.

Instructions

(a) Record income taxes for 2005, assuming that it is more likely than not that the future tax asset will be realized.

(b) 1. Assuming that it is more likely than not that $50,000 of the future tax asset will not be realized, prepare the journal entries to record income taxes for 2005. Scapriati does not use a valuation allowance account.

   2. In 2006, prospects for the company improved. While there was no change in the temporary deductible differences underlying the future tax asset account, it was now considered more likely than not that the company would be able to make full use of the temporary differences. Prepare the entry, if applicable, to adjust the future tax asset account.

E19-25 (Future Tax Asset—Different Amounts to Be Realized; Valuation Allowance)   Refer to the information provided about Scapriati Corp. in E19-24.

Instructions

(a) Assuming that it is more likely than not that $50,000 of the future tax asset will not be realized, prepare the journal entries to record income taxes for 2005. Scapriati uses a valuation allowance account.

(b) In 2006, prospects for the company improved. While there was no change in the temporary deductible differences underlying the future tax asset account, it was now considered more likely than not that the company would be able to make full use of the temporary differences. Prepare the entry, if applicable, to adjust the future tax asset and related account(s).

E19-26 (Intraperiod Tax Allocation)   Hamm Corp. had a profitable year on its regular operations in 2005, reporting $435,000 income before income taxes. Unfortunately, a major decision was handed down by the courts in late November 2005, holding Hamm responsible for environmental damage to prime farmland over the previous 10-year period. Hamm is not insured for such a risk and the company expects it will cost approximately $2.2 million to correct this problem. Hamm has reported this as an extraordinary item on its 2005 income statement. Part of this estimate, $150,000, is a fine levied by the province and it is not a deductible expense for tax purposes. The remainder is deductible, but not until 2006 when the costs will actually be incurred.

In completing the tax return for 2005, Hamm noted that its accounting income included $100,000 of dividends from taxable Canadian corporations, gross profit of $55,000 that is not taxable until 2007, and golf club dues for top management in the amount of $12,800. There were no future income tax assets or liabilities on the December 31, 2004 financial statements. The tax rate applicable to 2005 and future years is 38%.

Instructions

(a) Calculate income taxes payable and the amount of any future income tax asset or liability at the end of 2005.

(b) Prepare the journal entries to record income taxes for 2005.

(c) Indicate how income taxes will be reported on the income statement for 2005 by drafting the bottom portion of the statement, beginning with "Income before taxes and extraordinary items."

E19-27 **(Intraperiod Tax Allocation)** Yining Corp.'s operations in 2005 had mixed results. One division, Vista Group, continued to fail to earn income at a rate high enough to justify continuing to operate it, and the decision was made to close the division. Vista Group earned revenue of $112,000 during 2005 and recognized total expenses of $110,500. The remaining two divisions reported revenues of $268,000 and total expenses of $212,000 in 2005.

In preparing the annual income tax return, Yining's controller took into account the following information.

- The amortization expense exceeds CCA by $3,700. There were no amortizable assets in the Vista Group division.

- Included in Vista's expenses is an accrued loss of $5,000 that is not deductible for tax purposes until 2006.

- Included in the continuing divisions' expenses is the president's golf club dues of $4,500, and the revenues include $1,600 of dividends from taxable Canadian corporations.

- The tax rate for 2005 and future years is 25%.

Instructions

(a) Calculate income taxes payable by Yining Corp. in 2005.

(b) Prepare the journal entry(ies) to record income taxes for 2005.

(c) Indicate how income taxes will be reported on the income statement for 2005 by drafting the bottom portion of the statement, beginning with "Income before taxes and discontinued operations."

Problems

P19-1 Aneke Corp. reported the following differences between balance sheet carrying values and tax values at December 31, 2004.

	Book Value	Tax Value
Depreciable assets	$125,000	$93,000
Warranty liability (current liability)	18,500	0
Accrued pension liability (long-term liability)	34,600	0

The differences between the carrying amounts and tax values were expected to reverse as follows.

	2005	2006	after 2006
Depreciable assets	$17,500	$12,500	$2,000
Warranty liability	18,500	0	0
Accrued pension liability	11,000	11,000	12,600

Tax rates enacted at December 31, 2004 were 31% for 2004, 30% for 2005, 29% for 2006, and 28% for 2007 and later years.

During 2005, Aneke made four quarterly tax instalment payments of $8,000 each and reported income before taxes on its income statement of $109,400. Included in this amount were dividends from taxable Canadian corporations of $4,300 (nontaxable income) and $20,000 of expenses related to the executive team's golf dues (non-tax-deductible expenses). There were no changes to the enacted tax rates during the year.

As expected, book depreciation in 2005 exceeded the capital cost allowance claimed for tax purposes by $17,500 and there were no additions or disposals of property, plant, and equipment during the year. A review of the 2005 activity in the warranty liability account in the ledger indicated the following.

Balance, December 31, 2004	$18,500
Payments on 2004 product warranties	(18,900)
Payments on 2005 product warranties	(5,600)
2005 warranty accrual	28,300
Balance, December 31, 2005	$22,300

All warranties are valid for one year only.

The accrued pension liability account reported the following activity.

Balance, December 31, 2004	$34,600
Payment to pension trustee	(70,000)
2005 pension expense	59,000
Balance, December 31, 2005	$23,600

Pension expenses are deductible for tax purposes, but only as they are paid to the trustee, not as they are accrued for financial reporting purposes.

Instructions

(a) Calculate the future tax asset or liability account at December 31, 2004 and explain how it should be reported on the December 31, 2004 balance sheet.

(b) Prepare all 2005 income tax entries for Aneke Corp. for 2005.

(c) Identify the balances of all income tax accounts at December 31, 2005 and illustrate how they will be reported on the 2005 income statement and December 31, 2005 balance sheet.

P19-2   Information about Swanson Corporation's income before taxes of $633,000 for its year ended December 31, 2005 includes the following.

1. CCA reported on the 2005 tax return exceeded amortization reported on the income statement by $100,000. This difference plus the $150,000 accumulated taxable temporary difference at January 1, 2005 are expected to reverse in equal amounts over the four-year period from 2006 to 2009.

2. Dividends received from taxable Canadian corporations were $10,000.

3. Rent collected in advance on December 31, 2004 totalled $60,000 for a three-year period. Of this amount, $40,000 was reported as unearned for book purposes at December 31, 2005. Unearned revenue is reported as a current liability by Swanson.

4. Swanson paid a $3,500 interest penalty for late income tax instalments. The interest penalty is not deductible for income tax purposes at any time.

5. Equipment was disposed of during the year for $90,000. The equipment had a cost of $105,000 and accumulated amortization to the date of disposal of $37,000. The total proceeds on sale of these assets reduced the CCA class, i.e., no gain or loss is reported for tax purposes.

6. Swanson recognized a $75,000 writedown of a long-term investment whose value was considered impaired. The Income Tax Act only permits the loss to be deducted when the investment is sold and the loss is actually realized.

7. The tax rates are 40% for 2005 and 35% for 2006 and subsequent years. These rates have been enacted and known for the past two years.

Instructions

(a) Calculate the balance in the Future Income Tax Asset/Liability account at December 31, 2004.

(b) Prepare the journal entries to record income taxes for 2005.

(c) Indicate how the Future Income Tax Asset/Liability account(s) will be reported on the December 31, 2005 balance sheet.

(d) Prepare the income tax expense section of the income statement for 2005, beginning with "Income before income taxes."

P19-3   The accounting income of Kristali Corporation differs from its taxable income throughout each of four years as follows.

Year	Accounting Income	Taxable Income	Tax Rate
2005	$280,000	$180,000	35%
2006	320,000	225,000	40%
2007	350,000	270,000	40%
2008	420,000	580,000	40%

Accounting income for each year includes a non-deductible expense of $30,000 (never deductible for tax purposes). The remainder of the difference between accounting income and taxable income in each period is due to one amortization temporary difference. No future income taxes existed at the beginning of 2005.

Instructions

(a) Prepare journal entries to record income taxes for 2005. Assume that the change in the tax rate to 40% was enacted in 2004.

(b) Prepare journal entries to record income taxes in all four years. Assume that the change in the tax rate to 40% was not enacted until the beginning of 2006.

(c) Draft the income tax section of the income statement for 2006, under the assumption in part (b).

P19-4 The following information has been obtained for the Kerdyk Corporation.

1. Prior to 2004, taxable income and accounting income were identical.

2. Accounting income is $1.7 million in 2004 and $1.4 million in 2005.

3. On January 1, 2004, equipment costing $1 million is purchased. It is to be amortized on a straight-line basis over eight years for financial reporting purposes, and is a Class 8 - 20% asset for tax purposes.

4. Lottery winnings of $60,000 were won in 2005 on a ticket purchased out of petty cash. This type of windfall is not taxable.

5. Included in 2005 accounting income is an extraordinary gain of $200,000, which is fully taxable.

6. The tax rate is 35% for all periods.

7. Taxable income is expected in all future years.

Instructions

(a) Calculate taxable income and income tax payable for 2005.

(b) Prepare the journal entry(ies) to record 2005 income taxes.

(c) Prepare the bottom portion of Kerdyk's 2005 income statement, beginning with "Income before income taxes and extraordinary item."

(d) Indicate how future income taxes should be presented on the December 31, 2005 balance sheet.

P19-5 The accounting records of Andronni Corp, a real estate developer, indicated income before taxes of $850,000 for its year ended December 31, 2005 and $525,000 for the year ended December 31, 2006. The following data are available.

1. Andronni Corp. pays an annual life insurance premium of $9,000 covering the top management team. The company is the named beneficiary in each case.

2. The net book value of the company's property, plant, and equipment at January 1, 2005 was $1,256,000, and the UCC at that date was $998,000. Andronni recorded amortization expense of $175,000 and $180,000 in 2005 and 2006, respectively. CCA for tax purposes was $192,000 and $163,500 for 2005 and 2006, respectively. There were no asset additions or disposals over the two-year period.

3. Andronni deducted $211,000 as a restructuring charge in determining income for 2004. At December 31, 2004, an accrued liability of $199,500 remained outstanding relative to the restructuring. This expense is deductible for tax purposes, but only as the actual costs are incurred and paid for. As the actual restructuring of operations took place in 2005 and 2006, the liability was reduced to $68,000 at the end of 2005 and $0 at the end of 2006.

4. In 2005, property held for development was sold and a profit of $52,000 was recognized in income. Because the sale was made with delayed payment terms, the profit is taxable only as Andronni receives payment from the purchaser. A 10% down payment was received in 2005, with the remaining 90% expected in equal amounts over the following three years.

5. Nontaxable dividends of $2,250 were received from taxable Canadian corporations in 2005, and $2,750 in 2006.

6. In addition to the income before taxes identified above, Andronni reported a before-tax gain on discontinued operations of $18,800 in 2005.

7. A 30% rate of tax has been in effect since 2003.

Instructions

(a) Determine the balance of any future income tax asset or liability account at December 31, 2004.

(b) Determine 2005 and 2006 taxable income.

(c) Prepare the journal entries to record current and future income tax expense for 2005 and 2006.

(d) Identify how the future income tax asset or liability account(s) will be reported on the December 31, 2005 and 2006 balance sheets.

(e) Prepare partial income statements for the years ended December 31, 2005 and 2006, beginning with "Income from continuing operations before income tax."

P19-6   Mearat Inc. reported the following accounting income (loss) and related tax rates during the years 2000 to 2006.

Year	Accounting Income (Loss)	Tax Rate
2000	$ 40,000	30%
2001	25,000	30%
2002	60,000	30%
2003	80,000	40%
2004	(200,000)	45%
2005	70,000	40%
2006	90,000	35%

Accounting income (loss) and taxable income (loss) were the same for all years since Mearat began business. The tax rates from 2003 to 2006 were enacted in 2003.

Instructions

(a) Prepare the journal entries for the years 2004 to 2006 to record income taxes. Assume that Mearat uses the carryback provision where possible and expects to realize the benefits of any loss carryforward in the year that immediately follows the loss year.

(b) Indicate the effect the 2004 entry(ies) has on the December 31, 2004 balance sheet.

(c) Indicate how the bottom portion of the income statement, starting with Loss before income taxes, would be reported in 2004.

(d) Indicate how the bottom portion of the income statement, starting with Income before income taxes, would be reported in 2005.

(e) Prepare the journal entries for the years 2004 to 2006 to record income taxes, assuming that Mearat uses the carryback provision where possible but is uncertain about the ability to realize the benefits of any loss carryforward in the future. Mearat does not use a valuation allowance.

(f) Assume Mearat uses a valuation allowance account along with its future tax asset account. Identify which entries in (e) would differ and prepare the entries required.

(g) Based on your entries in (e), indicate how the bottom portion of the income statements for 2004 and 2005 would be reported, beginning with "Income (loss) before income taxes."

P19-7   Presented below are two independent situations related to future taxable and deductible amounts resulting from temporary differences existing at December 31, 2005.

1. Pirates Corp. has developed the following schedule of future taxable and deductible amounts.

	2006	2007	2008	2009	2010
Taxable amounts	$300	$300	$300	$ 200	$100
Deductible amount	—	—	—	(1,400)	—

Pirates reported a net future income tax liability of $540 at January 1, 2005.

2. Eagles Corp. has the following schedule of future taxable and deductible amounts.

	2006	2007	2008	2009
Taxable amounts	$300	$300	$ 300	$300
Deductible amount	—	—	(2,000)	—

Eagles Corp. reported a net future tax asset of $600 at January 1, 2005.

Both Pirates Corp. and Eagles Corp. have taxable income of $3,000 in 2005 and expect to have taxable income in all future years. The tax rates enacted as of the beginning of 2005 are 30% for 2005 to 2008 and 35% for years thereafter. All of the underlying temporary differences relate to noncurrent assets and liabilities.

Instructions

(a) For each of these two situations, prepare journal entries to record income taxes for 2005. Show all calculations.

(b) Determine the future income tax assets or liabilities that will be reported on each company's December 31, 2005 balance sheet and indicate their classification.

P19-8   The following information was disclosed during the audit of Muster Inc.

1.

Year	Amount Due per Tax Return
2004	$140,000
2005	112,000

2. On January 1, 2004, equipment costing $400,000 is purchased. For financial reporting purposes, the company uses straight-line amortization over a five-year life. For tax purposes, the company uses CCA at a 25% rate.

3. In January 2005, $225,000 is collected in advance rental of a building for a three-year period. The entire $225,000 is reported as taxable income in 2005, but $150,000 of the $225,000 is reported as unearned revenue in 2005 for financial reporting purposes. The remaining amount of unearned revenue will be earned equally in 2006 and 2007.

4. The tax rate is 40% in 2004 and all subsequent periods.

5. No temporary differences existed at the end of 2003. Muster expects to report taxable income in each of the next five years.

Instructions

(a) Determine the amount to report for future income taxes at the end of 2004 and indicate how it should be classified on the balance sheet.

(b) Prepare the journal entry(ies) to record income taxes for 2004.

(c) Draft the income tax section of the income statement for 2004 beginning with "Income before income taxes." (Hint: You must calculate taxable income and then combine that with changes in temporary differences to arrive at accounting income.)

(d) Determine the future income taxes at the end of 2005 and indicate how they should be classified on the balance sheet.

(e) Prepare the journal entry(ies) to record income taxes for 2005.

(f) Draft the income tax section of the income statement for 2005 beginning with "Income before income taxes."

P19-9   Kringe Corporation began operations in 2005. The following information pertains to this company.

1. Income before taxes on the income statement for 2005 is $100,000. In addition, Kringe reports an extraordinary loss of $46,000 for financial reporting purposes, as well as a tax-deductible $5,700 financing charge reported in the statement of retained earnings. The latter represents interest on a financial instrument that is legally debt but is (in substance) equity for financial reporting purposes.

2. The tax rate enacted for 2005 and future years is 40%.

3. Differences between the 2005 GAAP amounts and their treatment for tax purposes are listed below.

  (a) Warranty expense accrued for financial reporting purposes amounts to $5,000. Warranty deductions per the tax return amount to $2,000.

  (b) Of the extraordinary loss of $46,000, 25% will never be tax deductible. The remaining 75% will be deductible for tax purposes evenly over the years from 2006 to 2008.

  (c) Gross profit on construction contracts using the percentage-of-completion method for book purposes amounts to $92,000. Gross profit on construction contracts for tax purposes amounts to $62,000.

  (d) Amortization of property, plant, and equipment for financial reporting purposes amounts to $60,000. CCA charged on the tax return amounts to $80,000.

  (e) A $3,500 fine paid for violation of pollution laws was deducted in calculating accounting income.

  (f) Dividend revenue earned on an investment is tax-exempt and amounts to $1,400.

  (Assume (a) is short-term in nature; assume (c) is long-term in nature.)

4. Taxable income is expected for the next few years.

Instructions

(a) Calculate taxable income for 2005.

(b) Calculate the future taxes at December 31, 2005 that relate to the temporary differences described above. Clearly identify where they will be reported on the December 31, 2005 balance sheet.

(c) Prepare the journal entry to record income taxes for 2005.

(d) Draft a partial 2005 income statement beginning with "Income before income taxes and extraordinary items" and a statement of retained earnings, assuming no dividends were declared in 2005.

Illustration 20-4

*Projected Benefit Obligation—
Continuity Schedule*

Projected benefit obligation (PBO) beginning of period
+ Current service cost
+ Interest cost
+ Past service costs of plan amendments during period
− Benefits paid to retirees
± Actuarial gains (-) or losses (+) during period on the PBO
= Projected benefit obligation (PBO) end of period

Objective 7

Identify transactions and events that affect the balance of the plan assets.

The plan assets are the other major element. As can be seen from Illustration 20-5, the assets increase as a result of contributions from the employer (and employee, if the plan is contributory) and from the actual return generated on the assets invested. The pool of assets is reduced by payments to retirees. The relationship between the actual and expected return is also illustrated, indicating that the actual return is made up of two components: the expected return and the difference between the expected and the actual return. The plan trustee provides most of this information.

Illustration 20-5

*Plan Assets—
Continuity Schedule*

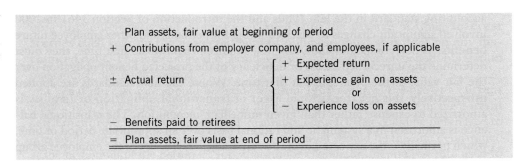

The difference between the projected benefit obligation and the pension assets' fair value at any point in time is known as the plan's **funded status**. A plan with liabilities that exceed assets is underfunded; a plan with accumulated assets in excess of the related obligation is overfunded.[22]

The amount of a company's contributions to the plan has a direct effect on its funded status. Who and what determine how much a company contributes to the plan?

In Canada, pension plans come under either federal or provincial pension legislation as well as regulations of the Canada Revenue Agency (CRA). The CRA stipulates the amount of the contributions that are tax-deductible to the company and the conditions on the payment of benefits out of the plan. Federal and provincial law dictate the funding requirements.

In general, the current service cost is required to be funded annually. If a plan is in a surplus position (overfunded), the company may be able to take a contribution holiday, i.e., temporarily not make any contributions. If there is a funding deficiency, the extent of the shortfall is determined by two different valuations: one based on a going concern and one based on a termination assumption. These dictate the additional funding required, with the deficiency to be funded over either a five-year or 15-year period. The accumulated benefit obligation (i.e., using current salary levels) is most often used to determine the minimum funding requirements.

While information about a company's future funding requirements for pensions would be very useful to users in assessing a company's future cash requirements, there is no requirement for companies to disclose this information under current standards.

What do the Numbers Mean?

Underlying Concept

Many plans are underfunded but still quite viable. For example, **Canadian Imperial Bank of Commerce** had a $1,043 million pension and other benefit plans shortfall. But CIBC at that time had earnings of $2,063 million and a net worth of $13,778 million. Thus, the going concern assumption permits us to ignore these pension underfundings in many cases because in the long run they are not significant.

---

[22] When **Air Canada** filed for protection under the Companies' Creditors Arrangement Act on April 1, 2003, a $1.5 billion unfunded pension liability was listed as one of the key factors behind the company's insolvency. As we saw in the opening vignette, the Office of the Superintendent of Financial Institutions had ordered the company to transfer assets to its pension funds in the latter part of March. How to deal with this underfunded plan and unbooked liability was central to Air Canada's restructuring negotiations.

Before covering the other pension expense components in detail, we will illustrate the basic accounting for the first three components: service cost, interest cost, and expected return on plan assets.

Basic Illustration

Essential to the accounting for pensions (and other similar future benefits) under *CICA Handbook* Section 3461 is the fact that it applies a noncapitalization approach. This means that several significant items related to the plan **are not recognized in the accounts and on the financial statements** of the employer, including the:

1. projected benefit obligation,

2. pension plan assets,

3. unrecognized past service costs,

4. unrecognized net actuarial gain or loss, and

5. unrecognized net transitional asset or liability.

As discussed later, the employer is required to disclose many of these balances in the notes to the financial statements, **but the balances are not recognized in the body of the financial statements**. Their amounts must be known at all times because they are used to calculate annual pension expense. Therefore, in order to track these off-balance-sheet pension items, supplementary information has to be maintained outside the formal general ledger system. As an example of how this could be done, a work sheet unique to pension accounting will be used to keep track of both the recognized and unrecognized balances and to illustrate the relationship among all the components.[23] Notice that it is changes in the PBO and fund assets that drive most of the work sheet entries, and an understanding of these changes is necessary to understand pension accounting. The work sheet format is shown in Illustration 20-6.

	General Journal Entries			Memo Record	
Items	Annual Pension Expense	Cash	Accrued Pension Asset/Liability	Projected Benefit Obligation	Plan Assets

Illustration 20-6

Basic Format of Pension Work Sheet

The left-hand "General Journal Entries" columns of the work sheet underlie entries in the general ledger accounts. The right-hand Memo Record columns maintain balances on the unrecognized (noncapitalized) pension items. On the first line of the work sheet, the beginning balances are recorded. Subsequently, transactions and events related to the pension plan are indicated, using debits and credits and using both sets of records as if they were one for recording the entries. For each transaction or event, the debits must equal the credits and the balance in the Accrued Pension Asset/Liability column must equal the net balance in the memo record.

8 Objective

Explain the usefulness of—and be able to complete—a work sheet to support the employer's pension expense entries.

2004 Entries and Work Sheet

To illustrate the use of a work sheet and how it helps in accounting for a pension plan, assume that on January 1, 2004, Zarle Corporation adopts *CICA Handbook* Section 3461 to

---

[23] The use of this pension entry work sheet is taken from Paul B. W. Miller, The New Pension Accounting (Part 2), *Journal of Accountancy*, February 1987, pp. 86-94.

account for its defined benefit pension plan. The following facts apply to the pension plan for the year 2004.

1. Plan assets, January 1, 2004 are $100,000 and at December 31, 2004 are $111,000.

2. Projected benefit obligation, January 1, 2004 is $100,000 and at December 31, 2004 is $112,000.

3. Annual service cost for 2004 is $9,000, accrued as of the end of 2004.

4. Interest (discount) rate on the liability for 2004 is 10%.

5. Expected and actual earnings on plan assets for 2004 is 10%.

6. Contributions (funding) in 2004 are $8,000, remitted at the end of 2004.

7. Benefits paid to retirees during the year are $7,000, paid at the end of 2004.

Using this data, Illustration 20-7 presents the work sheet, including the beginning balances and all of the pension entries needed by Zarle Corporation in 2004. The beginning balances of the projected benefit obligation and the pension plan assets are recorded on the work sheet's first line in the memo record. They are not recorded in the accounts and, therefore, are not reported as a liability and an asset in Zarle Corporation's financial statements. These two significant pension items are prime examples of off-balance-sheet amounts that directly affect pension expense but are not recorded as assets and liabilities in the employer's books.

Illustration 20-7

Pension Work Sheet—2004

| Items | General Journal Entries | | | Memo Record | |
	Annual Pension Expense	Cash	Accrued Pension Asset/Liability	Projected Benefit Obligation	Plan Assets
Balance, Jan 1, 2004				100,000 Cr.	100,000 Dr.
(a) Service cost	9,000 Dr.			9,000 Cr.	
(b) Interest cost	10,000 Dr.			10,000 Cr.	
(c) Expected return	10,000 Cr.				10,000 Dr.
(d) Contributions		8,000 Cr.			8,000 Dr.
(e) Benefits paid				7,000 Dr.	7,000 Cr.
Expense entry, 2004	9,000 Dr.		9,000 Cr.		
Contribution, 2004		8,000 Cr.	8,000 Dr.		
Balance, Dec. 31, 2004			1,000 Cr.	112,000 Cr.	111,000 Dr.

Entry (a) recognizes the service cost component, which increases pension expense by $9,000 and increases the projected benefit obligation by $9,000. Entry (b) accrues the interest cost, which increases both the PBO and pension expense by $10,000 (the beginning projected benefit obligation multiplied by the discount rate of 10%). Entry (c) records the expected return on plan assets, which increases the plan assets and decreases the pension expense. Entry (d) reflects Zarle Corporation's contribution (funding) of assets to the pension fund; cash is decreased by $8,000 and plan assets are increased by $8,000. Entry (e) records the benefit payments made to retirees, which results in equal $7,000 decreases to the plan assets and the projected benefit obligation.

The adjusting journal entry on December 31, 2004 to formally record the pension expense for the year is as follows.

A = L + SE
     +9,000   −9,000
Cash flows: No effect

| Pension Expense | 9,000 | |
| Accrued Pension Asset/Liability | | 9,000 |

When Zarle Corporation issued its $8,000 cheque to the pension fund trustee, the following entry was made.

Accrued Pension Asset/Liability	8,000	
Cash		8,000

A = L + SE
−8,000 −8,000

Cash flows: ↓ 8,000 outflow

The credit balance in the Accrued Pension Asset/Liability account of $1,000 represents the difference between the 2004 pension expense of $9,000 and the amount funded of $8,000. Because the full amount recognized as expense was not funded, an Accrued Pension Asset/Liability account credit balance remains. This account is reported as Accrued Pension Liability and is usually included with long-term liabilities. If the amount funded exceeded the pension expense recognized, the account would have a debit balance, be described as Accrued Pension Asset, and be included as an asset in the balance sheet, usually with the deferred charges. The balance in this account at any time indicates if the accumulated amounts charged to expense over the years exceeds the total amount of funding (a credit balance) or whether amounts contributed in the past exceed amounts charged to expense (a debit balance).

The Accrued Pension Liability account balance of $1,000 also equals the net of the balances in the memo accounts. A reconciliation of the off-balance-sheet items with the liability reported in the balance sheet is shown in Illustration 20-8.

Projected benefit obligation (Credit)	$(112,000)
Plan assets at fair value (Debit)	111,000
Funded status—net liability (Credit)	$ (1,000)
Accrued pension liability (Credit)	$ (1,000)

Illustration 20-8

Pension Reconciliation Schedule—December 31, 2004

If the net of the memo record balances is a credit, the reconciling amount in the Accrued Pension Asset/Liability column will be a credit that is equal in amount. If the net of the memo record balances is a debit, the Accrued Pension Asset/Liability amount will be a debit that is equal in amount. The work sheet is designed to highlight the relationships among these amounts—information that is useful later in preparing the notes related to pension disclosures.

PLANS WITH DEFINED BENEFITS THAT VEST OR ACCUMULATE: COMPLEXITIES

Past Service Costs (PSC)

When a defined benefit plan is either initiated (adopted) or amended, credit is often given to employees for years of service provided prior to the date of initiation or amendment. As a result of these credits for prior services, the actuary remeasures the projected benefit obligation, which is usually greater than it was before. The increase in the projected benefit obligation at the date of initiation or amendment is the cost of the retroactive benefits. This increase is often substantial. A simplified illustration of this is provided in Appendix A.

One question that arises is whether the expense and related liability for these past service costs should be fully recognized at the time the plan is initiated or amended. The AcSB has taken the position that no expense for these costs should be recognized at the time of the plan's adoption or amendment. The board's rationale is that the employer would not provide credit for past years of service unless it expected to receive benefits in

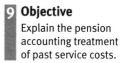

9 Objective
Explain the pension accounting treatment of past service costs.

International Insight

In Canada, past service cost is generally amortized over the average period to full eligibility. In Germany, it is recognized immediately. In the Netherlands, prior service cost may either be recognized immediately or directly charged to shareholders' equity.

the future. As a result, *CICA Handbook* Section 3461 specifies that the retroactive benefits' cost is recognized as an expense on a straight-line basis over the appropriate period benefiting, which normally is the expected period to full eligibility of the employee group covered by the plan.[24] This accounting treatment is consistent with the upper limit of the attribution period (i.e., the expected period to full eligibility) that is used for attributing current service cost to accounting periods. Alternatively, companies could conclude that the benefits are received over a shorter period of time, such as would be the case if it has a history of regular plan amendments. Regardless, amortization has the effect of smoothing the amount of pension expense from year to year.

To illustrate the amortization of unrecognized past service cost, assume that Zarle Corporation amends its defined benefit pension plan on January 1, 2005 to grant prior service benefits to certain employees. The company's actuaries determine that this causes an increase in the projected benefit obligation of $80,000. The affected employees are grouped according to expected remaining years of service to full eligibility and the expected remaining service period is calculated as follows.

Illustration 20-9

Calculation of Expected Period to Full Eligibility

Group	Number of Employees	Expected Remaining Years of Service to Full Eligibility	Total
A	40	1	40
B	20	2	40
C	40	3	120
D	50	4	200
E	20	5	100
	170		500

Expected period to full eligibility = 500 ÷ 170 = 2.94

Note: FASB prefers a "years-to-service" amortization method similar to a units-of-production calculation. In the first year, for example, 170 service years are worked by employees. Therefore, 170/500 of the past service cost is recognized in the first year.

The amortization of the unrecognized past service cost to be recognized in pension expense each year is $27,211 ($80,000 ÷ 2.94) in 2005, $27,211 in 2006, and the remainder of $25,578 in 2007. Note that although the projected benefit obligation is increased as soon as the company amends the plan on January 1, 2005, **the expense and associated liability are recognized on the books of Zarle over a three-year period, 2005 to 2007.** At the end of 2005 and 2006, therefore, a portion of the increased obligation has not been recognized in the financial statements, but is an off-balance-sheet amount.

If full capitalization of all pension plan elements had been adopted by the AcSB, the increase in the company's obligation would have been given accounting recognition immediately as a credit to the liability and a charge (debit) to an intangible asset. The intangible asset treatment assumes that the cost of additional pension benefits increases loyalty and productivity and reduces turnover among the affected employees. This account would have been amortized over its useful life.

IAS Note

IAS 19 requires that past service costs be recognized immediately to the extent that the benefits are already vested. Otherwise, they are amortized over the period to when they will be vested.

However, past service cost is accounted for off-balance sheet initially and may be called unrecognized (or unamortized) past service cost. Although not recognized on the balance sheet immediately, past service cost is a factor in calculating pension expense.

2005 Entries and Work Sheet

Continuing the Zarle Corporation illustration into 2005, we note that the January 1, 2005 amendment to the pension plan grants to employees prior service benefits having a pres-

---

[24] *CICA Handbook*, Section 3461.079.

ent value of $80,000. The annual amortization of $27,211 for 2005 as calculated in the previous section is carried forward in this illustration. The following facts apply to the pension plan for the year 2005.

1. On January 1, 2005, Zarle Corporation grants prior service benefits having a present value of $80,000.

2. Annual service cost for 2005 is $9,500.

3. Interest on the pension obligation (PBO) is 10%.

4. Expected and actual return on plan assets is 10%.

5. Annual contributions (funding) are $20,000.

6. Benefits paid to retirees in 2005 are $8,000.

7. Amortization of past service cost is $27,211.

8. At December 31, 2005, the PBO is $212,700 and plan assets are $134,100.

Note that unless otherwise specified, **it is assumed that current service cost is credited at year end and that contributions to the fund and benefits paid to retirees are year-end cash flows** in all chapter examples and end-of-chapter problem material.

Illustration 20-10 presents the entire pension "entries" and information used by Zarle Corporation in 2005. The work sheet's first line shows the beginning balances of the Accrued Pension Liability account and the memo accounts. Entry (f) records Zarle Corporation's granting of prior service benefits by adding $80,000 to the projected benefit obligation and to the unrecognized (noncapitalized) past service cost. Entries (g), (h), (i), (k), and (l) are similar to the corresponding entries in 2004. Entry (j) recognizes the 2005 amortization of unrecognized past service cost by including $27,211 in Pension Expense, reducing the Unrecognized Past Service Cost memo account by the same amount.

Illustration 20-10

Pension Work Sheet—2005

	General Journal Entries			Memo Record		
Items	Annual Pension Expense	Cash	Accrued Pension Asset/Liability	Projected Benefit Obligation	Plan Assets	Unrecognized Past Service Cost
Balance, Dec. 31, 2004			1,000 Cr.	112,000 Cr.	111,000 Dr.	
(f) Past service cost				80,000 Cr.		80,000 Dr.
Balance, Jan. 1, 2005			1,000 Cr.	192,000 Cr.	111,000 Dr.	80,000 Dr.
(g) Service cost	9,500 Dr.			9,500 Cr.		
(h) Interest cost	19,200 Dr.			19,200 Cr.		
(i) Expected return	11,100 Cr.				11,100 Dr.	
(j) Amortization of PSC	27,211 Dr.					27,211 Cr.
(k) Contribution		20,000 Cr.			20,000 Dr.	
(l) Benefits paid				8,000 Dr.	8,000 Cr.	
Expense entry, 2005	44,811 Dr.		44,811 Cr.			
Contribution, 2005		20,000 Cr.	20,000 Dr.			
Balance, Dec. 31, 2005			25,811 Cr.	212,700 Cr.	134,100 Dr.	52,789 Dr.

The journal entry on December 31, 2005 to formally record the pension expense for the year is as follows.

Pension Expense	44,811	
Accrued Pension Asset/Liability		44,811

A = L + SE
+44,811 −44,811

Cash flows: No effect

When the company made its contributions to the pension fund, the following entry was recorded.

A = L + SE
−20,000 −20,000

Cash flows: ↓ 20,000 outflow

| Accrued Pension Asset/Liability | 20,000 | |
| Cash | | 20,000 |

Because the expense exceeds the funding, the Accrued Pension Liability account increases by the $24,811 difference ($44,811 less $20,000). In 2005, as in 2004, the balance of the Accrued Pension Liability account ($25,811) is equal to the net of the balances in the memo accounts as shown in the following reconciliation schedule.

Illustration 20-11

Pension Reconciliation Schedule—December 31, 2005

Projected benefit obligation (Credit)	$(212,700)
Plan assets at fair value (Debit)	134,100
Funded status—net liability (Credit)	$ (78,600)
Unrecognized past service cost (Debit)	52,789
Accrued pension liability (Credit)	$ (25,811)

Actuarial Gains and Losses

Of great concern to companies that have pension plans are the uncontrollable and unexpected swings in pension expense that could be caused by (1) large and sudden changes in the market value of plan assets and (2) changes in actuarial assumptions that affect the amount of the projected benefit obligation. If these gains or losses were to be fully included in pension expense in the period in which they occurred, substantial fluctuations in pension expense would result. Therefore, the profession decided to reduce the volatility associated with pension expense by using smoothing techniques that dampen and in some cases fully eliminate the fluctuations.

Asset Gains and Losses

Objective 10

Explain the pension accounting treatment of actuarial gains and losses, including corridor amortization.

The return on plan assets is a component of pension expense that normally reduces the expense amount. A significant change in the actual return could substantially affect pension expense for the year. Assume a company has used 8% as an expected return on plan assets while the actual return experienced is 40%. Should this substantial and perhaps one-time event affect current pension expense?

Actuaries ignore short-term fluctuations when they develop a funding pattern to pay expected benefits in the future. They develop an expected rate of return and multiply it by an asset value weighted over a reasonable period of time to arrive at an expected return on plan assets. This return is then used to determine the funding pattern.

The AcSB adopted the actuaries' approach in order to avoid recording wide swings that might occur in the actual return: use of the expected return on plan assets is required as a component of pension expense. To achieve this goal, the fair value (or market-related value) of plan assets at the beginning of the year adjusted by additional contributions and payments to retirees during the year is multiplied by the expected long-term rate of return (the actuary's rate). The market-related value of plan assets is a calculated value that recognizes changes in fair value in a systematic and rational manner over no more than five years.[25]

---

[25] *CICA Handbook*, Section 3461.076 and .077. Different ways of calculating a market-related value may be used for different asset classes. For example, an employer might use fair value for bonds and a five-year moving average for equities, but the manner of determining market-related value should be applied consistently from year to year for each asset class.

Throughout our Zarle Corporation illustrations, market-related value and fair value of plan assets are assumed equal.

The difference between the expected return and the actual return is referred to as an asset experience gain or loss. A gain occurs when the actual return is greater than the expected return and a loss occurs when actual returns are less than expected.

The amount of asset gain or loss is determined at the end of each year by comparing the calculated expected return with the actual return earned. In the preceding example, the expected return on Zarle's pension fund assets for 2005 was $11,100. If the actual return on the plan assets for the year 2005 was $12,000, then an experience gain of $900 ($12,000 − $11,100) exists. Plan assets are increased by $12,000, annual expense is credited with $11,100, and an unrecognized actuarial gain of $900 is included in the memo accounts and combined with unrecognized gains and losses accumulated in prior years.

Liability Gains and Losses

In estimating the projected benefit obligation (the liability), actuaries make assumptions about such variables as mortality rate, retirement rate, turnover rate, disability rate, and salary amounts. Any difference between these assumed rates and amounts and those actually experienced changes the amount of the projected benefit obligation. Seldom does actual experience coincide exactly with actuarial predictions. Such an unexpected gain or loss that results in a change in the PBO is referred to as a liability experience gain or loss. Actuarial gains and losses also arise when the assumptions used by the actuary in calculating the PBO are revised, causing a change in the obligation amount. An example is the effect on the obligation calculation of a change in the interest rate used to discount the pension cash flows. Because experience gains and losses are similar to and affect the PBO in the same way as actuarial gains and losses, **both types are referred to as actuarial gains and losses**.

To illustrate, assume that the expected projected benefit obligation of Zarle Corporation was $212,700 at December 31, 2005. If the company's actuaries, using December 31, 2005 estimates, calculate a projected benefit obligation of $213,500, then the company has suffered an actuarial loss of $800 ($213,500 − $212,700). If the actuary calculates a reduced obligation, an actuarial gain results. The PBO is adjusted to its most recent estimate and the difference is included in the memo accounts as an unrecognized actuarial gain or loss.

Corridor Amortization for Net Actuarial Gains and Losses

Because the asset gains and losses and the liability gains and losses can and are expected to offset each other over time, the accumulated unrecognized net gain or loss may not grow very large. In fact, this is the reason given for not including these gains and losses directly in pension expense each year. But it is possible that no offsetting will occur and the balance of the unrecognized net gain or loss will continue to grow. To limit its growth, the corridor approach is used for amortizing the net unrecognized gain or loss. Under this approach, the unrecognized net gain or loss balance is considered too large and must be amortized **only when it exceeds the arbitrarily selected criterion of 10% of the larger of the beginning balance of the projected benefit obligation and the fair or market-related value of the plan assets**.

To illustrate the corridor approach, assume data on the projected benefit obligation and the plan assets over a six-year period as shown in Illustration 20-12.

Illustration 20-20

Illustrative Disclosure—CIBC

Employee Future Benefits

CIBC is the sponsor of a number of employee benefit plans. These plans include both defined benefit and defined contribution plans, and various other post-retirement and post-employment benefit plans.

Actuarial valuations of the obligations for employee future benefits are made periodically for accounting purposes by an independent actuary. These are based on the projected benefit method for valuing the obligations, prorated on service and are on management's best estimate assumptions about expected rate of return on plan assets, rate of salary growth, retirement age and health-care costs. These assumptions are selected such that they are long-term in nature. The discount rate used to value liabilities is based on market rates as at the measurement date. Plan assets and accrued benefit obligations are measured as at September 30, preceding each year-end.

The annual expense includes the estimated present value of the cost of future benefits payable in respect of services rendered in the current period; interest on projected obligations net of expected return on plan assets; amortization of past service costs, actuarial gains and losses, transitional assets and changes in valuation allowance. The expected rate of return on plan assets is based on a market-related value of plan assets, where investment (gains) losses versus the expected rate of return on investments are recognized over three years. Past service costs are amortized on a straight-line basis

over the expected average remaining service life of the employee groups covered by the plan, since it is expected that CIBC will realize economic benefit from these plan changes during this period. Net actuarial gains and losses that exceed 10% of the greater of the accrued benefit obligation or the fair value of plan assets are also amortized on a straight-line basis over the expected average remaining service life of the employee groups covered by the plan. Short-term experience will often deviate from the actuarial assumptions resulting in actuarial gains or losses. Recognizing these actuarial gains or losses over the expected average remaining service life of active employees who are expected to receive the benefits allows for the offsetting impact of gains and losses in other periods. Recognition of a valuation allowance is required when the accrued benefit asset for any plan is greater than the expected future benefit. A change in the valuation allowance is recognized in consolidated statements of income for the period in which the change occurs.

The accrued benefit asset or liability represents the cumulative difference between the expense and funding contributions and is included in other assets and other liabilities on the consolidated balance sheets.

Defined contribution expense is charged to employee compensation and benefits in the consolidated statements of income for services rendered during the period.

Note 16 — EMPLOYEE FUTURE BENEFITS

CIBC is the sponsor of pension plans for eligible employees in Canada, the U.S. and the U.K. These plans include registered funded pension plans, supplemental unfunded arrangements, which provide pension benefits in excess of statutory limits, and defined contribution plans. The pension plans are predominantly non-contributory, but some participants contribute to their respective plans and receive a higher pension. These benefits are, in general, based on years of

service and compensation near retirement. CIBC also provides certain health-care, life insurance and other benefits to employees and eligible pensioners, on a non-contributory basis. In addition, CIBC has a long-term disability plan to provide benefits to disabled employees.

The financial positions of the employee pension benefit plans and other benefit plans are as follows:

$ millions, for the years ended October 31	Pension benefit plans			Other benefit plans		
	2003	2002	2001	2003	2002	2001
Accrued benefit obligation[(1)]						
Balance at beginning of year	$ 2,537	$ 2,226	$ 2,013	$ 696	$ 609	$ 130
Adjustment for change in accounting policy	–	–	163	–	–	403
Adjustment for inclusion of subsidiary plans	–	216[(2)]	–	–	19	–
Current service cost	77	80	66	55	53	37
Employees' contributions	9	10	11	–	–	–
Interest cost	166	167	148	43	39	36
Benefits paid	(166)	(142)	(134)	(43)	(38)	(36)
Foreign exchange rate changes	(27)	7	–	(4)	–	–
Actuarial losses (gains)	281	(73)	(48)	68	14	39
Special termination benefits	8	–	–	–	–	–
Plan amendments	(7)	45	12	–	–	–
Divestitures	(46)	–	–	–	–	–
Corporate restructuring giving rise to:						
Settlements	(34)	–	–	(6)	–	–
Curtailments	–	1	(5)	(6)	–	–
Balance at end of year	**$ 2,798**	**$ 2,537**	**$ 2,226**	**$ 803**	**$ 696**	**$ 609**

Continued ...

Illustration 20-20

Illustrative Disclosure—CIBC
(continued)

Continued ...

$ millions, for the years ended October 31	Pension benefit plans			Other benefit plans		
	2003	2002	2001	2003	2002	2001
Plan assets[(1)(3)]						
Fair value at beginning of year	$2,188	$2,121	$2,545	$ 106	$ 103	$ 111
Adjustment for change in accounting policy	–	–	48	–	–	–
Adjustment for inclusion of subsidiary plans	–	211[(2)]	–	–	–	–
Actual return on plan assets	257	(106)	(364)	9	(4)	(3)
Employer contributions	253	88	15	44	45	31
Employees' contributions	9	10	11	–	–	–
Benefits paid	(166)	(142)	(134)	(43)	(38)	(36)
Foreign exchange rate changes	(19)	6	–	–	–	–
Divestitures	(46)	–	–	–	–	–
Corporate restructuring giving rise to settlements	(34)	–	–	–	–	–
Fair value at end of year	$2,442	$2,188	$2,121	$ 116	$ 106	$ 103
Funded status – plan deficit	$ (356)	$ (349)	$ (105)	$ (687)	$ (590)	$ (506)
Employer contribution received after measurement date	–	15	–	–	–	–
Unamortized net actuarial losses	953	786	506	118	59	39
Unamortized past service costs	42	54	12	–	–	–
Unamortized transitional obligation	(19)	(23)	–	5	6	–
Accrued benefit asset (liability)	620	483	413	(564)	(525)	(467)
Valuation allowance	(17)	(16)	–	–	–	–
Accrued benefit asset (liability), net of valuation allowance	$ 603	$ 467	$ 413	$ (564)	$ (525)	$ (467)
Current service cost	$ 77	$ 80	$ 66	$ 55	$ 53	$ 37
Interest cost	166	167	148	43	39	36
Expected return on plan assets	(188)	(199)	(191)	(7)	(8)	(8)
Amortization of past service costs	3	2	1	–	–	–
Amortization of net actuarial (gains) losses	15	2	–	5	5	–
Amortization of transitional asset	(2)	(2)	–	–	–	–
Curtailment losses (gains)	3	2	(5)	(6)	–	–
Settlement losses	20	–	–	–	–	–
Contractual termination benefits	8	–	–	–	–	–
Change in valuation allowance	1	(8)	–	–	–	–
Net benefit plan expense	$ 103	$ 44	$ 19	$ 90	$ 89	$ 65
Weighted-average assumptions at year-end						
Discount rate	6.2%	6.7%	6.75%	6.1%	6.4%	6.75%
Expected long-term rate of return on plan assets	7.0%	7.5%	7.5%	6.5%	7.0%	7.5%
Rate of compensation increase	3.6%	3.7%	4.0%	3.3%	3.4%	4.0%

(1) Plans are measured annually at September 30.
(2) Net of valuation allowance of $24 million.
(3) Plan assets of pension benefit plans include securities of CIBC having a fair value of $14 million at October 31, 2003 (2002: $15 million; 2001: $15 million).

Included in the accrued benefit obligation and fair value of the plan assets at year-end are the following amounts in respect of plans that are not fully funded:

$ millions, as at October 31	Pension benefit plans			Other benefit plans		
	2003	2002	2001	2003	2002	2001
Accrued benefit obligation	$2,755	$2,499	$ 120	$ 803	$ 696	$ 609
Fair value of plan assets	2,378	2,128	–	116	106	103
Funded status – plan deficit	$ (377)	$ (371)	$ (120)	$ (687)	$ (590)	$ (506)

A 10.1% weighted-average annual rate of increase in the per capita cost of covered health-care benefits was assumed for 2003 (2002: 9.2%; 2001: 9%). The rate was assumed to decrease gradually to 4.5% for 2011 and remain at that level thereafter. The effect of a 1% increase each year in the assumed health-care cost trend rate would be to increase the post-retirement benefit expense by $11 million (2002: $10 million; 2001: $7 million) and the accumulated post-retirement benefit obligation by $97 million (2002: $80 million; 2001: $60 million).

The accrued benefit asset (liability) is included in other assets and other liabilities as follows:

$ millions, as at October 31	Pension benefit plans			Other benefit plans		
	2003	2002	2001	2003	2002	2001
Other assets (Note 9)	$ 747	$ 604	$ 533	$ –	$ –	$ –
Other liabilities (Note 11)	(144)	(137)	(120)	(564)	(525)	(467)
Accrued benefit asset (liability), net of valuation allowance	$ 603	$ 467	$ 413	$ (564)	$ (525)	$ (467)

CIBC also maintains defined contribution plans for certain employees. The expense for CIBC's defined contribution pension plans totalled $19 million (2002: $25 million; 2001: $26 million). Expense for government pension plans (Canada Pension Plan/Quebec Pension Plan/U.S. Federal Insurance Contributions Act) totalled $82 million (2002: $87 million; 2001: $78 million).

KEY TERMS

accrued benefit
   obligation, 1068
accumulated benefit
   obligation, 1067
actual return, 1070
actuarial assumptions,
   1066
actuarial gains and
   losses, 1071
actuaries, 1066
asset experience gain
   or loss, 1079
attribution period, 1070
capitalization
   approach, 1068
contributory plans, 1064
corridor approach, 1079
defined benefit plan, 1065
defined contribution
   plan, 1064
EARSL, 1071
event accrual method,
   1093
expected average
   remaining service
   life, 1071
expected return, 1070
experience gains and
   losses, 1071
funded, 1063
funded status, 1072
liability experience gain
   or loss, 1079
market-related value of
   plan assets, 1078
noncapitalization
   approach, 1069
noncontributory plans,
   1064
past service cost, 1071
pension plan, 1063
projected benefit
   obligation (PBO), 1068
service cost, 1070
settlement rate, 1070
transitional asset, 1071

Summary of Learning Objectives

1 Distinguish between accounting for the employer's pension costs and accounting for the pension fund.

The company or employer is the organization sponsoring the pension plan. It incurs the cost and makes contributions to the pension fund. The fund or plan is the entity that receives the contributions from the employer, administers the pension assets, and makes the benefit payments to the pension recipients (retired employees). The fund should be a separate legal and accounting entity for which a set of books is maintained and financial statements are prepared.

2 Identify types of pension plans and their characteristics.

The two most common types of pension arrangements are: (1) Defined contribution plans: the employer agrees to contribute to a pension trust a certain sum each period based on a formula. This formula may consider such factors as age, length of employee service, employer's profits, and compensation level. Only the employer's contribution is defined; no promise is usually made regarding the ultimate benefits paid out to the employees. (2) Defined benefit plans: define the benefits that the employee will receive at the time of retirement. The formula typically used provides for the benefits to be a function of the employee's years of service and compensation level when he or she nears retirement.

3 Identify the accounting and disclosure requirements for defined contribution plans.

Defined contribution plans are accounted for on a cash basis. Companies are required to disclose the expense recognized for the period, the nature and effect of significant matters affecting comparability from period to period, and the total cash amount initially recognized in the period as paid or payable for that period in relation to the future benefits.

4 Explain alternative measures for valuing the pension obligation.

One measure of the pension obligation bases it only on the benefits vested to the employees. Vested benefits are those that the employee is entitled to receive even if the employee is no longer employed. The vested benefits pension obligation is calculated using current salary levels and includes only vested benefits. Another measure of the obligation, called the accumulated benefit obligation, bases the calculation of the deferred compensation amount on all years of service performed by employees under the plan, both vested and nonvested, using current salary levels. A third measure, called the projected benefit obligation, bases the calculation of the deferred compensation amount on both vested and nonvested service using future salaries.

5 Identify the components of pension expense.

Pension expense is a function of the following components: (1) service cost, (2) interest on the liability, (3) expected return on plan assets, (4) amortization of past service costs, (5) amortization of the net actuarial gain or loss, and (6) amortization of any transitional asset or obligation.

6 Identify transactions and events that affect the projected benefit obligation.

The projected benefit obligation is the actuarial present value of the accumulated pension benefits earned for employee services provided to date based on the pension formula, incorporating expected future salaries. The balance of the PBO is increased by the pension benefits earned by employees for services provided in the current period, by the interest cost on the outstanding obligation, by plan amendments that usually increase employee entitlements for prior services, and by actuarial losses. The balance is reduced by the payment of pension benefits and by actuarial gains.

7 Identify transactions and events that affect the balance of the plan assets.

Plan assets are the cash and investments set aside to meet retirement benefit payments when they become due. They are measured at fair value. Plan assets are increased by company and employee contributions and the actual return earned on fund assets (that is, the expected return plus the asset experience gain or minus the asset experience loss), and are reduced by pension benefits paid to retirees.

8 Explain the usefulness of—and be able to complete—a work sheet to support the employer's pension expense entries.

A pension work sheet accumulates all the information needed to calculate pension expense, including continuity schedules for the off-balance-sheet projected benefit obligation, fund assets, unrecognized past service costs, unrecognized actuarial gains and losses, and unrecognized transition amount. By completing the changes in the off-balance-sheet memo accounts and pulling out information that affects the calculation of pension expense, year-end balances are determined. The balances in the memo accounts reconcile to the reported accrued pension asset/liability account on the company's balance sheet.

9 Explain the pension accounting treatment of past service costs.

Past service costs arise from giving credit to employees for service provided prior to the date of initiation or amendment of a pension plan and, for defined benefit plans, are measured as the increase in the projected benefit obligation as a result of such change. Because the increased pension benefits are expected to benefit the employer as the employee group covered provides service to the company in the future, past service costs are amortized to pension expense over the expected period to full eligibility of the affected employee group.

10 Explain the pension accounting treatment of actuarial gains and losses, including corridor amortization.

Actuarial gains and losses represent the difference between the expected return on plan assets and the actual return earned, the change in the projected benefit obligation due to the difference between expected variables and actual outcomes, and changes in actuarial assumptions. If these changes were taken into pension expense each year in their entirety, reported pension expense would fluctuate widely. Because the actuary uses long-term rates to project amounts necessary to fund the estimated pension obligation, expected long-term rates are used to calculate pension expense. The net actuarial gain or loss is required to be amortized into pension expense only when it grows to an amount in excess of 10% of the greater of the PBO and the fair or market-related value of the fund assets. At a minimum, any excess is required to be amortized over the employee group's EARSL.

11 Identify the differences between pensions and post-retirement health care benefits.

Post-retirement health care benefits are more difficult to measure than pension benefits due mainly to the uncertainties associated with the changing health care environment and the variability of usage by those eligible for benefits.

12 Identify the financial reporting and disclosure requirements for defined benefit plans.

There are two levels of disclosure required by GAAP: all companies are required to report information about amounts recorded in the financial statements, the off-balance-sheet accounts, and underlying assumptions used; and public companies and others with broad public accountability have additional requirements. These include reconciliations of both the PBO and plan asset balances from one year to the next and additional information about the unamortized balances.

13 Identify the financial accounting and reporting requirements for defined benefit plans whose benefits do not vest or accumulate.

In this case, full accrual accounting cannot be applied as there is no specified service period over which to accrue the cost of and liability for the benefits. Instead, the "event accrual" method is applied: when the event obligating the employer to provide the benefit occurs, the total estimated expense and liability are recognized.

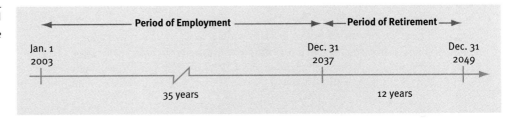

Example of a One-Person Plan

Objective 14

Explain the basics of what current service cost, projected benefit obligation, and past service cost represent.

The following simplified example is provided to enable students to better visualize and understand some of the new concepts introduced in this chapter.

Assume that Lee Sung, age 30, begins employment with HTSM Corp. on January 1, 2003 at a starting salary of $37,500. It is expected that Lee will work for HTSM Corp. for 35 years, retiring on December 31, 2037 when Lee is 65 years old. Taking into account estimated compensation increases of approximately 4% per year, Lee's salary at retirement is expected to be $150,000. Further assume that mortality tables indicate the life expectancy of someone age 65 in 2037 is 12 years.

The timeline in Illustration 20A-1 provides a snapshot of much of this information.

Illustration 20A-1

Timeline

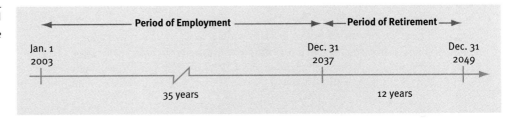

HTSM Corp. sponsors a defined benefit pension plan for its employees with the following **pension benefit formula**.

Annual pension benefit on retirement = 2% of salary at retirement for each year of service, or
= 2% × final salary × years of service

In order to measure 2003 pension amounts, dollars paid in the future must be discounted to their present values. Assume a **discount rate of 6%**, the current yield on high-quality debt instruments.

Current Service Cost

Year 2003

How much pension does Lee Sung earn for the one year of service in 2003? Applying the pension formula **using projected salaries**:

Annual pension benefit on retirement = 2% × \$150,000 × 1 year
= \$3,000 per year of retirement

That is, by virtue of working one year, Lee Sung has earned an entitlement to a pension of \$3,000 per year.

However, to determine the company's expense in 2003 related to this benefit, HTSM must discount these future payments to their present value at December 31, 2003. This is a two-step process. First, the pension annuity of \$3,000 per year for an estimated 12 years is discounted to its present value on December 31, 2037, the employee's retirement date. Because this is still 34 years in the future at December 31, 2003, the annuity's present value at the beginning of retirement is discounted to its present value at the end of 2003. The calculations are as follows.

PV of \$3,000 annuity ($n = 12$, $i = 6\%$) at Dec. 31, 2037 = \$3,000 × 8.38384 (Table A-4)
= \$25,151.52

PV of amount of \$25,151.52 ($n = 34$, $i = 6\%$) at Dec. 31, 2003 = \$25,151.52 × .13791 (Table A-2)
= \$3,469

Therefore the current service cost to HTSM of the pension benefit earned by Lee Sung in 2003 is \$3,469. This is a primary component of the period's pension expense.

Year 2004

The calculation of HTSM's current service cost for 2004 is identical to 2003, assuming a continuing discount rate of 6% and no change in the pension formula. The only difference is that the \$3,000 of pension benefit earned by Lee Sung in 2004 is discounted back to December 31, 2004 instead of 2003. The calculation is as follows.

Annual pension benefit on retirement = 2% × \$150,000 × 1 year
= \$3,000 per year of retirement

PV of \$3,000 annuity ($n = 12$, $i = 6\%$) at Dec. 31, 2037 = \$3,000 × 8.38384 (Table A-4)
= \$25,151.52

PV of amount of \$25,151.52 ($n = 33$, $i = 6\%$) at Dec. 31, 2004 = \$25,151.52 × .14619 (Table A-2)
= \$3,677

Therefore the current service cost to HTSM of the pension benefit earned by Lee Sung in 2004 is \$3,677.

Projected Benefit Obligation

At December 31, 2004

The projected benefit obligation calculation is similar to the current service cost except that it represents the present value of the pension benefits **accumulated for employee services provided to date as determined under the pension benefit formula**. Because 2003 was the first year of employment, we will assume that the accrued benefit obligation or PBO at December 31, 2003 is \$3,469, the same as the current service cost. At December 31, 2004, the PBO is determined as follows.

Effective Interest Method

Although the amounts initially capitalized as an asset and recorded as an obligation are calculated at the same present value, **the subsequent amortization of the asset and the discharge of the obligation are independent accounting processes**.

Over the term of the lease, the effective interest method is used to allocate each lease payment between principal and interest. This method produces a periodic interest expense equal to a constant percentage of the obligation's outstanding balance. The discount rate used by the lessee to determine the present value of the minimum lease payments is used by the lessee in applying the effective interest method to capital leases.

Capital Lease Method Illustrated

Lessor Corporation and Lessee Corporation sign a lease agreement dated January 1, 2005, which calls for Lessor Corporation to lease equipment to Lessee Corporation beginning January 1, 2005. The lease agreement's terms and provisions and other pertinent data are identified in Illustration 21-4.

Illustration 21-4

Lease Agreement Terms and Conditions

1. The lease term is five years, the lease agreement is non-cancellable, and requires equal rental payments of $25,981.62 at the beginning of each year (annuity due basis), beginning January 1, 2005.
2. The equipment has a fair value at the lease's inception of $100,000, an estimated economic life of five years, and no residual value.
3. Lessee Corporation pays all executory costs directly to third parties except for the property taxes of $2,000 per year, which are included in the annual payments to the lessor.
4. The lease contains no renewal options; the equipment reverts to Lessor Corporation at the termination of the lease.
5. Lessee Corporation's incremental borrowing rate is 11% per year.
6. Lessee Corporation amortizes similar equipment it owns on a straight-line basis.
7. Lessor Corporation set the annual rental to earn a rate of return on its investment of 10% per year; this fact is known to Lessee Corporation.

The lease meets the criteria for classification as a capital lease because (1) the lease term of five years, being equal to the equipment's estimated economic life of five years, satisfies the 75% test; or because (2) the minimum lease payments' present value ($100,000 as calculated below) exceeds 90% of the property's fair value ($100,000).

The **minimum lease payments** are $119,908.10 ($23,981.62 × 5), and the amount capitalized as leased assets is $100,000, the present value of the minimum lease payments determined as follows.

Illustration 21-5

Calculation of Capitalized Lease Payments

Capitalized amount = ($25,981.62 − $2,000) × present value of an annuity due of $1 for
　　　　　　　　　5 periods at 10% (Table A-5)
　　　　　　　= $23,981.62 × 4.16986
　　　　　　　= $100,000

The lessor's implicit interest rate of 10% is used instead of the lessee's incremental borrowing rate of 11% because (1) it is lower and (2) the lessee has knowledge of it.[9]

---

[9] If Lessee Corporation had an incremental borrowing rate of 9% (lower than the 10% rate used by Lessor Corporation) and it did not know the rate used by Lessor, the present value calculation yields a capitalized amount of $101,675.35 ($23,981.62 × 4.23972). Because this amount exceeds the equipment's $100,000 fair value, Lessee Corporation capitalizes the $100,000 and uses 10% as its effective rate for amortization of the lease obligation.

The entry to record the capital lease on Lessee Corporation's books on January 1, 2005 is:

Equipment under Capital Leases	100,000	
Obligations under Capital Leases		100,000

A = L + SE
+100,000 +100,000
Cash flows: No effect

The journal entry to record the first lease payment on January 1, 2005 is:

Property Tax Expense	2,000.00	
Obligations under Capital Leases	23,981.62	
Cash		25,981.62

A = L + SE
−25,981.62 −23,981.62 −2,000.00
Cash flows: ↓ 25,981.62 outflow

Each lease payment of $25,981.62 consists of three elements: (1) a reduction in the principal of the lease obligation, (2) a financing cost (interest expense), and (3) executory costs (property taxes). The total financing cost or interest expense over the lease's term is the difference between the lease payments' present value ($100,000) and the actual cash disbursed, net of executory costs ($119,908.10), or $19,908.10. The annual interest expense, applying the effective interest method, is a function of the outstanding obligation, as illustrated below.

LESSEE CORPORATION
Lease Amortization Schedule
(Annuity due basis)

Date	Annual Lease Payment	Interest (10%) on Unpaid Obligation	Reduction of Lease Obligation	Balance of Lease Obligation
	(a)	(b)	(c)	(d)
1/1/05				$100,000.00
1/1/05	$ 23,981.62	$ –0–	$ 23,981.62	76,018.38
1/1/06	23,981.62	7,601.84	16,379.78	59,638.60
1/1/07	23,981.62	5,963.86	18,017.76	41,620.84
1/1/08	23,981.62	4,162.08	19,819.54	21,801.30
1/1/09	23,981.62	2,180.32*	21,801.30	–0–
	$119,908.10	$19,908.10	$100,000.00	

(a) Lease payment as required by lease, excluding executory costs.
(b) 10% of the preceding balance of (d) except for 1/1/05; since this is an annuity due, no time has elapsed at the date of the first payment and no interest has accrued.
(c) (a) minus (b).
(d) Preceding balance minus (c).
*Rounded by 19 cents.

Illustration 21-6

Lease Amortization Schedule for Lessee—Annuity Due Basis

At Lessee Corporation's fiscal year end, December 31, 2005, accrued interest is recorded as follows.

Interest Expense	7,601.84	
Interest Payable		7,601.84

A = L + SE
+7,601.84 −7,601.84
Cash flows: No effect

Amortization of the leased equipment over its lease term of five years, applying Lessee Corporation's normal amortization policy (straight-line method), results in the following entry on December 31, 2005.

A	=	L	+	SE
−20,000				−20,000

Cash flows: No effect

Amortization Expense—Leased Equipment	20,000	
Accumulated Amortization—Leased Equipment		20,000
($100,000 ÷ 5 years)		

At December 31, 2005, the assets recorded under capital leases are separately identified on the lessee's balance sheet, or in a note cross-referenced to the balance sheet. Similarly, the related obligations are separately identified. The principal portion due within one year or the operating cycle, whichever is longer, is classified with current liabilities and the remainder with noncurrent liabilities. For example, the current portion of the December 31, 2005 total obligation of $76,018.38 in the lessee's amortization schedule **is the amount of the reduction in the principal of the obligation within the next 12 months,** or $16,379.78. The liability section as it relates to lease transactions at December 31, 2005 is as follows.

Illustration 21-7

Reporting Current and Noncurrent Lease Liabilities

Current liabilities	
Interest payable	$ 7,601.84
Obligations under capital leases	16,379.78
Noncurrent liabilities	
Obligations under capital leases	$59,638.60

The journal entry to record the lease payment on January 1, 2006 is as follows.

A	=	L	+	SE
−25,981.62		−23,981.62		−2,000.00

Cash flows: ↓ 25,981.62 outflow

Property Tax Expense	2,000.00	
Interest Payable[10]	7,601.84	
Obligations under Capital Leases	16,379.78	
Cash		25,981.62

Entries through 2009 follow the pattern above. Other executory costs (insurance and maintenance) assumed by Lessee Corporation are recorded the same way as the company records operating costs incurred on other assets it owns.

Upon expiration of the lease, the amount capitalized as leased equipment is fully amortized and the lease obligation is fully discharged. If not purchased, the equipment is returned to the lessor, and the leased equipment and related accumulated amortization accounts are removed from the books. If the equipment is purchased for $5,000 at the termination of the lease, and the equipment's estimated total life is changed from five to seven years, the following entry is made.

A	=	L	+	SE
0		0		0

Cash flows: ↓ 5,000 outflow

Equipment ($100,000 + $5,000)	105,000	
Accumulated Amortization—Leased Equipment	100,000	
Equipment under Capital Leases		100,000
Accumulated Amortization—Equipment		100,000
Cash		5,000

---

[10] This entry assumes the company does not prepare reversing entries. If reversing entries are used, the Interest Expense account is debited for this amount.

Reporting and Disclosure Requirements— Capital Leases

Consistent with the recognition of property, plant, and equipment and a long-term liability, most of the required disclosures are similar to those required in *CICA Handbook* Sections 3061 and 3210 for property, plant, and equipment and long-term liabilities. *CICA Handbook* Sections 3065.21 to .26 identify the following required disclosures:

1. The gross amount of assets recorded under capital leases and related accumulated amortization.

2. Amortization expense on leased assets, either disclosed separately or as part of amortization expense for fixed assets, and the methods and rates of amortization.

3. Separate disclosure of lease obligations from other long-term obligations, with separate disclosure of related details about interest rates, expiry dates, and any significant restrictions imposed as a result of the lease agreements.

4. The current portion, if any, of the lease obligations, as a current liability.

5. Future minimum lease payments, in the aggregate and for each of the five succeeding fiscal years, with a separate deduction for amounts included in the minimum lease payments representing executory costs and imputed interest. (The resulting net amount is the total lease obligation reported on the balance sheet.)

6. Interest expense related to lease obligations, disclosed separately or included in interest on long-term indebtedness.

Although not required, it may be appropriate to disclose separately total contingent rentals (rentals based on a factor other than the passage of time) as well as the amount of future minimum rentals receivable from non-cancellable sub-leases.

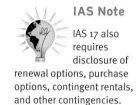

3 Objective
Identify the lessee's disclosure requirements for capital leases.

IAS Note

IAS 17 also requires disclosure of renewal options, purchase options, contingent rentals, and other contingencies.

Accounting for an Operating Lease

Under an operating lease, **neither the leased asset nor the obligation to make lease payments is given accounting recognition.** Instead, the lease payments are treated as rent expense, assigned to the accounting periods benefiting from the use of the leased asset.[11] Appropriate accruals or deferrals are made if the accounting period ends between cash payment dates.

Assume the capital lease described in Illustration 21-4 and accounted for above does not qualify as a capital lease and, by default, is accounted for as an operating lease. The charge to the income statement for rent expense each year is $25,981.62, the amount of the rental payment. The journal entry to record the payment each January 1 is as follows.

4 Objective
Identify the lessee's accounting and disclosure requirements for an operating lease.

Prepaid Rent	25,981.62	
Cash		25,981.62

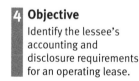

A = L + SE
0   0   0

Cash flows: ↓ 25,981.62 outflow

At each December 31 fiscal year end, the following entry is made, assuming adjusting entries are prepared only annually.

---

[11] *EIC-21*, "Accounting for Lease Inducements by the Lessee" (CICA: January 21, 1991) provides guidance on accounting for the benefits of lease inducements such as an upfront cash payment to the lessee, initial rent-free periods, etc. It is recommended that such benefits be taken into income over the lease's term on a straight-line or other basis that is representative of the pattern of benefits from the leased property.

A = L + SE
−25,981.62   −25,981.62
Cash flows: No effect

| Rent Expense | 25,981.62 | |
| Prepaid Rent | | 25,981.62 |

Reporting and Disclosure Requirements— Operating Leases

While disclosure of the amount of operating lease rentals charged against income and other details related to operating lease agreements may be desirable, there are only two required disclosures.

1. The future minimum lease payments, in total and for each of the next five years, and

2. A description of the nature of other commitments under such leases.[12]

These disclosures allow readers to assess the impact of such agreements on the organization.

Perspectives

Objective 5
Contrast the operating and capitalization methods of recording leases.

As indicated above, if the lease had been accounted for as an operating lease, the first-year charge to operations would have been $25,981.62, the amount of the rental payment. Treating the transaction as a capital lease, however, resulted in a first-year charge of $29,601.84: straight-line amortization of $20,000, interest expense of $7,601.84, and executory expenses of $2,000. Illustration 21-8 shows that while the total charges to operations are the same over the lease term whether the lease is accounted for as a capital lease or as an operating lease, the charges are higher in the earlier years and lower in the later years under the capital lease treatment. The higher charges in the early years are one reason lessees are reluctant to classify leases as capital leases. Lessees, especially when real estate leases are involved, claim that it is not more costly to operate the leased asset in the early years than in the later years; thus, they advocate an even charge similar to that provided by the operating method.

Illustration 21-8

Comparison of Charges to Operations—Capital vs. Operating Leases

LESSEE CORPORATION
Schedule of Charges to Operations
Capital Lease versus Operating Lease

| | Capital Lease | | | | Operating Lease | |
Year	Amortization	Executory Costs	Interest	Total Charge	Lease Charge	Difference
2005	$ 20,000	$ 2,000	$ 7,601.84	$ 29,601.84	$ 25,981.62	$ 3,620.22
2006	20,000	2,000	5,963.86	27,963.86	25,981.62	1,982.24
2007	20,000	2,000	4,162.08	26,162.08	25,981.62	180.46
2008	20,000	2,000	2,180.32	24,180.32	25,981.62	$(1,801.30)
2009	20,000	2,000	—	22,000.00	25,981.62	(3,981.62)
	$100,000	$10,000	$19,908.10	$129,908.10	$129,908.10	$ –0–

International Insight

In some countries, such as Germany, all leases can be off-balance-sheet.

If an accelerated amortization method is used, the differences between the amounts charged to operations under the two methods are even larger in the earlier and later years.

---

[12] *CICA Handbook*, Section 3065.31-.33.

The most important and significant difference between the two approaches, however, is the effect on the balance sheet. The capital lease approach results in an asset and related liability of $100,000 initially reported on the balance sheet, **whereas no such asset or liability is reported under the operating method.** Refer back to Illustration 21-1 to understand the significance of the amounts left off the statement of financial position for WestJet, Transforce, and Helijet. It is not surprising that the business community resists capitalizing leases, as the resulting **higher debt-to-equity ratio, reduced total asset turnover,** and **reduced rate of return on total assets** are perceived to have a detrimental effect on the company.

What do the Numbers Mean?

And resist this they have! While the intent of *CICA Handbook* Section 3065 was to have the accounting for leases based on whether or not the risks and benefits of ownership were transferred, specification of 75% of useful life and 90% of the fair value of the asset in the standard were interpreted by management as "rates to beat." That is, leases have been and continue to be specifically engineered to ensure ownership is not transferred and to have them come in just under the 75% and 90% hurdles so that the capitalization criteria are not triggered.

The experience with this standard remains one of the key reasons why the Accounting Standards Board shies away from identifying specific numerical criteria in its standards. Its preference is to rely on principles-based, rather than rules-based, guidance.

Whether this resistance is well founded is a matter of conjecture. From a cash flow point of view, the company is in the same position whether the lease is accounted for as an operating or a capital lease. The reasons managers often give when arguing against capitalization are that it can more easily lead to violation of loan covenants; it can affect the amount of compensation received (for example, a stock compensation plan tied to earnings); and it can lower rates of return and increase debt-to-equity relationships, thus making the company less attractive to present and potential investors.[13]

Illustration of Capital and Operating Lease Disclosures by the Lessee

The following excerpts from the financial statements of Transforce Income Fund for the year ended December 31, 2003 illustrate the disclosure by a lessee of both capital and operating leases. Transforce, based in Montreal, is a leading player in the freight transportation industry.

Transforce Income Fund (excerpts)
Notes to Consolidated Financial Statements

Year ended December 31, 2003 (Tabular amounts in thousands of dollars)	**2003**	2002
Fixed assets (note 5)	$200,455	$208,765
Current portion of long-term debt (note 8)	16,974	16,264
Long term debt (note 8)	73,430	57,490
Commitments and contingencies (note 14)		

Illustration 21-9

Capital and Operating Lease Disclosures by a Lessee—Transforce

Digital Tool

Student Toolkit— Additional Disclosures

www.wiley.com/canada/kieso

[13] One study indicates that management's behaviour did change as a result of the profession's requirements to capitalize certain leases. For example, many companies restructured their leases to avoid capitalization; others increased their purchases of assets instead of leasing; and others, faced with capitalization, postponed their debt offerings or issued shares instead. However, it is interesting to note that the study found no significant effect on share or bond prices as a result of capitalization of leases. A. Rashad Abdel-khalik, "The Economic Effects on Lessees of *FASB Statement No. 13,* Accounting for Leases," Research Report (Stamford, Conn.: FASB, 1981).

Illustration 21-9

Capital and Operating Lease Disclosures by a Lessee—Transforce
(continued)

2. **Significant accounting policies:** (in part)

Capital leases transferring substantially all the risks and benefits of ownership relating to property leased to the Fund are capitalized by recording as assets and liabilities the present value of payments provided for under these leases. Leased property capitalized under this policy is amortized over its estimated useful life. A portion of lease payments is accounted for as a reduction of the related liability, with the remainder accounted for as interest.

5. **Fixed assets:**

	2003		2002	
	Cost	Accumulated depreciation	Cost	Accumulated depreciation
Land	$ 29,886	$ —	$ 30,404	$ —
Buildings	45,877	12,066	44,758	10,860
Rolling stock	247,822	134,246	237,685	118,197
Furniture, machinery and hardware/software	63,035	45,181	60,739	40,611
Leasehold improvements	10,648	5,320	9,805	4,958
	397,268	196,813	383,391	174,626
Accumulated depreciation	(196,813)		(174,626)	
Net carrying value	$200,455		$208,765	

Fixed assets include property under capital leases which are recorded at the present value of the payments provided for under these leases. The cost of these assets, which consist of rolling stock and machinery totals $48,763,000 (2002—$43,045,000) and related accumulated depreciation amounts to $14,579,000 (2002—$11,206,000).

During the period, the Fund acquired fixed assets in the amount of $9,936,000 under capital leases and conditional sales contracts (2002—$5,924,000).

8. **Long-term debt:** (in part)

Obligations under capital leases, collateralized by rolling stock and machinery having a carrying value of $34,185,000 at interest rates varying between 4.44% and 8.51%, payable in monthly instalments of $808,000, principal and interest, maturing on various dates through August 2009 (see (c)):

	$30,339	$28,189

(c) The interest for the period on obligations under capital leases totalled $2,029,000 (2002—$1,915,000).

Minimum instalments payable under capital leases amounting to approximately $34,791,000, of which $4,452,000 is interest, for the subsequent years are as follows:

2004	$10,820
2005	8,020
2006	7,672
2007	6,177
2008	1,898
2009 and thereafter	204

14. **Commitments and contingencies:** (in part)

(a) The Fund entered into operating leases expiring on various dates through to January 2022, which call for lease payments of $88,916,000 with respect to rolling stock, computer hardware, machinery and premises. Minimum lease payments for the upcoming years are as follows:

2004	$26,387
2005	17,440
2006	10,737
2007	7,014
2008	3,956
2009 to 2022	23,382

ACCOUNTING BY LESSORS

Economics of Leasing

The lessor determines the rental amount based on the rate of return—the implicit rate—needed to justify leasing the asset.[14] The key variables considered in establishing the rate of return are the lessee's credit standing, the length of the lease, and the status of the residual value (guaranteed versus unguaranteed). In the Lessor Corporation/Lessee Corporation example in Illustration 21-4, the lessor wanted a 10% return, the investment in the equipment (and its fair value) was $100,000, and the estimated residual value at the end of the lease was zero. Lessor Corporation determined the amount of the rental payment in the following manner.

Net investment in leased equipment	$100,000.00
Less: Present value of the amount to be recovered through bargain purchase option or residual value at end of lease term	–0–
Present value of amount to be recovered through lease payments	$100,000.00
Five beginning-of-the-year lease payments to yield a 10% return ($100,000 ÷ 4.16986[a])	$ 23,981.62
[a]PV of an annuity due (Table A-5); i = 10%, n = 5	

Illustration 21-10

Calculation of Lease Payments by Lessor

If a bargain purchase option or other residual value is involved, the lessor does not have to recover as much through the rental payments. Therefore, the present value of such amounts is deducted before determining the lease payment. This is illustrated later in the chapter in more detail.

Classification of Leases by the Lessor

From the **lessor's** standpoint,[15] all leases are classified for accounting purposes as one of the following:

(a) Operating lease or

(b) Direct financing lease or sales-type lease.

Similar to the lessee's decision, where the risks and benefits are retained for the most part by the lessor, the lessor accounts for the agreement as an operating lease.[16] Where the risks and benefits of ownership related to the leased property are transferred from the lessor to the lessee, the lessor usually accounts for the lease as either a direct financing or a sales-type lease.

Whether a lease is a direct financing or a sales-type lease depends on the specific situation. Some companies enter into lease agreements as a means of selling their products

IAS Note

IAS 17 does not differentiate between direct financing and sales-type leases.

---

[14] In lease versus buy decisions and in determining the lessor's implicit rate, income tax consequences must be factored in. A major variable is whether the CRA requires the lease to be accounted for as a conditional sale, usually established by whether the title is transferred by the end of the lease term or the lessee has a bargain purchase option. Tax shields relating to the rental payment and capital cost allowance significantly affect the return and an investment's net present value.

[15] Not surprisingly, there are fewer lessors than lessee companies. *Financial Reporting in Canada—2003* (CICA) reports that only 10% of its 200 survey companies in 2003 provided information about their roles as lessors, while more than 75% had disclosures related to their activities as lessees.

[16] *CICA Handbook*, Section 3065.09-.10.

(usually a sales-type lease) while other companies are in business to finance a variety of assets in order to generate financing income (usually a direct financing lease).

Capitalization Criteria

If at the inception of the lease agreement the lease meets **one or more** of the following Group I criteria and **both** of the Group II criteria, the lessor classifies and accounts for the arrangement as either a direct financing lease or a sales-type lease.[17] **Note that the Group I criteria are identical to the criteria that must be met for a lease to be classified as a capital lease by a lessee.**

Group I

1. There is reasonable assurance that the lessee will obtain ownership of the leased property by the end of the lease term. If there is a bargain purchase option in the lease, it is assumed that the lessee will exercise it and obtain ownership.

2. The lease term is such that the lessee will receive substantially all of the economic benefits expected to be derived from the use of the leased property over its life. This is usually assumed to occur if the lease term is 75% or more of the economic life of the leased property.

3. The lease allows the lessor to recover its investment in the leased property and to earn a return on the investment. This is assumed to occur if the present value of the minimum lease payments (excluding executory costs) is equal to substantially all (usually 90% or more) of the fair value of the leased property.

Group II

1. The credit risk associated with the lease is normal when compared with the risk of collection of similar receivables.

2. The amounts of any unreimbursable costs that are likely to be incurred by the lessor under the lease can be reasonably estimated.

Why the Group II requirements? The answer is that the profession wants to make sure that the lessor has really transferred the risks and benefits of ownership. If collectibility of payments is not reasonably assured or if performance by the lessor is incomplete, then it is inappropriate to remove the leased asset from the lessor's books and recognize revenue. In short, **the Group II criteria are standard revenue recognition criteria** applied to a lease situation.

Computer leasing companies at one time used to buy IBM equipment, lease it out, and remove the leased assets from their balance sheets. In leasing the asset, the computer lessors stated that they would substitute new IBM equipment if obsolescence occurred. However, when IBM introduced a new computer line, IBM refused to sell it to the computer leasing companies. As a result, a number of computer leasing companies could not meet their contracts with their customers and were forced to take back the old equipment. What the computer leasing companies had taken off the books now had to be reinstated. Such a case demonstrates one reason for Group II requirements.

How do you distinguish between a sales-type and a direct financing lease? The difference for the lessor between these classifications **is the presence or absence of a manufacturer's or dealer's profit (or loss)**. A sales-type lease incorporates a manufacturer's or dealer's profit, but a direct financing lease does not. The profit (or loss) to the lessor is the difference between the fair value of the leased property at the lease inception, and the lessor's cost or carrying amount (book value). Normally, sales-type leases arise when manufacturers or dealers use leasing as a means of marketing their products. The present value of the pay-

---

[17] *CICA Handbook*, Section 3065.07.

ments to be received **is the sales price**, which is normally higher than the cost of the asset to the company. Thus a profit is earned on the "sale" as well as on the financing of the sale.

Direct financing leases, on the other hand, generally result from arrangements with lessors that are primarily engaged in financing operations, such as lease-finance companies, banks, insurance companies, and pension trusts. These lessors acquire assets specified by lessees. Their business model is to earn interest income on the financing arrangement with the lessee. However, it is the existence of the profit (or loss) at the inception of the lease that requires application of sales-type lease accounting, not the lessor's type of business.

All leases that do not qualify as direct financing or sales-type leases are classified and accounted for by the lessor as operating leases. The following flowchart shows the circumstances under which a lease is classified by the lessor as operating, direct financing, or sales-type.

Illustration 21-12

Flowchart of Lessor's Criteria for Lease Classification

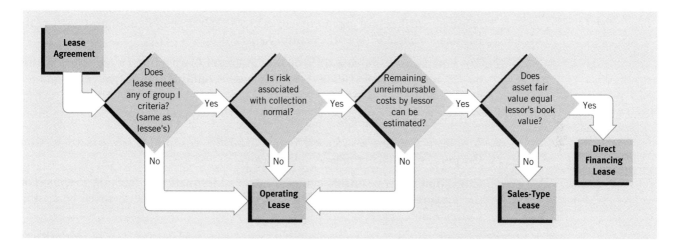

It is possible that a lessor that does not meet both Group II criteria will classify a lease as an **operating** lease while the lessee will classify the same lease as a **capital** lease. In such an event, both the lessor and lessee carry the asset on their books and both amortize the capitalized asset.

Accounting for a Direct Financing Lease

Leases that are in substance the financing of an asset purchase by a lessee require the lessor to remove the asset from its books and replace it with a receivable. The accounts and information needed to record a direct financing lease are as follows.

8 Objective
Describe the lessor's accounting for direct financing leases.

	DIRECT FINANCING LEASE TERMINOLOGY	
Term	**Account**	**Explanation**
Gross investment in lease	Lease Payments Receivable	The undiscounted lease payments (excluding executory costs) plus any residual value accruing to the lessor at the end of the lease term or any bargain purchase option.
Unearned finance revenue	Unearned Interest Revenue (contra account to Lease Payments Receivable)	The difference between the undiscounted Lease Payments Receivable and the carrying amount of the leased property.
Net investment in lease	Net of the two accounts above	The gross investment (the receivable) less the unearned finance or interest revenue included therein; i.e., the gross investment's present value.

The net investment is the present value of the items making up the gross investment. The difference between these two accounts is the unearned interest. The unearned interest revenue is amortized and taken into income over the lease term by applying the effective interest method. Thus, a constant rate of return is produced on the net investment in the lease.

Illustration of Direct Financing Lease (Annuity Due)

The following direct financing lease example uses the same data as the Lessor Corporation/Lessee Corporation example in Illustration 21-4, which is reproduced below. The information relevant to Lessor Corporation in accounting for this lease transaction is as follows.

1. The lease is for a **five-year term** that begins January 1, 2005, is non-cancellable, and requires equal **rental payments of $25,981.62** at the beginning of each year. Payments include **$2,000 of executory costs** (property taxes).

2. The equipment has a **cost of $100,000** to Lessor Corporation, a **fair value at the lease's inception of $100,000**, an estimated **economic life of five years**, and no residual value.

3. No initial direct costs were incurred in negotiating and closing the lease contract.

4. The lease contains no renewal options and the **equipment reverts to Lessor Corporation** at the termination of the lease.

5. **Collectibility is reasonably assured** and **no additional costs** (with the exception of the property taxes being reimbursed by the lessee) are to be incurred by Lessor Corporation.

6. Lessor Corporation set the annual lease payments to ensure a **rate of return of 10%** on its investment, shown previously in Illustration 21-10.

The lease meets the criteria for classification as a direct financing lease because (1) the lease term exceeds 75% of the equipment's estimated economic life, or (2) the minimum lease payments' present value exceeds 90% of the equipment's fair value, and (3) the credit risk is normal relative to similar receivables (collectibility of the payments is reasonably assured), and (4) there are no further unreimbursable costs to be incurred by Lessor Corporation. It is not a sales-type lease because **there is no dealer profit** between the equipment's fair value ($100,000) and the lessor's cost ($100,000).

The lease payments receivable (gross investment) is calculated as follows.

Illustration 21-13

Calculation of Lease Payments Receivable

Lease payments receivable = Lease payments (excluding executory costs) plus residual value
 or bargain purchase option
= [($25,981.62 − $2,000) × 5] + $0
= $119,908.10

The unearned interest revenue is the difference between the Lease Payments Receivable and the lessor's cost or carrying value of the leased asset, as shown below.

Illustration 21-14

Calculation of Unearned Interest Revenue

Unearned interest revenue = Lease payments receivable minus asset cost or carrying value
= $119,908.10 − $100,000
= $19,908.10

pattern
charge,
visions
indeper
amortiz

Illust

To illus
Lessee
fore cla
the $2,(

Cash
Re

An
a cost b

Amor
Ac

If
are the
rental r
If t
leased
an acco
nificant
are sep

Rep

For **di**
close o
current
culated
from th
Th
minim
income
income
next fi
Th
assess
erated.
of pro

The net investment in this direct financing lease is the lease payments' present value of $100,000 or the gross investment of $119,908.10 minus the unearned interest revenue of $19,908.10.

The acquisition of the asset by the lessor, its transfer to the lessee, the resulting receivable, and the unearned interest income are recorded on January 1, 2005 as follows.

Equipment Purchased for Lease	100,000	
Cash[18]		100,000
Lease Payments Receivable	119,908.10	
Equipment Purchased for Lease		100,000.00
Unearned Interest Revenue—Leases		19,908.10

A = L + SE
0   0   0
Cash flows: ↓ 100,000 outflow

A = L + SE
0   0   0
Cash flows: No effect

The unearned interest revenue is classified on the balance sheet as a contra account to the receivable account. Generally, the lease payments receivable, although **recorded** at the gross investment amount, is **reported** in the balance sheet at the "net investment" amount (gross investment less unearned interest revenue) and entitled "Net investment in capital leases."[19] It is classified either as current or noncurrent, depending on when the net investment is to be recovered.

The leased equipment with a cost of $100,000, representing Lessor Corporation's investment, is replaced with a net lease receivable. In a manner similar to the lessee's treatment of interest, Lessor Corporation applies the effective interest method and recognizes interest revenue as a function of the unrecovered net investment, as shown in Illustration 21-15.

Illustration 21-15

Lease Amortization Schedule for Lessor—Annuity Due Basis

LESSOR CORPORATION
Lease Amortization Schedule
(Annuity due basis)

Date	Annual Lease Payment	Interest (10%) on Net Investment	Net Investment Recovery	Net Investment
	(a)	(b)	(c)	(d)
1/1/05				$100,000.00
1/1/05	$ 23,981.62	$ –0–	$ 23,981.62	76,018.38
1/1/06	23,981.62	7,601.84	16,379.78	59,638.60
1/1/07	23,981.62	5,963.86	18,017.76	41,620.84
1/1/08	23,981.62	4,162.08	19,819.54	21,801.30
1/1/09	23,981.62	2,180.32*	21,801.30	–0–
	$119,908.10	$19,908.10	$100,000.00	

(a) Annual rental that provides a 10% return on net investment (exclusive of executory costs).
(b) Ten percent of the preceding balance of (d) except for 1/1/05.
(c) (a) minus (b).
(d) Preceding balance minus (c).
*Rounded by 19 cents.

[18] The lessor usually finances the purchase of this asset over a term generally coinciding with the term of the lease. Because the lessor's cost of capital is lower than the rate implicit in the lease, the lessor earns a profit generated by the interest spread.

[19] While lessees may record and report the lease obligation on a net basis, lessors tend to recognize the gross amount in receivables. Unlike the lessee, lessors may have hundreds or thousands of lease contracts to administer and the amounts to be collected are the gross receivables. Therefore, for administrative simplicity, amounts received are a direct reduction of the receivable and the interest is determined and adjusted for separately.

[20] CICA
[21] CICA

Further disclosure concerning minimum future rentals and contingent rentals included in income is at management's discretion.[22]

Illustration of Lease Disclosures by Lessors

Excerpts from the financial statements of **Bombardier Inc.** for its year ended January 31, 2004 are reproduced in Illustration 21-18 to provide a good example of the disclosures provided by a lessor for direct financing or sales-type leases as well as operating leases.

Illustration 21-18

Lease Disclosures by a Lessor—Bombardier

Digital Tool

Student Toolkit—
Additional
Disclosures

www.wiley.com/canada/kieso

Consolidated Balance Sheets (in part)
As at January 31
(millions of Canadian dollars)

	Notes	Bombardier Inc. consolidated 2004	2003
Assets			
Cash and cash equivalents		$ 1,619	$ 1,014
Receivables	3	2,438	2,259
Finance receivables	4	4,148	7,013
Assets under operating leases	5	740	1,358

BC - Significant accounting Policies

Financing revenues
Financing revenues are comprised of the following:

a)   Interest income
Interest income related to finance receivables is recognized on an accrual basis, computed on the average daily finance receivables outstanding balance.

b)   Finance lease income
Lease income related to finance leases is recognized over the terms of the applicable leases in a manner that produces a constant rate of return on the lease investment.

c)   Operating lease income
Operating lease income is recognized over the term of the lease on a straight-line basis.

Lease receivables
Assets leased under terms that transfer substantially all of the benefits and risks of ownership to customers are accounted for as direct financing leases and included in finance receivables.

Deferred origination costs
BC defers the direct origination costs of finance receivables. These costs are amortized on a yield basis over the expected term of the finance receivables.

[22] *CICA Handbook*, Section 3065.57-.59.

Illustration 21-18

4. Finance Receivables (in part)

BC's finance receivables were as follows as at January 31:

	Total	2004 Weighted average maturity (months)	Weighted average rate (%)	Total	2003 Weighted average maturity (months)	Weighted average rate (%)
Continued portfolios						
Inventory finance [1]	$ 2,474	5	8.7	$ 2,953	5	8.8
Receivable financing with BRP	84	2	5.2	-	-	-
	2,558			2,953		
Commercial aircraft						
Interim financing	685	7	4.6	786	6	4.5
Long-term leasing	100	68	5.7	136	73	5.6
	785			922		
Total [2]	3,343			3,875		
Allowance for credit losses	(38)			(44)		
Total continued portfolios	3,305			3,831		
Wind-down portfolios						
Manufactured housing [3]	310	245	11.6	434	258	11.6
Business aircraft	265	63	6.7	1,221	55	6.2
Consumer finance	195	88	11.0	342	89	11.4
Industrial equipment	42	37	8.8	59	42	8.8
Receivable factoring	-	-	-	1,039	3	4.3
Other [4]	69	15	8.5	194	21	9.0
Total [5]	881			3,289		
Allowance for credit losses	(38)			(107)		
Total wind-down portfolios	843			3,182		
	$ 4,148			$ 7,013		

[1] Includes $1,582 million securitized to third parties as at January 31, 2004 ($2,089 million as at January 31, 2003).

[2] Comprised of $669 million of loans, $2,558 million of receivables and $116 million of lease receivables as at January 31, 2004 ($771 million, $2,953 million and $151 million respectively, as at January 31, 2003).

[3] In addition, manufactured housing portfolios in public securitization vehicles amounting to $1,559 million as at January 31, 2004 ($2,096 million as at January 31, 2003) were serviced by BC.

[4] Includes the technology management and finance, mid-market equipment commercial finance and small ticket finance portfolios.

[5] Comprised of $690 million of loans and $191 million of lease receivables as at January 31, 2004 ($1,852 million of loans, $1,039 million of receivables and $398 million of lease receivables as at January 31, 2003).

Lease receivables

Lease receivables are mostly concentrated in the commercial aircraft long-term leasing and the business aircraft portfolios, as well as the "other" wind-down portfolios and consist of the following, before allowance for credit losses as at January 31:

	2004 Continued	2004 Wind-down	2003 Continued	2003 Wind-down
Total minimum lease payments	$ 167	$ 227	$ 181	$ 497
Unearned income	(51)	(43)	(30)	(110)
Unguaranteed residual value	-	7	-	11
	$ 116	$ 191	$ 151	$ 398

(or loss). The gross investment and the unearned interest revenue account are the same for both types of leases whether a guaranteed or an unguaranteed residual value is involved.

When recording sales revenue and cost of goods sold, however, there is a difference in accounting for guaranteed and unguaranteed residual values. A guaranteed residual value can be considered part of sales revenue because the lessor knows that the entire amount will be realized. There is less certainty, however, that any unguaranteed residual portion of the asset has been "sold" (i.e., will be realized); therefore, **sales and cost of goods sold are recognized only for the portion of the asset for which realization is assured**. The **gross profit amount on the asset's sale is the same**, however, whether a guaranteed or unguaranteed residual value is involved because **the present value of any unguaranteed residual is withheld from the calculation of both sales and cost of goods sold amounts.**

To illustrate a sales-type lease with and without a guaranteed residual value, assume the same facts as in the preceding examples: the estimated residual value is $5,000 (the present value of which is $3,104.60), the annual lease payments are $23,237.09 (the present value of which is $96,895.40), and the leased equipment has an $85,000 cost to the manufacturer, Lessor Corporation. At the end of the lease term, assume that the leased asset's fair value is $3,000.

The amounts relevant to a sales-type lease are calculated in Illustration 21-31.

Illustration 21-31

Calculation of Lease Amounts by Lessor Corporation— Sales-Type Lease

	Sales-Type Lease	
	Guaranteed Residual Value	Unguaranteed Residual Value
Gross investment	$121,185.45 ([$23,237.09 × 5] + $5,000)	Same
Unearned interest revenue	$21,185.45 ($121,185.45 − [$96,895.40 + $3,104.60])	Same
Sales	$100,000 ($96,895.40 + $3,104.60)	$96,895.40
Cost of goods sold	$85,000	$81,895.40 ($85,000 − $3,104.60)
Gross profit	$15,000 ($100,000 − $85,000)	$15,000 ($96,895.40 − $81,895.40)

The profit recorded by Lessor Corporation at the point of sale is the same, $15,000, whether the residual value is guaranteed or unguaranteed, but the amounts of **sales revenue and cost of goods sold are different.**

The 2005 and 2006 entries and the entry to record the asset's return at the end of the lease term are provided in Illustration 21-32. The only differences pertain to the original entry that recognizes the lease and the final entry to record the leased asset's return.

The estimated unguaranteed residual value in a sales-type lease (and a direct financing-type lease) must be reviewed periodically. If the estimate of the unguaranteed residual value declines, the accounting for the transaction must be revised using the changed estimate. The decline represents a reduction in the lessor's net investment and is recognized as a loss in the period in which the residual estimate is reduced. Upward adjustments in estimated residual value are not recognized.

Guaranteed Residual Value			Unguaranteed Residual Value		
To record sales-type lease at inception (January 1, 2005):					
Cost of Goods Sold	85,000.00		Cost of Goods Sold	81,895.40	
Lease Payments Receivable	121,185.45		Lease Payments Receivable	121,185.45	
Sales Revenue		100,000.00	Sales Revenue		96,895.40
Unearned Interest Revenue		21,185.45	Unearned Interest Revenue		21,185.45
Inventory		85,000.00	Inventory		85,000.00
To record receipt of the first lease payment (January 1, 2005):					
Cash	25,237.09		Cash	25,237.09	
Lease Payments Receivable		23,237.09	Lease Payments Receivable		23,237.09
Property Tax Expense		2,000.00	Property Tax Expense		2,000.00
To recognize interest revenue earned during the first year (December 31, 2005):					
Unearned Interest Revenue	7,676.29		Unearned Interest Revenue	7,676.29	
Interest Revenue		7,676.29	Interest Revenue		7,676.29
(See lease amortization schedule, Illustration 21-29)					
To record receipt of the second lease payment (January 1, 2006):					
Cash	25,237.09		Cash	25,237.09	
Lease Payments Receivable		23,237.09	Lease Payments Receivable		23,237.09
Property Tax Expense		2,000.00	Property Tax Expense		2,000.00
To recognize interest revenue earned during the second year (December 31, 2006):					
Unearned Interest Revenue	6,120.21		Unearned Interest Revenue	6,120.21	
Interest Revenue		6,120.21	Interest Revenue		6,120.21
To record receipt of residual value at end of lease term (December 31, 2009):					
Inventory	3,000		Inventory	3,000	
Cash	2,000		Loss on Capital Lease	2,000	
Lease Payments Receivable		5,000	Lease Payments Receivable		5,000

Bargain Purchase Options

A bargain purchase option allows the lessee to purchase the leased property for a future price that is substantially less than the property's expected future fair value. The price is so favourable at the lease's inception that the future exercise of the option is reasonably assured. **If a bargain purchase option exists, the lessee's accounting assumes it will be exercised and the title to the leased property will be transferred to the lessee**. Therefore, **the lessee includes the present value of the option price when calculating the amount to capitalize and recognize as a liability**.

For example, assume that Lessee Corporation in the continuing illustration had an option to buy the leased equipment for $5,000 at the end of the five-year lease term when the fair value is expected to be $18,000. The significant difference between the option price and the estimated fair value indicates this is a bargain purchase option, and exercising the option is reasonably assured. The following calculations are affected by a bargain purchase option **in the same way as they were by a guaranteed residual value**.

1. The amount of the five lease payments necessary for the lessor to earn a 10% return on net investment.

2. The amount of the minimum lease payments.

3. The amount capitalized as leased assets and lease obligation.

4. The amortization of the lease obligation.

Therefore, the lessee's calculations and amortization schedule necessary for a $5,000 **bargain purchase option** are identical to those shown previously for the $5,000 **guaranteed residual value**.

Illustration 21-32

Entries for Guaranteed and Unguaranteed Residual Values, Lessor Corporation— Sales-Type Lease

 Objective

Describe the effect of bargain purchase options on lease accounting.

Appendix 21A

Other Lease Issues

Sale-Leaseback Transactions

Objective 15

Describe the lessee's accounting for sale-leaseback transactions.

Sale-leaseback describes a transaction in which the property owner (the seller-lessee) sells the property to another party (the purchaser-lessor) and simultaneously leases it back from the new owner. The use of the property is generally continued without interruption. This type of transaction is fairly common.[32]

For example, a company buys land, constructs a building to its specifications, sells the property to an investor, and then immediately leases it back. The advantage of a sale and leaseback from the seller's viewpoint usually involves financing considerations. If an equipment purchase has already been financed, a sale-leaseback can allow the seller to refinance at lower rates if rates have decreased, or a sale-leaseback can provide additional working capital when liquidity is tight.

Underlying Concept

A sale-leaseback is similar in substance to the parking of inventories discussed in Chapter 8. The ultimate economic benefits remain under the control of the "seller," thus the definition of an asset is satisfied.

To the extent the seller-lessee's use of the asset sold continues after the sale, **the sale-leaseback is really a form of financing only**, and therefore no gain or loss should be recognized on the transaction. In substance, the seller-lessee is simply borrowing funds. On the other hand, if the seller-lessee gives up the right to use the asset sold, the transaction is in substance a sale, and gain or loss recognition is appropriate. Trying to ascertain when the lessee has given up the use of the asset is sometimes difficult, however, and complex rules have been formulated to identify this situation.[33] The profession's basic position in this area is that the lease should be accounted for as a capital, direct financing, or operating lease, as appropriate, by the seller-lessee and by the purchaser-lessor.[34]

Lessee Accounting

If the lease meets one of the three criteria for treatment as a capital lease, **the seller-lessee accounts for the transaction as a sale and the lease as a capital lease.** Any profit or loss experienced by the seller-lessee from the sale of the assets that are leased back under a capital lease **are deferred and amortized over the lease term** (or the economic life if criterion 1 is satisfied) in proportion to the amortization of the leased assets. If the leased asset is land only, the amortization is on a straight-line basis over the lease term.[35] If

---

[32] *Financial Reporting in Canada—2003* (CICA, 2003) reports that out of 200 companies surveyed, 9 companies in 2002, 11 in 2001, 9 in 2000, and 6 in 1999 disclosed information related to sale and leaseback transactions.

[33] Guidance is provided in *EIC-25* (CICA, April 22, 1991) for situations where the leaseback relates to only a portion of the property sold by the seller-lessee. A discussion of the issues related to these transactions is beyond the scope of this textbook.

[34] *CICA Handbook*, Section 3065.66.

[35] *CICA Handbook*, Section 3065.68.

Lessee, Inc. sells equipment having a book value of $580,000 and a fair value of $623,110 to Lessor, Inc. for $623,110 and leases the equipment back for $50,000 a year for 20 years, the profit of $43,110 (that is, $623,110 − $580,000) is deferred and amortized over the 20-year period at the same rate that the $623,110 leased asset is amortized. The $43,110 is credited originally to "Unearned Profit on Sale-Leaseback."

If not one of the capital lease criteria is satisfied, **the seller-lessee accounts for the transaction as a sale and the lease as an operating lease**. Under an operating lease, such profit or loss is deferred and amortized in proportion to the rental payments over the period of time the assets are expected to be used by the lessee.[36]

The profession requires, however, that when there is a legitimate loss on the sale of the asset—that is, when the asset's **fair value is less than the book value** (carrying amount)—the loss is recognized immediately.[37] For example, if Lessee, Inc. sells equipment having a book value of $650,000 and a fair value of $623,110, the difference of $26,890 is charged directly to a loss account.[38]

Lessor Accounting

If the lease meets one of the criteria in Group I and both the criteria in Group II (see Illustration 21-11), **the purchaser-lessor records the transaction as a purchase and a direct financing lease.** If the lease does not meet the criteria, the purchaser-lessor records the transaction as a purchase and an operating lease. **The criteria for a sales-type lease would not be met in a sale-leaseback transaction.**

Sale-Leaseback Illustration

To illustrate the accounting treatment accorded a sale-leaseback transaction, assume that Lessee Inc. on January 1, 2005 sells a used Boeing 767, having a cost of $85.5 million and a carrying amount on its books of $75.5 million, to Lessor Inc. for $80 million and immediately leases the aircraft back under the following conditions.

1. The term of the lease is 15 years, non-cancellable, and requires equal annual rental payments of $10,487,443 beginning January 1, 2005.

2. The aircraft has a fair value of $80 million on January 1, 2005, and an estimated economic life of 15 years.

3. Lessee Inc. pays all executory costs.

4. Lessee Inc. amortizes similar aircraft that it owns on a straight-line basis over 15 years.

5. The annual payments assure the lessor a 12% return, the same as Lessee's incremental borrowing rate.

6. The present value of the minimum lease payments is $80 million or $10,487,443 × 7.62817 (Table A-5: $i = 12$, $n = 15$).

This lease is a capital lease to Lessee Inc. because the lease term exceeds 75% of the aircraft's estimated remaining life or because the minimum lease payments' present value exceeds 90% of the aircraft's fair value. Assuming that collectibility of the lease payments is reasonably assured and that no important uncertainties exist in relation to unreim-

---

[36] *CICA Handbook*, Section 3065.69.

[37] There can be two types of losses in sale-leaseback arrangements. One is a real economic loss that results when the asset's carrying amount is higher than its fair value. In this case, the loss should be recognized. An artificial loss results when the sale price is below the asset's carrying amount but the fair value is above the carrying amount. In this case the loss is more in the form of prepaid rent and should be deferred and amortized in the future.

[38] *CICA Handbook*, Section 3065.70.

bursable costs yet to be incurred by the lessor, Lessor Inc. classifies this lease as a direct financing lease.

The journal entries to record the transactions related to this lease for both Lessee Inc. and Lessor Inc. for the first year are presented below.

	Lessee Inc.			Lessor Inc.		
Sale of Aircraft by Lessee to Lessor Inc., January 1, 2005, and leaseback transaction:						
Cash	80,000,000		Aircraft	80,000,000		
Accumulated amortization	10,000,000		Cash	80,000,000		
Aircraft (net)		85,500,000				
Unearned Profit on						
Sale-Leaseback		4,500,000	Lease Payments Receivable	157,311,645		
Aircraft under Capital Leases	80,000,000		Aircraft		80,000,000	
Obligations under Capital Leases		80,000,000	Unearned Interest Revenue		77,311,645	
			($10,487,443 × 15 = $157,311,645)			
First Lease Payment, January 1, 2002:						
Obligations under			Cash	10,487,443		
Capital Leases	10,487,443		Lease Payments			
Cash		10,487,443	Receivable		10,487,443	
Incurrence and Payment of Executory Costs by Lessee Inc. throughout 2005:						
Insurance, Maintenance,			(No entry)			
Taxes, etc. Expense	XXX					
Cash or Accounts Payable		XXX				
Amortization Expense for 2005 on the Aircraft, December 31, 2005:						
Amortization Expense	5,333,333		(No entry)			
Accumulated Amortization—						
Leased Aircraft		5,333,333				
($80,000,000 ÷ 15)						
Amortization of Deferred Profit on Sale-Leaseback by Lessee Inc., December 31, 2005:						
Unearned Profit on			(No entry)			
Sale-Leaseback	300,000					
Amortization Expense		300,000				
($4,500,000 ÷ 15)						
Note: A case might be made for crediting Revenue instead of Amortization Expense.						
Interest for 2005, December 31, 2005:						
Interest Expense	8,341,507[a]		Unearned Interest Revenue	8,341,507		
Interest Payable		8,341,507	Interest Revenue		8,341,507[a]	

[a] Partial Lease Amortization Schedule:

Date	Annual Rental Payment	Interest 12%	Reduction of Balance	Balance
1/1/05				$80,000,000
1/1/05	$10,487,443	$ –0–	$10,487,443	69,512,557
1/1/06	10,487,443	8,341,507	2,145,936	67,366,621

Although there are no specific disclosure requirements for a sale-leaseback transaction other than those required for leases in general, the following is an example of how **Helijet International Inc.**, based in British Columbia, reported such a transaction.

Illustration 21A-2

Example of a Sale-Leaseback Disclosure

HELIJET INTERNATIONAL INC.
Notes to Consolidated Financial Statements
August 31, 2003 and 2002

5. Deferred Gain on Sale and Leaseback

Effective August 25, 1998, March 1, 1999, and December 20, 2002, the Company completed sale and lease-back transactions involving three Sikorsky S76 helicopters. The proceeds received under the agreements were $4,091,931 in excess of the net book values of the helicopters (the "deferred gain"). The deferred gain of $4,091,931 is being amortized over the terms of the leases as a reduction of the related lease expense.

The transactions are represented by:

	2003	2002
Original deferred gain	$4,091,931	$2,574,270
Less, cumulative amount amortized as a reduction of helicopter lease expense	2,415,882	1,752,323
	$1,676,049	$ 821,947
Less, current portion	722,272	473,371
Non-current portion	$ 953,777	$ 348,576

Real Estate Leases

When a capital lease involves land whose ownership will not be transferred to the lessee, capitalization of the land on the lessee's balance sheet would result in no depreciation or other similar expense being recognized over the term of the lease, and a loss equal to the capitalized value of the land being recognized when it reverts to the lessor. **For this reason, special guidance is given for leases that involve land.**

16 Objective
Explain the classification and accounting treatment accorded leases that involve land as well as buildings and equipment.

Land

If land is the sole property leased, the **lessee** should account for the lease as a capital lease only if criterion 1 is met; that is, if the lease transfers ownership of the property or contains a bargain purchase option. Otherwise it is accounted for as an operating lease. The **lessor** accounts for a land lease either as a sales-type or direct financing lease, whichever is appropriate, provided the lease transfers ownership or contains a bargain purchase option and meets both the collectibility and uncertainties tests—otherwise the operating method is used.

Land and Building

If both land and building are involved and the lease transfers ownership or contains a bargain purchase option, the capitalized value of the land and the building should be separately classified by the **lessee**. The present value of the minimum lease payments is allocated between land and building in proportion to their fair values at the inception of the lease. The **lessor** accounts for the lease as a single unit, as a sales-type, direct financing lease, or operating lease, as appropriate.

In 2005, as the conventional banks again began to consider merger strategies among themselves, North Central felt the time was right to expand the number of its community branches throughout the province. The development and construction of more branches required significant financing, and North Central looked into selling the building that housed its head office and main branch as a source of cash. On June 29, 2005, Rural Life Insurance Company Ltd. purchased the building (but not the land) for $8 million and immediately entered into a 20-year lease with North Central to lease back the space occupied.

The terms of the lease were as follows.

1. Non-cancellable, with an option to purchase the building at the end of the lease for $1 million.

2. An annual rental of $838,380, payable on June 29 each year beginning on June 29, 2005.

3. Rural Life expects to earn a return of 10% on its net investment in the lease, the same as North Central's incremental borrowing rate.

4. North Central is responsible for maintenance, insurance, and property taxes.

5. Estimates of useful life and residual value have not changed appreciably since 1990.

Instructions

(a) Prepare all entries for North Central Credit Union from June 29, 2005 to December 31, 2006. North Central has a calendar year fiscal period.

(b) Assume instead that there was no option to purchase, that $8 million represents the building's fair value on June 29, 2005, and that the lease term was 12 years. Prepare all entries for North Central from June 29, 2005 to December 31, 2006.

*P21-16   Akbari Ltd. is a private corporation whose operations rely considerably on the technology companies that experienced operating difficulties from 2002 to 2004. As a result, Akbari suffered temporary cash flow problems that required it to look for innovative means of financing. As a result, in 2005 Akbari's management decided to enter into a sale and leaseback agreement with a major Canadian leasing company, Intranational Leasing.

Immediately after its September 30, 2005 year end, Akbari sold one of its major manufacturing sites to Intranational Leasing for $1,750,000, and entered into a 15-year agreement to lease back the property from them for $175,000 per year. The lease payment is due October 1 of each year, beginning October 1, 2005.

Akbari's carrying amount of the property when sold was $250,000. The lease agreement gives Akbari the right to purchase the property at the end of the lease for its expected fair value at that time of $2.5 million. In 2005, the land is estimated to be worth 40% of the total property value, and the building, 60%. Akbari uses a 10% declining-balance method of amortizing its buildings, and has a 7% incremental borrowing rate.

Instructions

(a) Prepare all entries needed by Akbari to recognize the sale and leaseback transaction on October 1, 2005, any adjusting entries required on September 30, 2006, and the October 1, 2006 transaction. Reversing entries are not used.

(b) Prepare all disclosures needed and amounts reported on the September 30, 2006 balance sheet including any notes, and the income statement and cash flow statement of Akbari for its year ended September 30, 2006.

(CICA adapted)

Writing Assignments

WA21-1   Cuby Corporation entered into a lease agreement for 10 photocopy machines for its corporate headquarters. The lease agreement qualifies as an operating lease in all terms except there is a bargain purchase option. After the five-year lease term, the corporation can purchase each copier for $1,000, when the anticipated market value is $2,500.

Glenn Beckert, the financial vice-president, thinks the financial statements must recognize the lease agreement as a capital lease because of the bargain purchase agreement. The controller, Tareek Koba, disagrees: "Although I don't know much about the copiers themselves, there is a way to avoid recording the lease liability." She argues that the corporation might claim that copier technology advances rapidly and that by the end of the lease term—five years in the future—the machines will most likely not be worth the $1,000 bargain price.

Instructions

Answer the following questions.

(a) What ethical issue is at stake?

(b) Should the controller's argument be accepted if she does not really know much about copier technology? Would it make a difference if the controller were knowledgeable about the pace of change in copier technology?

(c) What should Beckert do?

WA21-2

Part 1   Capital leases and operating leases are the two classifications of leases described in *CICA Handbook* Section 3065 from the lessee's standpoint.

Instructions

(a) What is the theoretical basis for the accounting standard that requires certain long-term leases to be capitalized by the lessee? Do not discuss the specific criteria for classifying a specific lease as a capital lease.

(b) Describe how a capital lease is accounted for by the lessee both at the inception of the lease and during the first year of the lease, assuming the lease transfers ownership of the property to the lessee by the end of the lease.

(c) Describe how an operating lease is accounted for by the lessee both at the inception of the lease and during the first year of the lease, assuming equal monthly payments are made by the lessee at the beginning of each month of the lease. Describe the change in accounting, if any, when rental payments are not made on a straight-line basis.

Do not discuss the criteria for distinguishing between capital leases and operating leases.

Part 2   Sales-type leases and direct financing leases are two of the classifications of leases described in *CICA Handbook* Section 3065 from the lessor's standpoint.

Instructions

Compare and contrast a sales-type lease with a direct financing lease as follows:

(a) Gross investment in the lease

(b) Amortization of unearned interest revenue

(c) Manufacturer's or dealer's profit

(d) Initial direct costs

Do not discuss the criteria for distinguishing between the leases described above and operating leases.

(AICPA adapted, in part)

WA21-3   On January 1, Shinault Corporation, a lessee, entered into three non-cancellable leases for brand new equipment: Lease L, Lease M, and Lease N. None of the three leases transfers ownership of the equipment to Shinault at the end of the lease term. For each of the three leases, the present value at the beginning of the lease term of the minimum lease payments, excluding that portion of the payments representing executory costs such as insurance, maintenance, and taxes to be paid by the lessor, is 75% of the equipment's fair value. The following information is peculiar to each lease.

  1. Lease L does not contain a bargain purchase option; the lease term is equal to 80% of the equipment's estimated economic life.

  2. Lease M contains a bargain purchase option; the lease term is equal to 50% of the equipment's estimated economic life.

  3. Lease N does not contain a bargain purchase option; the lease term is equal to 50% of the equipment's estimated economic life.

Instructions

(a) How should Shinault Corporation classify each of the three leases above, and why? Discuss the rationale for your answer.

(b) What amount, if any, should Shinault record as a liability at the lease's inception for each of the leases?

(c) Assuming that the rental payments are made on a straight-line basis, how should Shinault record each rental payment for each of the leases?

(AICPA adapted)

WA21-4   Brayes Corporation is a diversified company with nationwide interests in commercial real estate developments, banking, copper mining, and metal fabrication. The company has offices and operating locations in major cities throughout Canada. Corporate headquarters for Brayes Corporation is located in a metropolitan area of a western province, and executives connected with various phases of company operations travel extensively. Corporate management is currently evaluating the feasibility of acquiring a business aircraft that can be used by company executives to expedite business travel to areas not adequately served by commercial airlines. Proposals for either leasing or purchasing a suitable aircraft have been analysed, and the leasing proposal was considered more desirable.

The proposed lease agreement involves a twin-engine turboprop Viking that has a fair value of $1 million. This plane would be leased for a period of 10 years beginning January 14, 2005. The lease agreement is cancellable only upon accidental destruction of the plane. An annual lease payment of $141,780 is due on January 14 of each year; the first payment is to be made on January 14, 2005. Maintenance operations are strictly scheduled by the lessor, and Brayes Corporation will pay for these services as they are performed. Estimated annual maintenance costs are $6,900. The lessor will pay all insurance premiums and local property taxes, which amount to a combined total of $4,000 annually and are included in the annual lease payment of $141,780. Upon expiration of the 10-year lease, Brayes Corporation can purchase the Viking for $44,440. The plane's estimated useful life is 15 years, and its value in the used plane market is estimated to be $100,000 after 10 years. The residual value probably will never be less than $75,000 if the engines are overhauled and maintained as prescribed by the manufacturer. If the purchase option is not exercised, possession of the plane will revert to the lessor, and there is no provision for renewing the lease agreement beyond its termination on December 31, 2014.

Brayes Corporation can borrow $1 million under a 10-year term loan agreement at an annual interest rate of 12%. The lessor's implicit interest rate is not expressly stated in the lease agreement, but this rate appears to be approximately 8% based on 10 net rental payments of $137,780 per year and the initial market value of $1 million for the plane. On January 14, 2005, the present value of all net rental payments and the purchase option of $44,440 is $888,890 using the 12% interest rate. The present value of all net rental payments and the $44,440 purchase option on January 14, 2005 is $1,022,226 using the 8% interest rate implicit in the lease agreement. The financial vice-president of Brayes Corporation has established that this lease agreement is a capital lease as defined in *CICA Handbook* Section 3065 on "Leases."

Instructions

(a) *CICA Handbook* Section 3065 indicates that the crucial accounting issue is whether the risks and rewards (or benefits) of ownership are transferred from one party to the other, regardless of whether ownership is transferred. What is meant by "the risks and benefits of ownership," and what factors are general indicators of such a transfer?

(b) Have the risks and benefits of ownership been transferred in the lease described above? What evidence is there?

(c) What is the appropriate amount for Brayes Corporation to recognize for the leased aircraft on its balance sheet after the lease is signed?

(d) Without prejudice to your answer in part (c), assume that the annual lease payment is $141,780 as stated in the question, that the appropriate capitalized amount for the leased aircraft is $1 million on January 14, 2005, and that the interest rate is 9%. How will the lease be reported in the December 31, 2005 balance sheet and related income statement? (Ignore any income tax implications.)

(CMA adapted, in part)

*WA21-5   On October 30, 2005, Truttman Corp. sold six-month-old equipment at fair value and leased it back. There was a loss on the sale. Truttman pays all insurance, maintenance, and taxes on the equipment. The lease provides for eight equal annual payments, beginning October 30, 2006, with a present value equal to 85% of the equipment's fair value and sales price. The lease's term is equal to 80% of the equipment's useful life. There is no provision for Truttman to reacquire ownership of the equipment at the end of the lease term.

Instructions

(a) Why would Truttman have entered into such an agreement?

(b) 1.   Evaluate Truttman's leaseback of the equipment in terms of each of the three criteria for determining a capital lease.

   2.   Why is it important to compare the equipment's fair value with the present value of the lease payments and its useful life to the lease term? What does this information tell you?

(c) How should Truttman account for the sale portion of the sale-leaseback transaction on its financial statements for the year ended December 31, 2005?

(d) How should Truttman report the leaseback portion of the sale-leaseback transaction on its financial statements for the year ended December 31, 2005?

Cases

Refer to the Case Primer on the Digital Tool to help you with these cases.

CA21-1   Crown Inc. (CI) is a public company that manufactures a special type of cap that fits on a bottle. At present, it is the only manufacturer of this cap and therefore enjoys market security. The machinery used in production of this cap has been in use for 20 years and is due for replacement. CI has the option of buying the machine or leasing it. Currently, CI is leaning towards leasing the machine since it is expensive and funds would otherwise have to be borrowed from the bank. At present, the debt-to-equity ratio is marginal and if the funds were borrowed, the debt-to-equity ratio would surely worsen. CI's top management is anxious to maintain the ratio at its present level.

The dilemma for CI is that if the machine is leased, it may have to set up a long-term obligation under the lease and this would also affect the debt-to-equity ratio. Since this is clearly unacceptable, CI decided to see if the leasing company, Anchor Limited (AL), could do anything for it. After much negotiation, the following terms were agreed upon and written into the lease agreement:

- AL would manufacture and lease to CI a unique machine for making caps.
- The lease would be for a period of 12 years.
- The lease payments of $150,000 would be paid at the end of each year.
- CI would have the option to purchase the machine for $850,000 at the end of the lease term, which was equal to the FMV at that time; otherwise, the machine would return to the lessor.
- CI also had the option to lease the machine for another eight years at $150,000 per year.
- The rate implicit in the lease is 9%.

The machine was expected to last 20 years. Since it was a unique machine, AL had no other use for it if CI did not purchase it at the end of the lease or renew the lease. If CI had purchased the asset, it would cost $1.9 million. Although it was purposefully omitted from the written lease agreement, there was a tacit understanding that CI would either renew or exercise the option.

Instructions

Assume the role of CI's auditors and discuss the nature of the lease, noting how it should be accounted for. The controller of the company has confided in you that the machine will likely be purchased. Assume that you are aware of top management's position on adding debt to the balance sheet.

CA21-2   Eaton's used to be a major department store in Canada before it went bankrupt and was bought by Sears. Many of the stores were anchor tenants in medium to large sized retail shopping malls. This space was primarily leased under non-cancellable real estate leases as disclosed in note 16 to the consolidated financial statements. Aggregate commitments under both capital and operating leases amounted to over $1.3 million.

As part of Eaton's restructuring and downsizing plans prior to the bankruptcy, Eaton's announced in early 1997 that it planned to close down 31 of its 85 stores by June 30. Subsequently, it announced that it might keep certain stores open until February 1998 if the landlords were prepared to provide an appropriate level of financial support. Eaton's also announced that landlords who allowed the stores to close June 30 (the earlier date) would be given a bonus of three months free rent.

Instructions

Assume the role of management and discuss the financial reporting issues that the company had to deal with prior to the bankruptcy.

Integrated Cases

IC21-1   Air Canada (AC) is Canada's largest airline operating domestic and international flights on a full service basis. During 2003, the company ran into financial difficulty and took steps to reorganize its operations and rethink its business model. The company needed to obtain significant additional financing and was looking to undergo a financial reorganization under which the control of the company would likely change hands.

In March 2004, the company set up voluntary separation programs which allowed for up to 300 non-unionized employees to "retire" with severance payments. Unionized employees were covered by a separate similar plan. In addition, it was planned that certain employees would be terminated and receive severance payments under pre-existing contracts.

Many lease contracts were renegotiated and/or terminated. While operating under bankruptcy protection court orders, the company had ceased to pay its lessors. GE Capital Corporation and its subsidiaries (GE), leased, managed the leases or had an interest in 108 aircraft – the bulk of the company's aircraft. GE's lawyers notified the company that they must either pay the back rent or return the planes noting that the company should not be allowed to hide behind the bankruptcy protection and use the planes for free. The company had many of its leased planes recorded as operating leases. Aircraft operating lease rentals over the lease term were amortized to operating expense on a straight-line basis. The difference between the straight line aircraft rent expense and the payments as stipulated under the lease agreement was included in deferred charges and deferred credits ($1.8 billion).

($120,000). The restated balance is the amount the opening balance would have been if the new policy had always been in effect. In 2005, the beginning balance is adjusted for the $120,000 cumulative difference to January 1, 2004 plus the additional $12,000 for 2004. Again, the restated opening balance is what would have been in the accounts if the new policy had always been applied. As with the income statement (and any related balance sheets), if two prior years' statements were presented, the effect on the 2003 opening retained earnings would be shown as an adjustment to the balance previously reported as well. The 2003 income is adjusted for the income statement effect in that year. For any historical summaries, the statements are reported as if the percentage-of-completion method had always been used.

This may appear complicated at first. **Knowing what the objective is**, go back to the explanation of the change in Illustration 22-2 and the "before" statements in Illustrations 22-3 and 22-5. Try to develop the revised income and retained earnings statements on your own.

Illustration 2—Correction of an error affecting one prior year (retroactive, with restatement):   As soon as they are discovered, errors must be corrected retroactively by proper entries in the accounts and reflection in the financial statements. In the year in which the error is discovered, it is reported in the financial statements as an adjustment to the beginning balance of retained earnings. **If comparative statements are presented, the prior statements affected are restated to correct the error so they appear as if the error had never occurred.**

IAS Note

IAS 8 now requires retroactive restatement of prior financial statements for all errors and all non-mandated changes in accounting policy.

Because error correction requires retroactive restatement of all prior periods affected, the accounting is similar to the above illustration for a voluntary change in accounting policy. Assume that the bookkeeper for Selectric Corporation discovered in 2005 that in 2004 the company failed to record in the accounts $20,000 of amortization expense on a newly constructed building.

As a result of the $20,000 amortization error in 2004:

Amortization expense (2004) was understated	$20,000
Accumulated amortization at January 1, 2005 is understated	20,000
Income tax expense (2004) was overstated	
($20,000 × 40%)	8,000
Net income (2004) was overstated ($20,000 − $8,000)	12,000
Future income tax liability at January 1, 2005 is overstated	
($20,000 × 40%)	8,000

The entry needed in 2005 to correct the omission of $20,000 of amortization in 2004, assuming the books for 2004 have been closed, is:

A   =   L   +   SE
−20,000   −8,000   −12,000
Cash flows: No effect

Retained Earnings	12,000	
Future Income Tax Asset/Liability	8,000	
Accumulated Amortization—Buildings		20,000

The retained earnings account is adjusted because all 2004 income statement accounts were closed to retained earnings at the end of 2004. The journal entry to record the error correction is the same whether single-period or comparative financial statements are prepared; however, presentation on the financial statements will differ. If single-period financial statements are presented, the error is reported as an adjustment to the opening balance of retained earnings of the period in which the error is discovered, as reported in Illustration 22-7.

Retained earnings, January 1, 2005		
As previously reported (assumed)		$350,000
Correction of an error (amortization)	**$20,000**	
Less: Applicable income tax reduction	**8,000**	**(12,000)**
Restated balance of retained earnings, January 1, 2005		338,000
Add: Net income 2005 (assumed)		400,000
Retained earnings, December 31, 2005		$738,000

Illustration 22-7

Reporting an Error—Single-Period Financial Statements

If comparative financial statements are prepared, adjustments are made to correct the amounts for all affected accounts reported in the statements for all periods reported. The data for each year being presented are restated to the correct amounts, and any cumulative adjustment relating to periods prior to those reported is made to the opening balance of retained earnings for the earliest period reported. This is exactly the same as the previously illustrated retroactive-with-restatement treatment for a change in accounting policy. In the case of Selectric Corporation, the error of omitting the amortization of $20,000 in 2004, which was discovered in 2005, results in restating the 2004 financial statements when presented in comparison with those of 2005 but does not affect the January 1, 2004 retained earnings previously reported. The following accounts in the 2004 financial statements (presented in comparison with those of 2005) will be restated.

In the December 31, 2004 balance sheet:	
Accumulated amortization, buildings	$ 20,000 increase
Future income tax liability	$ 8,000 decrease
Retained earnings, Dec. 31, 2004	$12,000 decrease
In the 2004 income statement:	
Amortization expense, buildings	$ 20,000 increase
Income tax expense	$ 8,000 decrease
Net income	$12,000 decrease
In the 2004 retained earnings statement:	
Retained earnings, Jan. 1, 2004 balance	no change
2004 net income added in	$12,000 decrease
Retained earnings, Dec. 31, 2004 balance	
(due to lower net income for the period)	$12,000 decrease

Illustration 22-8

Reporting an Error—Comparative Financial Statements

The 2005 financial statements in comparative form with those of 2004 are prepared as if the error had not occurred, with the exception of correcting the opening balance of the previously reported opening retained earnings amount. The Statement of Retained Earnings would be identical to the statement in Illustration 22-7. In addition, a note to the 2005 financial statements is included, describing the error and disclosing the correction's effect on the current and prior years' financial statements and the fact that comparative information has been restated.

Illustration 3—Correction of an error affecting multiple years (retroactive, with restatement):   Assume when preparing the financial statements for the year ended December 31, 2005 that the controller of Shilling Corp. discovered that a property purchased in mid-2002 for $200,000 had been charged entirely to the "Land" account in error. The $200,000 cost should have been allocated between "Land" ($50,000) and "Building" ($150,000). The building was expected to be used for 20 years and then sold for $70,000 (building portion only). Prior to discovery of this error, Shilling Corp.'s accounting records indicated the following.

Illustration 22-9

*Accounting Records
before Restatement*

	2005 (books not closed)	2004
Revenues	$402,000	$398,000
Expenses	329,000	320,000
Income before tax	73,000	78,000
Income tax expense (30%)	21,900	23,400
Net income	$ 51,100	$ 54,600
Retained earnings, January 1	$294,000	$242,000
Net income for year	51,100	54,600
Dividends declared	(2,100)	(2,600)
Retained earnings, December 31	$343,000	$294,000

Retroactive restatement is required, so the first step is to determine the effect of this error on all prior periods. Preparing an appropriate analysis provides backup for the required correcting entry and helps in the restatement of the financial statements. The specific analysis will differ for each situation encountered. However, each analysis requires identifying what is in the books and records now and what would have been in the accounts if the error had not occurred. The correcting entry merely adjusts what is there now with what should be there. Illustration 22-10 indicates the analysis underlying the correcting entry to Shilling's accounts. Follow through each line, ensuring you understand the source of each number.

Illustration 22-10

*Analysis of Error on
Shilling's Records*

	Shilling Corp. Analysis of Accounting Error			
	2005	2004	2003	2002
Land reported, end of year	$200,000	$200,000	$200,000	$200,000
Correct Land balance, end of year	50,000	50,000	50,000	50,000
Building reported, end of year	–0–	–0–	–0–	–0–
Correct Building balance, end of year	150,000	150,000	150,000	150,000
Amortization expense reported for year	–0–	–0–	–0–	–0–
Correct amortization for year:	4,000	4,000	4,000	2,000
($150,000 − $70,000) ÷ 20 = $4,000 per year				
Accumulated amortization reported, end of year	–0–	–0–	–0–	–0–
Correct Accumulated Amortization, end of year	14,000	10,000	6,000	2,000
Income Tax reported related to Amortization Expense	–0–	–0–	–0–	–0–
Correct Tax benefit from Amortization Expense	1,200	1,200	1,200	600
= 30% of the Amortization Expense				
Future Tax Asset reported at end of year related to building	–0–	–0–	–0–	–0–
Correct Future Tax Asset at end of year = 30%	4,200	3,000	1,800	600
of Accumulated Amortization at end of year				
Summary effect:				
Overstatement of income reported in year	2,800	2,800	2,800	1,400
(Correct Amortization Expense after tax) − (Recorded Amortization Expense after tax)				
Overstatement of Retained Earnings, **first of year**	7,000	4,200	1,400	–0–
(cumulative income effect at first of year)				

The correcting entry needed at the 2005 year end when the error was discovered is taken directly from the analysis in Illustration 22-10.

Building (150,000 − 0)	150,000		
Amortization Expense (4,000 − 0)	4,000		
Future Tax Asset (4,200 − 0)	4,200		
Retained Earnings (Jan. 1, 2005)	7,000		
Land (200,000 − 50,000)		150,000	
Accumulated Amortization (14,000 − 0)		14,000	
Income Tax Expense (1,200 − 0)		1,200	

A = L + SE
−9,800   −9,800
Cash flows: No effect

Let's review this entry. The objective is to correct the accounts so the amounts in the records are the same as they would have been had there been no error. The Building account should have had a $150,000 balance, but now stands at $0, necessitating a $150,000 debit to Building. Amortization expense should have been taken on the building in 2005, so the current year's expense needs to be corrected. However, with income statement items, because all accounts get closed out each year end with balances transferred to Retained Earnings, the correction to amortization expense for 2002 to 2004 is to Retained Earnings. The expense for 2005 has not yet been closed out, so the correction is directly to the expense. The same explanation holds for why the correction for income tax expense for 2005 is to the expense account and for 2002 to 2004 is to Retained Earnings. In effect, the $7,000 adjustment to decrease the January 1, 2005 Retained Earnings balance represents the 2002 to 2004 Amortization Expense correction of $10,000 net of the related 2002 to 2004 Income Tax Expense correction of $3,000.

Three other balance sheet accounts need correcting. The Land account must be reduced to $50,000. The Accumulated Amortization now stands at $0 but should be $14,000, so it is credited for the difference. Lastly, the Future Tax Asset account related to the temporary (deductible) differences between the tax basis of the building and its revised carrying amount is recognized.

Now that the records have been adjusted, the controller has to report this accounting change on the financial statements for 2005 and the comparative statements for 2004. These financial statements must be presented "as if the error had never occurred, by correcting the error in the comparative information for the prior period(s) in which it occurred, including any income tax effects. The amount of the correction relating to errors that occurred in periods prior to those presented in comparative information in the financial statements is adjusted against the opening balance of retained earnings of the earliest period presented."[15]

The required financial statements, with the exception of any note disclosures, are presented in Illustration 22-11.

Income Statement	2005	2004 (restated)
Revenues	$402,000	$398,000
Expenses	333,000[a]	324,000[b]
Income before tax	69,000	74,000
Income tax expense	20,700[c]	22,200[d]
Net income	$ 48,300	$ 51,800

[a] $329,000 + $4,000   [b] $320,000 + $4,000
[c] $21,900 − $1,200   [d] $23,400 − $1,200

Statement of Retained Earnings		
Retained earnings, January 1, as previously reported	$294,000	$242,000
Cumulative effect of accounting error, net of tax benefit of $3,000 ($1,800 in 2004)	(7,000)	(4,200)
Retained earnings, January 1, as restated	287,000	237,800
Net income	48,300	51,800
Less: dividends declared	(2,100)	(2,600)
Retained earnings, December 31	$333,200	$287,000

Illustration 22-11

Retroactive Restatement of Comparative Statements— Shilling Corp.

[15] *CICA Handbook,* Section 1506.29.

The adjustments to the income statement are relatively straightforward as the expenses and income tax lines are changed to the corrected amounts. The adjustments to the statement of retained earnings are more complex.

For 2005, the previously reported opening retained earnings balance is adjusted for the effects on income prior to January 1, 2005. In this case, this cumulative adjustment is the additional $10,000 of amortization expense ($2,000 + $4,000 + $4,000) reduced by $3,000 of associated tax benefits ($600 + $1,200 + $1,200). The restated opening retained earnings for 2005 of $287,000 is, therefore, the balance that would have been reported if the error had never occurred. The revised net income for 2005 is added to this and the 2005 dividends are deducted to give the retained earnings at the end of 2005.

For the 2004 statement of retained earnings, the previously reported opening retained earnings balance (i.e., 2003 ending balance) is adjusted for the effects on income (and therefore retained earnings) prior to January 1, 2004. The cumulative adjustment at this date is $4,200. This reflects the $6,000 of additional amortization expense ($2,000 + $4,000) reduced by the $1,800 of related income tax benefit ($600 + $1,200) to January 1, 2004. If the error had not been made, the balance of retained earnings at January 1, 2004 would have been $237,800. The revised 2004 net income of $51,800 is added to this and the 2004 dividends are deducted in determining the corrected December 31, 2004 balance of retained earnings. **Note that this corresponds to the adjusted opening balance in the 2005 column.**

The comparative balance sheet for 2004 is also designated as "restated" as the Land, Building, Accumulated Amortization—Building, and Future Tax Asset accounts are restated, as well as Retained Earnings.

Retroactive-without-Restatement Accounting Method

As indicated earlier in the chapter, retroactively restating individual prior years' financial statements requires information that may, in many cases, be **impractical to obtain**, even though the cumulative effect can be determined. For example, when companies adopted the new accounting standards for post-retirement benefits other than pensions (Section 3461) for the first time, most companies accounted for the change retroactively. Prior to the new standard, companies recognized payments made for medical premiums for retirees as expense as the payments were made—a pay-as-you-go method. Under the new standard, the expense is required to be estimated and charged to the period in which the employees earn the entitlement to the future benefit—an accrual approach.

On a cost-benefit basis it was not practical to retroactively determine the effect of the new standard on specific prior years—a necessary condition for restatement. Therefore, the retroactive-without-restatement method was permitted by Section 3461's transitional provisions. If the effect can be determined for some of the prior periods, *CICA Handbook* Section 1506 requires that the policy be applied retroactively **with** restatement to as many consecutive years going back as practical, and then without restatement to the remainder.

Illustration 4—Change in accounting policy required by a primary source of GAAP (retroactive, without restatement): To illustrate the retroactive-without-restatement method, assume that Itwaru Corporation has accounted for its pensioner medical benefits on a pay-as-you-go basis. In 2004, the company changed to the accrual method required under the accounting standards in *CICA Handbook* Section 3461. The cumulative accrued medical benefits earned by employees but unrecognized in the accounts to December 31, 2003 were $220,000. For tax purposes (assume a 40% rate), only expenditures made for the medical premiums are tax deductible. Illustration 22-12 sets out the information for analysis.

Year	Cost of Medical Benefits Earned by Employees (accrual method)	Premiums Paid for Medical Benefits (Pay-as-you-go-method)	Difference	Tax Effect 40%	Effect on Net Incomes
Prior to 2004	$220,000	$75,000	**$145,000**	**$58,000**	**$87,000**
In 2004	$ 32,000	$15,000	$ 17,000	$ 6,800	$10,200

Illustration 22-12

Effect of Change in Accounting Policy to Comply with Section 3461

The entry to record the change effective January 1, 2004 is:

Future Income Tax Asset	58,000	
Retained Earnings—Change in Accounting Policy	87,000	
Accrued Post-retirement Medical Benefits Liability		145,000

A   =   L   +   SE
+58,000 +145,000 −87,000
Cash flows: No effect

The Accrued Post-retirement Medical Benefits Liability account is recognized effective January 1, 2004, representing the accrued but previously unrecognized obligation and expense. The Future Income Tax Asset account is used to recognize interperiod tax allocation. As the medical premiums are paid in the future, Itwaru can deduct these amounts in calculating taxable income. If the company had used the accrual method from the beginning in accounting for this employee benefit, retained earnings would have been $87,000 less than the amounts reported in its financial statements at January 1, 2004.

Because it was not practicable to determine this policy change's effect on any specific previous year, the change's cumulative effect is reported only as an adjustment to the opening balance of Retained Earnings for the current year, along with the related income tax effect, as illustrated below.

Illustration 22-13

Reporting a Change in Accounting Policy without Restatement

STATEMENT OF RETAINED EARNINGS

	2004	2003
Opening balance, as previously reported (assumed)	$1,696,000	$1,600,000
Less: Adjustment for the cumulative effect on prior periods of the change in accounting policy, net of income tax of $58,000 (Note A)	87,000	—
Opening balance, as restated	1,609,000	1,600,000
Net income (assumed)	120,000	96,000
Balance, end-of-year	$1,729,000	$1,696,000

Note A (in part)—Change in Accounting Policy: Effective January 1, 2004, the Company changed its method of accounting for post-retirement medical benefits for its employees to comply with *CICA Handbook* Section 3461. The costs of medical benefits are now accrued as earned by employees. Prior period financial statements have not been restated for the $87,000 after-tax additional costs recognized as it was impractical to determine the effect on specific prior years.

Note that this example is similar to the case involving restatement of prior periods' financial statements. The journal entries to record the accounting change are identical because, in each case, the change's cumulative effect on retained earnings is recorded as an adjustment to beginning Retained Earnings. The only difference between retroactive adjustment **with restatement** and **without restatement** is in the financial statements for prior periods issued for comparative purposes. **Restatement** provides financial statement readers with amounts for prior periods that would have been reported had the new policy been in effect originally. On the other hand, retroactive adjustment **without restatement** leaves the comparative financial statements as originally reported and presents the change's cumulative effect only as an adjustment to beginning Retained Earnings.

Assuming no previous 2005 amortization entry, the entry to record amortization for 2005 is:

A   =   L   +   SE
−10,000   −10,000
Cash flows: No effect

| Amortization Expense | 10,000 | |
| Accumulated Amortization—Building | | 10,000 |

The $10,000 amortization charge is calculated as follows.

Illustration 22-15

Amortization after Change in Estimate

$$\text{Amortization charge} = \frac{\text{Book value of asset} - \text{residual value}}{\text{Remaining service life}} = \frac{\$200,000 - \$0}{25 \text{ years} - 5 \text{ years}} = \$10,000$$

Disclosures—Changes in Accounting Estimates

Objective 7

Identify the disclosure requirements for changes in accounting estimates.

International Insight

In most nations, changes in accounting estimates are treated prospectively. International differences tend to be in the degree of disclosure required.

Disclosures for changes in estimates have the same objective as those for other types of changes: to provide information useful in assessing the effects of the change on the financial statements. Minimum disclosure, therefore, is the nature and amount of a change in an accounting estimate that affects the current period or is expected to affect future periods.[19] Materiality plays an important role here, as it does with other accounting standards.

Summary of Accounting Changes

Developing recommendations for reporting accounting changes has helped resolve several significant and long-standing accounting problems. Yet, because of diversity in situations and characteristics of the items encountered in practice, applying professional judgement is still of paramount importance. The primary objective is to serve the user of the financial statements. Achieving this requires full disclosure and an absence of misleading inferences. The principal distinction and treatments presented in the earlier discussion are summarized in Illustration 22-16.

Changes in accounting policies are considered appropriate only when dictated by a primary source of GAAP or the enterprise demonstrates that an alternative generally accepted accounting policy or its method of application is preferable to the existing one. Preferability among accounting policies is determined based on **whether the new policy results in a more relevant presentation in the financial statements**. Standard setters make this assessment in formulating or revising primary sources of GAAP, and the same test is required for voluntary changes.[20] But what is "more relevant" is not always obvious in financial reporting. How is relevance measured? One enterprise might argue that a change in accounting policy from FIFO to LIFO inventory valuation better matches current costs and current revenues and therefore provides better predictive, and therefore more relevant, information. Conversely, another enterprise might change from LIFO to FIFO because it wishes to report a more current and relevant ending inventory amount that also has better predictive value. How do you determine which is the better of these two arguments? The revised standards are an improvement over the previous ones because they provide a context for the decision; they relate the decision to qualitative characteristics agreed upon as financial statement concepts in *CICA Handbook* Section 1000. The problem of determining preferability, however, will continue to be an issue that requires exercising professional judgement.

[19] *CICA Handbook*, Section 1506.34 -.35.

[20] *AcSB Exposure Draft* "Background Information and Basis for Conclusions: Changes in Accounting Policies and Estimates, and Errors," CICA, September, 2003.

Illustration 22-16

Summary of Accounting Changes

CHANGE IN ACCOUNTING POLICY

General Rule 1. On adoption of a primary source of GAAP, apply the transitional provisions, if any, in that primary source of GAAP. If no transitional provisions are provided, apply retroactively following Rule 2.

General Rule 2. For a voluntary change in policy, use the retroactive-with-restatement approach by:

1. Reporting current and future results on the new basis.
2. Restating all prior period financial statements presented for comparison as if the new policy had always been in place.
3. Adjusting the opening balance of retained earnings for the earliest period presented to the balance it would have been had the new policy always been used.
4. Providing note disclosures that enable the users of the statements to understand the effects of the accounting policy change on the financial statements.
5. Applying the effect of the change to all applicable amounts in any historical summaries of financial data provided.

Exceptions. If restatement of comparative information presented for a particular prior period is impractical, use the retroactive-without-restatement approach by:

1. Applying the new policy to as many prior comparative periods as possible.
2. For the periods reported where application is impractical, applying the new policy to the assets and liabilities at the beginning of the next accounting period, and adjusting the opening retained earnings balance at the same point.
3. Providing note disclosures that enable the users of the statements to understand the effects of the accounting policy change on the financial statements.
4. Applying the effect of the change to all applicable amounts in any historical summaries of financial data provided, to the extent possible.

CHANGE IN ACCOUNTING ESTIMATE

Use the prospective approach by:

1. Reporting current and future results on the new basis.
2. Presenting prior period financial statements as previously reported.
3. Making no adjustment to current period opening balances and no catch-up provisions.
4. Providing note disclosures that enable the users of the statements to understand the effects of the changes in accounting estimate on the financial statements.

CORRECTION OF AN ERROR

Use the retroactive-with-restatement approach by:

1. Restating all prior period financial statements presented for comparison as if the error had never occurred.
2. Adjusting the opening balance of retained earnings for the earliest period presented to the balance it would have been had the error never occurred.
3. Providing note disclosures that enable the users of the statements to understand the effects of the error on the financial statements.
4. Applying the effect of the error to all applicable amounts in any historical summaries of financial data provided.

REPORTING ISSUES

Examples of Disclosures

Alliance Atlantis Communications Inc.'s financial statements for its year ended March 31, 2003 report a mix of accounting changes and a variety of methods of accounting for them. Even though these statements relate to a period prior to the recent revisions to *CICA Handbook* Section 1506, most of the detailed disclosure is still valid. Illustration 22-17 contains the company's comparative statement of retained earnings and most of the information from the financial statements that deal with its accounting changes. These are worth working through one at a time.

Illustration 22-17

*Accounting Changes
Disclosures—Alliance Atlantis*

CONSOLIDATED STATEMENTS OF RETAINED EARNINGS (DEFICIT)

ALLIANCE ATLANTIS COMMUNICATIONS INC.
FOR THE YEARS ENDED MARCH 31,
(IN MILLIONS OF CANADIAN DOLLARS)

	2003	2002	2001
		(REVISED)	(REVISED)
RETAINED EARNINGS (DEFICIT) –			
BEGINNING OF YEAR, AS PREVIOUSLY REPORTED (note 2)	(121.5)	(168.8)	50.1
Adjustment for revision of prior years' results (note 27)	(32.8)	(13.3)	-
Adjustment for adoption of new accounting pronouncement (note 2)	(10.2)	(9.9)	-
RETAINED EARNINGS (DEFICIT) – BEGINNING OF YEAR, RESTATED	(164.5)	(192.0)	50.1
Net earnings (loss) for the year	(18.8)	27.5	11.8
RETAINED EARNINGS (DEFICIT) – END OF YEAR	(183.3)	(164.5)	61.9

THE ACCOMPANYING NOTES FORM AN INTEGRAL PART OF THESE FINANCIAL STATEMENTS.

NOTES TO CONSOLIDATED FINANCIAL STATEMENTS (in part)
(IN MILLIONS OF CANADIAN DOLLARS - EXCEPT PER SHARE AMOUNTS)

The Company is a vertically integrated broadcaster, creator and distributor of filmed entertainment content. As described in note 24, the Company's principal business activities are carried out through three operating groups: the Broadcast Group, the Motion Picture Distribution Group and the Entertainment Group.

2. ACCOUNTING CHANGES

(a) During 2003, the Company adopted the following accounting policies:

Stock-based compensation and other stock-based payments On April 1, 2002, the Company adopted the recommendations of the new Canadian Institute of Chartered Accountants (CICA) Handbook Section 3870, "Stock-Based Compensation and Other Stock-Based Payments," on a prospective basis. The new standard requires that for all stock-based payments to non-employees and to employees when the stock-based awards call for settlement in cash or other assets, including stock appreciation rights, a compensation expense be recognized in the statement of earnings, determined using a fair value based method of accounting. There is no impact on the Company's net earnings or earnings per share for the year ended March 31, 2003 as a result of the adoption of this new standard. The Company was previously in compliance with this new standard as the compensation costs associated with such payments and awards were expensed in the statement of earnings.

Additionally, for stock options granted to its employees, the new standard does not require the Company to recognize a compensation expense if the Company chooses the disclosure-only method of adoption. Consideration paid by employees on the exercise of stock options is recorded as an increase in the Company's share capital accounts.

The Company has, however, chosen to record compensation expense related to the grant of stock options to its employees, determined using a fair value based method of accounting. For the year ended March 31, 2003, the expense related to the granting of stock options to employees was $0.2 and had no material impact on basic and diluted earnings per common share. (See note 13.)

As the provisions of the Section have not been applied to stock options granted to employees prior to April 1, 2002, the resulting compensation expense may not be representative of future amounts since the estimated fair value of these employee stock options on the date of grant is measured over the vesting period and additional options may be granted in future years.

Foreign currency translation On April 1, 2002, the Company retroactively adopted the recommendations of the revised CICA Handbook Section 1650, "Foreign Currency Translation." The revisions eliminate the deferral and amortization of foreign currency translation gains and losses on long-lived monetary items.

At March 31, 2002, the Company had $12.0 of unamortized foreign exchange losses related to the translation of U.S. dollar denominated senior subordinated notes. Accordingly, other assets have been reduced by $12.0, opening retained earnings have been reduced by $10.2 and future income taxes have been increased by $1.8. If the Company had not adopted this new standard in 2003, net earnings for the year ended March 31, 2003 would have been reduced by $10.2, net of income taxes of $1.8.

At March 31, 2001, the Company had $11.7 of unamortized foreign exchange losses related to the translation of U.S. dollar denominated senior subordinated notes. Accordingly, other assets as at March 31, 2001 have been reduced by $11.7, opening retained earnings reduced by $9.9 and future income taxes have been increased by $1.8. The impact of the adoption of this new standard on net earnings for the year ended

Illustration 22-17

*Accounting Changes
Disclosures—Alliance Atlantis*
(continued)

March 31, 2002 was a foreign exchange loss of $1.3, net of income tax recovery of $0.2. The impact of the adoption on basic and diluted earnings per share for the year ended March 31, 2002 was $0.03.

The impact of the adoption of this new standard on net earnings for the year ended March 31, 2001 was a foreign exchange loss of $11.0, net of income tax recovery of $1.9. The impact of the adoption on basic and diluted earnings per share for the year ended March 31, 2001 was $0.34.

Hedging relationships On April 1, 2002, the Company adopted the recommendations of Accounting Guideline AcG-13, "Hedging Relationships." The new standard establishes criteria for identification and documentation of hedging relationships. There was no impact on net earnings, basic earnings per share and diluted earnings per share as a result of the adoption of the new standard.

(b) During 2002, the Company adopted the following accounting policies: (in part)

Accounting for film and television programs In June 2000, the Accounting Standards Executive Committee of the American Institute of Certified Public Accountants issued Statement of Position 00-2, "Accounting by Producers or Distributors of Films" ("SOP 00-2"). SOP 00-2 establishes new accounting standards for producers or distributors of films, including changes in revenue recognition, capitalization and amortization of costs of films and television programs and accounting for development, overhead and other exploitation costs, including advertising and marketing expenses.

The Company has retroactively adopted SOP 00-2 effective as of April 1, 2001. Prior years' financial statements have not been restated, as the effect of the new policy on prior periods was not reasonably determinable. Accordingly, opening retained earnings for the year ended March 31, 2002 was reduced to reflect the cumulative effect of the accounting change in the amount of $253.9 (net of income taxes of $79.9).

The principal changes as a result of applying SOP 00-2 are as follows:

Cash outflows incurred to acquire, produce and develop film and television programs, which were previously presented under investing activities in the consolidated statement of cash flows, are presented under cash flows from operating activities.

Advertising and marketing costs, which were previously capitalized to investment in film and television programs and amortized using the individual film forecast method, are now expensed as incurred. This change resulted in a reduction of investment in film and television programs and retained earnings of $156.4.

Earnings per share Effective April 1, 2001, the Company adopted the revised CICA Handbook Section 3500, "Earnings per Share." As a result of adopting this Section, the Company now uses the treasury stock method to calculate diluted earnings per share. The adoption of this Section has been applied retroactively; however, it had no impact on the basic and diluted earnings per share for the year ended March 31, 2001. (See note 19.)

27. REVISION OF PRIOR YEARS' RESULTS

In accordance with the review of the accounting treatment of the Company's television productions as part of the annual audit process, it was concluded that the Company's interest in the two *CSI* television series should be accounted for as a 50% jointly controlled production. The Company has revised its financial statements for 2002 and 2001 to reflect a revision to the previous accounting with respect to the licence fees paid and contributions made by another party to this jointly controlled production. Based on this revision, the results of operations and financial position for the Company were revised for the fiscal years ended 2002 and 2001.

2002	AS PREVIOUSLY REPORTED	EFFECT OF REVISION	REVISED AMOUNT
Total assets	1,708.6	(8.1)	1,700.5
Total liabilities	1,143.7	24.7	1,168.4
Revenue	959.9	(47.1)	912.8
Direct operating profit	276.3	(21.7)	254.6
Earnings before undernoted	159.7	(21.7)	138.0
Net earnings (loss)	47.0	(19.5)	27.5
Basic earnings per common share	$ 1.19	$ (0.50)	$ 0.69
Diluted earnings per common share	$ 1.19	$ (0.50)	$ 0.69

2001	AS PREVIOUSLY REPORTED	EFFECT OF REVISION	REVISED AMOUNT
Total assets	1,759.0	(10.5)	1,748.5
Total liabilities	1,170.3	2.8	1,173.1
Revenue	806.1	(30.1)	776.0
Direct operating profit	225.8	(14.8)	211.0
Earnings before undernoted	133.6	(14.8)	118.8
Net earnings (loss)	25.1	(13.3)	11.8
Basic earnings per common share	$ 0.79	$ (0.42)	$ 0.37
Diluted earnings per common share	$ 0.79	$ (0.42)	$ 0.37

The effect of the change in accounting on fiscal 2003 was a decrease in revenue of $88.1, a decrease in direct operating profit and earnings (loss) before undernoted of $16.3, a decrease in net earnings (loss) of $14.7, a decrease in basic and diluted earnings (loss) per share of $0.34, a decrease in total assets of $0.6 and an increase in total liabilities of $46.9.

28. RECENT ACCOUNTING PRONOUNCEMENTS

(a) Impairment of Long-Lived Assets In 2002, the CICA issued Handbook Section 3063, "Impairment of Long-Lived Assets," which is effective for fiscal years beginning on or after April 1, 2003. Under this Section, an impairment loss is measured as the difference between the carrying value of an asset and its fair value. The Company does not expect the adoption of this Section to have a significant impact on its financial results.

(b) Disposal of Long-Lived Assets and Discontinued Operations In 2002, the CICA issued Handbook Section 3475, "Disposal of Long-Lived Assets and Discontinued Operations," which will be effective for all disposal activities initiated by a commitment to a plan on or after May 1, 2003. Under the new rules, (i) a long-lived asset to be disposed of other than by a sale continues to be classified as held and used until it is disposed of; (ii) a long-lived asset classified as held for sale is measured at the lower of its carrying amount or fair value less cost to sell; (iii) a loss recognized on classification of a long-lived asset as held for sale or a group of assets as a discontinued operation does not include future operating losses, other than to the extent they are included in the fair value of the asset; and (iv) discontinued operations are defined more broadly than under existing GAAP. The Company does not expect the adoption of this Section to have a significant impact on its financial results.

(c) Consolidation of Variable Interest Entities In June 2003, the CICA issued Accounting Guideline 15, "Consolidation of Variable Interest Entities," which will be effective for annual and interim periods beginning on or after January 1, 2004. This Guideline addresses the application of consolidation principles to entities that are subject to control on a basis other than ownership of voting interests. The Company does not expect the adoption of this Guideline to have a material impact on the Company's financial position or results of operations.

The statement of retained earnings for the year ended March 31, 2003 indicates two different adjustments to the opening balance previously reported, with the prior year's opening balance also restated. Note that both 2002 adjustments are less than the 2003 adjustments. Why is this? It is because the effect on 2002's income has been adjusted in the comparative 2002 income statement and is included in the $27.5 (million) net earnings added to retained earnings for 2002. It appears that the retroactive changes did not affect any periods prior to the 2001 fiscal period. Note that both 2002 and 2001 have been identified as "revised," as were the 2002 and 2001 columns on the income statement presented but not included in this illustration.

Note 2(a) identifies three new or revised accounting standards adopted in fiscal 2003 according to the transitional provisions of specific *CICA Handbook* sections. The stock-based compensation and other stock-based payments change was applied prospectively, and the foreign currency translation change was applied retroactively with restatement, making up the second adjustment on the retained earnings statement. It seems unusual that the change would not affect years prior to 2001, but no further information is provided. The third change relates to a new Accounting Guideline on hedging with no effect on earnings.

Note 2(b) includes information about two changes made in the year ended March 31, 2002. The first relates to a change in accounting for film and television programs based on an industry standard issued by the AICPA in the United States. What accounting method was applied to the change? The note indicates retroactive treatment without restatement on the basis that the effect on prior periods was not determinable. The last change described relates to the calculation of earnings per share. Although applied retroactively, the company indicates no material effect on the reported earnings per share (EPS).

Digital Tool

Student Toolkit— Additional Disclosures

www.wiley.com/canada/kieso

Note 27, Revision of Prior Years' Results, is very interesting. What type of accounting change is this? The note indicates that this is not related to anything reported in Note 2, but instead is a change in how the company's ownership interest in two television series is accounted for. The income statements and balance sheets for the two prior years have been restated along with the opening retained earnings balance previously reported. There is no explanation indicating whether this restatement results from an error, a change from an incorrect accounting method to a correct method, a change in circumstance, or a change from one acceptable accounting method to another. Under revised Section 1506, more detailed explanations would be required.

The last note included, on Recent Accounting Pronouncements, provides information about issued but not-yet-effective accounting standards. In all three cases, Alliance Atlantis does not expect their adoption to materially affect the company's financial results.

Illustration 22-18 provides an example of **CAE Inc.'s** reporting a change in estimate on its 2003 financial statements. CAE, a Canadian company employing more than 6,000 people, sells civil and military flight simulators and training, and marine control systems.

Illustration 22-18

*Change in Estimate
Disclosure—CAE Inc.*

Notes to Consolidated Financial Statements
Years ended March 31, 2003, 2002 and 2001 (amounts in millions of Canadian dollars)

Note 01—Summary of Significant Accounting Policies (in part)

Property, Plant and Equipment
Property, plant and equipment are stated at cost. The declining balance and straight-line methods are used in computing amortization over the estimated useful lives of the assets. Useful lives are estimated as follows:

Building and improvements	20 to 40 years
Machinery and equipment	3 to 10 years
Simulators	12 to 25 years

In fiscal year 2003, the Company has changed the amortization period for Civil simulation equipment from 20 years to 25 years, to reflect the approximate useful life of the simulators. This change reduced the amortization expense by $3.7 million on a year-to-year basis.

Motivations for Change

Difficult as it is to determine which accounting standards have the strongest conceptual support, other complications make the process even more complex. These complications stem from the fact that managers (and others) have a self-interest in how the financial statements make the company look. Managers naturally wish to show their financial performance in the best light. A favourable profit picture can influence investors, and a strong liquidity position can influence creditors. Too favourable a profit picture, however, can provide union negotiators with ammunition during bargaining talks. Also, if the federal government has established price controls, managers might believe that lower-trending profits might persuade the regulatory authorities to grant their company a price increase. Hence, managers might have varying profit motives depending on economic times and whom they seek to impress.

Research has provided additional insights into why companies may prefer certain accounting methods. Some of these reasons are as follows.

Objective 8
Identify economic motives for changing accounting methods.

1. **Political costs.** As companies become larger and more politically visible, politicians and regulators devote more attention to them. Some suggest that these politicians and regulators can "feather their own nests" by imposing regulations on these organizations for the benefit of their own constituents. Thus the larger the firm, the more likely it is to become subject to regulation such as anti-competition regulation and the more likely it is required to pay higher taxes. Therefore, companies that are politically visible may attempt to report income numbers that are low, to avoid the scrutiny of regulators. By reporting low income numbers, companies hope to reduce their exposure to the perception of monopoly power.[21] Other constituents are affected. For example, labour unions may be less willing to demand wage increases if reported income is low. Thus, researchers have found that the larger the company, the more likely it is to adopt approaches that decrease income when selecting accounting methods.[22]

---

[21] "There's an old saw on Bay Street that the Royal Bank earned a billion dollars three years before it told the world," indicates Kim Shannon of Sionna Investment Managers Inc. Although the comment was made in the context of a discussion on income smoothing, the authors believe that this was directly related to the optics of the situation at a time banks were heavily under fire for "gouging" consumers with fees and closing branches. Source: "A beautiful find," globeandmail.com, January 30, 2004.

[22] Ross Watts and Jerold Zimmerman, "Towards a Positive Theory of the Determination of Accounting Standards," *The Accounting Review*, January 1978.

2. **Capital structure**. A number of studies have indicated that a company's capital structure can affect the selection of accounting methods. For example, a company with a high debt-to-equity ratio is more likely to be constrained by debt covenants. That is, a company may have a debt covenant that indicates that it cannot pay any dividends if retained earnings fall below a certain level. As a result, this type of company is more likely to select accounting methods that will increase net income. For example, one group of researchers found that a company's capital structure affected its decision whether to expense or capitalize interest.[23] Others indicated that full cost accounting was selected instead of the successful efforts method by companies that have high debt-to-equity ratios.[24]

3. **Bonus payments.** If bonuses paid to management are tied to income, it has been found that management will select accounting methods that maximize their bonus payments. Thus, in selecting accounting methods, managers do concern themselves with the effect of accounting income changes on their compensation plans.[25]

4. **Smooth earnings**. Substantial increases in earnings attract the attention of politicians, regulators, and competitors. In addition, large increases in income create problems for management because the same results are difficult to achieve the following year. Compensation plans may adjust to these higher numbers as a baseline and make it difficult for management to achieve its profit goals and receive bonus compensation the following year. Conversely, large decreases in earnings might be viewed as a signal that the company is in financial trouble. Furthermore, substantial decreases in income raise concerns on the part of shareholders, lenders, and other interested parties about management's competency. Thus, companies have an incentive to manage or smooth earnings. Management typically believes that a steady growth of 10% per year is much better than 30% growth one year followed by a 10% decline the next. In other words, management usually prefers a gradually increasing income report (often referred to as "income smoothers") and sometimes changes accounting methods to ensure such a result. [26]

Management pays careful attention to the accounting it follows and often changes accounting methods not for conceptual reasons, but rather for economic reasons. As indicated throughout this textbook, such arguments have come to be known as economic consequences arguments, since they focus on the supposed impact of accounting on the behaviour of investors, creditors, competitors, governments, and the managers of the reporting companies themselves, rather than address the conceptual justification for accounting standards.[27]

---

[23] R. M. Bowen, E. W. Noreen, and J. M. Lacy, "Determinants of the Corporate Decision to Capitalize Interest," *Journal of Accounting and Economics*, August 1981.

[24] See, for example, Dan S. Dhaliwal, "The Effect of the Firm's Capital Structure on the Choice of Accounting Methods," *The Accounting Review*, January 1980; and W. Bruce Johnson and Ramachandran Ramanan, "Discretionary Accounting Changes from Successful Efforts to Full Cost Methods: 1970-1976," *The Accounting Review*, January 1988. The latter study found that firms that changed to full cost were more likely to exhibit higher levels of financial risk (leverage) than firms that retained successful efforts.

[25] See, for example, Mark Zmijewski and Robert Hagerman, "An Income Strategy Approach to the Positive Theory of Accounting Standard Setting/Choice," *Journal of Accounting and Economics*, August 1981.

[26] O. Douglas Moses, "Income Smoothing and Incentives: Empirical Tests Using Accounting Changes," *The Accounting Review*, April 1987. Findings provide evidence that smoothers are associated with firm size, the existence of bonus plans, and the divergence of actual earnings from expectations.

[27] Economic consequences arguments—and there are many of them—are manipulation through the use of lobbying and other forms of pressure brought on standard setters. We have seen examples of these arguments in the oil and gas industry about successful efforts versus full cost, in the technology area with the issue of mandatory expensing of research, most development costs, and stock options, and so on.

To counter these pressures, standard setters have declared, as part of their conceptual framework, that they will assess the merits of proposed standards from a position of neutrality. That is, the soundness of standards should not be evaluated on the grounds of their possible impact on behaviour. It is not the Accounting Standards Board's place to choose standards according to the kinds of behaviour they wish to promote or discourage. At the same time, it must be admitted that some standards will often have the effect of influencing behaviour, yet their justification should be conceptual, not behavioural.

Perspectives

What do the Numbers Mean?

What effect do accounting changes have on financial statement analysis? Not surprisingly, they often make it difficult to develop meaningful trend data, undermining one of the major reasons accounting information has been found useful in the past.

Consider the case of **Alliance Atlantis Communications**, whose disclosures were reported in Illustration 22-17. In the 2002 fiscal period, the company adopted three revised accounting policies, and during 2003, another three were adopted. All but one of these were required by primary sources of GAAP. The non-required change actually restated (downward) previous operating cash flows by hundreds of millions of dollars! The change identified in Note 27 is more disconcerting. Note 27 indicates that the company is changing the method of accounting for its "investment in the two *CSI* television series," but fails to adequately explain the reason. The confusing part is that while certain income (revenues of $77.1 million and income of $32.8 million) was reported in the financial statements in 2002 and 2001, these have been pulled out of retained earnings in 2003, and, one assumes, will again be reported in income at a later date.

Another example is provided by **International Hi-Tech Industries Inc.**, based in Vancouver. In September 2003, the company announced it was restating its aggregate revenue for the previous seven years by more than $6 million and reducing its income over the past two and one-half years by about $3 million. At issue was the fact the company had determined that revenue related to non-refundable fees and deposits had been recognized earlier than it should have been. Here, too, the restatement cancelled out previously reported earnings, leaving them available to be reported on the income statement again in the future! To be fair, the new revenue recognition policy appears to be a more appropriate policy. This situation underscores the difficulty experienced by standard setters in determining best practice for reporting accounting changes.

In general, financial statement readers should look closely at all accounting changes and adjust any trend data appropriately. Although most changes have no cash effect on the statement, some can end up converting previously reported operating cash flows to investment or financing flows. Most changes tend to shift earnings from one accounting period to another. Consider the case of **Quebecor Inc.**, a Quebec based giant, when it applied the revised recommendations on accounting for goodwill in 2002. Under the old standard, goodwill was amortized over its useful life; under the new standard, goodwill is kept on the books but is tested for impairment each year. The transitional provisions required companies to account for this change prospectively, but permitted them to carry out a transitional impairment test at the effective date of the new standard. Any transitional impairment loss on goodwill was treated as the effect of a change in accounting policy and accounted for retroactively without restatement. Quebecor Inc., which reported goodwill of $10.2 billion on its December 31, 2001 balance sheet, used the transitional provision to write off $2.2 billion of goodwill on January 1, 2002. It was reported as an adjustment to retained earnings at that date, relieving future income statements of $2.2 billion of costs! **BCE Inc.** similarly revised its goodwill policy at this time, retroactively adjusting its previously reported opening retained earnings balance of $712 million downward **by almost $8.2 billion.**

ERROR ANALYSIS

Objective 9
Analyse the effects of errors.

In the past, it was unusual to see the correction of material errors in the financial statements of large corporations. Internal control procedures coupled with the diligence of the accounting staff were ordinarily sufficient to find and correct any major errors in the system before the statements were released. However, in the first half of this decade, there have been a number of well publicized cases of major companies restating past results. As this text was written, **Nortel Networks'** Board of Directors was grappling with another set of restatements after issuing revised statement the previous year. **Atlas Cold Storage**, featured in the opening vignette to this chapter, is another company whose financial statements have been held up pending completion of a review. Whether these and other similar situations are errors or overly aggressive choices of accounting methods remains to be seen. Smaller businesses may face a different problem. These enterprises may not be able to afford an internal audit staff or to implement the necessary control procedures to ensure that accounting data are always recorded accurately.[28]

In practice, firms do not correct errors discovered that do not have a significant effect on the financial statements. For example, the failure to record accrued wages of $5,000 when the total payroll for the year is $1,750,000 and net income is $940,000 is not considered significant, and no correction is made. Obviously, defining materiality is difficult, and experience and judgement must be used to determine whether adjustment is necessary for a given error. All errors discussed in this section are assumed to be material and to require adjustment. The tax effects are ignored initially to simplify and allow you to zero in on the direct effects of the errors themselves.

The accountant must answer three questions in error analysis.

1. What type of error is involved?

2. What entries are needed to correct the error?

3. How are financial statements to be restated once the error is discovered?

As indicated earlier, the profession requires that errors be treated retroactively with restatement and reported in the current year as adjustments to the beginning balance of Retained Earnings, net of income tax effects. If comparative statements are presented, the prior statements affected are restated to correct the error. Three types of errors can occur. Because each type has its own peculiarities, it is important to differentiate among them.

Balance Sheet Errors

These errors affect only the presentation of an asset, liability, or shareholders' equity account. Examples are classifying a short-term receivable as part of the investment section, a note payable as an account payable, and plant assets as inventory. Reclassification of the item to its proper position is needed when the error is discovered. If comparative statements that include the error year are prepared, the balance sheet for the error year is restated correctly. No further corrections are needed.

Income Statement Errors

These errors affect only the presentation of the nominal accounts in the income statement. Errors involve the improper classification of revenues or expenses, such as recording

---

[28] See Mark L. DeFord and James Jiambalvo, "Incidence and Circumstances of Accounting Errors," *The Accounting Review*, July 1991, for examples of different types of errors and why these errors might have occurred.

interest revenue as part of sales, purchases as bad debt expense, or amortization expense as interest expense. An income statement classification error has no effect on the balance sheet or on net income. A reclassification entry is needed when the error is discovered, if it is discovered in the year it is made. If the error occurred in prior periods, no entry is needed at the date of discovery because the accounts for the year of the misclassification have all been closed to retained earnings and the current year is correctly stated. If comparative statements that include the error year are prepared, the income statement for the error year is restated correctly.

Balance Sheet and Income Statement Errors

The third type of error involves both the balance sheet and income statement. For example, assume that accrued wages payable were overlooked by the bookkeeper at the end of the accounting period. The error's effect is to understate expenses and liabilities, and overstate net income for that accounting period. **This type of error affects both the balance sheet and the income statement** and is classified in one of two ways: counterbalancing or noncounterbalancing.

Counterbalancing errors are errors that will be offset or self-corrected over two periods. In the previous illustration, the failure to record accrued wages is considered a counterbalancing error because over a two-year period, the error will no longer be present. In other words, failing to record accrued wages in the previous period means: (1) wages expense for the first period is understated, (2) net income for the first period is overstated, (3) accrued wages payable (a liability) at the end of the first period is understated, and (4) retained earnings at the end of the first period is overstated. In the next period, wages expense is overstated and net income is understated, but both accrued wages payable (a liability) and retained earnings at the end of the second period are now correct. **For the two years combined**, both wages expense and net income are correct, as are the ending balance sheet amounts of wages payable and retained earnings. Most errors in accounting that affect both the balance sheet and income statement are counterbalancing errors.

Noncounterbalancing errors are errors that are not offset in the next accounting period; for example, the failure to capitalize equipment that has a useful life of five years. If we expense this asset immediately, expenses will be overstated in the first period but understated in the next four periods. At the end of the second period, the error's effect is not fully offset. Net income is correct in the aggregate only at the end of five years, because the asset would have been fully amortized at this point, assuming no residual value. Thus, **noncounterbalancing errors are those that take longer than two periods to correct themselves.**

Only in rare instances is an error never reversed; for example, when land is initially expensed. Because land is not subject to amortization, the error is not offset until the land is sold.

Counterbalancing Errors

The usual types of counterbalancing errors are illustrated on the following pages. In studying these illustrations, a number of points should be remembered. **First**—and this is key—**the entries will differ depending on whether or not the books have been closed for the period in which the error is found.**

1. When **the books have been closed**:
   (a) If the error is already counterbalanced, no entry is necessary.
   (b) If the error is not yet counterbalanced, an entry is necessary to adjust the present balance of retained earnings and the other balance sheet account(s) affected.

2. When **the books have not been closed**:

(a) If the error is already counterbalanced and the company is in the second year, an entry is necessary to correct the current period income statement account(s) and to adjust the beginning balance of Retained Earnings.

(b) If the error is not yet counterbalanced, an entry is necessary to adjust the beginning balance of Retained Earnings, and correct the current period income statement account(s) and balance sheet account(s) affected.

Second, if comparative statements are presented, it is necessary to restate the amounts for comparative purposes. **Restatement is necessary even if a correcting journal entry is not required.** To illustrate, assume that Sanford Cement Ltd. failed to accrue revenue in 2003 when earned, but recorded the revenue in 2004 when received. The error is discovered in 2006. No entry is necessary to correct this error because the effects have been counterbalanced by the time the error is discovered in 2006. However, if comparative financial statements for 2003 through 2006 are presented, the accounts and related amounts for the years 2003 and 2004 are restated correctly for financial reporting purposes.

The following are examples of counterbalancing errors. **Income tax effects have been ignored for now.** Do not memorize these. Work with them until you understand each.

1. **Failure to record accrued wages.** On December 31, 2005, accrued wages of $1,500 were not recognized. The entry in 2006 to correct this error, assuming that the books have not been closed for 2006, is:

A = L + SE	
0 0 0	
Cash flows: No effect	

Retained Earnings	1,500	
Wages Expense		1,500

The rationale for this entry is as follows: When the accrued wages relating to 2005 are paid in 2006, an additional debit of $1,500 is made to 2006 Wages Expense, overstating this account by $1,500. Because 2005 accrued wages were not recorded as Wages Expense—2005, net income for 2005 was overstated by $1,500. Because 2005 net income is overstated by $1,500, the 2006 opening Retained Earnings is overstated by $1,500 because net income is closed to Retained Earnings.

If the books have been closed for 2006, no entry is made because the error is counterbalanced.

2. **Failure to record prepaid expenses.** In January 2005, a two-year insurance policy costing $1,000 was purchased; Insurance Expense was debited, and Cash was credited. No adjusting entries were made at the end of 2005. The entry on December 31, 2006 to correct this error, assuming that the books have not been closed for 2006, is:

A = L + SE	
0 0 0	
Cash flows: No effect	

Insurance Expense	500	
Retained Earnings		500

If the books are closed for 2006, no entry is made because the error is counterbalanced.

3. **Understatement of unearned revenue.** On December 31, 2005, cash of $50,000 was received as a prepayment for renting certain office space for the following year. The entry made when the rent payment was received was a debit to Cash and a credit to Rent Revenue. No adjusting entry was made as of December 31, 2005. The entry on December 31, 2006 to correct this error, assuming that the books have not been closed for 2006, is:

			A	=	L	+	SE
Retained Earnings	50,000		0		0		0
Rent Revenue		50,000					

Cash flows: No effect

If the books are closed for 2006, no entry is made because the error is counterbalanced.

4. **Overstatement of accrued revenue.** On December 31, 2005, interest revenue of $8,000 was accrued that applied to 2006. The entry made on December 31, 2005 was to debit Interest Receivable and credit Interest Revenue. The entry on December 31, 2006 to correct this error, assuming that the books have not been closed for 2006, is:

			A	=	L	+	SE
Retained Earnings	8,000		0		0		0
Interest Revenue		8,000					

Cash flows: No effect

If the books have been closed for 2006, no entry is made because the error is counterbalanced.

5. **Overstatement of purchases.** The accountant recorded a purchase of merchandise for $9,000 in 2005 that applied to 2006. The physical inventory for 2005 was correctly stated. The company uses the periodic inventory method. The entry on December 31, 2006 to correct this error, assuming that the books have not been closed for 2006, is:

			A	=	L	+	SE
Purchases	9,000		0		0		0
Retained Earnings		9,000					

Cash flows: No effect

If the 2006 books have been closed, no entry is made because the error is counterbalanced.

6. **Understatement of ending inventory.** On December 31, 2005, the physical inventory count was understated by $25,000 because the inventory crew failed to count one section of a merchandise warehouse. The entry on December 31, 2006 to correct this error, assuming the 2006 books have not yet been closed and the ending inventory has not yet been adjusted to the inventory account, is:

			A	=	L	+	SE
Inventory (beginning)	25,000		+25,000				+25,000
Retained Earnings		25,000					

Cash flows: No effect

If the books are closed for 2006, no entry would be made because the error has been counterbalanced.

7. **Overstatement of purchases and inventories.** Sometimes, both the physical inventory and the purchases are incorrectly stated. Assume that 2006 purchases of $9,000 were incorrectly recorded as 2005 purchases and that 2005 ending inventory was overstated by the same amount. The entry on December 31, 2006 to correct this error before the 2006 books are closed and the correct ending inventory is adjusted to the inventory account is:

			A	=	L	+	SE
Purchases	9,000		−9,000				−9,000
Inventory (beginning)		9,000					

Cash flows: No effect

The net income for 2005 is correct because the overstatement of purchases was offset by the overstatement of ending inventory in cost of goods sold. As with the other examples of counterbalancing errors, no entry is required if the 2006 books have already been closed.

Noncounterbalancing Errors

Because such errors do not counterbalance over a two-year period, the entries for non-counterbalancing errors are more complex and correcting entries are needed, even if the books have been closed. The best approach is to identify what the relevant account balances **are** in the accounts, what they **should be**, and then bring them to the correct balances through correcting entries.

1. **Failure to record amortization**. Assume that a machine with an estimated five-year useful life was purchased on January 1, 2005 for $10,000. The accountant incorrectly expensed this machine in 2005 and the error was discovered in 2006. If we assume that the company uses straight-line amortization on similar assets, the entry on December 31, 2006 to correct this error, given that the 2006 books are not yet closed, is:

A   =   L   +   SE
+6,000   +6,000

Cash flows: No effect

Machinery	10,000	
Amortization Expense (2006)	2,000	
Retained Earnings		8,000
Accumulated Amortization		4,000
Retained Earnings		
Expense reported in 2005	$10,000	
Correct amortization for 2005 (20% × $10,000)	(2,000)	
Retained earnings understated as of Dec. 31, 2005 by	$ 8,000	
Accumulated Amortization		
Accumulated amortization (20% × $10,000 × 2)	$ 4,000	

If the books are closed for 2006, the entry is:

A   =   L   +   SE
+6,000   +6,000

Cash flows: No effect

Machinery	10,000	
Retained Earnings		6,000
Accumulated Amortization		4,000
Retained Earnings		
Retained earnings understated as of Dec. 31, 2005 by	$ 8,000	
Correct amortization for 2006 (20% × $10,000)	(2,000)	
Retained earnings understated as of Dec. 31, 2006 by	$ 6,000	

2. **Failure to adjust for bad debts**. Assume a company has inappropriately been using the direct write-off method when the allowance method should have been applied. For example, assume that the following bad debt expense has been recognized as the debts have actually become uncollectible.

	2005	2006
From 2005 sales	$550	$690
From 2006 sales		700

The company estimates that an additional $1,400 will be written off in 2007, of which $300 is applicable to 2005 sales and $1,100 to 2006 sales. The entry on December 31, 2006 to correct the accounts for bad debt expense, assuming that the books have not been closed for 2006, is:

			A = L + SE
Bad Debt Expense	410		−1,400 −1,400
Retained Earnings	990		Cash flows: No effect
Allowance for Doubtful Accounts		1,400	

Allowance for doubtful accounts:
Additional $300 for 2005 sales and $1,100 for 2006 sales.

Bad debts and retained earnings balance:	**2005**	**2006**
Bad debt expense charged ($550 + $690 = $1,240)	$1,240	$ 700
Additional bad debts anticipated (Total of $1400)	300	1,100
Correct amount of bad debt expense	1,540	1,800
Charges currently included in each period	(550)	(1,390)
Bad debt expense adjustment	$ 990	$ 410

If the books have been closed for 2006, the entry is:

			A = L + SE
Retained Earnings	1,400		−1,400 −1,400
Allowance for Doubtful Accounts		1,400	Cash flows: No effect

Income Tax Effects

As previously indicated, the income tax effects have not been reported with the above correcting entries to allow you to focus on the effects of the errors themselves. Once you understand the correcting entries, you can add the income tax effects.

If a correction **increases a previous year's income** (either by an increase in revenue or a decrease in expense), the income tax expense for that period will usually be increased: more income, more tax. If the correction **reduces a previous year's income** (either by a decrease in revenue or an increase in expense), the income tax expense for that period will usually be reduced: less income, less tax. The net correction to Retained Earnings, therefore, is net-of-tax. Note that for counterbalancing errors, the income tax effects also offset each other over the two-year period, assuming tax rates have not changed.

Because the tax return for the previous period has already been filed, any adjustment of the previous year's balance sheet accounts and income for financial reporting purposes creates a temporary difference between tax values and the corrected book values. The tax effect, therefore, is captured in the Future Income Tax Asset/Liability account.

Illustration 22-19 identifies the correcting entries required, including the tax effects for the counterbalancing and noncounterbalancing examples provided on pages 1226 to 1229. A constant 40% income tax rate is assumed.

	BOOKS FOR 2006	
Error	**Not Closed**	**Closed**
COUNTERBALANCING ERRORS		
1. Accrued Wages		
Retained Earnings	900	−No Entry−
Future Tax Asset/Liability	600	
Wages Expense	1500	

Illustration 22-19

Correcting Entries with Income Tax Effects

Illustration 22-21
Work Sheet to Adjust Financial Statements

DICK & WALLY'S OUTLET
Work Sheet Analysis to Adjust Financial Statements for the Year 2006

	Trial Balance Unadjusted		Adjustments		Income Statement Adjusted		Balance Sheet Adjusted	
	Debit	Credit	Debit	Credit	Debit	Credit	Debit	Credit
Cash	3,100		(1) 1,000				4,100	
Accounts Receivable	17,600						17,600	
Notes Receivable	8,500						8,500	
Inventory, Jan. 1, 2006	34,000		(3) 5,400		39,400			
Property, Plant, and Equipment	112,000			(7) 10,000 ª			102,000	
Accumulated Amortization		83,500	(7) 6,000 ª					75,500
			(8) 2,000					
Investments	24,300						24,300	
Accounts Payable		14,500	(6) 6,000					8,500
Notes Payable		10,000		(6) 6,000				16,000
Share Capital		43,500						43,500
Retained Earnings		20,000	(4) 2,700 ᵇ	(3) 5,400				
			(7) 4,000 ª	(5) 600				
			(2) 2,500	(8) 800				17,600
Sales		94,000		(1) 1,000		95,000		
Purchases	21,000				21,000			
Selling Expenses	22,000			(4) 500 ᵇ	21,500			
Administrative Expenses	23,000		(2) 700	(5) 400	22,700			
			(5) 600	(8) 1,200				
Totals	265,500	265,500						
Wages Payable				(2) 3,200				3,200
Allowance for Doubtful Accounts				(4) 2,200 ᵇ				2,200
Unexpired Insurance			(5) 400				400	
Inventory, Dec. 31, 2006						(9) 40,000	(9) 40,000	
Net Income					30,400			30,400
Totals			31,300	31,300	135,000	135,000	196,900	196,900

Calculations:

ªMachinery		ᵇBad Debts		For Sales in	
				2005	2006
Proceeds from sale	$7,000	Bad debts charged		$2,400	$1,600
Book value of machinery	4,000	Additional bad debts anticipated		700	1,500
Gain on sale	3,000			3,100	3,100
Income credited	7,000	Charges currently made to each year		(400)	(3,600)
Retained earnings adjustment	$4,000	Bad debt adjustment		$2,700	$ (500)

Summary of Learning Objectives

1 Identify and differentiate among the types of accounting changes.

There are three different types of accounting changes. (1) Change in accounting policy: a change in the choice of specific principle or method used in applying a specific principle selected by an entity in the preparation of its financial statements. This could be imposed by the transitional provisions in new primary sources of GAAP, or a voluntary change. (2) Change in an accounting estimate: a change that occurs in the circumstances on which a previous estimate was based, or as the result of new information, more experience, or subsequent developments. (3) Correction of a prior period error: a change that occurs because of an error discovered in a prior period's financial statements resulting from mathematical mistakes, mistakes in applying accounting principles, fraud, or oversight or misinterpretation of facts that existed at the time financial statements were prepared.

Digital Tool

Glossary

www.wiley.com/canada/kieso

2 Identify and explain alternative methods of accounting for accounting changes.

Accounting changes could be accounted for retroactively, currently, or prospectively. The retroactive method requires restatement of prior periods as if the accounting change had been used from the beginning, with corrections of opening retained earnings balances previously reported. The current method calculates a catch-up adjustment related to the effect on all prior years, with this cumulative effect recognized in the current period. Prospective treatment requires making no adjustment for cumulative effects, but instead, beginning to use the new method in the current and future periods.

3 Identify the accounting standards for each type of accounting change.

A change in accounting policy is accounted for retroactively with restatement of comparative financial information unless this is impractical. If impractical, retroactive treatment without restatement may be used. A change in an accounting estimate is accounted for prospectively. Errors are corrected by retroactively restating all prior years affected.

4 Apply the retroactive application method of accounting for an accounting change.

The general requirement for changes in accounting policy and the required method for error correction is that the change's cumulative effect (net of tax) be shown as an adjustment to the beginning retained earnings. Income statements of the affected prior periods presented for comparison purposes are restated to show, on a retroactive basis, the effects of the new accounting policy. When historical summaries are reported, the adjustments are reported in each prior year affected. When a change in accounting policy's effects on particular prior periods is impractical to determine, the cumulative effect of the change (net of tax) is shown as an adjustment to the beginning retained earnings. Comparative financial statements of prior periods presented for comparison are not restated.

5 Identify the disclosure requirements for changes in accounting policies and for errors.

The objective of disclosure for all changes is to ensure that users of financial statements can determine the effect of the change on those financial statements. Required disclosures therefore include the provision of information to justify the change, the effect on each financial statement item presented and potentially affecting future periods, and the effects on financial statements prior to those presented. Information about the future effect of changes in primary sources of GAAP that are issued but not yet effective is also required.

6 Apply the prospective application method for an accounting change.

Accounting changes given prospective treatment affect only the current and future fiscal periods. There is no adjustment of current year opening balances and no attempt is made to "catch up" for prior periods.

7 Identify the disclosure requirements for changes in accounting estimates.

The nature and amount of a change in accounting estimate that affects the current period or is expected to affect future periods is required to be disclosed.

KEY TERMS

change in an accounting
   estimate, 1202
change in an accounting
   policy, 1201
correction of an accounting
   error, 1203
counterbalancing
   errors, 1225
impractical, 1205
noncounterbalancing
   errors, 1225
primary sources of
   GAAP, 1200
prospective
   treatment, 1204
retroactive
   treatment, 1203
retroactive-with-
   restatement
   method, 1205
retroactive-without-
   restatement
   method, 1212
transitional
   provisions, 1204

Research and Financial Analysis

RA22-1 Intrawest Corporation

Instructions

Refer to the financial statements and accompanying notes of **Intrawest Corporation** presented at the end of this volume, and answer the following questions or instructions.

(a) Identify the accounting changes reported by Intrawest during its fiscal year ending June 30, 2003. Indicate the effective date of each change and describe the nature of each.

(b) For each change in accounting policy, identify, if possible, the cumulative effect on prior years and the effect on operating results in the year of change.

(c) Where appropriate, prepare the journal entries likely made by Intrawest to recognize the changes in policy.

RA22-2 EnCana Corporation

According to **EnCana Corporation**'s 2003 Annual Report, the company "is one of the world's leading independent oil and gas companies and North America's largest independent natural gas producer and gas storage operator." EnCana reports a number of accounting changes in its financial statements for its year ended December 31, 2003.

Instructions

Obtain access to the financial statements of EnCana for its year ended December 31, 2003 through www.sedar.com or other source, and answer the following questions.

(a) Identify each type of accounting change reported by EnCana in 2003 as:

1. a change in accounting policy mandated by a change in a primary source of GAAP,

2. a voluntary change in accounting policy,

3. a change in estimate, or

4. a correction of an error.

(b) For changes 1. to 4. in (a) above, identify the *CICA Handbook* recommendation on how each should be accounted for.

(c) Were each of the actual changes identified by EnCana accounted for as recommended? Explain.

(d) The company adjusted the opening balance of Retained Earnings at January 1, 2003 by $66 million. How much of this change related to 2002? To 2001? Prior to 2001? What revenue and expense accounts do you think were affected in the prior years? Explain briefly.

(e) Does the company report any new but not yet effective changes in primary sources of GAAP? If so, how are they expected to affect the company's financial statements?

RA22-3 Comparative Analysis: Falconbridge Limited, Inco Limited, and Noranda Inc.

Instructions

From the SEDAR website (www.sedar.com) or other source, obtain the 2003 financial statements of **Falconbridge Limited**, **Inco Limited**, and **Noranda Inc.**, three companies in the metals and minerals industry. Answer the following questions or instructions.

(a) Identify the accounting changes reported by these companies in their 2003 fiscal year. Were similar changes made, accounted for, and reported in the same way by all three? Compare the extent of the disclosures by each company.

(b) Would you expect the accounting policy changes to have a similar effect on all three companies? Did they? Were the changes equally significant to all companies?

(c) Do the companies report what the effect is on the current year's income of these changes? Comment.

RA22-4   Research Case–Transitional Provisions 1

In July 2001, the CICA released its new recommendations on accounting for goodwill and other intangibles. Section 3062, entitled "Goodwill and Other Intangible Assets," effective for fiscal years beginning on or after January 2002 for public companies, includes very specific transitional provisions for the accounting and reporting of this revised accounting policy or accounting change.

Instructions

(a) Investigate what the accounting requirements are for this change in accounting policy.

(b) Suggest reasons why the Accounting Standards Board might have decided on this treatment.

(c) What disclosures are required when companies adopt the new recommendations?

RA22-5   Research Case–Transitional Provisions 2

With the Accounting Standards Board of the CICA working more closely with the FASB and IASB in recent years, the pace of change in primary sources of Canadian GAAP has accelerated. In almost every case, the AcSB includes transitional provisions to ensure that there is uniformity of practice between companies changing to the new or revised standards. Some of the more significant changes include the following.

Topic	*CICA Handbook* Section
Impairment of long-lived assets	3063
Asset retirement obligations	3110
Generally accepted accounting principles	1100
Variable interest entities	AcG-14
Changes in Accounting Policies and Estimates, and Errors	1506

Instructions

Review the transitional provisions for the topics identified above. Write a short report on the accounting requirements for each change in the year it becomes effective. Briefly discuss whether the requirements seem reasonable, and whether they are consistent from one standard to another.

Cash Flow is Key

Clearwater Seafoods Limited knows about maintaining a healthy cash flow, continuing to thrive and provide quality seafood products for more than 25 years. "The ability to sustain and grow cash flows is key," says Tyrone Cotie, director of corporate finance and investor relations at the Bedford, N.S.-based company. A vertically integrated company, Clearwater operates a large fleet of vessels and owns several processing plants throughout Eastern Canada.

The statement of cash flows ties together the information contained on the balance sheet and income statement, Cotie explains. It provides an accurate picture of cash flows by removing the non-cash items from the earnings statement and by adding the investments noted on the balance sheet to cash outflows. "It shows you the cash that was generated and what it was used for during the year," he says. And, for Clearwater, 2003 was an interesting year, with an increase in the volume of products sold and the acquisition of seafood quota from a competitor.

As an income fund, Clearwater has distributed a significant amount of cash to unit-holders since it went public in July 2002. For example, in 2003, the company generated $61.5 million in distributable cash and declared distributions of $58.5 million for a payout ratio of 95%. "Users of our financial statements look to the operations section of the cash flow statement in order to understand the cash flows that the business is generating, which in turn, after deducting certain items, is the basis for the payment of distributions," Cotie says.

The cash flows generated from operations are a key indicator of the company's health. "The sustainability of a business is ultimately linked to your ability to generate cash," Cotie says. ■

CHAPTER 23

Statement of Cash Flows

Learning Objectives

After studying this chapter, you should be able to:

1. Describe the purpose and uses of the statement of cash flows.

2. Define cash and cash equivalents.

3. Identify the major classifications of cash flows and explain the significance of each.

4. Contrast the direct and indirect methods of calculating net cash flow from operating activities.

5. Differentiate between net income and cash flows from operating activities.

6. Prepare a statement of cash flows.

7. Read and interpret a statement of cash flows.

8. Identify the financial reporting and disclosure requirements for the statement of cash flows.

After studying Appendix A, you should be able to:

9. Use a work sheet to prepare a statement of cash flows.

Examining a company's income statement may provide insights into its profitability, but it does not provide much information about its liquidity and financial flexibility. This chapter's purpose is to highlight the requirements of *CICA Handbook* Section 1540, "Cash Flow Statements," explain the main components of a statement of cash flows, the type of information it provides, and how to prepare, read, and interpret such a statement. The chapter's content and organization are as follows:

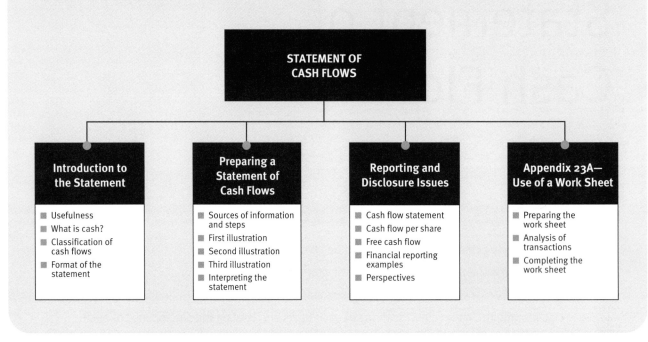

STATEMENT OF CASH FLOWS

Introduction to the Statement
- Usefulness
- What is cash?
- Classification of cash flows
- Format of the statement

Preparing a Statement of Cash Flows
- Sources of information and steps
- First illustration
- Second illustration
- Third illustration
- Interpreting the statement

Reporting and Disclosure Issues
- Cash flow statement
- Cash flow per share
- Free cash flow
- Financial reporting examples
- Perspectives

Appendix 23A— Use of a Work Sheet
- Preparing the work sheet
- Analysis of transactions
- Completing the work sheet

INTRODUCTION TO THE STATEMENT OF CASH FLOWS

Objective 1
Describe the purpose and uses of the statement of cash flows.

Will the company be able to continue to pay dividends? How did the company finance the acquisition of the new subsidiary this year? Will the company have sufficient cash to meet the significant debt maturing next year? How did cash increase when there was a net loss for the period? How were the bond issue proceeds used? How was the expansion in plant and equipment financed? Or, as the opening story alludes to, how sustainable are the company's operations? These questions cannot be answered by reviewing the balance sheet and income statement alone. A cash flow statement is needed.

The primary purpose of the **statement of cash flows** is to provide information about an entity's cash receipts and cash payments during a period. A secondary objective is to provide information on a cash basis about its operating, investing, and financing activities. The statement of cash flows therefore reports cash receipts, cash payments, and net change in cash resulting from an enterprise's operating, investing, and financing activities during a period, in a format that reconciles the beginning and ending cash balances.

Usefulness of the Statement of Cash Flows

The information in a statement of cash flows enables investors, creditors, and others to assess the following.

1. **Liquidity and solvency of an entity—its capacity to generate cash and its needs for cash resources.**   The timing and degree of certainty of expected cash inflows need to be determined in light of the entity's requirements for cash to pay maturing debt, maintain and increase productive capacity, and distribute a return to owners.[1]

2. **Amounts, timing, and uncertainty of future cash flows.**   Historical cash flows are often useful in helping to predict future cash flows. By examining relationships between items such as sales and net income and the cash flow from operating activities, or cash flow from operating activities and increases or decreases in cash, it is possible to make better predictions of the amounts, timing, and uncertainty of future cash flows than is possible using accrual basis data alone.

3. **Reasons for the difference between net income and cash flow from operating activities.**   The net income number is important, because it provides information on an enterprise's success or failure from one period to another. But some people are critical of accrual basis income because there are numerous estimates required in its calculation. As a result, the number's reliability is often challenged—usually not the case with cash. Readers of the financial statements benefit from knowing the reasons for the difference between net income and cash flow from operating activities. Then they can assess for themselves the income number's reliability.

Underlying Concept

The statement of cash flows is another example of relevant information—information that is useful in assessing and predicting future cash flows.

What Is Cash?

As part of a company's cash management system, short-term investments are often held instead of cash, thereby allowing the company to earn a return on cash balances in excess of its immediate needs. Also, it is common for an organization to have an agreement with the bank that permits the account to fluctuate between a positive balance and an overdraft. Because an entity's cash activity and position are more appropriately described by including these other cash management activities, the AcSB recommends that cash flows be defined as inflows and outflows of cash and cash equivalents.

Cash is defined as cash on hand and demand deposits. Cash equivalents are short-term, highly liquid investments that are readily convertible to known amounts of cash and are subject to an insignificant risk of change in value.[2] **Nonequity** investments acquired with short maturities and bank overdrafts repayable on demand, both of which result from and are an integral part of an organization's cash management policies, are included in cash and cash equivalents.[3]

Throughout this chapter, the use of the term "cash" should be interpreted to mean "cash and cash equivalents."

2 Objective
Define cash and cash equivalents.

---

[1] *CICA Handbook*, Section 1540.01.

[2] *CICA Handbook*, Section 1540.06(a), (b), and (c).

[3] *CICA Handbook*, Section 1540.08 suggests a maturity "of, say three months or less from the date of acquisition." Examples of cash equivalents are treasury bills, commercial paper, and money market funds purchased with cash that is in excess of immediate needs.

Classification of Cash Flows

Objective 3
Identify the major classifications of cash flows and explain the significance of each.

The statement of cash flows classifies cash receipts and cash payments according to whether they are a result of an operating, investing, or a financing activity. Transactions and other events characteristic of each kind of activity and the significance of each type of cash flow are as follows.

1. Operating activities are the enterprise's principal revenue-producing activities and other activities that are not investing or financing activities.[4] Operating flows generally involve the cash effects of transactions that determine net income, such as collections from customers on accounts receivable; and payments to suppliers on accounts payable, to CRA on income taxes payable, and to employees on salaries and wages payable.

   The level of cash provided from or used in operations is key information for financial statement users. Like blood flowing through the veins and arteries of our bodies, operating cash flows—derived mainly from receipts from customers—are needed to maintain the organization's systems: to meet payrolls, to pay suppliers, to cover rentals and insurance, and to pay taxes. In addition, surplus flows from operations are needed to repay loans, to take advantage of new investment opportunities, and to pay dividends without having to seek new external financing.

2. Investing activities cover the acquisition and disposal of long-term assets and other investments not included in cash equivalents.[5] They include such activities as making and collecting loans and acquiring and disposing of investments and productive long-lived assets.

   The use of cash in investment activities tells the financial statement reader whether the entity is ploughing cash back into additional long-term assets that will generate profits and increase cash flows in the future, or whether the stock of long-term productive assets is being decreased by conversion into cash.

3. Financing activities result in changes in the size and composition of the enterprise's equity capital and borrowings.[6] They include obtaining cash through the issuance of debt and repayment of amounts borrowed, and obtaining capital from owners and providing them with a return on, and a return of, their investment.

   Details of the cash flows related to financing activities allow readers to assess the potential for future claims to the organization's cash and to identify major changes in the form of financing, especially between debt and equity.

Illustration 23-1 identifies a business enterprise's typical cash receipts and payments and classifies them according to whether they are operating, investing, or financing activities. Note that the *operating* cash flows are related almost entirely to **working capital (current asset and current liability) accounts**, the *investing* cash flows generally involve **long-term asset items**, and the *financing* flows are derived principally from changes in **long-term liability and equity accounts**.

Some cash flows related to investing or financing activities are classified as operating activities. For example, **dividends and interest received and paid and included when determining net income** are classified as operating activities. Any **dividends or interest paid that are charged against retained earnings** are included as financing flows.[7]

IAS Note

IAS 7 permits interest and dividends received and paid to be reported as either operating, investing, or financing flows, but requires consistency from period to period.

---

[4] *CICA Handbook*, Section 1540.06(d).

[5] *CICA Handbook*, Section 1540.06(e).

[6] *CICA Handbook*, Section 1540.06(f).

[7] Dividend payments recognized in the income statement relate to equity securities that are determined to be liabilities in substance, and interest payments charged to retained earnings relate to debt securities that are judged to be equity instruments in substance. The statement of cash flows, therefore, treats returns to in-substance equity holders as financing outflows and to those designated as creditors as operating outflows.

Illustration 23-1

Classification of Typical Cash Inflows and Outflows

OPERATING
Cash inflows
 From cash sales and collections from customers on account
 From returns on loans (interest) and equity securities (dividends)
 From receipts for royalties, rents, and fees
Cash outflows
 To suppliers on account
 To employees for services
 To government for taxes
 To lenders for interest
 To others for expenses

         Generally non-cash current asset and current liability items

INVESTING
Cash inflows
 From sale of property, plant, and equipment
 From sale of debt or equity securities of other entities
 From collection of principal on loans to other entities
Cash outflows
 To purchase property, plant, and equipment
 To purchase debt or equity securities of other entities
 To make loans to other entities

         Generally long-term asset items

FINANCING
Cash inflows
 From issuance of equity securities
 From issuance of debt (bonds and notes)
Cash outflows
 To shareholders as dividends
 To redeem long-term debt or reacquire share capital
 To reduce capital lease obligations

         Generally long-term liability and equity items

Other items, although reported on the income statement, relate directly to investing and financing activities. For example, cash received from the sale of property, plant, and equipment is properly classified as an investing cash inflow. The gain or loss reported in the income statement, however, must be excluded in determining cash flows from operating activities. Similarly, a gain or loss on the repayment (extinguishment) of debt is not an operating cash flow. The cash outflow to redeem the debt, not the amount of the gain or loss, is the actual cash flow and the repayment is clearly a financing activity.

Outflows and proceeds on the sale of securities and loans acquired specifically for resale (trading securities) are treated the same as flows related to inventories acquired for resale—as operating cash flows.

Income taxes present another complexity. While income tax expense can be identified with specific operating, investing, and financing transactions, the related cash payments for taxes usually cannot. For this reason, income tax payments are classified as operating cash flows unless they can be specifically identified with financing and investing activities.[8]

How should **significant noncash transactions** that affect an organization's asset and capital structure be handled? Examples of such noncash transactions are:

1. acquisition of assets by assuming liabilities (including capital lease obligations) or by issuing equity securities,

2. exchanges of nonmonetary assets,

3. conversion of debt or preferred shares to common shares, and

4. issuance of equity securities to retire debt.

Underlying Concept

By rejecting the requirement to allocate taxes to the various activities, the Accounting Standards Board invoked the cost-benefit constraint. While the information is beneficial, the cost of providing it exceeds the benefits.

---

[8] *CICA Handbook*, Section 1540.38.

Because the cash flow statement reports only the cash effect of activities, significant investing and financing transactions that do not affect cash are excluded from the statement and are required to be disclosed elsewhere in the financial statements.[9]

Evaluation of overall cash flow requires examination of the alternative sources of cash and an understanding of where a company is in its product life cycle. Generally, companies move through several stages of development, which have implications for an evaluation of cash flow. As shown in the graph below, the pattern of cash flows from operating, financing, and investing activities will vary depending on the stage of the product life cycle.

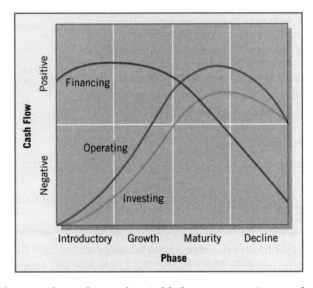

In the introductory phase, the product is likely not generating much revenue so operating cash flow is negative. Because the company is making heavy investments to get a product off the ground, cash flow associated with investing activities is also negative. Financing cash flows are positive as funds are raised to pay for the investments and cover the operating shortfall. As the product moves to the growth and maturity phases, these cash flow relationships reverse. The product generates more cash from operations, which can be used to cover investments needed to support the product, and less cash is needed from financing. So is a negative operating cash flow bad? Not always. It depends to a great extent on the product life cycle.

Source: Adapted from Paul D. Kimmel, Jerry J. Weygandt, and Donald E. Kieso, *Financial Accounting: Tools for Business Decision Making*, 2nd ed. (New York: John Wiley & Sons, 2000), p. 602.

Format of the Statement of Cash Flows

The three activities discussed in the preceding section constitute the general format of the statement of cash flows. The operating activities section usually appears first, followed by the investing and financing activities sections. The individual inflows and outflows from investing and financing activities are reported separately; that is, they are reported gross, not netted against one another. Thus, a cash outflow from the purchase of property is reported separately from the cash inflow from the sale of property. Similarly, the cash inflow from the issuance of debt is reported separately from the cash outflow for debt retirement. Not reporting them separately obscures the enterprise's investing and financing activities and makes it more difficult to assess future cash flows.[10]

---

[9] *CICA Handbook*, Section 1540.46.

[10] Netting is permitted in limited circumstances. See *CICA Handbook* Section 1540.25 to .27.

The skeleton format of a statement of cash flows is provided in Illustration 23-2. Note that it reconciles the beginning and ending cash balances reported in the comparative balance sheets.

Illustration 23-2

Format of the Statement of Cash Flows

COMPANY NAME
Statement of Cash Flows
Period Covered

Cash flows from operating activities		
Net income		XXX
Adjustments to reconcile net income to cash provided by (used in) operating activities: (List of individual items)	XX	XX
Net cash provided by (used in) operating activities		XXX
Cash flows from investing activities		
(List of individual inflows and outflows)	XX	
Net cash provided by (used in) investing activities		XXX
Cash flows from financing activities		
(List of individual inflows and outflows)	XX	
Net cash provided by (used in) financing activities		XXX
Net increase (decrease) in cash		XXX
Cash at beginning of period		XXX
Cash at end of period		XXX

Illustration 23-2 derives the net cash flow from operating activities indirectly by making the necessary adjustments to the net income reported on the income statement. This is referred to as the **indirect method** (or reconciliation method). The cash flow from operating activities could be calculated directly by identifying the sources of the cash receipts and payments. This approach is referred to as the **direct method** and is illustrated below.

4 Objective

Contrast the direct and indirect methods of calculating net cash flow from operating activities.

Illustration 23-3

Cash Flows from Operating Activities—Direct Method

Cash flows from operating activities	
Cash receipts from customers	XX
Cash receipts from other revenue sources	XX
Cash payments to suppliers for goods and services	(XX)
Cash payments to and on behalf of employees	(XX)
Cash payments of income taxes	(XX)
Net cash flow provided by (used in) operating activities	XX

There has been considerable controversy about which method should be recommended for use. The AcSB encourages use of the direct method because it provides additional information, but its use is not mandatory.[11]

Direct Versus Indirect

In general, reporting companies tend to prefer the indirect method, although commercial lending officers and other investors tend to express a strong preference for the direct method because of the additional information it provides.

---

[11] Unfortunately, use of the direct method is the exception in Canada. Prior to the AcSB stating a preference for the direct method in 1997, *Financial Reporting in Canada—1995* reported that 1 of 300 surveyed companies in 1994 used the direct method. In 2002, two companies out of 200 surveyed used the direct method. The authors expect a slow but consistent move toward the direct method.

In favour of the direct method.   The direct method's principal advantage is that it shows operating cash receipts and payments. That is, it is more consistent with the objective of a statement of cash flows—to provide information about cash receipts and cash payments— than the indirect method, which does not report operating cash receipts and payments.

Supporters of the direct method contend that knowing the specific sources of operating cash receipts and the purposes for which operating cash payments were made in past periods is useful in estimating future operating cash flows. Furthermore, information about amounts of major classes of operating cash receipts and payments is more useful than information only about their arithmetic sum (the net cash flow from operating activities). Such information is more revealing of an enterprise's ability to (1) generate sufficient cash from operating activities to pay its debts, (2) reinvest in its operations, and (3) make distributions to its owners.[12]

Many corporate providers of financial statements say that they do not currently collect information in a manner that allows them to determine amounts, such as cash received from customers or cash paid to suppliers. But supporters of the direct method contend that the incremental cost of assimilating such operating cash receipts and payments data is not significant.

International Insight

FASB also encourages the use of the direct method over the indirect. If the direct method is used, there is a requirement to also provide a reconciliation between net income and cash flow from operating activities.

In favour of the indirect method.   The indirect method's principal advantage is that it focuses on the differences between net income and cash flow from operating activities. That is, it provides a useful link between the statement of cash flows and the income statement and balance sheet.

Many providers of financial statements contend that it is less costly to adjust net income to net cash flow from operating activities (indirect) than it is to report gross operating cash receipts and payments (direct). Supporters of the indirect method also state that the direct method, which effectively reports income statement information on a cash rather than an accrual basis, may erroneously suggest that net cash flow from operating activities is as good as, or better than, net income as a measure of performance.

As the indirect method has been used almost exclusively in the past, both preparers and users are more familiar with it and this helps perpetuate its use. Each method provides different but useful information. The best solution may lie in mandating the direct method, which comes closer to meeting the statement's stated objectives, and requiring disclosure of the differences between net income and cash flow from operations.

PREPARING A STATEMENT OF CASH FLOWS

Sources of Information and Steps in the Process

The statement of cash flows was previously called the Statement of Changes in Financial Position for good reason.[13] By analysing the changes in all noncash accounts on the statement of financial position or balance sheet from one period to the next, the sources of all cash receipts and all cash disbursements can be identified and summarized. Illustration 23-4 explains why this is so.

---

[12] "The Statement of Cash Flows," *Statement of Financial Accounting Standards No. 95* (Stamford, Conn.: FASB, 1987), par. 107 and 111.

[13] Prior to the existing standard on cash flows, significant noncash transactions **were included** in the statement because of their effect on the entity's asset and capital structure. This difference illustrates the change in focus from a statement of changes in financial position (old terminology) to a statement of cash flows (new terminology), where only cash effects are reported.

$$A = L + OE$$
$$\Delta A = \Delta(L + OE)$$
$$\Delta A = \Delta L + \Delta OE$$
$$\Delta \text{ (Cash + noncash A)} = \Delta L + \Delta OE$$
$$\Delta Cash + \Delta noncash\ A = \Delta L + \Delta OE$$
$$\Delta Cash = \Delta L + \Delta OE - \Delta noncash\ A$$

Note: Δ is a symbol meaning "change in."

Therefore, unlike the other major financial statements that are prepared from the adjusted trial balance, the statement of cash flows is prepared **by analysing the changes in the balance sheet accounts over the accounting period**. Information to prepare this statement usually comes from the following three sources.

Comparative balance sheets provide the amount of the change in each asset, liability and equity account from the period's beginning to end.

The **current income statement** provides details about the change in the balance sheet retained earnings account, and information to help determine the amount of cash provided by, or used in, operations during the period.

Selected transaction data from the general ledger provide additional detailed information needed to determine how cash was provided or used during the period.

Preparing the statement of cash flows from the data sources above involves three major steps.

Step 1. Determine the change in cash. This procedure is straightforward because the difference between the beginning and ending cash and cash equivalents balances can easily be calculated by examining the comparative balance sheets. **Explaining this change is the objective of the subsequent analysis.**

Step 2. Record information from the income statement on the statement of cash flows. This is the starting point for calculating cash flows from operating activities. **Whenever subsequent analyses indicate that the operating cash flow and the amount reported on the income statement differ, the income statement number is adjusted.**

Most adjustments fit into one of three categories.

5 Objective
Differentiate between net income and cash flows from operating activities.

Category 1. Amounts reported as revenue and expense on the income statement are not the same as cash received from customers and cash paid to the suppliers of goods and services. Companies receive cash from customers for revenue reported in a previous year, and do not receive cash for all the revenue reported as earned in the current period. Similarly, cash payments are made in the current period to suppliers for goods and services acquired, used, and recognized as expense in a preceding period. In addition, not all amounts recognized as expenses in the current year are paid for by year end. Most of these adjustments are related to receivables, payables, and other working capital accounts.

Category 2. Some expenses, such as amortization, represent deferred costs incurred and paid for in a previous period. While there was a cash flow associated with the original acquisition of the asset (an investing flow), there is no cash flow associated with the amortization of these assets over their period of use.

Category 3. Amounts reported as gains or losses on the income statement are not usually the same as the cash flow from the transaction and, in many cases, the underlying activity is not an operating transaction. For example, gains and losses on the disposal of long-term assets and the early retirement of long-term debt are reported on the income statement. These result, respectively, from an investing and a financing transaction and the cash flow amounts are the **proceeds on disposal** of the asset and the **payment to retire the debt, not the amount of the reported gain or loss.**

(k) **Mortgage Payable.** The cash flow associated with part of the change in this account was identified above in item (d). If the account increased by $155,000 on the assumption of the mortgage, principal payments of $2,600 must have been made to reduce the balance to $152,400. The entry underlying this transaction is:

Mortgage Payable	2,600	
Cash		2,600

The outflow of $2,600 is a financing activity.

(l) **Bonds Payable.** The increase in this account is explained by the following entry.

Cash	10,000	
Bonds Payable		10,000

The $10,000 inflow of cash from the bond issue is a financing cash flow.

(m) **Common Shares.** The $8,000 increase in this account resulted from the issue of shares.

Cash	8,000	
Common Shares		8,000

The $8,000 inflow of cash is a financing flow.

(n) **Retained Earnings.** $59,900 of the increase in retained earnings is explained by net income. This has been recognized on the cash flow statement already as the starting point in calculating cash flows from operations. The remainder of the change is explained by the entry for dividends.

Retained Earnings	8,000	
Cash		8,000

The payment of dividends charged to retained earnings is a financing flow.

The changes in all balance sheet accounts have now been explained, all information required to prepare the statement of cash flows has been identified, and the statement can be completed.

Step 4. Complete the statement of cash flows. Subtotals are calculated for each section of the statement and the change in cash indicated is compared with the change calculated in Step 1. Both indicate a $22,000 decrease in EWPL's cash balance during 2006.

A statement in good form is then prepared from the working paper developed in Illustration 23-11, using more appropriate descriptions and explanations. Illustration 23-12 indicates what the final statement might look like if the indirect method is chosen. The additional disclosures provided are discussed in a later section of the chapter.

Illustration 23-12

EWPL Statement of Cash Flows, 2006—Indirect Method

EASTERN WINDOW PRODUCTS LIMITED
Statement of Cash Flows
Year Ended December 31, 2006

Cash provided by (used in) operations:		
Net income		$59,900
Add back noncash expense—amortization		15,000
Add (deduct) changes in noncash working capital*		
- accounts receivable	$10,000	
- inventory	(9,000)	
- prepaid expenses	1,500	
- accounts payable	10,900	
- income taxes payable	3,000	
- wages payable	(700)	15,700
		90,600
Cash provided by (used in) investing activities:		
Purchase of property, plant, and equipment		(120,000)
Cash provided by (used in) financing activities:		
Payment on mortgage payable	(2,600)	
Proceeds on issue of bonds	10,000	
Dividends paid	(8,000)	
Proceeds on issue of common shares	8,000	7,400
Decrease in cash		(22,000)
Cash balance, beginning of year		59,000
Cash balance, end of year		$37,000

Notes: 1. Cash consists of cash on hand and balances with banks.
  2. Cash outflows during the year for interest and income taxes were $16,200 and $36,900, respectively.
  3. During the year, property was acquired at a total cost of $275,000 (land $70,000; building $200,000; equipment $5,000) of which $155,000 was financed directly by the assumption of a mortgage.

*Many companies provide only the subtotal on the statement of cash flows and report the details in a note to the financial statements.

Where the direct method is preferred, the Operating Activities section of the cash flow statement would appear as follows.

Illustration 23-13

Operating Activities Section, EWPL, Direct Method

Cash provided by (used in) operations	
Received from customers	$602,000
Payments to suppliers	(402,600)
Payments to and on behalf of employees	(55,700)
Interest payments	(16,200)
Income taxes paid	(36,900)
	90,600

Third Illustration—Yoshi Corporation

The next step is to see how the same principles are applied to more complex situations. Some of these complexities are illustrated below for Yoshi Corporation, using the same approach as in the previous examples. Those who prefer a more structured method of accumulating the information for the cash flow statement should refer to the work sheet approach in Appendix A to the chapter or the T-account method illustrated on the Digital Tool.

The comparative balance sheets of Yoshi Corporation at December 31, 2006 and 2005, the statement of income and retained earnings for the year ended December 31, 2006, and selected additional information are provided in Illustrations 23-14, 23-15, and 23-16.

YOSHI CORPORATION
Comparative Balance Sheets
December 31, 2006 and 2005

	2006 $	2005 $	Change Increase/Decrease $
Assets			
Cash	20,000	32,000	12,000 Decrease
Short-term investments	39,000	34,000	5,000 Increase
Accounts receivable	106,500	52,700	53,800 Increase
Allowance for doubtful accounts	(2,500)	(1,700)	800 Increase
Inventories	303,000	311,000	8,000 Decrease
Prepaid expenses	16,500	17,000	500 Decrease
Investment in shares of Porter Corp.	18,500	15,000	3,500 Increase
Deferred development costs	190,000	30,000	160,000 Increase
Land	131,500	82,000	49,500 Increase
Equipment	187,000	142,000	45,000 Increase
Accumulated amortization—equipment	(29,000)	(31,000)	2,000 Decrease
Buildings	262,000	262,000	—
Accumulated amortization—buildings	(74,100)	(71,000)	3,100 Increase
Goodwill	7,600	10,000	2,400 Decrease
Total Assets	1,176,000	884,000	
Liabilities			
Accounts payable	130,000	131,000	1,000 Decrease
Dividends payable, term preferred shares	2,000	—	2,000 Increase
Accrued liabilities	43,000	39,000	4,000 Increase
Income taxes payable	3,000	16,000	13,000 Decrease
Bonds payable	100,000	100,000	—
Discount on bonds payable	(2,200)	(2,500)	300 Decrease
Term preferred shares	60,000	—	60,000 Increase
Future income tax liability	9,000	6,000	3,000 Increase
Total Liabilities	344,800	289,500	
Shareholders' Equity			
Common shares	247,000	88,000	159,000 Increase
Retained earnings	601,200	506,500	94,700 Increase
Treasury shares	(17,000)	—	17,000 Increase
Total Shareholders' Equity	831,200	594,500	
Liabilities and Shareholders' Equity	1,176,000	884,000	

YOSHI CORPORATION
Statement of Income and Retained Earnings
Year Ended December 31, 2006

Net sales		$924,500
Equity in earnings of Porter Corp.		5,500
		930,000
Expenses		
Cost of goods sold	$395,400	
Salaries and wages	200,000	
Selling and administrative	134,600	
Amortization	14,600	
Interest and dividend expense	11,300	
Impairment loss—goodwill	2,400	
Other expenses and losses	12,000	770,300
Income before income tax and extraordinary item		159,700

Income tax: Current	47,000	
Future	3,000	50,000
Income before extraordinary item		109,700
Extraordinary item: Gain on expropriation of land, net of tax of $2,500		8,000
Net income		117,700
Retained earnings, January 1		506,500
Less: Cash dividends, common shares	6,000	
Stock dividends, common shares	15,000	
Excess of cost of treasury shares over reissue price	2,000	(23,000)
Retained earnings, December 31		$601,200

Illustration 23-15

Statement of Income and Retained Earnings— Yoshi Corporation (continued)

YOSHI CORPORATION
Additional Information

1. Short-term investments represent held-for-trading money market instruments with original maturity dates of less than 90 days.
2. During 2006, bad debts written off amounted to $1,450.
3. Yoshi accounts for its 22% interest in Porter Corp. using the equity method. Porter Corp. paid a dividend in 2006.
4. During 2006, Yoshi incurred $200,000 of market development costs that met the criteria for deferral. $40,000 of deferred costs were amortized in the year.
5. Land in the amount of $54,000 was purchased by issuing term preferred shares. In addition, the municipality expropriated a parcel of land, resulting in a gain of $10,500 before tax.
6. An analysis of the Equipment account and related accumulated amortization indicates the following:

Equipment:	Balance, January 1, 2006	$142,000
	Cost of equipment purchased	53,000
	Cost of equipment sold (sold at a loss of $1,500)	(8,000)
	Balance, December 31, 2006	$187,000

Accumulated amortization:		
	Balance, January 1, 2006	$ 31,000
	Accumulated amortization on equipment sold	(2,500)
	Amortization expense, 2006	11,500
	Major repair charged to accumulated amortization	(11,000)
	Balance, December 31, 2006	$ 29,000

7. An analysis of the common shares account discloses the following:

Balance, January 1, 2006	$ 88,000
Issuance of a 2% stock dividend	15,000
Sale of shares for cash	144,000
Balance, December 31, 2006	$247,000

8. During 2006, Yoshi purchased its own common shares in the market at a cost of $34,000, holding them as treasury shares. Later in the year, half of these shares were reissued for proceeds of $15,000.
9. Changes in other balance sheet accounts resulted from usual transactions and events.

Illustration 23-16

Additional Information— Yoshi Corporation

Step 1. Determine the change in cash. Yoshi's cash and cash equivalents include temporary holdings of money market instruments as well as cash balances, with a decrease in cash of $7,000 to be explained. This is the difference between the opening cash and cash equivalents of $66,000 ($32,000 + $34,000) and the ending cash and cash equivalents of $59,000 ($20,000 + $39,000).

Step 2. Record information from the income statement on the statement of cash flows. Under the **indirect method,** the net income of $117,700 is "slotted in" as the starting point, as indicated in Illustration 23-17.

Using the **direct method**, skeleton headings that cover each type of cash flow—from customer receipts to the extraordinary gain—are set up within the Operating Activities section of the cash flow statement, as shown in Illustration 23-17. The description of each line may differ from situation to situation, but the income statement provides clues as to the types of operating cash flows and how they should be described. For example, the equity basis income from the investment in Porter Corp. is not a cash flow, but it will be replaced after adjustment with any dividends received from the investment.

Each amount making up the net income of $117,700 is transferred to the most appropriate skeleton heading on the cash flow statement work sheet. Amounts reported as cost of goods sold, selling and administrative expense, and other expenses and losses form the base for what will eventually be "cash paid to suppliers for goods and services." Income tax expense on ordinary income and on the extraordinary gain are both included on the line that will be adjusted to "income taxes paid." The extraordinary item is handled on a before-tax basis since the tax is reported separately.

Illustration 23-17

Statement of Cash Flows Working Paper— Yoshi Corporation

CASH FLOWS FROM OPERATING ACTIVITIES
Indirect Method

Net income		+117,700
Adjustments:	Increase in accounts receivable, net of write-offs	− 55,250 (a)
	Bad debt expense	+ 2,250 (b)
	Decrease in inventories	+ 8,000 (c)
	Decrease in prepaid expenses	+ 500 (d)
	Equity method investment income	− 5,500 (e)
	Dividend from equity method investment	+ 2,000 (e)
	Amortization of market development costs	+ 40,000 (f)
	Extraordinary gain on expropriation of land	− 10,500 (g)
	Loss on disposal of equipment	+ 1,500 (h)
	Amortization expense—equipment	+11,500 (h)
	Amortization expense—buildings	+ 3,100 (i)
	Impairment loss—goodwill	+ 2,400 (j)
	Decrease in accounts payable	− 1,000 (k)
	Increase in dividends payable on term preferred shares	+ 2,000 (i)
	Increase in accrued liabilities	+ 4,000 (m)
	Decrease in income taxes payable	− 13,000 (n)
	Amortization of bond discount	+ 300 (o)
	Increase in future income tax liability	+ 3,000 (q)
		+113,000

Direct Method

Receipts from customers	+924,500	−55,250 (a)	+869,250
Received from investment in Porter Corp.	+ 5,500	− 5,500 (e)	+ 2,000
		+ 2,000 (e)	
Payments for goods and services	−395,400	+ 2,250 (b)	
	−134,600	+ 8,000 (c)	
	− 12,000	+ 500 (d)	
		+40,000 (f)	−490,750
		+ 1,500 (h)	
		− 1,000 (k)	
Payments to employees	−200,000	+ 4,000 (m)	− 196,000
Interest and dividend payments	− 11,300	+ 2,000 (i)	− 9,000
		+ 300 (o)	
Income taxes paid	− 50,000	−13,000 (n)	− 62,500
	− 2,500	+ 3,000 (q)	
Other items:			
Amortization expense	− 14,600	+11,500 (h)	—
		+ 3,100 (i)	
Impairment loss	− 2,400	+ 2,400 (j)	—
Extraordinary gain, before tax	+ 10,500	−10,500 (g)	—
	+117,700		+113,000

CASH FLOWS FROM INVESTING ACTIVITIES

Market development costs incurred	− 200,000 (f)
Proceeds on expropriation of land (extraordinary item)	+ 15,000 (g)
Purchase of equipment	− 53,000 (h)
Proceeds on sale of equipment	+ 4,000 (h)
Major repair costs incurred	− 11,000 (h)
	− 245,000

CASH FLOWS FROM FINANCING ACTIVITIES

Proceeds on issue of term preferred shares	+ 6,000 (p)
Proceeds on issue of common shares	+ 144,000 (r)
Dividends paid on common shares	− 6,000 (s)
Proceeds on reissue of treasury shares	+ 15,000 (s)
Payment to acquire treasury shares	− 34,000 (t)
	+ 125,000
CHANGE IN CASH	− 7,000

Step 3. Analyse the change in each balance sheet account, identify any cash flows associated with a change in the account balance, and record the effect on the statement of cash flows. The analysis begins with accounts receivable because the short-term investments are considered cash equivalents.

(a) **Accounts Receivable.** Unlike the previous illustrations, Yoshi reports both the receivable and its contra allowance account. The receivable control account is increased by sales on account and reduced by the total of cash received from customers and accounts written off. During 2006, the receivable account increased by $53,800, indicating that the sales reported on the income statement exceeded the total of cash received on account and the accounts written off by $53,800. Because accounts written off explain $1,450 of the difference, the actual cash inflow from customers must have been $55,250 less than the sales revenue reported (i.e., $53,800 plus $1,450). Prepare a T account to verify this reasoning.

Accounts Receivable			
Jan.1	52,700		
Sales	924,500	1,450	Accounts written off (given)
		?	Cash receipts
Dec. 31	106,500		

The cash receipts must have been $869,250, an amount $55,250 less than the revenue reported on the income statement. Using the indirect approach, $55,250 is deducted from the net income reported because the cash received from customers was less than the revenue reported in net income. Under the direct method, the revenue of $924,500 is adjusted directly to convert it to cash received from customers.

(b) **Allowance for Doubtful Accounts.** This account had an opening balance of $1,700, was increased by bad debt expense, reduced by accounts written off, and ended the year at $2,500. With accounts written off of $1,450, bad debt expense must have been $2,250 ($1,700 + bad debt expense − $1,450 = $2,500; or prepare a T account to determine this). Because bad debt expense does not require the use of cash, the net income number in the Operating Activities section must be adjusted.

Under the indirect method, $2,250 is added back to net income. Under the direct method, the $2,250 adjustment reduces the expense line that includes bad debt expense. In this example, it is assumed to be in selling expenses.

The only time it is necessary to analyse the Accounts Receivable and the Allowance account separately is when the direct method is used. This is because two adjustments are needed: one to adjust the revenue reported ($55,250) and the other to adjust the noncash bad debt expense ($2,250). When the indirect method is used, both adjustments correct the net income number. The analysis is easier, therefore, if you zero in on the change in the net accounts receivable and make one adjustment to the net income number.[16]

(c) **Inventories.** Because the Inventory account is increased by the cost of goods purchased and decreased by the transfer of costs to cost of goods sold, the $8,000 decrease in the Inventory account indicates that cost of goods sold exceeded purchases by $8,000. Using the indirect approach, $8,000 is added back to the net income number because the cost of goods sold that was deducted to determine net income was higher than the purchases made in the year. The direct approach adjusts cost of goods sold directly to convert it to the cost of goods purchased. The analysis of Accounts Payable in step (k) will convert the purchases to cash paid to suppliers.

(d) **Prepaid Expenses.** The $500 decrease in this account resulted because the costs charged to the income statement were $500 greater than the costs of acquiring prepaid goods and services in the year. For reasons similar to the inventory analysis in step (c), $500 is either added back to net income under the indirect approach, or used to adjust the expense line associated with the prepaid expense under the direct approach. It is assumed in this case that the prepaid expenses were charged to selling and administrative expenses when they were used.

(e) **Investment in Shares of Porter Corp.** The journal entries that explain the increase of $3,500 in this account are:

Investment in Porter Corp.	5,500	
Equity in Earnings of Porter Corp.		5,500
(To record investment income in Porter Corp.		
using the equity method)		
Cash	2,000	
Investment in Porter Corp.		2,000
(To record the dividend received from Porter Corp.)		

The investment income amount is reported on the income statement and the dividend amount is determined from the change in the account balance. There was no cash flow as a result of the investment income; therefore, an adjustment is needed to reduce net income. Under the indirect method, the $5,500 is deducted to offset the $5,500 reported; under the direct approach, the $5,500 adjustment is made to the specific revenue line.

The second entry indicates an operating cash inflow of $2,000. An adjustment is needed to the net income reported because it does not include the dividend. Using the indirect method, $2,000 is added to net income; under the direct approach, $2,000 is added to the same line as the $5,500 deduction above to complete the adjustment of equity-basis income to cash received from the investment in Porter.

(f) **Deferred Development Costs.** Two types of transactions affected this account in the current year, summarized in the following journal entries.

---

[16] For Yoshi Corporation, net receivables increased $53,000, from $51,000 ($52,700 − $1,700) at the beginning of the year to $104,000 ($106,500 − $2,500) at year end. The increase means that $53,000 of income was recognized that did not result in a corresponding cash flow. On the cash flow statement under the indirect method, one adjustment to reduce net income by $53,000 is all that is needed.

Deferred Development Costs	200,000	
Cash		200,000
(To record capitalized development costs)		
Market Development Expenses	40,000	
Deferred Development Costs		40,000
(To record the amortization of deferred development costs)		

The first entry indicates a cash outflow of $200,000. This is an investing outflow and is recognized in the statement's investing activities section.

The second entry did not affect cash. As explained earlier, it is important to be alert to noncash amounts included in net income. This $40,000 expense did not require the use of cash; an adjustment to net income is therefore needed under the indirect approach. Under the direct method, the adjustment is made to the specific expense: in this case, to the selling and administrative expense line.

(g) **Land.**   This account increased by $49,500 during 2006. Because you know that land was purchased at a cost of $54,000 during the year, there must have been a disposal of land that cost $4,500. The entries that affect this account in 2006, therefore, were as follows.

Land	54,000	
Term Preferred Shares		54,000
(To record the purchase of land through		
the issue of term preferred shares)		
Cash	15,000	
Land		4,500
Gain on Disposal of Land		10,500
(To record the appropriation of land		
costing $4,500 by the municipality)		

The first entry indicates that there were no cash flows associated with this transaction. Although this investment and financing transaction is not reported on the statement of cash flows, information about such noncash transactions is required to be disclosed elsewhere in the financial statements.

The second entry identifies a cash inflow of $15,000 on land disposal. This is an investing inflow because it affects the company's stock of noncurrent assets. It is included on the cash flow statement, separately disclosed as the cash effect of an extraordinary item.

The second transaction also results in a gain on the income statement of $10,500. By starting with "net income" in the statement's Operating Cash Flow section in Step 2, the $10,500 gain is included in income as if the gain had generated $10,500 of operating cash flows. This is incorrect for two reasons. First, the cash inflow was $15,000, not $10,500. Second, the cash flow was an investing, not an operating flow. An adjustment is needed, therefore, to deduct $10,500 from the income reported using the indirect method or from the extraordinary item if the direct method is used.

(h) **Equipment and Accumulated Amortization—Equipment.**   All information needed to replicate the entries made to both these accounts in 2006 is provided.

Equipment	53,000	
Cash		53,000
Cash	4,000	
Loss on Disposal of Equipment	1,500	
Accumulated Amortization—Equipment	2,500	
Equipment		8,000

(r) **Common Shares.**   The following entries summarize the changes to this account in 2006.

Retained Earnings	15,000	
Common Shares		15,000
Cash	144,000	
Common Shares		144,000

The first entry records the stock dividend, which neither required nor generated cash. The issue of a stock dividend is not a financing and/or investing transaction, and therefore, is not required to be reported. The second entry records a $144,000 inflow of cash as a result of issuing shares, a financing activity. This is reported as a financing inflow on the cash flow statement.

(s) **Retained Earnings.**   The statement of income and retained earnings explains the $94,700 change in this account. The $117,700 increase due to net income and the cash flows associated with it already have been included in the Operating Activities section of the cash flow statement. The $6,000 decrease due to dividends paid on the common shares is reported as a financing outflow. The $15,000 decrease due to the stock dividend was analysed above as having no cash flow implications.

The remaining $2,000 decrease due to the excess of cost of treasury shares over the issue price needs to be examined more closely. The entry underlying this transaction is:

Cash	15,000	
Retained Earnings	2,000	
Treasury Shares ($34,000 × ½)		17,000

The $15,000 cash inflow on the reissue of treasury shares is reported as a financing activity.

(t) **Treasury Shares.**   The $17,000 increase during the year resulted from the company's purchase of its common shares as recorded in the entry below, and the subsequent sale of treasury shares as analysed in step (s) above.

Treasury Shares	34,000	
Cash		34,000

The purchase is a $34,000 financing outflow of cash. The cash inflow from the reissue of half these shares has been recognized on the cash flow statement already.

The changes in all balance sheet accounts have now been analysed and those with cash implications have been recorded on the cash flow statement working paper. **The following general statements summarize the approach to the analysis.**

1. For most current asset and current liability accounts, zero in on what increases and what decreases each account. Compare the effect on the income statement with the amount of the related cash flow and adjust the income number(s) in the operating activities section of the cash flow statement accordingly.

2. For noncurrent asset and noncurrent liability accounts in general, reconstruct summary journal entries that explain how and why each account changed. Analyse each entry in turn.

(a) The cash effect is the amount of the debit or credit to cash. Include each investing and financing cash flow or operating flow adjustment on the cash flow statement.

(b) Identify all debits or credits to income statement accounts where the operating cash flow is not equal to the amount of revenue, gain, expense, or loss reported. Each of these requires an adjustment to the net income number(s) originally reported in the operating activities classification.

While the transactions entered into by Yoshi Corporation represent a good cross section of common business activities, they do not encompass all possible situations. The general principles and approaches used in the above analyses, however, can be applied to most other transactions and events.

Step 4. Complete the statement of cash flows. Determine subtotals for each major classification of cash flow and ensure that the statement reconciles to the actual change in cash identified in Step 1.

The working paper prepared in Illustration 23-17 should be presented with more appropriate descriptions and complete disclosure to enable readers to better interpret the information and comply with GAAP. Illustration 23-18 presents the completed statement of cash flows, using the direct method to explain the operating flows.

YOSHI CORPORATION
Statement of Cash Flows
Year Ended December 31, 2006

Cash provided by (used in) operations:

Received from customers		$869,250
Dividends received on long-term equity investments		2,000
Payments to suppliers		(490,750)
Payments to and on behalf of employees		(196,000)
Payments for interest, and dividends on term preferred shares		(9,000)
Income taxes paid		(62,500)
		113,000

Cash provided by (used in) investing activities:

Investment in development costs	($200,000)	
Purchase of equipment	(53,000)	
Major repairs incurred	(11,000)	
Proceeds on expropriation of land, an extraordinary item	15,000	
Proceeds on sale of equipment	4,000	(245,000)

Cash provided by (used in) financing activities:

Proceeds on issue of common shares	$144,000	
Proceeds on issue of term preferred shares	6,000	
Purchase of treasury shares	(34,000)	
Proceeds on reissue of treasury shares	15,000	
Dividends paid on common shares	(6,000)	125,000
Decrease in cash and cash equivalents (Note 1)		(7,000)
Cash and cash equivalents, January 1		66,000
Cash and cash equivalents, December 31		$ 59,000

Note 1: Cash and cash equivalents are defined as cash on deposit and money market instruments included as short-term investments.

Note 2: Preferred shares valued at $54,000 were issued during the year as consideration for the purchase of land.

Illustration 23-18
Statement of Cash Flows—Yoshi Corporation (Direct Method)

For those who prefer the indirect method of reporting operating cash flows, Illustration 23-19 indicates how the statement's Operating Activities section might look.

Cash provided by (used in) operations:

Net income		$117,700
Add back noncash expenses:		
Amortization expense	$14,600	
Impairment loss—goodwill	2,400	
Amortization of bond discount	300	
Amortization of development costs	40,000	57,300
Equity in income of Porter Corp. in excess of dividends received		(3,500)
Deduct nonoperating gains (net)		
Extraordinary gain on land	(10,500)	
Loss on disposal of equipment	1,500	(9,000)
Deferral of income tax liability to future periods		3,000
Changes in noncash working capital accounts (see Note A)		(52,500)
		$113,000
Note A—changes in noncash working capital:		
Accounts receivable	($53,000)	
Inventory	8,000	
Prepaid expenses	500	
Accounts payable	(1,000)	
Dividends payable, term preferred shares	2,000	
Accrued liabilities	4,000	
Income taxes payable	(13,000)	
	($52,500)	

Interpreting the Statement

There is considerable flexibility in how information is reported in the cash flow statement. The way in which information is summarized and described can enhance the information content and help users interpret and understand the significance of the cash flow data. One approach to analysing the statement is to begin with the three subtotals and determine what they tell you about which activities (operating, investing, and financing) generated cash for the company and which used cash. After this general assessment, delve deeper into the details within each section.

The Yoshi Corporation statement in Illustrations 23-18 and 19 provides valuable information to financial statement readers. Excess operating cash flows of $113,000 allowed Yoshi to internally finance almost half of its investment activities during the year of $245,000. The remainder of cash required for investment was generated principally through financing activities, eating into existing cash balances only marginally ($7,000).

As far as **operations** are concerned, **it doesn't matter which method is used to determine cash flows from operating activities. The bottom line tells you the same thing — that cash receipts from customers and dividends from investments generated $113,000 more cash than needed to pay for operating expenditures.** The direct method provides more detail about the specific sources and uses of cash and is particularly useful in comparison with other years. A review of significant changes to each working capital account on the balance sheet is needed to complete this analysis. Alternatively, the indirect method identifies the $57,300 of noncash expenses deducted in calculating net income, and details are provided about the changes in the working capital accounts.

Yoshi **invested** an additional $264,000 in new investments while netting only $19,000 from the disposal of existing long-term assets. It appears the company is in a growth stage and the major expenditure of $200,000 in development activities provides the potential for increased operating cash flows in the future. The majority of new **financing** was achieved through the issue of common equity. This is reasonable given that the funds were invested in development costs—assets often difficult to finance through debt—but reduces the company's financial leverage. The resulting debt-to-equity ratio appears to be unreasonably low. Dividends have been held to only $6,000, a low payout on the company's $117,700 of net income and $113,000 operating cash flow.

Users must exercise care in interpreting cash flow statements. As mentioned earlier, companies in a growth or development stage will generally use more cash in their operating activities than they receive from customers, a situation that should reverse as the business life cycle matures. Users of financial statements should also look beyond the amount of cash generated or used in operations, and analyse the reasons for the operating cash flows. For example, are the cash flows from operations sustainable and likely to be replicated in the future, or are they the result of one-time events? Were collections on accounts receivable at an all-time high and accounts payable stretched to their limits? Consider **Axcan Pharma Inc.** Axcan reported cash flow from operating activities of more than $56.5 million (U.S.) in its year ended September 30, 2003, up substantially from $35.3 million (U.S.) the previous year. Almost $12.8 million (U.S.) of the increase, however, came from changes in working capital made up of greater than usual collections of accounts receivable and lower than usual payments on its payables. In this case, the operating cash flows in the period under review are probably not indicative of replicable operating cash flows.

Did new investment merely maintain the existing capacity, or were investments made in new assets that will increase future levels of operating cash flows? How were they financed? Details of cash flows related to financing activities allow readers to assess the potential for future claims to the organization's cash and to identify major changes in the form of financing, especially between debt and equity. Is the company continuing to increase equity financing, or is the level of debt increasing relative to equity? Will there be a demand for future cash for interest claims? Companies in a growth stage will usually report significant amounts of cash generated from financing activities—financing that is needed to handle the significant investment activity. As growth levels off and operations begin to generate positive cash flows, financing flows tend to reverse as debt is repaid and, if appropriate, shares are redeemed.

REPORTING AND DISCLOSURE ISSUES

Cash Flow Statement

In addition to requiring that cash flows be reported according to operating, investing, and financing classifications, *CICA Handbook* Section 1540 requires separate disclosure of the following:

8 Objective
Identify the financial reporting and disclosure requirements for the statement of cash flows.

1. cash flows (before tax) associated with extraordinary items, classified as operating, investing, or financing, as appropriate

2. cash outflows for interest and dividends paid and included as a component of net income (as operating flows), as well as those charged to retained earnings (as financing flows)

3. cash flows related to income taxes, classified as operating cash flows unless specifically identifiable with investing or financing activities

4. cash flows and other specified information from business combinations and disposals of business units (both as investing flows)

5. the policy for determining cash and cash equivalents; the components of cash and cash equivalents, with a reconciliation of the amounts reported on the cash flow statement with the amounts reported on the balance sheet; and the amount of cash and cash equivalents whose use is restricted[19]

---

[19] *CICA Handbook*, Section 1540.32-.50.

The recommendations leave the choice between the direct and indirect method up to the preparer, although the AcSB encourages reporting operating cash flows under the direct approach. The recommendations require the reporting of gross cash inflows and outflows from investing and financing activities rather than netted amounts, and separate disclosure in the financial statements about investing and financing transactions that did not generate or use cash resources. Other requirements related to financial institutions, foreign currency cash flows, and business combinations and disposals are left to a course in advanced financial accounting.

Cash Flow per Share Information

IAS Note

There is no IAS standard dealing with cash flow per share.

Because a number of companies had been reporting **cash flow per share** data in their financial statements, the Accounting Standards Board issued *EIC-34* in 1991 to ensure that readers were adequately informed about this statistic. The Emerging Issues Committee concluded that when companies provide cash flow per share information, it should not be reported as part of the income statement, where it might be given more prominence than it deserved and where it might be confused with earnings per share. In 2003, *EIC-34* was withdrawn, replaced by a recommendation within *CICA Handbook* Section 1540 that specifies that cash flow per share (or per unit) **should not be disclosed in financial statements.**[20] The AcSB's concern is that financial statement readers might confuse cash flow per share amounts as distributable to share or unitholders.

Free Cash Flow

A common measure introduced in Chapter 5 and publicized by many companies in recent years is **free cash flow (FCF)**. As the name suggests, this is an indicator of financial flexibility that uses information provided on the cash flow statement. Free cash flow is net operating cash flows reduced by the capital expenditures needed to sustain the current level of operations. The resulting cash flow is the amount of discretionary cash a company has available for increased capacity and new investments, paying dividends, retiring debt, purchasing treasury shares, or simply adding to its liquidity. The calculation varies by company as some deduct all capital expenditures on the basis that it is impossible to separate sustaining expenditures from the total. Others deduct current dividends in calculating FCF.

In general, companies with significant free cash flow have a strong degree of financial flexibility. They are able to take advantage of new opportunities or cope well during poor economic times without jeopardizing current operations.

Financial Reporting Examples

Digital Tool

Student Toolkit—
Additional
Disclosures

www.wiley.com/canada/kieso

Pacific Safety Products Inc.'s Consolidated Statements of Cash Flow for its years ended June 30, 2003 and 2002 are provided in Illustration 23-20. Note that this company uses the direct method in presenting its operating cash flows. Much of the additional information required is presented on the face of the statement itself, although most companies tend to provide it in notes to the financial statements. It is also interesting to note that the company incorporates bank indebtedness as part of its cash and cash equivalents, and had a negative cash balance at June 30, 2002. Review the statement for the differences in cash activity from one year to the next.

In contrast, the Operating Activities section of **Camco Inc.'s** Statement of Cash Flows for its year ended December 31, 2003 is provided in Illustration 23-21, along with Note 7 to its financial statements. Camco uses the indirect method to determine its operating cash flows. Compare the information provided with that of Pacific Safety Products above. It's difficult to believe that the cash flow from operations determined under two such different approaches actually has the same meaning.

---

[20] *CICA Handbook*, Section 1540.53. The only exception is for per share (or per unit) amounts payable to owners such as dividends paid or payable and cash distributions, in the case of income trusts.

Consolidated Statements of Cash Flow

For the years ended June 30th	2003	2002
Operating Activities		
Cash receipts from customers	$ 17,209,091	$ 17,293,165
Cash paid to suppliers and employees	(15,377,769)	(16,414,761)
Interest paid	(345,015)	(345,767)
Income taxes recovered (paid)	(88,376)	206,162
Cash Flow from Operating Activities	1,397,931	738,799
Investing Activities		
Purchase of property, plant and equipment	(257,632)	(107,603)
Proceeds on the sale of property, plant and equipment	—	4,702
Investment in new product development	(93,233)	(131,699)
Investment in intangible assets	(27,624)	(18,329)
Expenses related to abandoned business combination (Note 12)	—	(32,791)
Cash Flow from Investing Activities	(378,489)	(285,720)
Financing Activities		
Proceeds of long-term debt	4,170,175	27,391
Repayment of long-term debt	(2,057,638)	(388,423)
Costs related to financing	(166,782)	—
Return of capital stock to Treasury	—	(15,145)
Issue of capital stock	22,164	43,165
Cash Flow from Financing Activities	1,967,919	(333,012)
Increase in Cash and Cash Equivalents	2,987,361	120,067
Bank Indebtedness, Beginning	(2,729,742)	(2,849,809)
Cash and Cash Equivalents (Bank Indebtedness), ending	$ 257,619	$ (2,729,742)
Represented by:		
Cash and cash equivalents	$ 360,036	$ 223,351
Bank indebtedness	(102,417)	(2,953,093)
Cash and cash equivalents (Bank Indebtedness)	$ 257,619	$ (2,729,742)
Non-Cash Transactions		
Increase in property, plant and equipment due to the transfer from other assets held for resale	$ —	$ 94,080
Decrease in other assets held for sale due to transfer of property, plant and equipment held for resale	—	(94,080)
Debt forgiven by vendor according to purchase and sale agreement	30,797	81,850
Reduction of goodwill	(30,797)	(81,850)
Decrease in other assets due to long-term lease deposits now due within one year	(31,917)	—
Increase in prepaid expenses	31,917	—
	$ —	$ —

The accompanying notes are an integral part of these financial statements.

Illustration 23-20

Cash Flow Statement—Pacific Safety Products Inc.

Consolidated Statements of Cash Flows (in part)

Years ended December 31 (in thousands of dollars)	2003	2002
Operating Activities		
Net income (loss)	$(52,528)	$11,121
Add items not affecting cash		
Depreciation and amortization (Note 3)	47,482	16,498
Post employment benefits	49,191	7,514
Future income taxes	(25,856)	5,231
Writedown of retail advances	3,395	—
	21,684	40,364
Net decrease (increase) in working capital (Note 7)	4,191	(22,946)
Employee severence (Note 3)	6,177	—
Post employment benefits funding	(26,657)	(31,238)
Other non-current operating activities	964	(82)
	6,359	(13,902)

Illustration 23-21

Cash Flow from Operations—Camco Inc.

6 Prepare a statement of cash flows.

Preparing the statement involves determining the change in cash and cash equivalents during the period, slotting in either the net income (indirect method) or line items from the income statement (direct method) as the starting point within the statement's Operating Activities section, and analysing the changes in each balance sheet account to identify all transactions with a cash impact. Transactions with a cash impact are recorded on the cash flow statement. To ensure that all cash flows have been identified, the results recorded on the statement are compared with the change in cash during the period. The formal statement is then prepared, complete with appropriate descriptions and disclosures.

7 Read and interpret a statement of cash flows.

The first step is to look at the subtotals for the three classifications of activities and the overall change in cash. This provides a high level summary of the period's cash flows. Next, analyse the items within each section for additional insights, keeping alert for accounting policies that affect the type of cash flow reported.

8 Identify the financial reporting and disclosure requirements for the statement of cash flows.

Separate disclosure is required of cash flows associated with extraordinary items, interest and dividends received and paid, the components of cash and cash equivalents reconciled to the amounts reported on the balance sheet, and the amount of and explanation for cash and cash equivalents not available for use. All income tax cash flows are reported as operating flows unless they can be linked directly to investing or financing flows. Gross amounts should be reported except in specifically permitted circumstances, and noncash investing and financing transactions are excluded from the cash flow statement with details reported elsewhere on the financial statements.

Appendix 23A

Use of a Work Sheet

When numerous adjustments are necessary, or other complicating factors are present, a work sheet is often used to assemble and classify the data that will appear on the statement of cash flows. The work sheet (a spreadsheet when using computer software) is merely a device that aids in the preparation of the statement; its use is optional. The skeleton format of the work sheet for preparing the statement of cash flows using the indirect method is shown in Illustration 23A-1.

9 Objective
Use a work sheet to prepare a statement of cash flows.

Illustration 23A-1

Format of Work Sheet for Preparing Statement of Cash Flows

STATEMENT OF CASH FLOWS FOR THE YEAR ENDED...

Balance Sheet Accounts	End of Last Year Balances	Reconciling Items Debits	Reconciling Items Credits	End of Current Year Balances
Debit balance accounts	XX	XX	XX	XX
	XX	XX	XX	XX
Totals	XX			XXX
Credit balance accounts	XX	XX	XX	XX
	XX	XX	XX	XX
Totals	XX			XXX
Cash Flows				
Operating activities				
Net income		XX		
Adjustments		XX	XX	
Investing activities				
Receipts (dr.) and payments (cr.)		XX	XX	
Financing activities				
Receipts (dr.) and payments (cr.)		XX	XX	
Totals		XXX	XXX	
Increase (cr.) or decrease (dr.) in cash		XX or XX		
Totals		XXX	XXX	

The following guidelines are important in using a work sheet.

1. In the Balance Sheet Accounts section, accounts with debit balances are listed separately from those with credit balances. This means, for example, that Accumulated Amortization is listed under credit balances and not as a contra account under debit balances. The beginning and ending balances of each account are entered. As the analysis proceeds, each line pertaining to a balance sheet account should balance. That is, the beginning balance plus or minus the reconciling item(s) must equal the ending

deferred costs—a noncash expense—reported in net income. The adjustment adds back (debits) $40,000 to the net income number. Remember to enter the transactions that explain changes in the balance sheet accounts as you proceed.

7. **Land**.   The entries affecting the Land account are:

Land	54,000	
Term Preferred Shares		54,000
Cash	15,000	
Land		4,500
Gain on Disposal of Land (extraordinary item)		10,500

The first entry explains changes in both the Land and Term Preferred Shares accounts—a noncash transaction. The second entry identifies a $15,000 investing inflow of cash, a reduction of $4,500 in the Land account, and a gain reported in net income that does not correspond to the actual cash flow, and which results from an investing transaction. Net income is adjusted.

8. **Equipment**.   Entries affecting the Equipment account are reproduced below.

Equipment	53,000	
Cash		53,000
Cash	4,000	
Loss on Disposal of Equipment	1,500	
Accumulated Amortization—Equipment	2,500	
Equipment		8,000

The first entry identifies a $53,000 investing outflow of cash. The second entry explains the remainder of the change in the asset account and part of the change in the Accumulated Amortization account, reports a $4,000 investing inflow of cash, and a $1,500 noncash loss reported in net income that needs to be adjusted.

9. **Goodwill**.   The decrease in Goodwill is an impairment loss.

Impairment Loss—Goodwill	2,400	
Goodwill		2,400

The impairment loss is a noncash charge to the income statement. It therefore requires an adjustment to the net income included in the Operating Activities section.

10. **Discount on bonds payable**.   The entry to record discount amortization is:

Interest Expense	300	
Discount on Bonds Payable		300

Again, a noncash expense was deducted in determining income and must be adjusted.

11. **Treasury shares**.   The change in this account is explained in two entries.

Treasury Shares	34,000	
Cash		34,000
Cash	15,000	
Retained Earnings	2,000	
Treasury Shares ($34,000 × ½)		17,000

The first entry identifies a $34,000 financing outflow of cash to acquire the company's own shares. The second entry explains the remainder of the change in the Treasury Shares account and part of the change in retained earnings, and identifies a $15,000 inflow of cash from the reissue of the shares—a financing transaction.

12. **Allowance for doubtful accounts.** Part of the change in this account was explained previously in item 2 above. The remaining entry to this account recognized bad debt expense.

Bad Debt Expense	2,250	
Allowance for Doubtful Accounts		2,250

This completes the explanation of changes to the Allowance account. In addition, it identifies a noncash expense of $2,250, which requires an adjustment to net income in the Operating Activities section.

13. **Accumulated amortization—equipment.** One of the changes in the Accumulated Amortization account was explained previously in item 8. The remainder of the entries affecting this account are:

Amortization Expense	11,500	
Accumulated Amortization—Equipment		11,500
Accumulated Amortization—Equipment	11,000	
Cash		11,000

The first entry identifies an $11,500 noncash expense requiring an adjustment to net income and the cash flows from operations. The second entry explains the remainder of the change in the account—an investing outflow of cash.

14. **Accumulated amortization—buildings.** With no change in the Buildings account during the year, the only entry needed to explain the change in the Accumulated Amortization account is:

Amortization Expense	3,100	
Accumulated Amortization—Buildings		3,100

This $3,100 noncash expense requires an adjustment to the net income number in the Operating Activities section.

15. **Accounts payable.** The summary entry to explain the net change in this account is:

Accounts Payable	1,000	
Cash		1,000

The reduction in the payables balance resulted from paying out $1,000 more cash than purchases recorded. Cost of goods sold and other expenses have already been adjusted to represent the goods and services purchased, so a $1,000 credit adjustment is needed to convert the purchases to the amount paid, i.e., to the operating cash outflow.

16. **Dividends payable on term preferred shares.** The summary entry explaining the net change in this account follows.

E23-4   (Accounting Cycle, Financial Statements, Cash Account, and Statement of Cash Flows)   Listed below are the transactions of Isao Aoki, an interior design consultant, for the month of September 2005.

Sept. 1 Isao Aoki begins business as an interior design consultant, investing $30,000 for 5,000 common shares of the company, I.A. Design Limited.
  2 Purchases furniture and display equipment from Green Jacket Co. for $17,280.
  4 Pays rent for office space for the next three months at $680 per month.
  7 Employs a part-time secretary, Michael Bradley, at $300 per week.
  8 Purchases office supplies on account from Mann Corp. for $1,142.
  9 Receives cash of $1,690 from clients for services performed.
  10 Pays miscellaneous office expenses, $430.
  14 Invoices clients for consulting services, $5,120.
  18 Pays Mann Corp. on account, $600.
  19 Pays a dividend of $1.00 per share on the 5,000 outstanding shares.
  20 Receives $980 from clients on account.
  21 Pays Michael Bradley two weeks' salary, $600.
  28 Invoices clients for consulting services, $2,110.
  29 Pays the September telephone bill of $135 and miscellaneous office expenses of $85.

At September 30, the following information is available.

1. The furniture and display equipment have a useful life of five years and an estimated residual value of $1,500. Straight-line amortization is appropriate.

2. One week's salary is owing to Michael Bradley.

3. Office supplies of $825 remain on hand.

4. Two months' rent has been paid in advance.

5. The invoice for electricity for September of $195 has been received, but not paid.

Instructions

(a) Prepare journal entries to record the transaction entries for September. Set up a T account for the Cash account and post all cash transactions to the account. Find the balance of cash at September 30, 2005.

(b) Prepare any required adjusting entries at September 30, 2005.

(c) Prepare an adjusted trial balance at September 30, 2005.

(d) Prepare a balance sheet and income statement for the month ended September 30, 2005.

(e) Prepare a cash flow statement for the month of September 2005. Use the indirect method for the cash flows from operating activities.

(f) Recast the cash flow from operating activities section using the direct method.

(g) Compare the cash flow statement in (e) and (f) with the Cash account prepared in item (a) above.

E23-5   (Preparation of Operating Activities Section—Direct Method)   The income statement of Vincus Company is shown below.

Interactive
Homework

VINCUS COMPANY
Income Statement
for the Year Ended December 31, 2005

Sales		$6,900,000
Cost of goods sold		
Beginning inventory	$1,900,000	
Purchases	4,400,000	
Goods available for sale	6,300,000	
Ending inventory	1,600,000	
Cost of goods sold		4,700,000
Gross profit		2,200,000
Operating expenses		
Selling expenses	450,000	
Administrative expenses	700,000	1,150,000
Net income		$1,050,000

Additional information:

1. Accounts receivable increased $360,000 during the year.

2. Prepaid expenses increased $170,000 during the year.

3. Accounts payable to suppliers of merchandise decreased $275,000 during the year.

4. Accrued salaries payable increased $10,000 during the year.

5. Administrative expenses include amortization expense of $60,000.

6. Selling expenses include commissions and salaries of $280,000; administrative expenses include salaries of $525,000.

Instructions
Prepare the operating activities section of the statement of cash flows for the year ended December 31, 2005 for Vincus Company using the direct method.

E23-6 (Preparation of Operating Activities Section—Indirect Method) Data for the Vincus Company are presented in E23-5.

Instructions
Prepare the operating activities section of the statement of cash flows using the indirect method.

E23-7 (Preparation of Operating Activities Section—Direct Method) Krauss Corp.'s income statement for the year ended December 31, 2005 contained the following condensed information.

Revenue from fees		$840,000
Operating expenses (excluding amortization)	$624,000	
Amortization expense	60,000	
Loss on sale of equipment	26,000	710,000
Income before income taxes		130,000
Income tax expense		40,000
Net income		$ 90,000

Krauss' balance sheet contained the following comparative data at December 31.

	2005	2004
Accounts receivable	$37,000	$54,000
Accounts payable	41,000	31,000
Income taxes payable	4,000	8,500

Instructions
Prepare the operating activities section of the statement of cash flows using the direct method.

E23-8 (Preparation of Operating Activities Section—Indirect Method) Data for Krauss Corp. are presented in E23-7.

Instructions
Prepare the operating activities section of the statement of cash flows using the indirect method.

E23-9 (Convert Net Income to Operating Cash Flow—Indirect Method) Leung Limited reported net income of $36,500 for its latest year ended March 31, 2006.

Instructions
For each situation below, calculate the cash flow from operations assuming the following balance sheet amounts.

	Accounts Receivable March 31		Inventory March 31		Accounts Payable March 31	
	2006	2005	2006	2005	2006	2005
(a)	$20,000	$21,500	$16,500	$17,900	$ 9,000	$ 9,300
(b)	$23,000	$20,000	$17,300	$20,500	$14,600	$10,200
(c)	$20,000	–0–	$12,000	–0–	$ 7,000	–0–
(d)	$19,500	$21,000	$19,500	$15,600	$10,200	$14,100
(e)	$21,500	$24,000	$12,900	$14,000	$13,300	$11,300

Instructions

Calculate net cash provided (used) by:

(a) operating activities

(b) investing activities

(c) financing activities

E23-16   (Transactions, Statement of Cash Flows—Indirect Method and Balance Sheet)   Jobim Inc. had the following condensed balance sheet at the end of operations for 2005.

JOBIM INC.
Balance Sheet
December 31, 2005

Cash	$ 8,500	Current liabilities	$15,000
Current assets other than cash	29,000	Long-term notes payable	25,500
Investments	20,000	Bonds payable	25,000
Plant assets (net)	67,500	Share capital	75,000
Land	40,000	Retained earnings	24,500
	$165,000		$165,000

During 2006 the following occurred.

1. A tract of land was purchased for $9,000.

2. Bonds payable in the amount of $15,000 were retired at par.

3. An additional $10,000 of common shares were issued.

4. Dividends totalling $9,375 were paid to shareholders.

5. Net income for 2006 was $35,250 after allowing amortization of $13,500.

6. Land was purchased in exchange for $22,500 of bonds.

7. Jobim Inc. sold part of its investment portfolio for $12,875. This transaction resulted in a gain of $2,000 for the firm. The company classifies the investments as available-for-sale.

8. Both current assets (other than cash) and current liabilities remained at the same amount.

Instructions

(a) Prepare a statement of cash flows for 2006 using the indirect method.

(b) Prepare the condensed balance sheet for Jobim Inc. as it would appear at December 31, 2006.

E23-17   (Prepare Statement from Transactions, and Explain Changes in Cash Flow)   Ellwood House, Inc. had the following condensed balance sheet at the end of operations for 2004.

ELLWOOD HOUSE, INC.
Balance Sheet
December 31, 2004

Cash	$ 10,000	Current liabilities	$ 14,500
Current assets (noncash)	34,000	Long-term notes payable	30,000
Investments (available-for-sale)	40,000	Bonds payable	32,000
Plant assets	57,500	Share capital	80,000
Land	38,500	Retained earnings	23,500
	$180,000		$180,000

During 2005, the following occurred.

1. Ellwood House, Inc. sold part of its investment portfolio for $15,500, resulting in a gain of $500 for the firm. The company often sells and buys securities of this nature.

2. Dividends totalling $19,000 were paid to shareholders.

3. A parcel of land was purchased for $5,500.

4. Common shares with a fair value of $20,000 were issued.

5. $10,000 of bonds payable were retired at par.

6. Heavy equipment was purchased through the issuance of $32,000 of bonds.

7. Net income for 2005 was $42,000 after allowing amortization of $13,550.

8. Both current assets (other than cash) and current liabilities remained at the same amount.

Instructions

(a) Prepare a statement of cash flows for 2005 using the indirect method.

(b) Draft a one-page letter to Mr. Gerald Brauer, president of Ellwood House, Inc., briefly explaining the changes within each major cash flow category. Refer to your cash flow statement whenever necessary.

(c) Prepare a balance sheet at December 31, 2005 for Ellwood House, Inc.

(d) Comment briefly about why the cash flow statement used to be called a statement of changes in financial position.

E23-18 **(Partial Statement of Cash Flows—Indirect Method)** The accounts below appear in the ledger of Lazic Limited.

Retained Earnings		Dr.	Cr.	Bal.
Jan. 1, 2005	Credit balance			$ 42,000
Aug. 15	Dividends (cash)	$15,000		27,000
Dec. 31	Net income for 2005		$40,000	67,000

Machinery		Dr.	Cr.	Bal.
Jan. 1, 2005	Debit balance			$140,000
Aug. 3	Purchase of machinery	$62,000		202,000
Sept. 10	Cost of machinery constructed	48,000		250,000
Nov. 15	Machinery sold		$56,000	194,000

Accumulated Amortization—Machinery		Dr.	Cr.	Bal.
Jan. 1, 2005	Credit balance			$ 84,000
Apr. 8	Extraordinary repairs	$21,000		63,000
Nov. 15	Accum. amortization on machinery sold	25,200		37,800
Dec. 31	Amortization for 2005		$16,800	54,600

Instructions

From the postings in the accounts above, indicate how the information is reported on a statement of cash flows by preparing a partial statement of cash flows using the indirect method. The loss on sale of equipment (November 15) was $5,800.

E23-19 **(Analysis of Changes in Capital Asset Accounts and Related Cash Flows)** MacAskill Mills Limited engaged in the following activities in 2005.

1. The Land account increased by $50,000 over the year: Land that originally cost $12,000 was exchanged for another parcel of land valued at $30,000 and a lump sum cash receipt of $10,000. Additional land was acquired later in the year in a cash purchase.

2. The Furniture and Fixtures account had a balance of $67,500 at the beginning of the year and $62,000 at the end. The related Accumulated Amortization account decreased over the same period from a balance of $24,000 to $15,200. Fully amortized office furniture that cost $10,000 was sold to employees during the year for $1,000; fixtures that cost $3,000 with a net book value of $700 were written off; and new fixtures were acquired and paid for.

3. A five-year capital lease for specialized machinery was entered into halfway through the year whereby the company agreed to make five annual payments (in advance) of $25,000, after which the machinery will revert to the lessor. The present value of these lease payments at the 10% rate implicit in the lease was $104,247. The first payment was made as agreed.

Instructions

For each situation described above:

(a) Prepare the underlying journal entries made by MacAskill Mills during 2005 to record all information related to the changes in each capital asset and associated accounts over the year.

(b) Identify the amount(s) of the cash flows that result from the transactions and events recorded, and determine the classification of each.

P23-3   Seneca Corporation has contracted with you to prepare a statement of cash flows. The controller has provided the following information.

	December 31	
	2005	2004
Cash	$ 38,500	$13,000
Accounts receivable	12,250	10,000
Inventory	12,000	9,000
Investments	–0–	3,000
Building	–0–	29,750
Equipment	40,000	20,000
Patent	5,000	6,250
	$107,750	$91,000
Allowance for doubtful accounts	$ 3,000	$ 4,500
Accumulated amortization—equipment	2,000	4,500
Accumulated amortization—building	–0–	6,000
Accounts payable	5,000	3,000
Dividends payable	–0–	6,000
Notes payable, short-term (nontrade)	3,000	4,000
Long-term notes payable	31,000	25,000
Share capital	43,000	33,000
Retained earnings	20,750	5,000
	$107,750	$91,000

Additional data related to 2005 are as follows.

1. Equipment that cost $11,000 and was 40% amortized at time of disposal was sold for $2,500.

2. $10,000 of the long-term note payable was paid by issuing common shares.

3. Cash dividends paid were $6,000.

4. On January 1, 2005, the building was destroyed by a flood. Insurance proceeds on the building were $33,000 (net of $4,000 taxes).

5. Long-term investments (available-for-sale) were sold at $2,500 above their cost.

6. Cash of $15,000 was paid to acquire equipment.

7. A long-term note for $16,000 was issued in exchange for equipment.

8. Interest of $2,000 and income taxes of $5,000 were paid in cash.

Instructions

(a) Use the indirect method to analyse the above information and prepare a statement of cash flows for Seneca. Flood damage is unusual and infrequent in that part of the country. Ensure all required disclosures are provided.

(b) Prepare a short analysis of Seneca's cash flow activity for 2005 for submission to the controller.

(c) What would you expect to observe in the operating, investing, and financing sections of a statement of cash flows of:

1.   a severely financially troubled company?

2.   a recently formed company that is experiencing rapid growth?

P23-4   Cabanza Corporation has not yet prepared a formal statement of cash flows for the 2005 fiscal year. Comparative balance sheets as of December 31, 2004 and 2005, and a statement of income and retained earnings for the year ended December 31, 2005, are presented below.

CABANZA CORPORATION
Statement of Income and Retained Earnings
Year Ended December 31, 2005
($000)

Sales		$3,800
Expenses		
Cost of goods sold	$1,200	
Salaries and benefits	725	
Heat, light, and power	75	
Amortization—buildings and equipment	80	
Property taxes	19	
Patent amortization	25	
Miscellaneous expenses	10	
Interest	30	2,164
Income before income taxes		1,636
Income taxes		818
Net income		818
Retained earnings—January 1, 2005		310
		1,128
Stock dividend declared and issued		600
Retained earnings—December 31, 2005		$ 528

CABANZA CORPORATION
Comparative Balance Sheet
December 31
($000)

Assets	2005	2004
Current assets		
Cash	$ 383	$ 100
Canada T-Bills (60-day)	–0–	50
Accounts receivable	740	500
Inventory	720	560
Total current assets	1,843	1,210
Long-term assets		
Land	150	70
Buildings and equipment	910	600
Accumulated amortization	(200)	(120)
Patents (less amortization)	105	130
Total long-term assets	965	680
Total assets	$2,808	$1,890
Liabilities and Shareholders' Equity		
Current liabilities		
Accounts payable	$ 420	$ 340
Income taxes payable	40	20
Notes payable (trade)	320	320
Total current liabilities	780	680
Long-term notes payable—due 2007	200	200
Total liabilities	980	880
Shareholders' equity		
Common shares outstanding	1,300	700
Retained earnings	528	310
Total shareholders' equity	1,828	1,010
Total liabilities and shareholders' equity	$2,808	$1,890

Instructions

(a) Prepare a statement of cash flows using the direct method.

(b) Prepare a short analysis summarizing the year's cash flow activity.

(CMA adapted)

P23-5   Ashley Limited had the following information available at the end of 2005.

ASHLEY LIMITED
Comparative Balance Sheet
December 31, 2005 and 2004

	2005	2004
Cash	$ 15,000	$ —0—
Accounts receivable	17,500	16,950
Short-term working capital investments	20,000	30,000
Inventory	42,000	35,000
Prepaid rent	3,000	12,000
Prepaid insurance	2,100	900
Office supplies	1,000	750
Land	125,000	175,000
Building	350,000	350,000
Accumulated amortization	(105,000)	(87,500)
Equipment	525,000	400,000
Accumulated amortization	(130,000)	(112,000)
Patent	45,000	50,000
Total assets	$910,600	$871,100
Temporary bank overdraft	$ —0—	$ 12,000
Accounts payable	22,000	20,000
Income taxes payable	5,000	4,000
Wages payable	5,000	3,000
Short-term notes payable (trade)	10,000	10,000
Long-term notes payable (non-trade)	60,000	70,000
Future income tax liability	30,000	25,000
Bonds payable	375,000	375,000
Common shares	260,000	237,500
Retained earnings	143,600	114,600
Total liabilities and equity	$910,600	$871,100

ASHLEY LIMITED
Income Statement
Year Ended December 31, 2005

Sales revenue		$1,160,000
Cost of goods sold		(748,000)
Gross margin		412,000
Operating expenses		
Selling expenses	$ 19,200	
Administrative expenses	124,700	
Salaries and wages expense	92,000	
Amortization expense	40,500	
Total operating expenses		(276,400)
Income from operations		135,600
Other revenues/expenses		
Gain on sale of land	8,000	
Gain on sale of working capital investments	4,000	
Dividend revenue	2,400	
Interest expense	(51,750)	(37,350)
Income before taxes		98,250
Income tax expense		(39,400)
Net income		$ 58,850

Instructions

(a) Prepare a statement of cash flows for Ashley Limited using the direct method, accompanied by all required disclosures and a schedule reconciling net income to cash flow from operations. Assume the short-term investments are available-for-sale securities.

(b) Prepare a memo for top management that summarizes and comments on the cash activities of Ashley in 2005.

P23-6 You have completed the field work in connection with your audit of Casar Corporation for the year ended December 31, 2005. The following schedule shows the balance sheet accounts at the beginning and end of the year.

	Dec. 31, 2005	Dec. 31, 2004	Increase or (Decrease)
Cash	$ 267,900	$ 298,000	$ (30,100)
Accounts receivable	479,424	353,000	126,424
Inventory	731,700	610,000	121,700
Prepaid expenses	12,000	8,000	4,000
Investment in Amarill Ltd.	110,500	–0–	110,500
Cash surrender value of life insurance	2,304	1,800	504
Machinery	207,000	190,000	17,000
Buildings	535,200	407,900	127,300
Land	52,500	52,500	–0–
Patents	69,000	64,000	5,000
Goodwill	50,000	50,000	–0–
Bond discount and issue expense	4,502	–0–	4,502
	$2,522,030	$2,035,200	
Income taxes payable	$ 90,250	$ 79,600	$ 10,650
Accounts payable	299,280	280,000	19,280
Dividends payable	70,000	–0–	70,000
Bonds payable—8%	125,000	–0–	125,000
Bonds payable—12 %	–0–	100,000	(100,000)
Allowance for doubtful accounts	35,300	40,000	(4,700)
Accumulated amortization—buildings	424,000	400,000	24,000
Accumulated amortization—machinery	173,000	130,000	43,000
Common shares—no par value	1,285,200	1,455,600	(170,400)
Appropriation for plant expansion	10,000	–0–	10,000
Retained earnings—unappropriated	10,000	(450,000)	460,000
	$2,522,030	$2,035,200	

STATEMENT OF RETAINED EARNINGS

January 1, 2005	Balance (deficit)	$(450,000)
March 31, 2005	Net income for first quarter of 2005	25,000
April 1, 2005	Transfer from contributed capital	425,000
	Balance	–0–
December 31, 2005	Net income for last three quarters of 2005	90,000
December 31, 2005	Dividend declared payable January 21, 2006	(70,000)
December 31, 2005	Appropriation for plant expansion	(10,000)
	Balance	$ 10,000

Your working papers contain the following information.

1. On April 1, 2005, the existing deficit was written off against contributed capital (common shares).

2. On November 1, 2005, new common shares were sold for cash.

3. A patent was purchased for $15,000.

4. The following entry was made to record the payment of the president's life insurance premium.

Cash Surrender Value, Life Insurance	504	
Life Insurance Expense	1,336	
Cash		1,840

5. During the year, machinery that cost $16,400 and on which there was accumulated amortization of $5,200 was sold for $7,000. No other plant assets were sold during the year.

6. The 12%, 20-year bonds were dated and issued on January 2, 1993. Interest was payable on June 30 and December 31. They were sold originally at par. These bonds were retired at 102 plus accrued interest on March 31, 2005.

7. The 8%, 40-year bonds were dated January 1, 2005, and were sold on March 31 at 97 plus accrued interest. Interest is payable semi-annually on June 30 and December 31. Expense of issuance was $839.

8. Casar Corporation acquired a 40% interest in Amarill Ltd. on January 2, 2005 for $100,000. The income statement of Amarill Ltd. for 2005 shows a net income of $26,250, and no dividends were paid in the current year. Casar accounts for this investment using the equity method.

9. Extraordinary repairs to buildings of $7,200 were charged to Accumulated Amortization—Buildings.

10. Interest paid in 2005 was $10,500 and income taxes paid were $34,000.

Instructions

(a) From the information above, prepare a statement of cash flows using the indirect method. A work sheet is not necessary, but the principal calculations should be supported by schedules or skeleton ledger accounts. Include all required disclosures.

(b) Prepare a summary report explaining the $30,100 reduction in cash during the year, suitable for reporting to Casar's president.

P23-7   Presented below are the 2005 financial statements of Cymbala Corporation.

CYMBALA CORPORATION
Comparative Balance Sheet

	December 31,	
	2005	2004
Assets	$ in millions	
Current assets:		
Cash	$ 20.4	$ 7.5
Receivables (net of allowance for doubtful accounts of $5 million in 2005 and $4.6 million in 2004)	241.6	213.2
Inventories		
Finished goods	83.7	84.7
Raw materials and supplies	115.7	123.8
Prepaid expenses	6.2	6.7
Total current assets	467.6	435.9
Property, plant, and equipment:		
Plant and equipment	2,361.8	2,217.7
Less: Accumulated amortization	(993.4)	(890.1)
	1,368.4	1,327.6
Timberland, net	166.3	169.5
Property, plant, and equipment net	1,534.7	1,497.1
Other assets	74.7	34.7
Total assets	$2,077.0	$1,967.7
Liabilities and Shareholders' Equity		
Current liabilities:		
Bank overdrafts (temporary)	$ 25.5	$ 20.2
Accounts payable	102.2	91.3
Accrued liabilities		
Payrolls and employee benefits	73.5	73.9
Interest and other expenses	44.3	29.4
Federal and provincial income taxes	17.4	12.7
Current maturities of long-term debt	13.2	10.5
Total current liabilities	276.1	238.0
Long-term liabilities:		
Future income taxes	333.6	280.0
4.75% to 11.25% revenue bonds with maturities to 2025	174.6	193.4
Other revenue bonds at variable rates with maturities to 2032	46.3	26.6
7⅞% sinking fund debentures due 2011	19.5	21.0
8.70% sinking fund debentures due 2021	75.0	75.0
9½% convertible subordinated debentures due 2026	–0–	38.9
9¾% notes due 2008	50.0	50.0
Promissory notes	–0–	60.2
Mortgage debt and miscellaneous obligations	25.7	21.7
Other long-term liabilities	21.8	–0–
Total long-term liabilities	746.5	766.8

Shareholders' equity:
  Common shares (no par value, 60 million shares authorized,
    26,661,770 and 25,265,921 shares outstanding as of
    December 31, 2005 and 2004) .... 244.4 ... 196.9
  Retained earnings .... 810.0 ... 766.0
  Total shareholders' equity .... 1,054.4 ... 962.9
    Total liabilities and shareholders' equity . $2,077.0 ... $1,967.7

Statement of Income and Retained Earnings

$ in millions, except per share amounts	2005
Statement of Income	
Net sales	$2,044.2
Cost of sales	(1,637.8)
Gross margin	406.4
Selling, general, and administrative expense	(182.6)
Provision for reduced operations	(41.0)
Operating income	182.8
Interest on long-term debt	(33.5)
Other income—net	2.2
Income before tax	151.5
Income taxes	(61.2)
Net income	$ 90.3
Earnings per share	$ 3.39
Retained Earnings Statement	
Retained earnings at beginning of year	$ 766.0
Add: Net income	90.3
	856.3
Deduct: Dividends on common shares	
($1.76 a share in 2005)	(46.3)
Retained earnings at year end	$ 810.0

Additional information:

1. Amortization and cost of timberland harvested was $114.6 million.

2. The provision for reduced operations included a decrease in cash of $15.9 million.

3. Purchases of plant and equipment were $182.5 million, and purchases of other assets were $40 million.

4. Sales of plant and equipment resulted in cash inflows of $5.2 million. All sales were at book value.

5. The changes in long-term liabilities are summarized below.

Increase in future income taxes	$ 53.6
New borrowings	63.2
Debt retired by cash payments	(86.5)
Debt converted into shares	(37.4)
Reclassification of current maturities	(13.2)
Decrease in long-term liabilities	$(20.3)

6. The increase in common shares results from the issuance of shares for debt conversion, $37.4 million, and shares issued for cash, $10.1 million.

7. Interest paid during 2005 was $21.2 million and income tax paid was $2.9 million.

Instructions

(a) Prepare a statement of cash flows for the Cymbala Corporation using the indirect method, including all required disclosures.

(b) Prepare a brief memo that summarizes the company's cash activities during the year.

P23-8   Comparative balance sheet accounts of Secada Inc. are presented below:

SECADA INC.
Comparative Balance Sheet Accounts
December 31, 2005 and 2004

Debit Accounts	December 31 2005	December 31 2004
Cash	$ 45,000	$ 33,750
Accounts Receivable	67,500	60,000
Merchandise Inventory	30,000	24,000
Long-term Investments (available-for-sale)	22,250	38,500
Machinery	30,000	18,750
Buildings	67,500	56,250
Land	7,500	7,500
	$269,750	$238,750
Credit Accounts		
Allowance for Doubtful Accounts	$ 2,250	$ 1,500
Accumulated Amortization—Machinery	5,625	2,250
Accumulated Amortization—Buildings	13,500	9,000
Accounts Payable	30,000	24,750
Accrued Payables	2,375	1,125
Income Taxes Payable	1,000	1,500
Long-term Note Payable, non-trade	26,000	31,000
Common Shares, no par value	150,000	125,000
Retained Earnings	39,000	42,625
	$269,750	$238,750

Additional data:

1. Net income for the year was $42,500.

2. Cash dividends declared during the year were $21,125.

3. A 20% stock dividend was declared during the year. $25,000 of retained earnings was capitalized.

4. Investments that cost $20,000 were sold during the year for $23,750.

5. Machinery that cost $3,750, on which $750 of amortization had accumulated, was sold for $2,200.

Secada's 2005 income statement follows.

Sales		$640,000
Less cost of goods sold		380,000
Gross margin		260,000
Less: Operating expenses (includes $8,625 amortization, and $5,400 bad debts)		180,450
Income from operations		79,550
Other: Gain on sale of investments	$3,750	
Loss on sale of machinery	(800)	2,950
Income before taxes		82,500
Income tax expense		40,000
Net income		$ 42,500

Instructions

(a) Calculate net cash flow from operating activities using the direct method.

(b) Prepare a statement of cash flows using the indirect method.

(c) Assume your investment club is considering investing in Secada Inc. Write a memo to the other members of the club about the company's cash activities during 2005.

P23-9 Ivan Inc., a major retailer of bicycles and accessories, operates several stores and is a publicly traded company. The comparative Statement of Financial Position and Income Statement for Ivan as of May 31, 2006 are provided. The company is preparing its Statement of Cash Flows.

IVAN INC.
Statement of Financial Position
May 31, 2006 and May 31, 2005

	2006	2005
Current assets		
Cash	$ 33,250	$ 20,000
Accounts receivable	80,000	58,000
Merchandise inventory	210,000	250,000
Prepaid expenses	9,000	7,000
Total current assets	332,250	335,000
Plant assets		
Plant assets	600,000	502,000
Less: Accumulated amortization	150,000	125,000
Net plant assets	450,000	377,000
Total assets	$782,250	$712,000
Current liabilities		
Accounts payable	$123,000	$115,000
Salaries payable	47,250	72,000
Interest payable	27,000	25,000
Total current liabilities	197,250	212,000
Long-term debt		
Bonds payable	70,000	100,000
Total liabilities	267,250	312,000
Shareholders' equity		
Common shares	370,000	280,000
Retained earnings	145,000	120,000
Total shareholders' equity	515,000	400,000
Total liabilities and shareholders' equity	$782,250	$712,000

IVAN INC.
Income Statement
for the Year Ended May 31, 2006

Sales	$1,255,250
Cost of merchandise sold	722,000
Gross margin	533,250
Expenses	
Salary expense	252,100
Interest expense	75,000
Other expenses	8,150
Amortization expense	25,000
Total expenses	360,250
Operating income	173,000
Income tax expense	43,000
Net income	$ 130,000

The following is additional information concerning Ivan's transactions during the year ended May 31, 2006.

1. Plant assets costing $98,000 were purchased by paying $48,000 in cash and issuing 5,000 common shares.

2. The "other expenses" relate to prepaid items.

3. In order to supplement its cash, Ivan issued an additional 4,000 common shares.

4. There were no penalties assessed for the retirement of bonds.

5. Cash dividends of $105,000 were declared and paid at the end of the fiscal year.

Instructions

(a) Compare and contrast the direct method and the indirect method for reporting cash flows from operating activities.

(b) Prepare a statement of cash flows for Ivan Inc. for the year ended May 31, 2006 using the direct method. Support the statement with appropriate calculations, and provide all required disclosures.

(c) Using the indirect method, calculate only the net cash flow from operating activities for Ivan Inc. for the year ended May 31, 2006.

P23-10   Comparative balance sheet accounts of Jensen Limited are presented below.

JENSEN LIMITED
Balance Sheet Accounts
December 31, 2005 and 2004

Debit Balances	2005	2004
Cash	$ 80,000	$ 51,000
Accounts Receivable	138,500	119,000
Merchandise Inventory	75,000	61,000
Long-term Investments (available-for-sale)	55,000	85,000
Future Income Tax Asset	6,500	11,000
Equipment	70,000	48,000
Building	145,000	145,000
Land	40,000	25,000
	$610,000	$545,000

Credit Balances	2005	2004
Allowance for Doubtful Accounts	$ 10,000	$ 8,000
Accumulated Amortization—Equipment	21,000	14,000
Accumulated Amortization—Building	37,000	28,000
Accounts Payable	72,500	60,000
Income Taxes Payable	12,000	10,000
Long-term Notes Payable	62,000	70,000
Accrued Pension Liability	7,500	10,000
Common Shares	300,000	250,000
Retained Earnings	88,000	95,000
	$610,000	$545,000

Jensen's 2005 income statement is as follows.

Sales		$950,000
Less: Cost of goods sold		600,000
Gross profit		350,000
Less: Operating expenses (includes amortization and bad debt expense)		250,000
Income from operations		100,000
Other revenues and expenses		
Gain on sale of investments	$ 15,000	
Loss on sale of equipment	(3,000)	12,000
Income before taxes		112,000
Income taxes		45,000
Net income		$ 67,000

Additional data:

1. Equipment that cost $10,000 and was 40% amortized was sold in 2005.

2. Cash dividends were declared and paid during the year.

3. Common shares were issued in exchange for land.

4. Investments that cost $35,000 were sold during the year.

5. Cost of goods sold includes $115,000 of direct labour and benefits and $11,700 of pension costs, and operating expenses includes $76,000 of wages and $8,000 of pension expense.

Instructions

(a) Prepare a statement of cash flows using the indirect method, including all required disclosures.

(b) Prepare the "cash provided by (or used in) operating activities" section under the direct method.

(c) Comment on the company's cash activities during the year.

Writing Assignments

WA23-1 George Sundem and Bea Goldfarb are examining the following statement of cash flows for Tropical Clothing Store Ltd.'s first year of operations.

TROPICAL CLOTHING STORE LTD.
Statement of Cash Flows
for the Year Ended January 31, 2006

Sources of cash	
From sales of merchandise	$ 362,000
From sale of common shares	400,000
From sale of investment	120,000
From amortization	80,000
From issuance of note for truck	30,000
From interest on investments	8,000
Total sources of cash	1,000,000
Uses of cash	
For purchase of fixtures and equipment	340,000
For merchandise purchased for resale	253,000
For operating expenses (including amortization)	170,000
For purchase of investment	85,000
For purchase of truck by issuance of note	30,000
For purchase of treasury shares	10,000
For interest on note	3,000
Total uses of cash	891,000
Net increase in cash	$ 109,000

George claims that Tropical's statement of cash flows is an excellent portrayal of a superb first year, with cash increasing $109,000. Bea replies that it was not a superb first year, that the year was an operating failure, that the statement was incorrectly presented, and that $109,000 is not the actual increase in cash.

Instructions

(a) In general, what are the objectives of a statement of the type shown above for Tropical Clothing Store Ltd.?

(b) With whom do you agree: George or Bea? Explain your position.

(c) Using the data provided, prepare a statement of cash flows in proper indirect method form. The only noncash items in income are amortization and the gain on sale of the investments.

WA23-2 HTM Limited is a young and growing producer of electronic measurement instruments and technical equipment. You have been retained by HTM to advise it in preparing a statement of cash flows using the indirect method. For the fiscal year ended October 31, 2005, you have obtained the following information concerning certain HTM events and transactions.

1. Earnings reported for the fiscal year were $800,000, which included a deduction for an extraordinary loss of $110,000 (see item 5 below).

2. Amortization expense of $315,000 was included in the earnings reported.

3. Uncollectible accounts receivable of $40,000 were written off against the allowance for doubtful accounts. Also, $51,000 of bad debt expense was included in determining income for the year and was added to the allowance for doubtful accounts.

4. A gain of $9,000 was realized on the sale of a machine; it originally cost $75,000, of which $30,000 was amortized to the date of sale.

5. On April 1, 2005, lightning caused an uninsured building loss of $110,000 ($180,000 loss, less reduction in income taxes of $70,000). This extraordinary loss was included in determining income as indicated in 1. above.

6. On July 3, 2005, building and land were purchased for $700,000; HTM gave in payment $75,000 cash, $200,000 market value of its unissued common shares, and signed a $425,000 mortgage note payable.

7. On August 3, 2005, $800,000 face value of HTM's 10% convertible debentures were converted into common shares. The bonds were originally issued at face value.

8. Bonds payable with a par value of $100,000, on which there was an unamortized bond discount of $2,000, were redeemed at 99.5.

Instructions

(a) Explain whether each of the eight numbered items above is a source of cash, a use of cash, or neither a source nor a use.

(b) Explain how each item that is a source or use should be reported in HTM's statement of cash flows for the fiscal year ended October 31, 2005 using the indirect approach for the operating activities section.

(c) For items that are neither a source nor use, explain why this is so and indicate the disclosure, if any, that should be made of the item in the company's statement of cash flows for the year ended October 31, 2005.

WA23-3 The past few years have seen numerous changes in Canadian accounting standards, such as for investments, asset retirement obligations, and stock options.

Instructions

For each accounting situation listed below, identify whether there is a related cash flow(s) and explain how the cash flow statement is affected for companies with this type of transaction.

(a) Temporary investments of held-for-trading securities are held by a company. They do not meet the definition of cash equivalents, but are used to earn a return on excess cash until needed for operations. Small amounts of gains and losses on disposal, as well as interest and dividend income, are reported in income.

(b) A company holds long-term investments that are classified as available-for-sale. One security was disposed of at a gain during the year and the others have a fair value higher than at the previous year end. Dividends have been received and reported in income.

(c) An investment in another company's bonds is being held to maturity. The investment was acquired at a premium as the bond pays a higher than market rate of interest.

(d) A company began development activities related to a new mine site. As a result it incurred an obligation related to the mine's eventual retirement, reporting it as an asset retirement liability and as a portion of the mine's cost on its balance sheet. The following year the obligation was increased due to continuing mine activity as well as the accretion of the amount recognized in the preceding year due to the passage of time.

(e) Stock options with a two-year vesting period were issued to the top executive team at the beginning of the current fiscal period. The options' fair value exceeds the option price.

WA23-4 Durocher Guitar Corp. is in the business of manufacturing top-quality, steel-string folk guitars. In recent years the company has experienced working capital problems resulting from the procurement of factory equipment, the unanticipated buildup of receivables and inventories, and the payoff of a balloon mortgage on a new manufacturing facility. The founder and president of the company, Laraine Durocher, has attempted to raise cash from various financial institutions, but to no avail because of the company's poor performance in recent years. In particular, the company's lead bank, First Provincial, is especially concerned about Durocher's inability to maintain a positive cash position. The commercial loan officer from First Provincial told Laraine, "I can't even consider your request for capital financing unless I see that your company is able to generate positive cash flows from operations."

Thinking about the banker's comment, Laraine came up with what she believes is a good plan: with a more attractive statement of cash flows, the bank might be willing to provide long-term financing. To "window dress" cash flows, the company can sell its accounts receivables to factors, liquidate its raw material inventories, and arrange a sale and leaseback for major components of its equipment. These rather costly transactions would generate lots of cash. As the chief accountant for Durocher Guitar, it is your job to tell Laraine what you think of her plan.

Instructions

(a) Explain how each of these "solutions" would affect Durocher Guitar Corp.'s cash flow statement. Be specific.

(b) Are there any ethical issues related to Laraine Durocher's idea?

(c) How would you advise Laraine Durocher?

WA23-5   In 1974, the CICA's Accounting Research Committee issued a replacement to *CICA Handbook* Section 1540 on the Statement of Source and Application of Funds. The new section expanded the funds statement to include significant noncash exchanges affecting the entity's asset and capital structure. The statement could show changes in cash, working capital, or quick assets.

In 1985, Section 1540 was revised again. With a name change to the Statement of Changes in Financial Position, this revision required that changes in cash and cash equivalents be reported. In addition, the statement required that the information be categorized into operating, investing, and financing activities.

Most recently, in 1998, new requirements were put in place for Section 1540, harmonized with IAS 7 on Cash Flow Statements. These changes completed the move from a statement of changes in financial position to one clearly focused on cash flows.

Instructions

(a) Identify at least three reasons for developing the statement of cash flows.

(b) Explain the purposes of the cash flow statement.

(c) Identify and describe the three categories of activities that must be reported in the statement of cash flows. What is the relationship of these activities to a company's balance sheet?

(d) Identify two methods of reporting cash flows from operations. Are both permitted under GAAP? Explain. Which do you prefer? Why?

(e) Describe the financial reporting requirements for noncash investing and financing transactions, including two examples of such transactions.

(f) Assume you overhear the following comment made by an investor in the stock market: "You can't always trust the net income number reported because of all the estimates and judgement that go into its determination. That's why I only look at the cash flow from operations in analysing a company." Comment.

Cases

Refer to the Case Primer on the Digital Tool to help you with these cases.

Digital Tool

www.wiley.com/
canada/kieso

CA23-1   Papadopoulos Limited (PL) sells retail merchandise in Canada. The company was incorporated last year and is now in its second year of operations. PL is owned and operated by the Papadopoulos family, and Iris Papadopoulos, the president of the company, has decided to expand the company into the American marketplace. In order to do this, bank financing will be necessary.

The books have always been kept by Tonya, Iris' daughter. Tonya is presently studying accounting in university. Financial statements had only been prepared for tax purposes in the past. For the year-ended December 31, 2005, Tonya prepared the following statement showing cash inflows and cash outflows:

Sources of cash:	
From shareholder loan	$150,000
From sales of merchandise	350,000
From truck financing	50,000
From term deposit cashed in	100,000
From interest income	10,000
Total sources of cash	660,000
Uses of cash:	
For fixed asset purchases	$100,000
For inventory purchases	250,000
Operating expenses including depreciation of $70,000	160,000
For purchase of investment	55,000
For purchase of truck	50,000
For interest on debt	30,000
Total uses of cash	645,000
Net increase in cash	$15,000

Tonya showed the statement to her mother, noting that the bank was sure to give them a loan, especially since they were profitable in their second year and since cash had increased over the year, indicating that it had been a good year. Iris is not convinced and decides to have the statement looked at by a "real" accountant.

Instructions

Adopt the role of the accountant and redraft the statement, if necessary, in good form for the bank. Discuss the financial position of the company.

Integrated Cases

IC 23-1 Canadian Tire Corporation operates retail outlets, sells gasoline and provides financial services. There are 452 Canadian Tire retail outlets as well as 322 **Mark's Work Wearhouse** outlets. The Canadian Tire stores are owned by Associate Dealers who are essentially franchises. They own and operate the stores but benefit from centralized marketing and purchasing.

Below is an excerpt from the 2003 annual report of the company.

5.1 Expensing of stock options

Effective December 29, 2002, the Company elected early adoption, on a prospective basis, of the new recommendations issued by the Canadian Institute of Chartered Accountants (CICA) relating to stock-based compensation. In accordance with the new standard, stock options granted after adoption of the standard are measured on grant date using a fair-value based method and expensed over the vesting period. The earnings impact of options issued in 2003 at Canadian Tire using the fair-value based method was $0.01 per share, or 0.33 percent of the reported earnings of $3.06 per share. The offsetting accounting entry is recorded as contributed surplus. Any consideration paid by employees on exercise of stock options or purchase of shares is credited to share capital.

The Company has provided pro forma disclosure in Note 9 to the Consolidated Financial Statements, which indicates the impact on earnings, had the options granted in 2002 also been expensed.

Taking into account the movement by many issuers away from stock options as an appropriate form of compensation to align management and investor interests, Canadian Tire in recent years has been using other forms of long-term incentives, such as restricted share units and performance share units.

These alternate forms of compensation are full value share plans that more directly align management performance and shareholder value. These share plans are described in Note 9 to the Consolidated Financial Statements. All of the Company's compensation plans are expensed.

5.2 Variable interest entities (VIEs)

In June 2003, the CICA issued Accounting Guideline 15, "Consolidation of Variable Interest Entities" (AcG-15). Taking into account a recent announcement by the CICA, which deferred the effective dates of this guideline, AcG-15 requires consolidation of certain "variable interest entities" (VIEs) beginning in the first quarter of 2005 (for companies with calendar fiscal years). A VIE is any type of legal structure not controlled by voting equity, but rather by contractual or other financial arrangements. The Company has identified potential VIEs and is currently reviewing AcG-15 to determine to what extent, if at all, consolidation or note disclosure will be required. The rules are complex and views on interpretation are still evolving. Further clarification is expected and amendments to AcG-15 are forthcoming.

Based on the Company's current understanding of AcG-15, it has determined that the independent financing trusts described below that provide cost effective funds to the Company and its Associate Dealers are VIEs that would likely have to be consolidated with the Company unless structural changes are undertaken. In addition, certain corporations owned and operated by independent Associate Dealers, Mark's Work Wearhouse and PartSource franchisees and Petroleum agents may also be VIEs, a small number of which may have to be consolidated.

One such trust, GCCT, was formed in 1995 to purchase credit charge receivables from the Company. GCCT issues debt to third party investors to fund its receivables purchases. Financing outstanding through GCCT at January 3, 2004 was $1,865 million (December 28, 2002 – $1,364 million) as detailed earlier in this MD&A. In accordance with current CICA requirements (pre-AcG-15), sales of credit charge receivables to GCCT are recorded as sales in the Company's financial statements and the financial statements of GCCT are not consolidated with those of the Company. Disclosure of these transactions can be found in Note 2 to the Company's Consolidated Financial Statements.

In 1995, a major Canadian bank established another such trust (Trust) to facilitate financing for franchise operations. The Trust raises funds in public markets to finance loans it makes to franchisees. In 1997, the Trust began making loans to Associate Dealers to facilitate their purchase of inventory and fixed assets. Such loans at January 3, 2004 were $893 million (December 28, 2002 – $952 million). Several major Canadian banks have provided standby letters of credit in favour of the Trust to enable the Trust to maintain a high credit rating on the debt it issues to fund Associate Dealer loans. The Company has agreed to reimburse the banks for any amount drawn on those standby letters of credit to a maximum of $271 million as at January 3, 2004 (December 28, 2002 – $271 million) and to indemnify the Trust, and certain other parties dealing with the Trust, with respect to certain events. Those standby letters of credit have never been drawn. In accordance with current CICA requirements (pre-AcG-15), the financial statements of the Trust are not consolidated with those of the Company Disclosure of these arrangements can be found in Note 13 to the Company's Consolidated Financial Statement The Company is currently assessing whether to pursue structural changes to these VIEs. In any event, management believes that consolidation would not result in any material change in the underlying tax, legal or credit risks facing the Company.

Instructions

Adopt the role of a financial analyst and analyse the impact of the accounting policy changes and potential changes. Hint: use first principles to reason through the issues. You may want to work on this in a group.

Research and Financial Analysis

RA23-1 Intrawest Corporation

Instructions

Refer to the financial statements and accompanying notes and discussion of **Intrawest Corporation** presented at the end of this volume, or access the company's financial statements for its year ended June 30, 2003 from SEDAR (www.sedar.com), and answer the following questions.

(a) How does Intrawest define cash and cash equivalents? Do the cash and cash equivalents reported on the Statement of Cash Flows tie in to the balance sheet amounts reported?

(b) Provide a comparative statement of source and uses of cash at the level of operating, investing, and financing subtotals only. Comment on the similarities and differences between 2002 and 2003.

(c) In mid-2003, *The Globe & Mail* reported that Intrawest's 2004 goals were for free cash flow of between $250 million and $270 million. Based on the 2002 and 2003 financial statements, comment on the likelihood of this goal being attained.

(d) Note that Intrawest uses the indirect method of reporting its cash flows from operating activities. Assuming you were preparing a statement for this company using the direct method, suggest what line items you would report within the operating cash flow section. Which approach do you think provides more useful information to a potential investor? Explain briefly.

(e) Based on the information provided in Note 21, determine the balances of Amounts Receivable, Other Assets, Amounts Payable, and Deferred Revenue at June 30, 2001.

(f) Within the operating cash flow section, explain why future income taxes appear to use cash and the writedown of technology assets appears to be a source of cash.

(g) Based only on the information in the financing activities section of the statement of cash flows, can you tell whether the debt-to-equity ratio increased or decreased during the year ended June 30, 2003? 2002?

(h) Identify the extent of noncash investing and financing activities over the two-year period ending June 30, 2003.

(i) Comment briefly on the company's solvency and financial flexibility.

RA23-2   Abitibi-Consolidated Inc.

In early June 2003, Abitibi-Consolidated Inc. slashed its quarterly dividend by 75% from 10 cents per share to 2.5 cents, thus hoping to conserve its cash resources. The company was working in difficult market conditions, including having to contend with lower Canadian dollar inflows from forestry product sales priced in U.S. dollars as the Canadian dollar strengthened.

Instructions

Access the financial statements of Abitibi-Consolidated Inc. for its year ended December 31, 2003, either through the Digital Tool or SEDAR at www.sedar.com. Analyse the Statement of Cash Flows and notes to the financial statements and respond to the following questions.

(a) Review the Statement of Cash Flows for the three-year period ending December 31, 2003. What indication is there that the company might be experiencing cash flow problems?

(b) Although earnings from continuing operations were significantly higher in 2003 than in the previous two years, the cash flow from operations was considerably lower. Explain.

RA23-3   AnorMED Inc. versus Biomira Inc. Comparative Analysis

AnorMED Inc. and Biomira Inc. are both incorporated under the Canada Business Corporations Act and both are engaged in the biotechnology and pharmaceutical industry. AnorMED (British Columbia based) is primarily engaged in discovering and developing new therapeutic products for a variety of diseases, while Biomira (an Alberta company) researches and develops therapeutic products for the treatment of cancer.

Instructions

From the SEDAR website (www.sedar.com) or the company websites, obtain the comparative financial statements of AnorMED for its year ended March 31, 2003 and of Biomira for its year ended December 31, 2003. Review the financial statements and respond to the following questions.

(a) Compare the companies' statements of operations and comment on their results over the past two fiscal periods. What is the major reason for the results reported?

(b) How would you expect companies in this industry and stage of development to be financed? Why? Is this consistent with what is reported on their balance sheets? Comment.

(c) For the two most recent years reported by each company, write a brief explanation of their cash activities at the level of total operating, investing, and financing flows. Note any similarities and differences.

(d) How do the investments that AnorMED and Biomira make differ from the investments made by companies in other industries? Describe the difference in general and then how it affects each of the financial statements.

(e) Are the companies liquid? Explain. On what does the solvency and financial flexibility of companies in this industry depend?

RA23-4   Research Issue: EBITDA and Cash Flow

One accounting metric often used by companies and financial analysts over the past few years is EBITDA: earnings before interest, taxes, depreciation, and amortization. EBITDA is meant to be a "quick and dirty" surrogate for cash flow, but users should be cautioned about this interpretation.

Instructions

Research information about how EBITDA is used from at least two sources. Write a short report to your classmate, a finance major, about the limitations of this metric as a measure of cash flows.

RA23-5   Pacific Safety Products Inc.

According to the British Columbia company's releases, Pacific Safety Products Inc. "is an established industry leader in the production, distribution and sale of high-performance safety products such as: ballistic, stab and fragment protection vests; bomb and land mine retrieval suits; tactical clothing; emergency medical kits and rescue equipment." The company's statement of cash flows using the direct method for operating activities was referred to in the chapter and is provided in Illustration 23-20.

Instructions

Access Pacific Safety Products' financial statements for its year ended June 30, 2003 either on the Digital Tool or on SEDAR at www.sedar.com. From the information provided and to the fullest extent possible, construct the cash flows from operating activities section of a cash flow statement using the indirect method for the year ended June 30, 2003. To the extent you don't get the same result as reported under the direct method, suggest what might explain the difference.

Auditing for Accuracy

After several high-profile financial scandals in the United States and the subsequent increase in legislative and regulatory initiatives, full disclosure in financial reporting has become paramount for public companies.

"Companies are much more sensitive to disclosure issues than they were five years ago," says Doug Cameron, director of professional practice in Toronto with Ernst & Young LLP, which serves as an external auditor for clients such as large public entities, like banks and insurance companies, and small private operations. "They have a greater interest in what the external auditor is doing."

While companies are paying greater heed to the increased scrutiny placed on their financials, Cameron says that reporting irregularities are actually an anomaly. "Fraudulent financial reporting is receiving a lot of attention these days, but in my experience, it's not very common," he says. "Clients put a great deal of effort into doing the right thing. The consequences for not doing so are pretty serious."

The auditor's role is to determine whether the financial statements have been prepared according to GAAP, which requires more than knowledge of financial statement preparation. The auditor must also understand the client's business and apply accounting rules to its specifics, Cameron says.

When auditors find errors, they talk to the client to ensure accuracy of the information and to clarify the client's interpretation of the rules. Any misunderstandings are cleared up, with clients occasionally having to adjust their financial statements. Public companies are required by regulation to obtain an auditor's unqualified opinion on the accuracy of their statements, so they are usually willing to make any necessary adjustments, Cameron says.

Any irregularities that could be deemed fraudulent are reported to the company's senior management and the audit committee, Cameron says, adding that these situations are extremely rare. ■

CHAPTER 24

Other Measurement and Disclosure Issues

Learning Objectives

After studying this chapter, you should be able to:

1. Review the full disclosure principle and describe problems of implementation.
2. Explain the use of accounting policy notes in financial statement preparation.
3. Describe the disclosure requirements for major segments of a business.
4. Describe the accounting problems associated with interim reporting.
5. Discuss the accounting issues concerning related party transactions.
6. Identify the difference between the two types of subsequent events.
7. Identify issues related to financial forecasts and projections.
8. Identify the major disclosures found in the auditor's report.

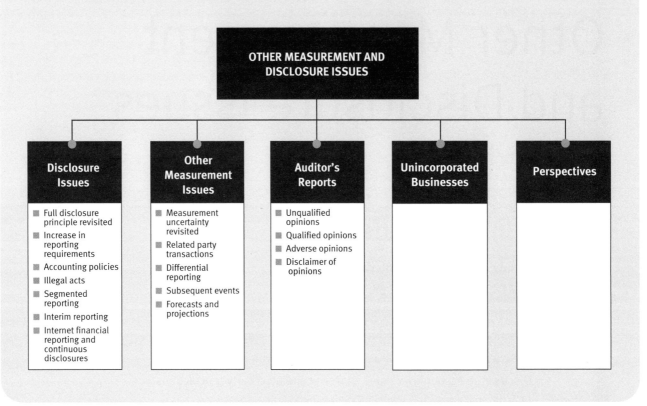

Preview of Chapter 24

It is very important to read not only a company's financial statements and related information, but also the president's letter and management discussion and analysis (MD&A). In this chapter we cover several disclosures that must accompany the financial statements so that they are not misleading. The content and organization of the chapter are as follows:

OTHER MEASUREMENT AND DISCLOSURE ISSUES

Disclosure Issues
- Full disclosure principle revisited
- Increase in reporting requirements
- Accounting policies
- Illegal acts
- Segmented reporting
- Interim reporting
- Internet financial reporting and continuous disclosures

Other Measurement Issues
- Measurement uncertainty revisited
- Related party transactions
- Differential reporting
- Subsequent events
- Forecasts and projections

Auditor's Reports
- Unqualified opinions
- Qualified opinions
- Adverse opinions
- Disclaimer of opinions

Unincorporated Businesses

Perspectives

DISCLOSURE ISSUES

Full Disclosure Principle Revisited

Some useful information is better provided in the financial statements and some is better provided by means of financial reporting other than financial statements. For example, earnings and cash flows are readily available in financial statements, but investors might do better to look at comparisons with other companies in the same industry, found in news articles or brokerage house reports.

Financial statements, notes to the financial statements, and supplementary information are areas directly affected by GAAP. Other types of information found in the annual report, such as management's discussion and analysis, are not subject to GAAP. Illustration 24-1 indicates these types of financial information.

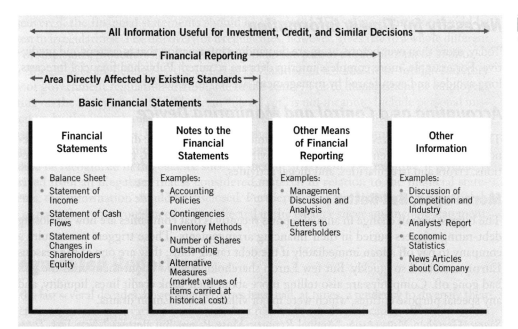

Illustration 24-1

Types of Financial Information

As indicated in Chapter 2, the profession has adopted a full disclosure principle that calls for financial reporting of any financial facts significant enough to influence the judgement of an informed reader. In some situations, the benefits of disclosure may be apparent but the costs uncertain, whereas in other instances the costs may be certain but the benefits of disclosure not as apparent. How much information is enough information? It is a difficult question to answer. While not enough information clearly is problematic, sometimes too much—often referred to as information overload—is equally as problematic.

Different users want different information, and it becomes exceedingly difficult to develop disclosure policies that meet their varied objectives.

Underlying Concept

Here is a good example of the trade-off between the cost/benefit constraint and the full disclosure principle.

Increase in Reporting Requirements

Disclosure requirements have increased substantially over the past several decades. One survey showed that in a sample of 25 large, well-known companies, the average number of pages of notes to the financial statements increased from 9 to 17 and the average number of pages for management's discussion and analysis went from 7 to 12 over a 10-year period. This result is not surprising because, as illustrated throughout this textbook, the accounting profession has issued many standards in the last two decades that have substantial disclosure provisions.[1] The reasons for this increase in disclosure requirements are varied. Some of them are as follows.

1 Objective

Review the full disclosure principle and describe problems of implementation.

Complexity of the Business Environment

The difficulty of distilling economic events into summarized reports has been magnified by the increasing complexity of business operations in such areas as derivatives, leasing, business combinations, pensions, financing arrangements, revenue recognition, and deferred taxes. As a result, notes to the financial statements are used extensively to explain these transactions and their future effects.

---

[1] The survey results were taken from Ray J. Groves, "Financial Disclosure: When More Is Not Better," *Financial Executive*, May/June 1994.

IAS Note

IAS 14 gives guidance on determining segments. The determination is based on the risks and returns approach, i.e., where the segment has different business risks and rewards.

In applying these tests, two additional factors must be considered. First, segment data must explain a significant portion of the company's business. Specifically, the segmented results must equal or exceed 75% of the combined sales to unaffiliated customers for the entire enterprise. This test prevents a company from providing limited information on only a few segments and lumping all the rest into one category.

Second, the profession recognizes that reporting too many segments may overwhelm users with detailed information and has therefore proposed 10 as an upper limit benchmark for the number of segments that a company should be required to disclose.

To illustrate these requirements, assume a company has identified six possible reporting segments (000 omitted).

Illustration 24-3

Data for Different Possible Reporting Segments

Segments	Total Revenue (Unaffiliated)	Operating Profit (Loss)	Assets
A	$100	$10	$60
B	50	2	30
C	700	40	390
D	300	20	160
E	900	18	280
F	100	(5)	50
	$2,150	$85	$970

The respective tests may be applied as follows.

Revenue test: 10% × $2,150 = $215; C, D, and E meet this test.

Operating profit (loss) test: 10% × $90 = $9 (note that the $5 loss is ignored); A, C, D, and E meet this test.

Assets tests: 10% × $970 = $97; C, D, and E meet this test.

The reportable segments are therefore A, C, D, and E, assuming that these four segments have enough sales to meet the 75% of combined sales test. The 75% test is calculated as follows.

75% of combined sales test: 75% × $2,150 = $1,612.50; the sales of A, C, D, and E total $2,000 ($100 + $700 + $300 + $900); therefore, the 75% test is met.

Measurement Principles

The accounting principles to be used for segment disclosure need not be the same as the principles used to prepare the consolidated statements. This flexibility may at first appear inconsistent. But, preparing segment information in accordance with generally accepted accounting principles would be difficult because some principles are not expected to apply at a segment level. Examples are accounting for the cost of company-wide employee benefit plans and accounting for income taxes in a company that files one overall tax return.

Allocations of joint, common, or company-wide costs solely for external reporting purposes are not required. Common costs are those incurred for the benefit of more than one segment and whose interrelated nature prevents a completely objective division of costs among segments. For example, the company president's salary is difficult to allocate to various segments. Allocations of common costs are inherently arbitrary and may not be meaningful if they are not used for internal management purposes. There is a presumption that allocations to segments are either directly attributable or reasonably allocable. Disclosure should be made regarding choices made in measuring segmented information.

Segmented Disclosures

The CICA requires that an enterprise report provide the following.[5]

1. **General information** about its reportable segments. This includes factors that management considers most significant in determining the company's reportable segments, and the types of products and services from which each operating segment derives its revenues.

2. **Segment profit and loss, assets, and related information.** This states total profit or loss and total assets for each reportable segment. In addition, the following specific information about each reportable segment must be reported if the amounts are regularly reviewed by management:

    (a) revenues from external customers

    (b) revenues from transactions with other operating segments of the same enterprise

    (c) interest revenue

    (d) interest expense

    (e) amortization of capital assets and goodwill

    (f) unusual items

    (g) equity in the net income of investees subject to significant influence

    (h) income tax expense or benefit

    (i) extraordinary items

    (j) significant noncash items other than amortization expense

    (k) other

3. **Reconciliations.** An enterprise must provide a reconciliation of the total of the segments' revenues to total revenues, a reconciliation of the total of the operating segments' profits and losses to its income before income taxes, discontinued operations and extraordinary items, and a reconciliation of the total of the operating segments' assets to total assets. Other reconciliations for other significant items disclosed should also be presented and all reconciling items should be separately identified and described for all of the above.

4. **Major customers.** If 10% or more of the revenues is derived from a single customer, the enterprise must disclose the total amount of revenues from each such customer by segment.

5. **Geographic areas.** Revenues from external customers (Canada versus foreign) and capital assets and goodwill (Canada versus foreign) should be stated. Disclose foreign information by country if material.

Interim Reporting

One further source of information for the investor is interim reports. As noted earlier, interim reports cover periods of less than one year. While at one time, annual reporting was considered sufficient in terms of providing timely information, demand quickly grew for quarterly information and now capital markets are moving rapidly to even more frequent disclosures. Illustration 24-4 presents the disclosure of selected quarterly data for Torstar.

---

[5] *CICA Handbook*, Section 1701.29 - .42.

Illustration 24-4

Disclosure of Selected Quarterly Data

Torstar Corporation
Consolidated Statements of Income

(unaudited)

Three months ended March 31

(thousands of dollars)	2004	2003
Operating revenue		
Newspapers	$215,261	$203,282
Book publishing	137,085	149,891
	$352,346	$353,173
Operating profit		
Newspapers	$18,610	$15,471
Book publishing	26,121	29,897
Corporate	(4,332)	(3,401)
	40,399	41,967
Interest	(2,782)	(2,998)
Foreign exchange	210	(1,222)
Unusual items (note 6)		2,066
Income before taxes	37,827	39,813
Income and other taxes	(14,600)	(14,300)
Income before loss of associated business	23,227	25,513
Loss of associated business	(189)	(398)
Net income	**$23,038**	**$25,115**
Earnings per Class A and Class B share (note 3(b)):		
Net income – Basic	**$0.29**	$0.33
Net income – Diluted	**$0.29**	$0.32

(See accompanying notes)

Objective 4

Describe the accounting problems associated with interim reporting.

Because of the short-term nature of the information in these reports, however, there is considerable controversy as to the general approach that should be employed. One group (which holds the discrete view) believes that each interim period should be treated as a separate accounting period; deferrals and accruals would therefore follow the principles employed for annual reports. Accounting transactions should be reported as they occur, and expense recognition should not change with the period of time covered. Another group (which holds the integral view) believes that the interim report is an integral part of the annual report and that deferrals and accruals should take into consideration what will happen for the entire year. In this approach, estimated expenses are assigned to parts of a year on the basis of sales volume or some other activity base. **The current *CICA Handbook* section on interim reporting, Section 1751, reinforces the discrete view with a few exceptions.**

One notable exception is in calculating tax expense. Normally a company would prepare its tax return at year end and assess taxes payable and related tax balances. It is neither cost effective nor feasible (since tax rates are often graduated and therefore increase with increasing taxable income) to do this for each interim period, so annual estimates are made. Specifically, an estimate is made of interim taxable income and temporary differences and then the annual estimated tax rate is applied. **Another exception relates to the employer's portion of payroll taxes.** Although these may be remitted by the employer early in the year (as required by law), they are assessed by the government on an annual basis. Therefore, for interim reporting periods, the total estimated annual amount is allocated to the interim periods such that the expense is recognized on an accrual basis as opposed to a cash basis. **Exceptions related to inventory are noted below.**

Interim Reporting Requirements

As a general rule, the profession indicates that the same accounting principles used for annual reports should be employed for interim reports. Revenues should be recognized in interim periods on the same basis as they are for annual periods. For example, if the instalment sales method is used as the basis for recognizing revenue on an annual basis, then the instalment basis should be applied to interim reports as well. Also, costs directly associated with revenues (product costs), such as materials, labour and related fringe benefits, and manufacturing overhead should be treated in the same manner for interim reports as for annual reports.

Companies generally should use the same inventory pricing methods (FIFO, LIFO, etc.) for interim reports that they use for annual reports. However, the following exceptions are appropriate at interim reporting periods.

International Insight

IASB GAAP requires that interim financial statements use the discrete method, except for tax charges.

1. When LIFO inventories are liquidated at an interim date and are expected to be replaced by year end, cost of goods sold should include the expected cost of replacing the liquidated LIFO base and not give effect to the interim liquidation.

2. Planned variances under a standard cost system that are expected to be absorbed by year end ordinarily should be deferred.[6]

Costs and expenses other than product costs, often referred to as period costs, are often charged to the interim period as incurred. But they may be allocated among interim periods based on an estimate of time expired, benefit received, or activity associated with the periods.

Underlying Concept

For information to be relevant, it must be available to decision-makers before it loses its capacity to influence their decisions (timeliness). Interim reporting is an excellent example of this concept.

At a minimum, the balance sheet, income statement, statement of retained earnings, statement of cash flows, and notes are required.[7] The balance sheet should be presented as at the end of the current interim period with a comparative balance sheet as of the end of the immediately preceding fiscal year. The income statement should be presented for the current interim period, interim year to date with like comparatives. For the statement of retained earnings, the information should be presented cumulatively for the current fiscal year to date with comparatives. Finally, for the cash flow statements, information should be presented for the current interim period, and cumulatively for the current fiscal year to date with like comparatives.[8] Earnings per share (EPS) information is also required where an enterprise must present this information in its annual information.[9]

---

[6] *CICA Handbook*, Section 1751.26.

[7] *CICA Handbook*, Section 1751.10.

[8] *CICA Handbook*, Section 1751.10 - .16.

[9] *CICA Handbook*, Section 1751.12.

Regarding disclosure, the following interim data should be reported as a minimum.[10]

1. When the statements do not comply with GAAP for the annual statements, so disclose. Disclose also that the statements should be read in conjunction with the annual statements.

2. A statement that the company follows the same accounting policies and methods as the most recent annual financial statements except for any new policy or method, any policies adopted to address the preparation of interim statements, or any special accounting methods adopted to address temporary costing fluctuations.

3. A description of any seasonality or cyclicality of interim period operations.

4. The nature and amount of changes in estimates.

5. Information about reportable segments.

6. Events subsequent to the interim period.

7. Specific information about business combinations; plans to exit an activity, restructure, integrate, or reorganize; discontinued operations; and extraordinary items.

8. Information about contingencies.

9. Any other information required for fair presentation.

Unique Problems of Interim Reporting

Changes in accounting.   What happens if a company decides to change an accounting principle in the third quarter of a fiscal year? Should the cumulative effect adjustment be charged or credited to that quarter? Presentation of a cumulative effect in the third quarter may be misleading because of the inherent subjectivity associated with the first two quarters' reported income. In addition, a question arises as to whether such a change might not be used to manipulate a given quarter's income. These changes should be reflected by retroactive application to prior interim periods unless the data are not available. The comparable interim periods of prior fiscal years should also be restated.[11]

Earnings per share.   Interim reporting of earnings per share has all the problems inherent in calculating and presenting annual earnings per share, and then some. If shares are issued in the third period, EPS for the first two periods will not be indicative of year-end EPS. If an extraordinary item is present in one period and new equity shares are sold in another period, the EPS figure for the extraordinary item will change for the year. On an annual basis, only one EPS figure is associated with an extraordinary item and that figure does not change; the interim figure is subject to change. For purposes of calculating earnings per share and making the required disclosure determinations, each interim period should stand alone. That is, all applicable tests should be made for that single period.[12]

Seasonality.   Seasonality occurs when sales are compressed into one short period of the year while certain costs are fairly evenly spread throughout the year. For example, the natural gas industry has its heavy sales in the winter, as contrasted with the beverage industry, which has its heavy sales in the summer.

---

[10] *CICA Handbook*, Section 1751.10 - .14.

[11] *CICA Handbook*, Section 1751.31.

[12] *CICA Handbook*, Section 1751, B35 and B36.

The problem of seasonality is related to the matching concept in accounting. Expenses should be matched against the revenues they create. In a seasonal business, wide fluctuations in profits occur because off-season sales do not absorb the company's fixed costs (for example, manufacturing, selling, and administrative costs that tend to remain fairly constant regardless of sales or production). Revenues and expenses should be recognized and accrued when they are earned or incurred according to GAAP. This also holds for interim periods. Thus, a company would only defer recognition of costs or revenues if it would be appropriate to do so at year end (i.e., the same tests are applied).

Continuing controversy.   The profession has developed the stringent standards noted above for interim reporting and this has alleviated much of the controversy that existed regarding the discrete and integral perspectives.

Controversy remains concerning the independent auditor's involvement in interim reports. Many auditors are reluctant to express an opinion on interim financial information, arguing that the data are too tentative and subjective. Conversely, an increasing number of individuals advocate some type of examination of interim reports. A compromise may be a limited review of interim reports that provides some assurance that an examination has been conducted by an outside party and that the published information appears to be in accord with generally accepted accounting principles.

Analysts want financial information as soon as possible, before it's old news. We may not be far from a continuous database system in which corporate financial records can be accessed by computer. Investors might be able to access a company's financial records via computer whenever they wish and put the information in the format they need. Thus, they could learn about sales slippage, cost increases, or earnings changes as they happen, rather than waiting until after the quarter has ended.[13]

A steady stream of information from the company to the investor could be very positive because it might alleviate management's continual concern with short-run interim numbers. It would also alleviate much of the allocation problems that plague current GAAP.

Internet Financial Reporting and Continuous Disclosures

How can companies improve the usefulness of their financial reporting practices? Many companies are using the Internet's power and reach to provide more useful information to financial statement readers. Recent surveys indicate that more than 80% of large companies have Internet sites, and a large proportion of these companies' websites contain links to their financial statements and other disclosures. The increased popularity of such reporting is not surprising, since the costs of printing and disseminating paper reports are reduced.

How does Internet financial reporting improve the overall usefulness of a company's financial reports? First, dissemination of reports via the Internet can allow firms to communicate with more users than is possible with traditional paper reports. In addition, Internet reporting allows users to take advantage of tools such as search engines and hyperlinks to quickly find information about the firm and, sometimes, to download the information for analysis, perhaps in computer spreadsheets. Finally, Internet reporting can help make financial reports more relevant by allowing companies to report expanded disaggregated data and more timely data than is possible through paper-based reporting.

IAS Note

IAS 34 deals with interim financial reporting.

---

[13] A step in this direction is the OSC's mandate for companies to file their financial statements electronically through SEDAR (similar to the SEC requirement to use EDGAR in the United States). SEDAR provides interested parties with computer access to financial information such as periodic filings, corporate prospectuses, and proxy materials.

For example, some companies voluntarily report weekly sales data and segment operating data on their websites.

Given these benefits and ever-improving Internet tools, will it be long before electronic reporting replaces paper-based financial disclosure? The main obstacles to achieving complete electronic reporting are related to **equality of access to electronic financial reporting and the reliability of the information distributed** via the Internet. Although companies may practise Internet financial reporting, they must still prepare traditional paper reports because some investors may not have Internet access. These investors would receive differential (less) information relative to wired investors if companies were to eliminate paper reports. In addition, at present, Internet financial reporting is a voluntary means of reporting. As a result, there are no standards as to the completeness of reports on the Internet, nor is there the requirement that these reports be audited. One concern in this regard is that computer hackers could invade a company's website and corrupt the financial information contained therein.

A great example of the use of technology and continuous reporting is the current practice of releasing the quarterly results via the company website using video and live streaming. Investors and analysts can visit the company website and hear the earnings announcements first hand.

Internet financial reporting is gaining in popularity; however, until issues related to differential access to the Internet and the reliability of web-based information are addressed, we will continue to see traditional paper-based reporting.

OTHER MEASUREMENT ISSUES

Measurement Uncertainty Revisited

As we have seen throughout the text, **increasing efforts are being made to standardize measurement of complex transactions through the use of measurement tools**. It is no longer acceptable to argue that complex transactions are not measurable and therefore should not be recognized in the financial statements. At the same time, **fair value accounting is becoming more and more acceptable** for more and more assets and liability accounts (versus the traditional historical cost focus).

Some examples of **measurement tools** are as follows.

Greater use of traditional approaches:

1. **Discounted cash flows and present value techniques**: measurement of impairment of assets and asset retirement obligations, estimation of pension obligations, valuation of leases

2. **Proportionate method and residual methods**: allocation of cost of bundled sales and measurement of components of compound instruments (debt and equity)

Non-traditional or newer approaches:

1. **Options pricing models such as the Black-Scholes or binomial tree models**: valuation of derivatives such as embedded options (used in conjunction with the proportionate and residual methods noted above)

2. **Probability weighted discounted cash flows**: cash flow test for recoverability of long-lived assets

Note that in the United States, FASB Concept Statement 7 deals with using cash flow information and present value in accounting measurements. It was issued in 2000. The CICA plans to issue a similar discussion paper on measurement objectives and concepts.

Historically, complex financial instruments such as derivatives were not recognized in the financial statements at all. This was partially due to the fact that they were not measurable and it was felt that they did not represent existing assets nor liabilities. **As executory contracts, they were felt to represent promises to do something in the future versus business transactions that had been effected.** Currently, however, as noted in Chapter 17, it will soon be mandatory to recognize derivatives. The acceptability of fair value accounting supports this decision as it allows better measurement and more relevant information to be presented.

Related Party Transactions

Related party transactions pose especially sensitive and difficult problems. The accountant or auditor who has responsibility for reporting on these types of transactions has to be extremely careful that the rights of the reporting company and the needs of financial statement users are properly balanced.

5 Objective
Discuss the accounting issues concerning related party transactions.

Related party transactions arise when a business engages in transactions in which one of the transacting parties has the ability to influence significantly the policies of the other, or in which a non-transacting party has the ability to influence the policies of the two transacting parties. Related parties include but are not limited to the following:

(a) companies or individuals who control, or are controlled by, or are under common control with the reporting enterprise

(b) investors and investees where there is significant influence or joint control

(c) company management

(d) members of immediate family of the above and

(e) the other party where a management contract exists.[14]

Transactions involving related parties cannot be presumed to be carried out at arm's length because the requisite conditions of competitive, free-market dealings may not exist. Transactions such as borrowing or lending money at abnormally low or high interest rates, real estate sales at amounts that differ significantly from appraised value, exchanges of nonmonetary assets, and transactions involving enterprises that have no economic substance ("shell corporations") suggest that related parties may be involved. **Because of the above, there is a measurement issue.** A basic assumption about financial information is that it is transactions based and that the transactions are between arm's-length parties. **Therefore, if this is not the case, these transactions should be at least disclosed. Furthermore, special measurement principles exist for related party transactions that may require the transaction to be remeasured.**

The accountant is expected to report the **economic substance rather than the legal form** of these transactions and to make adequate disclosures. The following disclosures are recommended:[15]

1. the nature of the relationship(s) involved

2. a description of the transactions

3. the recorded amounts of transactions

4. the measurement basis used

5. amounts due from or to related parties and the terms and conditions related thereto

6. contractual obligations with related parties and

7. contingencies involving related parties.

---

[14] *CICA Handbook*, Section 3840.04.

[15] *CICA Handbook*, Section 3840.43.

Certain related party transactions must be remeasured to the carrying amount of the underlying assets or services exchanged. **Carrying amount** is defined as the amount of the item transferred as recorded in the books of the transferor. **This is the case if the transaction is not in the normal course of business, there is no substantive change in ownership, and/or the exchange amount is not supported by independent evidence.** The argument to support remeasurement rests on the premise that if the transaction is not an ordinary transaction for the enterprise, there might not be a reasonable measure of fair value. Furthermore, if there is no change in ownership, *then* no bargaining has taken place and therefore, the price that is arrived at for the exchange may not represent a value that would have been arrived at had the transaction been arm's length.

Transactions that are in the normal course of business that have no commercial substance must also be remeasured. This argument rests on the premise that if the transaction is not bonafide, there is no real exchange of risks and rewards of ownership and therefore, no gain or loss should be recognized. **This is only an issue where the transaction is also a nonmonetary transaction.**

Illustration 24-5 is a decision tree[16] that reflects the judgement involved when determining how to treat related party transactions.

Where transactions are remeasured to carrying value, the difference between the carrying amounts of the items exchanged is booked as a charge or credit to equity.[17] To illus-

Illustration 24-5

Related Party Transactions— Decision Tree

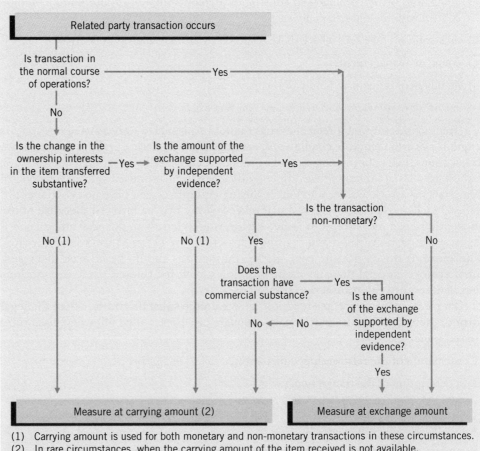

(1) Carrying amount is used for both monetary and non-monetary transactions in these circumstances.
(2) In rare circumstances, when the carrying amount of the item received is not available, a reasonable estimate of the carrying amount, based on the transferor's original cost, may be used to measure the exchange.

---

[16] *CICA Handbook*, Section 3840, Appendix (based on proposed amendments to the section).

[17] *CICA Handbook*, Section 3840.09.

trate, assume that Hudson Limited, a manufacturing company, sells land worth $20,000 to Bay Limited. The companies are related by virtue of the fact that the same shareholder has a 90% equity interest in each company (the rest of the shares are publicly traded). The land has a carrying value of $15,000 on Hudson's books. In exchange, Bay Limited, also a manufacturing company, transfers to Hudson a building that has a net book value of $12,000. This transaction is not in the **ordinary (normal) course of business** since both companies are manufacturers and would not normally be selling capital assets such as land and buildings. Therefore, the transaction is subject to further analysis.

Looking at the decision tree, the next question is **whether there has been a substantive change in ownership.** Do different parties own the items exchanged before and after the transaction? Since the same controlling shareholder owns both assets before and after the transaction (albeit indirectly, through the companies), there is no substantive change in ownership.[18] Therefore, the transaction would be remeasured to carrying values with the following journal entry on the Hudson books.

IAS Note

The recently added test for commercial substance harmonizes Canadian GAAP with international GAAP.

Property, plant, and equipment	12,000	
Retained earnings	3,000	
Land		15,000

A	= L	+	SE
−3,000			−3,000

Cash flows: No effect

Bay would record the land at $15,000 and take the building off its books. The resulting credit would be booked to Contributed Surplus. Note that the difference between the carrying values is generally viewed as an equity contribution or distribution and is therefore booked through equity.

Differential Reporting

The increasing amount and complexity of disclosures and measurement in financial reporting carries a significant cost. For companies whose financial instruments are publicly traded, the benefits of this additional information presumably exceed these costs since users of the financial statements need this information for decision-making. For private companies, however, where the owners of the company have greater access to information about the company, is the cost warranted?

The CICA has dealt with this issue by creating some relief for non-publicly accountable enterprises: those that do not have financial instruments that are traded in a public market.[19] Where the owners of these companies unanimously consent to the application of different accounting principles, differential reporting applies.

Differential reporting relates to the following financial reporting areas.

1. Subsidiaries: may elect to use the cost or equity methods for accounting for subsidiaries that would otherwise be consolidated. (This is beyond the scope of this text.)

2. Long-term investments: may elect to use the cost method rather than the equity method for those investments where significant influence exists. The cost method will disappear with the advent of proposed Section 3855 on Financial Instruments.

---

[18] As a benchmark, a substantive change in ownership may be deemed to have occurred if an unrelated party has gained or given up >20% interest in the items exchanged (*CICA Handbook*, Section 3840.31). In the example above, if the controlling shareholder only owned, say, 70% of both companies and the shares were publicly traded, then one might argue substantive change in ownership may be evident, i.e., the other 30% of the shareholders now own (indirectly, through their shareholdings) part of the asset where they did not prior. This is not so clear cut, however, Since the majority shareholders have controlling interest, no real bargaining would have happened between the minority shareholders and the majority shareholders. The resolution of this issue would be a matter of judgement.

[19] *CICA Handbook*, Section 1300.02.

Instructions

(a) Determine which of the segments are reportable based on the:

1. revenue test.

2. operating profit (loss) test.

3. assets test.

(b) Prepare the necessary disclosures.

P24-3   Lion Corporation is in the process of preparing its annual financial statements for the fiscal year ended April 30, 2005. The company manufactures plastic, glass, and paper containers for sale to food and drink manufacturers and distributors.

Lion Corporation maintains separate control accounts for its raw materials, work-in-process, and finished goods inventories for each of the three types of containers. The inventories are valued at the lower of cost or market.

The company's property, plant, and equipment are classified in the following major categories: land, office buildings, furniture and fixtures, manufacturing facilities, manufacturing equipment, and leasehold improvements. All fixed assets are carried at cost. The depreciation methods employed depend upon the type of asset (its classification) and when it was acquired.

Lion Corporation plans to present the inventory and fixed asset amounts in its April 30, 2005 balance sheet as shown below.

Inventories	$4,814,200
Property, plant, and equipment (net of amortization)	$6,310,000

Instructions

What information regarding inventories and property, plant, and equipment must be disclosed by Lion Corporation in the audited financial statements issued to shareholders, either in the body or the notes, for the 2004–2005 fiscal year?

(CMA adapted)

P24-4   Rem Inc. produces electronic components for sale to manufacturers of radios, television sets, and digital sound systems. In connection with her examination of Rem's financial statements for the year ended December 31, 2005, Maggie Zeen, CA, completed field work two weeks ago. Ms. Zeen now is evaluating the significance of the following items prior to preparing her auditor's report. Except as noted, none of these items have been disclosed in the financial statements or notes.

Item 1

A 10-year loan agreement, which the company entered into three years ago, provides that dividend payments may not exceed net income earned after taxes subsequent to the date of the agreement. The balance of retained earnings at the date of the loan agreement was $420,000. From that date through December 31, 2005, net income after taxes has totalled $570,000 and cash dividends have totalled $320,000. Based on these data the staff auditor assigned to this review concluded that there was no retained earnings restriction at December 31, 2005.

Item 2

Recently Rem interrupted its policy of paying cash dividends quarterly to its shareholders. Dividends were paid regularly through 2004, discontinued for all of 2005 to finance purchase of equipment for the company's new plant, and resumed in the first quarter of 2006. In the annual report, dividend policy is to be discussed in the president's letter to shareholders.

Item 3

A major electronics firm has introduced a line of products that will compete directly with Rem's primary line, now being produced in the specially designed new plant. Because of manufacturing innovations, the competitor's line will be of comparable quality but priced 50% below Rem's line. The competitor announced its new line during the week following completion of field work. Ms. Zeen read the announcement in the newspaper and discussed the situation by telephone with Rem executives. Rem will meet the lower prices that are high enough to cover variable manufacturing and selling expenses but will permit recovery of only a portion of fixed costs.

Item 4

The company's new manufacturing plant building, which cost $2.4 million and has an estimated life of 25 years, is leased from Ancient National Bank at an annual rental of $600,000. The company is obligated to pay property taxes, insurance, and maintenance. At the conclusion of its 10-year non-cancellable lease, the company has the option of purchasing the property for $1.00. In Rem's income statement, the rental payment is reported on a separate line.

Instructions

For each of the items above, discuss any additional disclosures in the financial statements and notes that the auditor should recommend to her client. (The four items' cumulative effect should not be considered.)

P24-5 You have completed your audit of Keesha Inc. and its consolidated subsidiaries for the year ended December 31, 2005, and were satisfied with the results of your examination. You have examined the financial statements of Keesha for the past three years. The corporation is now preparing its annual report to shareholders. The report will include the consolidated financial statements of Keesha and its subsidiaries and your short-form auditor's report. During your audit the following matters came to your attention.

1. A vice-president who is also a shareholder resigned on December 31, 2005 after an argument with the president. The vice-president is soliciting proxies from shareholders and expects to obtain sufficient proxies to gain control of the board of directors so that a new president will be appointed. The president plans to have a note prepared that would include information of the pending proxy fight, management's accomplishments over the years, and an appeal by management for the support of shareholders.

2. The corporation decides in 2005 to adopt the straight-line method of depreciation for plant equipment. The straight-line method will be used for new acquisitions as well as for previously acquired plant equipment for which depreciation had been provided on an accelerated basis. The new policy will result in more relevant financial reporting in order to be more consistent with the new standards.

3. The Canada Customs and Revenue Agency is currently examining the corporation's 2003 federal income tax return and is questioning the amount of a deduction claimed by the corporation's domestic subsidiary for a loss sustained in 2003. The examination is still in process, and any additional tax liability is indeterminable at this time. The corporation's tax counsel believes that there will be no substantial additional tax liability.

Instructions

(a) Prepare the notes, if any, that you would suggest for the items listed above.

(b) State your reasons for not making disclosure by note for each of the listed items for which you did not prepare a note.

(AICPA adapted)

P24-6 Presented below are three independent situations.

Situation 1

A company offers a one-year warranty for the product that it manufactures. A history of warranty claims has been compiled and the probable amounts of claims related to sales for a given period can be determined.

Situation 2

Subsequent to the date of a set of financial statements, but prior to the date of authorization for issue of the financial statements, a company enters into a contract that will probably result in a significant loss to the company. The loss amount can be reasonably estimated.

Situation 3

A company has adopted a policy of recording self-insurance for any possible losses resulting from injury to others by the company's vehicles. The premium for an insurance policy for the same risk from an independent insurance company would have an annual cost of $4,000. During the period covered by the financial statements, there were no accidents involving the company's vehicles that resulted in injury to others.

Instructions

Discuss the accrual or type of disclosure necessary (if any) and the reason(s) why such disclosure is appropriate for each of the three independent sets of facts above.

(AICPA adapted)

P24-7 At December 31, 2005, Brandt Corp. has assets of $10 million, liabilities of $6 million, common shares of $2 million (representing 2 million common shares of $1.00 par), and retained earnings of $2 million. Net sales for the year 2005 were $18 million, and net income was $800,000. As auditors of this company, you are making a review of subsequent events on February 13, 2006, and you find the following.

1. On February 3, 2006, one of Brandt's customers declared bankruptcy. At December 31, 2005, this company owed Brandt $300,000, of which $40,000 was paid in January 2006.

2. On January 18, 2006, one of the client's three major plants burned.

3. On January 23, 2006, a strike was called at one of Brandt's largest plants, which halted 30% of its production. As of today (February 13), the strike has not been settled.

4. A major electronics enterprise has introduced a line of products that would compete directly with Brandt's primary

line, now being produced in a specially designed new plant. Because of manufacturing innovations, the competitor has been able to achieve quality similar to that of Brandt's products, but at a price 50% lower. Brandt officials say they will meet the lower prices, which are high enough to cover variable manufacturing and selling costs but permit recovery of only a portion of fixed costs.

5. Merchandise traded in the open market is recorded in the company's records at $1.40 per unit on December 31, 2005. This price had prevailed for two weeks, after release of an official market report that predicted vastly enlarged supplies; however, no purchases were made at $1.40. The price throughout the preceding year had been about $2.00, which was the level experienced over several years. On January 18, 2006, the price returned to $2.00, after public disclosure of an error in the official calculations of the prior December, correction of which destroyed the expectations of excessive supplies. Inventory at December 31, 2005 was on a lower of cost or market basis.

6. On February 1, 2006, the board of directors adopted a resolution accepting the offer of an investment banker to guarantee the marketing of $1.2 million of preferred shares.

Instructions

State in each case how the 2005 financial statements would be affected, if at all.

P24-8　You are compiling the consolidated financial statements for Vender Corporation International (VCI). The corporation's accountant, Vincent Jones, has provided you with the following segment information.

Note 7: Major Segments of Business

VCI conducts funeral service and cemetery operations in the United States and Canada. Substantially all revenues of VCI's major segments of business are from unaffiliated customers. Segment information for fiscal 2005, 2004, and 2003 follows.

	Funeral	Floral	Cemetery	(thousands) Corporate	Dried Whey	Limousine	Consolidated
Revenues:							
2005	$302,000	$10,000	$ 83,000	$ —	$7,000	$14,000	$416,000
2004	245,000	6,000	61,000	—	4,000	8,000	324,000
2003	208,000	3,000	42,000	—	1,000	6,000	260,000
Operating Income:							
2005	$ 79,000	$ 1,500	$ 18,000	$ (36,000)	$ 500	$ 2,000	$ 65,000
2004	64,000	200	12,000	(28,000)	200	400	48,800
2003	54,000	150	6,000	(21,000)	100	350	39,600
Capital Expenditures[a]:							
2005	$ 26,000	$ 1,000	$ 9,000	$ 400	$ 300	$ 1,000	$ 37,700
2004	28,000	2,000	60,000	1,500	100	700	92,300
2003	14,000	25	8,000	600	25	50	22,700
Depreciation and Amortization:							
2005	$ 13,000	$ 100	$ 2,400	$ 1,400	$ 100	$ 200	$ 17,200
2004	10,000	50	1,400	700	50	100	12,300
2003	8,000	25	1,000	600	25	50	9,700
Identifiable Assets:							
2005	$334,000	$ 1,500	$162,000	$114,000	$ 500	$ 8,000	$620,000
2004	322,000	1,000	144,000	52,000	1,000	6,000	526,000
2003	223,000	500	78,000	34,000	500	3,500	339,500

[a] Includes $4,520,000, $111,480,000, and $1,294,000 for the years ended April 30, 2005, 2004, and 2003, respectively, for purchases of businesses.

Instructions

Determine which of the above segments must be reported separately and which can be combined under the category "Other." Then, write a one-page memo to the company's accountant, Vincent Jones, explaining the following:

(a) what segments must be reported separately and what segments can be combined

(b) what criteria you used to determine reportable segments

(c) what major items for each must be disclosed.

P24-9 Presented below is an excerpt from the financial statements of **H. J. Heinz Company** segment and geographic data.

The company is engaged principally in one line of business—processed food products—that represents more than 90% of consolidated sales. Information about the company business by geographic area is presented in the table below.

There were no material amounts of sales or transfers between geographic areas or between affiliates, and no material amounts of United States export sales.

(in thousands of U.S. dollars)	Domestic	United Kingdom	Canada	Foreign Western Europe	Other	Total	Worldwide
Sales	$2,381,054	$547,527	$216,726	$383,784	$209,354	$1,357,391	$3,738,445
Operating income	246,780	61,282	34,146	29,146	25,111	149,685	396,465
Identifiable assets	1,362,152	265,218	112,620	294,732	143,971	816,541	2,178,693
Capital expenditures	72,712	12,262	13,790	8,253	4,368	38,673	111,385
Depreciation expense	42,279	8,364	3,592	6,355	3,606	21,917	64,196

Instructions

(a) Why does H. J. Heinz not prepare segment information on its products or services?

(b) Why are revenues by geographical area important to disclose?

Writing Assignments

WA24-1 The following article appeared in *The Wall Street Journal*.

WASHINGTON—The Securities and Exchange Commission staff issued guidelines for companies grappling with the problem of dividing up their business into industry segments for their annual reports.

An industry segment is defined by the Financial Accounting Standards Board as a part of an enterprise engaged in providing a product or service or a group of related products or services primarily to unaffiliated customers for a profit.

Although conceding that the process is a "subjective task" that to a considerable extent, depends on the judgement of management, the SEC staff said companies should consider the nature of the products, the nature of their production and their markets and marketing methods to determine whether products and services should be grouped together or in separate industry segments.

Instructions

(a) What does financial reporting for segments of a business enterprise involve?

(b) Identify the reasons for requiring financial data to be reported by segments.

(c) Identify the possible disadvantages of requiring financial data to be reported by segments.

(d) Identify the accounting difficulties inherent in segment reporting.

WA24-2 J. J. Kersee Corporation, a publicly traded company, is preparing the interim financial data that it will issue to its shareholders and the Securities Commission at the end of the first quarter of the 2004–2005 fiscal year. Kersee's financial accounting department has compiled the following summarized revenue and expense data for the first quarter of the year.

Sales	$60,000,000
Cost of goods sold	36,000,000
Variable selling expenses	2,000,000
Fixed selling expenses	3,000,000

Included in the fixed selling expenses was the single lump sum payment of $2 million for television advertisements for the entire year.

Instructions

(a) J. J. Kersee Corporation must issue its quarterly financial statements in accordance with generally accepted accounting principles regarding interim financial reporting.

   1. Explain whether Kersee should report its operating results for the quarter as if the quarter were a separate reporting period in and of itself or as if the quarter were an integral part of the annual reporting period.

2. State how the sales, cost of goods sold, and fixed selling expenses would be reflected in Kersee Corporation's quarterly report prepared for the first quarter of the 2004–2005 fiscal year. Briefly justify your presentation.

(b) What financial information, as a minimum, must Kersee Corporation disclose to its shareholders in its quarterly reports?

(CMA adapted)

WA24-3   The following statement is an excerpt from a document on interim financial reporting.

Interim financial information is essential to provide investors and others with timely information as to the progress of the enterprise. The usefulness of such information rests on the relationship that it has to the annual results of operations. Accordingly, the Board has concluded that each interim period should be viewed primarily as an integral part of an annual period.

In general, the results for each interim period should be based on the accounting principles and practices used by an enterprise in the preparation of its latest annual financial statements unless a change in an accounting practice or policy has been adopted in the current year. The Board has concluded, however, that certain accounting principles and practices followed for annual reporting purposes may require modification at interim reporting dates so that the reported results for the interim period may better relate to the results of operations for the annual period.

Instructions

Listed below are six independent cases on how accounting facts might be reported on an individual company's interim financial reports. For each of these cases, state whether the method proposed to be used for interim reporting would be acceptable under generally accepted accounting principles applicable to interim financial data. Support each answer with a brief explanation.

(a) King Limited takes a physical inventory at year end for annual financial statement purposes. Inventory and cost of sales reported in the interim quarterly statements are based on estimated gross profit rates, because a physical inventory would result in a cessation of operations. The company does have reliable perpetual inventory records.

(b) Florence Limited is planning to report one-fourth of its pension expense each quarter.

(c) Lopez Corp. wrote inventory down to reflect lower of cost or market in the first quarter. At year end, the market exceeds the original acquisition cost of this inventory. Consequently, management plans to write the inventory back up to its original cost as a year-end adjustment.

(d) Witt Corp. realized a large gain on the sale of investments at the beginning of the second quarter. The company wants to report one-third of the gain in each of the remaining quarters.

(e) Marble Limited has estimated its annual audit fee. It plans to prorate this expense equally over all four quarters.

(f) McNeil Inc. was reasonably certain it would have an employee strike in the third quarter. As a result, it shipped heavily during the second quarter but plans to defer the recognition of the sales in excess of the normal sales volume. The deferred sales will be recognized as sales in the third quarter when the strike is in progress. McNeil management thinks this is more nearly representative of normal second- and third-quarter operations.

WA24-4   An article in *Barron's* noted:

Okay. Last fall, someone with a long memory and an even longer arm reached into that bureau drawer and came out with a moldy cheese sandwich and the equally moldy notion of corporate forecasts. We tried to find out what happened to the cheese sandwich—but, rats!, even recourse to the Freedom of Information Act didn't help. However, the forecast proposal was dusted off, polished up and found quite serviceable. The SEC, indeed, lost no time in running it up the old flagpole—but no one was very eager to salute. Even after some of the more objectionable features—compulsory corrections and detailed explanations of why the estimates went awry— were peeled off the original proposal.

Seemingly, despite the Commission's smiles and sweet talk, those craven corporations were still afraid that an honest mistake would lead down the primrose path to consent decrees and class action suits. To lay to rest such qualms, the Commission last week approved a "Safe Harbor" rule that, providing the forecasts were made on a reasonable basis and in good faith, protected corporations from litigation should the projections prove wide of the mark (as only about 99% are apt to do).

Instructions

(a) What are the arguments for preparing profit forecasts?

(b) What is the purpose of the safe harbour rule?

(c) Why are corporations concerned about presenting profit forecasts?

Cases

Refer to the Case Primer on the Digital Tool to help you answer these cases.

Digital Tool

www.wiley.com/
canada/kieso

CA24-1   Patty Gamble, the financial vice-president, and Victoria Maher, the controller, of Castle Manufacturing Corporation are reviewing the company's financial ratios for the years 2004 and 2005. The financial vice-president notes that the profit margin on sales ratio has increased from 6% to 12%, a hefty gain for the two-year period. Gamble is in the process of issuing a media release that emphasizes the efficiency of Castle Manufacturing in controlling cost. Victoria Maher knows that the difference in ratios is due primarily to an earlier company decision to reduce the estimates of warranty and bad debt expense for 2005. The controller, not sure of her supervisor's motives, hesitates to suggest to Gamble that the company's improvement is unrelated to efficiency in controlling cost. To complicate matters, the media release is scheduled in a few days.

Instructions

Adopt the role of Victoria Maher and discuss the financial reporting issues.

CA24-2   In June 2005, the board of directors for Holtzman Enterprises Inc. authorized the sale of $10 million of corporate bonds. Michelle Collins, treasurer for Holtzman Enterprises Inc., is concerned about the date when the bonds are issued. The company really needs the cash, but she is worried that if the bonds are issued before the company's year end (December 31, 2005), the additional liability will have an adverse effect on a number of important ratios. In July, she explains to company president Kenneth Holtzman that if they delay issuing the bonds until after December 31, the bonds will not affect the ratios until December 31, 2006. They will have to report the issuance as a subsequent event, which requires only footnote disclosure. Collins predicts that with expected improved financial performance in 2005, ratios should be better.

Instructions

Adopt the role of Michelle Collins and discuss any issues.

CA24-3   Below is an excerpt from the 1989 financial statements of **Exxon Corporation**. The note deals with a large oil spill caused by one of the company's oil tankers.

Note 14 to the 1989 annual financial statements of Exxon Corporation.

On March 24, 1989, The Exxon Valdez, a tanker owned by Exxon Shipping Company, a subsidiary of Exxon Corporation, ran aground on Bligh Reef in Prince William Sound off the port of Valdez, Alaska, and released approximately 260,000 barrels of crude oil. More than 170 lawsuits including class actions have been brought in various courts against Exxon Corporation and some of its consolidated subsidiaries. Most of these lawsuits seek unspecified compensatory and physical damages; several lawsuits seek damages in varying specified amounts. Some of the lawsuits seek injunctive relief.

The State of Alaska has filed a suit in Superior Court in Alaska against Exxon Shipping Company, Exxon Corporation and others seeking substantial civil penalties and unspecified damages arising from the oil spill. On February 27, 1990, an indictment was returned in the United States District Court in Anchorage Alaska, charging Exxon Shipping Company and Exxon Corporation with violation of the Refuse Act, the Migratory Bird Treaty Act, the Clean Water Act, the Ports and Waterways Safety Act and the Dangerous Cargo Act.

The potential total costs relating to the matters described above are difficult to predict and are not expected to be resolved for a number of years. It is believed that the ultimate outcome net of reserves already provided, will not have a materially adverse effect upon the corporation's operations or financial condition.

Instructions

(a) Why would the company want to disclose all the details given how it reflects negatively on the company?

(b) How much disclosure is necessary, and what level of detail is required?

Research and Analysis

RA 24-1 Thomson Corporation

In response to the investing public's demand for greater disclosure of corporate expectations for the future, safe harbour rules and legislation have been passed to encourage and protect corporations that issue financial forecasts and projections. Review the Management Discussion and Analysis for the Thomson Corporation.

Instructions

(a) What general expectation did the company have for the industry in 2003? How did the company plan to react to this expectation?

(b) Give examples of hard data forecasts (if any) that the company disclosed for the upcoming year (2003). Give some examples of soft data forecasts. ("Hard" means concrete and "soft" means open to judgement, interpretation, or change.)

(c) What caveats or other statements that temper its forecasts did the company make?

(d) What is the difference between a financial forecast and a financial projection?

RA24-2 Sears Canada Inc. versus Hudson's Bay Company

Instructions

Go to the Digital Tool and, using the annual reports for Sears Canada Inc. and the Hudson' Bay Company, answer the following questions.

(a) What specific items do the companies discuss in their Accounting Policies notes? (Prepare a list of the headings only.)

(b) Note the similarities and differences. Comment and tie into the nature of the businesses.

(c) For what lines of business or segments do the companies present segmented information?

(d) Note and comment on the similarities and differences between the auditors' reports submitted by the independent auditors.

RA 24-3 Canadian Financial Reporting

Al Rosen, a prominent forensic accountant in Canada, in his article entitled "Easy Prey" (*Canadian Business*, April 16, 2001), comments that Canadian investors are being swindled.

Instructions

Read the article and argue for this statement as well as against.

RA 24-4 GAAP

In an article entitled "Mind the GAAP," which appeared in *Canadian Business* on May 14, 2001, author Al Rosen argues that generally accepted accounting principles are not generally accepted. In the article he compares the differences between profit and loss for seven companies' Canadian GAAP versus U.S. GAAP.

Instructions

Obtain the financial statements of at least two of the companies and look at the note to the financial statements where the companies reconcile net income under Canadian to net income under U.S. GAAP. What are the major differences? Which earnings number is more useful to users? Why?

RA24-5 Measurement Uncertainty

Instructions

Go to the CICA website and download the discussion paper on Measurement Objectives. Alternatively, look up FASB Statement of Financial Accounting Concepts No. 7. Write a two-page summary of the paper, highlighting the important points.

RA24-6 Harmonization

The CICA AcSB has committed to harmonization of accounting standards.

Instructions

Go to the CICA website and note which major standards have been harmonized in the past few years. Identify harmonization initiatives that are outstanding. Comment on the success of the harmonization mandate.

Specimen Financial Statements

The following pages contain the financial statements, accompanying notes, and other information from the 2003 Annual Report of **Intrawest Corporation** (Intrawest), a significant resort operator in Canada. The company has 9 mountain resorts, 1 warm-weather resort, 25 golf courses under management, a vacation ownership business, and 6 world-class village resorts. One of the company's significant properties is Whistler Blackcomb, which generates significant cash flows.

The Business

Intrawest has three distinct businesses:

1. Mountain resort

2. Warm-weather resort, including golf courses

3. Real estate, including rental and development and sale

One of the key drivers of the mountain resort business is skier visits. Although the number of visits was up for Intrawest in the past year, mountain resort financial performance was affected by warmer weather in the east, a slower economy, and a decrease in international travellers due to the September 11 attack. This was partially offset by an increase in skiers who drove to the resorts.

Within the real estate division, the company develops resort properties such as condominiums, townhouses, and houses and operates a resort club. The company not only sells the units it develops but also rents them out, which contributes to more skiers. The sales represent one-time revenues whereas the rentals represent sustainable income. The resort club generates less than 10% of the company's real estate revenues and therefore is not reported separately. The real estate division performed well in the year.

We do not expect that you will comprehend the company's financial statements and the accompanying notes in their entirety at your first reading. But we expect that by the time you complete the material in this text, your level of understanding and interpretive ability will have grown.

At this point we recommend that you take 20 to 30 minutes to scan the statements and notes to familiarize yourself with the contents and accounting elements. Throughout the following chapters, when you are asked to refer to specific parts of Intrawest's financials, do so. Then, when you have completed reading this book, we challenge you to reread Intrawest's financials to see how much greater and more sophisticated is your understanding of them.

Management's Discussion and Analysis

(All dollar amounts are in United States currency, unless otherwise indicated)

The following discussion and analysis should be read in conjunction with our audited consolidated financial statements for the year ended June 30, 2003 and accompanying notes included in this annual report. The discussion of our business may include forward-looking statements about our future operations, financial results and objectives. These statements are necessarily based on estimates and assumptions that are subject to risks and uncertainties. Our actual results could differ materially from those expressed or implied by such forward-looking information due to a variety of factors including, but not limited to, our ability to implement our business strategies, seasonality, weather conditions, competition, general economic conditions, currency fluctuations, world events and other risks detailed in our filings with Canadian securities regulatory authorities and the U.S. Securities and Exchange Commission.

COMPANY OVERVIEW

Intrawest is the world's leading operator and developer of village-centered resorts. We have a network of 10 mountain resorts, geographically diversified across North America's major ski regions. Our resorts include Whistler Blackcomb (77% interest) and Panorama in British Columbia, Blue Mountain (50% interest) in Ontario, Tremblant in Quebec, Stratton in Vermont, Snowshoe in West Virginia, Copper and Winter Park in Colorado, Mammoth (59.5% interest) in California and Mountain Creek in New Jersey. We assumed control of Winter Park in December 2002 under a long-term capital lease arrangement. Our resorts hosted 8.2 million skier visits in fiscal 2003, 10.7% of the North American market and the most in the mountain resort industry.

We own and operate one warm-weather resort, Sandestin, in Florida. Our resort assets include 18 golf courses and we also manage an additional 11 golf courses for other owners. We have interests in several other leisure-related businesses, including Alpine Helicopters (45% interest) and the Breeze/Max retail store chain.

We are the largest mountain resort real estate developer in North America. We develop real estate at our resorts and at six third-party owned resorts (five in the United States and one in France). We develop real estate for the purpose of sale and to June 30, 2003 we have closed 10,490 residential units at 15 different resorts.

OPERATING SUMMARY

Our operating results in 2003 were below the expectations we set at the outset of the year. The travel and leisure industry continued to feel the impact of the challenges we faced in 2002, i.e., the slow economy and the aftermath of September 11, and it also had to deal with several unforeseen events, including the war in Iraq and the SARS outbreak.

Income from continuing operations was $34.8 million in 2003 compared with $58.6 million in 2002. The decline was caused primarily by reduced profits from our real estate business and a $12.3 million write-down of technology assets. Until the beginning of March our ski and resort operations were performing well, however concerns over the war in Iraq and the SARS outbreak had a dramatic impact on destination visits to our resorts at a time that has historically been the busiest part of our season. Consequently, in the third and fourth quarters, our ski and resort operations lost the ground they had gained earlier in the season.

In Colorado, real estate sales continued to be slow. In Whistler, we had planned to close the second phase of high-end, high-margin single-family lots at Kadenwood but the market for this product type has temporarily stalled. Notwithstanding these situations, demand for real estate has generally been very strong at our resorts, as evidenced by our record backlog of pre-sales. We will realize the benefit of these pre-sales when they close in 2004 and 2005. Our real estate profits were also impacted by delays in the completion of construction of two projects that pushed closings into fiscal 2004.

The write-down of technology assets resulted from our decision to standardize various business systems across our resorts and reflects the write-off of our investment in redundant systems. We expect to realize both efficiencies and cost savings as a consequence of this decision.

Total Company EBITDA was $209.2 million in 2003, down from $211.2 million in 2002. A reconciliation between earnings reported in our statements of operations and Total Company EBITDA is included in "Additional Information" at the end of this discussion and analysis.

REVIEW OF SKI AND RESORT OPERATIONS

Our ski and resort operations are segregated into two reportable segments: mountain resort operations and warm-weather resort operations. The mountain resort operations comprise all the operating activities at our 10 mountain resorts as well as the operations of Resort Reservations (RezRez), Alpine Helicopters and Breeze/Max Retail. The warm-weather resort operations comprise all the operating activities at Sandestin as well as operations at our five stand-alone golf courses.

The key drivers of the mountain resort operations business are skier visits, revenue per visit and margins. Our strategy to increase skier visits has two main elements: improving the quality of the resort experience by upgrading and expanding the on-mountain facilities and building villages at the base to provide accommodation for destination guests. By expanding the amenities on the mountain and in the village, we are able to broaden the customer mix, extend the length of stay and capture a higher percentage of guest spending, all of which increases revenue per visit. Building the accommodation also allows visits to be spread more evenly during the week and during the season, which improves margins since a significant proportion of operating expenses at a resort are fixed. The key drivers of the warm-weather resort operations business are similar; i.e., golf rounds, revenue per round and margins.

The following table highlights the results of our ski and resort operations.

	2003	2002	CHANGE (%)
Skier visits [1]	7,302,000	6,283,000	16.2
Revenue (Millions)	$ 571.5	$ 485.1	17.8
EBITDA (Millions)	$ 116.7	$ 107.3	8.8
Margin (%)	20.4	22.1	

[1] All resorts are at 100% except Mammoth at 59.5% and Blue Mountain at 50%.

Revenue from ski and resort operations was $571.5 million in 2003 compared with $485.1 million in 2002. Revenue from mountain resorts increased from $424.8 million to $506.5 million while revenue from warm-weather resorts increased from $60.3 million to $65.0 million.

MOUNTAIN RESORTS

On December 23, 2002, we closed on a transaction with the City and County of Denver to operate Winter Park on a long-term lease arrangement. Since the lease gives us control over the resort, for financial reporting purposes Winter Park is treated in the same manner as any of our directly owned resorts. This was an important transaction for us, not only because it adds a quality resort in the largest ski market in North America to our portfolio, but also because of the synergies that it will create with Copper and our other Colorado operations. Winter Park, combined with Copper, gives us an operation with over two million skier visits, similar in scale to Whistler Blackcomb, our most profitable resort. By sharing administrative services, collaborating on marketing initiatives, harmonizing operations and developing new product and service offerings, we expect to realize higher margins than either resort could achieve individually.

The results of Winter Park were consolidated from the closing date and accounted for $33.1 million of the increase in mountain resort revenue and 793,000 of the increase in skier visits. In February 2002 we sold our smallest resort, Mont Ste. Marie, which generated $1.6 million of revenue from 62,000 skier visits in fiscal 2002.

On a same-resort basis (i.e., excluding Winter Park and Mont Ste. Marie) mountain resort revenue increased by 11.8% or $50.1 million due to various factors:

(MILLIONS)	
Increase in skier visits	$ 15.9
Increase in revenue per skier visit	15.2
Increase in non-skier visit revenue	10.8
Impact of exchange rate on reported revenue	8.2
	$ 50.1

Same-resort skier visits increased by 4.6% from 6,221,000 in 2002 to 6,509,000 in 2003, despite the difficult conditions in the travel and leisure sector. Skier visits were higher at every resort except for Whistler Blackcomb, Panorama and Tremblant. Skier visits at our eastern resorts, which experienced excellent early-season conditions, were 18.7% ahead of last year through the first week of March but then declined by 7.5% to the end of the season. The changes were somewhat less significant at our western resorts, being 2.3% ahead through the first week of March and 3.9% below for the balance of the season. The decline in visits after the first week of March came entirely from the destination market as evidenced by the fact that during this period season pass visits increased 24.4%. We estimate that the increase in skier visits increased mountain resort revenue by $15.9 million in 2003.

Same-resort revenue per skier visit increased 4.2% from $55.07 in 2002 (after adjusting for the impact of the improvement in the Canadian dollar exchange rate) to $57.40 in 2003. Revenue per skier visit is a function of ticket prices and ticket yields, and revenue from non-ticket sources such as retail and rental stores, lodging, ski school, and food and beverage services. Ticket yields reflect the mix of ticket types (e.g., adult, child, season pass and group), the proportion of day versus destination visitors (destination visitors tend to be less price-sensitive), and the amount of discounting of full-price tickets in regional markets. Revenue per visit from non-ticket sources is also influenced by the mix of day versus destination visitors, the affluence of the visitor base, and the quantity and type of amenities and services offered at the resort.

Revenue per visit from ticket sales increased 1.4% from $27.60 to $27.99. There was a relative shift in the mix of visits from "paid" visits to season pass visits as we sold 16.6% more season passes and frequency cards in 2003 than 2002 and this tended to lower ticket yields. Over the past several seasons we have deliberately sought to increase season pass and frequency card sales in order to increase pre-committed revenue. Revenue per visit from non-ticket sources increased 7.1% from $27.46 to $29.41. This increase is less than we had expected due to softness in the retail business (which was an industry trend) and lower revenues from ski school and rental due to reduced destination visits after February. Approximately half of the increase in non-ticket revenue per visit came from lodging and property management due to a 12.9% increase in the number of occupied room nights, most notably at Blue Mountain, Stratton and Snowshoe. We estimate that the increase in revenue per visit increased mountain resort revenue by $15.2 million in 2003.

For the purposes of this analysis, non-skier visit revenue comprises revenue from golf and other summer activities and revenue from businesses such as RezRez, Alpine Helicopters and Breeze/Max. Revenue from golf and other summer activities increased 8.1% across the mountain resorts from $39.5 million in 2002 to $42.7 million in 2003. Summer lodging and property management revenue increased 20.1%, led by strong room night growth at Tremblant, Blue Mountain and Snowshoe. Our central reservations business, RezRez, expanded its operations into several new warm-weather destinations, leading to a 40.9% growth in revenue to $13.5 million in 2003. We had expected much higher revenues from RezRez, however increased competition in the on-line travel sector and reduced travel by U.S. customers (which account for over 80% of RezRez's business) significantly reduced bookings. Revenue at Alpine and Breeze/Max increased by 4.0% and 1.1%, respectively. Overall, non-skier visit revenue increased by $10.8 million in 2003.

The reported amount of mountain resort revenue was increased by $8.2 million in 2003 because of the increase in the value of the Canadian dollar against the U.S. dollar. In 2003 revenue from the Canadian resorts was translated for financial statement reporting purposes at an average rate of Cdn.$1.51 to U.S.$1.00 compared with an average rate of Cdn.$1.57 to U.S.$1.00 in 2002.

WARM-WEATHER RESORTS

Revenue from warm-weather resorts increased 7.9% from $60.3 million in 2002 to $65.0 million in 2003. Revenue at Sandestin increased by $6.4 million due mainly to a 12.6% increase in occupied room nights. The opening of the new village at Baytowne Wharf in July 2002 increased the accommodation base at Sandestin and added many new amenities to the resort, driving higher lodging, retail, and food and beverage revenue. The sale of the Sabino Springs golf course in Tuscon in June 2002 reduced warm-weather resort revenue by $3.2 million, however this was partially offset by $1.1 million more revenue from Big Island Country Club in Hawaii, which we acquired in January 2002.

REVENUE BREAKDOWN

The breakdown of ski and resorts operations revenue by business was as follows:

(MILLIONS)	2003 REVENUE	2002 REVENUE	INCREASE (DECREASE)	CHANGE (%)
Mountain operations	$ 228.6	$ 193.3	$ 35.3	18.3
Retail and rental shops	95.9	85.0	10.9	12.8
Food and beverage	74.9	63.0	11.9	18.9
Lodging and property management	81.7	61.0	20.7	33.9
Ski school	37.1	30.4	6.7	22.1
Golf	28.0	29.4	(1.4)	(4.9)
Other	25.3	23.0	2.3	10.3
	$ 571.5	$ 485.1	86.4	17.8

Assuming control of Winter Park in December 2002 increased revenue from mountain operations, retail and rental shops, food and beverage, and ski school by $20.7 million, $3.4 million, $4.8 million and $3.5 million, respectively.

The proportion of revenue from mountain operations has fallen from 49.3% of total ski and resort operations revenue in 1997 to 40.0% in 2003. This trend is likely to continue as we build out the villages at our resorts, expanding the inventory of lodging units and changing the customer mix in favor of destination visitors who spend more on retail and rental, ski school, and food and beverage.

SKI AND RESORT OPERATIONS EXPENSES AND EBITDA

Ski and resort operations expenses increased from $377.8 million in 2002 to $454.9 million in 2003. Mountain resort expenses increased by $71.4 million to $397.3 million while warm-weather resort expenses increased by $5.7 million to $57.6 million.

The net impact of assuming control of Winter Park and selling Mont Ste. Marie increased mountain resort expenses by $19.5 million, leaving same-resort expense growth of $51.9 million. The strengthening of the value of the Canadian dollar increased the reported amount of mountain resort expenses by $6.7 million. The strong start in the East in 2003 compared with a very late start in 2002 impacted our expense growth. In 2002 we had a "vertical" ramp-up at Blue Mountain, Stratton, Snowshoe and Mountain Creek with essentially no pre-Christmas season, resulting in abnormally low costs. By comparison, in 2003 these eastern resorts commenced operations much earlier, ramping up more gradually, resulting in higher costs supported by higher revenues. In addition, the impact of the war in Iraq and SARS occurred in our core-operating month of March and happened suddenly, reducing visits significantly. Since we were uncertain how long the decline in visits would last and how great it would be, we had limited ability to ramp down costs. Overall, increased business volumes at these four eastern resorts during the full 2003 season resulted in a 19.3% increase in operating expenses (equivalent to $13.1 million) and a 22.6% increase in revenues.

The expansion of RezRez into new locations added $10.5 million to ski and resort operations expenses. We had set up an organization and infrastructure at RezRez to deal with a significant expected increase in business volumes. With the majority of bookings typically occurring in the period from October to February, the revenue shortfall was evident too late to institute meaningful cost savings before year-end. We have now heavily downsized and reorganized RezRez to focus on the ski and golf destinations where we have inherent advantages and away from warm-weather destinations. We expect these expense reductions, combined with revenue opportunities from the significant interest we are receiving from other travel providers in the RezRez on-line booking engine, to return this business to profitability.

The increase in warm-weather resort expenses of $5.7 million was almost entirely due to Sandestin and the opening of the new village in July 2002. The revenue growth at Sandestin more than offset the growth in expenses.

EBITDA from ski and resort operations increased from $107.3 million in 2002 to $116.7 million in 2003. EBITDA from the mountain resorts increased from $98.9 million to $109.2 million while EBITDA from the warm-weather resorts declined from $8.4 million to $7.5 million.

On a same-resort basis, mountain resorts EBITDA was $96.8 million in 2003 compared with $98.6 million in 2002. EBITDA from the resorts increased by 8.3%, however this was offset by reduced EBITDA from the non-skier visit businesses, i.e., Alpine, RezRez and the Breeze/Max retail chain.

The decrease in warm-weather resort EBITDA was due mainly to reduced profits from our Arizona golf operations due to the sale of the Sabino Springs golf course last year.

REVIEW OF REAL ESTATE OPERATIONS

We have two real estate divisions – the resort development group and the resort club group. The resort development group develops and sells three main products: condo-hotel units (typically, small village-based units that owners occupy sporadically and put into a rental pool at other times), townhome units (typically, larger units outside the main village core that owners retain for their own use) and single-family lots (serviced land on which owners or other developers build homes). In order to broaden market appeal, condo-hotel and townhome units are sold on the basis of both whole ownership and fractional ownership. Currently most of the fractional product has been quarter-share but a high-end tenth-share project is under construction at Whistler and other fractions are under consideration. The resort club group's business is a flexible form of timeshare where owners purchase points that entitle them to use accommodation at different resorts. The resort club group currently generates less than 10% of our total real estate revenue and hence is not reported as a separate business segment in the financial statements.

Our business strategy for real estate has two major elements: the maximization of profits from the sale of real estate and the provision of accommodation for destination visitors, which represents an earnings annuity for the ski and resort operations. Visitors renting the accommodation generate lodging revenue as well as revenue from purchasing lift tickets or golf fees, food and beverage, and retail.

We recognize real estate sales revenue at the time of "closing," which is when title to a completed unit is conveyed to the purchaser and the purchaser becomes entitled to occupancy. Since our standard practice is to pre-sell our real estate, any proceeds received prior to closing are recorded as deferred revenue in our balance sheet.

The following table highlights the results of the real estate business.

	2003	2002	CHANGE (%)
Units closed	1,239	1,290	(4.0)
Revenue (Millions)	$ 512.7	$ 487.8	5.1
Operating profit (Millions)	$ 75.0	$ 85.1	(11.9)
Margin (%)	14.6	17.4	

Revenue from the sale of real estate increased 5.1% from $487.8 million in 2002 to $512.7 million in 2003. Revenue generated by the resort development group increased from $449.8 million to $472.8 million while revenue generated by the resort club group increased from $38.0 million to $39.9 million.

RESORT DEVELOPMENT GROUP REVENUE

We closed a total of 528 units at the Canadian resorts in 2003 compared with 589 units last year. The average price per unit increased from Cdn.$423,000 in 2002 to Cdn.$436,000 in 2003. We also closed the sale of the majority of our commercial properties at Tremblant in 2003, recognizing revenue of $21.5 million. Currently we have approximately 500,000 square feet of remaining commercial properties at nine different resorts. Our plan is to sell all of these properties in the normal course.

We closed 611 units at the U.S. resorts in 2003 compared with 701 units in 2002. The number of units that close in a particular period is dependent on both transacting sales and the timing of construction completion. We had expected to close more units in 2003, however construction delays, due mainly to difficult site conditions, the complicated building design and construction management issues (see below), were experienced on two projects at Lake Las Vegas and Squaw Valley. The average price per unit was $457,000 at the U.S. resorts in 2003 (after adjusting the number of units for the impact of joint ventures at Keystone and Three Peaks), up from $442,000 in 2002. In 2003 we also closed our first 100 units at Les Arcs in France for proceeds of $31.1 million.

The mix of product types (i.e., condo-hotel, townhome and single-family lot) closed was not materially different in 2003 than in 2002.

During 2003 we reorganized the resort development group from a resort-based structure to a regional structure. We have six regional offices providing development and construction services to 17 different resorts. This structure allows us to share resources between resorts and gives us the critical mass in each region to be able to engage specialized development and construction experts that might be uneconomical for an individual resort. The new structure also strengthens our control systems so that, for example, the construction management issues that affected the completion of two projects in 2003 are less likely to impact our business in the future.

RESORT CLUB GROUP REVENUE

The resort club group generated $39.9 million in sales revenue in 2003, up from $38.0 million in 2002. We had expected stronger revenue growth, however sales were impacted by the slow economy and the uncertainty created by recent world events. This product type is more of a consumer purchase than our resort development group product and confidence is an important factor in the purchase consideration. Furthermore, resort club product does not have the same sense of scarcity as other types of real estate so purchasers are under less pressure to buy.

REAL ESTATE OPERATING PROFIT

Operating profit from real estate sales decreased from $85.1 million in 2002 to $75.0 million in 2003. The profit margin was 14.6% in 2003 compared with 17.4% in 2002. The reduction in margin was due to a number of factors, including:

- The write-off of $3.3 million of costs at Copper in connection with various projects that are on hold pending a strengthening of the Colorado market.
- A write-down of $3.0 million in connection with two projects at Mountain Creek. Sales of these projects had slowed because of an environmental lawsuit (that has now been settled), resulting in increased holding costs. In addition we have projected more conservative sales prices for unsold inventory.
- Lower margins in 2003 for the resort club group. Marketing and sales costs increased to 57% of revenue in 2003 from 48% in 2002 as a result of the difficult market conditions.

  Excluding the impact of the factors listed above, the profit margin in 2003 would have been 16.7%.

REAL ESTATE PRE-SALES

At August 31, 2003, we had pre-sold real estate revenue of $460 million that we expect to close in fiscal 2004. This compares with pre-sold revenue this time last year of $370 million for delivery in fiscal 2003. In addition, we have $65 million of pre-sales for delivery in fiscal 2005. This does not include projects that will be undertaken by Leisura (see Liquidity and Capital Resources), which has $260 million of pre-sales for delivery in fiscal 2004 and 2005. Our strategy of pre-selling projects before the start of construction reduces market risk and increases the predictability of real estate earnings.

CAPITALIZATION OF COSTS TO REAL ESTATE

Generally accepted accounting practice for real estate requires that all costs in connection with the development of real estate be capitalized to properties under development and then expensed in the period when the properties are closed and the revenue is recognized. Such costs include land and building costs as well as overhead costs of personnel directly involved in the development, construction and sale of real estate, and interest on debt used to fund real estate costs. The capitalized interest comprises interest on specific real estate debt (i.e., construction financing) and interest on the portion of general corporate debt used to fund real estate development expenditures.

The book value of properties increased from $867.8 million at June 30, 2002 to $1,067.3 million at June 30, 2003. The strengthening of the value of the Canadian dollar from a year-end rate of Cdn$1.52:US$1.00 in 2002 to Cdn$1.35:US$1.00 in 2003 increased the reported book value of properties by $26.3 million. Other factors responsible for the increase include:

- A net increase of $73.3 million in the book value of commercial space resulting from the completion of new properties at Whistler, Mammoth, Sandestin, Squaw Valley, Lake Las Vegas and Blue Mountain and the sale of commercial properties at Tremblant.
- An increase of $26.1 million in the book value of resort club properties mainly due to the new resort club locations under construction at Blue Mountain and Zihuatanejo, Mexico.

  The book value of properties to be sold to Leisura was $73.8 million at June 30, 2003. We expect to transfer the majority of these properties in the first two quarters of fiscal 2004.

  With the completion and closing of projects currently under construction and with the development of most new projects to take place in Leisura, the book value of our properties is expected to decline significantly in 2004.

RENTAL PROPERTIES

Effective July 1, 2002, we changed our plans for commercial properties. Instead of holding them as long-term revenue-producing investments, existing commercial properties would be sold and commercial properties developed in the future would be developed for the purpose of sale. In 2003 we sold the majority of our commercial properties at Tremblant and we plan to sell our remaining portfolio of commercial properties. Rental revenue and rental expenses relating to these properties were capitalized during 2003. In 2002 rental property revenue of $8.0 million and rental property expenses of $5.0 million were included in the statement of operations.

REVIEW OF CORPORATE OPERATIONS

INTEREST AND OTHER INCOME

Interest and other income was $2.4 million in 2003, up from $1.1 million in 2002 due mainly to dividend income from Compagnie des Alpes (CDA) and higher interest income net of losses on asset disposals.

In July 2002 we sold 55% of our investment in CDA and at the same time ceased to exercise significant influence over CDA's affairs. In 2003 we therefore accounted for CDA on a cost basis, whereas in 2002 we used the equity basis and recorded income from equity accounted investment of $3.9 million. Subsequent to June 30, 2003, we sold the balance of our investment in CDA. Both the sale in July 2002 and the sale subsequent to June 30, 2003 were for proceeds approximately equal to the book value of our investment.

INTEREST COSTS

Interest expense increased from $43.1 million in 2002 to $47.1 million in 2003. We incurred total interest costs (including financing fees and amortization of deferred financing costs) of $102.9 million in 2003 compared with $83.4 million in 2002. The increase was due mainly to interest on the $137-million 10.5% senior unsecured notes issued in October 2002, partially offset by interest on the Cdn. $125-million 6.75% unsecured debentures repaid in December 2002. In addition we had higher construction loan interest due to increased construction activity and the Winter Park capital lease added $2.2 million of interest. In total, $55.5 million of this interest was capitalized to properties under development, $14.9 million of which was subsequently expensed in 2003 when the properties were closed.

DEPRECIATION AND AMORTIZATION

Depreciation and amortization expense increased from $65.4 million in 2002 to $67.5 million in 2003. The increase was due mainly to assuming control of Winter Park.

GENERAL AND ADMINISTRATIVE COSTS

All general and administrative (G&A) costs incurred by our resorts in connection with the ski and resort operations business are included in ski and resort operations expenses. Similarly, G&A costs incurred in the development of real estate are initially capitalized to properties, and then expensed to real estate costs in the period when the properties are closed. Corporate G&A costs, which mainly comprise executive employee costs, public company costs, audit and legal fees, corporate information technology costs and head office occupancy costs are disclosed as a separate line in the statement of operations. The breakdown of G&A costs for 2003 and 2002 was as follows:

(MILLIONS)		2003	PROPORTION (%)		2002	PROPORTION (%)
Corporate G&A costs	$	14.9	12.6	$	12.2	11.1
G&A expenses of ski and resort operations business		65.1	55.2		55.9	50.8
Previously capitalized G&A costs expensed in real estate cost of sales		16.5	14.0		15.4	14.0
Total G&A costs expensed during the year		96.5	81.8		83.5	75.9
Net G&A costs of real estate business capitalized to properties		21.5	18.2		26.6	24.1
Total G&A costs incurred during the year	$	118.0	100.0	$	110.1	100.0

Corporate G&A costs increased from $12.2 million in 2002 to $14.9 million in 2003 due mainly to higher compensation and pension costs, and increased insurance, legal and audit expenses. Including the G&A costs of our operations and real estate divisions, we expensed 81.8% of general and administrative expenses in 2003 compared with 75.9% in 2002.

WRITE-DOWN OF TECHNOLOGY ASSETS

When we acquired our network of resorts we inherited many different information technology (IT) systems. This impeded our ability to share information and build synergies across resorts. Where we introduced new IT systems, we used a standardized approach, however we recognized that we needed to move to greater standardization of legacy IT systems. During the fourth quarter of 2003 we therefore wrote off $9.1 million of IT systems that we plan to replace. Furthermore, in 2003 we reorganized and downsized RezRez, our central reservations business. RezRez had expanded into several warm-weather destinations but the expansion was not successful. We therefore decided to abandon these locations to focus on our core ski destinations. In light of this, we reviewed the value of RezRez assets and took a write-down of $3.2 million for various of its IT assets in the fourth quarter.

INCOME TAXES

We provided for income taxes of $6.2 million in 2003 compared with $9.5 million in 2002. This equates to an effective tax rate of 12.0% in both years. Note 13 to the consolidated financial statements provides a reconciliation between income tax at the statutory rate (38.0% and 41.2%, respectively, in 2003 and 2002) and the actual income tax charge.

NON-CONTROLLING INTEREST

We have a 23% limited partner in the two partnerships that own Whistler Blackcomb. The results of the two partnerships are fully consolidated with the outside partner's share of earnings shown as non-controlling interest. Non-controlling interest decreased from $11.7 million in 2002 to $11.3 million in 2003, reflecting reduced ski and resort operations earnings due to the slow start to the season and the impact of the war in Iraq and SARS on business, primarily in March.

DISCONTINUED OPERATIONS

Our consolidated financial statements disclose the results of our non-resort real estate business as discontinued operations. The discontinued operations incurred a loss of $0.6 million in 2003 compared with a loss of $0.1 million in 2002. Losses (or net income) from discontinued operations accrue to the holders of the non-resort preferred ("NRP") shares and any cash flows generated by the discontinued operations are paid to the NRP shareholders to redeem their shares. In December 2002 the discontinued operations were wound up and all the remaining NRP shares were redeemed.

LIQUIDITY AND CAPITAL RESOURCES

Generating free cash flow continues to be a high priority for us. Free cash flow does not have a standardized meaning prescribed by generally accepted accounting principles ("GAAP"). We calculate it as follows:

(MILLIONS)	2003		2002
Cash provided by (used in) continuing operating activities [1]	$ (26.6)	$	5.7
Investment in ski and resort operations assets ("capex")	(64.5)		(91.5)
Free cash flow	$ (91.1)	$	(85.8)

[1] A reconciliation between net earnings as determined by Canadian GAAP and cash provided by (used in) continuing operating activities is shown in the Consolidated Statements of Cash Flows.

In 2003 our results showed negative free cash flow of $91.1 million compared with negative free cash flow of $85.8 million in 2002. We had expected positive free cash flow in 2003, however the slowdown in the travel and leisure sector, made worse by concerns over the war in Iraq and SARS, reduced operating cash flow from our ski and resort operations businesses. Cash flow from our real estate business was impacted by delayed completions of some projects and slow sales in Colorado, although generally demand for our products has been robust. On the positive side we reduced resort capex to about $65 million, significantly below prior years, and we sold some non-core assets.

Over the past few years, as we started to build out our villages and install infrastructure, our real estate business has been a significant user of cash. In both 2003 and 2002 we were free cash flow positive before making investments to grow our real estate business. During 2003 we implemented a strategy – the Leisura partnerships – that will allow us to both reduce the capital required for real estate and to grow the business.

We are also focused on increasing cash flow from our ski and resort operations businesses. We have a number of initiatives at our resorts to increase revenue (e.g., customer relationship management (CRM) and E-commerce programs, more packaging of services and maximizing sales channels) and to reduce costs (e.g., shared-services model in Colorado and elsewhere, downsizing of RezRez and eliminating discretionary expenses). Given the strong competitive position of our resorts, we do not need to invest as much in capex as we did in 2002 and prior years. We expect future resort capex requirements to remain close to 2003 levels (at approximately the same amount as depreciation and amortization expense). We also plan to grow our fee-based businesses (e.g., golf course and lodging management) and we can do this by investing minimal capital.

We expect to generate free cash flow in fiscal 2004 and to use it to repay debt.

LEISURA PARTNERSHIPS

In 2003 we entered into two partnerships (one in Canada and one in the U.S., collectively referred to as "Leisura") that will have a significant impact on our capital structure and our capital requirements for real estate. Leisura is intended to carry out the ownership and financing of the bulk of our real estate production. By selling the bulk of our production-phase real estate to separate and independent entities we achieve several objectives, including:

- Significantly reducing the capital requirements needed to support the real estate business.
- Significantly reducing debt levels.
- Limiting our exposure to the risks of the production-phase real estate business.
- Implementing separate and appropriate capital structures for our resort business and our real estate business.

We will continue to undertake some development activity on our own account outside of the Leisura structure. This includes smaller townhome projects and single-family lots, which are not as capital intensive as condo-hotel and larger townhome projects, as well as resort club and fractional projects. In addition, we will carry out all development activity at certain resorts (e.g., Snowmass because it is a joint venture development or Les Arcs because construction is primarily purchaser-financed).

Intrawest is a minority partner in Leisura and we will account for our investment in Leisura on an equity basis. We will continue to identify land parcels for development and complete the master planning, project design and pre-sales process for all future real estate projects. Once a project has reached set pre-sale targets and construction is about to commence, Leisura will acquire the land parcels for the project from us at fair market value. By December 31, 2003, Leisura is expected to acquire land parcels for about 10 projects at seven resorts (none had been transferred at June 30, 2003). In future years, we expect to carry out the bulk of the real estate production at our resorts in a similar fashion. There is no guarantee, however, that Leisura will acquire more land parcels from us in future years. For the projects that are sold to Leisura, we will provide development management services on a fee basis.

The Leisura partnerships have sufficient capital to be strong credit-worthy entities that can comfortably finance and carry out their business on a freestanding basis. Construction financing will be secured by the projects with recourse only to Leisura.

The formation of Leisura will result in a significant reduction in our net debt in 2004. We will recover the bulk of our investment in projects currently under construction as they are completed over the next 12 months and our capital expenditures to support this part of our real estate business in future will be limited to our investment in Leisura. The difference between the large amount of capital recovered from current projects as they complete (approximately 80% of the units in these projects are pre-sold) and the much smaller investment in Leisura will generate significant cash flow that will be used to reduce debt.

CASH FLOWS IN 2003 COMPARED WITH 2002

The major sources and uses of cash in 2003 and 2002 are summarized in the table below. This table should be read in conjunction with the Consolidated Statements of Cash Flows, which are more detailed as prescribed by GAAP.

(MILLIONS)	2003	2002	CHANGE
Funds from continuing operations	$ 122.8	$ 128.6	$ (5.8)
Acquisitions, resort capex and other investments	(39.4)	(107.1)	67.7
Net cash flow from other net assets	14.6	44.3	(29.7)
Funds available before net investment in real estate	98.0	65.8	32.2
Net investment in real estate developed for sale	(163.8)	(163.2)	(0.6)
Net cash flow from operating and investing activities	(65.8)	(97.4)	31.6
Net financing inflows	115.9	87.7	28.2
Increase (decrease) in cash	$ 50.1	$ (9.7)	$ 59.8

Funds from continuing operations generated $122.8 million of cash flow in 2003, down from $128.6 million in 2002 as reduced real estate profits and increased interest and G&A expenses were partially offset by higher EBITDA from ski and resort operations.

Acquisitions, resort capex and other investments used $39.4 million of cash in 2003, down from $107.1 million in 2002. Acquisitions and resort capex used $6.0 million and $26.9 million, respectively, less cash in 2003 than 2002 while proceeds from asset disposals, net of other investments, generated $34.8 million more cash in 2003 than 2002.

Assuming control of Winter Park used $2.8 million cash in 2003 as the majority of the purchase price was financed through a capital lease. In 2002 we had acquired Big Island Country Club in Hawaii for a cash payment of $8.9 million. We do not plan to invest significant capital in acquisitions in the near term. We will continue to seek opportunities to expand our businesses but do so in ways (e.g., engaging in management contracts or entering joint ventures) that limit our capital requirements.

We spent $64.5 million on resort capex in 2003, down from $91.5 million in 2002. Each year we spend $25 million to $30 million on maintenance capex at our resorts. Maintenance capex is considered non-discretionary (since it is required to maintain the existing level of service) and comprises such things as snow grooming machine or golf cart replacement, snowmaking equipment upgrades and building refurbishments. Expansion capex (e.g., new lifts or new restaurants) is considered discretionary and the annual amount spent varies year by year. We expect maintenance and expansion capex to be approximately the same in 2004 as in 2003.

Proceeds from non-core asset sales (mainly 55% of our investment in Compagnie des Alpes and employee housing units at Whistler Blackcomb) net of new investments generated $28.0 million of cash in 2003. Subsequent to year-end we sold the balance of our investment in Compagnie des Alpes for $12.5 million. In 2002 we sold Mont Ste. Marie and Sabino Springs golf course but these sales were offset by new investments, resulting in a net investment in other assets of $6.7 million. We have identified other non-core assets for disposal and we will continue our program of selling these assets in the future.

Other net assets provided cash of $14.6 million in 2003 compared with $44.3 million in 2002. This represents the cash flow from changes in receivables, other assets, payables and deferred revenue.

Our businesses provided cash flow of $98.0 million in 2003 compared with $65.8 million in 2002, before net new investments in real estate. We invested $163.8 million in real estate in 2003, approximately the same as in 2002. We had expected our net investment to be lower in 2003, however the construction delays at Squaw Valley and Lake Las Vegas and slower transfers of properties to Leisura delayed cost recoveries until fiscal 2004. We expect to recover a portion of our investment in real estate in fiscal 2004 as units currently under construction are completed and closed and new real estate production moves to Leisura.

In total, our operating and investing activities used $65.8 million of cash in 2003, down from $97.4 million in 2002. We also paid $12.0 million and $11.3 million, respectively, in 2003 and 2002 for dividends to our shareholders and distributions to the limited partner in Whistler Blackcomb and we expect these payments to be approximately the same in 2004. Amounts paid to redeem and repurchase NRP shares were $6.7 million in 2003 and $0.4 million in 2002. We have now redeemed all the NRP shares. Net borrowings of $129.9 million and $46.3 million in 2003 and 2002, respectively, as well as proceeds of share issuances of $4.8 million and $53.0 million in 2003 and 2002, respectively, funded these cash flows.

DEBT AND LIQUIDITY POSITION

At June 30, 2003, we had net debt (i.e., bank and other indebtedness net of cash) of $1,134.1 million compared with $979.2 million at June 30, 2002. Part of the increase in net debt was due to the strengthening of the Canadian dollar, particularly in the fourth quarter. The change in the exchange rate from Cdn$1.52:US$1.00 at last year end to Cdn$1.35:US$1.00 at this year end increased the reported amount of Canadian dollar-denominated debt by $39.9 million at June 30, 2003.

As discussed above, we expect to generate significant free cash flow in fiscal 2004 and to reduce net debt. We are confident that we can achieve this objective because of the Leisura transaction and the current high level of pre-sales of real estate that is being completed within Intrawest. Not only does the Leisura transaction significantly reduce our capital requirements for real estate but it also reduces the risk that delays in construction completion will result in higher debt balances because these debt balances are obligations of Leisura, not Intrawest.

Over half of our bank and other indebtedness ($658.4 million) at June 30, 2003 is not due for repayment until after 2008. With respect to the balance of our bank and other indebtedness, $287.2 million is due to be repaid in fiscal 2004 of which $229.1 million, or approximately 80%, relates to construction financing that is covered more than 100% by real estate pre-sales. As these projects close, we will repay the construction loans as well as other debt. Our senior credit facility, which had a balance of $240.2 million at year-end, is due in fiscal 2005 and we expect to renew this facility on maturity.

We have a number of revolving credit facilities to meet our short-term capital needs. These include a $365-million facility at the corporate level, of which $240 million was drawn at June 30, 2003. In addition, several of our resorts have lines of credit in the range of $5 million to $10 million each to fund seasonal cash requirements. Since Leisura will be undertaking most of the future real estate development, we have not renewed the three revolving credit facilities that we had last year for real estate construction. Instead we will finance any projects that we develop through one-off project-specific loans. We believe that these credit facilities, combined with cash on hand and internally generated cash flow, are adequate to finance all of our normal operating needs.

BUSINESS RISKS

We are exposed to various risks and uncertainties in the normal course of our business that can cause volatility in our earnings. Our ski and resort operations and real estate businesses are managed to deal with risks that are common to most companies; i.e., the risks of severe economic downturn, competition and currency fluctuations, and the more industry-specific risks of unfavorable weather conditions, seasonality of operations and development issues.

ECONOMIC DOWNTURN

A severe economic downturn could reduce spending on resort vacations and weaken sales of recreational real estate.

Our results in both 2003 and 2002 (years that saw a significant slowdown in the economy) provide evidence of our ability to deal with an economic downturn. Ski and resort operations EBITDA for 2003 and 2002 were only 3.7% and 0.9%, respectively, below our record EBITDA in 2001, on a same-resort basis. There are two main reasons for this:

- The strong competitive position of each of our resorts due to the villages at their base and the quality of their on-mountain facilities. This has also created a loyal customer base that is strongly committed to our resorts.
- The profile of our customer base, who have incomes well above the national average and are therefore less likely to have their vacation plans impacted by a recession.

Real estate developers face two major risks from an economic downturn: land risk and completed inventory risk. Land risk arises when land is purchased with debt and economic conditions deteriorate resulting in higher holding costs and reduced profitability, or worse, loan defaults and foreclosure. We have reduced our land risk by generally acquiring land at low cost with the purchase of a resort or by securing land through options and joint ventures. Completed inventory risk arises when completed units cannot be sold and construction financing cannot be repaid. Often this risk arises because many developers are supplying units to the market and since we control most of the supply at our resorts, this risk is reduced. We have also mitigated this risk by pre-selling a significant portion of units prior to commencement of, and during, construction.

COMPETITION

The mountain resort industry has significant barriers to entry (e.g., very high start-up costs, significant environmental hurdles) that prevent new resorts from being created. Competition therefore is essentially confined to existing resorts. Our resorts compete for destination visitors with other mountain resorts in Canada, the United States, Europe and Japan, and with other leisure industry companies, such as cruise lines. They also compete for day skiers with other ski areas within each resort's local market area. Skier visits in North America have been relatively static over the past 10 years, which has increased competition between resort owners.

Our strategy has been to acquire resorts that have natural competitive advantages (e.g., in terms of location, vertical drop and quality of terrain) and to enhance those advantages by upgrading the facilities on the mountain and building resort villages at the base. Our principal strength compared with industry competitors is our ability to combine expertise in resort operations and real estate development, particularly in building master-planned resort villages. Increasingly the village has become the dominant attraction in generating visits to a resort.

We own substantially all of the supply of developable land at the base of our resorts and hence competition in real estate is somewhat restricted. Expertise in all aspects of the development process, including resort master-planning, project design, construction, sales and marketing, and property management also gives us a distinct competitive advantage.

CURRENCY FLUCTUATIONS

Over the past several years our Canadian resort operations have benefited from the lower Canadian dollar relative to other currencies, and particularly against the U.S. dollar. This has made vacationing in Canada more affordable for foreign visitors and it has encouraged Canadians to vacation at home. A significant shift in the value of the Canadian dollar, particularly against its U.S. counterpart, could impact earnings at Canadian resorts.

We finance our U.S. assets with U.S. dollar debt and our Canadian assets with Canadian dollar debt. Generally we service debt with revenue denominated in the same currency. In addition, cash flow generated by Canadian operations is generally retained in Canada and invested in expanding our Canadian assets. Similarly cash flow generated at our U.S. resorts is generally reinvested in the United States. Cross-border cash transactions and currency exchanges are kept to a minimum.

Since we report earnings in U.S. dollars but our income is derived from both Canadian and U.S. sources, we are exposed to foreign currency exchange risk in our reported earnings. Revenues and expenses of our Canadian operations will be impacted by changes in exchange rates when they are reported in U.S. dollars. We estimate that a 10% increase in the average value for the fiscal year of the Canadian dollar relative to the U.S. dollar would result in a 5% increase in our reported net income, while a 10% decline in the average value of the Canadian dollar would result in a 4% decrease in our reported net income. The impact of Canadian/U.S. dollar exchange rate changes on the balance sheet are reflected in the foreign currency translation amount included in shareholders' equity and does not affect reported earnings.

UNFAVORABLE WEATHER CONDITIONS

Our ability to attract visitors to our resorts is influenced by weather conditions and the amount of snowfall during the ski season.

We manage our exposure to unfavorable weather in three ways: by being geographically diversified, by seeking to spread visits to our resorts as evenly as possible through the season and by investing in snowmaking. Geographically diversified companies like ours can reduce the risk associated with a particular region's weather patterns. Every ski season since 1995, favorable and unfavorable weather conditions at different times across North America have offset one another, allowing us to come within 3% of our budgeted winter season ski and resort operations revenue on a same-resort basis. The more a resort can attract visitors evenly through the season the less vulnerable it is to unfavorable weather at a particular time. We seek to spread visits to our resorts by marketing to destination visitors who book in advance, stay several days and are less likely than day visitors to change their vacation plans, and by attempting to increase visits mid-week and at non-peak times. Investing in snowmaking also mitigates the impact of poor natural snow conditions. Snowmaking is particularly important in the East due to the number of competing resorts and less reliable snowfall. We have an average of 92% snowmaking coverage across our five eastern resorts.

SEASONALITY OF OPERATIONS

Ski and resort operations are highly seasonal. In fiscal 2003, 67% of our ski and resort operations revenue was generated during the period from December to March. Furthermore during this period a significant portion of ski and resort operations revenue is generated on certain holidays, particularly Christmas/New Year, Presidents' Day and school spring breaks, and on weekends. Conversely, Sandestin's peak operating season occurs during the summer months, partially offsetting the seasonality of the mountain resorts. Our real estate operations tend to be somewhat seasonal as well, with construction primarily taking place during the summer and the majority of sales closing in the December to June period. This seasonality of operations impacts reported quarterly earnings. The operating results for any particular quarter are not necessarily indicative of the operating results for a subsequent quarter or for the full fiscal year.

We have taken steps to balance our revenue and earnings throughout the year by investing in four-season amenities (e.g., golf) and growing summer and shoulder-season businesses. As a result of these initiatives, the proportion of ski and resort operations revenue earned outside the historically strong third fiscal quarter has increased to 45.2% in 2003 from 32.7% in 1997.

DEVELOPMENT ISSUES

As a real estate developer we face the following industry-specific risks:

- Zoning approvals or project permits could be withheld.
- Construction and other development costs could exceed budget.
- Project completion could be delayed.
- Purchasers could fail to close.

Our experience in resort master planning equips us to deal with municipal approval agencies. In addition, our approach of consulting with all community stakeholders during the planning process helps to ensure that we run into less resistance at public hearings.

We are not in the construction business – we engage general contractors to construct our real estate projects. Having fixed-price contracts with completion penalties reduces our exposure to cost overruns and construction delays. As our experience showed this year, some construction delays are inevitable in the real estate business, particularly given the location and variable weather conditions at our mountain resorts, however we do not anticipate that they would have a material impact on our earnings in any particular year.

Our pre-sales contracts require purchasers to put down 20% deposits, i.e., generally in the range of $50,000 to $150,000, which they forfeit if they do not close. Historically very few purchasers have failed to close.

Leisura rather than Intrawest is at risk for cost overruns, completion delays and purchaser contract defaults on any project that it purchases. We continue to be at risk for zoning and permit approvals since these approvals must be in hand before projects are sold to Leisura.

There is a risk that Leisura will not purchase land parcels from Intrawest in future years. The Leisura partners have, however, expressed a strong interest in extending their involvement in future years and we expect them to do so. In the event that the current partners decide not to participate in future projects we believe we will be able to identify alternative investors.

WORLD EVENTS

World events such as the terrorist attacks on September 11, 2001, the war in Iraq and the SARS outbreak disrupt domestic and international travel and reduce visits, or change the mix of visits, to our resorts. Often these types of events happen suddenly and cannot be prepared for. As we have shown over the past two years, we have been less impacted by these events than many other leisure and hospitality companies due to the high degree of commitment of our customers (e.g., as season pass holders or property owners), the significant proportion of our visitors who drive to our resorts (approximately 85% of all resort visits) and our ability to communicate with our database of customers and market products to them.

CRITICAL ACCOUNTING POLICIES

This discussion and analysis is based upon our consolidated financial statements, which have been prepared in accordance with GAAP in Canada. The preparation of these financial statements requires us to make estimates and judgments that affect the reported amounts of assets, liabilities, revenues and expenses and disclosure of contingencies. These estimates and judgments are based on factors that are inherently uncertain. On an ongoing basis, we evaluate our estimates based on historical experience and on various other assumptions that we believe are reasonable under the circumstances. Actual amounts could differ from those based on such estimates and assumptions.

We believe the following critical accounting policies call for management to make significant judgments and estimates.

USEFUL LIVES FOR DEPRECIABLE ASSETS　Ski and resort operations assets and administrative furniture, computer equipment, software and leasehold improvements are depreciated using both the declining balance and straight-line basis (depending on the asset category) over the estimated useful life of the asset. Assets may become obsolete or require replacement before the end of their estimated useful life in which case any remaining undepreciated costs must be written off.

FUTURE NET CASH FLOWS FROM PROPERTIES   **Properties under development and held for sale, which totaled $1,067.3 million at June, 30, 2003, are recorded at the lower of cost and net realizable value. In determining net realizable value it is necessary, on a non-discounted basis, to estimate the future cash flows from each individual project for the period from the start of land servicing to the sell-out of the last unit. This involves making assumptions about project demand and sales prices, construction and other development costs, and project financing. Changes in our assumptions could affect future cash flows from properties leading to reduced real estate profits or potentially property write-downs.**

RECOVERABILITY OF AMOUNTS RECEIVABLE   **At June 30, 2003, amounts receivable totaled $203.6 million. We regularly review the recoverability of amounts receivable and record allowances for any amounts that we deem to be uncollectible. Disputes with our customers or changes in their financial condition could alter our expectation of recoverability and additional allowances may be required.**

VALUE OF FUTURE INCOME TAX ASSETS AND LIABILITIES   **In determining our income tax provision, we are required to interpret tax legislation in a variety of jurisdictions and to make assumptions about the expected timing of the reversal of future tax assets and liabilities. In the event that our interpretations differed from those of the taxing authorities or that the timing of reversals is not as anticipated, the tax provision could increase or decrease in future periods.**

At June 30, 2003, we had accumulated $117.2 million of non-capital loss carryforwards which expire at various times through 2023. We have determined that it is more likely than not that the benefit of these losses will be realized in the future and we have recorded future tax assets of $35.8 million related to them. If it is determined in the future that it is more likely than not that all or a part of these future tax assets will not be realized, we will make a charge to earnings at that time.

OUTLOOK

As we move into fiscal 2004 we are focused on two primary financial objectives – to improve profitability and returns on capital from our existing businesses and to generate free cash flow.

Our goal is to increase profits in the ski and resort operations business by both growing revenue and containing costs. As we build more accommodation in our villages we will open up revenue-generating opportunities in lodging management and indirectly in our other businesses. We intend to utilize our capability in CRM and direct marketing to increase occupancy levels. Given the shortened booking window, these programs have the advantage that they can be introduced quickly and, since they are targeted to existing customers and good prospects, their rate of success is enhanced. They are also more cost-effective than other marketing programs.

We expect to reduce costs at our resorts by capitalizing on our network to take advantage of economies of scale. Standardized processes and technology will allow us to consolidate operations. The consolidation of our Colorado businesses in fiscal 2004 is the first step. Since new capex for ski and resort operations is expected to remain at about the same level as annual depreciation, these revenue growth and cost containment initiatives are expected to lead to a higher return on capital.

Our new organizational structure for the real estate development group is expected to improve our efficiency and our control, leading to stronger real estate margins in the future. This structure also facilitates growth since resources for multiple resorts are pooled.

As we assembled and improved our network of resorts we were significantly cash flow negative. We are now moving to a less capital-intensive business model with lower capital expenditures for our resorts and reduced infrastructure spending for real estate. We are also focused on growing our fee-based businesses (e.g., lodging, golf course and reservations management), which require minimal capital investment. We expect the Leisura transaction to produce free cash flow from our real estate business in fiscal 2004. This will occur as we recover the book value of current projects, and expenditures for the most capital-intensive projects in the future are restricted to our investment in Leisura. As we generate free cash flow we expect to pay down debt and improve our credit ratios.

ADDITIONAL INFORMATION

The term EBITDA does not have a standardized meaning prescribed by GAAP and may not be comparable to similarly titled measures presented by other publicly traded companies. A reconciliation between net earnings as determined in accordance with Canadian GAAP and Total Company EBITDA is presented in the table below.

(MILLIONS)	YEAR ENDED JUNE 30	
	2003	2002
Income before tax	$ 52.3	$ 79.8
Depreciation and amortization	67.5	65.4
Interest expense	47.1	43.1
Interest in real estate costs	32.4	27.9
Write-down of technology assets	12.3	—
Interest and other income	(2.4)	(5.0)
Total Company EBITDA	$ 209.2	$ 211.2

QUARTERLY FINANCIAL SUMMARY

(in millions of dollars, except per share amounts)

	2003 QUARTERS				2002 QUARTERS			
	1ST	2 ND	3RD	4TH	1ST	2ND	3RD	4TH
Total revenue	$ 112.7	$ 208.0	$ 402.6	$ 363.3	$ 93.7	$ 231.4	$ 342.1	$ 318.8
Income (loss) from continuing operations	(11.1)	3.4	56.8	(14.3)	(9.8)	6.0	56.2	6.2
Results of discontinued operations	0.0	(0.6)	0.0	0.0	0.2	(0.1)	0.0	(0.1)
Net income (loss)	(11.1)	2.8	56.8	(14.3)	(9.6)	5.9	56.2	6.0
PER COMMON SHARE:								
Income (loss) from continuing operations								
Basic	(0.23)	0.07	1.20	(0.30)	(0.22)	0.14	1.28	0.14
Diluted	(0.23)	0.07	1.19	(0.30)	(0.22)	0.14	1.25	0.13
Net income (loss)								
Basic	(0.23)	0.07	1.20	(0.30)	(0.22)	0.14	1.28	0.14
Diluted	(0.23)	0.07	1.19	(0.30)	(0.22)	0.14	1.25	0.13

Management's Responsibility

The consolidated financial statements of Intrawest Corporation have been prepared by management and approved by the Board of Directors of the Company. Management is responsible for the preparation and presentation of the information contained in the consolidated financial statements. The Company maintains appropriate systems of internal control, policies and procedures that provide management with reasonable assurance that assets are safeguarded and that financial records are reliable and form a proper basis for preparation of financial statements.

The Company's independent auditors, KPMG LLP, have been appointed by the shareholders to express their professional opinion on the fairness of the consolidated financial statements. Their report is included below.

The Board of Directors ensures that management fulfills its responsibilities for financial reporting and internal control through an Audit Committee which is composed entirely of outside directors. This committee reviews the consolidated financial statements and reports to the Board of Directors. The auditors have full and direct access to the Audit Committee.

Joe S. Houssian
Chairman, President and Chief Executive Officer
SEPTEMBER 2, 2003

Daniel O. Jarvis
Executive Vice President and Chief Financial Officer

Auditors' Report to the Shareholders

We have audited the consolidated balance sheets of Intrawest Corporation as at June 30, 2003 and 2002 and the consolidated statements of operations, retained earnings, and cash flows for the years then ended. These financial statements are the responsibility of the Company's management. Our responsibility is to express an opinion on these financial statements based on our audits.

We conducted our audits in accordance with Canadian generally accepted auditing standards. Those standards require that we plan and perform an audit to obtain reasonable assurance whether the financial statements are free of material misstatement. An audit includes examining, on a test basis, evidence supporting the amounts and disclosures in the financial statements. An audit also includes assessing the accounting principles used and significant estimates made by management, as well as evaluating the overall financial statement presentation.

In our opinion, these consolidated financial statements present fairly, in all material respects, the financial position of the Company as at June 30, 2003 and 2002 and the results of its operations and its cash flows for the years then ended in accordance with Canadian generally accepted accounting principles.

KPMG LLP
Chartered Accountants
Vancouver, Canada
SEPTEMBER 2, 2003

Consolidated Statements of Operations

For the years ended June 30, 2003 and 2002
(In thousands of United States dollars, except per share amounts)

	2003	2002
REVENUE:		
Ski and resort operations	$ 571,527	$ 485,142
Real estate sales	512,695	487,775
Rental properties	—	8,038
Interest and other income	2,417	1,115
Income from equity accounted investment	—	3,901
	1,086,639	985,971
EXPENSES:		
Ski and resort operations	454,861	377,801
Real estate costs	437,690	402,700
Rental properties	—	4,963
Interest (note 16)	47,142	43,072
Depreciation and amortization	67,516	65,434
Corporate general and administrative	14,889	12,175
Write-down of technology assets (note 8(b))	12,270	—
	1,034,368	906,145
Income before undernoted	52,271	79,826
Provision for income taxes (note 13)	6,243	9,549
Income before non-controlling interest and discontinued operations	46,028	70,277
Non-controlling interest	11,274	11,675
Income from continuing operations	34,754	58,602
Results of discontinued operations (note 4)	(578)	(122)
Net income	$ 34,176	$ 58,480
INCOME FROM CONTINUING OPERATIONS PER COMMON SHARE:		
Basic	$ 0.73	$ 1.33
Diluted	0.73	1.31
NET INCOME PER COMMON SHARE:		
Basic	0.73	1.33
Diluted	0.73	1.31

See accompanying notes to consolidated financial statements.

Consolidated Balance Sheets

June 30, 2003 and 2002
(In thousands of United States dollars)

	2003	2002
ASSETS		
CURRENT ASSETS:		
Cash and cash equivalents	$ 126,832	$ 76,689
Amounts receivable (note 7)	126,725	109,948
Other assets (note 8(a))	123,610	88,062
Resort properties (note 6)	662,197	399,572
Future income taxes (note 13)	10,619	7,536
	1,049,983	681,807
Ski and resort operations (note 5)	918,727	841,841
Properties (note 6):		
Resort	405,100	461,893
Discontinued operations	—	6,325
	405,100	468,218
Amounts receivable (note 7)	76,842	64,734
Other assets (note 8(b))	65,070	94,332
Goodwill	—	15,985
	$2,515,722	$2,166,917
LIABILITIES AND SHAREHOLDERS' EQUITY		
CURRENT LIABILITIES:		
Amounts payable	$ 218,444	$ 195,254
Deferred revenue (note 10)	134,878	99,484
Bank and other indebtedness (note 9):		
Resort	287,176	279,297
Discontinued operations	—	2,750
	640,498	576,785
Bank and other indebtedness (note 9):		
Resort	973,743	773,790
Discontinued operations	—	82
	973,743	773,872
Due to joint venture partners (note 14)	5,388	3,963
Deferred revenue (note 10)	43,609	23,069
Future income taxes (note 13)	94,986	75,843
Non-controlling interest in subsidiaries	46,359	36,116
	1,804,583	1,489,648
Shareholders' equity:		
Capital stock (note 12)	460,742	466,899
Retained earnings	264,640	241,665
Foreign currency translation adjustment	(14,243)	(31,295)
	711,139	677,269
	$2,515,722	$2,166,917

Contingencies and commitments (note 15)
Subsequent event (note 8(b))

Approved on behalf of the Board:

Joe S. Houssian
Director

Paul M. Manheim
Director

See accompanying notes to consolidated financial statements.

Consolidated Statements of Retained Earnings

For the years ended June 30, 2003 and 2002
(In thousands of United States dollars)

	2003	2002
Retained earnings, beginning of year:		
As previously reported	$ 241,665	$ 187,922
Adjustment to reflect change in accounting for goodwill and intangibles, net of tax (note 2(t)(i))	(6,150)	—
As restated	235,515	187,922
Net income	34,176	58,480
Dividends	(5,051)	(4,737)
Retained earnings, end of year	$ 264,640	$ 241,665

See accompanying notes to consolidated financial statements.

Consolidated Statements of Cash Flows

For the years ended June 30, 2003 and 2002
(In thousands of United States dollars)

	2003	2002
CASH PROVIDED BY (USED IN):		
OPERATIONS:		
Income from continuing operations	$ 34,754	$ 58,602
Items not affecting cash:		
Depreciation and amortization	67,516	65,434
Future income taxes	(3,914)	(2,873)
Income from equity accounted investment	—	(3,901)
(Gain) loss on asset disposals, net of write-offs	858	(323)
Write-down of technology assets	12,270	—
Non-controlling interest	11,274	11,675
Funds from continuing operations	122,758	128,614
Recovery of costs through real estate sales	437,690	402,700
Acquisition and development of properties held for sale	(601,524)	(565,863)
Increase in amounts receivable, net	(12,109)	(8,936)
Changes in non-cash operating working capital (note 21)	26,590	49,191
Cash provided by (used in) continuing operating activities	(26,595)	5,706
Cash provided by discontinued operations	140	3,898
	(26,455)	9,604
FINANCING:		
Proceeds from bank and other borrowings	599,112	351,259
Repayments on bank and other borrowings	(469,235)	(304,933)
Issue of common shares for cash, net of issuance costs	4,782	53,037
Redemption and repurchase of non-resort preferred shares (note 12(a))	(6,697)	(358)
Dividends paid	(5,051)	(4,737)
Distributions to non-controlling interests	(6,923)	(6,534)
	115,988	87,734
INVESTMENTS:		
Expenditures on:		
Revenue-producing properties	—	(2,353)
Ski and resort operations assets	(64,546)	(91,490)
Other assets	(11,778)	(8,463)
Business acquisitions (note 3)	(2,849)	(8,876)
Proceeds from asset disposals	39,783	4,103
	(39,390)	(107,079)
Increase (decrease) in cash and cash equivalents	50,143	(9,741)
Cash and cash equivalents, beginning of year	76,689	86,430
Cash and cash equivalents, end of year	$ 126,832	$ 76,689

Supplementary information (note 21)
See accompanying notes to consolidated financial statements.

Notes to Consolidated Financial Statements

For the years ended June 30, 2003 and 2002
(Tabular amounts in thousands of United States dollars, unless otherwise indicated)

1 OPERATIONS:

Intrawest Corporation was formed by an amalgamation on November 23, 1979 under the Company Act (British Columbia) and was continued under the Canada Business Corporations Act on January 14, 2002. Through its subsidiaries, the Company is engaged in the development and operation of mountain and golf resorts principally throughout North America.

2 SIGNIFICANT ACCOUNTING POLICIES:

(a) BASIS OF PRESENTATION:

The consolidated financial statements are prepared in accordance with generally accepted accounting principles in Canada as prescribed by The Canadian Institute of Chartered Accountants ("CICA"). Information regarding United States generally accepted accounting principles as it affects the Company's consolidated financial statements is presented in note 22.

(b) PRINCIPLES OF CONSOLIDATION:

The consolidated financial statements include:

(i)   the accounts of the Company and its subsidiaries; and

(ii) the accounts of all incorporated and unincorporated joint ventures, including non-controlled partnerships, to the extent of the Company's interest in their respective assets, liabilities, revenues and expenses.

The Company's principal subsidiaries and joint ventures are as follows:

SUBSIDIARIES	PERCENTAGE INTEREST HELD BY THE COMPANY (%)
Blackcomb Skiing Enterprises Limited Partnership	77
Whistler Mountain Resort Limited Partnership	77
Intrawest/Lodestar Limited Partnership	100
IW Resorts Limited Partnership	100
Mont Tremblant Resorts and Company, Limited Partnership	100
Copper Mountain, Inc.	100
Intrawest California Holdings, Inc.	100
Intrawest Golf Holdings, Inc.	100
Intrawest Resort Ownership Corporation	100
Intrawest Retail Group, Inc.	100
Intrawest Sandestin Company, L.L.C.	100
Intrawest/Winter Park Holdings Corporation (note 3)	100
Mountain Creek Resort, Inc.	100
Mt. Tremblant Reservations Inc.	100
Playground Real Estate Inc.	100
Resort Reservations Network Inc.	100
Snowshoe Mountain, Inc.	100
Intrawest Golf Management (Canada) Ltd.	100
The Stratton Corporation	100

Notes to Consolidated Financial Statements

2 SIGNIFICANT ACCOUNTING POLICIES: (CONTINUED)

JOINT VENTURES AND NON-CONTROLLED PARTNERSHIPS (note 14)	PERCENTAGE INTEREST HELD BY THE COMPANY (%)
Alpine Helicopters Ltd.	45
Blue Mountain Resorts Limited	50
Blue River Land Company L.L.C.	50
Chateau M.T. Inc.	50
Intrawest/Brush Creek Development Company L.L.C.	50
Intrawest/Lodestar Golf Limited Partnership	73.7
Keystone/Intrawest L.L.C.	50
Mammoth Mountain Ski Area	59.5
Resort Ventures Limited Partnership	50

All significant intercompany balances and transactions have been eliminated.

(c) ACCOUNTING FOR INVESTMENTS:

The Company accounts for investments in which it is able to exercise significant influence in accordance with the equity method. Under the equity method, the original cost of the shares is adjusted for the Company's share of post-acquisition earnings or losses, less dividends.

(d) USE OF ESTIMATES:

The preparation of financial statements in conformity with generally accepted accounting principles requires management to make estimates and assumptions that affect the reported amounts of assets and liabilities and disclosure of contingent assets and liabilities at the date of the financial statements and the reported amounts of revenues and expenses during the reporting period. Actual results could differ from those estimates.

The significant areas requiring management estimates include the estimates of future net cash flows from properties, useful lives for depreciation, the recoverability of amounts receivable, and the value of future income tax assets and liabilities.

(e) CASH EQUIVALENTS:

The Company considers all highly liquid investments with terms to maturity of three months or less when acquired to be cash equivalents.

(f) PROPERTIES:

(i) Properties under development and held for sale:

Properties under development and held for sale are recorded at the lower of cost and net realizable value. Cost includes all expenditures incurred in connection with the acquisition, development and construction of these properties. These expenditures consist of all direct costs, interest on specific debt, interest on that portion of total costs financed by the Company's pooled debt, and an allocation of indirect overhead. Incidental operations related specifically to properties under development are treated as an increase in or a reduction of costs.

Effective July 1, 2002, the Company determined that it would no longer retain the commercial properties that it developed as long-term revenue-producing properties. Instead existing commercial properties would be sold and commercial properties developed in the future would be developed for the purpose of sale. Consequently from July 1, 2002, commercial properties are classified as properties under development and held for sale and net rental income before depreciation is capitalized to the cost of the property. Properties held for sale are not depreciated.

Costs associated with the development of sales locations of the vacation ownership business, including operating and general and administrative costs incurred until a location is fully operational, are capitalized. The results of incidental operations related specifically to a location are treated as an increase in or a reduction of costs during the start-up period. These net costs are amortized on a straight-line basis over seven years.

The Company defers costs directly relating to the acquisition of new properties and resorts which, in management's judgment, have a high probability of closing. If the acquisition is abandoned, any deferred costs are expensed immediately.

The Company provides for write-downs where the carrying value of a particular property exceeds its net realizable value.

(ii) Classification:

Properties that are currently under development for sale and properties available for sale are classified as current assets. Related bank and other indebtedness is classified as a current liability.

(g) SKI AND RESORT OPERATIONS:

The ski and resort operations assets are stated at cost less accumulated depreciation. Costs of ski lifts, area improvements and buildings are capitalized. Certain buildings, area improvements and equipment are located on leased or licensed land. Depreciation is provided over the estimated useful lives of each asset category using the declining balance method at annual rates as follows:

	(%)
Buildings	3.3 to 5.0
Ski lifts	5.0 to 8.0
Golf courses	2.0 to 3.3
Area improvements	2.0 to 3.3
Automotive, helicopters and other equipment	10.0 to 50.0
Leased vehicles	20.0 to 25.0

Inventories are recorded at the lower of cost and net realizable value, and consist primarily of retail goods, food and beverage products, and mountain operating supplies.

(h) ADMINISTRATIVE FURNITURE, COMPUTER EQUIPMENT, SOFTWARE AND LEASEHOLD IMPROVEMENTS:

Administrative furniture, computer equipment and software are stated at cost less accumulated depreciation. Included in software costs are any direct costs incurred developing internal use software. Depreciation of administrative furniture is provided using the declining balance method at annual rates of between 20% and 30%. Depreciation of computer equipment and software is provided using the straight-line method at annual rates of between 10% and 33 ⅓%.

Leasehold improvements are stated at cost less accumulated amortization. Amortization is provided using the straight-line method over the lease term.

(i) DEFERRED FINANCING COSTS:

Deferred financing costs consist of legal and other fees directly related to the debt financing of the Company's ski and resort operations. These costs are amortized to interest expense over the term of the related financing.

(j) GOODWILL AND INTANGIBLE ASSETS:

Goodwill represents the excess of purchase price over the fair value of identifiable assets acquired in a purchase business combination. Intangible assets with indefinite useful lives represent costs that have been allocated to brand names and trademarks. Effective July 1, 2002, the Company no longer amortizes goodwill and intangible assets with indefinite useful lives, but they are subject to impairment tests on at least an annual basis (see note 2(t)(i)) and additionally, whenever events and changes in circumstances suggest that the carrying amount may not be recoverable.

Intangible assets with finite useful lives are costs that have been allocated to contracts and customer lists and are amortized on a straight-line basis over their estimated useful lives.

(k) DEFERRED REVENUE:

Deferred revenue mainly comprises real estate deposits, season pass revenue, club initiation deposits, government grants and the exchange gains arising on the translation of long-term monetary items that are denominated in foreign currencies (note 2(o)). Deferred revenue which relates to the sale of season passes is recognized throughout the season based on the number of skier visits. Deferred revenue which relates to club initiation deposits is recognized on a straight-line basis over the estimated membership terms. Deferred revenue which relates to government grants for ski and resort operations assets is recognized on the same basis as the related assets are amortized. Deferred revenue which relates to government grants for properties under development is recognized as the properties are sold.

Notes to Consolidated Financial Statements

2 SIGNIFICANT ACCOUNTING POLICIES: (CONTINUED)

(l) GOVERNMENT ASSISTANCE:
The Company periodically applies for financial assistance under available government incentive programs. Non-repayable government assistance relating to capital expenditures is reflected as a reduction of the cost of such assets.

(m) REVENUE RECOGNITION:
(i)   Ski and resort operations revenue is recognized as the service is provided. Commission revenues derived from airline ticket, hotel, car and cruise reservations are recognized when the customer first utilizes the service. Commission revenue is recorded at the net of the amount charged to the customer and the amount paid to the supplier.

(ii)   Revenue from the sale of properties is recorded when title to the completed unit is conveyed to the purchaser, the purchaser becomes entitled to occupancy and the purchaser has made a payment that is appropriate in the circumstances.

(iii) Points revenue associated with membership in the vacation ownership business of Club Intrawest (which revenue is included in real estate sales) is recognized when the purchaser has paid the amount due on closing, all contract documentation has been executed and all other significant conditions of sale are met.

(n) FUTURE INCOME TAXES:
The Company follows the asset and liability method of accounting for income taxes. Under such method, future tax assets and liabilities are recognized for future tax consequences attributable to differences between the financial statement carrying amounts of existing assets and liabilities and their respective tax bases.

Future tax assets and liabilities are measured using enacted or substantively enacted tax rates expected to apply to taxable income in the years in which those temporary differences are expected to be recovered or settled. The effect on future tax assets and liabilities of a change in tax rates is recognized in income in the period that includes the substantive enactment date. To the extent that it is not considered to be more likely than not that a future income tax asset will be realized, a valuation allowance is provided.

(o) FOREIGN CURRENCY TRANSLATION:
These consolidated financial statements are presented in U.S. dollars. The majority of the Company's operations are located in the United States and are conducted in U.S. dollars. The Company's Canadian operations use the Canadian dollar as their functional currency. The Canadian entities' financial statements have been translated into U.S. dollars using the exchange rate in effect at the balance sheet date for asset and liability amounts and at the average rate for the period for amounts included in the determination of income.

Cumulative unrealized gains or losses arising from the translation of the assets and liabilities of these operations into U.S. dollars are recorded as foreign currency translation adjustment, a separate component of shareholders' equity.

Effective July 1, 2002, exchange gains or losses arising on the translation of long-term monetary items that are denominated in foreign currencies to the applicable currency of measurement are included in the determination of net income (note 2(t)(ii)). Previously these gains and losses were deferred and amortized on a straight-line basis over the remaining terms of the related monetary item except for gains or losses related to foreign currency denominated long-term obligations designated as hedges of investments in self-sustaining foreign operations.

The actual exchange rates used for translation purposes were as follows:

CANADIAN DOLLAR TO U.S. DOLLAR EXCHANGE RATES	2003	2002
At June 30	1.3475	1.5162
Average during year	1.5112	1.5687

(p) PER SHARE CALCULATIONS:
Income per common share has been calculated using the weighted average number of common shares outstanding during the year. The dilutive effect of stock options is determined using the treasury stock method.

(q) STOCK OPTIONS AND STOCK-BASED COMPENSATION:

The Company has a stock option plan as described in note 12(c). Section 3870 of the CICA Accounting Handbook ("CICA 3870") requires a fair value-based method of accounting that is required for certain, but not all, stock-based transactions. CICA 3870 must be applied to all stock-based payments to non-employees, and to employee awards that are direct awards of shares, that call for settlement in cash or other assets, or are share appreciation rights that call for settlement by the issuance of equity instruments. As permitted by CICA 3870, the Company continues to account for employee stock option grants using the intrinsic value-based method under which no expense is recorded on grant and provides, on a pro forma basis, information as if a fair value methodology had been applied (note 12(h)). Accordingly, no compensation expense has been recognized for the periods presented. Any consideration paid on the exercise of options or purchase of shares is credited to capital stock.

(r) EMPLOYEE FUTURE BENEFITS:

The Company accrues its obligations under employee benefit plans and the related costs as the underlying services are provided.

(s) COMPARATIVE FIGURES:

Certain comparative figures for 2002 have been reclassified to conform with the financial statement presentation adopted in the current year.

(t) CHANGE IN ACCOUNTING POLICIES:

(i)   On July 1, 2002, the Company adopted the new recommendations of section 3062, "Goodwill and Other Intangible Assets," of the CICA Handbook, without restatement of prior periods. Under the new recommendations, goodwill and intangible assets with indefinite lives are no longer amortized but are subject to impairment tests on at least an annual basis by comparing the related reporting unit's carrying value to its fair value. Any write-down resulting from impairment tests made under the new section at adoption effective July 1, 2002 must be recognized as a charge to retained earnings at that date. Any impairment of goodwill or other intangible assets identified subsequent to July 1, 2002 will be expensed as determined. Other intangible assets with finite lives will continue to be amortized over their useful lives and are also tested for impairment by comparing carrying values to net recoverable amounts.

At June 30, 2002, the net carrying value of goodwill was $15,985,000. Upon adoption of these recommendations, it was determined that $179,000 needed to be reclassified from goodwill to ski and resort operations assets, and $3,813,000 needed to be reclassified from goodwill to depreciable intangible assets under CICA recommendations on business combinations. The Company completed its impairment testing on the balance of goodwill and intangible assets with indefinite lives as at July 1, 2002. As a result of this testing, an impairment loss of $6,150,000 (being net of taxes of $5,843,000) was required and has been recognized as an adjustment to opening retained earnings.

A reconciliation of previously reported net income and income per share (basic and diluted) to the amounts adjusted for the exclusion of goodwill amortization is as follows:

	2003	2002
Income as reported	$ 34,176	$ 58,480
Goodwill amortization	—	743
Adjusted income	$ 34,176	$ 59,223
Income per share (basic):		
Income as reported	$ 0.73	$ 1.33
Goodwill amortization	—	0.01
Adjusted income per share	$ 0.73	$ 1.34
Income per share (diluted):		
Income as reported	$ 0.73	$ 1.31
Goodwill amortization	—	0.02
Adjusted income per share	$ 0.73	$ 1.33

(ii)   On July 1, 2002, the Company retroactively adopted the new recommendations of section 1650, "Foreign Currency Translation," of the CICA Handbook which eliminated the requirement to defer and amortize unrealized translation gains and losses on long-term foreign currency denominated monetary items with a fixed or determinable life. Instead the exchange gains and losses on these items are included in the determination of income immediately. The adoption did not impact the financial position and results of operations of prior periods, or the results for the year ended June 30, 2003.

Notes to Consolidated Financial Statements

3 ACQUISITIONS:

On December 23, 2002, the Company assumed control of the assets and operations of Winter Park Resort, a major ski and resort operation in Colorado. For accounting purposes the assumption of control has been treated as a purchase of the resort. The fair value of the purchase price of the assets acquired was $47,204,000 of which $38,236,000 was assigned to ski and resort operations assets, $7,817,000 was assigned to real estate development properties and $1,151,000 was assigned to amounts receivable. The purchase was financed primarily through the issuance of a capital lease, the assumption of certain liabilities and the payment of $2,849,000 cash.

During the year ended June 30, 2002, the Company acquired the assets and business of Big Island Country Club Limited Partnership, which operates a golf course on the island of Hawaii, for cash consideration of $8,876,000.

4 DISCONTINUED OPERATIONS:

For reporting purposes, the results of operations and cash flow from operating activities of the non-resort real estate business have been disclosed separately from those of continuing operations for the periods presented.

The results of discontinued operations are as follows:

	2003	2002
Revenue	$ 441	$ 1,128
Loss before current income taxes	$ (578)	$ (104)
Provision for current income taxes	—	18
Loss from discontinued operations	$ (578)	$ (122)

5 SKI AND RESORT OPERATIONS:

	2003		
	COST	ACCUMULATED DEPRECIATION	NET BOOK VALUE
SKI OPERATIONS:			
Land	$ 58,679	$ —	$ 58,679
Buildings	300,351	59,124	241,227
Ski lifts and area improvements	443,889	140,260	303,629
Automotive, helicopters and other equipment	134,654	81,001	53,653
Leased vehicles	4,903	2,814	2,089
	942,476	283,199	659,277
RESORT OPERATIONS:			
Land	23,187	—	23,187
Buildings	68,178	7,486	60,692
Golf courses	124,919	21,173	103,746
Area improvements	95,256	23,431	71,825
	311,540	52,090	259,450
	$1,254,016	$ 335,289	$ 918,727

	2002		
	COST	ACCUMULATED DEPRECIATION	NET BOOK VALUE
SKI OPERATIONS:			
Land	$ 52,490	$ —	$ 52,490
Buildings	248,731	47,556	201,175
Ski lifts and area improvements	411,352	118,993	292,359
Automotive, helicopters and other equipment	120,681	70,499	50,182
Leased vehicles	4,614	2,311	2,303
	837,868	239,359	598,509
RESORT OPERATIONS:			
Land	21,925	—	21,925
Buildings	58,219	8,937	49,282
Golf courses	120,145	16,444	103,701
Area improvements	87,446	19,022	68,424
	287,735	44,403	243,332
	$1,125,603	$ 283,762	$ 841,841

The ski and resort operations have been pledged as security for certain of the Company's bank and other indebtedness (note 9).

6 PROPERTIES:

Summary of properties:

	2003	2002
Properties under development and held for sale	**$1,067,297**	$ 797,603
Revenue-producing properties	**—**	70,187
	$1,067,297	$ 867,790

Properties are classified for balance sheet purposes as follows:

	2003	2002
CURRENT ASSETS:		
Resort	**$ 662,197**	$ 399,572
LONG-TERM ASSETS:		
Resort	**405,100**	461,893
Discontinued operations	**—**	6,325
	$1,067,297	$ 867,790

Cumulative costs capitalized to the carrying value of properties under development and held for sale are as follows:

	2003	2002
Land and land development costs	**$ 205,709**	$ 187,269
Building development costs	**704,396**	478,175
Interest	**103,154**	80,082
Administrative	**54,038**	52,077
	$1,067,297	$ 797,603

During the year ended June 30, 2003, the Company capitalized interest of $55,525,000 (2002 – $38,850,000) (note 16).

Properties have been pledged as security for certain of the Company's bank and other indebtedness (note 9).

Breakdown of revenue-producing properties:

		2002	
	COST	ACCUMULATED DEPRECIATION	NET BOOK VALUE
REVENUE-PRODUCING PROPERTIES:			
Land	$ 8,217	$ —	$ 8,217
Buildings	68,298	11,340	56,958
Leasehold improvements and equipment	6,472	1,460	5,012
	$ 82,987	$ 12,800	$ 70,187

7 AMOUNTS RECEIVABLE:

	2003	2002
Receivables from sales of real estate	**$ 54,576**	$ 59,679
Ski and resort operations trade receivables	**34,427**	23,053
Loans, mortgages and notes receivable (note 20)	**89,189**	73,408
Funded senior employee share purchase plans (note 12(f))	**4,445**	4,475
Other accounts receivable	**20,930**	14,067
	203,567	174,682
Current portion	**126,725**	109,948
	$ 76,842	$ 64,734

Amounts receivable from sales of real estate primarily comprise sales proceeds held in trust which are generally paid out to the Company or to construction lenders within 60 days.

Total payments due on amounts receivable are approximately as follows:

YEAR ENDING JUNE 30,	
2004	$ 126,725
2005	19,129
2006	4,037
2007	3,310
2008	1,996
Subsequent to 2008	48,370
	$ 203,567

The loans, mortgages and notes receivable bear interest at both fixed and floating rates which averaged 10.71% per annum as at June 30, 2003 (2002 – 10.91%). Certain of these amounts have been pledged as security for the Company's bank and other indebtedness (note 9).

Notes to Consolidated Financial Statements

8 OTHER ASSETS:

(a) CURRENT:

	2003	2002
Ski and resort operations inventories	$ 34,640	$ 30,054
Restricted cash deposits	57,087	34,502
Prepaid expenses and other	31,883	23,506
	$ 123,610	$ 88,062

(b) LONG-TERM:

	2003	2002
Investment in Compagnie des Alpes	$ 12,257	$ 36,142
Deferred financing and other costs	20,053	16,481
Administrative furniture, computer equipment, software and leasehold improvements, net of accumulated depreciation of $19,644,000 (2002 – $15,769,000)	23,856	33,614
Other	8,904	8,095
	$ 65,070	$ 94,332

In July 2002 the Company sold 55% of its investment in Compagnie des Alpes ("CDA") for proceeds which approximated its carrying value. As a result, the Company changed from the equity to the cost method of accounting for its investment at the beginning of the current fiscal year. During July 2003 the Company sold its remaining interest in CDA for proceeds which approximated its carrying value.

During the year ended June 30, 2003, the Company decided to standardize certain information technology systems across its resorts in order to improve efficiencies and eliminate costs. In addition, the Company reorganized its central reservations business and assessed the value of the assets of that business. As a result, the Company wrote down the value of information technology assets by $12,270,000.

9 BANK AND OTHER INDEBTEDNESS:

The Company has obtained financing for its ski and resort operations and properties from various financial institutions by pledging individual assets as security for such financing. Security for general corporate debt is provided by general security which includes a floating charge on the Company's assets and undertakings, fixed charges on real estate properties, and assignment of mortgages and notes receivable. The following table summarizes the primary security provided by the Company, where appropriate, and indicates the applicable type of financing, maturity dates and the weighted average interest rate at June 30, 2003:

	MATURITY DATES	WEIGHTED AVERAGE INTEREST RATE(%)	2003	2002
SKI AND RESORT OPERATIONS:				
Mortgages and bank loans	Demand – 2017	3.68	$ 62,432	$ 124,578
Obligations under capital leases	2004 – 2052	9.09	45,070	3,869
			107,502	128,447
PROPERTIES:				
Interim financing on properties under development and held for sale	2004 – 2017	5.71	264,032	141,337
Resort club notes receivable credit facilities	2006	5.21	28,121	27,436
Mortgages on revenue-producing properties	2004 – 2011	nil	—	12,485
			292,153	181,258
General corporate debt	2004 – 2005	5.63	240,243	184,000
Unsecured debentures	2004 – 2010	10.20	621,021	562,214
		7.91	1,260,919	1,055,919
Current portion			287,176	282,047
			$ 973,743	$ 773,872

Principal repayments and the components related to either floating or fixed interest rate indebtedness are as follows:

YEAR ENDING JUNE 30.	INTEREST RATES		TOTAL
	FLOATING	FIXED	REPAYMENTS
2004	$ 252,630	$ 34,546	$ 287,176
2005	267,620	10,680	278,300
2006	19,257	12,836	32,093
2007	80	2,942	3,022
2008	1,278	653	1,931
Subsequent to 2008	5,231	653,166	658,397
	$ 546,096	$ 714,823	$ 1,260,919

The Company has entered into a swap agreement to fix the interest rate on a portion of its floating rate debt. The Company had $14,126,000 (2002 – $16,000,000) of bank loans swapped against debt with a fixed interest rate ranging from 4.70% to 5.58% (2002 – 4.70% to 5.58%) per annum.

Bank and other indebtedness includes indebtedness in the amount of $306,458,000 (2002 – $263,691,000) which is repayable in Canadian dollars of $412,952,000 (2002 – $399,808,000).

The Company is subject to certain covenants in respect of some of the bank and other indebtedness which require the Company to maintain certain financial ratios. The Company is in compliance with these covenants at June 30, 2003.

10   DEFERRED REVENUE:

	2003	2002
Deposits on real estate sales	$ 109,075	$ 76,239
Government assistance (note 11)	10,992	7,901
Club initiation deposits	24,845	13,431
Season pass revenue	14,989	13,883
Other deferred amounts	18,586	11,099
	178,487	122,553
Current portion	134,878	99,484
	$ 43,609	$ 23,069

11   GOVERNMENT ASSISTANCE:

The federal government of Canada and the Province of Quebec have granted financial assistance to the Company in the form of interest-free loans and forgivable grants for the construction of specified four-season tourist facilities at Mont Tremblant. Loans totaling $10,464,000 (Cdn.$14,100,000) (2002 – $9,300,000; Cdn.$14,100,000) have been advanced and are repayable over 17 years starting in 2000. The grants, which will total $43,052,000 (Cdn.$58,013,000) (2002 – $38,318,000; Cdn.$58,013,000) when they are fully advanced, amounted to $31,400,000 (Cdn.$42,312,000) at June 30, 2003 (2002 – $24,518,000; Cdn.$37,174,000). During the year ended June 30, 2003, grants received of $3,812,000 (Cdn.$5,138,000) (2002 – $3,513,000; Cdn.$5,326,000) were credited as follows: $1,138,000 (2002 – $1,010,000) to ski and resort operations assets, $573,000 (2002 – $1,461,000) to properties and $2,101,000 (2002 – $1,042,000) to deferred government assistance.

Notes to Consolidated Financial Statements

12 CAPITAL STOCK:

(a) SHARE CAPITAL REORGANIZATION:

Effective March 14, 1997, the Company completed a reorganization of its share capital designed to separate the remaining non-resort real estate assets from the rest of the Company's business. Under the reorganization, each existing common share was exchanged for one new common share and one non-resort preferred ("NRP") share. The new common shares have the same attributes as the old common shares.

On December 18, 2002, the Company redeemed all of the remaining NRP shares at a price of Cdn.$2.02 per share for a total of $6,697,000. As a result, the carrying value of the NRP shares was reduced to zero and contributed surplus was increased by $2,661,000 representing the difference between the redemption price and the assigned value of the NRP shares less the foreign currency translation adjustment related to the NRP shares.

(b) CAPITAL STOCK:

The Company's capital stock comprises the following:

	2003	2002
Common shares	$ 458,081	$ 453,299
NRP shares	—	13,600
Contributed surplus (note 12(a))	2,661	—
	$ 460,742	$ 466,899

(i) Common shares:

Authorized: an unlimited number without par value

Issued:

	2003 NUMBER OF COMMON SHARES	2003 AMOUNT	2002 NUMBER OF COMMON SHARES	2002 AMOUNT
Balance, beginning of year	47,255,062	$ 453,299	44,026,394	$ 400,262
Issued for cash under stock option plan	305,000	2,685	270,850	1,893
Amortization of benefit plan, net (g)	—	2,097	—	—
Purchased for benefit plan (g)	—	—	(292,182)	(4,807)
Issued for cash, net of issuance costs	—	—	3,250,000	55,951
Balance, end of year	47,560,062	$ 458,081	47,255,062	$ 453,299

(ii) NRP shares:

Authorized: 50,000,000 without par value

Issued:

	2003 NUMBER OF NRP SHARES	2003 AMOUNT	2002 NUMBER OF NRP SHARES	2002 AMOUNT
Balance, beginning of year	5,163,436	$ 13,600	5,513,936	$ 13,958
Redemption	(5,163,436)	(6,697)	—	—
Transferred to contributed surplus	—	(2,661)	—	—
Foreign currency adjustment	—	(4,242)	—	—
Purchased for cancellation	—	—	(350,500)	(358)
Balance, end of year	—	$ —	5,163,436	$ 13,600

(iii) Preferred shares:

Authorized: an unlimited number without par value

Issued: nil

(c) STOCK OPTIONS:

The Company has a stock option plan which provides for grants to officers and employees of the Company and its subsidiaries of options to purchase common shares of the Company. Options granted under the stock option plan are exercisable in Canadian dollars and may not be exercised except in accordance with such limitations as the Human Resources Committee of the Board of Directors of the Company may determine.

The following table summarizes the status of options outstanding under the Plan:

	2003		2002	
	SHARE OPTIONS OUTSTANDING	WEIGHTED AVERAGE PRICE	SHARE OPTIONS OUTSTANDING	WEIGHTED AVERAGE PRICE
Outstanding, beginning of year	3,697,900	$ 16.04	3,322,500	$ 15.24
Granted	445,000	15.89	711,800	16.17
Exercised	(305,000)	9.41	(270,850)	6.99
Forfeited	(34,000)	18.03	(65,550)	17.87
Outstanding, end of year	3,803,900	$ 18.68	3,697,900	$ 16.04
Exercisable, end of year	1,867,310	$ 18.20	1,753,950	$ 14.70

The following table provides details of options outstanding at June 30, 2003:

RANGE OF EXERCISE PRICES	NUMBER OUTSTANDING JUNE 30, 2003	WEIGHTED AVERAGE LIFE REMAINING (YEARS)	WEIGHTED AVERAGE PRICE	NUMBER EXERCISABLE JUNE 30, 2003	WEIGHTED AVERAGE PRICE
$ 8.56 – $ 10.74	134,100	1.8	$ 10.17	134,100	$ 10.17
$ 11.67 – $ 17.07	233,500	4.4	14.74	205,500	15.02
$ 17.66 – $ 21.56	3,436,300	6.8	19.28	1,527,710	19.19
	3,803,900	6.4	$ 18.68	1,867,310	$ 18.20

(d) EMPLOYEE SHARE PURCHASE PLAN:

The employee share purchase plan permits certain full-time employees of the Company and its subsidiaries and limited partnerships to purchase common shares through payroll deductions. The Company contributes $1 for every $3 contributed by an employee. To June 30, 2003, a total of 65,809 (2002 – 65,809) common shares have been issued from treasury under this plan. A further 100,000 common shares have been authorized and reserved for issuance under this plan.

(e) DEFERRED SHARE UNIT PLAN:

The company has a key executive Deferred Share Unit Plan (the "DSU Plan") that allows each executive officer to elect to receive all or any portion of his annual incentive award as deferred share units. A DSU is equal in value to one common share of the Company. The units are determined by dividing the dollar amount elected by the average closing price of the common shares on the Toronto Stock Exchange for the five trading days preceding the date that the annual incentive award becomes payable. The units also accrue dividend equivalents payable in additional units in an amount equal to dividends paid on Intrawest common shares. DSUs mature upon the termination of employment, whereupon an executive is entitled to receive the fair market value of the equivalent number of common shares, net of withholdings, in cash.

The Company records the cost of the DSU plan as compensation expense. As at June 30, 2003, 74,381 units were outstanding at a value of $981,000 (2002 – 49,351 units at a value of $827,000).

(f) FUNDED SENIOR EMPLOYEE SHARE PURCHASE PLANS:

The Company has two funded senior employee share purchase plans which provide for loans to be made to designated eligible employees to be used for the purchase of common shares. At June 30, 2003, loans to employees under the funded senior employee share purchase plans amounted to $4,445,000 with respect to 247,239 common shares (2002 – $4,475,000 with respect to 374,387 common shares and 26,939 NRP shares). The loans, which are included in amounts receivable, are non-interest bearing, secured by a promissory note and a pledge of the shares ($3,259,000 market value at June 30, 2003) and mature by 2012. A further 96,400 common shares have been authorized and reserved for issuance under one of the plans.

(g) KEY EXECUTIVE EMPLOYEE BENEFIT PLAN:

The Company has a key executive employee benefit plan which permits the Company to grant awards of common shares purchased in the open market to executive officers. To June 30, 2003, a total of 292,182 (2002 – 292,192) common shares were purchased under this plan. The common shares vest to the employees in part over time and the balance on the attainment of certain future earnings levels. The value of the shares amortized to income during the year ended June 30, 2003 was $2,097,000. None of the shares were vested as at June 30, 2003.

Notes to Consolidated Financial Statements

12 CAPITAL STOCK: (CONTINUED)

(h) STOCK COMPENSATION:

Had compensation expense for stock options granted subsequent to June 30, 2001 been determined by a fair value method using the Black-Scholes option pricing model at the date of the grant, the following weighted average assumptions would have been used for options granted in the current period:

	2003	2002
Dividend yield (%)	0.9	0.6
Risk-free interest rate (%)	3.11	4.38
Expected option life (years)	7	7
Expected volatility (%)	36	55

Using the above assumptions, the Company's net income for the year ended June 30, 2003 would have been reduced to the pro forma amount indicated below:

	2003	2002
Net income, as reported	$ 34,176	$ 58,480
Estimated fair value of option grants	(1,909)	(649)
Net income, pro forma	$ 32,267	$ 57,831
PRO FORMA INCOME PER COMMON SHARE FROM CONTINUING OPERATIONS:		
Basic	$ 0.69	$ 1.31
Diluted	0.69	1.29

The estimated fair value of option grants excludes the effect of those granted before July 1, 2001. The fair value of options granted during the year ended June 30, 2003 was $6.35 per option (2002 – $9.15) on the grant date on a weighted average basis.

(i) PER SHARE INFORMATION:

The reconciliation of the net income and weighted average number of common shares used to calculate basic and diluted income per common share is as follows:

	2003		2002	
	NET INCOME	SHARES (000)	NET INCOME	SHARES (000)
BASIC INCOME PER COMMON SHARE:				
Income from continuing operations	$ 34,754	47,364	$ 58,602	44,206
Dilutive effect of stock options	—	226	—	489
Diluted income per common share	$ 34,754	47,590	$ 58,602	44,695

Options aggregating 3,675,300 (2002 – 2,399,800) have not been included in the computation of diluted income per common share as they were anti-dilutive.

13 INCOME TAXES:

(a) The provision for income taxes from continuing operations is as follows:

	2003	2002
Current	$ 10,157	$ 12,422
Future	(3,914)	(2,873)
	$ 6,243	$ 9,549

The reconciliation of income taxes calculated at the statutory rate to the actual income tax provision is as follows:

	2003	2002
Statutory rate (%)	38.0	41.2
Income tax charge at statutory rate	$ 19,683	$ 32,888
Non-deductible expenses and amortization	326	53
Large corporations tax	2,574	1,159
Taxes related to non-controlling interest share of earnings	(4,284)	(4,804)
Reduction for enacted changes in tax laws and rates	—	(2,434)
Taxes related to equity accounted investment	—	(1,605)
Foreign taxes less than statutory rate	(13,182)	(15,589)
Other	1,126	(101)
	6,243	9,567
Current income taxes related to discontinued operations	—	18
Provision for income taxes	$ 6,243	$ 9,549

(b) The tax effects of temporary differences that give rise to significant portions of the future tax assets and future tax liabilities are presented below:

	2003	2002
FUTURE TAX ASSETS:		
Non-capital loss carryforwards	$ 35,823	$ 27,068
Differences in working capital deductions for tax and accounting purposes	5,465	4,004
Other	3,861	727
Total gross future tax assets	45,149	31,799
Valuation allowance	(17,559)	(16,206)
Net future tax assets	27,590	15,593
FUTURE TAX LIABILITIES:		
Differences in net book value and undepreciated capital cost of ski and resort assets and properties	81,824	80,021
Differences in book value and tax basis of bank and other indebtedness	28,844	3,879
Other	1,289	—
Total gross future tax liabilities	111,957	83,900
Net future tax liabilities	$ 84,367	$ 68,307

Net future tax liabilities are classified for balance sheet purposes as follows:

	2003	2002
CURRENT ASSETS:		
Future income taxes	$ 10,619	$ 7,536
LONG-TERM LIABILITIES:		
Future income taxes	94,986	75,843
	$ 84,367	$ 68,307

(c) At June 30, 2003, the Company has non-capital loss carryforwards for income tax purposes of approximately $117,200,000 (2002 – $101,960,000) that are available to offset future taxable income through 2023.

14 JOINT VENTURES:

The following amounts represent the Company's proportionate interest in joint ventures and non-controlled partnerships (note 2(b)):

	2003	2002
Properties, current	$ 53,993	$ 42,178
Other current assets	20,888	21,717
	74,881	63,895
Current liabilities	(59,629)	(49,487)
Working capital	15,252	14,408
Ski and resort operations	161,609	155,964
Properties, non-current	79,032	58,713
Bank and other indebtedness, non-current	(32,213)	(40,376)
Other, net	(14,856)	(14,924)
	$ 208,824	$ 173,785

	2003	2002
Revenue	$ 128,286	$ 131,122
Expenses	122,272	119,960
Income from continuing operations before income taxes	6,014	11,162
Results of discontinued operations	419	385
	$ 6,433	$ 11,547

	2003	2002
CASH PROVIDED BY (USED IN):		
Operations	$ (5,309)	$ 29,206
Financing	30,544	(15,267)
Investments	(25,003)	(20,425)
Increase (decrease) in cash and cash equivalents	$ 232	$ (6,486)

Due to joint venture partners is the amount payable to the Company's joint venture partners on various properties for costs they have incurred on the Company's behalf. Payments to the joint venture partners are governed by the terms of the respective joint venture agreement.

Notes to Consolidated Financial Statements

15 CONTINGENCIES AND COMMITMENTS:

(a) The Company holds licenses and land leases with respect to certain of its ski operations. These leases expire at various times between 2032 and 2051 and provide for annual payments generally in the range of 2% of defined gross revenues.

(b) The Company has estimated costs to complete ski and resort operations assets and properties currently under construction and held for sale amounting to $379,019,000 at June 30, 2003 (2002 – $397,642,000). These costs are substantially covered by existing financing commitments.

(c) In addition to the leases described in (a) above, the Company has entered into other operating lease commitments, payable as follows:

YEAR ENDING JUNE 30,	
2004	$ 10,478
2005	9,919
2006	8,987
2007	7,605
2008	7,024
Subsequent to 2008	65,785
	$ 109,798

(d) The Company is contingently liable for the obligations of certain joint ventures and partnerships. The assets of these joint ventures and partnerships, which in all cases exceed the obligations, are available to satisfy such obligations.

(e) The Company and its subsidiaries are involved in several lawsuits arising from the ordinary course of business. Although the outcome of such matters cannot be predicted with certainty, management does not consider the Company's exposure to lawsuits to be material to these consolidated financial statements.

(f) Canada Customs and Revenue Agency ("CCRA") has proposed certain adjustments to reduce the amount of capital cost allowance and non-capital losses claimed by the Company. No notice of reassessment has been issued. The Company has made submissions with respect to these proposals and intends to contest any adjustments, if made. The Company believes that it is unlikely that CCRA would be successful with the proposed challenge. Whether CCRA will ultimately proceed with such proposals, and the outcome of the issues under review if the proposals proceed, cannot be determined at this time. If all of the issues raised by CCRA in the proposals were reassessed as proposed, the Company would be required to pay total cash taxes of approximately $7,500,000 plus interest of approximately $5,000,000. For accounting purposes, the effect of any reassessment would be charged to income in the year the outcome of the proposals is determined.

16 INTEREST EXPENSE:

	2003	2002
Total interest incurred	$ 102,926	$ 83,439
Less:		
Interest capitalized to ski and resort operations assets	192	1,353
Interest capitalized to properties, net of capitalized interest included in		
real estate cost of sales of $14,872,000 (2002 – $13,314,000)	40,653	25,536
	$ 62,081	$ 56,550

Interest was charged to income as follows:

	2003	2002
Real estate costs	$ 14,872	$ 13,314
Interest expense	47,142	43,072
Discontinued operations	67	164
	$ 62,081	$ 56,550

Real estate cost of sales also include $17,581,000 (2002 – $14,525,000) of interest incurred in prior years.

Interest incurred and interest expense include commitment and other financing fees and amortization of deferred financing costs.

17 FINANCIAL INSTRUMENTS:

(a) FAIR VALUE:

The Company has various financial instruments including cash and cash equivalents, amounts receivable, certain amounts payable and accrued liabilities. Due to their short-term maturity or, in the case of amounts receivable, their market comparable interest rates, the instruments' book value approximates their fair value. Debt and interest swap agreements are also financial instruments. The fair value of the Company's long-term debt including interest swap agreements, calculated using current rates offered to the Company for debt at the same remaining maturities, is not materially different from amounts included in the consolidated balance sheets.

(b) INTEREST RATE RISK:

As described in note 9, $546,096,000 of the Company's debt instruments bear interest at floating rates. Fluctuations in these rates will impact the cost of financing incurred in the future.

(c) CREDIT RISK:

The Company's products and services are purchased by a wide range of customers in different regions of North America and elsewhere. Due to the nature of its operations, the Company has no concentrations of credit risk.

18 PENSION PLANS:

The Company has two non-contributory defined benefit pension plans, one registered and the other non-registered, covering certain of its senior executives. The number of senior executives included in the plan increased from five to 15 in 2002. The Company partially funded the accrued benefit obligation until December 2001. The estimated market value of the plans' assets (i.e., the funded amount) was $3,252,000 at June 30, 2003 (2002 – $2,857,000). A substantial portion of the unfunded benefit obligation, the estimated present value of which was $15,479,000 at June 30, 2003 (2002 – $10,783,000), has been secured by a letter of credit. This obligation is being expensed over a period of 13 years.

In addition to the plans mentioned above, one of the Company's subsidiaries has two defined benefit pension plans covering certain employees. The estimated market value of the plans' assets was $5,989,000 and the estimated present value of the unfunded benefit obligation was $2,229,000 at June 30, 2003. The obligation is being expensed over a period of 10 years.

For the year ended June 30, 2003, the Company charged to operations pension costs of $1,992,000 (2002 – $1,070,000).

19 SEGMENTED INFORMATION:

The Company has four reportable segments: mountain resort operations, warm-weather resort operations, real estate operations, and corporate and all other. The mountain resort segment includes all of the Company's mountain resorts and associated activities. The warm-weather segment includes Sandestin and all of the Company's stand-alone golf courses. The real estate segment includes all of the Company's real estate activities.

The Company evaluates performance based on profit or loss from operations before interest, depreciation and amortization, and income taxes. Intersegment sales and transfers are accounted for as if the sales or transfers were to third parties.

The Company's reportable segments are strategic business units that offer distinct products and services, and that have their own identifiable marketing strategies. Each of the reportable segments has senior executives responsible for the performance of the segment.

The following table presents the Company's results from continuing operations by reportable segment:

	2003	2002
SEGMENT REVENUE:		
Mountain resort	$ 506,483	$ 424,835
Warm-weather resort	65,044	60,307
Real estate	512,695	495,813
Corporate and all other	2,417	5,016
	$1,086,639	$ 985,971

Notes to Consolidated Financial Statements

19 SEGMENTED INFORMATION: (CONTINUED)

	2003	2002
SEGMENT OPERATING PROFIT:		
Mountain resort	$ 109,197	$ 98,935
Warm-weather resort	7,469	8,406
Real estate	75,005	88,150
Corporate and all other	2,417	5,016
	194,088	200,507
Less:		
Interest	47,142	43,072
Depreciation and amortization	67,516	65,434
Corporate general and administrative	14,889	12,175
Write-down of technology assets	12,270	—
	141,817	120,681
Income before income taxes, non-controlling interest and discontinued operations	$ 52,271	$ 79,826

	2003	2002
SEGMENT ASSETS:		
Mountain resort	$ 978,719	$ 912,642
Warm-weather resort	145,361	151,924
Real estate	1,311,079	1,032,296
Corporate and all other	80,563	60,720
Discontinued operations	—	9,335
	$2,515,722	$2,166,917

	2003	2002
CAPITAL EXPENDITURES:		
Mountain resort	$ 59,674	$ 81,658
Warm-weather resort	4,872	9,832
Corporate and all other	5,025	10,237
	$ 69,571	$ 101,727

GEOGRAPHIC INFORMATION:

	2003	2002
REVENUE:		
Canada	$ 474,865	$ 424,764
United States	611,774	561,207
	$1,086,639	$ 985,971

	2003	2002
SEGMENT OPERATING PROFIT:		
Canada	$ 102,871	$ 121,707
United States	91,217	78,800
	$ 194,088	$ 200,507

	2003	2002
IDENTIFIABLE ASSETS:		
Canada	$ 886,978	$ 753,885
United States	1,628,744	1,403,697
Discontinued operations	—	9,335
	$2,515,722	$2,166,917

20 RELATED PARTY TRANSACTIONS:

During the year ended June 30, 2002, $3,991,000 was repaid to the Company by a partnership, one of whose partners was a corporation controlled by an officer and a director of the Company.

21 CASH FLOW INFORMATION:

The changes in non-cash operating working capital balance consist of the following:

	2003	2002
CASH PROVIDED BY (USED IN):		
Amounts receivable	$ (17,208)	$ (29,720)
Other assets	(17,557)	20,819
Amounts payable	14,866	48,676
Due to joint venture partners	1,425	(4,788)
Deferred revenue	45,064	14,204
	$ 26,590	$ 49,191
SUPPLEMENTAL INFORMATION:		
Interest paid related to interest charged to income	$ 62,091	$ 56,550
Income, franchise and withholding taxes paid	11,067	11,596
NON-CASH INVESTING ACTIVITIES:		
Notes received on asset disposals	2,226	6,902
Bank and other indebtedness incurred on acquisition	35,172	—

22 DIFFERENCES BETWEEN CANADIAN AND UNITED STATES GENERALLY ACCEPTED ACCOUNTING PRINCIPLES:

The consolidated financial statements have been prepared in accordance with generally accepted accounting principles ("GAAP") in Canada. The principles adopted in these financial statements conform in all material respects to those generally accepted in the United States and the rules and regulations promulgated by the Securities and Exchange Commission ("SEC") except as summarized below:

	2003	2002
Income from continuing operations in accordance with Canadian GAAP	$ 34,754	$ 58,602
EFFECTS OF DIFFERENCES IN ACCOUNTING FOR:		
Depreciation and amortization pursuant to SFAS 109 (d)	(690)	(1,870)
Real estate revenue recognition (i)	(8,931)	4,089
Start-up costs (j)	3,101	(4,772)
Tax effect of differences	2,478	562
Foreign exchange pursuant to SFAS 52 (g)	—	(14)
Results of discontinued operations	(578)	(122)
Income before cumulative effect of change in accounting principle	30,134	56,475
Adjustment to reflect change in accounting for goodwill, net of tax (k)	(6,150)	—
Net income in accordance with United States GAAP	23,984	56,475
Opening retained earnings in accordance with United States GAAP (b)	275,101	223,363
Common share dividends	(5,051)	(4,737)
Closing retained earnings in accordance with United States GAAP	$ 294,034	$ 275,101
INCOME BEFORE CUMULATIVE EFFECT OF CHANGE IN ACCOUNTING PRINCIPLE PER COMMON SHARE (IN DOLLARS):		
Basic	$ 0.65	$ 1.28
Diluted	0.65	1.27
INCOME PER COMMON SHARE (IN DOLLARS):		
Basic	0.52	1.28
Diluted	0.52	1.27
WEIGHTED AVERAGE NUMBER OF SHARES OUTSTANDING (IN THOUSANDS):		
Basic	47,364	44,206
Diluted	47,590	44,695

Notes to Consolidated Financial Statements

22 DIFFERENCES BETWEEN CANADIAN AND UNITED STATES GENERALLY ACCEPTED ACCOUNTING PRINCIPLES: (CONTINUED)

	2003	2002
COMPREHENSIVE INCOME:		
Net income in accordance with United States GAAP	$ 23,984	$ 56,475
Other comprehensive income (h)	17,808	2,299
	$ 41,792	$ 58,774

	2003	2002
Total assets in accordance with Canadian GAAP	$2,515,722	$2,166,917
EFFECTS OF DIFFERENCES IN ACCOUNTING FOR:		
Shareholder loans (c)	(4,445)	(4,475)
Ski and resort assets (d)	1,948	2,525
Goodwill (d)	37,471	34,696
Properties (d)	640	650
Sale-leaseback (i)	14,080	—
Start-up costs (j)	(2,551)	(5,682)
Future income taxes on differences	4,222	1,744
Total assets in accordance with United States GAAP	$2,567,087	$2,196,375

	2003	2002
Total liabilities in accordance with Canadian GAAP	$1,804,583	$1,489,648
EFFECTS OF DIFFERENCES IN ACCOUNTING FOR:		
Revenue recognition (i)	24,096	—
Total liabilities in accordance with United States GAAP	$1,828,679	$1,489,648

	2003	2002
Capital stock in accordance with Canadian GAAP	$ 460,742	$ 466,899
EFFECTS OF DIFFERENCES IN ACCOUNTING FOR:		
Extinguishment of options and warrants (a)	1,563	1,563
Shareholder loans (c)	(4,445)	(4,475)
Capital stock in accordance with United States GAAP	457,860	463,987
Closing retained earnings in accordance with United States GAAP	294,034	275,101
Accumulated other comprehensive income (h)	(13,486)	(32,361)
Shareholders' equity in accordance with United States GAAP	$ 738,408	$ 706,727

(a) EXTINGUISHMENT OF OPTIONS AND WARRANTS:

Payments made to extinguish options and warrants can be treated as capital items under Canadian GAAP. These payments would be treated as income items under United States GAAP. As a result, payments made to extinguish options in prior years impact the current year's capital stock and retained earnings. No payments were made during the years ended June 30, 2003 and 2002.

(b) RETAINED EARNINGS:

Opening retained earnings in accordance with United States GAAP for the year ended June 30, 2002 includes the effects of:

(i)   adopting SFAS 109 as described in (d). The net increase in retained earnings was $40,685,000; and

(ii)   treating payments made to extinguish options and warrants as income items as described in (a). The net decrease in retained earnings was $1,563,000.

(c) SHAREHOLDER LOANS:

The Company accounts for loans provided to senior employees for the purchase of shares as amounts receivable. Under United States GAAP, these loans, totaling $4,445,000 and $4,475,000 as at June 30, 2003 and 2002, respectively, would be deducted from share capital.

(d) INCOME TAXES:

As described in note 2(n), the Company follows the asset and liability method of accounting for income taxes. Prior to July 1, 1999, the Company had adopted the Statement of Financial Accounting Standards No. 109, "Accounting for Income Taxes" ("SFAS 109"), for the financial statement amounts presented under United States GAAP. SFAS 109 requires that future tax liabilities or assets be recognized for the difference between assigned values and tax bases of assets and liabilities acquired pursuant to a business combination except for non tax-deductible goodwill and unallocated negative goodwill, effective from the Company's year ended September 30, 1994. The effect of adopting SFAS 109 increases the carrying values of certain balance sheet amounts at June 30, 2003 and 2002 as follows:

	2003	2002
Ski and resort operations assets	$ 1,948	$ 2,525
Goodwill	37,471	34,696
Properties	640	650

(e) JOINT VENTURES:

In accordance with Canadian GAAP, joint ventures are required to be proportionately consolidated regardless of the legal form of the entity. Under United States GAAP, incorporated joint ventures are required to be accounted for by the equity method. However, in accordance with practices prescribed by the SEC, the Company has elected for the purpose of this reconciliation to account for incorporated joint ventures by the proportionate consolidation method (note 14).

(f) STOCK COMPENSATION:

As described in note 2(q), the Company accounts for stock options by the intrinsic value-based method. In addition, in note 12(h) the Company provides pro forma disclosure as if a fair value-based method had been applied for grants made subsequent to June 30, 2001. For United States GAAP purposes, the pro forma disclosures would consider the fair value of all grants made subsequent to December 15, 1995.

Had compensation expense been determined in accordance with the timing of application provisions of United States GAAP using the Black-Scholes option pricing model at the date of the grant, the following weighted average assumptions would be used for option grants in:

	2003	2002
Dividend yield (%)	0.9	0.6
Risk-free interest rate (%)	3.11	4.38
Expected option life (years)	7	7
Expected volatility (%)	36	55

Using the above assumptions, the Company's net income under United States GAAP would have been reduced to the pro forma amounts indicated below:

	2003	2002
NET INCOME IN ACCORDANCE WITH UNITED STATES GAAP:		
As reported	$ 23,984	$ 56,475
Estimated fair value of option grants	(5,228)	(5,215)
Pro forma	$ 18,756	$ 51,260
PRO FORMA INCOME PER COMMON SHARE:		
Basic	$ 0.41	$ 1.16
Diluted	0.41	1.15

Notes to Consolidated Financial Statements

22 DIFFERENCES BETWEEN CANADIAN AND UNITED STATES GENERALLY ACCEPTED ACCOUNTING PRINCIPLES: (CONTINUED)

(g) FOREIGN EXCHANGE ON BANK AND OTHER INDEBTEDNESS:

Prior to July 1, 2002 under Canadian GAAP, the Company deferred and amortized foreign exchange gains and losses on bank and other indebtedness denominated in foreign currencies over the remaining term of the debt. Under United States GAAP, foreign exchange gains and losses are included in income in the period in which the exchange rate fluctuates.

(h) OTHER COMPREHENSIVE INCOME:

Statement of Financial Accounting Standards No. 130, "Reporting Comprehensive Income" ("SFAS 130"), requires that a company classify items of other comprehensive income by their nature in a financial statement and display the accumulated balance of other comprehensive income separately from retained earnings and capital stock in the equity section of the balance sheet.

The foreign currency translation adjustment in the amount of $14,243,000 (2002 – $31,295,000) presented in shareholders' equity under Canadian GAAP would be considered accumulated other comprehensive income under United States GAAP. The change in the balance of $17,808,000 would be other comprehensive income for the year (2002 – income of $2,299,000).

(i) REAL ESTATE REVENUE RECOGNITION:

The Company recognizes profit arising on the sale of a property, a portion of which is leased back by the Company, to the extent the gain exceeds the present value of the minimum lease payments. The deferred gain is recognized over the lease term. Under United States GAAP, the Company's continued involvement in the property precludes a sale-leaseback transaction from sale-leaseback accounting. As a result, the profit on the transaction is not recognized but rather the sales proceeds are treated as a liability and the property continues to be shown as an asset of the Company until the conditions for sales recognition are met.

In accordance with Canadian GAAP, the Company recognizes revenue from the sale of serviced lots after receiving a deposit and conveying title to the purchaser. Statement of Financial Accounting Standards No. 66, "Accounting for Sales of Real Estate" ("SFAS 66"), provides that a sale of real estate should not be recognized unless the deposit received from the purchaser is at least a major part of the difference between usual loan limits and the sales value of the property. Accordingly, no revenue and cost of sales would have been recognized under United States GAAP on certain lot sales for the year ended June 30, 2001 where the deposit received was less than 10% of the sales price. During the year ended June 30, 2002, the remainder of the loans receivable was collected.

(j) START-UP COSTS:

As described in note 2(f), the Company capitalizes for Canadian GAAP purposes certain costs incurred in the start-up period of specific operations. For United States GAAP purposes, such costs would be expensed as incurred.

(k) GOODWILL AND OTHER INTANGIBLE ASSETS:

As described in note 2(t)(i), the Company restated opening retained earnings for impairment losses calculated by comparing the carrying values to fair values of goodwill and intangible assets with indefinite lives. For United States GAAP, the Company adopted effective July 1, 2002 the provisions of SFAS 142, "Goodwill and Other Intangible Assets," which are similar to Canadian GAAP except that under this standard the impairment losses are recognized as a cumulative effect of a change in accounting principle and are treated as a charge to net income in the year of adoption.

(l) DERIVATIVES AND HEDGING ACTIVITIES:

For United States GAAP purposes, the Company adopted the provisions of SFAS 133, "Accounting for Derivative Instruments and Hedging Activities," as amended, effective July 1, 2000. Under this standard, derivative instruments are initially recorded at cost with changes in fair value recognized in income except when the derivative is identified, documented and highly effective as a hedge, in which case the changes in fair value are excluded from income to be recognized at the time of the underlying transaction. The only derivative instrument outstanding at June 30, 2003 and 2002 is the interest rate swap described in note 9. As the fair value of this swap is not materially different than its cost at both dates, no reconciliation adjustment is required.

(m) RECENTLY ANNOUNCED ACCOUNTING PRONOUNCEMENTS:

In the U.S., SFAS 143, "Accounting for Asset Retirement Obligations" ("SFAS 143"), addresses financial accounting and reporting for obligations associated with the retirement of long-lived assets and the associated asset retirement costs. SFAS 143 requires the Company to record the fair value of an asset retirement obligation as a liability in the period in which it incurs a legal obligation associated with the retirement of tangible long-lived assets that result from the acquisition, construction, development and/or normal use of the assets. The fair value of the liability is added to the carrying amount of the associated asset and this additional carrying amount is depreciated over the life of the asset. Subsequent to the initial measurement of the asset retirement obligation, the obligation will be adjusted at the end of each period to reflect the passage of time and changes in the estimated future cash flows underlying the obligation. If the obligation is settled for other than the carrying amount of the liability, the Company will recognize a gain or loss on settlement. The Company was required to adopt the provisions of SFAS 143 effective July 1, 2002. Certain of the land lease arrangements related to the Company's ski and resort operations require remediation steps be taken on termination of the lease arrangement. The Company plans to operate its resorts indefinitely and thus is unable to make a reasonable estimate of the fair values of the associated asset retirement obligations.

In the U.S., SFAS 144, "Accounting for the Impairment or Disposal of Long-Lived Assets" ("SFAS 144"), provides guidance for recognizing and measuring impairment losses on long-lived assets held for use and long-lived assets to be disposed of by sale. SFAS 144 also provides guidance on how to present discontinued operations in the income statement and includes a component of an entity (rather than a segment of a business). The provisions of SFAS 144 are required to be applied prospectively after the adoption date to newly initiated disposal activities. The Company was required to adopt SFAS 144 effective July 1, 2002. The adoption of SFAS 144 did not materially impact the Company's consolidated financial position or results of operations.

The FASB has issued SFAS 146, "Accounting for Costs Associated with Exit or Disposal Activities" ("SFAS 146"), which is effective for exit or disposal activities that are initiated after December 31, 2002. SFAS 146 requires that a liability be recognized for exit or disposal costs only when the liability is incurred, as defined in the FASB's conceptual frame-work, rather than when a company commits to an exit plan, and that the liability be initially measured at fair value. The Company expects the adoption of this standard will affect the timing of recognizing liabilities, and the amount recognized, in respect of future exit activities, if any.

The FASB has issued Interpretation No. 45, "Guarantor's Accounting and Disclosure Requirements for Guarantees, Including Indirect Guarantees of Indebtedness of Others" ("FIN 45"). FIN 45 requires additional disclosures as well as the recognition of a liability by a guarantor at the inception of certain guarantees entered into or modified after December 31, 2002. The initial measurement of this liability is the fair value of the guarantee at inception. The requirements of FIN 45 have been considered in the preparation of this reconciliation.

The FASB has issued Interpretation No. 46, "Consolidation of Variable Interest Entities" ("FIN 46"). Its consolidation provisions are applicable for all entities created after January 31, 2003, and for existing variable interest entities as of July 1, 2003. With respect to entities that do not qualify to be assessed for consolidation based on voting interests, FIN 46 generally requires consolidation by the entity that has a variable interest(s) that will absorb a majority of the variable interest entity's expected losses if they occur, receive a majority of the entity's expected residual returns if they occur, or both. The Company is currently evaluating the impact of adopting the requirements of FIN 46.

Directors and Management

DIRECTORS

R. THOMAS M. ALLAN [1]
Consultant

JOE S. HOUSSIAN
Chairman, President and Chief Executive Officer,
Intrawest Corporation

DANIEL O. JARVIS
Executive Vice President and
Chief Financial Officer, Intrawest Corporation

DAVID A. KING [1,2]
President, David King Corporation

GORDON H. MACDOUGALL [2,3]
Partner, CC&L Financial Services Group

PAUL M. MANHEIM [1,3]
President, HAL Real Estate Investments, Inc.

PAUL A. NOVELLY [2]
Chairman and Chief Executive Officer,
Apex Oil Company, Inc.

GARY L. RAYMOND
Chief Executive Officer, Resort
Development Group, Intrawest Corporation

BERNARD A. ROY [3]
Senior Partner, Ogilvy Renault

KHALED C. SIFRI [1]
Managing Partner, Hadef Al-Dhahiri & Associates

HUGH R. SMYTHE
President, Resort Operations Group,
Intrawest Corporation

NICHOLAS C.H. VILLIERS [2]
Consultant

[1] Audit Committee
[2] Corporate Governance and Nominating Committee
[3] Human Resources Committee

CORPORATE MANAGEMENT

JOE. S. HOUSSIAN
Chairman, President and Chief Executive Officer

DANIEL O. JARVIS
Executive Vice President
and Chief Financial Officer

  DAVID C. BLAIKLOCK
  Vice President and Corporate Controller

  JOHN E. CURRIE
  Senior Vice President, Financing and Taxation

JIM GREEHEY
Vice President, Corporate Insurance

MICHAEL M. HANNAN
Senior Vice President, Strategic
and Corporate Development

ROSS J. MEACHER
Corporate Secretary and Chief Privacy Officer

ANDREW C. MORDEN
Vice President,
Financial Planning and Systems

STEPHEN J. SAMMUT
Vice President, Project and Corporate Finance

STAN C. SPRENGER
President, Resort Reservations Network

ANDREW VOYSEY
Senior Vice President, Acquisitions

EWAN R. WILDING
Vice President, Internal Audit Services

RESORT OPERATIONS GROUP

HUGH R. SMYTHE
President, Resort Operations Group

  PAT ALDOUS
  Director, Canadian Mountain Holidays

  DAVID BARRY
  Senior Vice President, Intrawest Colorado

    GARY DEFRANGE
    Vice President/General Manager,
    Winter Park

    STEVE PACCAGNAN
    Vice President/General Manager, Copper

  DAVID B. BROWNLIE
  Senior Vice President, Finance,
  Whistler Blackcomb

    GORDON AHRENS
    Vice President and General Manager,
    Panorama Mountain Village

  DAVID A. CREASY
  Senior Vice President, Finance

  DOUG FORSETH
  Senior Vice President, Operations,
  Whistler Blackcomb

RUSTY GREGORY
Chief Executive Officer, Mammoth Mountain

DAVE HARTVIGSEN
Senior Vice President, Lodging

  R. SCOTT BUNCE
  Vice President, Sales – Lodging

  PETER A. COWLEY
  Vice President, Lodging
  Product Development

  MIKE STANGE
  Vice President and General Manager,
  Sandestin

EDWARD B. PITONIAK
Senior Vice President, Resort Enterprises

  LINDA DENIS
  Vice President,
  Customer Relationship Marketing

  MARK R. HULME
  Vice President, Retail/Rental Operations

  GRAHAM R. KWAN
  Vice President, Business Development

ANN M. MACLEAN
Vice President,
People and Organizational Development

TONY B. OSBORNE
Staff Vice President, Project Management

CATE THERO
Vice President, Marketing

STEPHEN K. RICE
Senior Vice President, Eastern Region

  MICHEL AUBIN
  President, Tremblant

  CHARLES BLIER
  Vice President and General Manager,
  Mountain Creek

  GORDON CANNING
  President, Blue Mountain

  SKY FOULKES
  Vice President and General Manager,
  Stratton

  BRUCE D. PITTET
  Vice President and General Manager,
  Snowshoe

RESORT DEVELOPMENT GROUP

GARY L. RAYMOND
Chief Executive Officer,
Resort Development Group

  LORNE D. BASSEL
  Executive Vice President,
  Northeast and Europe Regions

    ROBERT JÉRÔME
    Regional Vice President, Europe Region

  WILLIAM R. GREEN
  Regional Vice President, Northeast Region

    ROBIN CONNERS
    Vice President, Commercial,
    Northeast Region

    RICHARD LABONTÉ
    Vice President, Construction,
    Northeast Region

    CRAIG WATTERS
    Vice President, Development,
    Northeast Region

  MAX REIM
  Vice President, Commercial Development

  MICHAEL F. COYLE
  Executive Vice President

    GREG L. ASHLEY
    President, Playground

    DANAE JOHNSON
    Vice President, People Development

JIM ONKEN
President, Storied Places

DAVID S. GREENFIELD
Executive Vice President,
Northwest and Southwest Regions

  DONAL O'CALLAGHAN
  Vice President, Design

  DOUGLAS W. OGILVY
  Regional Vice President, Southwest Region

    FRED GOERS
    Vice President, Construction,
    Southwest Region

    TOM JACOBSON
    Vice President, Development,
    Southwest Region

  PAUL WOODWARD
  Vice President, Northwest Region

    ROBERT FRITZ
    Vice President, Construction,
    Northwest Region

    ERIC GERLACH
    Vice President, Development,
    Northwest Region

DAVID KLEINKOPF
Executive Vice President,
Southeast and Colorado Regions

  DON CARR
  Regional Vice President, Southeast Region

    JIM BOIVIN
    Vice President, Construction,
    Southeast Region

    TOM WALLINGTON
    Vice President, Development,
    Southeast Region

  MIKE O'CONNOR
  Vice President, Development,
  Colorado Region

  JOE WHITEHOUSE
  Vice President, Development,
  Colorado Region

  CONNIE WYNNE
  Vice President, Resort Planning,
  Southeast and Colorado Regions

JEFF STIPEC
President, Intrawest Golf

DREW STOTESBURY
Chief Financial Officer

  RASHA HODALY
  Vice President, Financial Reporting
  and Accounting

RESORT CLUB GROUP

JAMES J. GIBBONS
President, Resort Club Group

  RENÉ L. CARDINAL
  Senior Vice President,
  Finance and Administration

  R. JUDE CARRILLO
  Executive Vice President,
  Sales and Marketing

BARBARA J. JACKSON
Vice President,
Guest Experience and Communications

MICHAEL KAINE
Vice President, Technology

MURRAY PRATT
Vice President, Global Tour Generation

DOUG REGELOUS
Senior Vice President, Development

JEFF TISDALL
Vice President, Membership
Programs Marketing

RON. T. ZIMMER
Executive Vice President and
Chief Financial Officer

Table 1

FUTURE VALUE OF 1

(FUTURE VALUE OF A SINGLE SUM)

$$FVF_{n,i} = (1 + i)^n$$

(n) periods	2%	2½%	3%	4%	5%	6%	8%	9%	10%	11%	12%	15%
1	1.02000	1.02500	1.03000	1.04000	1.05000	1.06000	1.08000	1.09000	1.10000	1.11000	1.12000	1.15000
2	1.04040	1.05063	1.06090	1.08160	1.10250	1.12360	1.16640	1.18810	1.21000	1.23210	1.25440	1.32250
3	1.06121	1.07689	1.09273	1.12486	1.15763	1.19102	1.25971	1.29503	1.33100	1.36763	1.40493	1.52088
4	1.08243	1.10381	1.12551	1.16986	1.21551	1.26248	1.36049	1.41158	1.46410	1.51807	1.57352	1.74901
5	1.10408	1.13141	1.15927	1.21665	1.27628	1.33823	1.46933	1.53862	1.61051	1.68506	1.76234	2.01136
6	1.12616	1.15969	1.19405	1.26532	1.34010	1.41852	1.58687	1.67710	1.77156	1.87041	1.97382	2.31306
7	1.14869	1.18869	1.22987	1.31593	1.40710	1.50363	1.71382	1.82804	1.94872	2.07616	2.21068	2.66002
8	1.17166	1.21840	1.26677	1.36857	1.47746	1.59385	1.85093	1.99256	2.14359	2.30454	2.47596	3.05902
9	1.19509	1.24886	1.30477	1.42331	1.55133	1.68948	1.99900	2.17189	2.35795	2.55803	2.77308	3.51788
10	1.21899	1.28008	1.34392	1.48024	1.62889	1.79085	2.15892	2.36736	2.59374	2.83942	3.10585	4.04556
11	1.24337	1.31209	1.38423	1.53945	1.71034	1.89830	2.33164	2.58043	2.85312	3.15176	3.47855	4.65239
12	1.26824	1.34489	1.42576	1.60103	1.79586	2.01220	2.51817	2.81267	3.13843	3.49845	3.89598	5.35025
13	1.29361	1.37851	1.46853	1.66507	1.88565	2.13293	2.71962	3.06581	3.45227	3.88328	4.36349	6.15279
14	1.31948	1.41297	1.51259	1.73168	1.97993	2.26090	2.93719	3.34173	3.79750	4.31044	4.88711	7.07571
15	1.34587	1.44830	1.55797	1.80094	2.07893	2.39656	3.17217	3.64248	4.17725	4.78459	5.47357	8.13706
16	1.37279	1.48451	1.60471	1.87298	2.18287	2.54035	3.42594	3.97031	4.59497	5.31089	6.13039	9.35762
17	1.40024	1.52162	1.65285	1.94790	2.29202	2.69277	3.70002	4.32763	5.05447	5.89509	6.86604	10.76126
18	1.42825	1.55966	1.70243	2.02582	2.40662	2.85434	3.99602	4.71712	5.55992	6.54355	7.68997	12.37545
19	1.45681	1.59865	1.75351	2.10685	2.52695	3.02560	4.31570	5.14166	6.11591	7.26334	8.61276	14.23177
20	1.48595	1.63862	1.80611	2.19112	2.65330	3.20714	4.66096	5.60441	6.72750	8.06231	9.64629	16.36654
21	1.51567	1.67958	1.86029	2.27877	2.78596	3.39956	5.03383	6.10881	7.40025	8.94917	10.80385	18.82152
22	1.54598	1.72157	1.91610	2.36992	2.92526	3.60354	5.43654	6.65860	8.14028	9.93357	12.10031	21.64475
23	1.57690	1.76461	1.97359	2.46472	3.07152	3.81975	5.87146	7.25787	8.95430	11.02627	13.55235	24.89146
24	1.60844	1.80873	2.03279	2.56330	3.22510	4.04893	6.34118	7.91108	9.84973	12.23916	15.17863	28.62518
25	1.64061	1.85394	2.09378	2.66584	3.38635	4.29187	6.84847	8.62308	10.83471	13.58546	17.00000	32.91895
26	1.67342	1.90029	2.15659	2.77247	3.55567	4.54938	7.39635	9.39916	11.91818	15.07986	19.04007	37.85680
27	1.70689	1.94780	2.22129	2.88337	3.73346	4.82235	7.98806	10.24508	13.10999	16.73865	21.32488	43.53532
28	1.74102	1.99650	2.28793	2.99870	3.92013	5.11169	8.62711	11.16714	14.42099	18.57990	23.88387	50.06561
29	1.77584	2.04641	2.35657	3.11865	4.11614	5.41839	9.31727	12.17218	15.86309	20.62369	26.74993	57.57545
30	1.81136	2.09757	2.42726	3.24340	4.32194	5.74349	10.06266	13.26768	17.44940	22.89230	29.95992	66.21177
31	1.84759	2.15001	2.50008	3.37313	4.53804	6.08810	10.86767	14.46177	19.19434	25.41045	33.55511	76.14354
32	1.88454	2.20376	2.57508	3.50806	4.76494	6.45339	11.73708	15.76333	21.11378	28.20560	37.58173	87.56507
33	1.92223	2.25885	2.65234	3.64838	5.00319	6.84059	12.67605	17.18203	23.22515	31.30821	42.09153	100.69983
34	1.96068	2.31532	2.73191	3.79432	5.25335	7.25103	13.69013	18.72841	25.54767	34.75212	47.14252	115.80480
35	1.99989	2.37321	2.81386	3.94609	5.51602	7.68609	14.78534	20.41397	28.10244	38.57485	52.79962	133.17552
36	2.03989	2.43254	2.88928	4.10393	5.79182	8.14725	15.96817	22.25123	30.91268	42.81808	59.13557	153.15185
37	2.08069	2.49335	2.98523	4.26809	6.08141	8.63609	17.24563	24.25384	34.00395	47.52807	66.23184	176.12463
38	2.12230	2.55568	3.07478	4.43881	6.38548	9.15425	18.62528	26.43668	37.40434	52.75616	74.17966	202.54332
39	2.16474	2.61957	3.16703	4.61637	6.70475	9.70351	20.11530	28.81598	41.14479	58.55934	83.08122	232.92482
40	2.20804	2.68506	3.26204	4.80102	7.03999	10.28572	21.72452	31.40942	45.25926	65.00087	93.05097	267.86355

Table 2

PRESENT VALUE OF 1
(PRESENT VALUE OF A SINGLE SUM)

$$PVF_{n,i} = \frac{1}{(1+i)^n} = (1+i)^{-n}$$

(n) periods	2%	2½%	3%	4%	5%	6%	8%	9%	10%	11%	12%	15%
1	.98039	.97561	.97087	.96156	.95238	.94340	.92593	.91743	.90909	.90090	.89286	.86957
2	.96117	.95181	.94260	.92456	.90703	.89000	.85734	.84168	.82645	.81162	.79719	.75614
3	.94232	.92860	.91514	.88900	.86384	.83962	.79383	.77218	.75132	.73119	.71178	.65752
4	.92385	.90595	.88849	.85480	.82270	.79209	.73503	.70843	.68301	.65873	.63552	.57175
5	.90583	.88385	.86261	.82193	.78353	.74726	.68058	.64993	.62092	.59345	.56743	.49718
6	.88797	.86230	.83748	.79031	.74622	.70496	.63017	.59627	.56447	.53464	.50663	.43233
7	.87056	.84127	.81309	.75992	.71068	.66506	.58349	.54703	.51316	.48166	.45235	.37594
8	.85349	.82075	.78941	.73069	.67684	.62741	.54027	.50187	.46651	.43393	.40388	.32690
9	.83676	.80073	.76642	.70259	.64461	.59190	.50025	.46043	.42410	.39092	.36061	.28426
10	.82035	.78120	.74409	.67556	.61391	.55839	.46319	.42241	.38554	.35218	.32197	.24719
11	.80426	.76214	.72242	.64958	.58468	.52679	.42888	.38753	.35049	.31728	.28748	.21494
12	.78849	.74356	.70138	.62460	.55684	.49697	.39711	.35554	.31863	.28584	.25668	.18691
13	.77303	.72542	.68095	.60057	.53032	.46884	.36770	.32618	.28966	.25751	.22917	.16253
14	.75788	.70773	.66112	.57748	.50507	.44230	.34046	.29925	.26333	.23199	.20462	.14133
15	.74301	.69047	.64186	.55526	.48102	.41727	.31524	.27454	.23939	.20900	.18270	.12289
16	.72845	.67362	.62317	.53391	.45811	.39365	.29189	.25187	.21763	.18829	.16312	.10687
17	.71416	.65720	.60502	.51337	.43630	.37136	.27027	.23107	.19785	.16963	.14564	.09293
18	.70016	.64117	.58739	.49363	.41552	.35034	.25025	.21199	.17986	.15282	.13004	.08081
19	.68643	.62553	.57029	.47464	.39573	.33051	.23171	.19449	.16351	.13768	.11611	.07027
20	.67297	.61027	.55368	.45639	.37689	.31180	.21455	.17843	.14864	.12403	.10367	.06110
21	.65978	.59539	.53755	.43883	.35894	.29416	.19866	.16370	.13513	.11174	.09256	.05313
22	.64684	.58086	.52189	.42196	.34185	.27751	.18394	.15018	.12285	.10067	.08264	.04620
23	.63416	.56670	.50669	.40573	.32557	.26180	.17032	.13778	.11168	.09069	.07379	.04017
24	.62172	.55288	.49193	.39012	.31007	.24698	.15770	.12641	.10153	.08170	.06588	.03493
25	.60953	.53939	.47761	.37512	.29530	.23300	.14602	.11597	.09230	.07361	.05882	.03038
26	.59758	.52623	.46369	.36069	.28124	.21981	.13520	.10639	.08391	.06631	.05252	.02642
27	.58586	.51340	.45019	.34682	.26785	.20737	.12519	.09761	.07628	.05974	.04689	.02297
28	.57437	.50088	.43708	.33348	.25509	.19563	.11591	.08955	.06934	.05382	.04187	.01997
29	.56311	.48866	.42435	.32065	.24295	.18456	.10733	.08216	.06304	.04849	.03738	.01737
30	.55207	.47674	.41199	.30832	.23138	.17411	.09938	.07537	.05731	.04368	.03338	.01510
31	.54125	.46511	.39999	.29646	.22036	.16425	.09202	.06915	.05210	.03935	.02980	.01313
32	.53063	.45377	.38834	.28506	.20987	.15496	.08520	.06344	.04736	.03545	.02661	.01142
33	.52023	.44270	.37703	.27409	.19987	.14619	.07889	.05820	.04306	.03194	.02376	.00993
34	.51003	.43191	.36604	.26355	.19035	.13791	.07305	.05340	.03914	.02878	.02121	.00864
35	.50003	.42137	.35538	.25342	.18129	.13011	.06763	.04899	.03558	.02592	.01894	.00751
36	.49022	.41109	.34503	.24367	.17266	.12274	.06262	.04494	.03235	.02335	.01691	.00653
37	.48061	.40107	.33498	.23430	.16444	.11579	.05799	.04123	.02941	.02104	.01510	.00568
38	.47119	.39128	.32523	.22529	.15661	.10924	.05369	.03783	.02674	.01896	.01348	.00494
39	.46195	.38174	.31575	.21662	.14915	.10306	.04971	.03470	.02430	.01708	.01204	.00429
40	.45289	.37243	.30656	.20829	.14205	.09722	.04603	.03184	.02210	.01538	.01075	.00373

Table 3

FUTURE VALUE OF AN ORDINARY ANNUITY OF 1

$$FVF-OA_{n,\,i} = \frac{(1+i)^n - 1}{i}$$

(n) periods	2%	2½%	3%	4%	5%	6%	8%	9%	10%	11%	12%	15%
1	1.00000	1.00000	1.00000	1.00000	1.00000	1.00000	1.00000	1.00000	1.00000	1.00000	1.00000	1.00000
2	2.02000	2.02500	2.03000	2.04000	2.05000	2.06000	2.08000	2.09000	2.10000	2.11000	2.12000	2.15000
3	3.06040	3.07563	3.09090	3.12160	3.15250	3.18360	3.24640	3.27810	3.31000	3.34210	3.37440	3.47250
4	4.12161	4.15252	4.18363	4.24646	4.31013	4.37462	4.50611	4.57313	4.64100	4.70973	4.77933	4.99338
5	5.20404	5.25633	5.30914	5.41632	5.52563	5.63709	5.86660	5.98471	6.10510	6.22780	6.35285	6.74238
6	6.30812	6.38774	6.46841	6.63298	6.80191	6.97532	7.33592	7.52334	7.71561	7.91286	8.11519	8.75374
7	7.43428	7.54743	7.66246	7.89829	8.14201	8.39384	8.92280	9.20044	9.48717	9.78327	10.08901	11.06680
8	8.58297	8.73612	8.89234	9.21423	9.54911	9.89747	10.63663	11.02847	11.43589	11.85943	12.29969	13.72682
9	9.75463	9.95452	10.15911	10.58280	11.02656	11.49132	12.48756	13.02104	13.57948	14.16397	14.77566	16.78584
10	10.94972	11.20338	11.46338	12.00611	12.57789	13.18079	14.48656	15.19293	15.93743	16.72201	17.54874	20.30372
11	12.16872	12.48347	12.80780	13.48635	14.20679	14.97164	16.64549	17.56029	18.53117	19.56143	20.65458	24.34928
12	13.41209	13.79555	14.19203	15.02581	15.91713	16.86994	18.97713	20.14072	21.38428	22.71319	24.13313	29.00167
13	14.68033	15.14044	15.61779	16.62684	17.71298	18.88214	21.49530	22.95339	24.52271	26.21164	28.02911	34.35192
14	15.97394	16.51895	17.08632	18.29191	19.59863	21.01507	24.21492	26.01919	27.97498	30.09492	32.39260	40.50471
15	17.29342	17.93193	18.59891	20.02359	21.57856	23.27597	27.15211	29.36092	31.77248	34.40536	37.27972	47.58041
16	18.63929	19.38022	20.15688	21.82453	23.65749	25.67253	30.32428	33.00340	35.94973	39.18995	42.75328	55.71747
17	20.01207	20.86473	21.76159	23.69751	25.84037	28.21288	33.75023	36.97371	40.54470	44.50084	48.88367	65.07509
18	21.41231	22.38635	23.41444	25.64541	28.13238	30.90565	37.45024	41.30134	45.59917	50.39593	55.74972	75.83636
19	22.84056	23.94601	25.11687	27.67123	30.53900	33.75999	41.44626	46.01846	51.15909	56.93949	63.43968	88.21181
20	24.29737	25.54466	26.87037	29.77808	33.06595	36.78559	45.76196	51.16012	57.27500	64.20283	72.05244	102.44358
21	25.78332	27.18327	28.67649	31.96920	35.71925	39.99273	50.42292	56.76453	64.00250	72.26514	81.69874	118.81012
22	27.29898	28.86286	30.53678	34.24797	38.50521	43.39229	55.45676	62.87334	71.40275	81.21431	92.50258	137.63164
23	28.84496	30.58443	32.45288	36.61789	41.43048	46.99583	60.89330	69.53194	79.54302	91.14788	104.60289	159.27638
24	30.42186	32.34904	34.42647	39.08260	44.50200	50.81558	66.76476	76.78981	88.49733	102.17415	118.15524	184.16784
25	32.03030	34.15776	36.45926	41.64591	47.72710	54.86451	73.10594	84.70090	98.34706	114.41331	133.33387	212.79302
26	33.67091	36.01171	38.55304	44.31174	51.11345	59.15638	79.95442	93.32398	109.18177	127.99877	150.33393	245.71197
27	35.34432	37.91200	40.70963	47.08421	54.66913	63.70577	87.35077	102.72314	121.09994	143.07864	169.37401	283.56877
28	37.05121	39.85990	42.93092	49.96758	58.40258	68.52811	95.33883	112.96822	134.20994	159.81729	190.69889	327.10408
29	38.79223	41.85630	45.21885	52.96629	62.32271	73.63980	103.96594	124.13536	148.63093	178.39719	214.58275	377.16969
30	40.56808	43.90270	47.57542	56.08494	66.43885	79.05819	113.28321	136.30754	164.49402	199.02088	241.33268	434.74515
31	42.37944	46.00027	50.00268	59.32834	70.76079	84.80168	123.34587	149.57522	181.94343	221.91317	271.29261	500.95692
32	44.22703	48.15028	52.50276	62.70147	75.29883	90.88978	134.21354	164.03699	201.13777	247.32362	304.84772	577.10046
33	46.11157	50.35403	55.07784	66.20953	80.06377	97.34316	145.95062	179.80032	222.25154	275.52922	342.42945	644.66553
34	48.03380	52.61289	57.73018	69.85791	85.06696	104.18376	158.62667	196.98234	245.47670	306.83744	384.52098	765.36535
35	49.99448	54.92821	60.46208	73.65222	90.32031	111.43478	172.31680	215.71076	271.02437	341.58955	431.66350	881.17016
36	51.99437	57.30141	63.27594	77.59831	95.83632	119.12087	187.10215	236.12472	299.12681	380.16441	484.46312	1014.34568
37	54.03425	59.73395	66.17422	81.70225	101.62814	127.26812	203.07032	258.37595	330.03949	422.98249	543.59869	1167.49753
38	56.11494	62.22730	69.15945	85.97034	107.70955	135.90421	220.31595	282.62978	364.04343	470.51056	609.83053	1343.62216
39	58.23724	64.78298	72.23423	90.40915	114.09502	145.05846	238.94122	309.06646	401.44778	523.26673	684.01020	1546.16549
40	60.40198	67.40255	75.40126	95.02552	120.79977	154.76197	259.05652	337.88245	442.59256	581.82607	767.09142	1779.09031

Table 4

PRESENT VALUE OF AN ORDINARY ANNUITY OF 1

$$PVF - OA_{n,\,i} = \dfrac{1 - \dfrac{1}{(1+i)^n}}{i}$$

(n) periods	2%	2½%	3%	4%	5%	6%	8%	9%	10%	11%	12%	15%
1	.98039	.97561	.97087	.96154	.95238	.94340	.92593	.91743	.90909	.90090	.89286	.86957
2	1.94156	1.92742	1.91347	1.88609	1.85941	1.83339	1.78326	1.75911	1.73554	1.71252	1.69005	1.62571
3	2.88388	2.85602	2.82861	2.77509	2.72325	2.67301	2.57710	2.53130	2.48685	2.44371	2.40183	2.28323
4	3.80773	3.76197	3.71710	3.62990	3.54595	3.46511	3.31213	3.23972	3.16986	3.10245	3.03735	2.85498
5	4.71346	4.64583	4.57971	4.45182	4.32948	4.21236	3.99271	3.88965	3.79079	3.69590	3.60478	3.35216
6	5.60143	5.50813	5.41719	5.24214	5.07569	4.91732	4.62288	4.48592	4.35526	4.23054	4.11141	3.78448
7	6.47199	6.34939	6.23028	6.00205	5.78637	5.58238	5.20637	5.03295	4.86842	4.71220	4.56376	4.16042
8	7.32548	7.17014	7.01969	6.73274	6.46321	6.20979	5.74664	5.53482	5.33493	5.14612	4.96764	4.48732
9	8.16224	7.97087	7.78611	7.43533	7.10782	6.80169	6.24689	5.99525	5.75902	5.53705	5.32825	4.77158
10	8.98259	8.75206	8.53020	8.11090	7.72173	7.36009	6.71008	6.41766	6.14457	5.88923	5.65022	5.01877
11	9.78685	9.51421	9.25262	8.76048	8.30641	7.88687	7.13896	6.80519	6.49506	6.20652	5.93770	5.23371
12	10.57534	10.25776	9.95400	9.38507	8.86325	8.38384	7.53608	7.16073	6.81369	6.49236	6.19437	5.42062
13	11.34837	10.98319	10.63496	9.98565	9.39357	8.85268	7.90378	7.48690	7.10336	6.74987	6.42355	5.58315
14	12.10625	11.69091	11.29607	10.56312	9.89864	9.29498	8.24424	7.78615	7.36669	6.98187	6.62817	5.72448
15	12.84926	12.38138	11.93794	11.11839	10.37966	9.71225	8.55948	8.06069	7.60608	7.19087	6.81086	5.84737
16	13.57771	13.05500	12.56110	11.65230	10.83777	10.10590	8.85137	8.31256	7.82371	7.37916	6.97399	5.95424
17	14.29187	13.71220	13.16612	12.16567	11.27407	10.47726	9.12164	8.54363	8.02155	7.54879	7.11963	6.04716
18	14.99203	14.35336	13.75351	12.65930	11.68959	10.82760	9.37189	8.75563	8.20141	7.70162	7.24967	6.12797
19	15.67846	14.97889	14.32380	13.13394	12.08532	11.15812	9.60360	8.95012	8.36492	7.83929	7.36578	6.19823
20	16.35143	15.58916	14.87747	13.59033	12.46221	11.46992	9.81815	9.12855	8.51356	7.96333	7.46944	6.25933
21	17.01121	16.18455	15.41502	14.02916	12.82115	11.76408	10.01680	9.29224	8.64869	8.07507	7.56200	6.31246
22	17.65805	16.76541	15.93692	14.45112	13.16800	12.04158	10.20074	9.44243	8.77154	8.17574	7.64465	6.35866
23	18.29220	17.33211	16.44361	14.85684	13.48857	12.30338	10.37106	9.58021	8.88322	8.26643	7.71843	6.39884
24	18.91393	17.88499	16.93554	15.24696	13.79864	12.55036	10.52876	9.70661	8.98474	8.34814	7.78432	6.43377
25	19.52346	18.42438	17.41315	15.62208	14.09394	12.78336	10.67478	9.82258	9.07704	8.42174	7.84314	6.46415
26	20.12104	18.95061	17.87684	15.98277	14.37519	13.00317	10.80998	9.92897	9.16095	8.48806	7.89566	6.49056
27	20.70690	19.46401	18.32703	16.32959	14.64303	13.21053	10.93516	10.02658	9.23722	8.45780	7.94255	6.51353
28	21.28127	19.96489	18.76411	16.66306	14.89813	13.40616	11.05108	10.11613	9.30657	8.60162	7.98442	6.53351
29	21.84438	20.45355	19.18845	16.98371	15.14107	13.59072	11.15841	10.19828	9.36961	8.65011	8.02181	6.55088
30	22.39646	20.93029	19.60044	17.29203	15.37245	13.76483	11.25778	10.27365	9.42691	8.69379	8.05518	6.56598
31	22.93770	21.39541	20.00043	17.58849	15.59281	13.92909	11.34980	10.34280	9.47901	8.73315	8.08499	6.57911
32	23.46833	21.84918	20.38877	17.87355	15.80268	14.08404	11.43500	10.40624	9.52638	8.76860	8.11159	6.59053
33	23.98856	22.29188	20.76579	18.14765	16.00255	14.23023	11.51389	10.46444	9.56943	8.80054	8.13535	6.60046
34	24.49859	22.72379	21.13184	18.41120	16.19290	14.36814	11.58693	10.51784	9.60858	8.82932	8.15656	6.60910
35	24.99862	23.14516	21.48722	18.66461	16.37419	14.49825	11.65457	10.56682	9.64416	8.85524	8.17550	6.61661
36	25.48884	23.55625	21.83225	18.90828	16.54685	14.62099	11.71719	10.61176	9.67651	8.87859	8.19241	6.62314
37	25.96945	23.95732	22.16724	19.14258	16.71129	14.73678	11.77518	10.65299	9.70592	8.89963	8.20751	6.62882
38	26.44064	24.34860	22.49246	19.36786	16.86789	14.84602	11.82887	10.69082	9.73265	8.91859	8.22099	6.63375
39	26.90259	24.73034	22.80822	19.58448	17.01704	14.94907	11.87858	10.72552	9.75697	8.93567	8.23303	6.63805
40	27.35548	25.10278	23.11477	19.79277	17.15909	15.04630	11.92461	10.75736	9.77905	8.95105	8.24378	6.64178

Table 5

PRESENT VALUE OF AN ANNUITY DUE OF 1

$$PVF-AD_{n,i} = 1 + \frac{1 - \dfrac{1}{(1+i)^{n-1}}}{i}$$

(n) periods	2%	2½%	3%	4%	5%	6%	8%	9%	10%	11%	12%	15%
1	1.00000	1.00000	1.00000	1.00000	1.00000	1.00000	1.00000	1.00000	1.00000	1.00000	1.00000	1.00000
2	1.98039	1.97561	1.97087	1.96154	1.95238	1.94340	1.92593	1.91743	1.90909	1.90090	1.89286	1.86957
3	2.94156	2.92742	2.91347	2.88609	2.85941	2.83339	2.78326	2.75911	2.73554	2.71252	2.69005	2.62571
4	3.88388	3.85602	3.82861	3.77509	3.72325	3.67301	3.57710	3.53130	3.48685	3.44371	3.40183	3.28323
5	4.80773	4.76197	4.71710	4.62990	4.54595	4.46511	4.31213	4.23972	4.16986	4.10245	4.03735	3.85498
6	5.71346	5.64583	5.57971	5.45182	5.32948	5.21236	4.99271	4.88965	4.79079	4.69590	4.60478	4.35216
7	6.60143	6.50813	6.41719	6.24214	6.07569	5.91732	5.62288	5.48592	5.35526	5.23054	5.11141	4.78448
8	7.47199	7.34939	7.23028	7.00205	6.78637	6.58238	6.20637	6.03295	5.86842	5.71220	5.56376	5.16042
9	8.32548	8.17014	8.01969	7.73274	7.46321	7.20979	6.74664	6.53482	6.33493	6.14612	5.96764	5.48732
10	9.16224	8.97087	8.78611	8.43533	8.10782	7.80169	7.24689	6.99525	6.75902	6.53705	6.32825	5.77158
11	9.98259	9.75206	9.53020	9.11090	8.72173	8.36009	7.71008	7.41766	7.14457	6.88923	6.65022	6.01877
12	10.78685	10.51421	10.25262	9.76048	9.30641	8.88687	8.13896	7.80519	7.49506	7.20652	6.93770	6.23371
13	11.57534	11.25776	10.95400	10.38507	9.86325	9.38384	8.53608	8.16073	7.81369	7.49236	7.19437	6.42062
14	12.34837	11.98319	11.63496	10.98565	10.39357	9.85268	8.90378	8.48690	8.10336	7.74987	7.42355	6.58315
15	13.10625	12.69091	12.29607	11.56312	10.89864	10.29498	9.24424	8.78615	9.36669	7.98187	7.62817	6.72448
16	13.84926	13.38138	12.93794	12.11839	11.37966	10.71225	9.55948	9.06069	8.60608	8.19087	7.81086	6.84737
17	14.57771	14.05500	13.56110	12.65230	11.83777	11.10590	9.85137	9.31256	8.82371	8.37916	7.97399	6.95424
18	15.29187	14.71220	14.16612	13.16567	12.27407	11.47726	10.12164	9.54363	9.02155	8.54879	8.11963	7.04716
19	15.99203	15.35336	14.75351	13.65930	12.68959	11.82760	10.37189	9.75563	9.20141	8.70162	8.24967	7.12797
20	16.67846	15.97889	15.32380	14.13394	13.08532	12.15812	10.60360	9.95012	9.36492	8.83929	8.36578	7.19823
21	17.35143	16.58916	15.87747	14.59033	13.46221	12.46992	10.81815	10.12855	9.51356	8.96333	8.46944	7.25933
22	18.01121	17.18455	16.41502	15.02916	13.82115	12.76408	11.01680	10.29224	9.64869	9.07507	8.56200	7.31246
23	18.65805	17.76541	16.93692	15.45112	14.16300	13.04158	11.20074	10.44243	9.77154	9.17574	8.64465	7.35866
24	19.29220	18.33211	17.44361	15.85684	14.48857	13.30338	11.37106	10.58021	9.88322	9.26643	8.71843	7.39884
25	19.91393	18.88499	17.93554	16.24696	14.79864	13.55036	11.52876	10.70661	9.98474	9.34814	8.78432	7.43377
26	20.52346	19.42438	18.41315	16.62208	15.09394	13.78336	11.67478	10.82258	10.07704	9.42174	8.84314	7.46415
27	21.12104	19.95061	18.87684	16.98277	15.37519	14.00317	11.80998	10.92897	10.16095	9.48806	8.89566	7.49056
28	21.70690	20.46401	19.32703	17.32959	15.64303	14.21053	11.93518	11.02658	10.23722	9.54780	8.94255	7.51353
29	22.28127	20.96489	19.76411	17.66306	15.89813	14.40616	12.05108	11.11613	10.30657	9.60162	8.98442	7.53351
30	22.84438	21.45355	20.18845	17.98371	16.14107	14.59072	12.15841	11.19828	10.36961	9.65011	9.02181	7.55088
31	23.39646	21.93029	20.60044	18.29203	16.37245	14.76483	12.25778	11.27365	10.42691	9.69379	9.05518	7.56598
32	23.93770	22.39541	21.00043	18.58849	16.59281	14.92909	12.34980	11.34280	10.47901	9.73315	9.08499	7.57911
33	24.46833	22.84918	21.38877	18.87355	16.80268	15.08404	12.43500	11.40624	10.52638	9.76860	9.11159	7.59053
34	24.98856	23.29188	21.76579	19.14765	17.00255	15.23023	12.51389	11.46444	10.56943	9.80054	9.13535	7.60046
35	25.49859	23.72379	22.13184	19.41120	17.19290	15.36814	12.58693	11.51784	10.60858	9.82932	9.15656	7.60910
36	25.99862	24.14516	22.48722	19.66461	17.37419	15.49825	12.65457	11.56682	10.64416	9.85524	9.17550	7.61661
37	26.48884	24.55625	22.83225	19.90828	17.54685	15.62099	12.71719	11.61176	10.67651	9.87859	9.19241	7.62314
38	26.96945	24.95732	23.16724	20.14258	17.71129	15.73678	12.77518	11.65299	10.70592	9.89963	9.20751	7.62882
39	27.44064	25.34860	23.49246	20.36786	17.86789	15.84602	12.82887	11.69082	10.73265	9.91859	9.22099	7.63375
40	27.90259	25.73034	23.80822	20.58448	18.01704	15.94907	12.87858	11.72552	10.75697	9.93567	9.23303	7.63805

COMPANY INDEX

SUBJECT INDEX